WORLD TRADE ORGANIZATION

Dispute Settlement Reports

2012
Volume III

Pages 1249-1834

Shaftesbury Road, Cambridge CB2 8EA, United Kingdom

One Liberty Plaza, 20th Floor, New York, NY 10006, USA

477 Williamstown Road, Port Melbourne, VIC 3207, Australia

314–321, 3rd Floor, Plot 3, Splendor Forum, Jasola District Centre, New Delhi – 110025, India

103 Penang Road, #05–06/07, Visioncrest Commercial, Singapore 238467

Cambridge University Press is part of Cambridge University Press & Assessment,
a department of the University of Cambridge.

We share the University's mission to contribute to society through the pursuit of
education, learning and research at the highest international levels of excellence.

www.cambridge.org
Information on this title: www.cambridge.org/9781107051201

© World Trade Organization 2014

This publication is in copyright. Subject to statutory exception and to the provisions
of relevant collective licensing agreements, no reproduction of any part may take
place without the written permission of Cambridge University Press & Assessment.

First published 2014

A catalogue record for this publication is available from the British Library

ISBN   978-1-107-05120-1   Hardback

Cambridge University Press & Assessment has no responsibility for the persistence
or accuracy of URLs for external or third-party internet websites referred to in this
publication and does not guarantee that any content on such websites is, or will
remain, accurate or appropriate.

THE WTO DISPUTE SETTLEMENT REPORTS

The *Dispute Settlement Reports* of the World Trade Organization (the "WTO") include panel and Appellate Body reports, as well as arbitration awards, in disputes concerning the rights and obligations of WTO Members under the provisions of the *Marrakesh Agreement Establishing the World Trade Organization*. The *Dispute Settlement Reports* are available in English. Volumes comprising one or more complete cases contain a cumulative list of published disputes. The cumulative list for cases that cover more than one volume is to be found in the first volume for that case.

This volume may be cited as DSR 2012:III

TABLE OF CONTENTS

Page

United States - Measures Affecting Trade in Large Civil Aircraft (Second Complaint) (WT/DS353)

Report of the Panel (Part II)... 1251

US - Large Civil Aircraft (2nd Complaint)

UNITED STATES - MEASURES AFFECTING TRADE IN LARGE CIVIL AIRCRAFT (SECOND COMPLAINT)

Report of the Panel
WT/DS353/R*

*Adopted by the Dispute Settlement Body
on 23 March 2012
as Modified by the Appellate Body Report*

BCI DELETED, AS INDICATED [***]
TABLE OF CONTENTS

TABLE OF CONTENTS

			Page
4.	State of Illinois and municipalities therein		1275
	(a)	Introduction	1275
	(b)	The measures at issue	1275
	(c)	Whether a subsidy exists within the meaning of Article 1 of the SCM Agreement	1279
		(i) Arguments of the European Communities	1279
		(ii) Arguments of the United States	1280
		(iii) Evaluation by the Panel	1281
	(d)	Whether the subsidy is specific within the meaning of Article 2 of the SCM Agreement	1281
		(i) Arguments of the European Communities	1281
		(ii) Arguments of the United States	1282
		(iii) Evaluation by the Panel	1283
	(e)	The amount of the subsidy to Boeing's LCA division	1288

---

* Paragraphs 1.1 to 7.890 can be found in DSR 2012:II.

Report of the Panel

		(i)	Arguments of the European Communities 1288
		(ii)	Arguments of the United States............. 1288
		(iii)	Evaluation by the Panel......................... 1288
	(f)		Conclusion... 1292

2. National Aeronautics and Space Administration (NASA) aeronautics R&D.. 1292

(a) Introduction 1292

(b) The measures at issue 1293

(c) Whether a subsidy exists within the meaning of Article 1 of the SCM Agreement 1297

(i) Whether there is a financial contribution within the meaning of Article 1.1(a)(1) of the SCM Agreement.................................... 1298

Whether transactions properly characterized as "purchases of services" are excluded from the scope of Article 1.1(a)(1) of the SCM Agreement 1298

Whether NASA R&D contracts with Boeing are properly characterized as "purchases of services".......................... 1308

(ii) Whether there is a benefit within the meaning of Article 1.1(b) of the SCM Agreement 1338

Arguments of the European Communities 1338

Arguments of the United States.............. 1339

Evaluation by the Panel......................... 1341

(d) Whether the subsidy is specific within the meaning of Article 2 of the SCM Agreement.... 1343

(i) Arguments of the European Communities 1343

(ii) Arguments of the United States.............. 1343

(iii) Evaluation by the Panel......................... 1344

(e) The amount of the subsidy to Boeing's LCA division 1346

(i) Arguments of the European Communities 1346

1252

DSR 2012:III

| | | | US - Large Civil Aircraft (2nd Complaint) |

	(ii)	Arguments of the United States 1348
	(iii)	Evaluation by the Panel 1348
		Introduction 1348
		The United States' evidence regarding the maximum amount of the payments made to Boeing for aeronautics R&D over the period 1989-2006 1349
		The United States' evidence regarding the maximum value of the NASA facilities, equipment and employees provided to Boeing for aeronautics R&D over the period 1989-2006 1359
(f)		Conclusion 1371
3.		Department of Defense (DOD) aeronautics R&D 1371
(a)		Introduction....................................... 1371
(b)		The measures at issue....................................... 1371
(c)		Whether a subsidy exists within the meaning of Article 1 of the SCM Agreement.................... 1377
	(i)	Whether there is a financial contribution within the meaning of Article 1.1(a)(1) of the SCM Agreement 1377
		Arguments of the European Communities... 1377
		Arguments of the United States 1379
		Evaluation by the Panel 1381
	(ii)	Whether there is a benefit within the meaning of Article 1.1(b) of the SCM Agreement 1404
		Arguments of the European Communities... 1404
		Arguments of the United States 1405
		Evaluation by the Panel 1407
(d)		Whether the subsidy is specific within the meaning of Article 2 of the SCM Agreement 1409
	(i)	Arguments of the European Communities... 1409
	(ii)	Arguments of the United States 1410
	(iii)	Evaluation by the Panel 1411

DSR 2012:III   1253

Report of the Panel

		(e)	The amount of the subsidy to Boeing's LCA division 1413
			(i) Arguments of the European Communities 1413
			(ii) Arguments of the United States.............. 1414
			(iii) Evaluation by the Panel......................... 1414
		(f)	Conclusion... 1417
	4.		Department of Commerce (DOC) aeronautics R&D 1418
		(a)	Introduction 1418
		(b)	The measures at issue 1418
		(c)	Whether a subsidy exists within the meaning of Article 1 of the SCM Agreement 1422
			(i) Arguments of the European Communities 1422
			(ii) Arguments of the United States.............. 1422
			(iii) Evaluation by the Panel......................... 1423
		(d)	Whether the subsidy is specific within the meaning of Article 2 of the SCM Agreement.... 1424
			(i) Arguments of the European Communities 1424
			(ii) Arguments of the United States.............. 1425
			(iii) Evaluation by the Panel......................... 1426
		(e)	Conclusion... 1433
	5.		NASA/DOD intellectual property right waivers/transfers 1433
		(a)	Introduction 1433
		(b)	The measures at issue 1434
		(c)	Arguments of the European Communities......... 1436
		(d)	Arguments of the United States......................... 1439
		(e)	Evaluation by the Panel 1441
			(i) Patent rights... 1441
			(ii) Data rights and trade secrets.................. 1448
		(f)	Conclusion... 1455
	6.		NASA/DOD Independent Research & Development (IR&D) and Bid & Proposal (B&P) reimbursements ... 1455
		(a)	Introduction 1455
		(b)	The measures at issue 1456
		(c)	Arguments of the European Communities......... 1458

	(d)	Arguments of the United States	1461
	(e)	Evaluation by the Panel	1462

(i) The Panel's understanding of the nature of the claim of the European Communities and the scope of the measures at issue 1462

(ii) Whether the European Communities has established the existence of the measures it is challenging 1463

(f) Conclusion 1473

7. Department of Labor (DOL) 787 worker training grants 1473

(a) Introduction... 1473

(b) The measures at issue... 1473

(c) Whether a subsidy exists within the meaning of Article 1 of the SCM Agreement................... 1474

(i) Arguments of the European Communities.. 1474

(ii) Arguments of the United States.............. 1474

(iii) Evaluation by the Panel 1475

(d) Whether the subsidy is specific within the meaning of Article 2 of the SCM Agreement 1475

(i) Arguments of the European Communities.. 1475

(ii) Arguments of the United States.............. 1476

(iii) Evaluation by the Panel 1477

(e) Conclusion 1480

8. FSC/ETI and successor act subsidies 1481

(a) Introduction... 1481

(b) The measures at issue... 1481

(i) Provisions of the U.S. Internal Revenue Code relating to foreign sales corporations 1482

(ii) FSC Repeal and Extraterritorial Income Exclusion Act of 2000 1483

(iii) American Jobs Creation Act of 2004...... 1484

(iv) Tax Increase Prevention and Reconciliation Act of 2005 1485

Report of the Panel

	(c)	Whether a specific subsidy exists within the meaning of Articles 1 and 2 of the SCM Agreement	1485
		(i) Arguments of the European Communities	1485
		(ii) Arguments of the United States	1486
		(iii) Evaluation by the Panel	1487
	(d)	Amount of the subsidy to Boeing's LCA division	1490
		(i) Arguments of the European Communities	1490
		(ii) Arguments of the United States	1492
		(iii) Evaluation by the Panel	1493
	(e)	Conclusion	1496
9.		Summary of conclusions on whether the measures at issue constitute specific subsidies within the meaning of Articles 1 and 2 of the SCM Agreement	1496

E. Whether the FSC/ETI Measures and the Washington HB 2294 Tax Measures Are Prohibited Subsidies within the Meaning of Article 3 of the SCM Agreement 1500

1.	FSC/ETI and successor act subsidies	1500
	(a) Introduction	1500
	(b) The measures at issue	1500
	(c) Arguments of the European Communities	1500
	(d) Arguments of the United States	1503
	(e) Evaluation by the Panel	1505
	(f) Conclusion	1509
2.	State of Washington: HB 2294 tax incentives	1509
	(a) Introduction	1509
	(b) Measure at issue	1510
	(c) Arguments of the European Communities	1511
	(d) Arguments of the United States	1518
	(e) Arguments of third parties	1522
	(i) Australia	1522
	(ii) Canada	1523
	(iii) Korea	1524
	(f) Evaluation by the Panel	1525

| | (i) | European Communities' first legal argument | 1537 |

(i) European Communities' first legal argument 1537

(ii) European Communities' second and third legal arguments 1537

Grant of a subsidy in fact tied to *anticipated* exportation 1538

Grant of a subsidy in fact tied to *actual* exportation 1555

(g) Conclusion 1557

F. Whether the United States Causes, through the Use of the Subsidies at Issue, Adverse Effects within the Meaning of Article 5(c) of the SCM Agreement 1557

1. Introduction 1557

2. Whether the United States causes serious prejudice to the interests of the European Communities in the form of significant price suppression and significant lost sales, and a threat thereof, in the world market, and displacement and impedance, and a threat thereof, in the United States and third country markets 1558

(a) Main arguments of the parties and third parties 1558

(i) European Communities 1558

Effects of the aeronautics R&D subsidies on Boeing's development of technologies in relation to the 787 1562

Effects of the subsidies on Boeing's pricing behaviour with respect to the 737NG, 777 and 787 1565

(ii) United States 1576

Effects of the aeronautics R&D subsidies on Boeing's development of technologies in relation to the 787 1576

Effects of the subsidies on Boeing's pricing behaviour with respect to the 737NG, 777 and 787 1580

(iii) Third parties 1585

Australia 1585

Brazil 1586

Japan 1589

Report of the Panel

(b)		Preliminary considerations relating to the Panel's evaluation of the European Communities' claim under Articles 5(c) and 6.3(a), (b) and (c) of the SCM Agreement......... 1589	
	(i)	Interpretational and methodological issues 1589	
	(ii)	The organization of the European Communities' serious prejudice arguments 1594	
	(iii)	Relevant "markets", subsidized products, like products 1596	
	(iv)	Issues pertaining to the temporal scope of the European Communities' claim 1600	
	(v)	Use of order and delivery data 1602	
	(vi)	Overview of the LCA industry............... 1605	
	(vii)	European Communities' approach to the nature of the subsidies at issue and their consequent effects on the three products at issue 1609	
(c)		Evaluation... 1611	
	(i)	Whether the aeronautics R&D subsidies cause serious prejudice to the interests of the European Communities by reason of their effects on Boeing's development of technologies in relation to the 787 1611	
		Structure and design of the aeronautics R&D subsidies 1615	
		Operation of the aeronautics R&D subsidies 1628	
		The conditions of competition................ 1639	
		Effects of the aeronautics R&D subsidies on Airbus' sales and prices in the 200 – 300 seat wide-body LCA product market.. 1642	
		Conclusion... 1653	
	(ii)	Whether the subsidies at issue in this dispute cause serious prejudice to the interests of the European Communities by reason of their effect	

1258   DSR 2012:III

on Boeing's pricing behaviour with respect to the 737NG, 777 and 787. 1654

Effects on Boeing's pricing of subsidies alleged to affect Boeing's marginal unit costs 1654

Effects on Boeing's pricing of subsidies alleged to increase Boeing's non-operating cash flow 1664

Other causation arguments made by the European Communities.................... 1667

Conclusion 1669

Whether the subsidies at issue in this dispute cause a threat of significant price suppression in each of the three LCA product markets 1669

    (d)   Conclusion 1676

3.   The European Communities' claim that violation of the 1992 Agreement constitutes serious prejudice to the European Communities' interests within the meaning of Article 5(c) of the SCM Agreement........... 1677

    (a)   Arguments of the parties and third parties 1677

        (i)   European Communities 1677

        (ii)   United States.. 1683

        (iii)   Third Parties 1687

            Australia... 1687

            Brazil 1688

            Canada 1689

            Japan 1690

            Korea 1690

    (b)   Evaluation by the Panel 1691

    Appendix VII.F.1: Parties' arguments regarding the links between the U.S. Government funded R&D and the specific technologies applied to the 787... 1692

    Appendix VII.F.2: The Cabral Model.......................... 1728

VIII.   CONCLUSIONS AND RECOMMENDATION 1759

    A.   Conclusions 1759

    B.   Recommendation.. 1760

Report of the Panel

LIST OF ANNEXES

	Contents	Page
Annex A	Request for Consultations by the European Communities	1763
Annex B	Request for the Establishment of a Panel by the European Communities	1793
Annex C	Working Procedures of the Panel	1808
Annex D	BCI/HSBI Procedures of the Panel	1812
Annex E	Selected Rulings of the Panel concerning BCI/HSBI procedures and their application	1827

LIST OF ABBREVIATIONS

Abbreviation	Full Reference
1992 Agreement	Agreement concerning the application of the GATT Agreement on Trade in Civil Aircraft on trade in large civil aircraft
ACEE	NASA Aircraft Energy Efficiency Program
ACT	NASA Advanced Composites Technology Program
AD Agreement	Agreement on Implementation of Article VI of the General Agreement on Tariffs and Trade 1994
Airbus	Airbus S.A.S.
AJCA	American Jobs Creation Act
ASP	NASA Aviation Safety Program
AST	NASA Advanced Subsonic Technology Program
ATP	DOC Advanced Technology Program
B&O tax	Business and occupation tax, State of Washington
B&P	Bid and Proposal
BCA	Boeing Commercial Aircraft
BCI	Business Confidential Information
CBO	U.S. Congressional Budget Office
DOC	Department of Commerce
DOD	Department of Defense
DOL	Department of Labor

Abbreviation	Full Reference
DSB	Dispute Settlement Body
DSU	Understanding on Rules and Procedures Governing the Settlement of Disputes
EADS	European Aeronautic Defence and Space Company
EDGE tax credit	Economic Development for a Growing Economy tax credit, State of Illinois
ETI	Extraterritorial Income
FAA	Federal Aviation Administration
FSC	Foreign Sales Corporation
GATT 1994	The General Agreement on Tariffs and Trade 1994
HB 2294	House Bill 2294 in the State of Washington
HPCC	NASA High Performance Computing and Communications Program
HSBI	Highly Sensitive Business Information
HSR	NASA High Speed Research Program
IDS	Integrated Defense Systems
IP	Intellectual property
IR&D	Independent research and development
IR&D/B&P Program	Independent research and development/bid and proposal programme
IRB	Industrial Revenue Bonds of the City of Wichita, State of Kansas
IRS	U.S. Internal Revenue Service
ITAR	International Traffic in Arms Regulations
ITR	International Trade Resources
KDFA	Kansas Development Finance Authority
KDFA bonds	Kansas Development Finance Authority bonds, the State of Kansas
KSA	Kansas Statutes Annotated
LCA	Large Civil Aircraft
LERD	Limited exclusive rights data
MSA	Project Olympus Master Site Agreement between the State of Washington and Boeing
McDonnell Douglas or MD	McDonnell Douglas Corporation
NAC	NASA Advisory Council

Abbreviation	Full Reference
NASA	The National Aeronautics and Space Administration
PE	Programme Element
QAT	NASA Quiet Aircraft Technology Program
R&D	Research and development
R&T Base	NASA Research and Technology Base Program
Relocation Act	Corporate Headquarters Relocation Act, State of Illinois
RDT&E	Research, Development, Testing, and Evaluation
SAA	Space Act Agreement
SCM Agreement	Agreement on Subsidies and Countervailing Measures
TIPRA	Tax Increase Prevention and Reconciliation Act of 2005
USDOC	United States Department of Commerce
Vienna Convention	Vienna Convention On The Law Of Treaties
VSP	NASA Vehicle Systems Program

TABLE OF CASES

Short Title	Full Case Title and Citation
Argentina – Footwear (EC)	Panel Report, *Argentina – Safeguard Measures on Imports of Footwear*, WT/DS121/R, adopted 12 January 2000, as modified by Appellate Body Report WT/DS121/AB/R, DSR 2000:II, 575
Australia – Automotive Leather II	Panel Report, *Australia – Subsidies Provided to Producers and Exporters of Automotive Leather*, WT/DS126/R, adopted 16 June 1999, DSR 1999:III, 951
Australia – Salmon (Article 21.5 – Canada)	Panel Report, *Australia – Measures Affecting Importation of Salmon – Recourse to Article 21.5 of the DSU by Canada*, WT/DS18/RW, adopted 20 March 2000, DSR 2000:IV, 2031
Brazil – Aircraft	Appellate Body Report, *Brazil – Export Financing Programme for Aircraft*, WT/DS46/AB/R, adopted 20 August 1999, DSR 1999:III, 1161
Brazil – Aircraft	Panel Report, *Brazil – Export Financing Programme for Aircraft*, WT/DS46/R, adopted 20 August 1999, as modified by Appellate Body Report WT/DS46/AB/R, DSR 1999:III, 1221
Brazil – Aircraft (Article 21.5 – Canada II)	Panel Report, *Brazil – Export Financing Programme for Aircraft – Second Recourse by Canada to Article 21.5 of the DSU*, WT/DS46/RW/2, adopted 23 August 2001, DSR 2001:X, 5481
Canada – Aircraft	Appellate Body Report, *Canada – Measures Affecting the Export of Civilian Aircraft*, WT/DS70/AB/R, adopted 20 August 1999, DSR 1999:III, 1377
Canada – Aircraft	Panel Report, *Canada – Measures Affecting the Export of Civilian Aircraft*, WT/DS70/R, adopted 20 August 1999, as upheld by Appellate Body Report WT/DS70/AB/R, DSR 1999:IV, 1443
Canada – Aircraft Credits and Guarantees	Panel Report, *Canada – Export Credits and Loan Guarantees for Regional Aircraft*, WT/DS222/R and Corr.1, adopted 19 February 2002, DSR 2002:III, 849

Report of the Panel

Short Title	Full Case Title and Citation
Canada – Aircraft Credits and Guarantees (Article 22.6 – Canada)	Decision by the Arbitrator, *Canada – Export Credits and Loan Guarantees for Regional Aircraft – Recourse to Arbitration by Canada under Article 22.6 of the DSU and Article 4.11 of the SCM Agreement*, WT/DS222/ARB, 17 February 2003, DSR 2003:III, 1187
Canada – Autos	Appellate Body Report, *Canada – Certain Measures Affecting the Automotive Industry*, WT/DS139/AB/R, WT/DS142/AB/R, adopted 19 June 2000, DSR 2000:VI, 2985
Canada – Autos	Panel Report, *Canada – Certain Measures Affecting the Automotive Industry*, WT/DS139/R, WT/DS142/R, adopted 19 June 2000, as modified by Appellate Body Report WT/DS139/AB/R, WT/DS142/AB/R, DSR 2000:VII, 3043
Canada – Wheat Exports and Grain Imports	Appellate Body Report, *Canada – Measures Relating to Exports of Wheat and Treatment of Imported Grain*, WT/DS276/AB/R, adopted 27 September 2004, DSR 2004:VI, 2739
Canada – Wheat Exports and Grain Imports	Panel Report, *Canada – Measures Relating to Exports of Wheat and Treatment of Imported Grain*, WT/DS276/R, adopted 27 September 2004, as upheld by Appellate Body Report WT/DS276/AB/R, DSR 2004:VI, 2817
Chile – Price Band System	Appellate Body Report, *Chile – Price Band System and Safeguard Measures Relating to Certain Agricultural Products*, WT/DS207/AB/R, adopted 23 October 2002, DSR 2002:VIII, 3045 (Corr.1, DSR 2006:XII, 5473)
China – Auto Parts	Appellate Body Reports, *China – Measures Affecting Imports of Automobile Parts*, WT/DS339/AB/R, WT/DS340/AB/R, WT/DS342/AB/R, adopted 12 January 2009
China – Publications and Audiovisual Products	Appellate Body Report, *China – Measures Affecting Trading Rights and Distribution Services for Certain Publications and Audiovisual Entertainment Products*, WT/DS363/AB/R, adopted 19 January 2010
Colombia – Ports of Entry	Panel Report, *Colombia – Indicative Prices and Restrictions on Ports of Entry*, WT/DS366/R and Corr.1, adopted 20 May 2009

1264

DSR 2012:III

Short Title	Full Case Title and Citation
EC – Approval and Marketing of Biotech Products	Panel Report, *European Communities – Measures Affecting the Approval and Marketing of Biotech Products*, WT/DS291/R, WT/DS292/R, WT/DS293/R, Add.1 to Add.9, and Corr.1, adopted 21 November 2006, DSR 2006:III-VIII, 847
EC – Bananas III	Appellate Body Report, *European Communities – Regime for the Importation, Sale and Distribution of Bananas*, WT/DS27/AB/R, adopted 25 September 1997, DSR 1997:II, 591
EC – Bananas III (Ecuador)	Panel Report, *European Communities – Regime for the Importation, Sale and Distribution of Bananas, Complaint by Ecuador*, WT/DS27/R/ECU, adopted 25 September 1997, as modified by Appellate Body Report WT/DS27/AB/R, DSR 1997:III, 1085
EC – Bananas III (Guatemala and Honduras)	Panel Report, *European Communities – Regime for the Importation, Sale and Distribution of Bananas, Complaint by Guatemala and Honduras*, WT/DS27/R/GTM, WT/DS27/R/HND, adopted 25 September 1997, as modified by Appellate Body Report WT/DS27/AB/R, DSR 1997:II, 695
EC – Bananas III (Mexico)	Panel Report, *European Communities – Regime for the Importation, Sale and Distribution of Bananas, Complaint by Mexico*, WT/DS27/R/MEX, adopted 25 September 1997, as modified by Appellate Body Report WT/DS27/AB/R, DSR 1997:II, 803
EC – Bananas III (US)	Panel Report, *European Communities – Regime for the Importation, Sale and Distribution of Bananas, Complaint by the United States*, WT/DS27/R/USA, adopted 25 September 1997, as modified by Appellate Body Report WT/DS27/AB/R, DSR 1997:II, 943
EC – Chicken Cuts	Appellate Body Report, *European Communities – Customs Classification of Frozen Boneless Chicken Cuts*, WT/DS269/AB/R, WT/DS286/AB/R, adopted 27 September 2005, and Corr.1, DSR 2005:XIX, 9157
EC – Commercial Vessels	Panel Report, *European Communities – Measures Affecting Trade in Commercial Vessels*, WT/DS301/R, adopted 20 June 2005, DSR 2005:XV, 7713

Report of the Panel

Short Title	Full Case Title and Citation
EC – Computer Equipment	Appellate Body Report, *European Communities – Customs Classification of Certain Computer Equipment*, WT/DS62/AB/R, WT/DS67/AB/R, WT/DS68/AB/R, adopted 22 June 1998, DSR 1998:V, 1851
EC – Countervailing Measures on DRAM Chips	Panel Report, *European Communities – Countervailing Measures on Dynamic Random Access Memory Chips from Korea*, WT/DS299/R, adopted 3 August 2005, DSR 2005:XVIII, 8671
EC – Export Subsidies on Sugar (Australia)	Panel Report, *European Communities – Export Subsidies on Sugar, Complaint by Australia*, WT/DS265/R, adopted 19 May 2005, as modified by Appellate Body Report WT/DS265/AB/R, WT/DS266/AB/R, WT/DS283/AB/R, DSR 2005:XIII, 6499
EC – Export Subsidies on Sugar (Brazil)	Panel Report, *European Communities – Export Subsidies on Sugar, Complaint by Brazil*, WT/DS266/R, adopted 19 May 2005, as modified by Appellate Body Report WT/DS265/AB/R, WT/DS266/AB/R, WT/DS283/AB/R, DSR 2005:XIV, 6793
EC – Export Subsidies on Sugar (Thailand)	Panel Report, *European Communities – Export Subsidies on Sugar, Complaint by Thailand*, WT/DS283/R, adopted 19 May 2005, as modified by Appellate Body Report WT/DS265/AB/R, WT/DS266/AB/R, WT/DS283/AB/R, DSR 2005:XIV, 7071
EC – Hormones	Appellate Body Report, *EC Measures Concerning Meat and Meat Products (Hormones)*, WT/DS26/AB/R, WT/DS48/AB/R, adopted 13 February 1998, DSR 1998:I, 135
EC – Hormones (Canada)	Panel Report, *EC Measures Concerning Meat and Meat Products (Hormones), Complaint by Canada*, WT/DS48/R/CAN, adopted 13 February 1998, as modified by Appellate Body Report WT/DS26/AB/R, WT/DS48/AB/R, DSR 1998:II, 235
EC – Poultry	Appellate Body Report, *European Communities – Measures Affecting the Importation of Certain Poultry Products*, WT/DS69/AB/R, adopted 23 July 1998, DSR 1998:V, 2031
EC – Selected Customs Matters	Appellate Body Report, *European Communities – Selected Customs Matters*, WT/DS315/AB/R, adopted 11 December 2006, DSR 2006:IX, 3791

Short Title	Full Case Title and Citation
EC – Selected Customs Matters	Panel Report, *European Communities – Selected Customs Matters*, WT/DS315/R, adopted 11 December 2006, as modified by Appellate Body Report WT/DS315/AB/R, DSR 2006:IX-X, 3915
EC – Tariff Preferences	Panel Report, *European Communities – Conditions for the Granting of Tariff Preferences to Developing Countries*, WT/DS246/R, adopted 20 April 2004, as modified by Appellate Body Report WT/DS/246/AB/R, DSR 2004:III, 1009
EC – Trademarks and Geographical Indications (US)	Panel Report, *European Communities – Protection of Trademarks and Geographical Indications for Agricultural Products and Foodstuffs, Complaint by the United States*, WT/DS174/R, adopted 20 April 2005, DSR 2005:VIII, 3499
EC and certain member States – Large Civil Aircraft	Panel Report, *European Communities and Certain Member States – Measures Affecting Trade in Large Civil Aircraft*, WT/DS316/R, circulated to WTO Members 30 June 2010 (appeal in progress)
Guatemala – Cement I	Appellate Body Report, *Guatemala – Anti-Dumping Investigation Regarding Portland Cement from Mexico*, WT/DS60/AB/R, adopted 25 November 1998, DSR 1998:IX, 3767
Guatemala – Cement I	Panel Report, *Guatemala – Anti-Dumping Investigation Regarding Portland Cement from Mexico*, WT/DS60/R, adopted 25 November 1998, as modified by Appellate Body Report WT/DS60/AB/R, DSR 1998:IX, 3797
Guatemala – Cement II	Panel Report, *Guatemala – Definitive Anti-Dumping Measures on Grey Portland Cement from Mexico*, WT/DS156/R, adopted 17 November 2000, DSR 2000:XI, 5295
India – Additional Import Duties	Panel Report, *India – Additional and Extra-Additional Duties on Imports from the United States*, WT/DS360/R, adopted 17 November 2008, reversed by Appellate Body Report WT/DS360/AB/R
India – Patents (US)	Appellate Body Report, *India – Patent Protection for Pharmaceutical and Agricultural Chemical Products*, WT/DS50/AB/R, adopted 16 January 1998, DSR 1998:I, 9

Report of the Panel

Short Title	Full Case Title and Citation
India – Patents (US)	Panel Report, *India – Patent Protection for Pharmaceutical and Agricultural Chemical Products, Complaint by the United States*, WT/DS50/R, adopted 16 January 1998, as modified by Appellate Body Report WT/DS50/AB/R, DSR 1998:I, 41
Indonesia – Autos	Panel Report, *Indonesia – Certain Measures Affecting the Automobile Industry*, WT/DS54/R, WT/DS55/R, WT/DS59/R, WT/DS64/R and Corr.1 and 2, adopted 23 July 1998, and Corr. 3 and 4, DSR 1998:VI, 2201
Japan – Alcoholic Beverages II	Appellate Body Report, *Japan – Taxes on Alcoholic Beverages*, WT/DS8/AB/R, WT/DS10/AB/R, WT/DS11/AB/R, adopted 1 November 1996, DSR 1996:I, 97
Japan – DRAMs (Korea)	Appellate Body Report, *Japan – Countervailing Duties on Dynamic Random Access Memories from Korea*, WT/DS336/AB/R and Corr.1, adopted 17 December 2007
Japan – DRAMs (Korea)	Panel Report, *Japan – Countervailing Duties on Dynamic Random Access Memories from Korea*, WT/DS336/R, adopted 17 December 2007, as modified by Appellate Body Report WT/DS336/AB/R
Korea – Commercial Vessels	Panel Report, *Korea – Measures Affecting Trade in Commercial Vessels*, WT/DS273/R, adopted 11 April 2005, DSR 2005:VII, 2749
Mexico – Corn Syrup (Article 21.5 – US)	Appellate Body Report, *Mexico – Anti-Dumping Investigation of High Fructose Corn Syrup (HFCS) from the United States – Recourse to Article 21.5 of the DSU by the United States*, WT/DS132/AB/RW, adopted 21 November 2001, DSR 2001:XIII, 6675
Mexico – Corn Syrup (Article 21.5 – US)	Panel Report, *Mexico – Anti-Dumping Investigation of High Fructose Corn Syrup (HFCS) from the United States – Recourse to Article 21.5 of the DSU by the United States*, WT/DS132/RW, adopted 21 November 2001, as upheld by Appellate Body Report WT/DS132/AB/RW, DSR 2001:XIII, 6717
Mexico – Olive Oil	Panel Report, *Mexico – Definitive Countervailing Measures on Olive Oil from the European Communities*, WT/DS341/R, adopted 21 October 2008, DSR 2008:IX, 3179

1268

DSR 2012:III

Short Title	Full Case Title and Citation
Mexico – Taxes on Soft Drinks	Appellate Body Report, *Mexico – Tax Measures on Soft Drinks and Other Beverages*, WT/DS308/AB/R, adopted 24 March 2006, DSR 2006:I, 3
US – 1916 Act	Appellate Body Report, *United States – Anti-Dumping Act of 1916*, WT/DS136/AB/R, WT/DS162/AB/R, adopted 26 September 2000, DSR 2000:X, 4793
US – 1916 Act (EC)	Panel Report, *United States – Anti-Dumping Act of 1916, Complaint by the European Communities*, WT/DS136/R and Corr.1, adopted 26 September 2000, as upheld by Appellate Body Report WT/DS136/AB/R, WT/DS162/AB/R, DSR 2000:X, 4593
US – 1916 Act (Japan)	Panel Report, *United States – Anti-Dumping Act of 1916, Complaint by Japan*, WT/DS162/R and Add.1, adopted 26 September 2000, as upheld by Appellate Body Report WT/DS136/AB/R, WT/DS162/AB/R, DSR 2000:X, 4831
US – Continued Zeroing	Appellate Body Report, *United States – Continued Existence and Application of Zeroing Methodology*, WT/DS350/AB/R, adopted 19 February 2009
US – Corrosion-Resistant Steel Sunset Review	Appellate Body Report, *United States – Sunset Review of Anti-Dumping Duties on Corrosion-Resistant Carbon Steel Flat Products from Japan*, WT/DS244/AB/R, adopted 9 January 2004, DSR 2004:I, 3
US – Countervailing Duty Investigation on DRAMS	Appellate Body Report, *United States – Countervailing Duty Investigation on Dynamic Random Access Memory Semiconductors (DRAMS) from Korea*, WT/DS296/AB/R, adopted 20 July 2005, DSR 2005:XVI, 8131
US – Countervailing Duty Investigation on DRAMS	Panel Report, *United States – Countervailing Duty Investigation on Dynamic Random Access Memory Semiconductors (DRAMS) from Korea*, WT/DS296/R, adopted 20 July 2005, as modified by Appellate Body Report WT/DS296/AB/R, DSR 2005:XVII, 8243
US – Countervailing Measures on Certain EC Products	Appellate Body Report, *United States – Countervailing Measures Concerning Certain Products from the European Communities*, WT/DS212/AB/R, adopted 8 January 2003, DSR 2003:I, 5

Report of the Panel

Short Title	Full Case Title and Citation
US – Countervailing Measures on Certain EC Products	Panel Report, *United States – Countervailing Measures Concerning Certain Products from the European Communities*, WT/DS212/R, adopted 8 January 2003, as modified by Appellate Body Report WT/DS212/AB/R, DSR 2003:I, 73
US – Countervailing Measures on Certain EC Products (Article 21.5 – EC)	Panel Report, *United States – Countervailing Measures Concerning Certain Products from the European Communities – Recourse to Article 21.5 of the DSU by the European Communities*, WT/DS212/RW, adopted 27 September 2005, DSR 2005:XVIII, 8950
US – Export Restraints	Panel Report, *United States – Measures Treating Exports Restraints as Subsidies*, WT/DS194/R and Corr.2, adopted 23 August 2001, DSR 2001:XI, 5767
US – FSC	Appellate Body Report, *United States – Tax Treatment for "Foreign Sales Corporations"*, WT/DS108/AB/R, adopted 20 March 2000, DSR 2000:III, 1619
US – FSC	Panel Report, *United States – Tax Treatment for "Foreign Sales Corporations"*, WT/DS108/R, adopted 20 March 2000, as modified by Appellate Body Report WT/DS108/AB/R, DSR 2000:IV, 1675
US – FSC (Article 21.5 – EC)	Appellate Body Report, *United States – Tax Treatment for "Foreign Sales Corporations" – Recourse to Article 21.5 of the DSU by the European Communities*, WT/DS108/AB/RW, adopted 29 January 2002, DSR 2002:I, 55
US – FSC (Article 21.5 – EC)	Panel Report, *United States – Tax Treatment for "Foreign Sales Corporations" – Recourse to Article 21.5 of the DSU by the European Communities*, WT/DS108/RW, adopted 29 January 2002, as modified by Appellate Body Report WT/DS108/AB/RW, DSR 2002:I, 119
US – FSC (Article 21.5 – EC II)	Appellate Body Report, *United States – Tax Treatment for "Foreign Sales Corporations" – Second Recourse to Article 21.5 of the DSU by the European Communities*, WT/DS108/AB/RW2, adopted 14 March 2006, DSR 2006:XI, 4721

1270

DSR 2012:III

Short Title	Full Case Title and Citation
US – FSC (Article 21.5 – EC II)	Panel Report, *United States – Tax Treatment for "Foreign Sales Corporations" – Second Recourse to Article 21.5 of the DSU by the European Communities*, WT/DS108/RW2, adopted 14 March 2006, as upheld by Appellate Body Report WT/DS108/AB/RW2, DSR 2006:XI, 4761
US – FSC (Article 22.6 – US)	Decision by the Arbitrator, *United States – Tax Treatment for "Foreign Sales Corporations" – Recourse to Arbitration by the United States under Article 22.6 of the DSU and Article 4.11 of the SCM Agreement*, WT/DS108/ARB, 30 August 2002, DSR 2002:VI, 2517
US – Gambling	Appellate Body Report, *United States – Measures Affecting the Cross-Border Supply of Gambling and Betting Services*, WT/DS285/AB/R, adopted 20 April 2005, DSR 2005:XII, 5663 (Corr.1, DSR 2006:XII, 5475)
US – Gasoline	Appellate Body Report, *United States – Standards for Reformulated and Conventional Gasoline*, WT/DS2/AB/R, adopted 20 May 1996, DSR 1996:I, 3
US – Hot-Rolled Steel	Appellate Body Report, *United States – Anti-Dumping Measures on Certain Hot-Rolled Steel Products from Japan*, WT/DS184/AB/R, adopted 23 August 2001, DSR 2001:X, 4697
US – Hot-Rolled Steel	Panel Report, *United States – Anti-Dumping Measures on Certain Hot-Rolled Steel Products from Japan*, WT/DS184/R, adopted 23 August 2001 modified by Appellate Body Report WT/DS184/AB/R, DSR 2001:X, 4769
US – Lead and Bismuth II	Appellate Body Report, *United States – Imposition of Countervailing Duties on Certain Hot-Rolled Lead and Bismuth Carbon Steel Products Originating in the United Kingdom*, WT/DS138/AB/R, adopted 7 June 2000, DSR 2000:V, 2595
US – Lead and Bismuth II	Panel Report, *United States – Imposition of Countervailing Duties on Certain Hot-Rolled Lead and Bismuth Carbon Steel Products Originating in the United Kingdom*, WT/DS138/R and Corr.2, adopted 7 June 2000, upheld by Appellate Body Report WT/DS138/AB/R, DSR 2000:VI, 2623

Report of the Panel

Short Title	Full Case Title and Citation
US – Offset Act (Byrd Amendment)	Appellate Body Report, *United States – Continued Dumping and Subsidy Offset Act of 2000*, WT/DS217/AB/R, WT/DS234/AB/R, adopted 27 January 2003, DSR 2003:I, 375
US – Offset Act (Byrd Amendment)	Panel Report, *United States – Continued Dumping and Subsidy Offset Act of 2000*, WT/DS217/R, WT/DS234/R, adopted 27 January 2003, as modified by Appellate Body Report WT/DS217/AB/R, WT/DS234/AB/R, DSR 2003:II, 489
US – Shrimp	Appellate Body Report, *United States – Import Prohibition of Certain Shrimp and Shrimp Products*, WT/DS58/AB/R, adopted 6 November 1998, DSR 1998:VII, 2755
US – Shrimp (Article 21.5 – Malaysia)	Panel Report, *United States – Import Prohibition of Certain Shrimp and Shrimp Products – Recourse to Article 21.5 of the DSU by Malaysia*, WT/DS58/RW, adopted 21 November 2001, upheld by Appellate Body Report WT/DS58/AB/RW, DSR 2001:XIII, 6529
US – Softwood Lumber III	Panel Report, *United States – Preliminary Determinations with Respect to Certain Softwood Lumber from Canada*, WT/DS236/R, adopted 1 November 2002, DSR 2002:IX, 3597
US – Softwood Lumber IV	Appellate Body Report, *United States – Final Countervailing Duty Determination with Respect to Certain Softwood Lumber from Canada*, WT/DS257/AB/R, adopted 17 February 2004, DSR 2004:II, 571
US – Softwood Lumber IV	Panel Report, *United States – Final Countervailing Duty Determination with Respect to Certain Softwood Lumber from Canada*, WT/DS257/R and Corr.1, adopted 17 February 2004, as modified by Appellate Body Report WT/DS257/AB/R, DSR 2004:II, 641
US – Softwood Lumber IV (Article 21.5 – Canada)	Panel Report, *United States – Final Countervailing Duty Determination with Respect to Certain Softwood Lumber from Canada – Recourse by Canada to Article 21.5 (of the DSU)*, WT/DS257/RW, adopted 20 December 2005, upheld by Appellate Body Report WT/DS257/AB/RW, DSR 2005:XXIII, 11401

Short Title	Full Case Title and Citation
US – Underwear	Appellate Body Report, *United States – Restrictions on Imports of Cotton and Man-made Fibre Underwear*, WT/DS24/AB/R, adopted 25 February 1997, DSR 1997:I, 11
US – Upland Cotton	Appellate Body Report, *United States – Subsidies on Upland Cotton*, WT/DS267/AB/R, adopted 21 March 2005, DSR 2005:I, 3
US – Upland Cotton	Panel Report, *United States – Subsidies on Upland Cotton*, WT/DS267/R, Corr.1, and Add.1 to Add.3, adopted 21 March 2005, as modified by Appellate Body Report WT/DS267/AB/R, DSR 2005:II, 299
US – Upland Cotton (Article 21.5 – Brazil)	Appellate Body Report, *United States – Subsidies on Upland Cotton – Recourse to Article 21.5 of the DSU by Brazil*, WT/DS267/AB/RW, adopted 20 June 2008
US – Upland Cotton (Article 21.5 – Brazil)	Panel Report, *United States – Subsidies on Upland Cotton – Recourse to Article 21.5 of the DSU by Brazil*, WT/DS267/RW and Corr.1, adopted 20 June 2008, as modified by Appellate Body Report WT/DS267/AB/RW
US – Upland Cotton (Article 22.6 – US I)	Decision by the Arbitrator, *United States – Subsidies on Upland Cotton – Recourse to Arbitration by the United States under Article 22.6 of the DSU and Article 4.11 of the SCM Agreement*, WT/DS267/ARB/1, 31 August 2009
US – Wheat Gluten	Appellate Body Report, *United States – Definitive Safeguard Measures on Imports of Wheat Gluten from the European Communities*, WT/DS166/AB/R, adopted 19 January 2001, DSR 2001:II, 717
US – Wheat Gluten	Panel Report, *United States – Definitive Safeguard Measures on Imports of Wheat Gluten from the European Communities*, WT/DS166/R, adopted 19 January 2001, as modified by Appellate Body Report WT/DS166/AB/R, DSR 2001:III, 779
US – Wool Shirts and Blouses	Appellate Body Report, *United States – Measure Affecting Imports of Woven Wool Shirts and Blouses from India*, WT/DS33/AB/R, adopted 23 May 1997, and Corr.1, DSR 1997:I, 323

Report of the Panel

Short Title	Full Case Title and Citation
US – Wool Shirts and Blouses	Panel Report, *United States – Measure Affecting Imports of Woven Wool Shirts and Blouses from India*, WT/DS33/R, adopted 23 May 1997, as upheld by Appellate Body Report WT/DS33/AB/R, DSR 1997:I, 343
US – Zeroing (Japan) (Article 21.5 – Japan)	Appellate Body Report, *United States – Measures Relating to Zeroing and Sunset Reviews – Recourse to Article 21.5 of the DSU by Japan*, WT/DS322/AB/RW, adopted 31 August 2009
US – Zeroing (Japan) (Article 21.5 – Japan)	Panel Report, *United States – Measures Relating to Zeroing and Sunset Reviews – Recourse to Article 21.5 of the DSU by Japan*, WT/DS322/RW, adopted 31 August 2009, upheld by Appellate Body Report WT/DS322/AB/RW

4. State of Illinois and municipalities therein

(a) Introduction

7.891 The European Communities argues that each of the four measures at issue is a subsidy within the meaning of Article 1 of the SCM Agreement, and is specific within the meaning of Article 2 of the SCM Agreement. The European Communities estimates that the total amount of the four subsidies to Boeing's LCA division is approximately $25 million over the period 2002-2021.

7.892 The United States accepts that these measures are subsidies within the meaning of Article 1 of the SCM Agreement, but argues that three of the four subsidies are not specific within the meaning of Article 2 of the SCM Agreement. In addition, the United States asserts that any amounts that Boeing receives after 2006 are "speculative" and fall outside of the Panel's terms of reference, and asserts that the total value of the four subsidies to Boeing's LCA division is [***] million over the period 2002-2006.

(b) The measures at issue

7.893 The European Communities' claim concerns four separate incentives that the State of Illinois and municipalities therein (i.e. Cook County and the City of Chicago[2306]) provided to Boeing in consideration for Boeing's decision to relocate its corporate headquarters from Seattle to Chicago in 2001. The first three incentives are derived from the *Corporate Headquarters Relocation Act*[2307] ("CHRA"). The CHRA was signed into law on 1 August 2001, approximately one month before Boeing relocated its headquarters to Chicago. The CHRA authorized the granting of certain incentives to an "eligible business" undertaking a "qualifying project". The CHRA incentives included the following:

(a)   the reimbursement of up to 50 per cent of the relocation expenses incurred by an "eligible business"[2308];

(b)   the granting of 15-year Economic Development for a Growing Economy ("EDGE") tax credits to an "eligible business", instead of the normal 10-year tax credit available under the EDGE Tax Credit Act[2309]; and

---

[2306] The City of Chicago is located within Cook County.
[2307] Corporate Headquarters Relocation Act, 2001 Ill. Pub. Act 92-0207, Exhibit EC-216.
[2308] 20 ILCS § 611/20, Exhibit EC-223.
[2309] 35 ILCS § 10/5-45(b), Exhibit EC-224.

Report of the Panel

(c)   the abatement or refund of a portion of property taxes of an "eligible business" for up to 20 years.[2310]

7.894 Under the CHRA, an "eligible business" is defined as a business that:

(a)   is engaged in interstate or intrastate commerce;

(b)   maintains its corporate headquarters in a state other than Illinois as of 1 August 2001;

(c)   had annual worldwide revenues of at least $25 billion for the year immediately preceding its application for the benefits authorized by the CHRA; and

(d)   is prepared to commit contractually to relocating its corporate headquarters to the State of Illinois in consideration of the benefits authorized by this Act.[2311]

7.895 The CHRA defines a "qualifying project" to mean:

"... the relocation of the corporate headquarters of an eligible business from a location outside of Illinois to a location within Illinois, whether to an existing structure or otherwise. When the relocation involves an initial interim facility within Illinois and a subsequent further relocation within 5 years after the effective date of this Act to a permanent facility also within Illinois, all those activities collectively constitute a 'qualifying project' under this Act."[2312]

7.896 To qualify as an "eligible business" with a "qualifying project", a company must meet all of these requirements. In addition, the CHRA provides that in order to obtain the reimbursement for relocation costs, an "eligible business" had to propose a "qualifying project" by 1 July 2004.[2313] The CHRA likewise provides that, to receive a 15-year EDGE tax credit, an "eligible business" had to propose a "qualifying project" no later than 1 July 2004.[2314] The CHRA granted both the City of Chicago and Cook County, as taxing districts, the authority to abate or refund certain property taxes, so long as such property tax abatements/refunds were approved by 1 August 2006.[2315]

7.897 The CHRA indicates that its purpose is to encourage the relocation of the international headquarters of large, multinational corporations to a location

---

[2310] 35 ILCS § 200/18-165(a)(8), Exhibit EC-225.
[2311] 20 ILL. COMP. STAT. § 611/10, Exhibit EC-226.
[2312] *Ibid.*
[2313] 20 ILCS § 611/20(a), Exhibit EC-223.
[2314] 35 ILCS § 10/5-45(b), Exhibit EC-224; 20 ILCS § 611/20(a), Exhibit EC-223.
[2315] See 35 ILCS § 200/18-165(a)(8), Exhibit EC-225.

1276   DSR 2012:III

US - Large Civil Aircraft (2nd Complaint)

within Illinois "through the use of incentives ... that would otherwise not be available through existing incentives programs".[2316]

7.898 Boeing has made use of all of these incentives provided under the CHRA.

7.899 First, Boeing and the State of Illinois entered into a "Corporate Headquarters Relocation Act Master Agreement" in March 2002, under which the State of Illinois agreed to reimburse Boeing for a portion of its relocation expenses.[2317] The reimbursement for corporate relocation costs is provided through one or more grants issued annually for (i) a period of up to 10 years or (ii) until 50 per cent of the expenses of an "eligible business" have been reimbursed, whichever comes first.[2318] The amount of the annual grant, however, cannot exceed 50 per cent of the total amount of income taxes withheld by an "eligible business" during the preceding calendar year from its employees at the headquarters.[2319] These reimbursements are issued from the Corporate Headquarters Relocation Assistance Fund. This Fund is generated from the personal income taxes paid by the employees of an "eligible business". In particular, 50 per cent of the aggregate amount of income taxes withheld from the employees of an "eligible business" at the corporate headquarters during the preceding calendar year is transferred to the Fund.[2320]

7.900 Second, Boeing and the State of Illinois entered into an EDGE tax agreement on 27 March 2002.[2321] The tax credit that Boeing received lowered the company's state income tax liability by the amount of the credit. Pursuant to the EDGE Agreement, the EDGE credit is equal to 60 per cent of the state payroll taxes of Boeing's employees.[2322]

7.901 Third, Boeing applied for and received the property tax abatements provided for in the CHRA. These tax abatements entered into force upon the City and County passing two separate ordinances[2323], and completing two associated agreements with Boeing.[2324] Pursuant to the tax reimbursement agreement between the City of Chicago and Boeing, and the accompanying

---

[2316] Corporate Headquarters Relocation Act, 2001 Ill. Pub. Act 92-0207, Exhibit EC-216.

[2317] See Corporate Headquarters Relocation Act Master Agreement between The Illinois Department of Commerce and Community Affairs and The Boeing Company, 27 March 2002, Exhibit EC-228.

[2318] 20 ILCS § 611/20(b)(6), Exhibit EC-223.

[2319] 20 ILCS § 611/20(b)(7), Exhibit EC-223.

[2320] 20 ILCS § 611/30, Exhibit EC-232.

[2321] EDGE Tax Credit Agreement between the State of Illinois and The Boeing Company, 27 March 2002, Exhibit EC-237.

[2322] EDGE Tax Credit Agreement between the State of Illinois and The Boeing Company, 27 March 2002, Exhibit EC-237, p. 5, § 2.B.

[2323] An Ordinance of the City of Chicago, Illinois Approving Execution of a Tax Reimbursement Payment Agreement with the Boeing Company, Exhibit EC-244; An Ordinance of the County of Cook, Illinois Approving Execution of a Tax Reimbursement Payment Agreement with the Boeing Company, Exhibit EC-245.

[2324] Tax Reimbursement Payment Agreement between the County of Cook and The Boeing Company, 1 November 2001, Exhibit EC-246; Tax Reimbursement Payment Agreement by and between the City of Chicago and The Boeing Company, 1 November 2001, Exhibit EC-247.

DSR 2012:III

Report of the Panel

approval ordinance passed by the City Council, the City of Chicago has been providing Boeing with the abatement of property taxes since 2002.[2325] In particular, the City of Chicago committed to provide Boeing, on an annual basis from 2002 through 2021 (or until the Boeing lease expires, whichever comes first)[2326], reimbursements for the applicable shares of the Boeing General Real Estate Taxes[2327] paid to the City of Chicago, the School Finance Authority, the Board of Education, and the City's Library Fund.[2328] Pursuant to the tax reimbursement agreement between Cook County and Boeing, and the accompanying approval ordinance passed by Cook County's Board of Commissioners, Cook County has also provided Boeing with property tax refunds since 2002.[2329] In particular, Cook County committed to reimburse Boeing for the Boeing General Real Estate Taxes paid to the County and the Forest Preserve District on its corporate headquarters building for 20 years – that is, from 2002 until 2021, or until the last year of the Boeing lease, whichever comes first.[2330]

7.902 In addition to the three incentives provided under the CHRA, the City of Chicago also agreed to pay $1 million to retire the lease of the previous tenant of Boeing's new headquarters building. Chicago made the payment in order to enable Boeing to move into its office space by September 2001. Immediately after the City agreed to the $1 million payment, on 10 May 2001, the Landlord and Boeing executed a 15-year lease agreement (the "Boeing Lease").[2331] The City made the actual payment on 15 January 2003 pursuant to the Lease Termination Compensation Agreement between 100 North Riverside, LLC, and the City of Chicago. This Agreement notes that the City made the payment in order to "induce the Landlord to consent to the termination of Morton's {the previous tenant's} long-term, above market lease".[2332] This served to "make floors 25-28 available to Boeing and finalize the Boeing relocation".[2333]

[2325] Tax Reimbursement Payment Agreement by and between the City of Chicago and The Boeing Company, 1 November 2001, Exhibit EC-247, pp. 2-3.

[2326] Tax Reimbursement Payment Agreement by and between the City of Chicago and The Boeing Company, 1 November 2001, Exhibit EC-247, pp. 5-6.

[2327] Boeing General Real Estate Taxes are defined as the general *ad valorem* real estate taxes Boeing is obligated to pay with respect to the two private tax parcels applicable to Boeing's Property and Building in Chicago. Tax Reimbursement Payment Agreement by and between the City of Chicago and The Boeing Company, 1 November 2001, Exhibit EC-247, p. 4.

[2328] Tax Reimbursement Payment Agreement by and between the City of Chicago and The Boeing Company, 1 November 2001, Exhibit EC-247, p. 2-3.

[2329] See Tax Reimbursement Payment Agreement between the County of Cook and The Boeing Company, 1 November 2001, Exhibit EC-246.

[2330] Tax Reimbursement Payment Agreement between the County of Cook and The Boeing Company, 1 November 2001, Exhibit EC-246, pp. 8-9, § 4.2.

[2331] Lease Termination Compensation Agreement between 100 North Riverside, LLC and the City of Chicago, 15 January 2003, Exhibit EC-217, p. 2.

[2332] *Ibid.*

[2333] Lease Termination Compensation Agreement between 100 North Riverside, LLC and the City of Chicago, 15 January 2003, Exhibit EC-217, p. 2.

1278   DSR 2012:III

US - Large Civil Aircraft (2nd Complaint)

(c) Whether a subsidy exists within the meaning of Article 1 of the SCM Agreement

(i) Arguments of the European Communities

7.903 The European Communities provides a separate financial contribution analysis for each of these four measures. First, the European Communities argues that the reimbursements to Boeing for its relocation expenses constitute a direct transfers of funds within the meaning of Article 1.1(a)(1)(i) of the SCM Agreement.[2334] Alternatively, the European Communities argues that "by using income tax withholdings to finance the grant, the State of Illinois is also foregoing tax revenue that would otherwise be available to it within the meaning of Article 1.1(a)(1)(ii)".[2335] Second, the European Communities argues that through the 15-year EDGE tax credits, the State of Illinois is required to forego tax revenue that it otherwise would have collected from Boeing, as Boeing's tax liability is reduced by the amount of the credit. According to the European Communities, such government revenue foregone or not collected constitutes a financial contribution within the meaning of Article 1.1(a)(1)(ii).[2336] Third, the European Communities argues that the combined contributions of the City of Chicago and Cook County pursuant to the tax reimbursement agreements and ordinances can be considered either as a direct transfer of funds within the meaning of Article 1.1(a)(1)(i), or as the foregoing of government revenue that is otherwise due pursuant to Article 1.1(a)(1)(ii).[2337] Fourth, the European Communities argues that the lease retirement payment from the City of Chicago to Boeing's landlord constitutes a direct transfer of funds within the meaning of Article 1.1(a)(1)(i).[2338]

7.904 The European Communities also provides a separate benefit analysis for each of these four measures. However, the arguments that it advances for each of the four measures are very similar. With respect to the existence of a benefit within the meaning of Article 1.1(b) of the SCM Agreement, the European Communities argues in respect of each of the four measures that: (i) the financial contributions provide Boeing's LCA division with "advantages on non-market terms"[2339]; (ii) Boeing "is not required to pay anything in return" for these financial contributions[2340]; (iii) advantages conferred on Boeing's LCA division by these financial contributions "result in a reduction in Boeing's overhead costs"[2341]; (iv) these types of financial contributions are not available on the market because by definition they can be granted "only by a government"[2342];

[2334] European Communities' first written submission, para. 381.
[2335] European Communities' first written submission, para. 382.
[2336] European Communities' first written submission, para. 402.
[2337] European Communities' first written submission, para. 427.
[2338] European Communities' first written submission, para. 448.
[2339] European Communities' first written submission, paras. 386, 407, 432 and 451.
[2340] European Communities' first written submission, paras. 387, 408, 433 and 452.
[2341] European Communities' first written submission, paras. 388, 409, 434 and 453.
[2342] *Ibid.*

DSR 2012:III
1279

Report of the Panel

and (v) a portion of these reimbursements "relate to Boeing's production of commercial aircraft".[2343]

7.905 In its second written submission, the European Communities notes that the United States does not dispute that each of the four measures constitutes a financial contribution within the meaning of Article 1.1(a)(1)(i) or (ii) of the SCM Agreement[2344], and that the United States does not dispute that each of the financial contributions confers a benefit within the meaning of Article 1.1(b) of the SCM Agreement.[2345]

(ii)   Arguments of the United States

7.906 In its first written submission, the United States argues, under the sub-heading "Financial Contribution/Benefit", that the European Communities has overestimated the value of the subsidies provided to Boeing.[2346] However, the United States does not dispute that each of the four measures provides a financial contribution within the meaning of Article 1.1(a)(1) of the SCM Agreement, and the United States does not dispute that each of these four financial contributions confers a benefit within the meaning of Article 1.1(b) of the SCM Agreement. Furthermore, in its responses to questions 13[2347], 14[2348], and 368[2349] from the Panel, the United States agrees that each of the four measures challenged by the European Communities is a subsidy within the meaning of Article 1 of the SCM Agreement.

[2343] European Communities' first written submission, paras. 389, 410, 435 and 454.

[2344] European Communities' second written submission, paras. 272, 286, 297, and 308.

[2345] European Communities' second written submission, paras. 277, 290, 302, and 309.

[2346] United States' first written submission, paras. 662-663 (concerning the amount of the relocation expenses reimbursed to Boeing), 669 (concerning the amount of the EDGE tax credit claimed by Boeing), and 679 (concerning the amount of the property tax abatements claimed by Boeing). The United States does not dispute the European Communities' estimate of the amount of the subsidy to Boeing's LCA Division arising from the lease termination payment. United States' first written submission, para. 682.

[2347] United States' response to question 13, para. 29 ("The retirement of the lease by the City of Chicago is a subsidy that is specific within the meaning of Articles 1 and 2 of the SCM Agreement.")

[2348] United States' response to question 14, paras. 34-35 ("The reimbursement of certain relocation expenses by the State of Illinois pursuant to the Corporate Headquarters Relocation Act ("CHRA") constitutes a subsidy under Article 1 of the SCM Agreement. ... The property tax abatement provided by the City of Chicago to Boeing can be considered a subsidy within the meaning of Article 1 of the SCM Agreement ...").

[2349] In its response to question 368, the United States confirmed that with respect to the reimbursement of corporate relocation expenses, the EDGE tax credit, and the property tax abatements, the arguments in the United States' first written submission regarding the "speculative nature" of these tax credits, abatements, and reimbursements are aimed at challenging the European Communities' "quantification" of the alleged subsidies, rather than the "existence of the alleged subsidies under Article 1.1".

1280   DSR 2012:III

(iii)   Evaluation by the Panel

7.907 In this case, the European Communities provides evidence and legal argument as to why each of the four challenged measures constitutes a financial contribution within the meaning of Article 1.1(a)(1) of the SCM Agreement, and why each financial contribution confers a benefit within the meaning of Article 1.1(b) of the SCM Agreement. The United States does not contest that each of the four challenged measures constitutes a subsidy within the meaning of Article 1. Having reviewed the evidence presented by the European Communities, the Panel sees nothing that would support a different conclusion.

7.908 Accordingly, the Panel finds that each of the four challenged measures constitutes a subsidy within the meaning of Article 1 of the SCM Agreement.

(d)   Whether the subsidy is specific within the meaning of Article 2 of the SCM Agreement

(i)   Arguments of the European Communities

7.909 The European Communities argues that each of the four subsidies is specific within the meaning of Article 2 of the SCM Agreement.

7.910 With respect to the three subsidies provided to Boeing under the CHRA, the European Communities asserts that: (i) Boeing is the only company that has met the definition of an "eligible business" under the CHRA, and therefore Boeing is the only company that has ever received these subsidies[2350]; (ii) as a result of the expiry of the statutory time limits for applying for these subsidies, no company other than Boeing will ever receive these subsidies[2351]; and (iii) numerous government publications, statements by members of the Illinois General Assembly, press reports, and other sources demonstrate that the CHRA was tailored specifically for Boeing.[2352] The European Communities therefore argues that the CHRA subsidies, i.e. (i) the reimbursement of relocation expenses (ii) the 15-year EDGE tax credits and (iii) the abatement or refund of property taxes, are all de facto specific within the meaning of Article 2.1(c) of the SCM Agreement.[2353] In addition, the European Communities argues that the property tax abatements are specific within the meaning of Article 2.1(a) of the SCM Agreement because "the two ordinances at issue here are specific only to Boeing, as are the tax agreements that Boeing entered into with the City and County".[2354]

7.911 The European Communities argues that the lease retirement grant is *de jure* specific within the meaning of Article 2.1(a) of the SCM Agreement, because the Lease Termination Agreement, by its terms, applies only to Boeing.

[2350] European Communities' first written submission, paras. 390-391, 411, 415 and 441.
[2351] European Communities' first written submission, paras. 391, 412 and 443.
[2352] European Communities' first written submission, paras. 392-395, 412-414 and 442-443.
[2353] European Communities' first written submission, paras. 390, 411 and 442.
[2354] European Communities' first written submission, para. 436.

Report of the Panel

The European Communities notes that this payment was purely a one-time grant from the City of Chicago.[2355] In the alternative, the European Communities argues that the subsidy is nonetheless de facto specific under Article 2.1(c) of the SCM Agreement, because it benefits only one company, i.e. Boeing.[2356]

(ii) Arguments of the United States

7.912 The United States argues that the three subsidies provided to Boeing under the CHRA are not specific within the meaning of Article 2 of the SCM Agreement.

7.913 First, the United States argues that the relocation expense reimbursements are not specific because: (i) the CHRA is not *de jure* specific under Article 2.1(a) of the SCM Agreement because "it is not explicitly limited to Boeing or similar enterprises"; (ii) the CHRA is non-specific under Article 2.1(b) of the SCM Agreement because it "contains objective criteria governing the eligibility for and the amount of costs that may be reimbursed"; and (iii) although Boeing was the only company that ever received relocation expense reimbursements pursuant to the CHRA, this does not indicate de facto specificity under Article 2.1(c) of the SCM Agreement because of "the size of the neutrally defined benefit group and the short length of time for this program".[2357]

7.914 Second, the United States argues that the 15-year EDGE tax credits provided to Boeing pursuant to CHRA are not specific because: (i) the EDGE Tax Credit Act "is not explicitly limited to certain enterprises under Article 2.1(a)"; (ii) the EDGE Tax Credit Act "contains objective criteria that govern the eligibility for, and the amounts of, the tax credits" under Article 2.1(b); (iii) EDGE tax credits are "broadly available to a variety of companies in Illinois that meet the {EDGE Tax Credit} Act's requirements" and therefore are not de facto specific under Article 2.1(c); and (iv) only during the five-year extension provided by the Relocation Act is there an EDGE tax credit that is unavailable to non-CHRA companies, but since this is in the future, it is irrelevant to this dispute.[2358]

7.915 Third, the United States argues that the property tax abatements are not specific "because Illinois law permits any taxing district in the State to abate the property taxes of numerous types of enterprises".[2359]

7.916 The United States does not dispute that the lease retirement payment is specific within the meaning of Article 2.[2360]

[2355] European Communities' first written submission, para. 455.

[2356] European Communities' first written submission, para. 456.

[2357] United States' first written submission, para. 664.

[2358] United States' first written submission, paras. 670-672.

[2359] United States' first written submission, para. 680.

[2360] United States' first written submission, para. 683; United States' response to question 13, para. 29 ("The retirement of the lease by the City of Chicago is a subsidy that is specific within the meaning of Articles 1 and 2 of the SCM Agreement.")

(iii) Evaluation by the Panel

7.917 The parties agree that one of the four subsidies, i.e. the lease retirement payment, is specific within the meaning of Article 2.[2361] The main point of disagreement is whether the three subsidies provided to Boeing pursuant to the CHRA are de facto specific within the meaning of Article 2.1(c) of the SCM Agreement. In the Panel's view, the three subsidies provided to Boeing under the CHRA are clearly de facto specific within the meaning of Article 2.1(c) of the SCM Agreement.

7.918 First, Boeing is the only company that has met the statutory definition of an "eligible business" with a "qualifying project", and it is not in dispute that Boeing is the only company that has ever received these subsidies.[2362] The fact that Boeing was the only company that ever received these subsidies is perhaps not surprising, given the European Communities' unrebutted assertions that only a limited group of U.S. companies (less than 75) located outside of Illinois had revenues of over $25 billion in 2002, and that none of those had announced plans to move to Illinois in the pertinent timeframe.[2363]

7.919 Second, as a result of the expiry of the statutory time limits for applying for these subsidies, no company other than Boeing will ever receive these subsidies.[2364] As we have explained above, the CHRA provides that in order to obtain the reimbursement for relocation costs, an "eligible business" had to propose a "qualifying project" by 1 July 2004. The CHRA likewise provides that, to receive a 15-year EDGE tax credit, an "eligible business" had to propose a "qualifying project" no later than 1 July 2004. The CHRA granted both the City of Chicago and the County of Cook, as taxing districts, the authority to abate or refund certain property taxes, so long as such property tax abatements/refunds were approved by 1 August 2006.

7.920 Third, the fact that Boeing is the only company that has ever received and the only company that will ever receive these subsidies is no coincidence, given the numerous government publications, statements by members of the Illinois General Assembly, press reports, and other sources that demonstrate that the CHRA was tailored specifically for Boeing.[2365] Among other things, an Illinois Department of Commerce and Community Affairs publication explains that the CHRA "was endorsed in concept by the four legislative leaders during

---

[2361] United States' first written submission, para. 683; United States' response to question 13, para. 29 ("The retirement of the lease by the City of Chicago is a subsidy that is specific within the meaning of Articles 1 and 2 of the SCM Agreement.")

[2362] European Communities' first written submission, paras. 390-391, 411, 415, 441.

[2363] European Communities' first written submission, footnote 607 (citing The 500 Largest U.S. Corporations, Fortune, 15 April 2002, Exhibit EC-230, F-1).

[2364] European Communities' first written submission, paras. 391, 412, 443.

[2365] European Communities' first written submission, paras. 392-395, 412-414, 442-443.

Report of the Panel

negotiations with the Boeing Company in April {2001}".[2366] An Illinois Economic and Fiscal Commission publication explains that "{i}n addition to financial and tax incentives, some states have used customized, company-specific incentives to engage in bidding wars which other states, such as Illinois did in obtaining Boeing's headquarters".[2367] Legislators referred to the CHRA as the "Boeing package"[2368], or otherwise made clear that they understood that the law was being created specifically for Boeing.[2369] A press report issued by the Illinois Government upon Boeing's announcement that it would move its headquarters to Chicago indicates that "the Governor said the General Assembly would be asked to make minor modifications to existing incentive programs to meet Boeing's specific needs. Legislation would be introduced this session".[2370]

7.921 The United States does not dispute any of those facts. Rather, it argues that notwithstanding these facts, the European Communities has failed to demonstrate that the subsidies are specific. The Panel considers the United States' arguments to be unpersuasive.

7.922 The United States argues that the definition of "eligible business" and "qualifying project" is not *de jure* specific under Article 2.1(a) of the SCM Agreement because "it is not explicitly limited to Boeing or similar enterprises", and is non-specific under Article 2.1(b) of the SCM Agreement because it "contains objective criteria governing the eligibility for and the amount of costs that may be reimbursed". In the Panel's view, even if these arguments were correct, they are not relevant given the fact that the European Communities argues that the subsidies are de facto specific under Article 2.1(c) of the SCM Agreement. Article 2.1(c) provides that a subsidy may be de facto specific "notwithstanding" any "appearance" of non-specificity under sub-paragraphs (a) and (b). The use of the term "notwithstanding" indicates that if such an analysis leads to a finding of de facto specificity, any appearance of non-specificity under

---

[2366] Memo to Honorable Members of the General Assembly from Pam McDonough, Director, Department of Commerce and Community Affairs, regarding the Corporate Headquarters Relocation Act, 23 May 2001.

[2367] Illinois Economic and Fiscal Commission, Corporate Incentives in the State of Illinois, August 2001, Exhibit EC-221, p. 20.

[2368] See e.g. State of Illinois, 92nd General Assembly, House of Representatives, Transcription Debate, 69th Legislative Day, 31 May 2001, Exhibit EC-234, p. 105.

[2369] See e.g. State of Illinois, 92nd General Assembly, House of Representatives, Transcription Debate, 69th Legislative Day, 31 May 2001, Exhibit EC-234, p. 103 (Floor Statement of Representative Franks) ("I think it's important that the state does provide incentives for Boeing."), p. 98 (Floor Statement of Representative Wojcik) ("I compliment the Governor and I compliment DCCA for their fine efforts in recruiting Boeing to Illinois."), p. 97 (Floor Statement of Representative Mulligan) ("What we need to do is to continue to work to have companies like Boeing move here."), p. 95 (Floor Statement of Representative Fritchey) ("I have a lot of respect for the people involved in the negotiation of the Boeing package, people from the city, people from the state, people from DCCA, the Legislators involved.").

[2370] Press Release from the Office of Illinois Governor George Ryan, "Governor Ryan, Mayor Daley Welcome Boeing's Global Headquarters to Chicago", 10 May 2001, Exhibit EC-215.

US - Large Civil Aircraft (2nd Complaint)

sub-paragraphs (a) and (b) can be disregarded. Therefore, if a subsidy is de facto specific under Article 2.1(c), this is dispositive of the matter.

7.923 The United States argues that although Boeing was the only company that ever received the CHRA subsidies, this does not indicate de facto specificity under Article 2.1(c) of the SCM Agreement because of "the short length of time for this program".[2371] The Panel agrees that Article 2.1(c) mandates that in considering de facto specificity, a Panel must take into account "the length of time during which the subsidy programme has been in operation". We have taken this consideration into account. However, rather than calling into question the conclusion that the subsidies are de facto specific to Boeing, the 2001-2006 statutory "window" for applying for CHRA subsidies simply reinforces that the CHRA subsidies were designed specifically for Boeing.

7.924 The United States argues that only during the five-year extension provided by the CHRA is there an EDGE tax credit that is unavailable to non-CHRA companies, i.e. to companies other than an "eligible business" under the CHRA.[2372] In other words, the Panel understands the United States to argue that for the first 10 years of the EDGE tax credit, the subsidy is not specific, and that it is only for the last five years of the 15-year EDGE tax credit that there would be a specific subsidy. Leaving aside the question of whether the 15-year EDGE tax credits granted to Boeing under the CHRA can be split into a 10-year subsidy and five-year subsidy for the purposes of Article 2 of the SCM Agreement, the United States' argument rests on a false premise, namely, that "for the first ten years, benefits to Boeing are the same as to any other recipient of the EDGE tax credits".[2373] First, the CHRA provides that when an "eligible business" makes use of the 15-year EDGE tax credit, it "applies against its State income tax liability, during the entire 15-year period, *no more than 60%* of the maximum credit per year that would otherwise be available under this Act".[2374] Thus, the *amount* of the EDGE tax credit that an "eligible business" receives is also different. Second, while the EDGE Tax Credit Act provides that the credit may generally not be claimed "with respect to any jobs that the taxpayer relocates from one site in Illinois to another site in Illinois", the CHRA provides that "any-full time employee of an eligible business relocated to Illinois in connection with that of a qualifying project *is deemed to be a new employee* for purposes of this Act".[2375] Thus, the *kinds* of tax credits that an "eligible business" may claim under the EDGE tax credit are different. In sum, it is clear that for "the first ten years", benefits to Boeing are *not* the same as to any other

---

[2371] United States' first written submission, para. 664.

[2372] United States' first written submission, paras. 670-672.

[2373] United States' response to question 261, para. 454.

[2374] 35 ILCS § 10/5-45(b), Exhibit EC-224 (emphasis added). See also, Illinois Economic and Fiscal Commission, Corporate Incentives in the State of Illinois, August 2001, Exhibit EC-221, p. 19 (explaining that "{u}nder the original deal with Boeing, the 60% provision was not included, but legislators wanted this provision included in the bill, which Boeing later accepted").

[2375] Corporate Headquarters Relocation Act, 2001 Ill. Pub. Act 92-0207, Exhibit EC-216.

DSR 2012:III

Report of the Panel

recipient of the EDGE tax credits. The Panel recalls that the CHRA indicates that its purpose is to encourage the relocation of the international headquarters of large, multinational corporations to a location within Illinois "through the use of incentives ... that would otherwise not be available through existing incentives programs".[2376]

7.925 Finally, the United States argues that the property tax abatements are not specific "because Illinois law permits any taxing district in the State to abate the property taxes of numerous types of enterprises".[2377] In support of this argument, the United States refers the Panel to the provision of the Illinois tax code that authorizes taxing districts to abate the property taxes of "commercial and industrial firms", "academic or research institutes", "historical societies", "recreational facilities", "housing for older persons", "property used for horse or auto racing", and "relocated corporate headquarters".[2378] The Panel accepts that Illinois law permits any taxing district in the State to abate the property taxes of numerous types of industries. However, the Panel fails to see the relevance of that fact because the Panel observes that the provision of the Illinois tax code that contains this authorization makes clear that each one of the listed enterprises and industries is subject to a *different set of terms, conditions and limitations*.

7.926 For instance, the *duration* of these property tax abatements differ from one another: not more than 10 years in the case of most "commercial and industrial firms" (except a development of at least 500 acres, in which case it is not more than 20 years), "horse and auto racing", and "recreational firms"; not more than 15 years in the case of "housing for older persons"; at least 15 years in the case of "academic or research institutes"; and not more than 20 years in the case of "relocated corporate headquarters". To take another example, the *maximum dollar amount* that may be claimed differs: not more than $3 million for "housing for older persons"; generally not more than $4 million in the case of "commercial and industrial firms" (except a development of at least 500 acres, in which case not more than $12 million); not more than $5 million in the case of "horse racing" and "academic or research institutes"; no stated maximum dollar limit in the case of "auto racing" or "historical society" or "recreational facilities". Furthermore, this provision sets forth *different methods for calculating the applicable property tax abatements* for the different enterprises and industries that are listed. In some cases (e.g. "commercial and industrial"), there is a very detailed methodology. In others, no calculation methodology is set forth. As the United States itself notes, the methods for calculating the applicable property tax abatements for Boeing are memorialized in the two separate agreements that it entered into with Chicago and Cook County.[2379] In

---

[2376] *Ibid.*

[2377] United States' first written submission, para. 680.

[2378] 35 ILL. COMP. STAT. § 200/18-165, Exhibit EC-225.

[2379] United States' first written submission, para. 674. The United States elaborates upon the formula at paragraphs 675-677 of its first written submission:

US - Large Civil Aircraft (2ⁿᵈ Complaint)

addition, the provision sets forth different rules regarding what *types of property* may be subject to the property tax abatement granted to the particular type of enterprise or industry.

7.927 In our view, the fact that Illinois law permits taxing authorities to grant different property tax abatements to different enterprises and industries subject to different sets of terms, conditions and limitations does not call into question that the property tax abatements granted to "eligible businesses" (i.e. Boeing) under the CHRA are de facto specific under Article 2.1(c) of the SCM Agreement. The Panel again recalls that the CHRA indicates that its purpose is to encourage the relocation of the international headquarters of large, multinational corporations to a location within Illinois "through the use of incentives ... that would otherwise not be available through existing incentives programs".[2380]

"The two agreements – which by their terms are substantially identical – set out a formula for determining the value of the property tax abatements Boeing may receive as a result of its occupancy of its corporate headquarters at 100 North Riverside Plaza in Chicago. Specifically, the value of the property tax abatements is the product of: (a) the portion of the property's total property tax bill that Boeing has paid in a given year; and (b) the "allocable share" of the property's total property tax bill that is attributable to City of Chicago or Cook County taxes, as the case may be. Thus, for example, if Boeing's share of the property's total tax bill in a given year were $50 out of $150 and the "allocable share" of the property's total tax bill attributable to the City of Chicago (as opposed to other jurisdictions) was 80 per cent, Boeing would be entitled to a property tax abatement of $40 from the City of Chicago.

The two agreements, however, provide certain limitations on Boeing's entitlement to property tax abatements. First, the value of Boeing's tax abatement may not exceed – as a percentage of the property's total property tax bill – the ratio of rentable square feet leased to and occupied by Boeing and the total number of rentable square feet in the property. Under the agreements, this ratio is 0.3573. In other words, notwithstanding the formula discussed in the paragraph above, Boeing's total property tax abatement may not exceed 35.73 per cent of the property's total property tax bill. Thus, if Boeing occupied half of the property, such that it paid $50 of the property's total tax bill of $100 (and still assuming that the "allocable share" of the property's total tax bill attributable to the City of Chicago were 80 per cent), Boeing would be entitled to a property tax abatement of only $35.73 from the City of Chicago, rather than a $40 property tax abatement.

Second, Boeing's entitlement to abatement of its property taxes further depends on the number of employees it maintains at its corporate headquarters in the 100 North Riverside building. If Boeing maintains 500 or more employees at that location, it may receive 100 per cent of the figure calculated according to the formula in the above paragraphs. If, however, it employs fewer than 500 people, its property tax abatement is reduced as follows {...} Thus, to take again the example cited above, if Boeing employed only 450 people in its corporate headquarters in a given year (and still assuming that the "allocable share" of the property's total tax bill attributable to the City of Chicago were 80 per cent), Boeing would be entitled to a property tax abatement of only $36 from the City of Chicago, or 90 per cent of the $40 tax abatement it would otherwise receive if it had met the 500-employee threshold."

[2380] Corporate Headquarters Relocation Act, 2001 Ill. Pub. Act 92-0207, Exhibit EC-216.

DSR 2012:III

Report of the Panel

7.928 For these reasons, the Panel finds that the CHRA subsidies to Boeing are de facto specific under Article 2.1(c) of the SCM Agreement, and that it is therefore not necessary to make a finding on whether the property tax abatements and refunds are also *de jure* specific under Article 2.1(a) of the SCM Agreement. The Panel recalls that the parties agree that the lease retirement payment is specific within the meaning of Article 2.[2381]

(e)   The amount of the subsidy to Boeing's LCA division

(i)   Arguments of the European Communities

7.929 The European Communities estimates that the total amount of the four subsidies to Boeing's LCA division is approximately $25 million over the period 2002-2021. More specifically, the European Communities estimates that: (i) the amount of the subsidy to Boeing's LCA division from the relocation reimbursements from 2002 through 2011 (or until the relocation costs are paid in full) is $4.3 million; (ii) the amount of the subsidy to Boeing's LCA division from the EDGE tax credits is $8.5 million from 2003 through 2017; (iii) the amount of the subsidy to Boeing's LCA division from the local property tax abatements provided by the City of Chicago and Cook County is $11.5 million from 2002 through 2021; and (iv) the amount of the subsidy to Boeing's LCA division from the lease retirement payment is $0.5 million in 2003.[2382]

(ii)   Arguments of the United States

7.930 The United States argues that any amounts that Boeing receives after 2006 are "speculative" and fall outside of the Panel's terms of reference. The United States asserts that the total value of the four subsidies to Boeing's LCA division is [***] million over the period 2002-2006.

(iii)   Evaluation by the Panel

7.931 Before addressing the relatively narrow point of disagreement between the parties, the Panel will first set forth the points in respect of which the parties appear to be in agreement.

7.932 First, there is no disagreement on the question of whether and if so how much of the subsidies provided to The Boeing Company by the State of Illinois and municipalities therein should be allocated to Boeing's LCA division. The European Communities argues that 50 per cent of the total amount of the subsidies provided to The Boeing Company by the State of Illinois and

---

[2381] United States' first written submission, para. 683; United States' response to question 13, para. 29 ("The retirement of the lease by the City of Chicago is a subsidy that is specific within the meaning of Articles 1 and 2 of the SCM Agreement.")

[2382] European Communities' first written submission, paras. 384 and 387, 405 and 408, 430 and 433; 449 and 452; State and Local Subsidies to Boeing LCA Division, Exhibit EC-27, pp. 1-2.

municipalities therein should be allocated to Boeing's LCA division because, over time, approximately 50 per cent of Boeing's total sales have related to LCA.[2383] The United States agrees that 50 per cent of the value of these four subsidies should be allocated to Boeing's LCA division.[2384] The Panel sees no reason to disagree with the European Communities' allocation methodology, and will therefore allocate 50 per cent of any subsidies provided to The Boeing Company to Boeing's LCA division.

7.933 Second, there is no disagreement regarding the amount of the subsidy provided to The Boeing Company (and hence the total amount of the subsidy allocable to Boeing's LCA division) for three of the four measures over the period 2002-2006. The parties agree that the amount of the subsidy to Boeing's LCA division arising from the reimbursement of relocation expenses is [***] over the period 2002-2006, that the amount of the subsidy to Boeing's LCA division arising from the property tax abatements is [***] million over the period 2002-2006, and that the amount of the subsidy to Boeing's LCA division arising from the lease payment is $0.5 million over the period 2002-2006.[2385] The Panel sees no reason to disagree, given that each of these figures is sufficiently substantiated by evidence submitted by the United States and/or the European Communities.[2386]

7.934 Third, neither party argues that it is necessary for the Panel to arrive at an estimate of the post-2006 amounts of the subsidies provided to Boeing by the three CHRA measures. The European Communities explains that "the estimates of future {i.e. post-2006} payments from all three subsidies referenced in the Panel's question have *no* impact on the European Communities' analysis of present adverse effects. These particular subsidy amounts are applied to the year

---

[2383] European Communities' first written submission, para. 384 and footnote 615, para. 405 and footnote 643, para. 430 and footnote 676, and para. 449 and footnote 697 (citing Boeing/MD LCA Allocation Charts, Exhibit EC-18.)

[2384] United States' first written submission, paras. 663, 679, and 682.

[2385] United States' first written submission, paras. 661-663, 678-679, 682; European Communities' second written submission, paras. 276, 301 and 308.

[2386] Regarding the amount of the subsidy arising from the reimbursement for relocation expenses, the information is found in Illinois Corporate Headquarters Relocation Act Relocation Grant Expenses, 2002-2006, Exhibit US-255 (BCI). For each year, the amounts claimed by Boeing are indicated on the first page of "Exhibit B", within Exhibit US-255. The pages that include the amounts of reimbursement claimed by Boeing each year are signed by an Executive Officer of the Boeing Company who states that "under penalty of perjury, I certify that the above information is true and correct". Regarding the amount of the property tax abatements, see City of Chicago Property Tax Abatements 2002-2006, Exhibit US-262 and Cook County Property Tax Abatements 2002-2006, Exhibit US-263 (BCI), which contain the "Annual Reimbursement Forms" submitted by Boeing to the City of Chicago and the County of Cook, pursuant to the "Tax Reimbursement Payment Agreement". Regarding the amount of the lease payment, see Lease Termination Compensation Agreement between 100 North Riverside, LLC and the City of Chicago, 15 January 2003, Exhibit EC-217, p. 2, which indicates the amount paid by the City to the landlord.

Report of the Panel

that the subsidy was received".[2387] The European Communities estimates that the total amount of the subsidy to Boeing's LCA division from the reimbursement of relocation expenses would be $4.3 million over the period 2002-2011, that the total amount of the subsidy to Boeing's LCA division from the EDGE tax credits would be approximately $17 million over the period 2003-2017, and that the total amount of the subsidy to Boeing's LCA division from the local property tax abatements would be $11.5 million over the period 2002-2021.[2388] According to the United States, the post-2006 amounts are "speculative", and are "not within the Panel's terms of reference" because they were not "a measure in existence at the time this Panel was established".[2389] Because it appears to be unnecessary for the Panel to arrive at an estimate of the post-2006 amounts of the subsidies provided to Boeing by the three CHRA measures, the Panel considers it unnecessary to resolve these other issues.

7.935 The point of disagreement concerns the amount of the EDGE tax credit subsidy to Boeing over the period 2002-2006. The European Communities estimates that the total amount of the subsidy to Boeing's LCA division from the EDGE tax credits would be approximately $17 million over the period 2003-2017, including $2.4 million over the period 2003-2006.[2390] The European Communities bases its estimate on the figures contained in two publicly available documents, both prepared and dated 2001, setting forth the State of Illinois' own estimate of the amount of the EDGE tax credit subsidy to

---

[2387] European Communities' comments on United States' response to question 368, para. 201 (emphasis original).

[2388] European Communities' first written submission, paras. 384, 405 and 430. The European Communities' estimates of the amounts of these subsidies on a yearly basis is set forth in International Trade Resources LLC, Calculating on a Per-Aircraft Basis the Magnitude of the Subsidies Provided to US Large Civil Aircraft, 20 February 2007, Exhibit EC-13, Appendix A, and also in State and Local Subsidies to Boeing LCA Division, Exhibit EC-27. After the United States provided information indicating that the actual amount of the relocation expenses reimbursed to Boeing during the period 2002-2006 was higher than the European Communities estimate of the amount that Boeing received over the period 2002-2006, the European Communities submitted that the amount of the subsidy to Boeing's LCA Division from the reimbursement of relocation expenses over the period 2007-2011 "may be as high as [***]". The European Communities calculates this by noting that the figures provided by the United States indicate that total reimbursement to Boeing [***] by approximately [***] between 2004 and 2005 and by approximately [***] between 2005 and 2006. According to the European Communities, if Boeing's annual reimbursement continues to [***] at this pace, Boeing may receive the maximum possible reimbursement for its relocation costs by 2011, namely 50 per cent of its relocation expenses. Therefore, the European Communities concludes that the total financial contribution to Boeing is [***] from 2002 through 2011. European Communities' second written submission, para. 276.

[2389] United States' first written submission, para. 663; United States' first written submission, para. 669; United States' first written submission, para. 679. In its response to question 368, the United States confirms the Panel's understanding that the United States' arguments relating to post-2006 measures concern the amount of the subsidies, rather than the existence of the subsidies.

[2390] The European Communities' estimates of the amounts of these subsidies on a yearly basis is set forth in International Trade Resources LLC, Calculating on a Per-Aircraft Basis the Magnitude of the Subsidies Provided to US Large Civil Aircraft, 20 February 2007, Exhibit EC-13, Appendix A, and also in State and Local Subsidies to Boeing LCA Division, Exhibit EC-27.

US - Large Civil Aircraft (2nd Complaint)

Boeing.[2391] The European Communities indicates that it attempted to obtain more precise figures through the Freedom of Information Act, but that the State of Illinois refused to provide it with such information.[2392] The United States asserts that the State of Illinois made [***] financial contribution to Boeing in relation to the EDGE tax credits between 2003-2006 because [***].[2393] However, the United States notes that in 2002 [***].[2394] At paragraph 289 of its second written submission, the European Communities responds that:

> "Finally, as to the amount of financial contribution to Boeing's LCA division from these EDGE tax credits, the United States has offered no support for its assertion that the amount is less than the $17 million from 2003 through 2017 claimed by the European Communities. The United States simply asserts that [***] without providing Boeing's Illinois corporate income tax returns for those years. Absent such concrete evidence, there is no basis to accept the United States' assertion. ..."

7.936 The Panel asked the United States to respond to the European Communities' arguments at paragraph 289 of its second written submission, but the United States only indicated that "{a}s ... stated previously, Boeing has [***]".[2395]

7.937 The Panel considers that the European Communities' estimate is supported by evidence, and that the United States assertions are not supported by any evidence. We recall that the European Communities relies on the State's 2001 estimates of the amount of revenue it will forego under the EDGE tax credit scheme.[2396] In contrast, the United States does not provide any evidence to support its assertion that [***]. The Panel provided the United States with an opportunity to respond to the European Communities' argument on this very point, and it did not do so. We consider the European Communities' estimate to be based on the best publicly available information and we accept it. Consequently, we quantify the value of the tax credits received by Boeing in the

---

[2391] Illinois Economic and Fiscal Commission, Corporate Incentives in the State of Illinois, August 2001, Exhibit EC-221, p. 19; Testimony of Pam McDonough to the Illinois House Revenue Committee, 23 May 2001, Exhibit EC-233, p. 3.

[2392] European Communities' first written submission, para. 403.

[2393] United States' first written submission, para. 669.

[2394] United States' first written submission, para. 669, footnote 863. We note that the United States provides Boeing's Corporate Income Tax Return in the State of Illinois for 2002, and this tax return indicates that in 2002 Boeing claimed an EDGE tax credit to the value of [***]. See Boeing 2002 Illinois Corporate Income Tax Return, Exhibit US-259 (BCI), p.2.

[2395] United States' response to question 260, para. 453.

[2396] Illinois Economic and Fiscal Commission, Corporate Incentives in the State of Illinois, August 2001, Exhibit EC-221, p. 19; Testimony of Pam McDonough to the Illinois House Revenue Committee, 23 May 2001, Exhibit EC-233, p. 3.

DSR 2012:III   1291

Report of the Panel

period 2003-2006 as $2.4 million.[2397] Adding to this 50 per cent of the value of the EDGE tax credit that Boeing received in 2002[2398], we estimate that the amount of the subsidy to Boeing's LCA division arising from the EDGE tax credit over the period 2002-2006 is [***], i.e. $2.4 million + [***].

7.938 In sum, the Panel estimates that the amount of the subsidy to Boeing's LCA division arising from the four measures at issue is [***].

(f)   Conclusion

7.939 For these reasons, the Panel finds that the four incentives that the State of Illinois and municipalities therein provided to Boeing in consideration for Boeing's decision to relocate its corporate headquarters to Chicago constitute specific subsidies within the meaning of Articles 1 and 2 of the SCM Agreement, and estimates that the amount of the subsidy provided to Boeing's LCA division is approximately $11 million over the period 2002-2006.

2.   *National Aeronautics and Space Administration (NASA) aeronautics R&D[2399]*

(a)   Introduction

7.940 The European Communities asserts that NASA provides Boeing with funding and support for aeronautics R&D pursuant to a number of R&D programmes. The European Communities argues that this funding and support constitutes a subsidy within the meaning of Article 1 of the SCM Agreement, and is specific within the meaning of Article 2 of the SCM Agreement. The European Communities estimates that NASA provided $10.4 billion in subsidies to Boeing over the period 1989-2006.[2400]

[2397] European Communities' first written submission, para. 404. The European Communities estimates that Boeing will receive $1.13 million per year in EDGE tax credits, and submits that 50 per cent of this should be allocated to the Boeing LCA Division.

[2398] As noted above, in 2002 Boeing claimed an EDGE tax credit of [***]. The parties agree that only 50 per cent of the value of these should be allocated to Boeing's LCA Division. 50 per cent of [***] is [***].

[2399] The European Communities discusses the payments and access to "facilities, equipment and employees" that NASA allegedly granted to Boeing in two different parts of its first written submission. In Section VI:E.2, the European Communities discusses them both under the heading "NASA Aeronautics Research and Development". In Section VI:H of its first written submission, the European Communities elaborates on the latter under the heading "NASA/DOD Facilities, Equipment and Employees". In its first written submission, the United States addresses both in one section, entitled "NASA R&D". Likewise, in its second written submission the European Communities addresses both in only one section, entitled "NASA Aeronautics Research and Development". The Panel addresses the European Communities' arguments relating to payments and "facilities, equipment and employees" together in this section of its Report. The Panel will follow this same approach in respect of "Department of Defense (DOD) Aeronautics R&D".

[2400] NASA/DOD/DOC Aeronautics R&D Subsidies to Boeing LCA Division, Exhibit EC-25, p. 20.

1292   DSR 2012:III

US - Large Civil Aircraft (2nd Complaint)

7.941 The United States does not dispute that, under the eight NASA aeronautics R&D programmes at issue in this dispute, NASA made payments to Boeing, and that NASA provided Boeing with access to government facilities, equipment and employees for the purpose of performing aeronautics-related research. However, the United States argues that the payments and access to facilities, equipment and employees that NASA provided to Boeing are not subsidies within the meaning of Article 1 of the SCM Agreement. The United States further argues that NASA's granting Boeing access to wind tunnels is not specific within the meaning of Article 2 of the SCM Agreement. In addition, the United States argues that the European Communities has overestimated the amount of any subsidy provided to Boeing by NASA. According to the United States, the total amount of payments made to Boeing under NASA R&D contracts and agreements entered into under the eight aeronautics R&D programmes at issue was $1.05 billion, out of which less than $775 million was LCA-related. According to the United States, the total value of the NASA facilities, equipment and employees provided to Boeing under these R&D contracts and agreements was less than $80 million.

(b)   The measures at issue

7.942 From 1969 to 2002, aeronautics research each year accounted for between two and seven percent of NASA's total budget.[2401] It is common ground between the parties that most of NASA's budget is related to *space* activities, and it is also common ground between the parties that most of NASA's contracts with Boeing are unrelated to aeronautics.[2402] The scope of the European Communities claim is limited to *aeronautics*-related R&D.

7.943 The pertinent items of the European Communities' panel request[2403] read as follows:

"a.   allowing the US LCA industry to participate in research programmes, making payments to the US LCA industry under those programmes, or enabling the US LCA industry to exploit the results thereof by means including but not limited to the foregoing or waiving of valuable patent rights, the granting of limited

---

[2401] United States' first written submission, footnote 266.

[2402] The European Communities estimates that the value of payments and goods and services provided to Boeing for aeronautics R&D over the period 1989-2006 was $10.4 billion. In Boeing's Share of NASA Contracts, FY 1991-FY 2004, Exhibit EC-19, the European Communities indicates that the value of "Total NASA Contract Awards to Boeing/MD" over the period FY1991-FY2004 was approximately $32.064 billion. Note 1 to Exhibit EC-19 indicates that the information is drawn from NASA Annual Procurement Report, FY 1991-FY 2004, "One Hundred Principal Contractors", Exhibit EC-341. Thus, it appears that by the European Communities' estimate, the value of the payments and goods and services that NASA provided to Boeing for aeronautics-related R&D is roughly equal to one third of the total amount of payments that NASA made to Boeing over the period 1991-2004.

[2403] WT/DS353/2, items 2(a) and 2(b), pp. 6-8.

DSR 2012:III

exclusive rights data ("LERD") or otherwise exclusive or early access to data, trade secrets and other knowledge resulting from government funded research. The following are examples of such NASA programmes:

(i)   *High Speed Research Program*

...

(ii)   *Advanced Subsonic Technology Program*

...

(iii)   *Aviation Safety Program/Aviation Safety & Security Program/Aviation Security & Safety Program*

...

(iv)   *Quiet Aircraft Technology Program*

...

(v)   *High Performance Computing and Communications Program*

...

(vi)   *Research & Technology Base Program*

...

(vii)   *Advanced Composites Technology Program*

...

(viii)   *Vehicle Systems Program*

...

(ix)   *Materials and Structures Systems Technology Program, including advanced composites materials and structures research*

...

(x)   *Aircraft Energy Efficiency Program, including Composite Primary Aircraft Structures, Transport Aircraft Systems Technology, and Advanced Composite Structures Technology Programs*

...

b.   providing the services of NASA employees, facilities, and equipment to support the R&D programmes listed above and paying salaries, personnel costs, and other institutional support, thereby providing valuable services to the US LCA industry on terms more favourable than available on the market or not at arm's length"

US - Large Civil Aircraft (2nd Complaint)

7.944 On the basis of the European Communities' panel request, written submissions and responses to questions, the Panel understands that the measures challenged by the European Communities in this dispute are the "payments"[2404] and "free access to NASA facilities, equipment and employees"[2405] that NASA provided to Boeing through R&D contracts and agreements entered into with Boeing[2406] under the following aeronautics R&D programmes: Advanced Composites Technology ("ACT"), High Speed Research ("HSR"), Advanced Subsonic Technology ("AST"), High Performance Computing and Communications ("HPCC"), Aviation Safety, Quiet Aircraft Technology ("QAT"), Vehicle Systems ("VSP"), and Research and Technology Base ("R&T Base").[2407]

7.945 NASA and Boeing entered into a number of R&D contracts and agreements with Boeing under the eight aeronautics R&D programmes at issue. The contracts and agreements essentially fall into two different categories: (i) "procurement contracts", (as distinguished from "assistance" instruments[2408]) and

---

[2404] In its Panel Request, the European Communities refers to NASA "making payments" to Boeing. In its first written submission, the European Communities refers to the "direct R&D funding" provided to Boeing in the form of "grants". European Communities' first written submission, paras. 524, 548, 572, 588, 603, 618, 631, and 650.

[2405] See e.g. European Communities' first written submission, paras. 890-891 ("In addition to funding the R&D efforts of the US LCA industry over the years, NASA and DOD have provided Boeing and McDonnell Douglas with substantial R&D support through free access to NASA/DOD facilities, equipment, and employees ... NASA, in particular, has provided Boeing with substantial benefit by giving Boeing free access to its facilities, equipment, and employees."); European Communities' response to question 148, para. 172 ("The European Communities uses the term "facilities, equipment, and employees" as a shorthand to describe the types of "goods and services" provided by NASA. For purposes of the European Communities' claim, the terms "facilities, equipment, and employees" and "goods and services" are interchangeable. The European Communities has described the "facilities, equipment, and employees" provided by NASA in detail in its prior submissions by citing to specific NASA Space Act Agreements and other contracts.") and European Communities' response to question 148, paras. 180-182 ("the European Communities' claim is that NASA provides "facilities, equipment, and employees" to Boeing for LCA-related R&D. This claim is captured by the first element of item 2(b) of the European Communities' Panel Request. The second element of item 2(b) ... is intended to point out that "institutional support" reflects *part of* the value of the "facilities, equipment, and employees" provided by NASA. ... Item 2(d) serves as a more specific example of the types of facilities provided by NASA.").

[2406] See e.g. European Communities' first written submission, para. 457 ("NASA and DOD generally provide funding for LCA-related R&D through what they call "contracts," but what are in reality grants to Boeing/MD for LCA-related R&D expenses.") and European Communities' response to question 148, para. 171 ("NASA provides these "goods and services" in conjunction with the various contractual instruments (i.e. Space Act Agreements and other contracts) it enters into with Boeing under the eight NASA aeronautics R&D programs challenged in this dispute").

[2407] European Communities' first written submission, para. 476.

[2408] The Panel notes that the vast majority of the transactions between NASA and Boeing under the eight aeronautics R&D programmes at issue are "procurement contracts". However, in a few cases, the transactions between NASA and Boeing (or entities purchased by Boeing) under these programmes have been in the form of what are termed "assistance" instruments under U.S. law, and more specifically "cooperative agreements". According to the United States, there were only three cooperative agreements between Boeing and NASA, and a total of less than $5 million was allotted to

---

DSR 2012:III   1295

Report of the Panel

(ii) Space Act Agreements. U.S. laws and regulations establish legal conditions for using "procurement contracts". Specifically, this type of instrument may be used only where the "principal purpose" of the activity is the "acquisition of goods or services" for the "direct benefit or use" of the U.S. Government.[2409] In addition, NASA regulations provide that the types of Space Act Agreements challenged by the European Communities in this case, i.e. "non-reimbursable" or "partially reimbursable" Space Act Agreements, may only be entered into when the R&D conducted pursuant to the agreement will "further the Agency's missions".[2410] In this Report, we use the expression "NASA R&D contracts" to

---

these agreements. According to the United States, there were no other types of "assistance" instruments between NASA and Boeing. See Exhibit US-1245; United States' response to question 20(a), para. 46; United States' response to question 214, para. 345 and footnote 464; United States' response to question 328, paragraph 38 and footnote 55.

[2409] See, e.g. United States' first written submission, footnote 100 (citing 32 C.F.R. § 22.205(a) (Exhibit US-22) and 48 C.F.R. § 35.003) (Exhibit US-23)); *NASA Grants and Cooperative Agreement Handbook,* § 1260.12(b)(1) (Exhibit US-94); parties' responses and related comments to questions 20, 151, 154 and 191.

[2410] NASA policy regarding Space Act Agreements is set out in NASA Policy Directive 1050.1H, Exhibit US-108. The Space Act authorizes NASA "to enter into and perform such contracts, leases, cooperative agreements, or other transactions as may be necessary in the conduct of its work and on such terms as it may deem appropriate, with any agency or instrumentality of the United States, or with any State, territory, or possession, or with any political subdivision thereof, or with any person, firm, association, corporation, or educational institution". The term "Space Act Agreements" refers to agreements that NASA enters into pursuant to the "other transactions" authority provided by the Space Act. NASA's policy directive governing Space Act Agreements explains:

> Under its Space Act authority, NASA has entered into a great number of agreements with diverse groups of people and organizations, both in the private and public sector, *in order to meet wide-ranging NASA mission and program requirements and objectives.* It is NASA's policy to utilize the broad authority granted to the Agency in the Space Act to further the Agency's missions.

NASA uses three different types of Space Act Agreement – reimbursable, partially reimbursable, and non-reimbursable. NASA provides goods and services under *reimbursable* Space Act Agreements when it "has unique goods, services, and facilities, not being fully utilized to accomplish mission needs, which it can make available to others on a non-interference basis, consistent with the Agency's missions". NASA requires full reimbursement, defined as "full cost recovery" for the goods services or facilities provided, where it does not receive any "benefit" from the use of its facilities. NASA also has the authority to accept *partial* reimbursement where a proposed contribution of the Agreement Partner is fair and reasonable compared to the NASA resources to be committed, NASA programme risks, and corresponding "benefits to NASA". Where NASA is "obtaining rights to intellectual property or data or some other benefit", there is a presumptive NASA interest that may justify partial reimbursement. In partial reimbursement situations, NASA policy is that "{a} determination to charge less than full cost should: (1) be accomplished consistent with NASA's written regulations and policies, (2) articulate the market pricing analysis, benefit to NASA, or other legal authority that supports less than full cost recovery, and (3) account for recovered and unrecovered costs in accordance with NASA financial management policy". NASA uses *non-reimbursable* Space Act Agreements where it works with "one or more Agreement Partners in a mutually beneficial activity that furthers the Agency's missions". In these situations, "each party bears the cost of its participation and there is no exchange of funds between the parties". NASA requires, under all non-reimbursable Space Act Agreements, that "the respective contributions of each Agreement Partner must be fair and reasonable compared to the NASA resources to be committed, NASA programme risks, and corresponding benefits to NASA."

1296

DSR 2012:III

mean NASA's procurement contracts with Boeing under the eight aeronautics R&D programmes at issue, "agreements" to mean NASA's non-reimbursable and partially reimbursable Space Act Agreements with Boeing under the eight aeronautics R&D programmes at issue, and "NASA R&D contracts and agreements" to cover both.

7.946 In response to a question from the Panel, the European Communities clarifies that it does not challenge NASA allowing Boeing to "participate" in research programmes as a distinct measure.[2411] With respect to NASA "enabling the US LCA industry to exploit the results thereof by means including but not limited to the foregoing or waiving of valuable patent rights, the granting of limited exclusive rights data ('LERD') or otherwise exclusive or early access to data, trade secrets and other knowledge resulting from government funded research", the European Communities addresses these measures primarily in the sections of its submissions regarding "NASA/DOD Intellectual Property Rights Transfers/Waivers".[2412]

7.947 We discuss the challenged measures in greater detail in the context of our evaluation of whether these measures constitute specific subsidies within the meaning of Articles 1 and 2 of the SCM Agreement, and in the context of estimating the amount of any subsidy to Boeing's LCA division.

(c)   Whether a subsidy exists within the meaning of Article 1 of the SCM Agreement

7.948 In this section, we address whether the payments and access to facilities, equipment and employees that NASA provided to Boeing under the eight aeronautics R&D programmes at issue constitute a subsidy within the meaning of Article 1 of the SCM Agreement. We begin by addressing the question of whether the transactions involve a financial contribution covered by Article 1.1(a)(1) of the SCM Agreement. The two main issues raised by the arguments of the parties are: (i) whether transactions properly characterized as "purchases of services" are excluded from the scope of Article 1.1(a)(1); and (ii) whether NASA's R&D contracts with Boeing are properly characterized as "purchases of services". We will address these two issues in turn. If we find that the challenged measures provide financial contributions to Boeing, we will then address the question of whether those financial contributions are provided on terms that confer a benefit within the meaning of Article 1.1(b) of the SCM Agreement.

[2411] European Communities' response to question 149.
[2412] European Communities' response to question 215.

Report of the Panel

> (i) Whether there is a financial contribution within the meaning of Article 1.1(a)(1) of the SCM Agreement
>
> Whether transactions properly characterized as "purchases of services" are excluded from the scope of Article 1.1(a)(1) of the SCM Agreement

Arguments of the European Communities

7.949 The European Communities argues that transactions involving purchases of services are not excluded from the scope of Article 1.1(a)(1). Rather, the European Communities considers that Article 1.1(a)(1)(i) can be interpreted so as to cover any transaction involving a monetary payment to a recipient, regardless of whether or not the transaction involves a "purchase of services". Regarding the interpretation of Article 1.1(a)(1), the principal arguments of the European Communities are as follows: (i) the plain meaning of the terms of Article 1.1(a)(1)(i) ("a government practice involves a direct transfer of funds...") is broad enough to encompass a direct transfer of funds made pursuant to contracts for services; (ii) one can only speculate on why the drafters omitted the reference to purchases of services in the final draft of the SCM Agreement, as there is more than one possible explanation; (iii) Article 8.2(a) of the SCM Agreement confirms that purchases of services, at least with respect to contractual R&D support, are covered by Article 1.1(a)(1); (iv) excluding purchases of services from the scope of Article 1.1(a)(1) would create an enormous loophole in the coverage of and run counter to the overall object and purpose of the SCM Agreement; (v) the potential for partial overlap between the second part of Article 1.1(a)(1)(iii) ("or purchases goods") and different sub-paragraphs of Article 1.1(a)(1) does not, contrary to the United States argument, render the reference to purchases of goods in Article 1.1(a)(1)(iii) redundant or inutile; (vi) the reference to "equity infusion" (i.e. a purchase of shares) as an example of a "direct transfer of funds" in Article 1.1(a)(1)(i) confirms that purchases may be covered by Article 1.1(a)(1)(i); and (vii) what a government receives in exchange for its funding and support is an issue properly addressed under the "benefit" inquiry.[2413]

Arguments of the United States

7.950 The United States argues that governmental purchases of services are excluded from the scope of Article 1.1(a)(1). The principal arguments of the United States are as follows: (i) the ordinary meaning of the terms of Article

---

[2413] European Communities' second written submission, paras. 349-364; European Communities' responses (and/or comments on United States responses) to questions 15, 17, 113, 114, 115, 116, 117, 118, 119, and 120.

1298

DSR 2012:III

US - Large Civil Aircraft (2nd Complaint)

1.1(a)(1)(i) must be interpreted "in their context" and may not be interpreted so as to render other provisions of Article 1 meaningless; (ii) Article 8.2(a) of the SCM Agreement, which concerns "assistance" for research activities, does not support the view that "purchases" of services are covered by Article 1.1(a)(1); (iii) the European Communities misconstrues the object and purpose of the SCM Agreement, and ignores the fact that the definition of "financial contribution" was meant to exclude some measures from the disciplines of the SCM Agreement; (iv) the only defensible conclusion that flows from a review of the drafting history of Article 1.1(a)(1)(iii) is that the negotiators deleted the explicit reference to purchases of services because they intended that those types of transactions not be treated as a financial contribution; (v) the European Communities' interpretation of subparagraphs (i) and (iii) would render the reference to purchases of goods in Article 1.1(a)(1)(iii) redundant or inutile, and the examples to the contrary provided by the European Communities do not demonstrate otherwise; (vi) the fact that "equity infusion" is included as an example of a "direct transfer of funds" does not imply that purchase of goods or services are covered by subparagraph (i); and (vii) giving effect to the omission of purchases of services from Article 1.1(a)(1) does not collapse the distinction between financial contribution and benefit.[2414]

Arguments of Third Parties

7.951 Australia and Brazil submit that "purchases of services" are not excluded from the scope of Article 1.1(a)(1) of the SCM Agreement.[2415] These third parties advance arguments that are essentially the same as those advanced by the European Communities. Among other things, both of these parties argue that excluding purchases of services from the scope of Article 1.1(a)(1) could create an "enormous loophole" in the coverage of and run counter to the overall object and purpose of the SCM Agreement.[2416]

7.952 Canada, Japan, and Korea take the position that purchases of services are excluded from the scope of Article 1.1(a)(1) of the SCM Agreement.[2417] These third parties advance arguments that are essentially the same as those advanced by the United States. Among other things, these third parties argue that the

---

[2414] United States' first written submission, paras. 48 and 218; United States' responses (and/or comments on European Communities responses) to questions 15, 17, 113, 114, 115, 116, 117, 118, 119, and 120.

[2415] Australia's written submission, paras. 19-26; Australia's response to questions 1, 5, and 6; Australia's oral statement, paras. 5-27; Brazil's written submission, paras. 9-15; Brazil's response to questions 1, 5, and 6; Brazil's oral statement, paras. 7-12.

[2416] See e.g. Brazil's written submission, para. 10 ("Obviously, such an enormous loophole was not intended by the drafters, and, accordingly, the Panel should reject the U.S. interpretation"); Australia's oral statement, para. 6 ("Australia finds force in the European Communities' argument that 'accepting the US argument that LCA-related R&D is a purchase of services simply because it is funded through contracts would create an enormous loophole in the SCM Agreement'").

[2417] Canada's response to questions 1 and 5; Canada's oral statement, paras. 3-11; Japan's response to question 1; Japan's oral statement, paras. 2-4; Korea's response to question 1.

DSR 2012:III

Report of the Panel

omission of any reference to the purchase of services in Article 1.1(a)(1)(iii) of the SCM Agreement reflected a deliberate choice by the drafters and must be given meaning.[2418]

Evaluation by the Panel

7.953 As the Panel sees it, the issue before it is whether transactions properly characterized as purchases of services are excluded from the scope of Article 1.1(a)(1)(i) of the SCM Agreement. This issue has not been addressed in any prior WTO panel or Appellate Body Report.[2419] There is no "subsequent agreement" regarding this issue between WTO Members within the meaning of Article 31(3)(a) of the Vienna Convention, and there is no "subsequent practice" establishing the agreement of WTO Members regarding this issue within the meaning of Article 31(3)(b) of the Vienna Convention.[2420] Thus, to answer this

---

[2418] See e.g. Canada's response to question 1, para. 3 ("the omission of any reference to the purchase of services in Article 1.1(a) (1) (iii) reflected a deliberate choice by the drafters"); Japan's oral statement, para. 2 ("Through this obvious omission, the SCM Agreement plainly exempts the government purchase of services from the definition of financial contribution"); Korea's response to question 1, para. 1 ("the SCM Agreement should be interpreted and applied as it was agreed upon at the Uruguay Round negotiations").

[2419] The issue before the Panel is not whether there are certain transactions that can be covered simultaneously by different sub-paragraphs of Article 1.1(a)(1), or covered simultaneously by both the SCM Agreement and the GATS. We do not exclude the possibility that certain transactions "might be covered simultaneously by different sub-paragraphs of Article 1.1(a)(1)" (Panel Report, *Japan – DRAMs (Korea)*, para. 7.439). Likewise, we understand that "measures that involve a service relating to a particular good or a service supplied in conjunction with a particular good" constitute a "category of measures that could be found to fall within the scope of both the GATT 1994 and the GATS" (Appellate Body Report, *EC – Bananas III*, para. 221), and see little difficulty with the proposition that measures that involve a service relating to a particular good or a service supplied in conjunction with a particular good constitute a category of measures that could be found to fall within the scope of both the SCM Agreement and the GATS.

[2420] In question 118, the Panel asked the United States and the European Communities whether there was an any subsequent practice, within the meaning of Article 31(3)(b) of the Vienna Convention, which establishes the agreement of Members on whether transactions involving the "purchase of a service" fall within the scope of Article 1.1(a)(1). In its response to question 118, the United States refers the Panel to the U.S. Court of Appeals for the Federal Circuit's ruling that the plain meaning of the text of the U.S. countervailing duty law implementing Article 1 of the SCM Agreement was "unambiguous" because:

> "Section 1677(5) is clear as to what constitutes a subsidy--and the purchase of a service by a foreign public entity, however related to the manufacture of a good, is not contemplated in the statute as being a subsidy. While the provision of services by a government entity to another entity for less than adequate compensation may be considered a subsidy, the plain language of § 1677(5) does not allow for the *purchase* of services by a government entity from another entity to be considered a subsidy. Furthermore, § 1677(5)(D)(iii) clearly shows that Congress was aware of the distinction between contracts for services and contracts for goods. Aware of the distinction, Congress could have easily included the purchase of services by public entities in the statutory definition of a subsidy. Because it did not, we must assume that the omission was intentional. *See Clay v. United States*, 537 U.S. 522, 528, 155 L. Ed. 2d 88, 123 S. Ct. 1072 (2003) ("When Congress includes particular language in one section of a statute but omits it in another section of the same Act, we have

---

1300

DSR 2012:III

US - Large Civil Aircraft (2nd Complaint)

question, the Panel must examine the ordinary meaning of the terms of Article 1.1(a)(1)(i), their context, and the object and purpose of the SCM Agreement, as required by Article 31(1) of the Vienna Convention. The Panel will also have recourse to supplementary means of interpretation under Article 32 of the Vienna Convention to confirm the meaning that arises from the application of Article 31 of the Vienna Convention.

7.954 Article 1.1(a)(1)(i) provides in relevant part that a financial contribution exists where "a government practice involves a direct transfer of funds (e.g. grants, loans, and equity infusion)". We accept that if the terms of Article 1.1(a)(1)(i) of the SCM Agreement are read in isolation, the ordinary meaning of the words "a government practice involves a direct transfer of funds" might be broad enough to cover purchases of services. First, there is nothing in the dictionary definitions of these terms to suggest that transactions properly characterized as purchases of services fall outside of their scope: the definition of "transfer" is "a conveyance from one person to another"[2421], and the definition of "funds" is "a stock or sum of money, *esp.* one set apart for a particular purpose" or "financial resources".[2422] Second, there is no qualifying or limiting language in the text of this provision. Third, one of the examples of a "direct transfer of funds" given in Article 1.1(a)(1)(i) is that of "equity infusion", which refers to a situation in which a government "purchases" something (i.e. shares in a company).[2423] Fourth, previous panels and the Appellate Body have not given a

---

recognized, it is generally presumed that Congress acts intentionally and purposely in the disparate inclusion or exclusion". *Eurodif, S.A. v. United States*, pp. 17-18 (Court of Appeals for the Federal Circuit, 3 Mar. 2005) (emphasis original) (footnotes omitted), Exhibit US-1264.

However, the United States indicates that it is "unaware of any other examples of subsequent practice that would establish an agreement of the Members as to whether transactions involving the purchase of a service fall within the scope of Article 1.1(a)(1)". United States' response to question 118, para. 26.

The European Communities comments that "The fact that the United States refers to the practice of *only one* WTO Member – itself – can be taken as an implicit acknowledgment that there is no "subsequent practice in the application of the treaty which establishes *the agreement of the parties* regarding its interpretation" pursuant to Article 31(3)(b) of the *Vienna Convention*. The unilateral actions/decisions of *one party* clearly do not reflect the "agreement *of the parties*". Therefore, the wording of the US countervailing duty law, and its interpretation by the US Court of Appeals for the Federal Circuit ("Federal Circuit"), are simply irrelevant for purposes of Article 31(3)(b) of the *Vienna Convention*". European Communities' comments on United States' response to question 18, para. 32 (emphasis original).

[2421] *Shorter Oxford English Dictionary*, L. Brown (ed.) (Clarendon Press, 2002), Vol. II, p. 3367. See also, *Webster's Online Dictionary*, defining "transfer" to mean, among other things, the "conveyance of right, title, or property, either real or personal, from one person to another, whether by sale, by gift, or otherwise".

[2422] *Shorter Oxford English Dictionary*, L. Brown (ed.) (Clarendon Press, 2002), Vol. I, p. 1042. See also, *Webster's Online Dictionary*, defining "funds" to mean, among other things, "Assets in the form of money" and "A reserve of money set aside for some purpose".

[2423] Panel Report, *EC – Countervailing Measures on DRAM Chips*, para. 7.92 ("Article 1.1(a)(1)(i) of the *SCM Agreement* provides that there is a financial contribution where a government practice involves a direct transfer of funds, such as in the case of a grant, loan and equity infusion for

---

DSR 2012:III

Report of the Panel

restrictive interpretation to these terms.[2424] However, the terms of Article 1.1(a)(1)(i) must be read in their context.

7.955 The immediate context of Article 1.1(a)(1)(i) includes Article 1.1(a)(1)(iii) and Article 14(d) of the SCM Agreement. Article 1.1(a)(1)(iii) reads in its entirety, "a government *provides goods or services* other than general infrastructure, or *purchases goods*". Likewise, Article 14(d) of the SCM Agreement, which forms part of the context of Article 1 of the SCM Agreement[2425], mirrors the wording of Article 1.1(a)(1)(iii) in providing that "the *provision of goods or services* or *purchase of goods* by a government shall not be considered as conferring a benefit unless the provision is made for less than adequate remuneration, or the purchase is made for more than adequate remuneration". The omission must have some meaning.[2426] In other words, a textual analysis in accordance with the Vienna Convention requires an interpreter to consider both what is in the text, and at the same time what is *not* in the text. The glaring difference between the first and second parts of sub-paragraph (iii) necessarily implies that the parties intended to exclude purchases of services from the definition of Article 1.1(a)(1) of the SCM Agreement. Moreover, we recall that "omissions in different contexts" may carry different meanings.[2427] Article 1.1(a)(1) is a definitional provision that sets forth an exhaustive, closed list ("... i.e. where ...") of the types of transactions that constitute financial contributions under the SCM Agreement. The omission of the words "or services" in the context of a provision that sets forth an exhaustive, closed list of the kinds of transactions covered by the SCM Agreement only reinforces the implication that the parties intended to exclude purchases of services from the definition of "financial contribution" in Article 1.1(a)(1) of the SCM Agreement.[2428]

7.956 It must be emphasized that if the Panel were to invent a line of reasoning to support the view that transactions involving purchases of services are covered by other sub-paragraphs and elements of Article 1.1(a)(1) of the SCM Agreement, whether as a "direct transfer of funds" under Article 1.1(a)(1)(i) or

---

example. *The purchase of corporate bonds* is such a direct transfer of funds, and therefore constitutes a financial contribution.") (emphasis added)

[2424] Appellate Body Report, *Japan – DRAMs (Korea)*, para. 250 ("In our view, the term "funds" encompasses not only "money" but also financial resources and other financial claims more generally. The concept of "transfer of funds" adopted by Korea is too literal and mechanistic because it fails to encapsulate how financial transactions give rise to an alteration of obligations from which an accrual of financial resources results.")

[2425] Appellate Body Report, *Canada – Aircraft*, paras. 155 and 158.

[2426] See e.g. Appellate Body Report, *Canada – Autos*, para. 138, citing Appellate Body Report, *Japan – Alcoholic Beverages II*, p. 18.

[2427] Appellate Body Report, *Canada – Autos*, para. 138.

[2428] We note that the omission of purchases of "services" from Article 14(d) not only implies that the parties intended to excluded purchases of services from the scope of the SCM Agreement, but means also that there is no standard for determining whether purchases of "services" provide a "benefit" under Article 1.1(b).

1302   DSR 2012:III

US - Large Civil Aircraft (2nd Complaint)

otherwise, this would necessarily mean that transactions involving purchases of goods must also be covered by those same other sub-paragraphs and elements. That would mean that the term "purchases goods" in Article 1.1(a)(1)(iii) is redundant and inutile, because the scope and coverage of Article 1.1(a)(1) of the SCM Agreement would be precisely the same if those words had not been added to Article 1.1(a)(1)(iii). The Panel is not free to adopt a reading of Article 1 that would result in reducing key terms of that provision to "redundancy or inutility".[2429] Accordingly, the Panel is not free to accept the argument that transactions involving purchases of services (along with transactions involving purchases of goods) are covered by other sub-paragraphs and elements of Article 1.1(a)(1).

7.957 The context of Article 1.1(a)(1)(i) also includes (now lapsed) Article 8.2(a) of the SCM Agreement.[2430] The European Communities reasons that:

> "Article 8.2(a) states 'the following *subsidies* shall be non-actionable'[2431], and the first item on the list is 'assistance for research activities conducted by firms or by higher education for research on a contract basis with firms if {certain conditions are met}.' As correctly noted by Australia in its third party submission[2432], although this provision is no longer in force, and indeed never applied to civil aircraft pursuant to footnote 24, it expressly provides that government support of R&D on a contract basis is a 'subsidy,' and therefore by definition qualifies as a financial contribution."[2433]

7.958 We do not find this reasoning persuasive, and believe that the European Communities' argument is to some extent based on a misreading of the text of Article 8.2(a), which concerns "assistance" for research activities conducted by firms, including "assistance" for higher education or research establishments that conduct research for firms on a contract basis. In addition, Article 8.2(a) does not state that "government support of R&D on a contract basis" is a subsidy. Rather, Article 8.2(a) refers to government assistance for research activities conducted by firms "or by higher education or research establishments on a contract basis with firms". If the terms of Article 8.2(a) gave rise to the

---

[2429] See e.g. Appellate Body Report, *US – Gasoline*, p. 23; Appellate Body Report, *Japan – Alcoholic Beverages II*, p. 12; Appellate Body Report, *US – Underwear*, p. 16.

[2430] Panel Report, *US – Upland Cotton*, footnotes 1086 ("We realize that this provision has now lapsed, by virtue of the operation of Article 31 of the *SCM Agreement*. ... However, these provisions can nevertheless be instructive in understanding the overall architecture of the Agreement with respect to the different types of subsidies it sought and seeks to address. We recall that the Decision by the Arbitrator in *US – FSC (Article 22.6 – US)*, footnote 66, expressed a similar view.")

[2431] Emphasis added.

[2432] Australia's written submission, paras. 20-21.

[2433] European Communities' response to question 15(a); European Communities' second written submission, para. 355.

DSR 2012:III

1303

Report of the Panel

necessary implication that certain types of transactions necessarily constitute subsidies within the meaning of the SCM Agreement, we would of course agree that those types of transactions must logically involve a financial contribution within the meaning of Article 1.1(a)(1). The problem with the European Communities' argument is that there does not appear to be anything in Article 8.2(a) to suggest that governmental purchases of R&D services from firms fall within the scope of the SCM Agreement. By its own terms, Article 8.2(a) concerns "assistance" for research conducted by firms. If the only manner in which a government could provide "assistance" for research conducted by firms was by purchasing R&D services from firms, then the European Communities argument would rest on solid ground. However, this strikes us as a false premise.

7.959 Turning to "object and purpose", we recall that the Appellate Body has clarified that "the object and purpose of the SCM Agreement ... reflects a *delicate balance* between the Members that sought to impose more disciplines on the use of subsidies and those that sought to impose more disciplines on the application of countervailing measures".[2434] In addition, we find useful guidance in the reasoning of the panel in *US – Export Restraints*. In that case, the panel concluded that the type of measure at issue did not involve a financial contribution within the meaning of Article 1 of the SCM Agreement. In the course of interpreting Article 1, the Panel explained that:

> "we do not see any contradiction between the said object and purpose of the SCM Agreement and the fact that certain measures that might be commonly understood to be subsidies that distort trade might in fact be *excluded* from the scope of the Agreement. Indeed, while the object and purpose of the Agreement clearly is to discipline subsidies that distort trade, this object and purpose can only be in respect of 'subsidies' *as defined* in the Agreement. This definition, which incorporates the notions of 'financial contribution', 'benefit', and 'specificity', was drafted with the express purpose of ensuring that not every government intervention in the market would fall within the coverage of the Agreement."[2435]

7.960 The Panel has given very careful consideration to the argument advanced by the European Communities, Brazil and Australia that excluding purchases of

---

[2434] Appellate Body Report, *US – Countervailing Duty Investigation on DRAMS*, para. 115 (emphasis added).

[2435] Panel Report, *US – Export Restraints*, para. 8.63 (emphasis original). See also, Panel Report, *US – Softwood Lumber IV*, para. 7.29 (citing Panel Report, *US – Export Restraints*, para. 8.63, and reiterating that "the definition of a subsidy in Article 1 SCM Agreement reflects the Members' agreement that only certain types of government action are subject to the SCM Agreement, and also that not all government actions that may affect the market come within the ambit of the SCM Agreement.")

1304

DSR 2012:III

US - Large Civil Aircraft (2nd Complaint)

services from the scope of Article 1.1(a)(1) "would run counter to the overall object and purpose of the *SCM Agreement*" by creating "an enormous loophole in the coverage of the *SCM Agreement* and provide WTO Members with a roadmap for distorting trade in goods through "service contracts" with their goods producers".[2436] If a finding that purchases of services are excluded from the scope of the SCM Agreement necessarily led to the manifestly absurd result that a Member could turn a grant into an excluded "purchase of services" simply by that Member "labelling"[2437] the transaction a "contract" or "purchase of services", then such an interpretation would indeed run counter to the object and purpose of the SCM Agreement. However, a finding that transactions *properly characterized* as purchases of services are excluded from the scope of Article 1.1(a)(1) would not lead to such a result. There is every reason to believe that WTO panels and national investigating authorities will be able to detect transactions that are not properly characterized as purchases of services.

7.961 To confirm the meaning that arises from the application of Article 31 of the Vienna Convention, we now turn to "supplementary means" of interpretation under Article 32 of the Vienna Convention.

7.962 First, an examination of the preparatory work of Article 1.1(a)(1)(iii) and Article 14(d) of the SCM Agreement reveals that a reference to governmental "purchases of services" originally appeared in and was subsequently removed from the text of both of these provisions in the final draft. More specifically, the first and second drafts of Article 1.1(a)(1)(iii) referred to the *provision* of "goods or services", but not to *purchases* of either goods or services.[2438] In the third draft, an additional reference to *purchases* of "goods or services" was added to Article 1.1(a)(1)(iii), which was mirrored in the draft of Article 14(d).[2439] In this regard, Articles 1.1(a)(1)(iii) and 14(d) remained unchanged in the fourth draft, and in the first draft of the Final Act of the Uruguay Round.[2440] However, in the second draft of the Final Act, the reference to *purchases* of "services" was removed from both Article 1.1(a)(1)(iii) and Article 14(d), but the reference to purchases of "goods" was retained.[2441] In our view, the preparatory work confirms that the parties intended to exclude purchases of services from the scope of Article 1.1(a)(1).

7.963 According to the European Communities, "one can only speculate on why the drafters omitted the reference to purchases of services in the final draft of the

---

[2436] European Communities' response to question 15(a), para. 51; Brazil's written submission, para. 10; Australia's oral statement, para. 6.

[2437] European Communities' second written submission, paras. 356-361.

[2438] MTN/GNG/NG10/W/38 (dated 18 July 1990); MTN/GNG/NG10/W/38/Rev.1 (4 September 1990).

[2439] MTN/GNG/NG10/W/38/Rev.2 (2 November 1990).

[2440] MTN/GNG/NG10/W/38/Rev.3 (6 November 1990); MTN.TNC/W/35/Rev.1 (3 December 1990).

[2441] MTN/TNC/W/FA (20 December 1991).

DSR 2012:III

Report of the Panel

SCM Agreement, as there is more than one possible explanation".[2442] The Panel considers that the European Communities has failed to provide the Panel with any plausible explanation of why the drafters deleted the reference to purchases of services from Article 1.1(a)(1)(iii) and Article 14(d) of the SCM Agreement. First, with respect to the hypothesis that the negotiators wished "to clarify that the *SCM Agreement* does not discipline subsidies that exclusively distort trade in services", excluding purchases of services does not convey this meaning, as the negotiators retained other types of financial contributions, which could just as easily exclusively distort trade in services. In addition, we agree with the United States that "one would think that if the negotiators sought to 'clarify' the complete exclusion of subsidies to 'services', they would pick a less oblique textual device".[2443] Second, with respect to the hypothesis that "the negotiators sought to be clear that the SCM Agreement applies only to those purchases of services that fall within other clauses of Article 1.1(a)(1)", the European Communities does not explain why the negotiators would seek such a result for purchases of services, but not purchases of goods. It is not plausible that purchases of services were omitted from Article 1.1(a)(1)(iii) in order to clarify that the SCM Agreement applies only to those purchases of "services" that fall within other clauses of Article 1.1(a)(1) (e.g. a purchase of services effected through a monetary payment), but that purchases of *goods* are covered by Article 1.1(a)(1) even *in the absence* of the payment of any consideration of the type that would otherwise fall within the scope of one of the other sub-paragraphs of Article 1.1(a)(1). Rather, as we have concluded above, the necessary implication of a finding that purchases of services are covered by other sub-paragraphs and elements of Article 1.1(a)(1) is that the words "or purchases goods" in Article 1.1(a)(1)(iii) are redundant and inutile.

7.964 Second, the "circumstances of {the} conclusion" of the SCM Agreement[2444], which include both pre-existing GATT disciplines regarding government procurement, relevant dispute settlement proceedings that took place under those disciplines, and also the negotiations that were underway to establish new disciplines regarding government procurement, including government procurement in respect of services, suggest to us that the drafters of Article 1 of the SCM Agreement would have understood the consequences of removing the reference to purchases of "services" in Article 1.

7.965 The scope of the 1979 Procurement Code was limited to the "procurement of products", and did not extend to "services contracts *per se*".[2445]

[2442] European Communities' response to question 15(a), paras. 52-53.

[2443] United States' comments on European Communities' response to question 15(a), para. 55.

[2444] With regard to "the circumstances of {the} conclusion" of a treaty, the Appellate Body has explained that "this permits, in appropriate cases, the examination of the historical background against which the treaty was negotiated." Appellate Body Report, *EC – Computer Equipment*, para. 86.

[2445] Paragraph 1(a) of Article I (Scope and Coverage) stated that "any law, regulation, procedure and practice regarding the procurement of products by the entities subject to this Agreement. This

1306   DSR 2012:III

In Article IX:6(b), the parties to the Procurement Code committed themselves to explore the possibilities of expanding the coverage of the Code to cover purchases of services.[2446] Article V:15(e) of the Procurement Code specifically addressed "contract{s} for research, experiment, study or original development".

7.966 At the time that the SCM Agreement was being negotiated, there were two GATT panel proceedings underway examining the meaning of these provisions. In *US - Sonar Mapping*[2447], the United States argued that the procurement at issue involved the procurement of a product under a "service contract", and was therefore excluded from the scope of the Procurement Code. The European Communities disagreed. The panel proceeded to analyse the meaning of the phrase "service contracts *per se*" in Article I:1(a). The panel ultimately rejected the United States' position, and found that the procurement at issue fell within the scope of the Code, based on its interpretation of the scope of Article I:1(a). In *Norway – Trondheim Toll Ring*[2448], the question before the panel was whether, under the contract in question, the Norwegian entity had procured prototypes which had been developed at its request in the course of, and for, a particular "contract for research or original development". The panel examined the different interpretations of Norway and the United States of the phrase "contract for research ... or original development" in Article V:15(e). The panel ultimately concluded that the procurement fell within the scope of the Procurement Code.

7.967 While these panel proceedings were underway, and while the SCM Agreement was being negotiated, the parties to the plurilateral Tokyo Round Procurement Code were in the process of extending the scope and coverage of that agreement to cover purchases of services. The renegotiation of the Code led to the WTO Agreement on Government Procurement.[2449] The WTO Agreement on Government Procurement "expand{s} the coverage of the Agreement to include service contracts".[2450]

7.968 While the SCM Agreement was being negotiated, parallel negotiations on trade in services were also taking place. Article XIII:2 and XV of the GATS reflect the fact that the negotiators of the GATS were unable to reach agreement

---

includes services incidental to the supply of products if the value of these incidental services does not exceed that of the products themselves, but not service contracts *per se*".

[2446] Article IX:6(b) stated that "Not later than the end of the third year from the entry into force of this Agreement and periodically thereafter, the Parties thereto shall undertake further negotiations, with a view to broadening and improving this Agreement on the basis of mutual reciprocity, having regard to the provisions of Article III relating to developing countries. In this connection, the Committee shall, at an early stage, explore the possibilities of expanding the coverage of this Agreement to include service contracts".

[2447] GATT Panel Report, *US – Sonar Mapping*, circulated 23 Apr 1992 (not adopted).

[2448] GATT Panel Report, *Norway – Trondheim Toll Ring*, adopted 13 May 1992.

[2449] The Agreement on Government Procurement, a plurilateral agreement, is included in Annex 4 to the WTO Agreement.

[2450] Agreement on Government Procurement, preamble. See also, Article I (Scope and Coverage).

DSR 2012:III

1307

Report of the Panel

on disciplines regarding governmental purchases of services, or on disciplines governing the provision of subsidies to service suppliers.

7.969 When the omission of "purchases" of "services" is read against this historical background, it becomes clear that the drafters could not have removed the express reference to "purchases" of "services" in Article 1.1(a)(1)(iii) on the understanding that the reference was superfluous, and that it would be understood and intended that such transactions were implicitly covered by Article 1.1(a)(1)(i). Rather, the exclusion of "purchases" of "services" from Article 1 can only be seen as a deliberate choice.

7.970 The Panel is not entitled to assume that the disappearance of certain terms from the text of Article 1 of the SCM Agreement "was merely accidental or an inadvertent oversight on the part of either harassed negotiators or inattentive draftsmen".[2451] The Panel must "read and interpret the words actually used" in Article 1, not the words that the Panel "may feel should have been used".[2452] It is not open to the Panel to impute into Article 1 "words that are not there".[2453] Having considered the ordinary meaning of the terms of Article 1.1(a)(1)(i), their context, the object and purpose of the SCM Agreement, and the preparatory work and circumstances of the conclusion of the SCM Agreement, the Panel finds that transactions *properly characterized* as purchases of services are excluded from the scope of Article 1.1(a)(1)(i) of the SCM Agreement.

> Whether NASA R&D contracts with Boeing are properly characterized as "purchases of services"

Arguments of the European Communities

7.971 In the introduction to the section of its first written submission addressing NASA, DOD and DOC aeronautics R&D, the European Communities asserts that "NASA and DOD generally provide funding for LCA-related R&D through what they call "contracts", but what are in reality grants to Boeing/MD for LCA-related R&D expenses".[2454] In the sections of its first written submission addressing NASA aeronautics R&D in particular, the European Communities argues in respect of each of the eight programmes that "NASA directly transferred funds in the form of grants to Boeing's LCA division".[2455] The European Communities argues that this "direct R&D funding"[2456] constitutes a

---

[2451] Appellate Body Report, *US – Underwear*, p. 17.

[2452] Appellate Body Report, *EC – Hormones*, para. 181.

[2453] Appellate Body Report, *India – Patents (US)*, para. 45.

[2454] European Communities' first written submission, para. 457.

[2455] European Communities' first written submission, paras 524, 548, 572, 588, 603, 618, 631, and 650.

[2456] *Ibid.*

1308

DSR 2012:III

direct transfer of funds within the meaning of Article 1.1(a)(1)(i) of the SCM Agreement.

7.972 The European Communities further argues, in respect of each of the eight programmes, that NASA provided Boeing with access to government "facilities, equipment and employees", which constitutes a provision of goods or services within the meaning of Article 1.1(a)(1)(iii) of the SCM Agreement.[2457] According to the European Communities, the value of these "facilities, equipment and employees" is partly captured in NASA's "institutional support" budgets, and the European Communities occasionally refers to the provision of access to facilities, equipment and employees as "institutional support".[2458]

7.973 In its second written submission, the European Communities responds to the United States' argument that NASA's R&D contracts with Boeing are "purchases of services" that fall outside of the scope of Article 1.1(a)(1) of the SCM Agreement. The European Communities argues that NASA's R&D contracts with Boeing cannot be characterized as "purchases of services", and that "purchases of services" are in any event not excluded from the scope of Article 1.1(a)(1).[2459]

7.974 In its response to question 15 from the Panel, the European Communities argues that NASA R&D contracts with Boeing are not properly characterized as "purchases of services" for four reasons. First, because "NASA R&D contracts do not ultimately aim at the acquisition of a service for the direct benefit and own use of the government". Rather, with regard to the NASA R&D contracts, the R&D that Boeing performs under the aspects of the eight aeronautics R&D programmes in question "ultimately benefits Boeing, and is not a service for the direct benefit and use of NASA". NASA is undisputedly "not in the business of manufacturing LCA or its parts, and therefore has no demonstrable need for the LCA-related R&D that Boeing performs under the programs in question".[2460] Second, because "NASA R&D contracts do not contain the typical elements of a purchase". In this regard, the European Communities reiterates that because NASA's contracts with Boeing "are intended to primarily and ultimately benefit Boeing's LCA manufacture", they deviate from a typical purchase where one would expect the purchased service to be of primary interest for the purchaser. The European Communities reiterates that "NASA, however, receives virtually nothing of value from these contracts, since it is not in the business of acquiring

---

[2457] European Communities' first written submission, paras 524, 548, 572, 588, 603, 618, 631, 650, and 890-901.

[2458] See e.g. European Communities' response to question 148, para. 181 ("the European Communities' claim is that NASA provides "facilities, equipment, and employees" to Boeing for LCA-related R&D. This claim is captured by the first element of item 2(b) of the European Communities' Panel Request. The second element of item 2(b) ... is intended to point out that "institutional support" reflects *part of* the value of the "facilities, equipment, and employees" provided by NASA.")

[2459] European Communities' second written submission, paras. 329-365.

[2460] European Communities' response to question 15(c), para. 61.

DSR 2012:III

Report of the Panel

or manufacturing LCA or its parts".[2461] Third, because "NASA R&D contracts do not exclusively affect trade in services". The European Communities argues that the "R&D services" that Boeing performed under the aspects of the NASA R&D programs in question "relate directly to the production of LCA – i.e. goods".[2462] Fourth, because "Boeing is not a genuine provider of LCA-related R&D services". In this regard, the European Communities argues that "Boeing does not offer such R&D services to anybody else but NASA and DOD" and that "Boeing has not advertised itself as a service provider for LCA-related R&D in the market".[2463]

Arguments of the United States

7.975 With respect to the existence of a financial contribution, the United States submits that NASA's R&D contracts with Boeing are not "grants", as the European Communities asserts, but are rather "purchases of services". The United States argues that "purchases of services" are not covered by Article 1.1(a)(1) of the SCM Agreement. Accordingly, any payments and/or access to facilities, equipment and employees provided to Boeing under NASA R&D contracts are not financial contributions within the meaning of Article 1.1(a)(1). With regard to the European Communities' assertions, it is true that NASA does not acquire or produce large civil aircraft. However, NASA does acquire, produce, and disseminate knowledge. And, accordingly, the "true purpose" of the NASA programmes is to develop and disseminate the greatest amount of information to the broadest group in the shortest amount of time possible, and not to "convey resources to Boeing". That information is used both within government, by U.S. government agencies, such as the Federal Aviation Administration ("FAA") and DOD, and airport authorities, and outside of government by industry and academia. NASA's contracts with Boeing and its actions provide evidence that this is the case, and that the challenged measures are purchases of services – not just in name, but in substance. NASA formulates its own goals, based on consultations with a wide variety of stakeholders. NASA seeks proposals from contractors on how to meet those goals, and accepts the bid that presents the best value. NASA and its contractors negotiate over the terms of the contract. The contractor must then carry out all of the terms of the contract in return for payment by NASA. This process, documented by the citations to U.S. procurement regulations, the numerous examples of individual contracts and modifications, and the huge volume of publicly disseminated literature generated by these programmes, demonstrates that NASA's contracts with

---

[2461] European Communities' response to question 15(c), para. 63.
[2462] European Communities' response to question 15(c), para. 65.
[2463] European Communities' response to question 15(c), para. 67.

Boeing are not, as the European Communities would have the Panel believe, a "sham".[2464]

7.976 While the United States argues in its first written submission that Space Act Agreements should be analyzed as "purchases of services", it has subsequently adopted the view that both reimbursable and non-reimbursable Space Agreements involve a provision of goods and services by NASA.[2465] The United States accepts that the provision of (access to) facilities, equipment and employees provided to Boeing through the Space Act Agreements at issue constitutes a provision of goods or services within the meaning of Article 1.1(a)(1)(iii) of the SCM Agreement.

Evaluation by the Panel

7.977 Having concluded that purchases of services are excluded from the scope of Article 1.1(a)(1), the next question before the Panel is whether NASA R&D contracts are properly characterized as "purchases of services". The parties agree that NASA provides goods and services to Boeing, within the meaning of Article 1.1(a)(1)(iii) of the SCM Agreement, under Space Act Agreements.[2466] However, the parties disagree on the question of whether the payments and access to facilities, equipment and employees provided to Boeing through its R&D contracts with NASA are covered by the definition of "financial contribution" in Article 1.1(a)(1) of the SCM Agreement. In this regard, the United States argues that NASA's R&D contracts with Boeing are "purchases of services" that fall outside of the scope of Article 1.1(a)(1). As the Appellate Body has recognized, "{a}n evaluation of the existence of a financial contribution involves consideration of the *nature of the transaction* through which something of economic value is transferred by a government".[2467] In this case, the Panel's task is to reach a conclusion regarding the nature of NASA's aeronautics R&D contracts with Boeing.

[2464] United States' first written submission, paras. 213-225; United States' second written submission, paras. 60-64; United States' responses (and/or comments on European Communities' responses) to questions 15(c), 16, 19, 20, 151, 154, 155, and 327.

[2465] United States' response to question 18, para. 39. See also, United States' response to question 161.

[2466] The European Communities has provided specific examples in its submissions of the "facilities, equipment and employees" provided to Boeing under NASA Space Act Agreements. European Communities' first written submission, para. 524, footnote 827; para. 614; para. 618, footnote 1020; para. 650, footnote 1071; para. 645; and para. 892; European Communities' second written submission, paras. 389, 390. In its response to question 148, the European Communities states that it "has described the 'facilities, equipment and employees' provided by NASA in detail in its prior submissions by citing to specific NASA Space Act Agreements and other contracts". European Communities' response to question 148, para. 172, footnote 161. See also, European Communities' response to question 148, para. 188, footnote 172.

[2467] Appellate Body Report, *US – Softwood Lumber IV*, para. 52 (emphasis added). The "nature" of something is generally defined as the basic or inherent features, character or quality of something; *Oxford Dictionary of English*, 2ed (rev), 2005, p. 1172.

Report of the Panel

7.978 In the Panel's view, whether or not NASA's R&D contracts with Boeing are properly characterized as a "purchase of services" depends on *the nature of the work* that Boeing was required to perform under the contracts, and more specifically, *whether the R&D that Boeing was required to conduct was principally for its own benefit and use, or whether it was principally for the benefit and use of the U.S. Government (or unrelated third parties)*. This for several reasons. First, the Panel considers that NASA's R&D contracts with Boeing should be characterized based on their *terms*, and the core term[2468] of these contracts is the work that Boeing was required to perform. Second, it is inherent in the ordinary meaning of the concept of a "service" that the work performed be for the benefit and use of the entity funding the R&D (or unrelated third parties).[2469] Third, characterizing the transactions on the basis of whether the R&D that Boeing was required to conduct was principally for its own benefit and use, or whether it was principally for the benefit and use of the U.S. Government (or unrelated third parties), is broadly consistent with the arguments of the parties and third parties in this case.[2470] Fourth, focusing on whether the work performed was principally for the benefit and use of the government (or unrelated third parties) is consistent with prior GATT panel reports examining the question of whether a transaction was properly characterized as a government procurement.[2471]

[2468] The Panel uses the word "term" in its ordinary sense, i.e. "Conditions under which some action may be undertaken ... *stipulated requirememts* or limitations", and specifically, "Conditions with regard to payment for goods or services", and "A condition, a prerequisite of something." *Shorter Oxford English Dictionary*, p. 3215 (5th ed. 2002).

[2469] The *Shorter Oxford English Dictionary* defines "service" to mean, "An act of helping or benefiting *another* ... The action of serving, helping, or benefiting *another*; behaviour conducive to the welfare or advantage of *another*". *Shorter Oxford English Dictionary*, p. 2768 (5th ed. 2002) (emphasis added).

[2470] According to the European Communities, whether or not a transaction is properly characterized as a purchase of services depends, *inter alia*, on whether "the ultimate purpose of the transaction would need to be the acquisition of a service for the direct benefit and own use of the government". European Communities' response to question 15(b), para. 55. Canada notes that in general terms, "a service is the performance of duties or work for someone else", such that the relevant question is whether the government has "procured the performance of duties or work for itself or anyone else (other than the service seller)". Canada's response to question 5(c), paras. 4-7.

[2471] In *US – Sonar Mapping*, the panel stated that "{w}hile not intending to offer a definition of government procurement within the meaning of Article I:1(a) {of the Tokyo Round Agreement on Government Procurement}, the Panel felt that in considering the facts of any particular case the following characteristics, none of which alone could be decisive, provide guidance as to whether a transaction should be regarded as government procurement within the meaning of Article I:1(a): payment by government, *governmental use of or benefit from the product*, government possession and government control over the obtaining of the product". The panel concluded that in that case, the government agency would "*enjoy the benefits* of the system's purchase - Antarctic research and the preparation of seabed maps – which were clearly *for government purposes*, and the Government can thus be regarded as the *ultimate beneficiary* of the system". (GATT Panel Report, *US – Sonar Mapping*, paras. 4.7 and 4.10 (emphasis added). See also, GATT Panel Report, *Norway – Trondheim*, paras. 4.8-4.13.)

1312

DSR 2012:III

US - Large Civil Aircraft (2nd Complaint)

7.979 Having formulated the question that needs to be asked and answered, the Panel now turns to the question of what kinds of evidence it will consider for the purpose of answering that question. In general, the Panel has eschewed any notion of focusing on one single fact for the purpose of reaching a conclusion on that question. Rather, the Panel believes that it should review all of the evidence regarding the terms and surrounding context of NASA's aeronautics R&D contracts with Boeing, with a view to reaching a conclusion on whether NASA's aeronautics R&D contracts with Boeing are, in essence, purchases of services. In the Panel's view, there is no reason why, for example, the type of instrument and so-called "formal" features of the transaction would be disregarded *if* they shed light on the question of the nature of the R&D activities required of Boeing under the contracts; there is likewise no reason why, for example, evidence of the purpose and motives of the programmes under which they were entered into would be disregarded *if* they shed light on the question of the nature of the R&D activities required of Boeing under the contracts. In both cases, they are not extraneous features divorced from the "terms" of the transactions; rather, they could be central to understanding the core *term* of the transaction. That is, this is evidence that could be very helpful in understanding whether the nature of the work performed under Boeing's R&D contracts with NASA (the core terms of the transactions) was principally for the U.S. Government's benefit or use (and/or for the benefit or use of unrelated third parties), or rather for Boeing's own benefit or use. That is the question that needs to be answered for the purpose of determining whether the transactions are properly characterized as purchases of services.

7.980 More specifically, the Panel will consider, *inter alia*, the legislation authorizing the programmes at issue, the types of instruments entered into between NASA and Boeing, whether NASA has any demonstrable use for the R&D performed under these programmes, the allocation of intellectual property rights under these transactions, and whether the transactions at issue had the typical elements of a "purchase of services".[2472]

7.981 When considered in its totality[2473], the evidence relating to NASA aeronautics R&D, some of which is individually discussed below, leads to the conclusion that the work that Boeing performed under its aeronautics R&D contracts with NASA was principally for its own benefit or use, rather than for the benefit or use of the U.S. Government (or unrelated third parties).

[2472] As will become clear in our review of some of the evidence before the Panel, these different considerations overlap to a certain extent.

[2473] The Appellate Body has on a number of occasions stressed that a panel must consider the evidence before it "in its totality". See e.g. Appellate Body Report, *US – Continued Zeroing*, para. 331 ("Article 11 requires a panel to consider evidence before it in its totality, which includes consideration of submitted evidence in relation to other evidence. A particular piece of evidence, even if not sufficient by itself to establish an asserted fact or claim, may contribute to establishing that fact or claim when considered in conjunction with other pieces of evidence".)

DSR 2012:III

Report of the Panel

Accordingly, the Panel concludes that NASA's R&D contracts with Boeing are not properly characterized as "purchases of services".

7.982 We begin with NASA's statutory basis for performing aeronautical research, which is found in the *National Aeronautics and Space Act of 1958*.[2474] The Space Act provides that:

> "(d) The aeronautical and space activities of the United States shall be conducted so as to contribute materially to one or more of the following objectives:
>
> > (1) The expansion of human knowledge of the Earth and of phenomena in the atmosphere and space;
> >
> > (2) *The improvement of the usefulness, performance, speed, safety, and efficiency of aeronautical and space vehicles*;
> >
> > (3) The development and operation of vehicles capable of carrying instruments, equipment, supplies, and living organisms through space;
> >
> > (4) The establishment of long-range studies of the potential benefits to be gained from, the opportunities for, and the problems involved in the utilization of aeronautical and space activities for peaceful and scientific purposes;
> >
> > (5) *The preservation of the role of the United States as a leader in aeronautical and space science and technology* and in the application thereof to the conduct of peaceful activities within and outside the atmosphere;
> >
> > (6) The making available to agencies directly concerned with national defense of discoveries that have military value or significance, and the furnishing by such agencies, to the civilian agency established to direct and control nonmilitary aeronautical and space activities, of information as to discoveries which have value or significance to that agency;

[2474] National Aeronautics and Space Act of 1958, Pub. L. No. 85-568, as amended, Exhibit EC-286 (emphasis added).

US - Large Civil Aircraft (2nd Complaint)

(7)   Cooperation by the United States with other nations and groups of nations in work done pursuant to this Act and in the peaceful application of the results thereof;

(8)   The most effective utilization of the scientific and engineering resources of the United States, with close cooperation among all interested agencies of the United States in order to avoid unnecessary duplication of effort, facilities, and equipment;

(9)   *The preservation of the United States preeminent position in aeronautics and space through research and technology development related to associated manufacturing processes.*"[2475]

7.983 We note that Sec. 203(a) of the *Space Act* provides that NASA must, in order to carry out the objectives of the *Space Act*, "provide for the widest practicable and *appropriate* dissemination of information concerning its activities and the results thereof".

7.984 We now turn to an examination of the *types of instruments* entered into between NASA and Boeing. In the case of NASA aeronautics R&D, we consider that NASA's decision to provide payments and access to facilities to Boeing through "procurement contracts" rather than "assistance instruments" does not shed very much light on the nature of the transactions. Our reasoning on this issue is as follows. NASA considers that a "direct benefit or use" to NASA exists when it initially drafts a scope of the work to advance research under one of its programmes and defines the delivery of the end products. In the case of the procurement contracts awarded to Boeing at issue in this dispute, the research under the contract advanced one of NASA's research programmes and NASA determined particular work that it needed, so it solicited proposals under a request for proposals, and awarded contracts.[2476] Thus, the United States explains that NASA considers R&D to have "direct benefit or use" for NASA where that R&D "advances research under one of its programmes". Likewise, NASA considers R&D conducted pursuant to a Space Act Agreement to be of "benefit" to NASA where that R&D advances its "program requirements and objectives".

7.985 We turn now to the question of whether NASA has any demonstrable use for the R&D performed under the eight aeronautics programmes at issue. Based on the Panel's review of all of the evidence before it, it appears that a principal purpose of NASA's aeronautics R&D in general, and of the eight aeronautics

---

[2475] *Ibid.*
[2476] United States' response to question 151(a), para. 137.

DSR 2012:III   1315

Report of the Panel

programmes at issue, is to transfer technology to U.S. industry with a view to improving U.S. competitiveness vis-à-vis foreign competitors.

7.986 In a 1992 congressional meeting on Federal Support for U.S. Aeronautics Industry, NASA's Richard Petersen, Associate Administrator of Office of Aeronautics, Exploration and Technology, stated that:

> "The current *U.S. leadership* in aeronautics has not happened by accident. It is the result of a successful industry and government partnership that has evolved since the founding of the NACA, over 77 years ago. In this partnership, there is a shared responsibility between NASA, Industry, DOD and FAA for technology development and in *securing U.S. leadership.* NASA plays a central role in developing and *transferring technology,* a responsibility we take very seriously."[2477]

7.987 In a statement to a Senate subcommittee in 2001, Daniel Goldin, former Administrator of NASA, explained that past NASA research is already incorporated into Boeing planes and that NASA's partnership with Boeing will continue well into the future:

> "{I}f the Europeans are going to make small, marginal improvements with what we're saying here, we'll whip them. Money is not the magic ingredient. The partnership is. It is absolutely clear. We have been talking to Boeing and working with Boeing and I think it's important you talk to the Boeing representative David Swain here today. We've been talking to Pratt & Whitney and GE, who are the backbone of our commercial aviation. They don't want us to do the near-term things that will impact the next five years. The die is cast for the next five years. The things we have already done are into their products and we're now looking, what can we do now for a decade from now. ... {I}n talking to Pratt & Whitney, GE and Boeing, looking at a futuristic program like that {i.e. the HSR Program} where the government does the high-risk, high-payoff research and then transitions it to industry, they say that they're interested. ... With Boeing, we need to look at new ways of building wings, new tools so they can get

---

[2477] Federal Support for U.S. Aeronautics Industry: Hearing before the House Subcomm. on Government Activities and Transportation of the Comm. on Government Operations, 102nd Cong. (1992) (statement of Richard Petersen, Associate Administrator, Office of Aeronautics, Exploration and Technology, NASA), Exhibit EC-326, p. 182 (emphasis added).

US - Large Civil Aircraft (2nd Complaint)

the cycle time by a factor of two, down by a factor of two. The cycle time is too long for building planes."[2478]

7.988 In a 1993 Senate hearing, Mr. Goldin stated that:

"As global competition increases, we will have to improve our ability to assist industry to commercialize technology. *We are all painfully aware that Airbus beat us to the punch* in commercializing, among other advanced technologies, fly-by-wire controls, a technology invented in the United States by NASA and DOD. *To prevent this kind of occurrence in the future*, we are now working harder at developing and validating new technologies for industry to commercialize, and *we intend to do it faster, better, and cheaper than our competitors*. NASA's Aeronautics Program can contribute by ensuring that commercialization by industry is an integral part of program planning from the very beginning, accomplished in cooperation with our partners. This is a change from the way we have done business in recent years – a much needed change – and exactly the tack we are taking."[2479]

In response to written questions, Administrator Goldin stated:

Question 1. Do you believe that *American manufacturers* are behind Airbus in terms of technology?

Answer. ... The principal shortfall in *U.S. technology development* has been insufficient validation and risk reduction to allow *U.S. manufacturers* to take full and early advantage of technology availability. The proposed NASA aeronautics enhancements for FY 1994 focus on cooperation with industry through the technology validation phase.

...

Question 3. You have discussed the importance of NASA's aeronautics research programs to the aircraft manufacturing industry. What steps has NASA taken to ensure that technology development under these programs is effectively transferred to

---

[2478] NASA's Aeronautics Program: Hearing before the Senate Subcomm. on Science, Technology and Space of the Comm. on Commerce, Science and Transportation, 107th Cong. (2001), FDCH Political Transcripts, 24 April 2001, Exhibit EC-292, pp. 13-18.

[2479] Competitiveness of the Aerospace Industry: Hearing on S. 419 Before the Senate Comm. on Commerce, Science, and Transportation, 103rd Cong. 81 (1993), Exhibit EC-1365, p. 34 (emphasis added).

DSR 2012:III

1317

Report of the Panel

industry? How does NASA ensure that *American manufacturers have access to these technologies before foreign companies*?

Answer. NASA generally performs its research in cooperation with the aeronautics industry, thereby providing some direct mechanisms for technology transfer. However, we are stepping up our efforts to increase and improve industry involvement both in planning and implementing our programs. Additionally, much of the Aeronautics investment, beginning in FY 1994, is aimed at developing technologies to a more advanced stage, reducing the risks sufficiently for industry commercialization. Industry's partnership in the NASA program should allow manufacturers to easily continue the technology development through commercialization, as desired. Furthermore, the natural advantage *U.S. industry* is afforded through direct partnership in the NASA technology development program will be supported by NASA contracts and cooperative agreements *which include provisions to protect commercially valuable and/or sensitive technology from premature foreign dissemination.*"[2480]

7.989 In a 1994 hearing, Wesley L. Harris, NASA Associate Administrator for Aeronautics, stated that:

"NASA's objective in the Advanced Subsonic Technology (AST) program is to *provide U.S. industry with a competitive edge to recapture market share*, maintain a strongly *positive balance of trade*, and *increase U.S. jobs*. The program has been planned and is being implemented in close coordination with *U.S. industry* and the Federal Aviation Administration (FAA) to address critical technology needs for a new generation of *superior U.S. subsonic aircraft* and engines, an efficient global air transportation system, and an expanded role for advanced short-haul aircraft in the civil transportation system."[2481]

Mr. Harris went on to state that:

"Also funded from our R&T base is the research we conduct with high performance aircraft, which supports both military and civil applications. In FY 1993, we demonstrated the use of throttles

---

[2480] Competitiveness of the Aerospace Industry: Hearing on S. 419 Before the Senate Comm. on Commerce, Science, and Transportation, 103rd Cong. 81 (1993), Exhibit EC-273, pp. 80-81 (emphasis added).

[2481] Statement of Wesley L. Harris, NASA Associate Administrator for Aeronautics, before the House Subcommittee on Technology, Environment, and Aviation, 10 February 1994, Exhibit EC-359, p. 4 (emphasis added).

1318   DSR 2012:III

US - Large Civil Aircraft (2ⁿᵈ Complaint)

only for flight control by landing our F- 1 5 aircraft with a specially designed propulsion control system. The NASA research team was honored for this Propulsion Controlled Aircraft (PCA) project by Popular Science magazine with a "Best of What's New' Award. The technology is now being extended to civil transport aircraft. This is *an example of how we have worked with our DoD partners to transfer technologies developed from our integrated flight and propulsion controls research to our commercial customers*, which improves safety *and makes them more competitive.* ... the R&T Base supports our unique national aeronautics research facilities which include wind tunnels, simulators, computational capability and research aircraft. These provide strong tools for aeronautics research and help increase *the U.S. aerospace industry's competitiveness.*"[2482]

7.990 In 1996, NASA Langley Center Director Paul Holloway stated that "{i}t is really important to us at Langley when *a customer like the Boeing Company uses and appreciates our technology.* This is the *reason for our existence*".[2483] Along the same lines, in 1998, Langley Director Dr. J.F. Creedon stated that:

> "*The reason that there is a NASA Langley and the other aeronautics centers is to contribute technology to assure the pre-eminence of US aeronautics.* When Boeing brings out a flagship product like the 777, that uses as many products of NASA technology as are on this plane, it reaffirms *the reason that we exist* and it is very gratifying to us."[2484]

7.991 At a 2005 hearing, Dr. J. Victor Lebacqz, NASA Associate Administrator for Aeronautics Research, stated that:

> "{t}he revolutionary technologies developed by NASA within the next decade will form the basis for a new generation of environmentally friendly aircraft and will enhance *U.S. competitiveness* 20 years from now."[2485]

7.992 The evidence contains similar statements from senior Boeing officials. For example, in a 1994 hearing, Robert Spitzer, Vice President of Technology with BCA, explained that:

[2482] *Ibid.*, pp. 8-9 (emphasis added).

[2483] NASA News Release No. 96-33, "Boeing says 'thanks' with visit of innovative 777 airliner to NASA Langley," 8 May 1996, Exhibit EC-1362 (emphasis added).

[2484] Video clip of Langley Director Dr. J.F. Creedon on visit of Boeing 777, Langley Research Center, LV-1998-00023, Exhibit EC-287 (emphasis added).

[2485] Statement of Dr. J. Victor Lebacqz, NASA Associate Administrator for Aeronautics Research, before the House Subcommittee on Space and Aeronautics, 16 March 2005, Exhibit EC-289, pp. 2-3 (emphasis added).

DSR 2012:III

Report of the Panel

"The NASA aeronautics role is different from the space role within NASA where they are the customer and industry is the supplier. In the commercial aeronautics the *manufacturer of airplanes is the customer and NASA is the supplier.*"[2486]

7.993 A 1994 NASA document entitled *Achieving Aeronautics Leadership, NASA Aeronautics Strategic Enterprise Plan, 1995-2000*[2487] states that the "Aeronautics Industry" is one of its main "customers" (along with DOD, FAA, the academic community, and non-aerospace industries). The document defines "customers" as "entities that require NASA-developed technologies, facilities, and/or technical expertise to enhance the economic competitiveness, military security, and air transportation infrastructure of the United States".[2488] It goes on to state that while each of NASA's "customer segments" is facing its own challenges, there are several factors which have severely affected the "industry" (i.e. the "industry" that is NASA's "customer") as a whole, including the following:

"*Foreign Competition.* During the same period in which domestic producers have been facing this "profit squeeze" between cost-conscious customers and escalating production costs, foreign competition, often subsidized by their host governments, has captured *a large share of previously U.S. dominated markets.* For example, *U.S. manufacturers* held 80 percent of the large commercial transport market in 1974, but only 68 percent in 1993. And in 1994, for the first time ever, Europe's Airbus Industrie consortium posted more new orders than did Boeing. Similar losses are working their way through the lower-tier supplier industries. Although subsequent trade negotiations have been addressing this situation, concerns still remain about future foreign support in aircraft development and production."[2489]

The document goes on to state that NASA will:

"Emphasize Technology Transfer. The Aeronautic Enterprise has long recognized the importance of ensuring that our customers actually use the products that we develop. The Enterprise will continue *to emphasize technology transfer to the aerospace community through joint program planning and execution,* and to all U.S. industry through proactive commercial technology

---

[2486] Hearing Before the Subcommittee on Technology, Environment and Aviation of the Committee on Science, Space, and Technology, US House of Representatives, 10 February 1994, Exhibit EC-1363, p. 128 (emphasis added).

[2487] NASA, Achieving Aeronautics Leadership, NASA Aeronautics Strategic Enterprise Plan, 1995-2000, Exhibit EC-302 (emphasis added).

[2488] *Ibid.*, p. 11.

[2489] *Ibid.*, p. 12 (emphasis added).

1320

DSR 2012:III

US - Large Civil Aircraft (2nd Complaint)

utilization outreach efforts. *The Enterprise will also continue to protect sensitive research and technology as appropriate."*

7.994 A 1991 study prepared by the Office of Technology Assessment, a research entity of the US Congress, states that:

"NASA's aeronautics R&D program also benefits *U.S. aircraft producers*, though it does not *always* bestow a competitive advantage. The program helps *U.S. aircraft manufacturers* develop and adopt new technologies by conducting research inhouse and then transferring the results to companies and by contracting with companies to perform specific research tasks, usually in cooperation with inhouse NASA research. Further, NASA researchers act as a free consulting service for industry engineers having technical problems. The availability of technologies developed and tested at NASA's expense and risk helps aircraft manufacturers incorporate new capabilities into their products at diminished cost or risk, just as military developments do."[2490]

7.995 A 1997 report by the Congressional Budget Office states that:

"The National Aeronautics and Space Administration (NASA) funds the development of technology and systems intended for use in commercial airliners—both subsonic and supersonic-*with the explicit objective of preserving the U.S. share of the current and future world airliner market.* ... NASA justifies the supersonic part of its aeronautical research and technology program the same way it justifies the program's subsonic component: the agency needs to support *U.S. businesses* that produce large commercial aircraft for the world market. ... Although a case can be made for federal support of R&D that ultimately benefits private businesses and is consistent with an economically efficient allocation of resources, it applies only weakly, or not at all, to the production of large aircraft. The benefits from the R&D supported by the NASA programs in question {the AST and HSR programs} fall almost exclusively to aircraft manufacturers, their suppliers, and airlines."[2491]

[2490] Office of Technology Assessment of the Congress of the United States, Competing Economies: America, Europe, and the Pacific Rim, Chapter 8 (selections): Government Support of the Large Commercial Aircraft Industries of Japan, Europe, and the United States, 1991, Exhibit EC-306, p. 347 (emphasis added).

[2491] Congressional Budget Office, Reducing the Deficit: Spending and Revenue Options, March 1997, Exhibit EC-307, pp. 152-153 (emphasis added).

DSR 2012:III   1321

Report of the Panel

7.996 In 2003, Langley catalogued some of the contributions it had made to US large civil aircraft in a publication entitled *Concept to Reality: Contributions of the NASA Langley Research Center to the US Civil Aircraft of the 1990's*. This publication states that:

> "A high priority is placed by NASA on the rapid, timely dissemination of information to *appropriate U.S. organizations*, while being extremely sensitive to proprietary interests and the protection of technology and critical intellectual property. ... Numerous NASA focused programs for civil aircraft have emerged and delivered unprecedented opportunities for the maturation of key technologies to *the U.S. airframe, propulsion, and avionics and flight controls industries* for the design of advanced aircraft."[2492]

This same publication states that Boeing "flew the first 777 to Langley for a 'thank you' visit" as "a gesture of thanks for NASA's technology contributions to its creation".[2493] According to this publication, Langley research contributed to several advances in aerodynamics, flight dynamics, structures and materials, flight systems, noise reduction, and operating problems.[2494]

7.997 A 2003 Langley *Economic Impact Report* highlights numerous contributions made by Langley to aircraft design.[2495] This report states, in a section entitled "Direct Impact of NASA Langley on Government and *U.S. Industry*", that:

> "Within the manufacturing sector, aerospace is the only industry with a positive contribution to the *U.S. balance of trade*. It provides a net annual contribution of more than $21 billion. However, *the U.S. faces strong competition*. Prior to 1974, the U.S. had more than 90 percent of the commercial transport market share. Today, the U.S. share is around 60 percent. To preserve our nation's economic health and the welfare of the traveling public, *NASA has set bold research objectives and goals to sustain U.S. leadership* in aeronautics and space. NASA Langley's leadership and technology advancements in aviation safety, advanced subsonic technology, airframe systems and high-speed research play a pivotal role in accomplishing these goals."[2496]

[2492] Joseph R. Chambers, Concept to Reality: Contributions of the NASA Langley Research Center to U.S. Civil Aircraft of the 1990s (2003), Exhibit EC-293, p. 1 (emphasis added).

[2493] *Ibid.*, pp. 166-167.

[2494] *Ibid.*, pp. 249-258.

[2495] NASA Langley Research Center, Economic Impact, Fiscal Year 1998, Exhibit EC-303, p. 17.

[2496] *Ibid.*, p. 16 (emphasis added).

US - Large Civil Aircraft (2nd Complaint)

7.998 A 1994 NASA "Facts Online" publication entitled "NASA's B-737 Flying Laboratory" catalogues a number of "Advanced Technologies Tranferred *To U.S. Industry*".[2497] It proceeds to discuss "Technology Transfer Lessons":

"Gone are the days when successful technology transfer is as simple as writing a report on research results after the work is completed. There is a growing consensus ... that technology transfer efforts stand a much better chance of success if they occur as a part of the technology development process, through personal contact between NASA and industry engineers. By involving industry earlier in the process, NASA Langley B-737 program managers have helped insure that their efforts are relevant to industry's needs. Also, flight testing new concepts on the airplane has provided unassailable proof that the technology will work."[2498]

7.999 The ACT Program Budget states that:

"*The goal of the Advanced Composites Technology (ACT) program is to increase the competitiveness of the U.S. aeronautics industry by putting the commercial transport manufacturers* in a position to expand the application of composites beyond the secondary structures in use today to wings and fuselages by the end of this decade. Industry's resistance to using composites is one of economics. While the current demonstrated level of composites technology can promise improved aircraft performance and lower operating costs through reduced structural weight, it does so with increased manufacturing costs, currently twice the cost of aluminum. The goal of this program is to verify composite structure designs that will have acquisition costs 20-25% less and weigh 30-50% less than an aluminum aircraft sized for the same payload and mission."[2499]

7.1000 NASA Contract NAS1-20546, funded under NASA's ACT Program, states that:

"The objectives of this contract are to perform design, analysis, fabrication and testing verification of a full-scale composite wing structure *for commercial transport aircraft. The contract results are expected to provide the technical data required for the*

[2497] NASA Facts Online, "NASA's B-737 Flying Laboratory," May 1994, Exhibit EC-1389, pp. 1-3 (emphasis added).
[2498] *Ibid.*, pp. 4-5.
[2499] NASA ACT Budget Estimates, FY 1989-FY 1997, Exhibit EC-321, FY 1997, SAT 4-21 (emphasis added).

DSR 2012:III
1323

Report of the Panel

application of composite wing structures in new 21ˢᵗ Century commercial transport aircraft."[2500]

This contract goes on to require that the Contractor, in that case MD, directly transfer the new manufacturing technology "to other *U.S. aircraft builders".*[2501]

7.1001 Certain contracts between NASA and Boeing under the ACT Program contained a "For Early Domestic Dissemination" (FEDD) clause, stating that:

> "It has been determined that performance under this contract may result in the generation of data having *significant commercial potential.* In recognition of this agency's *policy of enhancing the opportunities for U.S. economic benefits by providing for early dissemination of such data in the US Government and U.S. domestic industry prior to general publication* ... It is agreed that the Contractor will not grant permission to publish this data or release said data to foreign parties, or transfer this information to foreign parties, or associates in any form without prior concurrence of the Contracting Officer .... Information for general release will be two (2) years from publication date indicated on the document."[2502]

7.1002 Space Act Agreements entered into between NASA and Boeing under the ACT Program state that:

> "The NASA Program has been structured around definitions of success for the *commercial industry* .... {M}any of the deliverables from the NASA program will directly benefit *Boeing."*[2503]

> "The principal technical objectives of the program {include}: ... {t}ransfer the technology to *U.S. industry* through technology transfer workshops...."[2504]

> "*NASA has a goal under its Advanced Composites Technology (ACT) program to help establish United States leadership in this field.* Toward this goal, MDC and NASA LaRC agree to

---

[2500] NASA Contract NAS1-20546 with McDonnell Douglas regarding Technology Verification of Composite Primary Wing Structures for Commercial Transport Aircraft, 18 September 1995, Exhibit EC-324, p. 3 (emphasis added).

[2501] *Ibid.* (emphasis added).

[2502] See e.g. NASA Contract NAS1-18862 with McDonnell Douglas Corporation regarding Innovative Composite Aircraft Primary Structures (ICAPS), 31 March 1989, Exhibit EC-331, Article H-6 (emphasis added).

[2503] SAA 214: Aging Aircraft Research and Technology Development, Exhibit US-500, Article 4.0 (emphasis added)

[2504] SAA 288: Aging Aircraft Research and Technology Development, Exhibit US-501, Article 3.0 (emphasis added)

US - Large Civil Aircraft (2nd Complaint)

coordinate {their} two programs to develop and demonstrate engineering and manufacturing readiness for composite wing structure on new commercial transports."[2505]

7.1003 A NASA technical report prepared under the ACT Program states:

"The timely development of advanced composite technologies for wing and fuselage structures will ensure that *U.S. manufacturers maintain a majority share of the world market for transport aircraft.* The US government currently finances such developments under the NASA funded Advanced Composite Technology (ACT) program. Developmental funding such as ACT is *crucial to the future of the U.S. aircraft industry* and, since a large number of commercial aircraft manufactured in the U.S. are sold abroad, provides long term national benefits. ...

World dominance in transport aircraft sales by US industry is threatened by foreign competitors {...}

Boeing has remained the only US aircraft manufacturer to meet the Airbus challenge without loss of market share. US government research funding, such as the NASA ACT program, helps *Boeing and other US aircraft manufacturers* develop advanced technology and remain competitive in world markets."[2506]

7.1004 NASA also explained that "{t}he program will help accomplish one of NASA's new technology goals for aeronautics – to reduce the costs of air travel by 25 percent within 10 years, and by 50 percent within 20 years".[2507]

7.1005 The HSR Program Budget states that:

"The HSR program continues to develop technologies to establish the viability of an economical and environmentally sound High Speed Civil Transport (HSCT), a vehicle that - *if built by U. S. industry - could provide U. S. leadership in the long-range commercial air travel markets of the next century*, offering returns of billions of dollars in sales and numerous high-quality jobs for the *U.S. workers.* In FY 1999, NASA has proposed an extension to the program, HSR Phase IIA, which will mitigate risk in two critical areas-propulsion and airframe materials and structures. HSR Phase IIA will enable American taxpayers to continue to

---

[2505] SAA 331: Composite Wing Structure Research, Exhibit US-503, Article 1.0 (emphasis added).
[2506] L. Ilcewicz, et al., Advanced Technology Composite Fuselage, printed in Sixth NASA/DOD ACT Conference, Exhibit EC-279, pp. 21, 22, 76, and 98 (emphasis added).
[2507] NASA Facts Online, "The Advanced Stitching Machine: Making Composite Wing Structures of the Future", Exhibit EC-336, p. 2.

DSR 2012:III

1325

Report of the Panel

receive a return on their investment in high-speed research and will be essential to *enabling U. S. industry* to make its decisions on whether the 21st Century commercial aircraft market will call for an HSCT."[2508]

7.1006 NASA's HSR Program was a focused technology development programme intended to enable development of a high-speed (i.e. supersonic) civil transport ("HSCT").[2509] The programme proceeded in two phases, with Phase I commencing in 1990 and Phase II commencing in 1994.[2510] Phase II of the programme was directed at "addressing *essential technologies needed by the U.S. aeronautics industry* in order to make informed decisions regarding future HSCT development and production".[2511]

7.1007 The "Technology Transfer" *Handbook* for the HSR Program states the reason behind the "Limited Exclusive Rights Data" (LERD) clauses used in certain contracts: "{b}ecause it is critical for the *U.S. to maintain its lead over foreign competition in aerospace technology*, access to sensitive information ... generated in this program will be restricted to the extent permitted by applicable Federal law".[2512] NASA further stated that "{o}pen dissemination of critical technology developed under this Program could severely impact the competitiveness of *the U.S. aeronautics industry*".[2513] The HSR Handbook states that:

"The intent in the application of the controls to be described in this section is to control the transfer of sensitive information to *foreign competitors*."[2514]

7.1008 The HSR "*Program Plan*" states that:

"The projected High-Speed Civil Transport (HSCT) market is substantial, and successful development and production of an HSCT by *foreign competitors* would significantly reduce the *U.S. aerospace industry* world market share of civil transport aircraft. Technology development is essential. The NASA HSR program is being conducted in two phases with the ultimate objective of

---

[2508] NASA HSR Budget Estimates, FY 1991-FY 2001, Exhibit EC-343, FY 1999, SAT 4.1-30 (emphasis added).

[2509] National Research Council, Committee on High Speed Research, U.S. Supersonic Commercial Aircraft: Assessing NASA's High Speed Research Program, 1997, Exhibit EC-319, p. 1.

[2510] NASA HSR Budget Estimates, FY 1991-FY 2001, Exhibit EC-343, FY 1994, RD 9-31 and RD 9-33.

[2511] NASA HSR Budget Estimates, FY 1991-FY 2001, Exhibit EC-343,FY 1994, RD 9-33.

[2512] NASA Langley Research Center, High-Speed Research Program: Technology Transfer Control Handbook, April 1998, Exhibit EC-344, p. 1 (emphasis added).

[2513] NASA Langley Research Center, High-Speed Research Program: Technology Transfer Control Handbook, April 1998, Exhibit EC-344, p. 17 (emphasis added).

[2514] *Ibid.* (emphasis added).

1326   DSR 2012:III

US - Large Civil Aircraft (2nd Complaint)

helping to assure *U.S. industry's* continued preeminence in aeronautics well into the next century by developing technology that will enable an environmentally compatible and economically viable HSCT aircraft."[2515]

7.1009 A Space Act Agreement entered into between NASA and Boeing states:

"Through this commitment each Party agrees to focus HSR and HSCT funding on the high-priority technologies required to develop a commercially viable supersonic transport."[2516]

7.1010 Other programme objectives included addressing "environmental issues and developing the basis for evaluating technology advances that can provide the necessary environmental compatibility"[2517], providing "as strong a technical basis as possible for establishing suitable {environmental} standards" for high speed flight[2518], to "understand better the potential environment effects" of high speed flight and carry out studies to "lead to environmental certification requirements for future high speed transports" and "working on ways to soften the sonic boom to ensure minimal or no harmful effects on human and animal life from its operation".[2519]

7.1011 The AST Program Budget states that:

"The goal of NASA's Advanced Subsonic Technology (AST) Program is to develop, in cooperation with the Federal Aviation Administration (FAA) and *the United States aeronautics industry*, high payoff technologies to enable a safe, highly productive global air transportation system that includes a new generation of environmentally compatible, economical *U.S. subsonic aircraft* that are *superior to foreign products*. To improve the *technological competitiveness of the U.S.,* the objective of the AST program is to accelerate subsonic technology development in several key areas in which the focus is on the economic value of the technologies to the airframe and engine manufacturers, airlines and FAA.

With competition from foreign competitors greatly increasing, technology is critically needed to help preserve the U.S. aeronautics industry market share, jobs, and balance of trade.

[2515] NASA High Speed Research Program Plan, April 1998, Exhibit EC-1208, p. 1 (emphasis added).
[2516] SAA 249: High Speed Technology Research, Exhibit US-502, Article 1.0; SAA 404: High Speed Technology Research, Exhibit US-506, Article 1.0.
[2517] NASA HSR Budget Estimates, FY 1991-FY 2001, Exhibit EC-343, FY 1991, RD 12-35; FY 1992, RD 12-22, FY 1993, RD 12-23.
[2518] NASA High Speed Research Program Plan, April 1998, Exhibit EC-1208, p. 4.
[2519] Statement of Daniel S. Goldin, Administrator, National Aeronautics and Space Administration, US Senate Committee on Commerce, Science, and Transportation, 19 May 1993, Exhibit EC-1365.

DSR 2012:III

Report of the Panel

> Exports in large commercial transports make a significant contribution to the U.S. balance of trade. However, according to industry estimates, the *U.S. world-wide market share* has slipped from a high of 91% during the 1960's to about 67% today."[2520]

7.1012 The objectives for the composites element of the AST Program were described as follows:

> "The aircraft industry's resistance to using composites is one of economics. While the current demonstrated level of composites technology can promise improved aircraft performance and lower operating costs through reduced structural weight, it does so with increased manufacturing costs, currently twice the cost of aluminum. The goals of the composites element are to reduce the weight of civil transports by 30-50% and their cost by 20-25% compared to today's metallic transports. This translates into a potential 16% direct operating cost-savings to the airlines and *increases the competitiveness of the U.S. built transports*. In cooperation with industry and the FAA, research is performed to validate the technology for the application of new composites manufacturing techniques, such as through-the-thickness stitching and resin transfer moulding, textile preforms and advanced fiber placement, on transport wings."[2521]

7.1013 The HPCC Program consisted of four components, one of which was the computational aerosciences project ("CAS"), the component most relevant to the aeronautics industry.[2522] The aim of the CAS project has been described variously as "to significantly shorten the design cycle time for advanced aerospace products such as future high-speed civil transports"[2523] and to "accelerate the development, availability and use of high-performance computing technology *by the U.S. aerospace industry*, and to hasten the

---

[2520] NASA AST Budget Estimates, FY 1992-FY 2001, Exhibit EC-357, FY 1996 (emphasis added).

[2521] NASA AST Budget Estimates, FY 1992-FY 2001, Exhibit EC-357, FY 1996, SAT4-38. In FY 1997, this objective was modified to recognize industry's concern not just with the comparative costs of composites, but also the robustness and reparability of composites. In addition, the weight and cost reduction targets were modified as follows: reduce the weight of civil transports by 10-30 per cent and their cost by 10-20 per cent, translating into a potential 5 per cent direct operating cost-savings to the airlines; NASA AST Budget Estimates, FY 1997, SAT4-37, Exhibit EC-357.

[2522] Dominik Wacht, An Analysis of Selected NASA Research Programs and Their Impact on Boeing's Civil Aircraft Programs, November 2006, Exhibit EC-15 (BCI), p. 122. The other components of HPCC were the Earth and Space Sciences project, the Information Infrastructure and Technology and Applications component, and the Remote Exploration and Experimentation project, Exhibit EC-372.

[2523] NASA HPCC Budget Estimates, FY 1992-FY 2003, Exhibit EC-373, FY 1996, SAT 4-18.

1328   DSR 2012:III

US - Large Civil Aircraft (2nd Complaint)

emergence of a viable commercial market for hardware and software vendors *to exploit this lead*".[2524] In other words:

> "The CAS objectives are: to accelerate development and availability of high-performance computing technology of use to *the U.S. aerospace community*; to facilitate adoption and use of this technology by *the U.S. aerospace industry;* and to hasten emergence of a viable commercial market for hardware and software vendors to exploit this lead. CAS targets advances in aeroscience algorithms and applications, system software, and computing machinery that will enable more than 1000-fold increases in system performance early in the Twenty-first Century. These computational capabilities will be sufficiently characterized such that they can be rapidly integrated into economical design and development processes for use *by U.S. industry*. Although CAS does not develop production computing systems, CAS technology and the characterization of existing hardware and software will enable the development of full-scale systems by industry and will make commercial ventures into this area more attractive."[2525]

7.1014 Further, according to the HPCC Budget estimates:[2526]

> "CAS targets advances in aeroscience algorithms and applications, system software and machinery that will enable more than 1000-fold increases in system performance early in the twenty-first century. These computational capabilities will be sufficiently characterized such that they can be rapidly integrated into economical design and development processes *for use by the U.S. industry*. Although CAS does not develop production computing systems, CAS technology and the characterization of existing hardware and software will enable the development of full-scale systems by industry and will make commercial ventures into this area more attractive."

7.1015 The HPCC fact sheet provides:[2527]

> "*The U.S. aerospace industry can effectively respond to increased international competition* only by producing across-the-board

---

[2524] The National Aeronautics and Space Administration's (NASA) High Performance Computing and Communications (HPCC) Program, Exhibit EC-372, p. 3 (emphasis added).
[2525] NASA HPCC Budget Estimates, FY 1992-FY 2003, Exhibit EC-373, FY 2000, SAT 4.1-24 (emphasis added).
[2526] *Ibid.*
[2527] The National Aeronautics and Space Administration's (NASA) High Performance Computing and Communications (HPCC) Program, Exhibit EC-372, p. 3 (emphasis added).

DSR 2012:III

1329

Report of the Panel

better quality products at affordable prices. High performance computing capability is a key to the creation of a competitive advantage, by reducing product cost and design cycle times; its introduction into the design process is, however, a risk to a commercial company that NASA can help mitigate by performing this research. The CAS project catalyzes these developments in aerospace computing, while at the same time pointing out the future way to aerospace markets for domestic computer manufacturers."

7.1016 A Space Act Agreement between NASA and Boeing states that:

"This effort will provide an excellent opportunity to transfer NASA HPCC technology to the *U.S. aerospace industry.*"[2528]

7.1017 NASA's HPCC *Program Plan* states that the "principal industry customers" of the CAS project are "aerospace vehicle and engine manufacturers".[2529] It goes on to state that "NASA center management, working with industry and NASA HPCC researchers, are responsible for identifying sensitive technologies. These technologies are handled in such a way that their dissemination to *foreign* persons, companies, laboratories, and universities is restricted".[2530]

7.1018 The Aviation Safety Program, which commenced in FY 2000, funds the development of technologies that are intended to reduce aviation accident and fatality rates. The programme grew out of aviation safety research conducted under the R&T Base Program prior to FY 2000.[2531] The *Program Plan* for the Aviation Safety Program states that:

"The NASA Office of Aero-Space Technology (OAT) Enterprise is focused on long-term, high-risk, high-payoff research and technology. The Enterprise seeks to promote economic growth and security and to *enhance U.S. economic competitiveness* through leadership in the global aircraft market by revolutionizing air travel and the way in which aircraft are designed, built, and operated and by providing low-cost space transportation technologies. ...

[2528] NASA SAA2-B0001.3, Exhibit US-512, Article 1.2 (emphasis added).
[2529] NASA High Performance Computing and Communications Program Plan, 25 April 2000, Exhibit EC-1211, p. 14 (emphasis added).
[2530] NASA High Performance Computing and Communications Program Plan, 25 April 2000, Exhibit EC-1211, p. 48 (emphasis added).
[2531] NASA Aviation Safety Budget Estimates, FY 2000-FY 2007, Exhibit EC-382, FY 2000, SAT 4.1-49.

1330

DSR 2012:III

US - Large Civil Aircraft (2ⁿᵈ Complaint)

NASA may use formal agreements to establish partnerships with the *U.S aviation industry*, FAA, DoD and other NASA Programs, such as the six R&T Base Programs and the Aviation System Capacity Programs. These agreements leverage existing programs within these organizations, as well as identify the means through which the technology can be realized *in U.S. industry production.*

...

The Aviation Safety program will emphasize rapid and effective dissemination of the technology to the U.S. industry. Technology transfer mechanisms depend on the maturity of the technology. A variety of technology transfer mechanisms will be employed. The most important is direct involvement of the Users in the formulation of the program described in this plan and direct contract of R&D. AvSP resources fund R&D contracts and grants, which help ensure direct transfer of technology *to the U.S. industry* and thus increase the likelihood of direct input into near-term products. Technology exchange will also occur among the participants through special technical working group meetings. Presentations at technical conferences sponsored by the American Institute of Aeronautics and Astronautics, American Society of Mechanical Engineers, and other similar professional societies will be limited to discussion of *non-competitively sensitive information.* Other methods of technology transfer include technical reports, cooperative programs, and personnel exchanges between NASA, industry and other government agencies through memoranda of agreement (MOA's), and technical demonstrations at NASA and user facilities."[2532]

7.1019 The QAT Program built upon the Noise Reduction portion of the AST Program, which according to NASA was "a focused technology program for developing noise reduction technology *for the US commercial aircraft industry to enhance its competitiveness* to meet national and international environmental requirements and to facilitate market growth".[2533] The QAT Program funded the development of technologies to reduce aircraft noise levels by a factor of two within 10 years, by a factor of four within 25 years, and to create a transportation system "with no need for curfews, noise budgets, or noise abatement procedures."[2534] NASA described the goal of the QAT Program as follows:

[2532] NASA Aviation Safety Program Plan, 1 August 1999, Exhibit EC-1209, pp. 2, 4 and 35 (emphasis added).
[2533] NASA Memorandum to Research and Focused Programs Contracts Branch, 23 May 1996, Exhibit EC-365, p. 4 (emphases added).
[2534] NASA QAT Budget Estimates, FY 2001-FY 2007, Exhibit EC-384, FY 2002, SAT 4.1-74.

DSR 2012:III   1331

Report of the Panel

> "The goal of the Quiet Aircraft Technology program is to contribute to the 10-year noise objective of the Global Civil Aviation enabling technology goals, as stated in the Office of Aero-Space Technology Enterprise Strategic Plan, 'Reduce the perceived noise levels of future aircraft by a factor of two from today's subsonic aircraft within ten years, and by a factor of four within 25 years.' The Quiet Aircraft Technology program is the next step in achieving the very ambitious and desirable 25-year goal for the public good. Achievement of the 25-year goal will fulfill NASA's vision of a noise constraint-free air transportation system with the objectionable aircraft noise contained within the airport boundaries. Part of this vision is a transportation system with no need for curfews, noise budgets, or noise abatement procedures. Benefits to the public of achieving these goals include increased quality of life, readily available and affordable air travel, and *continued U.S. global leadership.*"[2535]

7.1020 NASA also formulated the objectives of the QAT Program in terms of "fulfull{ing} NASA's vision of a noise constraint-free air transport system with objectionable noise contained within airport boundaries" and leading "the technology development necessary to meet national community noise impact reduction requirements"[2536], and developing "technology that, when implemented, reduce the impact of aircraft noise to benefit airport neighbors, the aviation industry, and travellers".[2537]

7.1021 The VSP, which began as a separate programme in FY 2003 based on components from the QAT and R&T Base Programs, focuses on "the development of key enabling technologies to enable capabilities for future air vehicles".[2538] In particular, it is "developing enabling technologies to expand the availability of air travel that will satisfy the public's demand for increased air travel without affecting safety or degrading the environment".[2539] NASA has described the goal of this programme as follows:

> "*U.S. competitors* are targeting aviation leadership as a stated strategic goal. Without careful planning and investment in new technologies, near- term gridlock, constrained mobility, unrealized economic growth, and the continued erosion of U.S. aviation

---

[2535] NASA QAT Budget Estimates, FY 2001-FY 2007, Exhibit EC-384, FY 2001, p. 4/55 (emphasis added).

[2536] NASA QAT Budget Estimates, FY 2001-FY 2007, Exhibit EC-384, FY 2001 and FY 2002, SAT 4.1-74.

[2537] NASA Vehicle Systems Budget Estimates, FY 2003-FY 2007, Exhibit EC-396, FY 2003, SAT 4-24.

[2538] NASA Vehicle Systems Budget Estimates, FY 2003-FY 2007, Exhibit EC-396, FY 2005, ESA 16-16.

[2539] *Ibid.*

1332   DSR 2012:III

US - Large Civil Aircraft (2ⁿᵈ Complaint)

leadership could result. ... Breakthrough Vehicle Technologies investigates and develops breakthrough technologies *to maintain the superiority of U.S. aircraft*, to ensure the long-term environmental compatibility of aircraft systems, and to improve their safety and efficiency."[2540]

7.1022 NASA also formulated the objectives of the VSP in terms of ensuring the "long-term environmental compatibility of aircraft systems, and to improve their safety and efficiency",[2541] as research that would "focus on embryonic technologies to further increase the quality of life for our citizens"[2542], and demonstrations of "breakthrough of aeronautics technologies for protecting the Earth's environment and enabling science missions".[2543]

7.1023 The R&T Base Program Budget states that:

"The aerodynamics research and technology program: ... Is advancing the understanding of fundamental fluid mechanics and aero acoustics phenomena and providing new, validated aerodynamics technology applicable to future U.S. military and civil aircraft from subsonic to hypersonic speeds. ...

Through basic and applied research in partnership with industry, academia, and other government agencies, *NASA develops critical high-risk technologies and advanced concepts for U.S. aircraft and engine industries*. ...

These efforts provide the enabling technology that ultimately leads to future focused technology programs and advanced systems development *by U.S. industry*. The majority of the research is captured in the principal aeronautics disciplines of aerodynamics, propulsion, materials, structures, controls and guidance, human factors, and flight systems. A significant portion of the base program is performed in cooperative agreements with the aerospace industry and other Government agencies *to facilitate rapid technology transfer*. ...

The program seeks to provide the technology which, *when applied by the U.S. aerospace industry*, will enable the development of economical, safe quiet globally competitive aircraft for all speed

---

[2540] NASA Vehicle Systems Budget Estimates, FY 2003-FY 2007, Exhibit EC-396, FY 2003, SAT 4-23 (emphasis added).
[2541] *Ibid.*
[2542] NASA Vehicle Systems Budget Estimates, FY 2003-FY 2007, Exhibit EC-396, FY 2004, SAE 15-19 and FY 2005, ESA 16-16.
[2543] NASA Vehicle Systems Budget Estimates, FY 2003-FY 2007, Exhibit EC-396, FY 2006, SAE 11-14.

DSR 2012:III

1333

Report of the Panel

ranges. Further, the program includes the development of multidisciplinary methodologies to enable *the U. S. industry* to reduce design cycle time and cost in the development of future aircraft. The primary objective of the program is to provide the fundamental viscous aerodynamic expertise and facilities to meet the ongoing and future design requirements of the U.S. industry, the NASA, the DoD, the FAA, and other Government agencies. ...

In FY 1994, a computer code for designing and analyzing thermal ice protection systems will be made available to U.S. industry, a joint NASA / FAA / Industry Program to address the problem of ice-induced tail plane stalls will be initiated, and a joint NASA/Industry Program to develop requirements for ice protection for Hybrid Laminar Flow Control (HLFC) systems will be initiated. ...

The associated design databases, and design methods are effectively transferred to industry and DoD for the development of safe and *superior U.S. civil and military aircraft.* ...

Each element of the R&T Base Program has an objective to develop methods that will contribute to the *U.S. aerospace industry* goal of reducing design cycle time by at least 50%."[2544]

7.1024 The Panel has also examined the allocation of intellectual property rights under the R&D contracts between NASA and Boeing. The allocation of intellectual property rights under a number of NASA's R&D contracts with Boeing, in particular with respect to data rights (as opposed to patent rights) differed from the standard data rights clauses in U.S. government R&D procurement contracts. Boeing, as the contractor, retained rights to any inventions (i.e. patent rights) that it conceived of in the course of performing research funded by NASA; however the U.S. Government receives a royalty-free, "government use/purpose" license to use the subject invention. Boeing as the contractor also retained rights to use any data (i.e. data rights) that it produced in the course of performing research funded by NASA; however, the U.S. Government receives a royalty-free, "unlimited rights" license to use any data produced by the contractor in the course of performing research funded by NASA. Boeing was not required to pay any royalties to NASA for any resulting commercial rewards. Under some of the R&D programmes at issue, however, NASA included "Limited Exclusive Data Rights" (LERD) clauses in its R&D contracts with Boeing. The clauses limited the otherwise "unlimited rights" that the U.S. Government would normally have in the data developed in the course of

---

[2544] NASA R&T Base Budget Estimates, FY 1991-FY 2004, Exhibit EC-398, FY 1992, 1995, 1999 (emphasis added).

1334

DSR 2012:III

US - Large Civil Aircraft (2nd Complaint)

the contracted research. The LERD clauses granted Boeing exclusive rights to exploit critical technologies developed under certain NASA contracts for at least five years from the date the data was reported. Technologies were categorized as "sensitive" and protected through LERD restrictions if they were considered to affect the competitive position of US industry.[2545] The NASA R&D contracts that contained LERD clauses involved "joint funding situation{s}", i.e. contractors were "contributing a significant amount of their own resources to contract research efforts". In a statement to a Senate subcommittee in 2001, Daniel Goldin, former Administrator of NASA, explained a link between the allocation of intellectual property rights and objectives NASA was pursuing under the programmes at issue:

> *Question 1.* Do you believe that *American manufacturers* are behind Airbus in terms of technology?
>
> *Answer.* ... The principal shortfall in *U.S. technology development* has been insufficient validation and risk reduction to allow *U.S. manufacturers* to take full and early advantage of technology availability. The proposed NASA aeronautics enhancements for FY 1994 focus on cooperation with industry through the technology validation phase.
>
> ...
>
> *Question 3.* You have discussed the importance of NASA's aeronautics research programs to the aircraft manufacturing industry. What steps has NASA taken to ensure that technology development under these programs is effectively transferred to industry? How does NASA ensure that *American manufacturers* have access to these technologies before *foreign companies*?

[2545] European Communities' first written submission, para. 838 (citing NASA Langley Research Center, High-Speed Research Program: Technology Transfer Control Handbook, April 1998, Exhibit EC-344, p. 17; Advanced Subsonic Technology Program, Technology Transfer Control Handbook, August 1998, Exhibit EC-370, p. 18). These LERD and other data rights provisions have appeared in several NASA contracts with Boeing. See, e.g. NASA Contract NAS1-20267 with Boeing Commercial Airplane Group regarding Integrated Wing Design, 12 September 1994, Exhibit EC-360, pp. 11-19; NASA Contract NAS1-20268 with McDonnell Douglas regarding Integrated Wing Design, 12 September 1994, Exhibit EC-361, pp. 11-17. NASA's R&D solicitations have also advertised to potential contractors that data produced under the project would be protected by LERD and other data rights provisions. See e.g. NASA Final Solicitation 1-063-DIG.1299, Flight Critical Systems Research, 27 August 1999, Exhibit EC-588, at I-7 to I-10; NASA Solicitation 1-49-3400.0408, High Speed Research Program Systems Studies, 11 June 1990, Exhibit EC-589, pp. 8-10 and 26-36; NASA Solicitation 1-50-0140.0001, High-Speed Research Airframe Technology, 11 August 1993, Exhibit EC-570, pp. 34-41.

DSR 2012:III

1335

Report of the Panel

> Answer. NASA generally performs its research in cooperation with the aeronautics industry, thereby providing some direct mechanisms for technology transfer. However, we are stepping up our efforts to increase and improve industry involvement both in planning and implementing our programs. Additionally, much of the Aeronautics investment, beginning in FY 1994, is aimed at developing technologies to a more advanced stage, reducing the risks sufficiently for industry commercialization. Industry's partnership in the NASA program should allow manufacturers to easily continue the technology development through commercialization, as desired. Furthermore, the natural advantage *U.S. industry* is afforded through direct partnership in the NASA technology development program will be supported by NASA contracts and cooperative agreements *which include provisions to protect commercially valuable and/or sensitive technology from premature foreign dissemination.*"[2546]

7.1025 Although the United States does not assert that NASA's Space Act Agreements with Boeing constitute "purchases of services", we note that a number of these agreements contained provisions "to maintain any data that was generated in confidence for at least 2 to 5 years".[2547]

7.1026 Another relevant consideration is whether the transactions at issue involve the typical elements of a purchase of services. In this regard, we observe that a number of the R&D procurement contracts between NASA and Boeing provide that Boeing would receive no fee or profit.[2548] Under the "no fee" contracts, Boeing received no fee/profit for the R&D that it performed, because of NASA's determination that Boeing stood to benefit commercially from the R&D that it performed under the contract. For example, the selection statement for one of the R&D contracts at issue indicates that the fee provisions were deleted from the proposed procurement "based on a determination by the NASA Administrator that the benefits {are} to be derived by the U.S. aerospace

---

[2546] Competitiveness of the Aerospace Industry: Hearing on S. 419 Before the Senate Comm. on Commerce, Science, and Transportation, 103rd Cong. 81 (1993), Exhibit EC-273, pp. 80-81 (emphasis added).

[2547] European Communities' second written submission, para. 396, citing SAA 331: Composite Wing Structure Research, Exhibit US-503, Article 5.3; SAA 401: CADDRAD II Developments, Exhibit US-505, Article 5.3; SAA 404: High Speed Technology Research, Exhibit US-506, Article 5.3; SAA 1-506: Advanced Methodologies for Aerospace Analysis and Optimization, Exhibit US-508, Article 5.4; SAA 2-B0001.3: Advanced Aeroelastic Design Procedures, Exhibit US-512, Article 7.7; SAA 469: Study of High Reynolds Number Aerodynamics and Ground-to-Flight Scaling for Aerospace Vehicles, Exhibit US-521 (BCI), Article 5.3.

[2548] Based on our own review of 16 R&D contracts between NASA and Boeing that the European Communities submitted in its first written submission, it appears that nine of the R&D contracts involved a payment of a fee, and that seven of the contracts were "no fee" procurement contracts.

1336   DSR 2012:III

industry".[2549] Documents related to another R&D contract between NASA and Boeing indicate that there would be no fee because "Boeing stands to benefit commercially from efforts conducted as a result of the proposed contract".[2550]

7.1027 For the reasons given above, the Panel considers that the question of whether or not a transaction is properly characterized as a "purchase of services" depends on whether or not the work performed was principally for the benefit or use of the government (or unrelated third parties), or rather principally for the benefit or use of the "service" "seller" itself. The evidence relating to NASA aeronautics R&D, reviewed above, leads to the conclusion that the work that Boeing performed under its aeronautics R&D contracts with NASA was principally for its own benefit or use, rather than for the benefit or use of the U.S. Government (or unrelated third parties).[2551] While NASA's aeronautics R&D contracts take the form of a governmental procurement of services, the totality of the evidence before the Panel leads to the conclusion that the

---

[2549] Selection Statement, Phase II High-Speed Research Airframe Technology, 9 September 1994, Exhibit EC-356, p. 1.

[2550] Prenegotiation Position – Proposed Contract to Boeing Commercial Airplane Group for AST Noise Reduction Research, 13 December 1996, Exhibit EC-371, pp. 1-2 ("Prior to solicitation issuance, several discussions between procurement, technical and {Boeing Commercial Aircraft Group} were conducted to determine and agree that a no-fee procurement was appropriate. It was discussed that {sic} NASA technical personal have identified that {sic} Boeing stands to benefit commercially from efforts conducted as a result of the proposed contract. Further, NASA technical personnel cited their understanding of Dan Goldin's (NASA Administrator's) edict that "focused programmes" shall not be fee-bearing. BCAG orally informed the Contract Specialist that they would accept a no-fee contract for this programme, notwithstanding historical precedence of earning fee {sic} for this type of effort.")

[2551] In conducting this analysis, the Panel has found guidance in the Appellate Body report in *China – Auto Parts:*

> "We consider that a panel's determination of whether a specific charge falls under Article II:1(b) or Article III:2 of the GATT 1994 must be made in the light of the characteristics of the measure and the circumstances of the case. *In many cases this will be a straightforward exercise. In others, the picture will be more mixed, and the challenge faced by a panel more complex.* A panel must thoroughly scrutinize the measure before it, both in its design and in its operation, and identify its *principal characteristics.* Having done so, the panel must then seek to identify the *leading or core features of the measure at issue,* those that define its *"centre of gravity"* for purposes of characterizing the charge that it imposes as an ordinary customs duty or an internal charge. It is not surprising, and indeed to be expected, that the same measure may exhibit *some characteristics* that suggest it is a measure falling within the scope of Article II:1(b), and *others* suggesting it is a measure falling within the scope of Article III:2. In making its objective assessment of the applicability of specific provisions of the covered agreements to a measure properly before it, a panel must identify *all relevant characteristics of the measure,* and *recognize which features are the most central* to that measure itself, and *which are to be accorded the most significance* for purposes of characterizing the relevant charge and, thereby, properly determining the discipline(s) to which it is subject under the covered agreements."

> Appellate Body Report, *China – Auto Parts,* para. 171 (emphasis added, footnote omitted).

Report of the Panel

substance of these transactions cannot properly be characterized as a "purchase of services" for the purpose of Article 1.1(a)(1) of the SCM Agreement. Therefore, the Panel finds that the payments made to Boeing under these contracts are covered by Article 1.1(a)(1)(i) of the SCM Agreement as a direct transfer of funds.[2552] The Panel further finds that the access to NASA facilities, equipment and employees provided to Boeing through the R&D contracts and agreements at issue constitutes a provision of goods or services within the meaning of Article 1.1(a)(1)(iii) of the SCM Agreement.

(ii) Whether there is a benefit within the meaning of Article 1.1(b) of the SCM Agreement

Arguments of the European Communities

7.1028 Regarding the existence of a benefit within the meaning of Article 1.1(b) of the SCM Agreement, the European Communities argues that the NASA "subsidies" confer "benefits" upon Boeing's LCA division. More specifically, the European Communities argues that: (i) the financial contributions "relate to the production of Boeing LCA"; (ii) the financial contributions "provide Boeing's LCA division with advantages on non-market terms"; (iii) "Boeing is not required to pay anything in return" for the funding and support, and "has not been required to repay the US Government for any resulting commercial rewards"; (iv) Boeing has received valuable "knowledge and experience" from the aeronautics R&D, and (v) it is "axiomatic that such R&D funding and support are not available on the market."[2553]

7.1029 In its second written submission, the European Communities responds to the United States' argument that NASA R&D contracts constitute "value-for-value" exchanges. First, NASA, which "is not in the business of manufacturing LCA or its parts", receives nothing in real value from the contracts and agreements with Boeing. Whereas Boeing receives research experience and valuable technology, NASA receives "summary research reports and license rights that are of no apparent use to it".[2554]

7.1030 Second, in a commercial transaction, one entity will pay another entity to conduct research and development only if it intends to actually utilize the research to some end, i.e. if it can obtain the full rights to the resulting technology and will not pay another entity to conduct research and development "in exchange for nominal research reports to disseminate to the public and license rights to hold onto *ad infinitum*". By contrast, under the NASA R&D

[2552] We do not accept that the payments to Boeing are outright "grants". We address this issue in the context of estimating the amount of the subsidy to Boeing's LCA division. See below, para. 7.1100.

[2553] European Communities' first written submission, paras. 526-528, 550-552, 574-576, 590-592, 605-607, 620-622, 633-635 and 652-654.

[2554] European Communities' second written submission, paras. 375 and 377.

1338   DSR 2012:III

contracts, "Boeing can utilize the results of the R&D and keep the technology for itself in exchange for only nominal remuneration".[2555] The European Communities argues that in a market transaction one entity will pay another entity to conduct research and development only if that entity acquires full ownership of any intellectual property rights to the technologies that result from the research and development. The European Communities refers[2556] to an article on intellectual property rights and stem cell research[2557] and a Declaration of Regina Dieu, Legal Counsel in the Airbus SAS Industrial Procurement Legal Department, which states that when Airbus funds an R&D project it exclusively and solely owns any and all Intellectual Property generated or acquired in connection with and during the performance of the R&D project.[2558] In addition, in support of the same argument made in the context of its claim regarding the NASA/DOD waiver/provision of intellectual property rights, the European Communities refers[2559] to an article on collaborative research[2560], a WIPO Training Course[2561] and a contract concluded by Boeing with the National Institute for Aviation Research at Wichita State University.[2562]

7.1031 Third, a commercial entity will not pay another entity to conduct research and development for the public policy objectives pursued by NASA, i.e. preserving the prominent position and increasing the competitiveness of the U.S. aeronautics industry. The argument of the United States that "NASA receives adequate remuneration from Boeing in furtherance of government objectives" is circular in that the objective pursued by NASA is to enhance the competitiveness of the US LCA industry.[2563]

7.1032 Finally, not all the results of the NASA R&D programmes are published, and the results that are made available to the public are of little value to companies that did not participate in the research.[2564]

Arguments of the United States

7.1033 In its first written submission, the United States does not explicitly address the issue of whether the payments made to Boeing under R&D contracts confer a benefit within the meaning of Article 1.1(b) of the SCM Agreement.

[2555] European Communities' second written submission, paras. 376 and 379.

[2556] European Communities' second written submission para. 376.

[2557] Sean M. O'Connor, "Intellectual Property Rights and Stem Cell Research: Who Owns the Medical Breakthroughs?" 39 New Eng. L. Rev. 665 (2005), Exhibit EC-1212, p. 669.

[2558] Declaration of Regina Dieu, 8 November 2007, Exhibit EC-1178.

[2559] European Communities' second written submission, paras. 553-556.

[2560] Rochelle Cooper Dreyfuss, "Collaborative Research: Conflicts on Authorship, Ownership and Accountability", 53 Vand. L. Rev. 1161 (2000), Exhibit EC-1228, p. 1212.

[2561] WIPO-MOST, "Intermediate Training Course on Practical Intellectual Property Issues in Business", 13 November 2003, Exhibit-EC 1229, pp. 42-43.

[2562] Contract Between Boeing Commercial Airplane Group Wichita Division and Wichita State University, Contract No. 000051728, 4 November 2002, Exhibit EC-1231.

[2563] European Communities' second written submission, paras. 378 and 380.

[2564] European Communities' second written submission, para. 381.

Report of the Panel

However, in addressing the argument of the European Communities that NASA contracts are grants, the United States rejects the assertion that because the U.S. Government is not in the business of manufacturing LCA or its parts, it cannot possibly receive anything of value in return for the R&D payments made to Boeing.[2565] In its first written submission, the United States argues that NASA's provision of goods and services to Boeing is "always adequately remunerated". The United States recalls that NASA provides goods and services to Boeing pursuant to Space Act Agreements. More specifically, the United States explains that NASA provides Boeing with wind tunnel services, as well as "non-wind tunnel" goods and services. The United States argues that NASA' provision of goods and services to Boeing pursuant to Space Act Agreements is always in exchange for adequate remuneration.[2566]

7.1034 In its second written submission, the United States argues that the European Communities has failed to support its assertions as to the benefit associated with the NASA-Boeing transactions. The argument that NASA received "nothing in return" for the payments made to Boeing pursuant to the R&D contracts is incorrect because in exchange for the money that NASA pays Boeing, the U.S. Government receives a commensurate value. The U.S. Government receives the labour of Boeing scientists and engineers directed to the objectives of the U.S. Government, can disseminate the knowledge they generate for the public benefit and receives intellectual property rights with regard to inventions and data that it would not otherwise hold.[2567]

7.1035 The United States also submits that the European Communities erroneously asserts "that no commercial entity would ever pay another entity to conduct R&D primarily for the other entity's benefit, receiving only nominal research reports to disseminate to the public and license rights it never plans to utilize in return". First, the research reports generated in these transactions are not "nominal", as evidenced by the amount of public information generated by NASA aeronautics research and the wide dissemination of that information.[2568] Second, the European Communities provides no evidence that the U.S. Government never plans to use the patents and licenses acquired under the research contracts. These rights are government rights that can be utilized by any U.S. government agency, including the FAA, DOD or NASA itself in further research conducted by NASA employees. The fact that NASA is not in the business of acquiring or manufacturing LCA "is as irrelevant as it is correct" in this regard.[2569] Third, the R&D conducted at NASA's request is not primarily for Boeing's benefit, as alleged by the European Communities, but for the broader

---

[2565] United States' first written submission, paras. 219-225.
[2566] United States' first written submission, paras. 230-267.
[2567] United States' second written submission, para. 65.
[2568] United States' second written submission, para. 67.
[2569] United States' second written submission, para. 68.

1340

DSR 2012:III

public good.[2570] Fourth, the European Communities provides no support for its assertion that a commercial entity will not pay another entity to conduct services that also provide benefit to that other entity. Such a benefit is a normal occurrence in commercial transactions.[2571]

7.1036 In its response to questions 21 and 22 from the Panel, the United States argues that the European Communities has failed to demonstrate that the treatment of intellectual property rights under NASA/DOD R&D contracts constitutes a deviation from normal commercial practice that confers a benefit within the meaning of Article 1.1(b) of the SCM Agreement. In this regard, the United States argues that commercial practice differs from case to case. Commercial entities seek to buy the intellectual property rights they *need*, and do not operate from a single paradigm, as the European Communities suggests. While certain commercial transactions may assign the buyer ownership of intellectual property generated in the performance of a contract, there are commercial entities that purchase R&D services in exchange for a limited license to use the resulting intellectual property. By way of example, the United States provides four contracts in which Boeing pays for major research universities to conduct R&D on its behalf, and receives in exchange a license – not ownership – of the intellectual property developed under the contract.

Evaluation by the Panel

7.1037 A financial contribution confers a benefit within the meaning of Article 1.1(b) of the SCM Agreement if the terms of the financial contribution are more favourable than the terms available to the recipient in the market.[2572] Thus, in order to determine whether NASA's financial contributions to Boeing confer a benefit upon Boeing within the meaning of Article 1.1(b), the Panel must begin by recalling what the *terms* of those financial contributions are. Only then can the Panel proceed to compare *those* terms with the terms of a market transaction.

7.1038 As the Panel has already concluded above in its analysis of the existence of a financial contribution, NASA has made payments to Boeing and granted Boeing access to NASA facilities, equipment and employees *on the condition that Boeing perform aeronautics R&D work that is principally for Boeing's own benefit and use*, rather than principally for the benefit or use of the U.S. Government (or unrelated third parties). While the R&D contracts and agreements of course contain numerous other terms (for example, the contracts and agreements contain or incorporate by reference numerous standardized

---

[2570] United States' second written submission, para. 69. The United States emphasizes that while NASA does not acquire or produce large civil aircraft, it acquires, produces and disseminates knowledge and that the purpose of the NASA R&D programs is "to develop and disseminate the greatest amount of information to the broadest group in the shortest amount of time possible, and not to 'convey resources to Boeing'". United States' second written submission, paras. 62-64.

[2571] United States' second written submission, para. 70.

[2572] See paras. 730-731 of this Report.

DSR 2012:III

1341

Report of the Panel

clauses governing miscellaneous matters), this is, in the Panel's view, the core "term" upon which the financial contributions are provided, i.e. that Boeing use the payments and access to facilities, equipment and employees that it receives from NASA for the purpose of conducting aeronautics R&D work that is principally for Boeing's own benefit and use. The Panel has concluded above that a transaction in which the work performed is principally for the benefit and use of the "seller" cannot properly be characterized as a "purchase of services".

7.1039 In this case, both parties agree that, with regard to the financial contributions that Boeing receives under the NASA R&D programmes, "the relevant market benchmark would be the terms of a commercial transaction in which one entity pays another entity to conduct R&D".[2573] The question, then, is whether, in a commercial transaction, one entity would pay another entity to conduct R&D on these same terms, i.e. on the term that the entity receiving the financial contributions conducts R&D that is principally for the benefit and use of the entity receiving the payment. The Panel believes that no commercial entity, i.e. no private entity acting pursuant to commercial considerations, would provide payments (and access to its facilities and personnel) to another commercial entity on the condition that the other entity perform R&D activities principally for the benefit and use of that other entity. At a minimum, it would be expected that some form of royalties or repayment would be required in the event that financial contributions were provided on such terms. Thus, with respect to the financial contributions provided by NASA to Boeing, which were provided on these terms, we consider that it was not necessary for the European Communities to present benchmark evidence of the terms and conditions of specific market-based R&D financing in order to establish, at least on a prima facie basis, that these NASA transactions conferred a benefit upon Boeing. Rather, it would fall upon the United States, if it wished to rebut this prima facie case, to identify examples of transactions in which commercial entities have paid other commercial entities to perform R&D on these terms, i.e. to perform R&D that is principally for the benefit or use of the entity receiving the funding. The United States has not provided any evidence or examples of commercial transactions in which one entity pays another entity to conduct R&D that is principally for the benefit and use of the entity receiving the funding.

7.1040 Accordingly, the Panel concludes that the financial contributions provided to Boeing under its aeronautics R&D contracts and agreements with NASA confer a benefit within the meaning of Article 1.1(b) of the SCM Agreement.

7.1041 For these reasons, we find that the payments and access to facilities, equipment and employees that NASA provided to Boeing through the eight aeronautics R&D programmes at issue constitute subsidies within the meaning of Article 1 of the SCM Agreement.

[2573] European Communities' response to question 21, para. 76; United States' response to question 136, para. 85.

1342

DSR 2012:III

US - Large Civil Aircraft (2nd Complaint)

(d) Whether the subsidy is specific within the meaning of Article 2 of the SCM Agreement

(i) Arguments of the European Communities

7.1042 In its first written submission, the European Communities argues that each of the NASA aeronautics R&D programmes at issue is *de jure* specific within the meaning of Article 2.1(a) of the SCM Agreement, or, in the alternative, de facto specific within the meaning of Article 2.1(c) of the SCM Agreement.[2574] The European Communities argues that the programmes are *de jure* specific by virtue of the subject matter of the research. More specifically, the European Communities argues that the eight NASA aeronautics R&D programmes at issue are specific within the meaning of Article 2.1(a) because they are explicitly limited to certain enterprises that participate in aeronautics-related R&D. The European Communities argues that because the legislative authority for each of the eight programmes at issue derives from the Space Act, the programmes are also limited "to those industries that can satisfy the objectives of that Act". The European Communities also argues that the programmes are de facto specific because Boeing has received a disproportionate amount of the funding provided under NASA R&D programmes. The European Communities argues that, in addition to receiving a disproportionate amount of the funding awarded by NASA under each of the programmes, Boeing has also received a disproportionate amount of all contracts awarded by NASA.[2575] Finally, the European Communities asserts that "Boeing's active participation at the highest levels of the NASA Advisory Council and its subcommittees reveals that NASA exercises discretion in granting subsidies in a manner that takes full account of Boeing's views and needs".

7.1043 In its second written submission, the European Communities observes that the United States "does not dispute the conclusion that NASA's aeronautics R&D support for Boeing is specific within the meaning of Article 2.1 of the *SCM Agreement*".[2576]

(ii) Arguments of the United States

7.1044 The United States does not respond to the European Communities' arguments on specificity, except in the context of the wind tunnel access that Boeing received pursuant to a number of Space Act Agreements. In this regard,

---

[2574] European Communities' first written submission, paras. 529-530; 553-554; 577-578; 593-594; 608-609; 623-624; 636-637 and 655-656.

[2575] The European Communities cites to Boeing's Share of NASA Contracts, FY 1991-FY 2004, Exhibit EC-19, which indicates that Boeing received, on average, 23.4 per cent of all NASA contracts over the period 1991-2004. Note 1 to Exhibit EC-19 indicates that the information is drawn from NASA Annual Procurement Report, FY 1991-FY 2004, "One Hundred Principal Contractors", Exhibit EC-341.

[2576] European Communities' second written submission, para. 383.

DSR 2012:III
1343

Report of the Panel

the United States asserts that NASA's wind tunnel services are "used by a wide range of industries across the U.S. economic spectrum".[2577]

(iii) Evaluation by the Panel

7.1045 In this case, the United States does not dispute that each of the eight aeronautics R&D programmes at issue would, if found to provide subsidies within the meaning of Article 1, be specific under Article 2.1(a) of the SCM Agreement. It is not in dispute that the Space Act explicitly limits the scope of NASA's R&D activities (i.e. to aeronautics and space). It is also not in dispute that each of the eight programmes at issue involves R&D aimed at the "improvement of the usefulness, performance, speed, safety, and efficiency of aeronautical and space vehicles".[2578]

7.1046 The United States' only argument with respect to specificity is that NASA's wind tunnel services are "used by a wide range of industries across the U.S. economic spectrum".[2579] In its response to question 162[2580] from the Panel, the United States indicates that it has provided the following evidence to support this assertion:

"(1) RAND National Defense Research Institute, Wind Tunnel and Propulsion Test Facilities (Exhibit US-116): found that primary users of NASA wind tunnels are aerospace related, but cover a wide range of applications, including spacecraft, launch vehicles, missiles, fixed-wing and rotorcraft (both military and commercial applications, including fighters, transports, business jets, and operating at all speeds, including hypersonic, supersonic and subsonic speeds), as well as engines.

(2) NASA Langley Research Center, Wind Tunnel Enterprise, The Enterprise (Exhibit US-93): wind tunnels are used by "traditional commercial and DoD ground testing community" and being positioned to attract "non-traditional customers e.g. automotive, submersible, recreational, etc."

By way of example, NASA reviewed its usage records for two wind tunnels, the 11-foot Transonic Wind Tunnel and the

---

[2577] United States' first written submission, para. 251.

[2578] National Aeronautics and Space Act of 1958, Pub. L. No. 85-568, as amended, Exhibit EC-286, s. 102(d)(2).

[2579] United States' first written submission, para. 251

[2580] Question 162 reads, "In its FWS, the United States submits that NASA's provision of wind tunnel services is not specific under Article 2. (United States' first written submission, para. 251) In this regard, the United States asserts that NASA's wind tunnel services are "used by a wide range of industries across the U.S. economic spectrum". Has the United States provided any evidence to support that assertion?"

1344

DSR 2012:III

US - Large Civil Aircraft (2nd Complaint)

Transonic Dynamics Tunnel, which show usage by the following entities: Bell Helicopters, General Dynamics, Georgia Institute of Technology, Jet Propulsion Laboratories, Lockheed Martin, the U.S. Navy, NextGen Aeronautics, Northrop Grumman, Orbital Sciences, Sandia, and Sikorsky."[2581]

7.1047 The Panel considers that the evidence provided by the United States does not support its assertion that NASA's wind tunnel services are "used by a wide range of industries across the U.S. economic spectrum". In fact, the evidence submitted by the United States, and its own summary of that evidence in response to question 162, seems to the Panel to actually contradict that assertion: it confirms that the "primary users of NASA wind tunnels are aerospace related". What the United States evidence seems to demonstrate is that enterprises other than *Boeing* use NASA wind tunnels. However, that does not call into question the fact that NASA's provision of wind tunnel services is specific to "an enterprise *or industry or group of enterprises or industries*".[2582]

7.1048 Apart from the United States' argument relating to wind tunnel services, which the Panel has rejected, the European Communities is correct in observing that the "United States offers no response to the European Communities' *prima facie* case that the eight NASA aeronautics R&D programmes at issue are specific within the meaning of Article 2.1(a) of the SCM Agreement because they are explicitly limited to certain enterprises that participate in aeronautics-related R&D".[2583]

7.1049 For these reasons, the Panel finds that the NASA aeronautics R&D subsidies at issue are specific subsidies within the meaning of Article 2.1(a) of the SCM Agreement. Having concluded that the subsidies are specific within the meaning of Article 2.1(a), it is not necessary for the Panel to address the European Communities' alternative argument that the NASA R&D subsidies at issue are de facto specific within the meaning of Article 2.1(c) of the SCM Agreement "because Boeing receives a share of funding pursuant to these programmes that is disproportionate to its 0.5% share of the US economy"

[2581] United States' response to question 162, paras. 155-156.

[2582] If there were any evidence to support the assertion that NASA wind tunnel services are provided to a "wide range of industries across the U.S. economic spectrum" that is so diverse that it cannot be considered a "group of enterprises or industries" for the purpose of Article 2.1 of the SCM Agreement, it would then be necessary to proceed to examine the point in dispute between the parties, which is whether the Panel should confine its analysis and focus only on those entities that received access to NASA wind tunnel services under the eight programmes at issue (as the European Communities argues), or whether it should take a wider analysis of the terms upon which NASA provides wind tunnel services outside of the context of the eight programmes at issue (as the United States argues). However, because the Panel believes that the user of NASA wind tunnel services would either way constitute a "group of enterprises or industries" for the purpose of Article 2.1, we think that it is unnecessary for the Panel to resolve that point.

[2583] European Communities' second written submission, para. 383.

DSR 2012:III

1345

Report of the Panel

and/or "because NASA exercises discretion in granting these subsidies to Boeing".[2584]

        (e)   The amount of the subsidy to Boeing's LCA division

        (i)   Arguments of the European Communities

7.1050 The European Communities estimates that NASA provided $10.4 billion in subsidies to Boeing over the period 1989-2006.[2585] The European Communities allocates approximately $3 billion[2586] of that total to the 2004-2006 period, which is the "reference period" suggested by the European Communities for the purpose of determining whether NASA and other challenged subsidies caused serious prejudice within the meaning of Articles 5 and 6 of the SCM Agreement.

7.1051 The European Communities asserts that the United States has failed to fully disclose information regarding all of the NASA R&D contracts pursuant to which Boeing received LCA-related R&D funding, and that as a result, the European Communities is unable to undertake a comprehensive "bottom-up" analysis of the U.S. Government's R&D support for Boeing. The European Communities explains that, because it does not have information regarding the amount of the "direct R&D funding" and "goods and services" provided to Boeing, it must rather rely on a "top-down", industry-level allocation methodology for the purpose of estimating the amount of the subsidies provided to Boeing through each programme. The European Communities asks the Panel to accept this methodology, and the resulting estimate, as the "best information available"[2587].

7.1052 The European Communities uses a "top down" approach, based on aggregated data in NASA's programme budgets and figures regarding the "U.S. civil aircraft industry", to estimate the amount of the subsidy to Boeing. The European Communities begins by estimating the total cost of the eight aeronautics R&D programmes at issue, based on NASA programme budgets. The European Communities then subtracts, from that total, certain estimated amounts for non-LCA related research conducted under the programmes. Specifically, the European Communities seeks to identify and then deduct estimated amounts for (i) engine-specific research; (ii) research related to air traffic; and (iii) research related to other miscellaneous non-LCA related projects

---

[2584] *Ibid.*

[2585] NASA/DOD/DOC Aeronautics R&D Subsidies to Boeing LCA Division, Exhibit EC-25, p. 20.

[2586] International Trade Resources LLC, Calculating on a Per-Aircraft Basis the Magnitude of the Subsidies Provided to US Large Civil Aircraft, 20 February 2007, Exhibit EC-13, p. 22. The European Communities allocates $993 million to 2004, $992 million to 2005, and $983 million to 2006.

[2587] European Communities' first written submission, paras. 63-68 and paras. 525, 549, 573, 589, 604, 619, 632 and 651.

1346   DSR 2012:III

US - Large Civil Aircraft (2nd Complaint)

(e.g. space-related research[2588]). The European Communities then allocates the remainder exclusively to the "U.S. civil aircraft industry", which includes producers of large civil aircraft (i.e. Boeing), small civil aircraft, helicopters, and their suppliers. The European Communities then allocates a share of that total to Boeing, based on Boeing's share of the "U.S. civil aircraft industry". Using this methodology, the European Communities estimates that $10.4 billion, out of the $18.7 billion in total programme costs, should be allocated to Boeing. The European Communities explains its methodology as follows:

> "For NASA, the EC analysis started with budget data that reflected total annual spending on a programme-by-programme basis, with no indication of how much NASA spent to support any particular company. Based on the budgets themselves and other available facts regarding the eight NASA programmes at issue, it was clear that the budgets reflected R&D spending related to: (1) civil aircraft airframes and components (for all eight programmes at issue); (2) aircraft engines (for some of the eight programmes at issue); and (3) other technologies unrelated to airframes, such as air traffic control or space launch technology (for some of the eight programmes at issue). To arrive at its estimate of the subsidy to Boeing's LCA division from each NASA programme, the European Communities started by isolating the portion of each budget related to item (1) by subtracting items (2) and (3) from the total budget figures where applicable. This resulted in budget figures for each programme that reflected the total amount spent by NASA on R&D related to exclusively civil aircraft airframes and components. Then, recognising that some of this R&D spending likely supported entities in the US civil aircraft industry other than Boeing's LCA division, the European Communities allocated only a portion of the resulting figures to Boeing's LCA division. In performing this allocation, the European Communities considered it reasonable to use a ratio derived by dividing (i) the sum of all Boeing and McDonnell Douglas LCA and parts sales for each year by (ii) the amount of all US civil aircraft and parts sales for that year. The rationale for doing so was that Boeing's LCA division (including McDonnell Douglas' LCA division) is a subset of the larger US civil aircraft and parts industry, in support of which NASA spent the budgeted amounts being allocated."[2589]

[2588] More specifically, the European Communities deducts estimated amounts for costs relating to the following elements of the R&T Base Program: "Space Transfer and Launch Technology", "Minority University Research and Education Program", "Construction of Facilities", and "Future Space Launch Studies".

[2589] European Communities response to question 163, para. 243.

DSR 2012:III

1347

Report of the Panel

7.1053 In its second written submission, the European Communities argues that the United States has failed to demonstrate that the funding to Boeing under these programmes was worth less than $750 million, and that $6.48 billion actually went to entities unrelated to Boeing. The European Communities submits that, unless and until the United States discloses all of the contracts (and Space Act Agreements) and sub-contracts pursuant to which Boeing and McDonnell Douglas received "funding and support" under the eight programmes at issue, "including all relevant dollar figures, statements of work, indications and values of goods and services provided by NASA under the contracts, etc.", there is no way to conduct an adequate "bottom-up" analysis of the financial contribution to Boeing from these NASA aeronautics R&D programmes.[2590]

(ii) Arguments of the United States

7.1054 The United States asserts that the European Communities has overestimated the amount of any subsidy provided to Boeing by NASA. According to the United States, the total amount of payments made to Boeing under NASA R&D contracts and agreements entered into under the eight aeronautics programmes at issue was $1.05 billion, out of which less than $775 million was LCA-related. The United States estimates that the total value of the NASA facilities, equipment and employees provided to Boeing under these R&D contracts and agreements was less than $80 million. According to the United States, the remainder of the funding was provided to other NASA contractors, grantees and partners to conduct research under the programmes, as well as the direct costs of NASA's in-house R&D, and "program support" costs that NASA incurs under each programme.[2591]

(iii) Evaluation by the Panel

Introduction

7.1055 The European Communities has demonstrated that the payments and access to facilities, equipment and employees provided to Boeing through aeronautics R&D contracts and agreements are subsidies within the meaning of Article 1 of the SCM Agreement. The Panel will now address the amount of the subsidy to Boeing's LCA division.

7.1056 The European Communities presents the Panel with an estimate of the amount of the subsidy provided to Boeing's LCA division. The European Communities' estimate is based on the publicly available information regarding the total budgeted costs of the eight R&D programmes at issue, and Boeing's share of the U.S. civil aircraft industry. The European Communities argues that the Panel should adopt this "top down" estimate, unless the United States

---

[2590] European Communities' second written submission, paras. 365-373.
[2591] United States' first written submission, para. 198.

1348   DSR 2012:III

discloses evidence indicating the actual value of the payments and access to facilities, equipment and employees provided to Boeing. The United States submits that it has done exactly that. In the Panel's view, if the United States were able to provide the Panel with the actual information and figures regarding the amount of those subsidies, or information from which the maximum amount of those subsidies could be derived, then such information would necessarily prevail over the European Communities' "top down" estimate. Therefore, the Panel will begin by reviewing the evidence provided by the United States.

> The United States' evidence regarding the maximum amount of the payments made to Boeing for aeronautics R&D over the period 1989-2006

7.1057 The United States initially asserted that NASA records indicate that NASA "disbursements" to Boeing under the challenged programmes amounted to less than $750 million."[2592] The United States set forth, in paragraph 212 of its first written submission, a list of the eight R&D programmes, and the corresponding total disbursements to Boeing under those programmes, which added together, came to $715 million, or "less than $750 million".[2593] The United States adds that much of the "less than $750 million" that was directly provided to Boeing was actually passed along to other companies who performed work as sub-contractors.[2594]

7.1058 In its first set of questions to the parties, the Panel asked the United States to explain how it arrived at the figure of "less than $750 million". The United States responded that NASA reached this estimate by:

(a)   Identifying the relevant contracts with Boeing that were awarded under the eight R&D programmes at issue between 1989 and 2006

[2592] United States' first written submission, para. 212. The United Status explains that "disbursements" are the cumulative amounts actually paid to Boeing and MDD under research contracts. There are several points to note about the disbursement information: First, according to the United States, "disbursements" offer very close approximations of the true amount of payments, although they may not be exact due to changes in record keeping over the period 1989-2006; second, disbursements for a particular contract are allocated to a single program, even if multiple programs use the same contract; and third, actual disbursements to Boeing may differ from the amounts planned to be paid at the beginning of each period and appearing in the contract documents; e.g. amounts actually paid under time and materials contracts may vary from anticipated amounts if contracted tasks take more or less time than anticipated and amounts may differ where budget pools are exhausted or contracted work is cancelled; United States' first written submission, para. 212, footnote 303.

[2593] The figure of $715 million includes an estimate of disbursements of $66 million to Boeing pursuant to the ACEE program which predate 1989, and for which company-specific records were not available due to the age of the program.

[2594] United States' first written submission, para. 226, footnote 328. In this regard, the United States provides the example of the HSR program, which had 40 major subcontracts. According to the United States, the structure of the program was such that Boeing effectively served as consortium leader, disbursing funding to the other entities.

Report of the Panel

through a search of the Federal Procurement Data Base (FPDS) of all awards (whether contracts, cooperative agreements, or grants) made to Boeing for the years 1989-2006.[2595] For the years 2004-2006, the relevant database was the Federal Procurement Data Base – Next Generation (FPDS-NG) which had superseded the FPDS.

(b)   Eliminating awards that "clearly did not pertain to any NASA Aeronautics programs, such as those related to manned space flight, the International Space Station or space science".[2596]

(c)   Calculating the amounts disbursed to Boeing for each such contract from disbursement information obtained from NASA's internal financial databases which, prior to 2004, accumulated data, performed checks and then fed the information into FPDS. NASA's system was known as the NASA Procurement Management System (NPMS).[2597]

7.1059 The United States also submitted *Exhibit US-1202* as part of its response to the Panel's question. Exhibit US-1202 sets forth the amounts disbursed under each contract, grouped by R&D programme, as determined based on the above methodology.[2598]

7.1060 The Panel sought to confirm the above understanding of the methodology that the United States used to calculate the amount of payments made to Boeing pursuant to contracts under the eight R&D programmes in its second set of questions to the parties. The Panel also sought additional details from the United States on: (i) the list of relevant contracts obtained from the FPDS database searches of awards to Boeing between 1989 and 2006; (ii) the awards that were determined not to pertain to any NASA aeronautics programmes; and (iii) identification of amounts disbursed under each relevant

---

[2595] The United States explains that the FPDS is the database of record for procurements for the United States Government and is the only reliable and comprehensive source for data on NASA procurements. The United States explains that, whenever a federal agency awards a procurement action with an obligation greater than $3,000, it must be reported to the Office of Management and Budget in the Executive Office of the President via the FPDS. Following the award, the FPDS is updated over its life with additional obligations as they occur. United States' response to question 7, para. 12.

[2596] United States' response to question 7, para. 14.

[2597] United States' response to question 7, para. 15. According to the United States, the FPDS did not record *disbursement* data. However, prior to 2005, NASA routinely accumulated disbursement data in its NPMS. The United States submits that for each action identified for Boeing, NASA could accurately identify amounts obligated and disbursed for each contract, by year. The FPDS-NG also did not record disbursement data for the years 2005 and 2006, however, the United States indicates that NASA obtained disbursement data for these years from NASA's internal financial records.

[2598] The United States notes that the ACEE Program is so old that no disbursement data were available on either FPDS or NPMS. NASA therefore derived an estimate for disbursements to Boeing through contracts under the ACEE Program based on Boeing's share of the NASA program budget for the next oldest program, ACT. United States' response to question 7, para. 15.

1350   DSR 2012:III

US - Large Civil Aircraft (2nd Complaint)

contract award on the basis of information contained in the NPMS and NASA's internal financial records.

7.1061 The United States responded as follows. First, it confirmed the Panel's basic understanding as outlined above. Second, it indicated that NASA did not print out the FPDS list of all awards to Boeing between 1989 and 2006 because the FPDS and FPDS-NG contain entries for individual purchase orders and task orders issued under each contract, and therefore contain thousands of entries for such awards. According to the United States, NASA used the list as the basis for additional steps to weed out instruments not related to the European Communities' claims.[2599] Third, it explained in greater detail than previously had been provided to the Panel the process by which NASA "eliminated" awards that it ascertained did not pertain to the eight R&D programmes.

7.1062 The first, and most important, step in the elimination process was to identify awards issued by NASA research centers that perform aeronautics research. In this regard, the United States explained that NASA conducts all of its research activities at nine research centers. Four of those centers; namely, Langley Research Center, Glenn Research Center, Ames Research Center and Dryden Research Center, are responsible for all aeronautics research conducted by NASA. These four research centers administer the eight R&D programmes and perform all aeronautics research required in support of NASA's other programmes. According to the United States, each research center awards its own contracts for work performed in support of its projects.[2600] Because the FPDS record for each award contains a code that indicates the center that awarded the instrument in question, NASA was able to filter the FPDS list of Boeing contracts to remove all contracts awarded by the five NASA research centers that do not perform aeronautics research.

7.1063 The second part of the elimination process involved elimination of contracts that, although awarded by one of the four NASA research centers that perform aeronautics research, nevertheless pertained to non-aeronautics research (e.g. contracts whose subject matter pertained to space, atmospheric science, airspace hypersonics, vertical take-off and landing and short takeoff and landing, and aircraft support related to the maintenance and upkeep of NASA's aircraft).[2601] Identification of the subject matter of the contracts was based on the FPDS and FPDS-NG fields that describe the subject matter of each contract.

7.1064 In response to the Panel's request for additional detail as to its identification of amounts disbursed under each relevant award on the basis of data in the NPMS and NASA's internal financial records, the United States further explained that the FPDS databases contain only data on the amounts "obligated" for funding a particular contract (i.e. budgeted funds provided to a

---

[2599] United States' response to question 179, para. 179.

[2600] United States' response to question 179, para. 180.

[2601] United States' response to question 179, para. 181. The United States explains that the four aeronautics research centers also conduct some non-aeronautics research.

DSR 2012:III

1351

Report of the Panel

prime contract for costs to be expended in the performance of that contract).[2602] Funds "obligated" are not "disbursed" to the contractor until the contractor has demonstrated an entitlement to payment.[2603] The NPMS database, in addition to containing information on funds obligated, also recorded the amounts actually disbursed for all disbursements prior to 2005. For the disbursement figures for 2005 and 2006, NASA used data from NASA's SAP/BW system.[2604]

7.1065 The Panel also asked the United States to explain how the Panel could satisfy itself that the information submitted by the United States as to the universe of R&D contracts and agreements between NASA and Boeing is accurate and complete. The United States responded by explaining that NASA had conducted the following verification exercise:

(a)   NASA conducted a FPDS/FPDS-NG database search of all contracts with Boeing and Boeing subsidiaries (i.e. not limited to aeronautics-related contracts, or contracts pursuant to the challenged R&D programs) as identified in the list of 100 Principal Contractors published in NASA's Annual Procurement Reports for the 1989-2006 period.

(b)   NASA compared the values of awards identified from that search (a total of **$30.4 billion** for 1989-2006) with the total value of awards to Boeing published in the NASA Annual Procurement Reports. According to the United States, in no case was the variation in values of awards to Boeing in the Top 100 contractors list as reported by FPDS and FPDS-NG to the value reported in the Annual Procurement Reports more than 2.1 per cent.[2605]

7.1066 The United States contends that this part of the check verifies that the NASA's contract data set, based on its search of its FPDS/FPDS-NG databases, closely matches the published data from the Annual Procurement Reports which are accepted by the United States and the European Communities as a valid and complete representation of all NASA contracts with Boeing.[2606]

[2602] United States' response to question 179, para. 184.

[2603] United States' response to question 179, para. 184, footnote 196.

[2604] United States' response to question 179, para. 184.

[2605] The results of the comparison are at Exhibit US-1301. The United States appears to have based its valuations on the amounts obligated under the awards as reported in the FPDS/FPDS-NG, rather than the actual disbursements made under the contracts, unlike its original estimate, which relied on the actual disbursements as indicated from the NPMS and SAP/BW internal databases. The United States explains that the actual funds disbursed under a contract may be (i) less than the funds allotted (e.g. where the contractor finishes the work before the funds run out); or (ii) more than the amount shown in the final contract modification (e.g. if adjustments are necessary when the contract is closed out). According to the United States, the funds allotted under the contract modifications allow an estimate of the maximum that NASA was authorized to spend under the contract. United States' response to question 6, para. 3, footnote 7.

[2606] United States' response to question 188, para. 217. We note, however, that the United States indicates that the FPDS/FPDS-NG databases were the source for the Annual Procurement Report data, so this verification step does not address the European Communities' criticisms of the reliability

US - Large Civil Aircraft (2nd Complaint)

7.1067 The United States continued this "verification" exercise to arrive at what it contends is the "maximum value" of contracts with Boeing under the eight R&D programmes:

(c)   From the FPDS/FPDS-NG database search of all contracts with Boeing and its subsidiaries (including any that were not in the 100 Principal Contractor's List), NASA then filtered out contracts awarded by NASA centers that perform no aeronautics research. The value of the eliminated contracts (i.e. contracts with non-aeronautics NASA centers) for 1989-2006 was **$29 billion for 1989-2006**. According to the United States, this amount represents 96.5 per cent of the value of all of Boeing's contracts with NASA. In other words, the "vast majority" of Boeing's contracts with NASA are related to *non-aeronautics activities* (i.e. NASA facilities, NASA research activities and NASA programs supporting NASA's space and exploration objectives), none of which have been challenged in this dispute.

7.1068 The United States contends that, once contracts issued by NASA facilities that conduct no aeronautics research are factored out, there are only **$1.05 billion** in contracts remaining for the 1989-2006 period that are even *potentially* related to the European Communities' claims regarding aeronautics research.[2607]

(d)   Finally, NASA personnel manually reviewed the descriptions of the research conducted under each Boeing contract *awarded by the four centers that conduct aeronautics research*. The result identified every Boeing contract with the four aeronautics centers, not simply those related to aeronautics R&D. Then NASA personnel assigned contracts to 13 various subject categories and excluded only those contracts within nine of the clearly non-LCA-related categories.[2608] The remaining group of contracts had a value of **$775 million**, which according to the United States, represents the "maximum value" of Boeing contracts related to EC-challenged R&D.[2609]

---

of the FPDs/FPDS-NG databases as the starting point for the identification of relevant contracts. The European Communities makes this point also. European Communities' comments on United States' response to question 188, para. 207.

[2607] United States' response to question 188, para. 219. The United States further notes that the contract set at this stage still includes contracts relating to engine research, research into hypersonics and air traffic control, which the European Communities has stated are not related to its claims, as well as research funded by programs other than the eight aeronautics R&D programs.

[2608] See United States' response to question 188, paras. 218 and 220.

[2609] The United States contends that this list of remaining contracts is over-inclusive (and therefore the value of such contracts is certainly larger than the actual value of NASA research contracts related to the European Communities' challenge) because, for purposes of this verification exercise, where the description of research under a contract involved both aeronautics and non-aeronautics

DSR 2012:III   1353

Report of the Panel

7.1069 The United States argues that, while the value of the contracts identified in this verification exercise is approximately $116 million higher than the value of contracts reported by the United States at paragraph 212 of its first written submission, the difference is not significant.[2610]

7.1070 Certain of the European Communities' criticisms of the United States' "payments" estimate of $750 million relate to the *scope* of transactions included in the estimate; i.e. that (i) the estimate excludes payments made to Boeing as a sub-contractor, and (ii) does not include the value of goods and services provided to Boeing through Space Act Agreements. Both of these criticisms are without foundation. Leaving aside the strongly disputed issue of whether any payments that Boeing received as a sub-contractor pursuant to contracts between NASA and third parties are financial contributions covered by Article 1.1(a)(1) of the SCM Agreement[2611], including such payments within the scope of the transactions in the "payments" estimate would not increase the total amount. It would actually *reduce* the total amount. If a proper estimate of the total amount of the payments received by Boeing should include/add payments that Boeing received as a sub-contractor, then that estimate must logically exclude/subtract payments that Boeing made to its sub-contractors when it was Boeing that was the prime contractor. The parties appear to agree that the total amount of the payments that Boeing received as a sub-contractor is likely far less than the total amount of the payments that Boeing paid out to its own sub-contractors. Therefore, adding the value of the payments that Boeing received as a sub-contractor would actually lead to a reduction – likely a significant reduction – in the total amount of the payments that should be included in the estimate of the amount of the subsidy to Boeing. As for the exclusion of the value of "goods and services" from the United States' $750 million estimate, the United States acknowledges that its payments estimate relates only to *payments* to Boeing under NASA R&D contracts and agreements, and does not include the value of any *goods and services* provided to Boeing through R&D contracts or agreements. It provides a separate valuation of the goods and services provided by NASA pursuant to Space Act Agreements with Boeing, which the Panel addresses below. Therefore, this criticism is also without foundation.

7.1071 The European Communities argues that the United States has offered no means of verifying that NASA has properly identified and counted all of the

---

related R&D, NASA treated the whole contract as related to the dispute. United States' response to question 188, para. 222.

[2610] The United States explains that in order to compare the estimate at paragraph 212 of its first written submission, with the estimate arrived at through the verification exercise in response to Panel question 188, it is appropriate to subtract from the $715 million initial estimate the estimated $66 million in respect of the ACEE program. United States' response to question 188, para. 222, footnote 239. If we do this, we find that the difference between the two estimates is $126 million, not $116 million as indicated by the United States.

[2611] The arguments of the parties on this issue are found in their responses, and corresponding comments, to questions 3(b), 130, 131 and 132.

1354

DSR 2012:III

US - Large Civil Aircraft (2ⁿᵈ Complaint)

LCA-related contracts with Boeing (i.e. the completeness of the contract data set)[2612]; and has provided no basis for concluding that its "disbursements" estimate captures all of the funds actually disbursed to Boeing under the R&D programmes at issue.

7.1072 As to the criticisms directed towards the completeness of the relevant contract data set, the European Communities alleges that the FPDS/FPDS-NG database is a flawed and unreliable source for identifying the contracts between NASA and Boeing.[2613] In this regard, the European Communities refers to a Congressional Research Service Report and a General Accounting Office (GAO) report critical of the FPDS database.[2614] The European Communities also alleges that the United States failed to include four contracts with Boeing in its contract data set in Exhibit US-1202 (worth $41 million) and that this omission of relevant contracts from the contract data set on which the disbursement estimate is based also calls into question whether the estimate includes all of the relevant contracts between NASA and Boeing.[2615]

7.1073 The Panel has reviewed the exhibits submitted by the European Communities to support its contention that the FPDS/FPDS-NG databases cannot be relied upon to produce a complete set of relevant contracts. The Panel is not persuaded that the evidence supports the European Communities' contentions in this regard.[2616] Moreover, the Panel notes that there do not appear to be any practical alternatives for the Panel, or for NASA, to reliance on the FPDS/FPDS-NG database to generate an initial list of contracts between NASA and Boeing. We are inclined to agree with the United States that a list of contracts generated by FPDS/FPDS-NG inquiries would be the starting point for compiling any list of contracts between NASA and Boeing. Although not perfect, it is not only the best source, but the only practical source of information on the universe of contracts between NASA and Boeing.

7.1074 In relation to the European Communities' allegation that the United States had failed to include four relevant contracts between NASA and Boeing in the list of contracts in Exhibit US-1202 that formed the basis for the United States' disbursement estimate, the United States explains that one of the contracts in question was included in the list in Exhibit US-1202 but was mislabelled as a

---

[2612] European Communities' comments on United States' response to question 7, para. 6.

[2613] European Communities' response to question 173(b), para 301.

[2614] CRS Report for Congress, The Federal Funding Accountability and Transparency Act: Background, Overview, and Implementation Issues, 6 October 2006, Exhibit EC-1375; GAO, Improvements Needed to the Federal Procurement Database System-Next Generation, GAO 05-960R, 27 September 2005, Exhibit EC-1376. See also, GAO, Reliability of Federal Procurement Data, GAO-04-295R, 30 December 2003, Exhibit EC-1377.

[2615] European Communities' comments on United States' response to question 6, para. 8.

[2616] More specifically, we consider that the European Communities has taken the comments made in the reports out of context, and that the criticisms of the FPDS system do not pertain to whether or not the FPDS would be a reliable source of NASA-specific contract information.

DSR 2012:III

1355

Report of the Panel

different contract[2617] and that the other three contracts were "apparently missed in the initial analysis", although they were captured in the calculation of the "maximum value" of Boeing contracts in the United States' verification exercise performed in response to Panel question 188 and set forth in *Exhibit US-1305*.[2618] The United States does not elaborate on exactly how the three contracts were apparently missed in the initial analysis, although it is reasonable to assume that they were erroneously omitted by NASA personnel as part of the elimination of contracts whose subject matter indicated that they pertained to non-aeronautics research.

7.1075 If the United States' verification exercise correctly portrays the relative value of contracts awarded to Boeing by the four NASA research centers that perform aeronautics research ($1.05 billion) compared to all contracts awarded to Boeing by the NASA research centers that do not perform aeronautics research ($29 billion), then it appears that the most significant element of the United States' methodology for identifying the relevant contracts is its filtering of the FPDS/FPDS-NG databases to eliminate the latter category of contracts.

7.1076 It was in response to questions 179 and 188 from the Panel that the United States explained that, once contracts issued by NASA facilities that conduct no aeronautics research were filtered out of the "all Boeing contracts" set, there are only **$1.05 billion** in contracts remaining for the 1989-2006 period that are even potentially related to the European Communities' claims regarding aeronautics research.[2619] In its comments on the United States' response to questions 179 and 188, the European Communities did not criticise this aspect of the United States' methodology for identifying the relevant contracts. Given that this seems to be the most significant element of the United States methodology for identifying the maximum value of contractual payments made to Boeing, the Panel subsequently sought further submissions from the parties. In its response to question 339, the United States confirmed, among other things, that the Panel was correct in understanding that, as a factual matter, all contracts that are related to the European Communities' challenges to non-engine aeronautics research must have been awarded by the four NASA centers (Langley, Glenn (formerly Lewis), Ames, and Dryden) that are responsible for all aeronautics research conducted by NASA and cannot have been awarded by any other NASA center or unit:

[2617] United States' response to question 184, para. 191. Contract NAS1-20553 was mislabelled as NAS1-20550. The United States also indicates that, although the amount awarded under this contract was originally $22 million (as alleged by the European Communities), the amount actually disbursed was $1.8 million.

[2618] United States' response to question 184, para. 191. According to the United States, the combined value of disbursements under these three contracts was $15.2 million.

[2619] United States' response to question 179, para. 180; United States' response to question 188, para. 219.

1356 DSR 2012:III

US - Large Civil Aircraft (2nd Complaint)

> "... The EC challenge relates to a group of named research programs, all of them involving aeronautics research. All of NASA's expenditures, including procurements, cooperative agreements, and grants, are administered through one of the various centers. Only four of the centers – Langley Research Center, Glenn Research Center (formerly known as Lewis), Ames Research Center, and Dryden Flight Research Center – perform aeronautics research. These centers administered all of the aeronautics research under the programs challenged by the EC. The remaining centers were not responsible for administering any of the programs challenged by the EC. It is NASA policy that the center implementing a research program is responsible for awarding any contracts, cooperative agreements, or grants to perform research under that program. Therefore, all contracts (and cooperative agreements) that are related to the EC challenges to non-engine aeronautics research must have been awarded by those four NASA centers, and cannot have been awarded by any other NASA center or unit."[2620]

7.1077 In its comments on the United States' response to question 339, the European Communities advances two arguments in response to the United States' assertion that all contracts that are related to the European Communities' challenges must have been awarded by those four NASA centers, and cannot have been awarded by any other NASA center or unit.

7.1078 First, that "{t}he European Communities challenges non-engine aeronautics-related R&D conducted by NASA at any of its facilities. The specific facility that conducts such R&D is immaterial to the EC claims and arguments".[2621] The Panel understands that the European Communities has challenged payments and access to facilities, equipment and employees provided to Boeing under the eight R&D programmes at issue, regardless of the specific NASA center involved. However, in the Panel's view, this still does not respond to the United States' contention that, as a factual matter, all contracts that are related to the European Communities' challenge to aeronautics research must have been awarded by Langley, Glenn (formerly Lewis), Ames, or Dryden.

7.1079 Second, the European Communities argues that "{w}hile the bulk of NASA's expenditures related to aeronautics may have been undertaken by Langley, Glenn (formerly Lewis), Ames, and Dryden, the United States is incorrect that *all* NASA aeronautics expenditures were undertaken by these four centers". The European Communities notes that "{e}ven a cursory review of NASA's "aeronautical research and technology" budget summaries reveals that some of NASA's aeronautics funding was in fact spent by NASA centers other

---

[2620] United States' response to question 339, para. 82 (footnote omitted).
[2621] European Communities' comments on United States' response to question 339, para. 78.

DSR 2012:III   1357

Report of the Panel

than these four".[2622] In this connection, the European Communities refers the Panel to "NASA Aeronautical Research and Technology, Budget Summaries, FY 1991-FY 2000" (Exhibit EC-1440). The "NASA Aeronautical Research and Technology, Budget Summaries, FY 1991-FY 2000" submitted by the European Communities identifies aggregate, yearly figures on the "resource requirements" for the R&T Base Program and other "Aeronautical focused programs", followed by a breakdown of the "Distribution of Program Amount by Installation". What this document shows is that while "some of NASA's aeronautics funding was in fact spent by NASA centers other than these four", i.e. other than Langley, Glenn (formerly Lewis), Ames, and Dryden, as asserted by the European Communities, it appears that over the period 1989-2006, these four centres accounted for more than 99 per cent of "Aeronautical Research & Technology Resources". Thus, rather than calling into question the United States' assertion, this information appears to offer confirmation that *substantially all* NASA aeronautics expenditures were undertaken by these four centers.

7.1080 As for the accuracy of the disbursement information related to each of the identified contracts, the Panel notes, first, that the European Communities does not challenge the use of "disbursements" data as a close approximation of the amount of "payments" made to Boeing under the research contracts. The European Communities does challenge the reliability of NASA's "financial databases", which presumably include the NPMS and SAP/BW systems that were the source of the disbursements data. In this regard, the European Communities cites from a report of the GAO that indicates that NASA had been on GAO's "high-risk" list since 1990 because of its failure to effectively oversee its contracts, due in part to NASA's lack of accurate and reliable information on contract spending.[2623] The Panel has reviewed this GAO Report and notes that it does not refer to the NPMS or SAP/BW systems specifically, nor does it suggest that those systems would be unreliable sources of information as to actual disbursements made by NASA. We are therefore not persuaded that the European Communities has adequately supported its allegations that NASA's financial databases are unreliable for purposes of estimating the value of NASA's R&D subsidies to Boeing.

7.1081 It is clear to the Panel that NASA has made mistakes in compiling the relevant information, and that NASA's records are not perfect (and as we discuss below, in relation to Space Act Agreements, far from perfect). However, the European Communities has not demonstrated that the United States' estimate involved any "methodological" errors. The Panel therefore estimates that the

---

[2622] European Communities' comments on United States' response to question 339, para. 79.

[2623] European Communities' response to question 173(b), paras. 300-302; Statement of Gregory D. Kutz, NASA Long-standing Financial Management Challenges Threaten the Agency's Ability to Manage its Programs, 27 October 2005, Exhibit EC-1313. The European Communities also quotes from a 2006 Congressional Research Service Report which noted that the GAO had noted that FPDS users lacked confidence in the data provided because there was no rigorous system in place to ensure the accuracy and completeness of the data; Exhibit EC-1375.

1358

DSR 2012:III

total amount of payments to Boeing through R&D contracts under the eight R&D programmes over the period 1989-2006 was **$1.05 billion**.

> The United States' evidence regarding the maximum value of the NASA facilities, equipment and employees provided to Boeing for aeronautics R&D over the period 1989-2006

7.1082 The United States estimates that the value of goods and services supplied to Boeing under non-reimbursable and partially reimbursable SAAs was $79.7 million.[2624] The United States' estimate reflects the value of facilities, equipment and employees captured in "Estimated Price Reports" prepared by NASA in connection with the Space Act Agreements that it entered into with Boeing.

7.1083 The United States provided an original list of relevant Space Act Agreements as *Exhibit US-74*.[2625] In the second set of questions, the Panel asked the United States to explain the methodology that it used to develop the list of Space Act Agreements in Exhibit US-74. The United States responded that the list of relevant Space Act Agreements set forth in Exhibit US-74 was obtained by searching NASA's "physical and electronic records" to identify Boeing Space Act Agreements, and then taking the relevant information from the hard copy documents. At that time, NASA had not sought to determine which programme funded the particular Space Act Agreements in Exhibit US-74, and the United States subsequently explained during the second meeting with the Panel, that Exhibit US-74 included some Space Act Agreements that on closer inspection, had not in fact been funded under the challenged R&D programmes.[2626]

7.1084 At the second meeting with the Panel, the United States submitted Exhibit US-1256, "The Value of NASA Facilities, Equipment, and Employees

---

[2624] United States' response to question 175, para. 160. The Panel recalls that NASA provides goods and services under *reimbursable* Space Act Agreements when it has unique goods, services and facilities that are not being fully utilized to accomplish mission needs, which it can make available to others on a non-interference basis. United States' first written submission, para. 233, footnote 336. NASA requires full reimbursement, defined as "full cost recovery" for the goods, services or facilities provided. NASA also has the authority to accept *partial reimbursement* where a proposed contribution of the SAA partner is fair and reasonable compared to the NASA resources to be committed, NASA program risks and corresponding benefits to NASA. The European Communities does not challenge the supply of goods and services under Space Act Agreements to the extent that Boeing pays cash in exchange for those goods and services.

[2625] The United States first referred to this list of Space Act Agreements at para. 201 of its first written submission (footnote 283), in the context of its criticism of the inclusion of $3.3 billion from NASA's "institutional support" budgets in the European Communities' $10.4 billion estimate. According to the United States, from the $3.3 billion in "institutional support" challenged by the European Communities, NASA has only provided limited goods and services to Boeing pursuant to 35 Space Act Agreements that cover discrete uses by Boeing of NASA wind tunnels and work on other jointly undertaken R&D projects.

[2626] United States' response to question 183, para. 190; United States' non-confidential oral statement at the second meeting with the Panel, para. 63.

Report of the Panel

under Selected Space Act Agreements". Exhibit US-1256 lists the relevant Space Act Agreements for which the United States was able to obtain valuation information.[2627] The total non-reimbursable value of the instruments listed there was estimated to be $82.9 million. However, the United States also explained during the Second Meeting that Exhibit US-1256 was not yet "final" (and also that some of the Space Act Agreements that had been listed in Exhibit US-74 were not, on closer examination, related to the challenged R&D programmes).

7.1085 The United States subsequently *revised Exhibit US-1256* in response to the Panel's Question 185 to add two SAAs and remove two cooperative agreements that were inadvertently included on the original list of SAAs in Exhibit US-1256. The United States indicated in response to Panel question 185 that revised Exhibit US-1256 contains all of the SAAs "for which the United States has value information".[2628] The total of "NASA Planned Contributions" under the 21 Space Act Agreements listed in the revised Exhibit US-1256 was $79.9 million.

7.1086 In response to a question from the Panel as to how the value of NASA facilities, equipment and employees provided through Space Act Agreements set forth in Exhibit US-1256 was calculated, the United States indicated that these figures are based on "Estimated Price Reports" contained in either the physical files related to an SAA, or in NASA's TechTrackS System, which includes data on the Estimated Price Reports for SAAs.

7.1087 The TechTrackS System is an electronic database that also contains data on the R&D programme that is the source of funding for particular SAAs. The United States advises that, in compiling Exhibit US-1256, NASA removed SAAs that were funded by programmes other than the eight R&D programmes at issue in this dispute. The United States indicated that the list of Space Act Agreements in revised Exhibit US-1256 contains all of the Space Act Agreements "for which the United States has value information".[2629] In other words, Exhibit US-1256 does not purport to be a comprehensive valuation of all relevant Space Act Agreements. Rather, in the light of the difficulties accessing value information for Space Act Agreements that are not recorded in the TechTrackS system (i.e. Space Act Agreements entered into prior to 1993 by all research centers except the Langley Research Center, which apparently entered onto the electronic database information for its pre-1993 contracts), revised Exhibit US-1256 is a listing of the relevant Space Act Agreements for which

---

[2627] United States' non-confidential oral statement at the second meeting with the Panel, para. 63. See also, United States' comments on European Communities' response to question 172, para. 299, where the United States explains that the value information in Exhibit US-1256 that was based on corresponding value information reported in Exhibit US-74 was based on documents submitted to the Panel (these are listed in footnote 489), while the remaining value information was based on information in the TechTrackS database.

[2628] United States' response to question 185, para. 193.

[2629] United States' response to question 185, para. 193; United States' comments on European Communities' response to question 172, para. 300.

1360

DSR 2012:III

Estimated Price Reports were available, or for which other value information was available.[2630]

7.1088 The European Communities advances a number of arguments concerning the United States' valuation of goods and services provided pursuant to Space Act Agreements, including the following:

- First, it alleges that the United States has not submitted copies of all relevant Space Act Agreements between NASA and Boeing.[2631] In support of this contention, the European Communities alleges that NASA failed to submit into evidence copies of two relevant Space Act Agreements that the European Communities was able to identify through FOIA requests.[2632]

- Second, the European Communities has complained that in estimating the values of Space Act Agreements in revised Exhibit US-1256, the United States has *failed to tabulate values* for all of the Space Act Agreements that have been identified as relevant Space Act Agreements by either the European Communities or the United States (these are set forth in *Exhibit EC-1374,* which lists 21 such Space Act Agreements).[2633]

- Moreover, the European Communities argues that the United States' valuation of the facilities, equipment and employees provided to Boeing through Space Act Agreements is unsupported as the United States has failed to submit the Estimated Price Reports and the results of its inquiries of the TechTrackS system that form the basis for the estimate.[2634]

7.1089 The United States explains that six of the 21 SAAs for which it had not tabulated a value were signed prior to 1993 and were not included on the

---

[2630] As indicated previously, in United States' comments on European Communities' response to question 172, para. 299 (footnote 489), the United States lists the Exhibits (all of which are BCI) from which the other value information was drawn, namely, Exhibits US-70 (BCI), US-109 (BCI), US-113 (BCI), US-120 (BCI), US-122 (BCI).

[2631] Exhibit US-1245 was provided by the United States in response to a question from the Panel (issued on 17 December 2007) requesting the United States to submit a list of NASA contracts for which Exhibits have been submitted by the United States, along with other information related to the contract and the relationship of the contract to the U.S. submissions.

[2632] The European Communities identifies Exhibits EC-1314 and EC-1315 as "examples" of such Space Act Agreements; see European Communities' comments on United States' response to question 6, para. 14.

[2633] European Communities' response to question 172, para. 297. The European Communities argues that the unavailability of data on estimated price reports through the TechTrackS system for Space Act Agreements signed before 1993 does not excuse the United States from submitting information about the value of goods and services provided through the relevant Space Act Agreements. European Communities' comments on United States' response to question 184, para. 187.

[2634] European Communities' comments on United States' response to question 183, para. 185.

DSR 2012:III

Report of the Panel

TechTrackS System.[2635] However, the United States notes that Langley Research Center entered historical (i.e. pre-1993) SAA data on the TechTrackS System, and asserts that the Langley Center originated the greatest number of agreements related to the European Communities' allegations, with greater value than those originated by other centers, so the data in revised Exhibit US-1256 can be considered to be "substantially complete".[2636]

7.1090 According to the United States, nine of the remaining 17 SAAs[2637] that the European Communities had identified were valued at a total of $8.1 million and were sponsored by a NASA office that provided general support for putting such agreements into effect, and were possibly related to one of the eight R&D programmes.[2638] The United States makes no mention of the possible value of the other eight (or six) SAAs on which there is no value information.

7.1091 The United States considers that the Panel can have a high degree of confidence that the United States has identified "all of the available Boeing Space Act Agreements that are related to the eight challenged programs".[2639] The United States suggests that, should the Panel consider that any Space Act Agreement was improperly excluded, it assign a value to it equal to the average value of SAAs listed in the revised Exhibit US-1256 (i.e. $4.7 million).

7.1092 The Panel notes that, although the United States was subsequently able to advise that the value of nine SAAs for which value information was not tabulated in revised Exhibit US-1256, was approximately $8.1 million in total, it did not revise the total value of SAAs set forth in its revised version to Exhibit US-1256 to reflect the values of those SAAs. Leaving that point to one side, the position appears to be:

- the United States has identified 38 relevant Space Act Agreements, copies of which it has submitted to the Panel. The list of these Space Act Agreements is at *Exhibit US-1245*.

- the United States has tabulated value information for 21 of the 38 Space Act Agreements, this valuation appearing in revised Exhibit US-1256 and amounting to $79.9 million.

- the United States has estimated in addition that nine Space Act Agreements whose values were not part of the $79.9 million estimate, are worth approximately $8.1 million.

[2635] The TechTrackS system was not operational prior to 1993, so data pertaining to Space Act Agreements entered into prior to 1993 are not necessarily retrievable using TechTrackS.

[2636] United States' comments on European Communities' response to question 172, para. 300.

[2637] By the Panel's calculation, there are 15 (not 17) remaining SAAs from the original 21 if we subtract from 21 the six that were signed prior to 1993.

[2638] United States' comments on European Communities' response to question 172, para. 300.

[2639] United States' comments on European Communities' response to question 172, para. 301. This statement is qualified in a way that suggests that there may be other SAAs that are no longer available.

1362   DSR 2012:III

7.1093 As indicated above, the United States has only been able to tabulate value information for 21 of the 38 known Space Act Agreements between NASA and Boeing. Second, the United States' valuation of goods and services provided to Boeing does not capture the value of NASA facilities, equipment and employees provided to Boeing in conjunction with R&D contracts (as distinguished from Space Act Agreements).

7.1094 As a result of these limitations in the information available concerning the value of NASA facilities, equipment and employees provided to Boeing, the United States has advanced an alternative methodology for estimating the maximum value of the free access to facilities, equipment and employees provided to Boeing. Specifically, in its responses to question 175, the United States argues that the Panel could, for the purpose of estimating the maximum value of this financial contribution, use Boeing's share of total payments made to all of NASA's aeronautics R&D contractors, partners, and grantees. In other words, an estimate of the maximum value of the use of NASA facilities, equipment and employees to Boeing would be derived from the value of NASA's payments to Boeing. The United States explained in its response to question 175[2640] that:

> "The United States estimates that the value of goods and services supplied to Boeing under non-reimbursable Space Act Agreements was $57.7 million and the value under nonreimbursable Space Act Agreements was $21.9 million.
>
> NASA's databases and internal information did not allow a valuation of goods and services provided to all other contractors. With regard to Space Act Agreements that might have been used to provide goods and services, the only way to determine with certainty whether an agreement relates to large civil aircraft more generally or to the eight challenged programs in particular is to review the physical copy of the contract. That is simply not possible in light of the hundreds of Space Act Agreements signed with companies other than Boeing. With regard to the EC allegations that NASA facilities and personnel referenced in procurement contracts were separate provisions of personnel and facilities to Boeing, NASA's records do not allow the linking of personnel to contracts in a way that would allow quantification and valuation.
>
> Should the Panel feel constrained to perform an estimate, it could use the Boeing share of payments made under contracts, cooperative agreements, grants, and government agreements to

---

[2640] United States' response to question 175, paras. 160-162.

DSR 2012:III

Report of the Panel

estimate the Boeing share of any overall provisions of goods or services that it finds to exist."

7.1095 The Panel requested clarification from the United States, and in response to question 352, the United States explained that:

"Despite the many objections to a methodology that treats NASA facilities, equipment, and employees as working for private enterprises, the U.S. response to Question 175 sought to assist the Panel in valuing the facilities, equipment, and employees related to contracts if it nonetheless found that they were 'provided' to contractors in the sense of Article 1.1(a)(1)(iii) of the SCM Agreement and conferred a benefit. The suggestion was that if the Panel considered a class of NASA personnel or other expenditures to be in reality a good or service provided to contractors, it could determine the share attributable to Boeing based on the company's 10.4 percent,[2641] share of the total value of NASA aeronautics research contracts in the 1989-2006 period.

To take an example, for most of the period, NASA divided its budget between program budgets (covering expenditures under contracts, cooperative agreements, and grants with outside suppliers) and 'Institutional Expenses' (which covered primarily personnel costs).[2642] If the Panel were to conclude that some portion of one of these budgets represented facilities, equipment, or employees provided to contractors, it could allocate part of that value to Boeing based on the company's share of contracting.

To give a numerical example, the EC asserts that the sum of program budgets under the challenged programs from 1989 to 2006 was \$12,235 million.[2643] NASA's data show that the agency paid contractors (including Boeing) \$7,446 million to conduct aeronautics research during that period,[2644] indicating that

---

[2641] (footnote original) United States' response to question 175, para. 155.

[2642] (footnote original) "Institutional expenses", comprised civil servant salaries, benefits, costs of administrative buildings, travel, maintenance, office equipment, electricity, library services, and vehicles. Payments to non-NASA entities under contracts, cooperative agreements, government agreements, and grants represented a large portion of program budgets. The HSR program budget had \$1.00 in contracts and grants spending for every 52 cents of non-contract costs, meaning that approximately 2/3 of all spending was for payments under contracts or grants. US Comment on European Communities' response to question 148, paras. 164 & 171; US Comment on European Communities' response to question 158(h), para. 253; US Comment on European Communities' response to question 166, paras. 263 and 265.

[2643] (footnote original) See U.S. response to Question 334 (\$12,365 million total, minus \$130 million on the ACEE program, all of which predated 1989.

[2644] (footnote original) United States' response to question 175, para. 155.

1364

DSR 2012:III

US - Large Civil Aircraft (2nd Complaint)

payments under other types of contracts were $4,789 million. If the Panel decided that some portion of these expenses were a financial contribution to contractors within the meaning of Article 1.1(a)(1) of the SCM Agreement,[2645] it could multiply the value of that portion by Boeing's 10.4 percent share of the total value of aeronautics research contracts, to estimate a value to Boeing. Because this approach is based on real data on NASA's expenditures, it would estimate Boeing's share of any NASA costs more accurately than the EC's approach based on Boeing's share of sales of civil aircraft and parts. The Panel could take a similar approach if it decided that some portion of the Institutional Expenses budget, which the EC alleges was $6,469 million in the 1989-2006 period, also constituted a financial contribution within its terms of reference.[2646, 2647]

7.1096 The Panel accepts the U.S. argument that if Boeing received only 10.4 per cent of payments made to all programme participants, there is no basis for allocating to Boeing more than 10.4 per cent of the total costs incurred by NASA in maintaining and providing facilities, equipment and employees for aeronautics R&D. In fact, the European Communities itself sought to estimate the value of NASA "facilities, equipment and employees" to Boeing based on Boeing's share of NASA funding. As the European Communities explained in its comments on the United States response to question 175:

"... the US suggestion that the Panel use 'the Boeing share of payments made under contracts, cooperative agreements, grants, and government agreements to estimate the Boeing share of any overall provisions of goods and services' is analogous to the approach used by the European Communities in deriving its own estimates of the NASA R&D subsidies."

7.1097 More specifically, the European Communities has explained that it "allocates total aerospace institutional support" to Boeing "by using the percent of overall NASA aerospace/aeronautics funding" going to Boeing.[2648]

[2645] *(footnote original)* The United States notes that any such valuation would have to take account of the fact that the large (but unsegregable) majority of NASA budgets not devoted to funding of contracts is used to fund NASA's own in-house research independent of contractors, with results disseminated to the broader public.

[2646] *(footnote original)* Any calculation attempting to relate NASA's non-contract costs to Boeing would have to avoid double counting the Space Act Agreements reported in Exhibit US-1256(revised). Any NASA contribution of employee time under those agreements is paid through the Institutional Support budget, while facilities or equipment would be paid through the relevant program budget.

[2647] United States' response to question 352, paras. 172-174.

[2648] "NASA/DOD/DOC Aeronautics R&D Subsidies to Boeing LCA Division", Exhibit EC-25, Note 2, p. 6.

DSR 2012:III

1365

Report of the Panel

7.1098 In its comments on the United States' response to question 352, the European Communities argues that the Panel should not follow the United States' suggestion for estimating the value of the access to facilities, equipment and employees provided to Boeing under the NASA programmes at issue. The European Communities argues that

> "the US calculations that (i) Boeing's share of aeronautics research contracts under the programmes at issue is 10.4 per cent, (ii) the amount of the programme budgets that relate to aeronautics research contracts with Boeing is $775 million, (iii) the amount of the programme budgets that relate to total aeronautics research contracts is $7,446 million, and (iv) the amount of the programme budgets that do not relate to payments to contractors is $4,789 million, are not supported by any actual evidence".[2649]

The Panel has already concluded, for the reasons given above, that the United States' calculations are supported by sufficient evidence.

7.1099 For the reasons given above, the Panel has estimated that the total amount of payments to Boeing through R&D contracts entered into under the eight R&D programmes over the period 1989-2006 is $1.05 billion. If the Panel were to use the $775 million figure advanced by the United States, this would mean that Boeing received 10.4 per cent of payments made under the programmes. Using the programme budget figures set out in the United States' response to question 352 (which are in turn derived from the figures submitted by the European Communities in Exhibit EC-25), this would yield an estimate of approximately $1.17 billion for "facilities, equipment and employees". However, the Panel has estimated that the value of the payments made to Boeing is $1.05 billion. When this figure is used, it leads to the conclusion that Boeing received 14 per cent, not 10.4 per cent, of payments made to programme participants. Using this figure, the Panel estimates that the value of the free access to facilities, equipment and employees under the eight R&D programmes at issue was $1.55 billion.

7.1100 As indicated above[2650], the Panel does not agree with the European Communities that the transactions are properly characterized as outright "grants". Among other things, the Panel accepts that NASA publicly disseminated the reports that summarized the results of the research conducted under the eight programmes at issue, and that this represents a situation in which Boeing has given up something of value in exchange for the funds and access to facilities, equipment and employees that it receives. The Panel agrees with the reasoning by the panel in *EC – DRAMs*:

[2649] European Communities' comments on United States' response to question 352, para. 142.
[2650] See above, footnote 2552.

1366

DSR 2012:III

> "In our view, there is a basic problem with the EC's grant methodology, and that is, simply put that a loan, a loan guarantee, a debt-to-equity swap that requires the recipient to repay the money or to surrender an ownership share in the company is not the same as a grant and can not reasonably be considered to have conferred the same benefit as the provision of funds without any such obligation. For the recipient, a loan clearly has a different value than a grant as it involves a debt that is owed to someone and will appear as such in a company's balance sheet. It is thus obviously less beneficial for a company to be given a loan than it is to be given a grant. Similarly, the issuance of new equity, directly or through a debt-to-equity swap dilutes the ownership claims of existing shareholders. We note that, in a benefit analysis, it is the perspective of the recipient that is important, not that of the provider of the financial contribution. In that sense, we find erroneous the starting point of the EC's calculation of the amount of benefit, which focuses on the expectation of the provider of the funds to see his money back. The question of benefit is not about the cost to the provider of the financial contribution, it is about the benefit to the recipient."[2651]

7.1101 Having said this, there are two reasons why we shall treat the full amount of the financial contributions provided to Boeing as a subsidy to Boeing's LCA division. First, this is a case involving claims of serious prejudice under Part III of the SCM Agreement, not a countervailing duty investigation. It is well established that in a case brought under Part III of the SCM Agreement, a panel is under no obligation to "quantify precisely the amount of the subsidy".[2652] Second, in addition to this legal consideration, the United States has advanced no argument or evidence to support any alternative approach to calculating the

---

[2651] Panel Report, *EC – Countervailing Measures on DRAM Chips*, para. 7.212.

[2652] Appellate Body Report, *US – Upland Cotton*, para. 467 ("In sum, reading Article 6.3(c) in the context of Article 6.8 and Annex V suggests that a panel should have regard to the magnitude of the challenged subsidy and its relationship to prices of the product in the relevant market when analyzing whether the effect of a subsidy is significant price suppression. In many cases, it may be difficult to decide this question in the absence of such an assessment. Nevertheless, this does not mean that Article 6.3(c) imposes an obligation on panels to quantify precisely the amount of a subsidy benefiting the product at issue in every case. A precise, definitive quantification of the subsidy is not required"). We note that Article VI:3 of the GATT 1994 and footnote 36 to Article 10 of the SCM Agreement provide that the term "countervailing duty" shall be understood to mean "a special duty levied for the purpose of offsetting any bounty or subsidy bestowed, directly, or indirectly, upon the manufacture, production or export of any merchandise". Article 19.4 of the SCM Agreement provides that no countervailing duty shall be levied on any imported product in excess of the amount of the subsidy found to exist "calculated in terms of subsidization per unit of the subsidized and exported product". These provisions do not apply in cases brought under Part III of the SCM Agreement. The reason is that cases brought under Part III of the SCM Agreement do not result in the imposition of countervailing duties.

Report of the Panel

amount of the subsidy to Boeing. In such circumstances, it is not for the Panel to invent its own calculation methodology.

7.1102 We turn now to an argument advanced by the European Communities that would, if accepted, render all of the foregoing irrelevant. Following its first and second written submissions, and in response to the United States' information and evidence regarding the maximum value of the payments and access to facilities, equipment and employees challenged, the European Communities advanced the argument that the amount of the payments and the value of free access to facilities, equipment and employees provided to Boeing was actually irrelevant. The European Communities argued, for the first time in response to a question from the Panel in the second set of questions, that this was because NASA shared the results of the R&D performed by other contractors and by NASA in-house with Boeing. Thus, the European Communities argued that the Panel should reject the U.S. information on the amount of the subsidies and accept the European Communities top down estimate, because the U.S. estimate did not account for the fact that NASA allegedly provided Boeing with access to the results of the R&D performed by these other contractors, and by NASA in-house. According to the European Communities:

> ".... NASA spent some of this funding on in-house LCA-related R&D activities, and shared the results (e.g. technologies and data) with Boeing, thereby providing goods and services to Boeing. Further, to the extent NASA spent some of this funding on R&D by entities such as military aircraft manufacturers or universities, it did so to bring about technologies for use on civil aircraft, and it made the results of that R&D available to Boeing, thereby also providing goods and services to Boeing. The bottom line is that *regardless of the precise recipient of the funding* under these programs, the non-engine civil aircraft components of this funding provided *support* to the US civil aircraft industry. ... {T}he purpose of the non-engine civil aircraft components of the other NASA programmes at issue was to develop technologies specifically for use by Boeing and other entities in the US civil aircraft industry, *regardless of the precise recipient of NASA's funding*"[2653]

7.1103 By way of background, we recall that in its first and second written submissions, the European Communities focused exclusively on the payments and the free access to facilities, equipment and employees that NASA provided to Boeing through R&D contracts and agreements for the purpose of enabling Boeing to conduct R&D. The European Communities argued that these were the two financial contributions provided to Boeing. It was in respect of these

---

[2653] European Communities' response to question 163, paras. 252-253 (emphasis added).

1368   DSR 2012:III

two alleged financial contributions, and only in respect of these two financial contributions, that the European Communities provided any analysis of the existence of a subsidy under Article 1 of the SCM Agreement. The European Communities sought to estimate the value of these two financial contributions. It argued that unless the United States provided complete information on the value of these two challenged financial contributions to Boeing, the Panel should adopt the European Communities' top down estimate of $10.4 billion.

7.1104 The United States subsequently provided the Panel with information, taken from contemporaneous NASA records and databases, regarding the maximum amount of the payments made to Boeing under the eight aeronautics R&D programmes at issue. The United States also provided the Panel with an estimate of the value of facilities, equipment and employees provided to Boeing, and submitted that the Panel could derive its own estimate based on Boeing's share of total payments.[2654] The United States explained that the remainder of the funding that the European Communities had included in its estimate of the subsidy to Boeing captured payments made to other programme participants, the cost of NASA's in-house research, and the cost of providing access to facilities, equipment and employees to third parties. The Panel put a large number of very detailed questions to the United States on how it arrived at these figures.[2655]

7.1105 Against this background, the Panel is not persuaded by the European Communities' argument that programme funding provided to other contractors (and funding used by NASA itself for in-house R&D) and programme funding used to cover the cost of providing facilities, equipment and employees to other contractors (and used by NASA itself for in-house R&D) should be included in the estimate of the amount of the subsidies provided to Boeing.

7.1106 First, the factual and legal arguments set out in the first and second written submissions of the European Communities to identify the particular measures which the European Communities considers to be subsidies within the meaning of Article 1 of the SCM Agreement do not include an allegation that NASA provides a financial contribution to Boeing in the form of early or

---

[2654] The United States acknowledged that its $80 million estimate only covered the amount of access to facilities, equipment and employees provided to Boeing under Space Act Agreements, and did not include the value of any such goods and services provided to Boeing through R&D contracts. The United States argued that its $80 million estimate was substantially accurate though, because as the European Communities itself recognized, the "bulk" (European Communities' second written submission, para. 389) of the free access to facilities, equipment and employees was provided to Boeing through Space Act Agreements. The United States submitted, however, that because the value of the facilities, equipment and employees could not be determined with the same degree of precision and certainty as the value of the payments made to Boeing, an alternative way of estimating the cost of the access to facilities, equipment and employees granted to Boeing would be to arrive at an estimate based on Boeing's share of total payments made. See e.g. United States' response to questions 175 and 352).

[2655] The questions to the United States on this issue include Questions 6, 7, 175, 176, 177, 178, 179, 180, 181, 182, 183, 184, 185, 186, 187, 188, 336, 337, 338, 339, 340, 341, 342, 343, 344, 345, 351, 352, and 353.

Report of the Panel

exclusive access to the results of R&D performed by other programme participants. The "financial contributions" identified in the "legal considerations" section are clearly limited to "grants to Boeing's LCA division" and NASA's provision of "free access to facilities, equipment and employees" to Boeing.

7.1107 Second, the European Communities does not identify the particular transactions or types of transactions through which NASA provides to the U.S. civil aircraft industry access to the results of research performed by entities outside that industry. In this regard, the Panel notes that the one technology transfer mechanism on which the European Communities has actually provided detailed information in this case – the allocation of intellectual property rights under NASA R&D contracts and agreements – concerns the transfer of technology from the government *to the entity that performed the research*. To take the case of patent rights, it is the entity that performs the research (whether it is Boeing, a third party, etc.) that takes title to patents (with a limited government-purpose license granted to the U.S. Government). As the European Communities correctly notes, a patent right accords the rights to "*exclude others* from making, using, offering for sale, or selling" the invention for a minimum of 20 years from date of application.[2656] Likewise, the European Communities' arguments relating to Limited Exclusive Data Rights (LERD) clauses focus on the "critical commercial data *developed by Boeing* through NASA-funded research were protected pursuant to the LERD restrictions".[2657]

7.1108 Third, the logic of an argument that NASA's R&D funding to other entities is a subsidy to Boeing is fundamentally incompatible with the logic of the principal argument of the European Communities in its first and second written submissions, namely that through R&D contracts NASA pays Boeing to conduct R&D that is principally for its own benefit and use. The allocation of the entire amount of the R&D funding as a subsidy to entities other than the entity that performs the research necessarily implies that the R&D funding is not principally for the benefit and use of the entity that performs the R&D, i.e. is not a subsidy to the entity that performs the research.

7.1109 For these reasons, the Panel estimates that the amount of the subsidy provided to Boeing's LCA division in the form of payments under R&D contracts is **$1.05 billion** over the period 1989-2006, and that the amount of the subsidy provided to Boeing's LCA division in the form of access to NASA facilities, equipment and employees under R&D contracts and agreements is **$1.55 billion** over this same period. Thus, the Panel estimates that the total amount of the subsidy provided to Boeing's LCA division through the eight R&D programmes at issue is **$2.6 billion**.

[2656] European Communities' first written submission, para. 812 (emphasis added).
[2657] European Communities' first written submission, para. 838 (emphasis added).

1370   DSR 2012:III

US - Large Civil Aircraft (2nd Complaint)

(f) Conclusion

7.1110 For these reasons, the Panel finds that the payments and access to facilities, equipment and employees that NASA provided to Boeing through the eight aeronautics R&D programmes at issue constitute specific subsidies within the meaning of Articles 1 and 2, and estimates that the amount of the subsidy to Boeing's LCA division is $2.6 billion over the period 1989-2006.

3. *Department of Defense (DOD) aeronautics R&D*

(a) Introduction

7.1111 The European Communities argues that DOD makes payments to Boeing (and grants Boeing access to facilities, equipment and employees) to perform R&D related to "dual-use" technologies – i.e. technologies applicable to both military and commercial aircraft. The European Communities argues that these payments (and access to facilities, equipment and employees) are subsidies within the meaning of Article 1 of the SCM Agreement, and are specific within the meaning of Article 2 of the SCM Agreement. The European Communities estimates that DOD provided $4.3 billion in "dual use" funding to Boeing over the period 1991-2006, and argues that $2.4 billion of that total should be treated as a subsidy to Boeing's LCA division.[2658]

7.1112 The United States argues that DOD R&D contracts and agreements with Boeing are not subsidies within the meaning of Article 1 of the SCM Agreement, and are not specific within the meaning of Article 2 of the SCM Agreement. In addition, the United States argues that the European Communities has overestimated the amount of "dual use" research conducted under the programmes at issue. According to the United States, the total amount of payments made to Boeing under DOD R&D contracts and agreements to perform R&D with even theoretical "dual uses" was only $308 million.

(b) The measures at issue

7.1113 The pertinent items of the European Communities' panel request[2659] read as follows:

> "a.   allowing the US LCA industry to participate in DOD-funded research, making payments to the US LCA industry for such research, or enabling the US LCA industry to exploit the results of such research, by means including but not limited to the foregoing or waiving of valuable patent rights, and the granting of exclusive or early access to data, trade secrets and other

---

[2658] NASA/DOD/DOC Aeronautics R&D Subsidies to Boeing LCA Division, Exhibit EC-25, p. 20.
[2659] WT/DS353/2, item 3(a) and 3(b), pp. 9-10.

DSR 2012:III   1371

knowledge resulting from government funded research, through, for example:

(i)   A number of Research, Development, Test, and Evaluation ("RDT&E") Programs of the US Air Force, Navy, Army, and the Defense Advanced Research Projects Agency ("DARPA") including, but not limited to:

- Defense Research Sciences (PE# 0601102F)

- Materials (PE# 0602102F)

- Aerospace Flight Dynamics and Aerospace Vehicle Technologies (PE# 0602201F)

- Aerospace Propulsion (PE# 0602203F)

- Aerospace Sensors (PE# 0602204F)

- Dual Use Applications and Dual Use Science & Technology (PE# 0602805F)

- Advanced Materials for Weapon Systems (PE# 0603112F)

- Flight Vehicle Technology (PE# 0603205F)

- Aerospace Structures and Aerospace Technology Dev/Demo (PE# 0603211F)

- Aerospace Propulsion & Power Technology (PE# 0603216F)

- Flight Vehicle Technology Integration (PE# 0603245F)

- RDT&E For Aging Aircraft (PE# 0605011F)

- Manufacturing Technology/Industrial Preparedness (PE# 0603771F/0708011F/0708011N)

- C-17 (PE# 0401130F/0604231F)

- CV-22 (PE# 0401318F)

- Joint Strike Fighter (PE#0603800F/0603800N/0603800E/0604800F/0604800N)

- AV-8B Aircraft (PE# 0604214N)

- Comanche (PE# 0604223A)

- F-22 (PE# 0604239F)

- B-2 Advanced Technology Bomber (PE# 0604240F)

- V-22 (PE# 0604262N)

US - Large Civil Aircraft (2nd Complaint)

- A-6 Squadrons (PE# 0204134N)

- F/A-18 Squadrons (PE# 0204136N)

- Dual Use Applications Program (including its predecessor, the Technology Reinvestment Project).

...

b. allowing the US LCA industry to use research, test and evaluation facilities owned by the US Government, including the Major Range Test Facility Bases."

7.1114 The European Communities distinguishes "general aircraft" RDT&E programmes from "military aircraft" RDT&E programmes:

- **"general aircraft" RDT&E programmes:** Defense Research Sciences (PE# 0601102F), Materials (PE# 0602102F), Aerospace Flight Dynamics and Aerospace Vehicle Technologies (PE# 0602201F), Aerospace Propulsion (PE# 0602203F), Aerospace Sensors (PE# 0602204F), Dual Use Applications and Dual Use Science & Technology (PE# 0602805F), Advanced Materials for Weapon Systems (PE# 0603112F), Flight Vehicle Technology (PE# 0603205F), Aerospace Structures and Aerospace Technology Dev/Demo (PE# 0603211F), Aerospace Propulsion & Power Technology (PE# 0603216F), Flight Vehicle Technology Integration (PE# 0603245F), RDT&E For Aging Aircraft (PE# 0605011F), and Manufacturing Technology/Industrial Preparedness (PE# 0603771F/0708011F/0708011N); and

- **"military aircraft" RDT&E programmes**[2660]: CV-22 (PE# 0401318F), V-22 (PE# 0604262N), and F/A-18 Squadrons (PE#

[2660] The European Communities challenges funding provided to Boeing under 13 "general aircraft" programmes, and under 10 "military aircraft" programmes. However, of the 10 military aircraft programmes identified in the European Communities' Panel Request (WT/DS353/2), and para. 677 of its first written submission, only five are discussed in CRA International, U.S. Department of Defense (DoD) Research, Development, Test and Evaluation (RDT&E) Funding Support to The Boeing Company for Dual-Use Aircraft R&D, November 2006, Exhibit EC-7. CRA's estimate of the funding provided to Boeing under the DOD military aircraft programmes, adopted by the European Communities in its submissions, is limited to these five military aircraft programmes. At footnote 16 of its report, CRA indicates that:

"Other RDT&E PEs related to military aircraft, such as the F-22, B-2, Comanche, A-6, and AV-8B, likely also contributed dual-use LCA technologies to Boeing, but CRA was unable to find adequate publicly available information to allow it to provide a high-fidelity estimate of the amount of dual-use aircraft-related RDT&E funding to Boeing from these PEs. Thus, it chose to focus its analysis on the V-22 / CV-22, F/A-18, JSF and C-17."

DSR 2012:III 1373

Report of the Panel

0204136N), Joint Strike Fighter (PE#0603800F / 0603800N / 0603800E / 0604800F / 0604800N), C-17 (PE# 0401130F/0604231F).

7.1115 It is not in dispute that DOD made payments to Boeing (and granted Boeing access to government facilities) to perform R&D pursuant to two different categories of R&D arrangements. First, DOD entered into "procurement contracts" with Boeing, the stated purpose of which was to acquire goods or services for the "*direct benefit or use* of the United States Government". Second, DOD entered into different types of "assistance instruments" (including cooperative agreements, technology investment agreements, and certain other transactions) with Boeing, the stated purpose of which was "*to transfer a thing of value to the recipient ... instead* of acquiring property or services for the direct benefit or use of the United States Government". In this Report, we use the expression "DOD R&D contracts" to mean DOD's procurement contracts with Boeing under the 23 aeronautics R&D programmes at issue, "agreements" to mean DOD assistance instruments with Boeing under the 23 aeronautics R&D programmes at issue, and "DOD R&D contracts and agreements" to cover both.

7.1116 The scope of the European Communities' claim relating to DOD R&D measures is clear: it challenges the payments (and access to facilities) provided to Boeing through R&D contracts and agreements entered into under the 23 programmes identified in the European Communities' panel request. The scope of the European Communities claim is relatively narrow in several respects.

7.1117 First, the European Communities does not challenge the RDT&E Program as a whole. Rather, it challenges only certain funding provided to Boeing under the 23 RDT&E programmes at issue. In addition, the European Communities does not challenge all of the funding that Boeing received under these 23 programmes. Rather, it challenges only the subset of funding that is, in the European Communities' view, related to "dual use" technologies.

7.1118 Second, the European Communities' challenge is limited to the "payments" (and, as discussed further below, access to government "facilities") that DOD provided to Boeing for the purpose of performing *R&D* – it does not challenge DOD's *purchase* of military aircraft from Boeing. In its panel request, the European Communities does refer to DOD "entering into procurement contracts, including those for the purchase of goods, from the US LCA industry for more than adequate remuneration ...".[2661] However, the

---

The European Communities has also "focused" its analysis on these five military aircraft programmes: following a separate discussion of each of the five military aircraft programmes analysed in the CRA report, the European Communities briefly discusses "other military aircraft" programmes at paras. 721-723 of its first written submission.

[2661] WT/DS353/2, p. 11 ("entering into procurement contracts, including those for the purchase of goods, from the US LCA industry for more than adequate remuneration, including in particular but not limited to the US Air Force contract with Boeing for the purchase of certain spare parts for its

1374   DSR 2012:III

US - Large Civil Aircraft (2nd Complaint)

European Communities did not subsequently advance arguments or evidence on DOD's purchases of aircraft or other goods.[2662] For example, the European Communities has not provided the Panel with any information regarding the price that DOD paid Boeing for the articles specified in this item of its panel request.

7.1119 Third, the scope of the European Communities claim is clearly limited to payments (and access to facilities) provided to *Boeing* – as distinguished from a broader challenge to the DOD R&D programmes *per se*, and as distinguished from a challenge to a subsidy provided to a broader industry, e.g. the U.S. military aircraft industry. This is made clear by many aspects of the European Communities' argumentation, including but not limited to the methodology followed by CRA in its 96-page report that seeks to estimate "the amount of Research, Development, Test and Evaluation ("RDT&E") funding received by The Boeing Company ("Boeing") from the United States Department of Defense ("DOD") that can be considered relevant to both military and commercial aircraft (i.e. "dual-use" RDT&E)".[2663]

7.1120 Finally, whereas the scope of the European Communities' claim relating to NASA R&D covers NASA "facilities, equipment and employees", the scope of the European Communities' claim relating to DOD only covers DOD "facilities". As with NASA aeronautics R&D, the European Communities has advanced arguments regarding DOD "facilities, equipment and employees".[2664] Unlike NASA R&D, however, the European Communities' panel request only identifies DOD "facilities", and not DOD "equipment" and/or "employees". To illustrate the differences, we provide a side-by-side comparison of the pertinent items of the European Communities' panel request regarding NASA and DOD R&D:

Airborne Warning and Control System (AWACS) aircraft, the National Polar-orbiting Operational Environmental Satellite System-Conical Microwave Imager Sensor, the C-22 Replacement Program (C-40), the KC-135 Programmed Depot Maintenance, the C-40 Lease and Purchase Program, the C-130 avionics modernisation upgrade program, the C-17 H22 contract (Boeing BC-17X), the US Navy contract with Boeing for the production and maintenance of 108 civil B-737 and their conversion into long-range submarine hunter Multi-Mission Aircraft, the Missile Defense Agency's Airborne Laser (ABL) Program, and the Army's Comanche Program").

[2662] In its submissions, the European Communities makes certain observations and assertions related to DOD's purchases of aircraft from Boeing. However, the European Communities does not advance any claim in this regard. See e.g. European Communities' first written submission, paras. 658-662, discussing the "close and cosy relationship between the DOD and Boeing".

[2663] CRA International, U.S. Department of Defense (DoD) Research, Development, Test and Evaluation (RDT&E) Funding Support to The Boeing Company for Dual-Use Aircraft R&D, November 2006, Exhibit EC-7, p. 1.

[2664] European Communities' first written submission, paras. 762, 895 and 896-901; European Communities' second written submission, paras. 496-510.

DSR 2012:III

1375

Report of the Panel

"2. NASA Subsidies	"3. Department of Defense Subsidies
b. providing the services of NASA employees, facilities, and equipment to support the R&D programmes listed above and paying salaries, personnel costs, and other institutional support, thereby providing valuable services to the US LCA industry on terms more favourable than available on the market or not at arm's length d. allowing the US LCA industry to use the research, test and evaluation facilities owned by the US Government, including NASA wind tunnels, in particular the Langley Research Center."	b. allowing the US LCA industry to use research, test and evaluation facilities owned by the US Government, including the Major Range Test Facility Bases"

7.1121 Article 6.2 of the DSU provides that a panel request must "*identify the specific measures at issue* and provide a brief summary of the legal basis of the complaint sufficient to present the problem clearly". To the extent that a measure is not identified in the complaining party's panel request, that measure falls outside of the scope of the panel's terms of reference.

7.1122 In response to a question from the Panel, the European Communities has clarified that it does not challenge DOD allowing Boeing to "participate" in research programmes as a distinct measure.[2665] With respect to DOD "enabling the US LCA industry to exploit the results of such research, by means including but not limited to the foregoing or waiving of valuable patent rights, and the granting of exclusive or early access to data, trade secrets and other knowledge resulting from government funded research", the European Communities addresses these measures primarily in the sections of its submissions regarding "NASA/DOD Intellectual Property Rights Transfers/Waivers".[2666]

7.1123 We discuss the challenged measures in greater detail in the context of our evaluation of whether these measures constitute specific subsidies within the meaning of Articles 1 and 2 of the SCM Agreement, and in the context of estimating the amount of any subsidy to Boeing's LCA division.

[2665] European Communities' response to question 149.

[2666] European Communities' response to question 215.

1376   DSR 2012:III

(c) Whether a subsidy exists within the meaning of Article 1 of the SCM Agreement

7.1124 In this section, we address whether the payments and access to facilities that DOD provided to Boeing under the 23 RDT&E programmes at issue constitute a subsidy within the meaning of Article 1 of the SCM Agreement. We begin by addressing the question of whether the transactions involve a financial contribution covered by Article 1.1(a)(1) of the SCM Agreement. We have already concluded that transactions properly characterized as "purchases of services" are excluded from the scope of Article 1.1(a)(1).[2667] Thus, the main issue addressed here is whether DOD's R&D contracts and agreements with Boeing are in fact properly characterized as "purchases of services". If we find that the challenge measures are not properly characterized as "purchases of services" and therefore provide financial contributions to Boeing, we will then address the question of whether those financial contributions are provided on terms that confer a benefit within the meaning of Article 1.1(b) of the SCM Agreement.

(i) Whether there is a financial contribution within the meaning of Article 1.1(a)(1) of the SCM Agreement

Arguments of the European Communities

7.1125 In the introduction to the section of its first written submission addressing NASA, DOD and DOC aeronautics R&D, the European Communities asserts in general terms that "NASA and DOD generally provide funding for LCA-related R&D through what they call 'contracts', but what are in reality grants to Boeing/MD for LCA-related R&D expenses".[2668] In the section of its first written submission addressing DOD R&D in particular, the European Communities argues that DOD, directly transfers funds in the form of "grants" to Boeing to support dual-use aeronautics research, and that this "direct R&D funding" constitutes a financial contribution within the meaning of Article 1.1(a)(1)(i) of the SCM Agreement.[2669]

7.1126 The European Communities argues that DOD also dedicates federal personnel and research facilities to support the RDT&E programmes, and that the Government's provision of these goods and services constitutes a financial contribution within the meaning of Article 1.1(a)(1)(iii) of the SCM Agreement.[2670]

[2667] See above, para. 7.970 of this Report.
[2668] European Communities' first written submission, para. 457.
[2669] European Communities' first written submission, para. 762.
[2670] *Ibid.*

Report of the Panel

7.1127 In its second written submission, the European Communities responds to the United States' argument that DOD's RDT&E contracts with Boeing constitute "purchases of services" and therefore are not financial contributions within the meaning of Article 1.1(a)(1) of the SCM Agreement. The European Communities argues that it would circumvent the object and purpose of the SCM Agreement if DOD RDT&E contracts were considered to be entirely excluded from the definition of financial contribution in Article 1.1(a)(1) of the SCM Agreement based on the United States labelling them as "purchases of services". The European Communities argues that DOD RDT&E contracts have helped Boeing develop technology that it utilizes toward its LCA. The European Communities argues that DOD RDT&E contracts are not properly characterised as "purchases of services" for the reasons set out in its responses to questions 15, 16, 19 and 20.[2671] The European Communities also argues that DOD's transfers of funds to Boeing for RDT&E "in fact relate to DOD's purchase of *goods*" – i.e. the military aircraft and other defence systems that DOD ultimately procures".[2672] The European Communities explains that while a commercial customer of a good would pay for R&D costs and acquisition costs through one purchase price, DOD pays these costs separately by first transferring funds for R&D through its RDT&E budgets, and then procuring a related aircraft or defence system through its procurement budgets.[2673]

7.1128 In its response to Panel question 15, the European Communities argues that DOD RDT&E contracts are not properly characterized as "purchases of services" for four reasons. First, because "DOD RDT&E contracts do not ultimately aim at the acquisition of a service for the direct benefit and own use of the government". Rather, the European Communities argues, "the ultimate purpose of DOD RDT&E is not the purchase of services, but rather the purchase of goods – i.e. military aircraft and other defence systems".[2674] Second, because "DOD RDT&E contracts do not contain the typical elements of a purchase". In this regard, the European Communities argues among other things that under the cooperative agreements entered into between Boeing, "DOD does not receive the entire fruits of the labour generated with DOD's resources pursuant to these agreements. ... Boeing does not make a profit pursuant to these agreements, while the seller in a typical 'purchase' transaction would undoubtedly expect to make a profit."[2675] Third, because "DOD RDT&E contracts do not exclusively affect trade in services". In this regard, the European Communities again argues that the DOD RDT&E contracts "ultimately aim at the purchase of military aircraft and other defence systems, necessarily implying the production of goods" and that "the transactions are directly related to the manufacture of

---

[2671] European Communities' second written submission, para. 457.

[2672] European Communities' second written submission, para. 454 (emphasis added).

[2673] European Communities' second written submission, para. 455.

[2674] European Communities' response to question 15(c), para. 62.

[2675] European Communities' response to question 15(c), and European Communities' comments on United States' response to question 20(a), para. 75.

1378　　　　　　　　　　　　　　　　　　　　　　　　　　DSR 2012:III

US - Large Civil Aircraft (2nd Complaint)

goods, affect trade in goods, and therefore cannot properly be characterised as 'purchases of services'".[2676] Finally, because "Boeing is not a genuine provider of LCA-related R&D services". In this regard, the European Communities argues that "Boeing does not offer such R&D services to anybody else but NASA and DOD" and that "Boeing has not advertised itself as a service provider for LCA-related R&D in the market".[2677]

7.1129 With respect to the alleged provision of goods and services, the European Communities responds to the United States' argument that the European Communities has failed to provide any specific evidence that DOD grants Boeing access to DOD facilities, equipment and employees. In its second written submission, the European Communities points to several contracts and agreements through which Boeing received the "rent-free use of facilities".[2678]

Arguments of the United States

7.1130 In its first written submission, the United States argues that the contracts submitted by the European Communities "show conclusively that under these instruments, DoD purchased research services from Boeing". The United States argues that the further contracts and agreements included among the U.S. exhibits support the same conclusion. According to the United States, research is a service, which accordingly makes these contracts purchases of services. Purchases of services are not financial contributions for purposes of Article 1.1(a)(1). Therefore, the only evidence on the Panel record regarding the nature of these transactions establishes that they are not a financial contribution, and that no subsidy exists. The United States submits that the Panel's review of the entire issue should end there.[2679]

7.1131 The United States observes that "{u}nder U.S. government contracting law, some of these instruments are formally termed 'contracts,' and others 'other transactions', 'cooperative agreements', or 'technology investment agreements'".[2680] The United States notes that some of the "contracts" submitted by the European Communities are "procurement contracts", and some are "cooperative agreements, technology investment agreements, or other transactions".[2681] The United States acknowledges that contracts are used only when the "principal purpose" is the acquisition of supplies or services for the "direct benefit or use" of the federal government, and that an "agreement" will "often have a clause specifying that its principal purpose is not the acquisition of goods or services for direct use by the U.S. government". However, the United States asserts that such a clause only "reflects that the contract does not have as

---

[2676] European Communities' response to question 15(c), para. 66.
[2677] European Communities' response to question 15(c), para. 67.
[2678] European Communities' second written submission, para. 500.
[2679] United States' first written submission, para. 90.
[2680] United States' first written submission, footnote 75.
[2681] United States' first written submission, para. 91.

DSR 2012:III

1379

Report of the Panel

its immediate goal the development of a particular technology for a particular weapon system" and "is not meant to reflect on the nature of the effort by the private party". The United States argues that "in any event, the Appellate Body has found that "municipal law classifications are not determinative" as to whether a measure is a financial contribution.[2682]

7.1132 The United States then sets out some of the similarities and differences between these two different types of transactions.[2683] The United States concludes that in respect of all of the contracts and agreements, "it is clear that the government is not providing a grant to the contractor and is, instead, engaging the contractor to perform research of interest to the government for government purposes".[2684] The United States argues that "Research and Development" is widely recognized as a "service".[2685]

7.1133 In its second written submission, the United States reiterates that "the contracts make clear that what DOD purchased was Boeing's RDT&E services, a transaction that is not a financial contribution within the meaning of Article 1.1 of the SCM Agreement".[2686] It then responds to several arguments advanced by the European Communities in its oral statement at the first meeting with the Panel. First, the United States responds to the European Communities' argument that the contracts are not properly characterized as purchases of services because DOD R&D "benefits Boeing's commercial division".[2687] The United States responds that the European Communities' theory mixes two concepts that are separate under the SCM Agreement – financial contribution and benefit. The identification of a financial contribution under Article 1.1(a)(1) depends on the type of the transaction that allegedly confers a subsidy. The question of whether there is a benefit comes only *after* the establishment of a financial contribution. Thus, the EC's assertion that technologies researched under some contracts have civil application is irrelevant to a determination of whether the contracts convey a financial contribution in the first place.[2688]

7.1134 Second, the United States responds to the European Communities' reference to the fact that some of the contracts and agreements contain statements to the effect that "the principal purpose of this agreement is for *the government to support and stimulate the recipient* to provide reasonable efforts in advanced research and technology development and *not for the acquisition of property or services for the direct benefit or use of the government*".[2689] The

---

[2682] United States' first written submission, footnote 100 (citing Appellate Body Report, *US – Softwood Lumber IV*, para. 56.)
[2683] United States' first written submission, paras. 91-92 and 96-97.
[2684] United States' first written submission, para. 92.
[2685] United States' first written submission, para. 95.
[2686] United States' second written submission, para. 31.
[2687] European Communities' oral statement at the first meeting with the Panel, para. 12.
[2688] United States' second written submission, para. 32.
[2689] European Communities' non-confidential oral statement at the first meeting with the Panel, para. 70 (emphasis original), citing F33615-95-2-5019 with McDonnell Douglas regarding Affordable

1380

DSR 2012:III

US - Large Civil Aircraft (2nd Complaint)

United States responds by noting, among other things, that "{t}he document cited by the EC (and others containing similar statements) are cooperative agreements, technology investment agreements, or 'other transactions,'...".[2690]

7.1135 Finally, the United States responds to the European Communities' argument that "DoD's ultimate aim is to purchase *goods* – i.e. the military aircraft and other defense systems eventually purchased by DoD".[2691] The United States argues that the ultimate aim of a purchase "does not change the nature of the item purchased", and provides the examples of a manufacturer hiring an advertising agency to create a marketing campaign to sell a new good (which does not make the advertising service into a good), and the example of a company buying picks and shovels for a contractor to use in landscaping (which does not make the picks and shovels into a service). The United States concludes that the "R&D services contracts are discrete transactions that cannot be equated with any goods that may result".[2692]

Evaluation by the Panel

7.1136 It is not in dispute that DOD made payments to Boeing and granted Boeing access to DOD facilities pursuant to aeronautics R&D contracts and agreements.[2693] Having concluded that purchases of services are excluded from the scope of Article 1.1(a)(1)[2694], the question before the Panel is whether DOD R&D contracts and agreements are properly characterized as "purchases of services". As the Appellate Body has recognized, "{a}n evaluation of the existence of a financial contribution involves consideration of the *nature of the transaction* through which something of economic value is transferred by a

---

Tooling for Rapid Prototyping and Limited Production of Composite Structures, 1 February 1995, Exhibit EC-512, Article 2.C.

[2690] United States' second written submission, para. 34.

[2691] European Communities' non-confidential oral statement at the first meeting with the Panel, para. 70 (emphasis added).

[2692] United States' second written submission, para. 35.

[2693] In its first written submission, the United States argues that the European Communities failed to provide any specific evidence that DOD grants Boeing access to DOD facilities. (United States' first written submission, para. 177.) However, the United States does not actually deny that DOD does so, and even refers the Panel to several such instances under Agreements F33615-97-2-3400 and F33615-98-3-5104. (United States' first written submission, para. 179.) In its second written submission, the European Communities points to several contracts and agreements through which Boeing received the "rent-free use of facilities". (European Communities' second written submission, para. 500, citing: F33615-94-C-3400: Extended Life Tire (EXLITE) Batch Queue Capability and Grid Generation Enhancements for 3-Dimensional Design Optimization, Exhibit US-622 (HSBI), clause 15; F33615-98-2-5113: Structural Repair of Aging Aircraft (1 of 2), Exhibit US-636 (HSBI), Article 32; F33615-96-C-1958: Low Cost Insertion of Commercial Technology into Legacy Aircraft, Exhibit US-618 (HSBI), clause 16.)

[2694] See above, paras. 7.953-7.970

DSR 2012:III

1381

Report of the Panel

government".[2695] In this case, the Panel's task is to reach a conclusion regarding the nature of DOD's aeronautics R&D contracts and agreements with Boeing.

7.1137 For the reasons already given above[2696], the Panel considers that whether or not DOD's R&D contracts and agreements with Boeing are properly characterized as a "purchase of services" depends on *the nature of the work* that Boeing was required to perform under the contracts, and more specifically, *whether the R&D that Boeing was required to conduct was principally for its own benefit and use, or whether it was principally for the benefit and use of the U.S. Government (or unrelated third parties)*. As with its analysis of NASA aeronautics R&D, the Panel considers that it should review all of the evidence that sheds light on this issue. Again, the Panel sees no reason why, for example, the type of instrument and so-called "formal" features of the transaction would be disregarded *if* they shed light on the nature of the R&D activities required of Boeing under the contracts and agreements; there is likewise no reason why, for example, evidence of the purpose and motives of the programmes under which they were entered into would be disregarded *if* they shed light on the question on the nature of the R&D activities required of Boeing under the contracts and agreements. In both cases, they are not extraneous features divorced from the "terms" of the transactions; rather, they could be central to understanding the core *term* of the transaction. That is, this is evidence that could be very helpful in understanding whether the nature of the work performed under Boeing's R&D contracts and agreements with DOD (the core terms of the transactions) was principally for the U.S. Government's benefit or use (and/or for the benefit or use of unrelated third parties), or rather for Boeing's own benefit or use. That is the question that needs to be answered for the purpose of determining whether the transactions are properly characterized as purchases of services.

7.1138 More specifically, the Panel will consider, *inter alia*, the legislation authorizing the programmes at issue, the types of instruments entered into between DOD and Boeing, whether DOD has any demonstrable use for the R&D performed under these programmes, the allocation of intellectual property rights under these transactions, and whether the transactions at issue had the typical elements of a "purchase of services".

7.1139 When considered in its totality, the evidence relating to DOD aeronautics R&D, some of which is individually discussed below, leads to the conclusion that *some* of the work that Boeing performed under its aeronautics R&D contracts and agreements with DOD was principally for its *own* benefit or use, rather than for the benefit or use of the U.S. Government (or unrelated third parties), and that *some* of the work that Boeing performed under its aeronautics R&D contracts and agreements with DOD was principally for the

---

[2695] Appellate Body Report, *US – Softwood Lumber IV*, para. 52 (emphasis added). The "nature" of something is generally defined as the basic or inherent features, character or quality of something; *Oxford Dictionary of English*, 2ed (rev), 2005, p. 1172.

[2696] See above, para. 7.978.

1382   DSR 2012:III

benefit or use of the U.S. Government (or unrelated third parties). A transaction in which the work performed is principally for the benefit and use of the "seller" cannot properly be characterized as a "purchase of services". Accordingly, the Panel concludes that some of DOD's R&D contracts and agreements with Boeing are not properly characterized as "purchases of services", whereas others are. Thus, the Panel rejects the European Communities' position that none of the DOD R&D contracts and agreements at issue are properly characterized as "purchases of services", and we reject the United States' position that all of the DOD R&D contracts and agreements at issue are properly characterized as purchases of services.

7.1140 We begin with the legislation authorizing the programmes and transactions at issue. 10 U.S.C. § 2358[2697] is the general statutory authority for all research and development (R&D) in which DOD engages by "contract", "grant", or "cooperative agreement".[2698] Section 2358 states:

> "§ 2358. Research and development projects
>
> (a)   Authority.— The Secretary of Defense or the Secretary of a military department may engage in basic research, applied research, advanced research, and development projects that—
>
>> (1)   are necessary to the responsibilities of such Secretary's department in the field of research and development; and
>>
>> (2)   either —
>>
>>> (A)   relate to weapon systems and other military needs; or
>>>
>>> (B)   are of potential interest to the Department of Defense.
>
> (b)   Authorized Means.-The Secretary of Defense or the Secretary of a military department may perform research and development projects—
>
>> (1)   by contract, cooperative agreement, or grant, in accordance with chapter 63 of title 31;

[2697] 10 U.S.C. (Armed Forces), Sub-Part A (General Military Law), Part IV (Service, Supply and Procurement), Chapter 139 (Research and Development), § 2358, Exhibit US-1205.

[2698] See United States' response to question 20(a). The United States explains that 10 U.S.C. § 2371 is the authority for R&D projects using "other transactions", that is, transactions other than contracts, cooperative agreements, and grants.

Report of the Panel

(2)   through one or more military departments;

(3)   by using employees and consultants of the Department of Defense; or

(4)   by mutual agreement with the head of any other department or agency of the Federal Government.

(c)   Requirement of Potential Department of Defense Interest.- Funds appropriated to the Department of Defense or to a military department may not be used to finance any research project or study unless the project or study is, in the opinion of the Secretary of Defense or the Secretary of that military department, respectively, of potential interest to the Department of Defense or to such military department, respectively.

(d)   Additional Provisions Applicable to Cooperative Agreements.- Additional authorities, conditions, and requirements relating to certain cooperative agreements authorized by this section are provided in sections 2371 and 2371a of this title."

7.1141 Thus, section 2358 gives DOD authority to fund certain kinds of R&D (§ 2358(a)), identifies "contracts", "cooperative agreements", and "grants" as the different means through which DOD can generally provide funding to perform R&D (§ 2358(b)), requires that any R&D funded be of "potential interest" to DOD (§ 2358(c)), and identifies the special and additional rules that apply to R&D funded through the means of "cooperative agreements" (§ 2358(d)) as distinguished from "contracts". Sections 2371 and 2371a, referenced above in § 2358(d), authorized the use of certain "other transactions".

7.1142 We turn now to the different types of instruments entered into between DOD and Boeing. The DOD Grant and Agreement Regulations are set forth in Sub-Chapter C (Parts 21 to 37) of 32 C.F.R. Part 21 of the DOD Grant and Agreement Regulations sets forth general policies and procedures related to "assistance and certain other nonprocurement instruments" that are subject to the Grant and Agreement Regulations (§ 21.100(b)). These "assistance" and "other nonprocurement instruments" are defined to include "grants, cooperative agreements, and technology investment agreements", as well as certain other "nonprocurement instruments" (§ 21.205(a) and (b)). Subpart F of Chapter 21 defines certain terms:

"§ 21.605 *Acquisition*

The acquiring (by purchase, lease, or barter) of property or services for the *direct benefit or use* of the United States Government (see more detailed definition at 48 CFR 2.101). In accordance with 31 U.S.C. 6303, *procurement contracts* are the

US - Large Civil Aircraft (2nd Complaint)

appropriate legal instruments for acquiring such property or services.

...

§ 21.615 *Assistance.*

The *transfer of a thing of value* to a recipient to carry out a public purpose of support or stimulation authorized by a law of the United States (see 31 U.S.C. 6101(3)). *Grants, cooperative agreements, and technology investment agreements* are examples of legal instruments used to provide assistance.

...

§ 21.640 *Cooperative agreement.*

A legal instrument which, consistent with 31 U.S.C. 6305, is used to enter into the *same kind of relationship as a grant* (see definition "grant"), except that substantial involvement is expected between the Department of Defense and the recipient when carrying out the activity contemplated by the cooperative agreement. The term does not include "cooperative research and development agreements" as defined in 15 U.S.C. 3710a.

§ 21.670 Procurement contract.

A legal instrument which, consistent with 31 U.S.C. 6303, reflects a relationship between the Federal Government and a State, a local government, or other recipient when the *principal purpose* of the instrument is to acquire property or services for the *direct benefit or use* of the Federal Government. See the more detailed definition for contract at 48 CFR 2.101."[2699]

(emphasis added)

7.1143 32 CFR part 37 (i.e. a part of the DOD *Grant and Agreement Regulations*) is entitled "Technology investment agreements". § 37.205 provides that a TIA may be used where the "grants officer" concludes:

"... that the *principal purpose* of the project is stimulation or support of research (*i.e., assistance*), *rather than acquiring goods*

[2699] The text of 48 CFR 2.101 has already been reproduced above.

DSR 2012:III

1385

Report of the Panel

or services for the benefit of the Government (*i.e.,* acquisition)".
(emphasis added)

7.1144 §22.205[2700] of the *DOD Grant and Agreement Regulations* ("Distinguishing assistance from procurement") provides, in accordance with 31 U.S.C. chapter 63, that before using a "grant or cooperative agreement", the "grants officer" must make a positive judgment that an "assistance instrument", rather than a procurement contract, is the appropriate instrument. More specifically:

> "the grants officer must judge that the *principal purpose* of the activity to be carried out under the instrument is to stimulate or support a public purpose (i.e., to provide assistance), rather than acquisition (i.e., to acquire goods and services for the direct benefit of the United States Government). If the principal purpose is acquisition, then the grants officer shall judge that a procurement contract is the appropriate instrument" (§22.205(a)(1)). (emphasis added)

7.1145 All of the instruments submitted to the Panel clearly indicate, on the title page, whether they are a "Contract", a "Cooperative Agreement", a "Technology Investment Agreement", or an "Other Transaction". Some of the DOD cooperative agreements with Boeing submitted by the European Communities contain a clause within the agreement itself that explicitly states:

> "This agreement is a 'Cooperative Agreement' under 10 USC 2358 (Pursuant to 10 USC2371). The parties agree that the principal purpose of this agreement is for the government to support and stimulate the recipient to provide reasonable efforts in advanced research and technology development and not for the acquisition of property or services for the direct benefit or use of the government. The Federal Acquisition Regulation (FAR) and Department of Defense FAR Supplement (DFARS) apply only as specifically referenced herein. This is not a procurement contract." (see F33615-95-2-5019 (EC-512) and F33615-96-2-5051 (EC-513))

7.1146 All of the cooperative agreements, TIAs, and "other transactions" submitted by the European Communities repeatedly and consistently use the terminology of "Grants Officer" and "Grants Administration Office". All of these instruments (like the corresponding regulations above) refer to the other party as the "recipient", and not a "contractor".

7.1147 We turn now to an examination of whether DOD has any demonstrable use for the R&D performed under the 23 programmes at issue. Unlike NASA

[2700] 32 CFR § 22.205, Exhibit US-22.

aeronautics R&D programmes, the declared purposes of the DOD programmes at issue do not generally demonstrate that DOD aimed to transfer technology to Boeing and the wider U.S. aircraft industry. Generally, the purpose of these programmes was to conduct R&D aimed at designing more advanced weapons or other defense systems or to reduce the cost of such systems.[2701] The more specific purpose of each of these programmes is set out below, drawn from the "Mission Description" statement contained in the programme budgets:

- **Defense Research Sciences:** "This Basic Research program, managed by the Air Force Office of Scientific Research (AFOSR), supports Air Force research efforts comprised of in-house investigations in Air Force laboratories and extramural activities in academia and industry. The program element funds broad-based scientific and engineering basic research in technologies critical to the Air Force mission. These technologies include aerospace structures, aerodynamics, materials, propulsion, power,

---

[2701] United States' first written submission, para. 72. Both of these aims – technological improvement, and cost reduction – are readily apparent and feature prominently in DOD's annual budgets, reviewed below, describing the nature of the research conducted under the RDT&E Program Elements at issue. Regarding the cost reduction aim, see e.g. **Defense Research Sciences**: "... leading to *cost-effective* development and safe and reliable operation of superior weapons and defensive systems"; **Materials**: "... advanced materials and processes *to reduce life cycle costs* and improve performance, *affordability*, supportability, reliability, and survivability of current and future ... . Develops materials technologies for aircraft, spacecraft, and missiles with improved *affordability*, maintainability, and enhanced performance of current and future Air Force systems. Advanced thermal protection and carbon-carbon (C-C) composites materials are developed that are *affordable* ..."; **Aerospace Flight Dynamics/Aerospace Vehicle Technologies**: "... *to reduce life cycle costs and* improve the performance of existing and future manned and unmanned aerospace vehicles, and the maintenance and survivability of air bases. The payoffs from these technology programs include: decreased vulnerability, and *increased affordability* ..."; **Aerospace Propulsion**: "... Power conditioning, thermal management, and power source improvements will significantly enhance reliability, reduce weight, and *lower life cycle costs*"; **Aerospace Avionics/Aerospace Sensors:** "... will also *reduce life cycle costs*, facilitate affordable modernization of aging and future aerospace platforms ..."; **Dual Use Science & Technology**: "... stimulate the development of dual-use technologies that will provide greater access to commercial technologies, and will result in *affordable* defense systems..."; **Advanced Materials for Weapons Systems**: "Reducing risk in materials technology improves the *affordability*, supportability, reliability, survivability, and operational performance of current and future warfighting systems"; **Flight Vehicle Technology**: "... technologies for improved performance, reliability, maintainability, and supportability while increasing *affordability* ..."; **Aerospace Structures/Aerospace Technology Dev/Demo**: "... demonstrates affordable aerospace vehicle structures by utilizing innovative metallic and composite structures technologies to *reduce the cost* of airframe ownership ..."; **Aerospace Propulsion and Power Technology**: "... develops and demonstrates *affordable* turbine engine high pressure core components ..."; **Flight Vehicle Technology Integration**: "... provides proven aerospace vehicle technologies for allweather, day or night operations, and technologies for improved *affordability*"; **Industrial Preparedness/Manufacturing Technology**: "... ManTech provides *cost reduction processes and practices* and new manufacturing capabilities applicable to existing as well as new weapon systems under development" (emphasis added).

Report of the Panel

electronics, computer science, directed energy, conventional weapons, life sciences, and atmospheric and space sciences".[2702]

- **Materials:** "This Applied Research program is the primary source of advanced materials and processes to reduce life cycle costs and improve performance, affordability, supportability, reliability, and survivability of current and future Air Force systems. Structural, propulsion, and sub-systems materials and processes are developed for aircraft, missile, space, satellite, and launch systems applications. Electronic and optical, advanced electromagnetic, and laser protection materials and processes are developed for application in Air Force aircraft, missile, space, and personnel protection systems. Advanced nondestructive materials evaluation methods, materials design data, pollution prevention materials, materials failure analysis, and materials repair methods are developed to improve the sustainment of Air Force systems for the current and future warfighters".[2703]

- **Aerospace Flight Dynamics/Aerospace Vehicle Technologies:** "This Applied Research program determines the technical feasibility of aerospace vehicle technologies in aeromechanics, structures, flight control, air vehicle-pilot interface, vehicle subsystems, and air base technologies to reduce life cycle costs and improve the performance of existing and future manned and unmanned aerospace vehicles, and the maintenance and survivability of air bases. The payoffs from these technology programs include: decreased vulnerability, and increased affordability, reliability, maintainability, and supportability for aerospace vehicles and subsystems; improved air base operations; and safe aerospace vehicle allweather operations".[2704]

- **Aerospace Propulsion:** "This Applied Research program develops airbreathing propulsion and aerospace power technologies. The prime areas of focus are turbine engines, dual-mode ramjets, combined cycle engines, fuels, lubricants, and aerospace power technologies. ... Power system technologies are focused to eliminate troublesome, centralized hydraulic systems by replacement with highly reliable electric systems. Power conditioning, thermal management, and power source improvements will significantly enhance reliability, reduce weight, and lower life cycle costs".[2705]

[2702] Defense Research Sciences Budgets for FY 1993-FY 2007 (PE# 0601102F), Exhibit EC-419.

[2703] Materials Budgets for FY 1993-FY 2007 (PE #0602102F), Exhibit EC-420.

[2704] Aerospace Flight Dynamics/Aerospace Vehicle Technologies Budgets for FY 1993-FY 2007 (PE# 0602201F), Exhibit EC-421.

[2705] Aerospace Propulsion Budgets for FY 1993-FY 2007 (PE# 0602203F), Exhibit EC-422.

US - Large Civil Aircraft (2nd Complaint)

- **Aerospace Avionics/Aerospace Sensors**: "This Applied Research program develops the technology base for Air Force aerospace sensors. Advances in aerospace sensors are required to increase combat effectiveness by providing "anytime, anywhere" surveillance, reconnaissance, precision targeting, and electronic warfare capabilities for ground, air, and space platforms. Advances in aerospace sensor technology will also reduce life cycle costs, facilitate affordable modernization of aging and future aerospace platforms, and provide protection against emerging hostile threat systems. Meeting these needs necessitates simultaneous advances in multiple, interrelated disciplines including: airborne and spaceborne sensors (e.g. infrared, radar, etc.); multi-function high-power electronic devices; target detection, classification, and recognition techniques; fire control; sensor fusion methods; communication and navigation subsystems; and electronic warfare technologies".[2706]

- **Dual Use Science & Technology**: "This program allows the Air Force to leverage industry investments in advanced technologies that are mutually advantageous to both the Air Force and industry. One of the program's objectives is to establish a tool for the Air Force to stimulate the development of dual-use technologies that will provide greater access to commercial technologies, and will result in affordable defense systems that maintain battlefield superiority. A key component of the program is the costsharing requirement from both industry and the Air Force, which affirms commitment to the development effort. Specific projects are determined through annual competitive solicitation(s). A second objective is to use FY 1997 Defense Authorization Act Section 804, Other Transactions Authority, as part of the Dual Use S&T program to educate the Air Force S&T workforce in non-traditional or commercial contracting practices. Technology development areas considered include advanced materials and manufacturing, affordable sensors, advanced propulsion, power and fuel efficiency, information and communications systems, and weapons systems sustainment".[2707]

- **Advanced Materials for Weapons Systems**: "This Advanced Technology Development program demonstrates materials technology options for application into Air Force weapon systems. Developing materials technologies for the broadband laser

---

[2706] Aerospace Avionics/Aerospace Sensors Budgets for FY 1993-FY 2007 (PE# 0602204F), Exhibit EC-423.
[2707] Dual Use Science & Technology Budgets for FY 2000-FY 2007 (PE# 0602805F), Exhibit EC-424.

DSR 2012:III   1389

Report of the Panel

protection of aircrews and sensors from a variety of threats is a high priority of the Air Force. The Non-Destructive Inspection/Evaluation (NDI/E) techniques for fighter, bomber, and transport aircraft are critical to the logistics centers as well as the operational fleet as the service lives of these systems increase. This program provides critical data for prospective users to make engineering decisions on both structural and non-structural materials for air and space. Reducing risk in materials technology improves the affordability, supportability, reliability, survivability, and operational performance of current and future warfighting systems".[2708]

- **Flight Vehicle Technology**: "This Advanced Technology Development program develops and demonstrates advanced aerospace vehicle subsystems, aerodynamic/flight controls, and vehicle-pilot interface technologies for improved aerospace vehicle performance, decreased vulnerability, and reduced logistics support. This program also demonstrates technologies for fixed and bare base assets, including airfield pavements, energy systems, air base survivability, air base recovery, protective systems, fire protection, and crash rescue".[2709]

- **Aerospace Structures/Aerospace Technology Dev/Demo**: "This Advanced Technology Development program develops and demonstrates affordable aerospace vehicle structures by utilizing innovative metallic and composite structures technologies to reduce the cost of airframe ownership. Innovative structural concepts integrate these two types of materials with design and monitoring techniques to develop and demonstrate solutions and repairs for corrosion fatigue, multi-site damage fatigue, and other damage to which aging aircraft are susceptible. The goal of this program is to develop technologies to restore structural integrity, extend life, and improve survivability of the current fleet, and future fleet of manned and unmanned aerospace vehicles. The results are less maintenance intensive, more durable, and more dependable structures for current and future aerospace systems. This yields lower cost of ownership (by delaying acquisition and by reducing support and maintenance costs), restored and improved sortie rates (due to durability, damage or threat

---

[2708] Advanced Materials for Weapons Systems Budgets for FY 1993-FY 2007 (PE# 0603112F), Exhibit EC-425.
[2709] Flight Vehicle Technology Budgets for FY 1993-FY 2006 (PE# 0603205F), Exhibit EC-426.

1390

DSR 2012:III

tolerance, and design for supportability), and reduced observability (both radar cross section and infrared)".[2710]

- **Aerospace Propulsion and Power Technology**: "This Advanced Technology Development program develops and demonstrates affordable turbine engine high pressure core components, advanced airbreathing engine concepts, high heat sink and thermally stable fuels, and power technology for aerospace vehicles".[2711]

- **Flight Vehicle Technology Integration**: "This Advanced Technology Development program integrates and demonstrates advanced flight vehicle technologies that will improve the performance and supportability of existing and future manned and unmanned aerospace vehicles. System level integration brings together the aerospace vehicle technologies along with avionics, propulsion, and weapon systems to flight demonstrate them in a near-realistic operational environment. Integration and flight test demonstrations reduce the risk and time required to transition technologies into operational aircraft. This program provides proven aerospace vehicle technologies for allweather, day or night operations, and technologies for improved affordability".[2712]

- **RDT&E for Aging Aircraft**: "This program is comprised of multiple efforts which will transition needed technologies from laboratory research and commercial technology development into fieldable tools or capabilities. Projects will target critical needs of the aging fleet such as corrosion, structural integrity, and improved nondestructive inspection (NDI) methods".[2713]

- **Industrial Preparedness/Manufacturing Technology**: "The Manufacturing Technology (ManTech) program is a corporate Air Force program that establishes and demonstrates advancements in manufacturing process technologies, manufacturing engineering systems, and industrial practices, and transitions these advancements into weapon systems design, development, acquisition, and/or sustainment. ManTech provides cost reduction processes and practices and new manufacturing capabilities applicable to existing as well as new weapon systems under development. ManTech strives to make superior mission enabling

---

[2710] Aerospace Structures/Aerospace Technology Dev/Demo Budgets for FY 1993-FY 2007 (PE# 0603211F), Exhibit EC-427.

[2711] Aerospace Propulsion and Power Technology Budgets for FY 1993-FY 2007 (PE# 0603216F), Exhibit EC-428.

[2712] Flight Vehicle Technology Integration Budgets for FY 1993-FY 2003 (PE# 0603245F), Exhibit EC-429.

[2713] RDT&E for Aging Aircraft Budgets for FY 2000-FY 2007 (PE# 0605011F), Exhibit EC-430.

Report of the Panel

technologies an affordable life cycle reality by expanding access to a capable, responsible, multi-use industrial base with efficiencies comparable to world class enterprises".[2714]

- **V-22/CV-22**: "This program element funds the development of a replacement aircraft to meet the medium lift needs of the United States Marine Corps (USMC) and the special operations needs of the United States Special Operations Command (USSOCOM). ... The CV-22 is a Special Operations Forces (SOF) variant of the V-22 vertical lift, multi-mission aircraft. The CV-22 will provide critical capability to insert, extract, and resupply special operation forces into denied or sensitive territory, not currently provided by existing aircraft. This aircraft will be baselined upon the V-22 aircraft (MV-22 configuration) with added terrain following radar, fuel tanks, radios and flare/chaff dispensers, radar warning receiver and jammer, and infrared countermeasures (CV-22 Block 0 configuration). CV-22 production buys will begin in FY04. This RDT&E funding is required to continue the design, integration, testing and certification of CV-22-required GANS/GATM components for compliance with the GANS/GATM Capstone Requirements Document (CRD)".[2715]

- **F/A-18 Squadrons**: "... The capabilities of the F/A-18 weapon system can be upgraded to accommodate and incorporate new or enhanced weapons as well as advances in technology to respond effectively to emerging future threats. Continued development capability is required to successfully optimize new F/A-18 weapon system capabilities in the Fleet. Additionally, continued improvements in reliability and maintainability are necessary to ensure maximum benefit is achieved through reduced cost of ownership and to provide enhanced availability".[2716]

- **Joint Strike Fighter**: "The Joint Strike Fighter (JSF) programme will develop and field an affordable, highly common family of next generation strike fighter aircraft for the USN, USMC, USAF and allies. Current program emphasis is on facilitating the evolution of fully validated and affordable joint operational requirements, and demonstrating cost leveraging technologies and concepts to lower risk prior to entering Engineering and Manufacturing Demonstration (E&MD) in FY 2001. This is a joint

---

[2714] Air Force Industrial Preparedness/Manufacturing Technology Budgets for FY 1993, FY 1996-FY 2007 (PE# 0708011F for FY 1993, FY 1997-FY 2007; PE# 0603771F for FY 1996), Exhibit EC-431.

[2715] V-22 Budgets for FY 1994-FY 2007 (PE# 0604262N), Exhibit EC-433; CV-22 Budgets for FY 2002-FY 2007 (PE# 0401318F), Exhibit EC-435.

[2716] F/A-18 Squadrons Budgets for FY 1993-FY 2007 (PE# 0204136N), Exhibit EC-436.

1392

DSR 2012:III

US - Large Civil Aircraft (2nd Complaint)

program with no executive service. Navy and Air Force each provide approximately equal shares of annual funding for the program. The United Kingdom (UK) is a collaborative partner in this phase of the program and several other countries also participate".[2717]

- **C-17**: "Airlift provides essential flexibility when responding to contingencies on short notice anywhere in the world. It is a major element of America's national security strategy and constitutes the most responsive means of meeting U.S. mobility requirements. Additional airlift capability is needed for rapid deployment of combat forces in support of national objectives. Specific tasks associated with the airlift mission include deployment, employment (airland and airdrop), sustaining support, retrograde, and combat redeployment. The C-17 can perform the entire spectrum of airlift missions and is specifically designed to operate effectively and efficiently in both strategic and theatre environments. The C-17 provides a vast increase in overall airlift capability necessary to replace and exceed the capabilities lost from retiring the aging C-141 fleet from the Air Force inventory. ... RDT&E efforts support producibility enhancements and product improvements".[2718]

7.1148 The European Communities does not dispute that, in the case of DOD, the R&D performed is of some benefit and use to DOD. The foregoing confirms this. However, of the 13 different "general aircraft" programmes at issue, it would appear that at least two had the explicit objective of developing "dual use" R&D. These are: (i) the Dual Use Applications and Dual Use Science & Technology Program (PE# 0602805F); and (ii) the Manufacturing Technology/Industrial Preparedness Program (PE# 0603771F / 0708011F / 0708011N). In its first written submission, the European Communities provides a brief overview of all of the programmes at issue, and then discusses these two particular programmes – "DUS&T" and "ManTech" – in considerable detail.[2719] These two programmes were funded through cooperative agreements or other cost-shared arrangements.[2720]

[2717] Joint Strike Fighter Budgets for FY 1995-FY 2003 (PE# 0603800F), Exhibit EC-437.

[2718] C-17 Budgets for FY 1993-FY 2007 (PE# 0604231F for FY 1993-FY 1997; PE# 0401130F for FY 1997-FY 2007), Exhibit EC-438.

[2719] European Communities' first written submission, paras. 724-749 ("Additional Details Related to Selected RDT&E PEs").

[2720] See e.g. Department of Defense, Guidelines for Dual Use Science and Technology Program, Fiscal Year 2002, Exhibit EC-484, December 2000, p. 6 ("Projects must be awarded using Technology Investment Agreements or "Other Transactions" for prototypes. Intellectual property rights are often a stumbling block that prevent commercial firms from participating in defense programs. The BAA must clearly state that Agreements Officers have maximum flexibility to negotiate intellectual property rights that are appropriate for the program. Agencies are encouraged to

DSR 2012:III

Report of the Panel

7.1149 We turn now to the allocation of intellectual property rights under DOD R&D contracts and agreements with Boeing. The R&D procurement contracts between DOD and Boeing differ from the R&D assistance instruments with Boeing with regard to the allocation of intellectual property rights. This appears to derive from the fact that under assistance instruments, the "recipient" is required to contribute its own funds to the R&D on a cost-shared basis. While the allocation of patents is uniform across all U.S. government R&D contracts and agreements, the allocation of "data rights" differs (depending on the extent to which there is cost-sharing.) Any data delivered under an R&D *procurement* contract funded solely by the government is "*unlimited* rights data". This means that the license acquired by the U.S. Government gives it "unlimited rights" to use the technical data "as it sees fit, both inside and outside of the government", i.e. to "use, disclose, reproduce, prepare derivative works, distribute copies to the public, and perform publicly and display publicly, in any manner and for any purpose, and to have or permit others to do so".[2721] A typical "Unlimited Rights" Data Clause reads:

> "With the exception of the technical data or computer software set out below, all technical data and computer software to be delivered under this contract shall be furnished with unlimited rights as defined in Section I clause of DFARS 252.227-7013.
>
> {list of selected technical data items developed at private expense follows below}"[2722]

7.1150 However, in the case of *assistance* instruments, the government acquires only "limited rights" data. In such transactions, the government generally "may release or disclose the data outside the government *only* for government purposes (government purpose rights)".[2723] The term for these "government purpose rights" is negotiable, with five years being the baseline, subject to

---

negotiate for the minimum intellectual property rights for the Government that are necessary for program execution, which could result in the award of an Other Transaction agreement". See also, European Communities' first written submission, paras. 725 and 733 ("TRP awarded funds, on a cost-shared basis, to industry-led projects working to create new dual-use technologies", and "As with TRP, DOD established DUS&T for the purposes of jointly funding, with industry, the development of dual-use technologies ...").

See e.g. Manufacturing Technology Program, 10 U.S.C. § 2521 (2003), Exhibit EC-445, p. 6 ("For any grant awarded or contract, cooperative agreement, or other transaction entered into on a basis other than a cost-sharing basis because of a determination made under subparagraph (A), the transaction file for the project concerned must document the rationale for the determination.")

[2721] United States' first written submission, para. 350; United States' second written submission, para. 64 and accompanying footnote.

[2722] Air Force Contract F33615-91-C-5716 with Boeing regarding Design and Manufacturing of Low Cost Composite Fuselage, 24 July 1991, Exhibit EC-507, p. 24.

[2723] 48 C.F.R. §§ 227.7100 - 227.7103-17, § 227.7103-4(a)(1), Exhibit EC-590 (emphasis added). The Government may, however, "use, modify, release, reproduce, perform, display or disclose" such jointly-funded data "within the government without restriction". *Ibid.* at § 227.7103-4(a)(1).

1394

DSR 2012:III

negotiation between the parties.[2724] DOD regulations state that "{l}onger periods should be negotiated when a five-year period does not provide sufficient time to apply the data for commercial purposes ...".[2725] During the term of the "government purpose rights", the government "may not use, or authorize other persons to use, technical data marked with government purpose rights legends for commercial purposes".[2726]

7.1151 Another relevant consideration is whether the transactions at issue involve the typical elements of a purchase of services. In this regard, we observe that the R&D procurement contracts between DOD and Boeing differ from the R&D assistance instruments with Boeing with regard to the payment of a fee or profit. The DOD R&D assistance instruments with Boeing do not provide for any fee or profit. All of the procurement contracts submitted to the Panel appear to provide for the payment of a fee. §22.205 of the *DOD Grant and Agreement Regulations*[2727] ("Distinguishing assistance from procurement") explains that the payment of a "fee or profit":

> "is consistent with an activity whose principal purpose is the acquisition of goods and services for the direct benefit or use of the United States Government, rather than an activity whose principal purpose is assistance." (§ 22.205(b))

7.1152 §22.205 of the *DOD Grant and Agreement Regulations* therefore mandates that a procurement contract, rather than an assistance instrument, be used in all cases where: (i) a fee or profit is to be paid to the recipient of the instrument; or (ii) the instrument is to be used to carry out a programme where a fee or profit is necessary to achieving programme objectives (§22.205(b)). Along the same lines, Part 34 ("Administrative Requirements for Grants and Agreements with For-Profit Organizations") states in § 34.18: "In accordance with 32 CFR 22.205(b), grants and cooperative agreements shall not: (a) Provide for the payment of fee or profit to the recipient. (b) Be used to carry out programs where fee or profit is necessary to achieving program objectives". The payment of a fee or profit is also prohibited under technology investment agreements.[2728]

7.1153 Based on the foregoing, it appears to the Panel that DOD "assistance instruments" are not properly characterized as "purchases of services", but that there does not appear to be any reason for treating DOD "procurement contracts"

[2724] 48 C.F.R. § 227.7103-5(b)(2), Exhibit EC-590.

[2725] *Ibid.*

[2726] 48 C.F.R. § 227.7103-5(b)(4), Exhibit EC-590.

[2727] 32 CFR § 22.205, Exhibit US-22.

[2728] § 37.230 provides that, in accordance with 32 CFR 22.205(b), a TIA may not be used if any participant is to receive fee or profit. As noted below, 32 CFR 22.205(b) provides that the payment of a fee/profit "is consistent with an activity *whose principal purpose is the acquisition of goods and services for the direct benefit or use of the United States Government,* rather than an activity *whose principal purpose is assistance".* (§ 22.205(b))

Report of the Panel

as something other than a "purchase of services". The Panel would further note that the distinction between DOD "procurement contracts" and DOD "assistance instruments" is not one of the Panel's own making. In its first written submission, the United States draws the Panel's attention to the fact that there are two different categories of transactions between DOD and Boeing. Specifically, the United States draws the Panel's attention to the fact that "{u}nder U.S. government contracting law, some of these instruments are formally termed 'contracts', and others 'other transactions', 'cooperative agreements', or 'technology investment agreements'".[2729] The United States notes that some of the "contracts" submitted by the European Communities are "procurement contracts", and some are "cooperative agreements, technology investment agreements, or other transactions".[2730] The United States acknowledges that R&D contracts are used only when the "principal purpose" is the acquisition of supplies or services for the "direct benefit or use" of the federal government, and that an "agreement" will "often have a clause specifying that its principal purpose is not the acquisition of goods or services for direct use by the U.S. government".[2731] The Panel has put a number of questions to the parties on this distinction, and asked the parties to explain the differences between the two categories of transactions.[2732] In response to these questions, the European Communities generally argues that what matters "is the substance of the transaction, not its form"[2733], and that the Panel should not be guided by the "label" of the transactions.[2734] The United States counters that "the EC fails to recognize that the type of vehicle (that is, cooperative agreement, procurement contract, or Other Transaction) used will determine some of the substantive features of the contract".[2735] Along the same lines, in response to the European Communities' argument that consideration of the types of instrument is "too formalistic" to guide the analysis, the United States indicates that it is "difficult to square this position with the EC view that the terms of the contracts are relevant, since under the U.S. system, the type of instrument will determine which contract clauses are available".[2736]

7.1154 Notwithstanding the foregoing, the United States argues that all of the DOD R&D contracts and agreements at issue are properly characterized as "purchases of services", and the European Communities argues that none of the DOD R&D contracts and agreements at issue are properly characterized as "purchases of services". We will consider some of the arguments advanced by the parties, in support of their respective positions, below.

[2729] United States' first written submission, footnote 75.
[2730] United States' first written submission, para. 91.
[2731] United States' first written submission, footnote 70.
[2732] See questions 19, 20, 151, 152, 154, 191, 192, 195, 197, and 321.
[2733] See e.g. European Communities' response to question 20(b).
[2734] European Communities' response to question 154, para. 217.
[2735] United States' comments on European Communities' response to question 20, para. 76.
[2736] United States' comments on European Communities' response to question 19, para. 75.

1396　　　　　　　　　　　　　　　　　　　　　　　　　　　　　　DSR 2012:III

7.1155 The United States argues that the DOD assistance instruments at issue are properly characterized as genuine "purchases of services" because:

> "these instruments typically committed Boeing to a coordinated research and development program in accordance with a detailed statement of work. These agreements set a schedule for performance of research, and tied payments to completion of the requisite tasks. The agreements specified that costs would be governed by the same rules applicable to contracts, and that Boeing would provide a final report, as well as quarterly reports and reports upon the achievement of certain milestones."[2737]

7.1156 In the Panel's view, it is reasonable to assume that similar or identical legal terms and characteristics are found in most if not all instruments through which governments around the world provide R&D grants. For example, it seems unlikely that a government would provide an R&D grant to a firm in the absence of an agreed statement of work / R&D.[2738] The fact that the "terms and conditions of a cooperative agreement are enforceable, including by actions in U.S. courts, in the same way as contracts"[2739] is also hardly surprising. In this regard, we note that Department of Commerce (DOC) cooperative agreements – which the United States acknowledges are "grants" – have similar if not identical features. Among other things:

- As with DOD cooperative agreements, under DOC cooperative agreements (as with all U.S. government R&D contracts, agreements, and grants) the U.S. Government acquires a royalty-free license to use any patents developed as a result of the R&D;[2740]

[2737] United States' first written submission, para. 92.

[2738] For example, we note that both parties agree that the "Department of Labour 787 Worker Training Grants", which we will examine further below in this Report, constitute "grants" within the meaning of Article 1.1(a)(1)(i) of the SCM Agreement. These "grants" contained a "Statement of Work". See e.g. Edmonds Community College Grant Notification, Exhibit EC-622, p. 1 ("The Grantee is approved for this project up to $1,475,045 as specified in the attached Statement of Work with an additional increment of $725,045"). See also, European Communities' second written submission, para. 348 ("It is normal practice among governments all over the world to provide R&D support on the basis of contracts – this does not make such contracts conventional transactions whereby R&D services are purchased by NASA. For instance, the European Commission provides funds to consortia of EC companies under its R&D Framework Programme to cover a portion of costs (and only a portion) incurred in projects selected through calls for tender. This support is regulated by a contract under which both parties have obligations – the companies to carry out the work, and the European Commission to provide the funds.")

[2739] United States' response to question 20, para. 51.

[2740] European Communities' first written submission, para. 784 ("The US Government itself retains some rights with respect to the intellectual property developed with ATP funding. As with NASA and DOD patent waivers/transfers, the US Government reserves a nonexclusive, nontransferable license to use the invention on its own behalf. It also retains march-in rights").

Report of the Panel

- As with DOD cooperative agreements, DOC cooperative agreements are legally binding instruments;

- As with DOD cooperative agreements, DOC requires that recipients conduct the work set out in an agreed upon work statement and does not allow the recipient to unilaterally modify the scope of work;[2741]

- As with DOD cooperative agreements, DOC "closely monitors the ongoing progress of the project and ensures that it maintains appropriate technical and financial oversight of the project"[2742]; and

- As with DOD cooperative agreements, DOC cooperative agreements require that the recipients provide technical and other reports.[2743]

7.1157 None of these features make DOC cooperative agreements "purchases of services". If that is so, then it necessarily follows that these same features do not make DOD R&D cooperative agreements and other assistance instruments with Boeing "purchases of services".

7.1158 The Panel is not persuaded by the United States' general arguments that technologies developed under the DOD R&D programmes are neither "technologically applicable" to commercial aircraft (because of the different missions and cost-sensitivities of military and commercial aircraft), nor "legally applicable" to commercial aircraft (because of Boeing's decision to ensure that the 787 is "ITAR free").

7.1159 With respect to the first of these arguments, we believe that the United States has failed to substantiate its assertion that only a miniscule amount of the R&D conducted by Boeing under the DOD R&D programmes at issue was "technologically applicable" to commercial aircraft. Among other things, the United States' argument that DOD-funded research on military aircraft is designed to fulfil military functions, and does not translate well to the different commercial imperatives of commercial aircraft production (in terms of FAA

[2741] United States' first written submission, para. 377 ("The PMT, which includes both a technical expert and a business expert, is responsible for monitoring the progress of the project and *ensuring its consistency with the project proposal*") (emphasis added). See also, United States' first written submission, para. 378 ("In certain circumstances it may become necessary to modify a project's technical plan in light of such developments. In such cases, the PMT ensures that modified plans remain consistent with the approved goals and objectives of the project proposal and equivalent to the original merit of the project with respect to the ATP selection criteria").

[2742] United States' first written submission, para. 376. See also, United States' first written submission, para. 378 ("PMT continuously reevaluates the progress of a project to determine how technological or industrial developments affect the project and to ensure that the project remains on course for a successful conclusion").

[2743] United States' first written submission, para. 378 ("In addition, the ATP General Terms and Conditions require all award recipients to submit quarterly technical and business performance reports. The PMT reviews all such reports and tracks project developments on an ongoing basis").

1398   DSR 2012:III

US - Large Civil Aircraft (2nd Complaint)

certification/maintenance requirements and efficiency of production) overlooks the fact that at least some of the DOD programmes, for example, the ManTech Composites Affordability Initiative related to Advanced Fibre Placement, had the *explicit objective* of funding R&D to be applied towards both military and civil aircraft and emphasized the development of lower cost technologies. In this regard, we also recall the United States' explanation that there exists a link between "assistance instruments" and "dual use" technologies: according to the United States, the reason that Boeing and other firms agree to enter into cost-sharing cooperative agreements with DOD is because of the benefit (or potential benefit) of the R&D *for their commercial operations*. For example, the United States explains that, "{t}here are some small areas of overlap, which produce "dual-use" technologies, but in these areas, DOD generally tries to use the *potential civil application* to motivate commercial companies to contribute their resources to lessen DOD's cost of reaching its military objective".[2744] The United States explains elsewhere that "where a DoD contracting agency sees *additional direct applications* for purchased technology, it seeks to obtain private sector contribution for the development of the technology".[2745] The United States further explains that, "the incentive for private participation is the opportunity to share the cost of developing some technology of mutual interest to both the contractor and the government".[2746]

7.1160 With respect to the second of these arguments, we consider that the United States has failed to substantiate its assertion that the *International Traffic in Arms Regulations* ("ITAR") make it effectively impossible for Boeing to utilize any of the R&D performed under DOD R&D contracts and agreements towards LCA. Among other things, while we accept the United States' assertions that the ITAR restrict Boeing's ability to use certain R&D performed for DOD towards its civil aircraft, and while we accept that Boeing complies with ITAR in general and took steps to ensure that the 787 will be "ITAR free", and while we further accept that the situation with respect to the scope and coverage of the ITAR is not entirely clear, the United States has failed to explain how its assertions regarding the ITAR can be reconciled with the fact that some of the R&D funded by DOD – including R&D performed by Boeing under assistance instruments entered into under the ManTech and DUS&T Programs, which were subject to the ITAR - had the *explicit objective* of being applied towards civil aircraft.

7.1161 The European Communities has advanced a number of arguments as to why, in its view, the DOD R&D contracts at issue cannot be characterized as genuine "purchases of services".

7.1162 The European Communities argues that the DOD R&D contracts at issue are not properly characterized as "purchases of services" because the DOD R&D

[2744] United States response to question 208, para. 266 (emphasis added).
[2745] United States' first written submission, para. 132 (emphasis added).
[2746] United States' first written submission, footnote 119 and para. 112.

DSR 2012:III

1399

Report of the Panel

contracts in fact "relate to DOD's purchase of goods" – i.e. the military aircraft and other defence systems that DOD ultimately procures.[2747] The Panel is not persuaded by this argument. While we accept that the military aircraft that Boeing produces for DOD are goods within the meaning of Article 1.1(a)(1)(iii) of the SCM Agreement, and while the R&D contracts clearly "relate" to these goods, we do not see how it follows that these contracts are themselves properly characterized as "purchases of goods". Most R&D is either directly or indirectly related in some way to the development of new products. However, "Research and Development Services", including R&D services on natural sciences, are also one of the sectors with regard to which WTO Members may undertake commitments under the General Agreement on Trade in Services, indicating that they are "services" for purposes of the GATS. "Research and development" is similarly categorized in the United Nations Provisional Central Product Classification. R&D is also widely classified as a "service" under national procurement regimes. For example, the U.S. government procurement regime classifies "Research and development" as a service under Federal Service Classification Code A, which is then further divided into subcodes based on the area of research. The European Communities similarly treats R&D as a "service" under Division 73 of its "Common Procurement Vocabulary".[2748]

7.1163 The European Communities argues that there is a degree of artificiality in how DOD finances R&D:

> "DOD does not simply pay one purchase price for its goods; rather DOD first pays for R&D through its RDT&E budgets, and then pays for acquisition costs through its procurement budgets. In theory, one could construct a total purchase price for the goods that DOD acquires by summing up the amounts DOD pays through its RDT&E and procurement budgets."[2749]

7.1164 We consider that the European Communities could have framed its case in terms of the "total purchase price" paid to Boeing for the aircraft it acquired, and it was open to the European Communities to provide evidence that this "total purchase price" was higher than the "total purchase price" that a commercial purchaser (e.g. airlines) would pay for a similar product (e.g. LCA). In this way, the European Communities could have focused on the "broader" transaction, rather than focusing narrowly on DOD's R&D contracts with Boeing. And had the European Communities advanced that kind of analysis, then the Panel might have found the existence of a financial contribution in the form of a "purchase of goods" within the meaning of Article 1.1(a)(1)(iii). However, the European Communities did not advance this analysis. Among other things, there is no

---

[2747] European Communities' second written submission, para. 454.
[2748] See United States' first written submission, para. 95; European Communities' response to question 116, para. 51.
[2749] European Communities' second written submission, paras. 475-476.

1400

DSR 2012:III

US - Large Civil Aircraft (2nd Complaint)

evidence before the Panel on the "total purchase price" that DOD pays Boeing. Instead, the European Communities has focused more narrowly on the payments and access to facilities that DOD provided to Boeing under R&D contracts and agreements.

7.1165 The European Communities also argues that the DOD R&D contracts at issue are not properly characterized as "purchases of services" because DOD conveys monetary resources to Boeing "for the purpose of conducting dual-use R&D".[2750] In our view, if it were the case that DOD R&D contracts between DOD and Boeing had as their purpose conducting "dual use" R&D, then this might well serve as a basis for finding that those procurement contracts are not properly characterized as "purchases of services". However, as noted above, it appears that only two of the 23 R&D programmes at issue in this dispute – the DUS&T and ManTech Programs – had a declared purpose of funding "dual use" R&D (and, as was also indicated above, it appears that both of these programmes were, as consequence, funded primarily if not exclusively through cooperative agreements or other cost-shared "assistance instruments").

7.1166 The European Communities further argues that the DOD R&D contracts at issue are not properly characterized as "purchases of services" because "DOD RDT&E contracts do not contain the typical elements of a purchase". In this regard, the European Communities argues among other things that under the cooperative agreements entered into between Boeing, "Boeing does not make a profit pursuant to these agreements, while the seller in a typical "purchase" transaction would undoubtedly expect to make a profit".[2751] As discussed above, the "atypical" elements that the European Communities emphasizes are not found in procurement contracts. Rather, they are elements found in cooperative agreements and other assistance instruments. Thus, this argument does nothing to undermine, and would seem to reinforce, the conclusion that the DOD procurement contracts at issue are "purchases of services" and that the DOD assistance instruments are not purchases of services.

7.1167 The European Communities argues that the DOD R&D contracts at issue are not properly characterized as "purchases of services" because "Boeing does not offer such R&D services to anybody else but NASA and DOD". We accept the European Communities' factual assertion that Boeing does not provide similar R&D services to commercial entities on the market, and we do not believe that the United States has adequately rebutted this factual assertion.[2752]

[2750] European Communities' second written submission, para. 453.

[2751] European Communities' response to question 15(c), and European Communities' comments on United States' response to question 20(a), para. 75.

[2752] The United States asserts that Boeing does offer certain "services" to customers other than the government, "including financing services and lifecycle solution and support services". In support of that assertion, the United States cites a Boeing Company annual report and a section of the Boeing website that describes certain "lifecycle solutions and support" services that Boeing offers to its "aviation and transport industry customers". United States' comments on European Communities' response to question 15, paras. 63 and 65. The United States does not, however, contest the

DSR 2012:III
1401

Report of the Panel

However, we do not see how this is relevant to whether the DOD R&D contracts with Boeing are properly characterized as "purchases of services". It seems clear that there are certain "services" that governments "purchase", and that no entities other than governments purchase. This does not call into question that these are "purchases of services".

7.1168 The European Communities argues that the DOD R&D contracts at issue are not properly characterized as "purchases of services" because the "DOD RDT&E contracts do not exclusively affect trade in services", but rather "affect trade in goods".[2753] In our view, the problem with this argument is that it imports into the Article 1.1(a)(1) analysis considerations that are germane to a later step in the analysis, in this instance, the analysis of the "effects" of the subsidy under Articles 5 and 6 of the SCM Agreement. The extent to which the measures challenged in this dispute affect trade in goods – i.e. "the effect of the subsidy" – is the question that arises in the context of the analysis of serious prejudice under Articles 5 and 6. To find that DOD R&D procurement contracts with Boeing provide a "financial contribution" by reference to their *effect* on trade in goods, the Panel would essentially have to make a finding on the "effect of the subsidy" (i.e. the extent to which DOD and other federal measures affect trade in goods is the issue in dispute under Articles 5 and 6) and then, on the basis of that finding, reason that there is a financial contribution.

7.1169 The European Communities argues that what matters "is the substance of the transaction, not its form"[2754], and that "the manner in which the municipal law of a WTO Member classifies a transaction cannot, in itself, be determinative for the purpose of applying any provision of the WTO covered agreements".[2755] It is difficult to disagree with either proposition. And it is because we agree with both propositions that we have gone beyond the simple "labels" of the transactions, and examined, in detail, the different substantive features of these contracts and agreements, as reflected, *inter alia*, in U.S. laws and regulations and in the contracts and agreements themselves. The conclusion reached is that there are significant, substantive differences between DOD's R&D procurement contracts and DOD's R&D assistance instruments with Boeing. This is not an analysis that rests on the label "contract". There is more to our analysis than the label or form of the transactions.

European Communities' assertions that Boeing does not offer "LCA-related R&D services" to anybody else but NASA and DOD, and/or that Boeing has not advertised itself as a service provider for "LCA-related R&D" in the market.

[2753] European Communities' response to question 15(c), para. 66.

[2754] See e.g. European Communities' response to question 20(b).

[2755] Appellate Body Report, *US – Softwood Lumber IV*, paras. 56 and 65; Appellate Body Report, *US – Corrosion-Resistant Steel Sunset Review*, footnote 87 to para. 87. See also, Panel Report, *India – Additional import Duties*, footnote 320 ("we would agree that the purpose stated in a Member's legislation is not determinative, by itself, for WTO purposes. Nevertheless, it is a relevant factual element which we may consider together with others in coming to an overall conclusion ...") and para. 7.32.

7.1170 Finally, the European Communities argues that the DOD R&D contracts at issue are not properly characterized as "purchases of services" because "DOD RDT&E contracts have helped Boeing develop technology that it utilizes toward its LCA".[2756] As an initial matter, we believe that this argument is inextricably linked to, and is in fact about, the allocation of intellectual property rights under the R&D contracts and agreements at issue. That is, the reason that Boeing may be able to utilize the technology developed under DOD R&D contracts towards its LCA is that under these R&D contracts and agreements, Boeing retains certain intellectual property rights. If DOD acquired complete intellectual property rights over the results of the R&D, then Boeing would not be able to utilize the results for any purpose. Thus, this argument is equivalent to arguing that the DOD R&D contracts at issue cannot be characterized as purchases of services by virtue of the allocation of intellectual property rights under the contracts.

7.1171 For the reasons given above, the Panel considers that the question of whether or not a transaction is properly characterized as a "purchase of services" depends on whether or not the work performed was principally for the benefit or use of the government (or unrelated third parties), or rather principally for the benefit or use of the "service" "seller" itself. The evidence relating to DOD aeronautics R&D, reviewed above, leads to the conclusion that the work that Boeing performed under its aeronautics R&D contracts with DOD was principally for the benefit and use of DOD, and is therefore properly characterized as a "purchase of services". Therefore, the Panel finds that the payments and access to facilities provided to Boeing under DOD contracts are not financial contributions within the meaning of Article 1.1(a)(1). However, the evidence demonstrates that the work Boeing performed under its aeronautics R&D "assistance instruments" with DOD was principally for the benefit and use of Boeing itself. Accordingly, the Panel concludes that DOD's R&D agreements (i.e. "assistance instruments") with Boeing are not properly characterized as "purchases of services". Therefore, the Panel finds that the payments made to Boeing under these agreements are covered by Article 1.1(a)(1)(i) of the SCM Agreement as a direct transfer of funds.[2757] The Panel further finds that the access to DOD facilities provided to Boeing under these agreements constitutes a provision of goods or services within the meaning of Article 1.1(a)(1)(iii) of the SCM Agreement.

[2756] European Communities' second written submission, para. 457.

[2757] As with NASA, we do not accept that these DOD payments to Boeing constitute outright "grants".

Report of the Panel

> (ii) Whether there is a benefit within the meaning of Article 1.1(b) of the SCM Agreement
>
> Arguments of the European Communities

7.1172 Regarding the existence of a benefit within the meaning of Article 1.1(b) of the SCM Agreement, the European Communities argues that the DOD "subsidies" confer "benefits" upon Boeing's LCA division. More specifically, the European Communities argues that: (i) the financial contributions "relate to the production of all Boeing LCA"; (ii) the financial contributions "provide Boeing's LCA division with advantages on non-market terms"; (iii) "Boeing is not required to pay anything in return" for the funding and support, and "has not been required to repay the US Government for any resulting commercial rewards"; (iv) Boeing has received valuable "knowledge and experience" from the aeronautics R&D, and (v) it is "axiomatic that such R&D funding and support, which provide commercial rewards for nothing in return, are not available on the market".[2758]

7.1173 In its second written submission, the European Communities responds to the United States' argument that DOD's RDT&E contracts with Boeing do not confer a benefit within the meaning of Article 1.1(b). The European Communities argues, among other things, that "the critical point is that Boeing maintains the results of and technology from the R&D for use throughout its military and civil divisions, without adequately paying DOD back for their commercial value".[2759]

7.1174 The European Communities then contrasts the manner in which DOD directly finances R&D from the manner in which commercial buyers of civil aircraft (e.g. airlines) indirectly finance R&D. The European Communities argues that in the commercial market, the cost of R&D that is directly applied toward developing or building a particular product is generally linked to the cost of that product. In other words, R&D directly used toward the development of a military aircraft would be recovered through the price of the military aircraft, and R&D directly used toward the development of a commercial aircraft would be recovered through the price of the commercial aircraft. The European Communities argues that DOD practice, however, departs from this commercial benchmark: DOD does not simply pay one purchase price for its goods; rather DOD first pays for R&D through its RDT&E budgets, and then pays for acquisition costs through its procurement budgets. In theory, one could construct a total purchase price for the goods that DOD acquires by summing up the amounts DOD pays through its RDT&E and procurement budgets.[2760]

[2758] European Communities' first written submission, paras. 764-766.
[2759] European Communities' second written submission, para. 474.
[2760] European Communities' second written submission, paras. 475-476.

1404

DSR 2012:III

US - Large Civil Aircraft (2nd Complaint)

7.1175 The European Communities then argues that "{t}he overwhelming evidence already reviewed above and discussed in the EC First Written Submission shows that Boeing does in fact use R&D results funded through DOD's RDT&E programme toward the development of its LCA. However, DOD fails to recoup the RDT&E funding and support that relates to Boeing LCA, and therefore confers a benefit on Boeing's LCA division".[2761]

7.1176 In addition, the European Communities argues that "a commercial entity that pays for R&D retains the full rights to the technologies that result", and that if "the entity performing the R&D wishes to utilize the R&D in this fashion, it is required to negotiate some form of license rights from the entity paying for the R&D, thereby ensuring that the paying entity recoups the value of the R&D being used by the performing entity for some other purpose".[2762] The European Communities refers[2763] to an article on intellectual property rights and stem cell research[2764] and a Declaration of Regina Dieu, Legal Counsel in the Airbus SAS Industrial procurement Legal Department, which states that when Airbus funds an R&D project it exclusively and solely owns any and all Intellectual Property generated or acquired in connection with and during the performance of the R&D project.[2765] The European Communities also points to DOD's recoupment policy prior to June 1992, as evidence of a benchmark pursuant to which, in the words of DOD's own recoupment regulations, the Department of Defense intended 'to recover a fair share of its investment in nonrecurring costs related to products, and/or a fair price for its contribution to the development of related technology, when the products are sold, and/or when technology is transferred.'[2766]

Arguments of the United States

7.1177 In its first written submission, the United States argues that even if the Panel were to find that the payments made to Boeing under the R&D contracts constitute a financial contribution covered by Article 1.1(a)(1), the European Communities has not met its burden of proof with regard to the existence of a benefit within the meaning of Article 1.1(b).[2767]

7.1178 First, the United States responds to the European Communities' argument that Boeing "pays" nothing to DOD in return for RDT&E funding.[2768] The United States argues that whether under a R&D contract or agreement, when Boeing conducts research for the government, it "pays" DOD value

---

[2761] European Communities' second written submission, para. 477.
[2762] European Communities' second written submission, para. 483.
[2763] European Communities' second written submission, para. 376.
[2764] Sean M. O'Connor, "Intellectual Property Rights and Stem Cell Research: Who Owns the Medical Breakthroughs?" 39 New Eng. L. Rev. 665 (2005), Exhibit EC-1212, p. 669.
[2765] Declaration of Regina Dieu, 8 November 2007, Exhibit EC-1178.
[2766] European Communities' second written submission, para. 479.
[2767] United States' first written submission, para. 100.
[2768] United States' first written submission, paras. 101-103.

DSR 2012:III

1405

Report of the Panel

commensurate with the funds expended. It puts Boeing's scientists at DOD's disposal, to conduct research designed by DOD. It reports periodically on results and makes presentations, educating DOD personnel on the outcome of the work. DOD's patent and data rights mean that if another contractor on a subsequent government project (whether with DOD or any other government agency) needs to make use of the technology or data, it may do so without making any payment or receiving any permission from Boeing. Accordingly, it is plainly untrue to assert that Boeing pays nothing in return for government funding.[2769]

7.1179 The United States proceeds to argue that DOD ensures that it pays no more than "adequate remuneration" for its purchases in the RDT&E contracts at issue in this dispute by reimbursing the contractor – Boeing – only enough to cover the costs that Boeing actually incurred in conducting the research activities subject to the contract, along with a reasonable profit margin.[2770] In the context of its discussion of the amount of the profit paid under DOD contracts, the United States notes that "agreements do not allow for payment of a fee", and that under cooperative agreements, other transactions, and technology investment agreements, "the incentive for private participation is the opportunity to share the cost of developing some technology of mutual interest to both the contractor and the government".[2771]

7.1180 The United States concludes by addressing the relevance of the possible "spillover" effects from DOD R&D to Boeing's LCA division. The United States recalls that the European Communities ends its argument on benefit with an "axiom", namely, that DOD's purchases of R&D, "which provide commercial rewards for nothing in return, are not available on the market". This "axiom", too, is untrue. In its civil aviation division, Boeing also conducts research aimed at developing new products. It recovers the cost of that research through revenue gained from selling aircraft to customers, who are in every real sense funding the research. Technology developed in this effort does sometimes have military application. However, these customers do not insist that Boeing reimburse them when it uses civil technology on military products. Rather, they recognize that this sort of "spillover" of knowledge is a natural outcome of a commercial business relationship. Thus, even if a DOD RDT&E contract resulted in a true dual-use technology, and that technology was not barred from use on large civil aircraft by U.S. export laws, that rare example of such military-to-civil synergy would be completely commercial in nature.

7.1181 In its second written submission, the United States reiterates that even if the Panel were to find that the payments made to Boeing under the R&D contracts constitute a financial contribution covered by Article 1.1(a)(1), they did not confer a benefit because "any payment to Boeing was no more than adequate remuneration for what Boeing did, which, under the analysis provided

---

[2769] United States' first written submission, para. 103.
[2770] United States' first written submission, paras. 104-105, and 108-115.
[2771] United States' first written submission, footnote 119 and para. 112.

1406 DSR 2012:III

in Article 14(d), establishes that the payments do not confer a benefit".[2772] It then responds to several arguments advanced by the European Communities in its Oral Statement at the first meeting with the Panel. With respect to the DOD's former "recoupment" policy, the United States repeats its earlier argument that the European Communities misunderstands what was covered by this policy and that "the old policy did not have the effect that the EC asserts". The United States then adds that the more important point is that during the period covered by the European Communites' allegations, DOD used cost-contribution agreements (cooperative agreements, technology investment agreements, and other transactions) to require contractors to make an up-front contribution to any research with applicability beyond DOD's direct requirements. Therefore, there was no need to try to "recoup" money from subsequent commercial transactions. Rather, "{w}hen DoD perceives a project as having usefulness to both DoD and Boeing, it requires the company to share the costs of that project".[2773]

Evaluation by the Panel

Payments and access to facilities provided to Boeing through DOD assistance instruments

7.1182 It is well established that a financial contribution confers a benefit within the meaning of Article 1.1(b) of the SCM Agreement if the terms of the financial contribution are more favourable than the terms available to the recipient in the market.[2774] Thus, in order to determine whether the financial contributions to Boeing provided under DOD assistance instruments confer a benefit upon Boeing within the meaning of Article 1.1(b), the Panel must begin by recalling what the *terms* of those financial contributions are. Only then can the Panel proceed to compare *those* terms with the terms of a market transaction.

7.1183 As the Panel has already concluded above in its analysis of the existence of a financial contribution, DOD has made payments to Boeing and granted Boeing access to DOD facilities *on the condition that Boeing perform aeronautics R&D work that is principally for Boeing's own benefit and use*, rather than principally for the benefit or use of the U.S. Government (or unrelated third parties). While the R&D agreements of course contain numerous other terms (for example, the contracts and agreements contain or incorporate by

---

[2772] United States' second written submission, para. 37. At paragraph 107 of its first written submission, the United States observes with respect to Article 14(d) that "this standard for measuring a benefit covers only the government purchase of a good, or provision of a good or service, thereby emphasizing that purchase of a service, such as R&D, is not a financial contribution for which determination of a benefit is necessary. However, if DoD's RDT&E contracts were assumed *arguendo* to constitute financial contributions, the standard set out in Article 14(d) would provide useful context for confirming there was no benefit in light of the fact that Boeing received no more than adequate remuneration for its work".

[2773] United States' second written submission, paras. 42-43.

[2774] See paras. 7.30-7.31 of this Report.

DSR 2012:III   1407

Report of the Panel

reference numerous standardized clauses governing miscellaneous matters), this is, in the Panel's view, the core "term" upon which the financial contributions are provided – i.e. that Boeing use the payments and access to facilities it receives from DOD for the purpose of conducting aeronautics R&D work that is principally for Boeing's own benefit and use. The Panel has concluded above that a transaction in which the work performed is principally for the benefit and use of the "seller" cannot properly be characterized as a "purchase of services".

7.1184 In this case, both parties agree that, with regard to the financial contributions that Boeing receives under the DOD R&D programmes, "the relevant market benchmark would be the terms of a commercial transaction in which one entity pays another entity to conduct R&D".[2775] The question, then, is whether, in a "commercial transaction", one entity would pay another entity to conduct R&D on these same terms, i.e. on the term that the entity receiving the financial contributions conduct R&D that is principally for the benefit and use of the entity receiving the payment. The Panel believes that no commercial entity, i.e. no private entity acting pursuant to commercial considerations, would provide payments (and access to its facilities and personnel) to another commercial entity on the condition that the other entity perform R&D activities principally for the benefit and use of that other entity. At a minimum, it is to be expected that some form of royalties or repayment would be required in the event that financial contributions were provided on such terms. Thus, with respect to the financial contributions provided by DOD to Boeing, which were provided on these terms, we consider that it was not necessary for the European Communities to present benchmark evidence of the terms and conditions of specific market-based R&D financing in order to establish, at least on a prima facie basis, that these DOD transactions conferred a benefit upon Boeing. Rather, it would fall upon the United States, if it wished to rebut this prima facie case, to identify examples of transactions in which commercial entities have paid other commercial entities to perform R&D on these same terms, i.e. to perform R&D that is principally for the benefit or use of the entity receiving the funding. The United States has not provided any evidence or examples of commercial transactions in which one entity pays another entity to conduct R&D that is principally for the benefit and use of the entity receiving the funding.

7.1185 Accordingly, the Panel finds that the financial contributions provided to Boeing under its aeronautics R&D assistance instruments with DOD confer a benefit within the meaning of Article 1.1(b) of the SCM Agreement.

[2775] European Communities' response to question 21, para. 76; United States' response to question 136, para. 85.

1408

DSR 2012:III

Payments and access to facilities provided to Boeing through R&D procurement contracts

7.1186 Having found that these transactions do not provide a financial contribution to Boeing that is covered by Article 1.1(a)(1) of the SCM Agreement, it is not necessary for the Panel to address the issue of whether or not these alleged financial contributions confer a benefit within the meaning of Article 1.1(b) of the SCM Agreement.

7.1187 For these reasons, the Panel concludes that the payments and access to facilities granted to Boeing under assistance instruments are provided on terms that confer a benefit within the meaning of Article 1.1(b) of the SCM Agreement. In the light of its conclusion that the payments and access to facilities granted to Boeing under R&D procurement contracts are properly characterized as "purchases of services" that fall outside of the scope of Article 1.1(a)(1) of the SCM Agreement, the Panel makes no finding on whether the different set of terms upon which those alleged financial contributions are provided confer a benefit.

7.1188 For these reasons, we find that some of the payments and access to facilities that DOD provided to Boeing through the 23 aeronautics R&D programmes at issue constitute subsidies within the meaning of Article 1 of the SCM Agreement.

  (d) Whether the subsidy is specific within the meaning of Article 2 of the SCM Agreement

  (i) Arguments of the European Communities

7.1189 In its first written submission, the European Communities argues that the "DOD RDT&E Program" is *de jure* specific within the meaning of Article 2.1(a) of the SCM Agreement, or, in the alternative, de facto specific within the meaning of Article 2.1(c) of the SCM Agreement.[2776] The European Communities argues that the programmes are *de jure* specific by virtue of the subject matter of the research. More specifically, the European Communities argues that the "RDT&E Program funds only those enterprises in the research-based defence and aerospace industries that are capable of conducting specified activities: (1) basic research; (2) applied research; (3) advanced technology development; (4) advanced component development and prototypes; (5) system development and demonstration; (6) RDT&E management support; and (7) operational system development".[2777] According to the European Communities, these "activities may be performed only by a limited number of enterprises", and the "DOD RDT&E Program" is "explicitly limited to the companies in the US

[2776] European Communities' first written submission, paras. 767-770.
[2777] European Communities' second written submission, para. 767.

Report of the Panel

defence industry capable of conducting these specialized activities".[2778] The European Communities argues that the programmes are de facto specific because Boeing has received a "disproportionate" amount of the funding provided under DOD RDT&E programmes. In this regard, the European Communities asserts that from 1991 through 2005, Boeing has received on average 12.6 per cent of all DOD RDT&E awards, and as much as 17.7 per cent of all such funding in 2001. In fact, only four other companies – Lockheed Martin, Northrop Grumman, Raytheon, and United Technologies – received more than $1.0 billion in RDT&E funding in FY 2005. On average, Boeing and these four other companies have together received 45.2 per cent of all DOD RDT&E awards from 1991 through 2005. The European Communities notes that all RDT&E funding went to "research-based defence and aerospace companies".[2779]

7.1190 In its second written submission, the European Communities responds to the United States' argument that the "DOD RDT&E Program" is not specific within the meaning of Article 2 of the SCM Agreement. The European Communities clarifies that "what is at issue in this dispute are *the 13 general aircraft RDT&E PEs* and *10 military aircraft RDT&E PEs* that gave rise to dual-use technologies, and an examination *at the PE level* confirms that *each PE* was explicitly limited to a group of enterprises, and therefore each PE is *de jure* specific within the meaning of Article 2.1(a)". In this regard, the European Communities explains that "only enterprises capable of conducting RDT&E in narrow areas such as defense research sciences, materials, aerospace flight dynamics, etc., and only enterprises capable of supporting or building military aircraft such as the V-22/CV-22, F/A-18, JSF, C-17, etc., could receive RDT&E funding and support from DOD under the PEs at issue. As such, each PE is *de jure* specific pursuant to Article 2.1(a) of the *SCM Agreement*".[2780]

(ii)   Arguments of the United States

7.1191 In its first written submission, the United States argues that the "DOD RDT&E program" covers "a huge number of areas, and involves a huge number of companies, universities, and other research entities"[2781], and that the DOD "RDT&E program" is therefore neither *de jure* specific within the meaning of Article 2.1(a) of the SCM Agreement nor de facto specific within the meaning of Article 2.1(c) of the SCM Agreement.[2782]

7.1192 In its second written submission, the United States reiterates that the DOD RDT&E programme is not specific because "DoD contracts for RDT&E

[2778] European Communities' first written submission, paras. 768-769.
[2779] European Communities' first written submission, para. 770.
[2780] European Communities' second written submission, para. 490 (emphasis added).
[2781] United States' first written submission, para. 118.
[2782] United States' first written submission, paras. 118-123.

1410   DSR 2012:III

on a large variety of topics, with thousands of enterprises, in a large number of industries".[2783]

(iii)   Evaluation by the Panel

7.1193 The European Communities advances three different lines of argument in support of its contention that the subsidies provided to Boeing are specific. First, the European Communities argues that the entire DOD "RDT&E Program" is *de jure* specific within the meaning of Article 2.1(a) of the SCM Agreement by virtue of the fact that DOD provides RDT&E funding only to those entities capable of carrying out the types of activities enumerated in DOD's regulations. Second, the European Communities argues that the entire DOD "RDT&E Program" is de facto specific within the meaning of Article 2.1(c) of the SCM Agreement because the top five U.S. aerospace companies – Boeing, Lockheed Martin, Northrop Grumman, Raytheon, and United Technologies – have received, on average, 45.2 per cent of total DOD RDT&E funding over the period 1991 through 2005. Third, the European Communities argues that each of the individual RDT&E programmes at issue in this dispute is *de jure* specific within the meaning of Article 2.1(a).

7.1194 We recall, at the outset, that we have not found that all of the funding provided to Boeing under the so-called DOD "RDT&E Program" is a subsidy within the meaning of Article 1 of the SCM Agreement, or even that all of the funding provided to Boeing under the 23 RDT&E programmes at issue is a subsidy. Rather, the Panel has concluded, on the basis of the evidence and arguments before it, that some of the funding (and access to government facilities) provided to Boeing under the programmes at issue is a subsidy, whereas other funding (and access to government facilities) provided to Boeing under these programmes is not a subsidy. Accordingly, while we will conduct our analysis of specificity under Article 2 of the SCM Agreement as the parties have, i.e. by examining whether R&D funding provided to entities under the aforementioned programmes is limited to "certain enterprises" within the meaning of Article 2 of the SCM Agreement, in following this line of analysis we do not mean to suggest that either the "RDT&E Program" as a whole, or the individual RDT&E programmes at issue as a whole, is a subsidy within the meaning of Article 1.

7.1195 The first issue that arises from the arguments of the parties is whether, for the purposes of analysing DOD R&D subsidies to Boeing under Article 2 of the SCM Agreement, the focus should be on the "RDT&E Program" as a whole, or rather on the 23 individual RDT&E programmes at issue (which may be termed "programme elements", "project elements", or "PEs") into which the broader "RDT&E Program" is subdivided. The Panel considers that it is appropriate to analyse specificity at the level of the individual programmes,

---

[2783] United States' second written submission, para. 44.

Report of the Panel

rather than at the level of the entire "RDT&E Program". First, the descriptions of the "PEs" themselves refer to the R&D activities covered by each PE as an individual "program", and these programmes each have a defined purpose.[2784] Second, the European Communities has pointed to an official DOD document which explains that "the program element ... is the major aggregation, at which RDT&E efforts are organized, budgeted and reviewed".[2785] Third, what the parties refer to as the "RDT&E Program" appears to be the aggregate of all R&D activities in all areas, by all of the individual branches of the U.S. armed forces (Army, Navy, and Air Force) and the Department of Defense.[2786] It is not clear that this aggregation constitutes a "programme" for the purposes of Article 2 of the SCM Agreement. In this regard, we disagree with the United States that "a determination as to the specificity of DoD RDT&E cannot be made at the PE level, as the EC contends, because the PEs challenged by the European Communities are, for the most part, not themselves programs, or even groupings below the program level, and do not create a frame of reference".[2787] In our view, it is the so-called "RDT&E Program" that creates no "frame of reference" for the specificity analysis under Article 2 of the SCM Agreement.

7.1196 Given that we consider that the individual programmes appear to be the relevant frame of reference for the purpose of Article 2 of the SCM Agreement, the question that we ask is not whether the "RDT&E Program" as a whole is specific under Article 2 of the SCM Agreement; rather, the relevant question is

---

[2784] See above, para. 7.1147 of this Report.

[2785] DoD Financial Management Regulation, Volume 2B, Chapter 5, June 2006, Exhibit EC-1324, p. 5-3. The United States responds that this statement "comes from a two-page segment of the DoD Financial Management Regulations, which address the policy, regulations, and procedures that are the responsibility of the Comptroller of DoD. This document deals with the organization and review of the *DoD budget*, not of the research efforts themselves". United States' response to question 140, para. 117. Like the European Communities, the Panel "fails to see how this explanation does anything to refute the understanding that DOD organises its own R&D efforts based on PEs". European Communities' comments on United States' response to question 140, para. 125.

[2786] The Department of Defense's (DOD) budget is divided into five broad budget categories: Military Personnel; Operations & Maintenance; "Procurement"; "Research, Development, Test, & Evaluation (RDT&E)"; and Military Construction. The "RDT&E" budget category funds research, development, test and evaluation spending by DOD toward designing and developing military systems or technology, while the "Procurement" budgets fund the actual acquisition costs of parts and labour of military systems that are in production. RDT&E funding focused on a particular military aircraft may continue even after procurement spending commences on the same military aircraft. This funds the further design or development of advanced technologies that can later be incorporated into a military system that is already in production. The DOD RDT&E programme is executed by the individual branches of the U.S. armed forces (Army, Navy and Air Force), as well as by DOD generally. The broader RDT&E programme is subdivided into numerous "program elements" or "PEs". We will simply refer to these as "programmes" here. The programmes into which the broader RDT&E programme is subdivided include what the European Communities terms "general aircraft" R&D programmes (which are not specific to a particular military aircraft, such as the "Defense Research Sciences" programme), as well as "military aircraft" programmes (specific to a particular military aircraft, e.g. the "C-17" programme). Each of these programmes has its own "PE#"; for example, the "Defense Research Sciences" programme is identified as "PE# 0601102F".

[2787] United States' response to question 50, para. 146.

1412

DSR 2012:III

whether the individual programmes at issue are specific under Article 2. Given the fairly narrow focus of R&D performed under the 23 individual programmes (i.e. PEs) challenged by the European Communities, we conclude that the subsidies provided to Boeing through DOD R&D assistance instruments entered into under the 23 programmes at issue are specific within the meaning of Article 2.1(a) of the SCM Agreement.

7.1197 In any event, even if it were necessary to examine specificity at the level of the "RDT&E Program" as a whole, we believe that the European Communities has demonstrated de facto specificity under Article 2.1(c) of the SCM Agreement. The European Communities has substantiated its assertion that Boeing, Lockheed Martin, Northrop Grumman, Raytheon, and United Technologies have received on average 45.2 per cent of total DOD RDT&E funding over the period 1991 through 2005.[2788] The United States' has responded that this does not establish the existence of "disproportionately" large amounts being granted to "certain enterprises or industries". In our view, it is not necessary for us to resolve the issue of whether this demonstrates "disproportionately" large amounts for the purpose of Article 2.1(c), or what the proper "baseline" is for determining whether these five contractors have received "disproportionately" large amounts of R&D funding. The reason is that, leaving aside this particular factor in Article 2.1(c), this evidence demonstrates that almost half of all RDT&E funding went to five enterprises, all of which form part of the same industry. In our view, this is more than enough to confirm that RDT&E funding goes "predominantly" to firms in the defense industry, and this is enough to establish de facto specificity under Article 2.1(c).

7.1198 We conclude that the payments and access to facilities provided to Boeing through the 23 programmes at issue are subsidies that are sufficiently limited to "a group of enterprises or industries" within the meaning of Article 2.

(e)   The amount of the subsidy to Boeing's LCA division

(i)   Arguments of the European Communities

7.1199 The European Communities estimates that DOD provided Boeing with $4.3 billion in funding and support for "dual use" R&D over the period 1991-2006. The European Communities argues that $2.4 billion of that total should be treated as a subsidy to Boeing's LCA division.[2789]

[2788] See European Communities' first written submission, para. 770; European Communities' second written submission, para. 491. Top Contractors' Share of DOD RDT&E, FY 1991-FY 2005, Exhibit EC-29.

[2789] NASA/DOD/DOC Aeronautics R&D Subsidies to Boeing LCA Division, Exhibit EC-25, p. 20.

Report of the Panel

(ii) Arguments of the United States

7.1200 The United States argues that the European Communities has overestimated the amount of "dual use" research conducted under the programmes at issue. According to the United States, the total amount of any subsidy to Boeing's LCA division under DOD R&D contracts and agreements is significantly less than $308 million over the period 1991-2006.

(iii) Evaluation by the Panel

7.1201 The European Communities has demonstrated that some of the DOD payments and access to facilities, equipment and employees provided to Boeing through aeronautics R&D contracts and agreements are subsidies within the meaning of Article 1 of the SCM Agreement. The Panel will now consider the amount of the subsidy to Boeing's LCA division.

7.1202 It is not in dispute that DOD provided Boeing with $45 billion in RDT&E funding over the period 1991-2005.[2790] The European Communities does not assert that the entirety of this funding constitutes a subsidy to Boeing. Rather, the European Communities' claim relates to DOD R&D funding and support to Boeing for "dual use" R&D.

7.1203 At the outset, we note that there is no publicly available information setting forth the amount of DOD "dual use" R&D funding to Boeing. Thus, the European Communities has presented the Panel with an estimate of the amount of the DOD subsidy provided to Boeing's LCA division. The European Communities estimates that out of the $45 billion in RDT&E funding that Boeing received from DOD over the period 1991-2005, approximately $4.3 billion related to "dual use" R&D. The European Communities' estimate is based on a detailed expert report prepared by CRA International.[2791] The European Communities argues that $2.4 billion of this "dual use" R&D funding and support should be treated as a subsidy to Boeing's LCA division. The European Communities argues that the Panel should adopt its estimate of the amount of DOD R&D subsidies to Boeing 's LCA division, unless the United States discloses evidence indicating the actual value of the payments and access to facilities, equipment and employees that DOD provided to Boeing for the purpose of conducting "dual use" R&D. The United States submits that it has done so. In the Panel's view, if the United States were able to provide the Panel with the actual information and figures regarding the amount of DOD R&D subsidies to Boeing, or information from which the maximum amount of those subsidies could be derived, then such information would necessarily prevail over

---

[2790] See European Communities' second written submission, para. 471; Top Contractors' Share of DOD RDT&E, FY 1991-FY 2005, Exhibit EC-29, p. 1.

[2791] CRA International, U.S. Department of Defense (DoD) Research, Development, Test and Evaluation (RDT&E) Funding Support to The Boeing Company for Dual-Use Aircraft R&D, November 2006, Exhibit EC-7.

1414

DSR 2012:III

US - Large Civil Aircraft (2nd Complaint)

the European Communities' estimate. Therefore, the Panel will begin by reviewing the evidence provided by the United States.

7.1204 The United States initially indicated that the total funding provided to Boeing under the 23 programmes at issue that met the European Communities' criteria of "dual use" R&D was not more than $529 million.[2792] The United States provided the Panel with a list of 43 R&D contracts and agreements in the form of Exhibit US-41. However, the United States subsequently indicated that Exhibit US-41 contained several mistakes, and that the actual maximum amount is only $308 million.[2793] Furthermore, the United States has argued that this represents the maximum possible amount of DOD subsidies to Boeing, and that many of the R&D contracts and agreements that comprise this $308 million estimate do not, in fact, involve any "dual use" R&D.[2794] In addition, in respect of a number of the few remaining contracts and agreements on its list, the United States argues that some had "elements" with "no civil applicability".[2795] Finally, the United States' estimate of the amount of any DOD subsidy (i.e. significantly less than $308 million) concerns the total amount of the subsidy to Boeing as a whole: if we were to apply the European Communities' methodology for allocating DOD subsidies to Boeing's "LCA division", then whatever remained of the United States' estimate following all of these reductions would then need to be further split in half. Thus, while the United States has never provided an exact figure regarding the actual amount of any DOD subsidy to Boeing's LCA division, it is clear that any such estimate would be significantly less than $308 million, and, it seems, significantly less than $100 million over the period 1991-2006.

7.1205 The Panel cannot accept the United States' estimate that the total amount of any DOD subsidy to Boeing for "dual use" R&D is significantly less than $308 million over the period 1991-2006. First, we note that the United States' estimate completely excludes all funding provided to Boeing under the "military aircraft" RDT&E programmes at issue, which accounts for $3.1 billion out of the European Communities' $4.3 billion estimate. Second, the United States' assertions regarding the maximum value of DOD R&D contracts and agreements with Boeing related to "dual use" R&D is not supported by the same kind of evidence as the United States' estimate of the amount of NASA payments to Boeing: among other things, while the United States has provided the Panel with evidence demonstrating that the maximum amount of the NASA payments to Boeing for aeronautics R&D cannot be more than $1.05 billion, the United States has advanced no similar argument or evidence in respect of the maximum amount of DOD R&D. In addition, the United States' estimate of the amount of

---

[2792] United States' first written submission, paras 160-161.

[2793] See United States' response to question regarding U.S. Exhibits (10 January 2008), p. 2.

[2794] See United States' first written submission, paras. 161-162; United States' response to question 208, para. 290; United States' comments on European Communities' response to question 190(b), para. 326.

[2795] United States' response to question 208(b), para. 290 and footnote 376.

DSR 2012:III
1415

Report of the Panel

DOD R&D subsidies to Boeing does not account for the value of any access to DOD facilities granted to Boeing. In addition, the Panel does not consider it credible that less than 1 per cent of the $45 billion in aeronautics R&D funding that DOD provided to Boeing over the period 1991-2005 had any potential relevance to LCA.[2796]

7.1206 However, while the Panel cannot accept the United States' estimate of the total amount of DOD R&D subsidies to Boeing, we are also unable to accept the European Communities' estimate of the amount of the subsidy to Boeing's LCA division. The reason is that the European Communities' estimate is based on a methodology and analysis that do not distinguish payments and access to facilities provided to Boeing under procurement contracts from payments and access to facilities provided to Boeing through assistance instruments.

7.1207 The parties have informed the Panel that it is not possible to perform such an analysis on the basis of the information before us.[2797] Based on the Panel's careful review of the parties' responses to question 321, and of the evidence submitted by the parties relating to the measures at issue, we agree with the parties that it is not possible to perform such an analysis on the basis of the information before us.

7.1208 In *US – Upland Cotton*, the Appellate Body clarified that while a panel should endeavour to arrive at an estimate of the order of the "magnitude" of the subsid(ies) alleged to cause price suppression within the meaning of Article 6.3(c) of the SCM Agreement, a "precise, definitive quantification is not required".[2798] Although the Appellate Body was focusing in that case on

---

[2796] We recognize that the concept of "dual use" R&D can be interpreted relatively broadly or narrowly. For example, under a relatively broad understanding, research with "theoretical" or "potential" civil applications might be considered "dual use". Under a narrower conception of what constitutes "dual use", it might be considered that only R&D giving rise to tangible technologies actually applied on civil aircraft should be considered "dual use". We are not taking a position on this definitional issue here. We understand the United States' estimate of the amount of DOD R&D that is "dual use" to reflect the broadest understanding of "dual use" R&D; applying a narrower definition of what constitutes "dual use", the United States' estimate would be even less.

[2797] See e.g. parties' responses to question 321 (the United States explains why "it is not possible to conclude that a given program element funds exclusively assistance agreements or exclusively procurement contracts" (para. 23); the European Communities likewise indicates that "PEs cannot necessarily be divided into a group of PEs funded through cooperative agreements or other "assistance" instruments, and a group of PEs funded through procurement contracts; rather, any of these instruments may be utilised under any RDT&E PE" (para. 29)).

[2798] Appellate Body Report, *US – Upland Cotton*, para. 467 ("In sum, reading Article 6.3(c) in the context of Article 6.8 and Annex V suggests that a panel should have regard to the magnitude of the challenged subsidy and its relationship to prices of the product in the relevant market when analyzing whether the effect of a subsidy is significant price suppression. In many cases, it may be difficult to decide this question in the absence of such an assessment. Nevertheless, this does not mean that Article 6.3(c) imposes an obligation on panels to quantify precisely the amount of a subsidy benefiting the product at issue in every case. A precise, definitive quantification of the subsidy is not required").

1416   DSR 2012:III

Article 6.3(c), we believe that the same conclusion must also hold true with respect to the other forms of serious prejudice set forth in Article 6.3.[2799]

7.1209 In this case, where we have determined that a measure constitutes a specific subsidy within the meaning of Articles 1 and 2 of the SCM Agreement, we have attempted to determine the amount of the subsidy that is properly allocated to Boeing's "LCA division". However, in the case of DOD R&D subsidies to Boeing, while we do not accept the United States' estimate that the total amount of any DOD subsidy to Boeing for "dual use" R&D is significantly less than $308 million over the period 1991-2006, we also cannot accept the European Communities' estimate, and any attempt by the Panel to go further and arrive at our own estimate of the amount of the subsidy to Boeing's LCA division would be speculative.[2800]

(f)   Conclusion

7.1210 For these reasons, the Panel finds that some of the payments and access to facilities that DOD provided to Boeing through the 23 aeronautics

---

[2799] We see nothing in the Appellate Body's analysis to suggest that a different conclusion would apply to any other forms of serious prejudice set out in Article 6.3 of the SCM Agreement. Among other things, the Appellate Body referred generally to the differences between Parts III and V of the SCM Agreement in reaching this conclusion. See e.g. Appellate Body Report, *US – Upland Cotton*, para. 464.

[2800] However, we see no evidence to suggest that the value of the payments and access to government facilities that DOD provided to Boeing through assistance instruments would have been greater than the value of the payments and access to government facilities that DOD provided to Boeing through procurement contracts. In this regard, we observe that the European Communities submitted a number of DOD R&D contracts and agreements with Boeing along with its first written submission. Of these, nine were procurement contracts. See Exhibit EC-507, Exhibit EC-508, Exhibit EC-509, Exhibit EC-510, Exhibit EC-511, Exhibit EC-514, Exhibit EC-827, Exhibit EC-838 and Exhibit EC-1143. The remaining seven were cooperative agreements, technology investment agreements or other assistance instruments. See Exhibit EC-406, Exhibit EC-512, Exhibit EC-513, Exhibit EC-515, Exhibit EC-517, Exhibit EC-518 and Exhibit EC-830. We have reviewed all of these R&D contracts and agreements to ascertain the face value indicating the total amount of government funds "committed" or "obligated" under each. It appears that $72 million was committed under these nine procurement contracts , and that $48 million was committed under these seven assistance instruments. Thus, funding committed under assistance instruments ($48 million) accounts for 40 per cent of the total amount of funding committed under the contracts and agreements submitted by the European Communities. Exhibit US-41 (revised) lists 42 different DOD assistance instruments and procurement contracts with Boeing, totalling $308 million. This list includes 14 assistance instruments, and 28 procurement contracts. The list indicates that the "amount" provided through assistance instruments is approximately $44 million. Thus, funding provided through assistance instruments accounts for 14 per cent of the total amount indicated in Exhibit US-41(revised).

Therefore, if the Panel were to accept the various steps in the European Communities' analysis leading to its estimate that DOD provided a $2.4 billion subsidy to Boeing's LCA division, and if the Panel were to consider that there is no evidence to support the conclusion that the value of the payments and access to government facilities that DOD provided to Boeing through "assistance instruments" would have been greater than the value of the payments and access to government facilities that DOD provided to Boeing through procurement contracts, then the Panel might estimate that the amount of the subsidy to Boeing's LCA division would not be more than half of what the European Communities estimates, i.e. not more than $1.2 billion.

Report of the Panel

R&D programmes at issue constitute specific subsidies within the meaning of Articles 1 and 2. While the Panel does not accept the United States' estimate that the total amount of any DOD subsidy to Boeing for "dual use" R&D is significantly less than $308 million over the period 1991-2006, the amount of the subsidy to Boeing's LCA division is unclear.

4. Department of Commerce (DOC) aeronautics R&D

(a) Introduction

7.1211 The European Communities argues that DOC makes payments to Boeing (and grants Boeing access to facilities, equipment and employees) to perform R&D under the Advanced Technology Program (ATP). The European Communities argues that these payments (and access to facilities, equipment and employees) are subsidies within the meaning of Article 1 of the SCM Agreement, and are specific within the meaning of Article 2 of the SCM Agreement. The European Communities estimates that DOC provided $7.5 million in R&D funding to Boeing over the period 1991-2004, and submits that $4.6 million of that total should be treated as a subsidy to Boeing's LCA division.[2801]

7.1212 The United States accepts that DOC R&D funding to Boeing is a subsidy within the meaning of Article 1 of the SCM Agreement. However, the United States argues that the subsidy is not specific within the meaning of Article 2 of the SCM Agreement. In addition, the United States asserts that Boeing only received [***] million under the eight projects at issue.[2802]

(b) The measures at issue

7.1213 The pertinent item of the European Communities' panel request[2803] reads:

> "The US Department of Commerce ("DOC") transfers economic resources to the US LCA industry on terms more favourable than available on the market or not at arm's length, through the Advanced Technology Program operated pursuant to the Omnibus Trade and Competitiveness Act of 1988, Pub. L. No. 100-418, as amended, and the American Technology Preeminence Act of 1991, Pub. L. No. 102-245 and 15 CFR §§ 295.1 *et seq.*, by allowing the US LCA industry to participate in this programme, making payments to the US LCA industry under this programme, or allowing the US LCA industry to exploit the results of this programme, including but not limited to the foregoing or waiving of valuable patent rights, and the granting of exclusive or early

---

[2801] NASA/DOD/DOC Aeronautics R&D Subsidies to Boeing LCA Division, Exhibit EC-25, p. 21.
[2802] United States' first written submission, para. 395.
[2803] WT/DS353/2, item 4, pp. 11-12.

1418   DSR 2012:III

access to data, trade secrets and other knowledge resulting from government funded research. In particular, economic resources are transferred to the US LCA industry through a number of projects, including, but not limited to, the following:

- Project 93-01-0089 (CVD Diamond-Coated Rotating Tools for Machining Advanced Composite Materials);
- Project 95-12-0024 (An Agent-Based Framework for Integrated Intelligent Planning – Execution);
- Project 95-01-0108 (Precision Optoelectronics Assembly);
- Project 91-01-0267 (Pre-competitive Advanced Manufacturing of Electrical Products);
- Project 97-05-0020 (Extended Enterprise Coalition for Integrated Collaborative Manufacturing Systems);
- Project 98-01-0168 (Hot Metal Gas Forming);
- Project 90-01-0126 (Solid-State Laser Technology for Point Source X-Ray Lithography);
- Project 95-02-0036 (Plasma-Based Processing of Lightweight Materials for Motor-Vehicle Components and Manufacturing Applications)."

7.1214 Thus, the European Communities has not challenged the ATP as a whole. Rather, it has challenged only the eight ATP "projects" through which DOC has provided funding to Boeing/MD for LCA-related research.[2804] This is clear, and is not in dispute.

7.1215 What also seems clear is that the European Communities' argument that DOC provides goods and services to Boeing in the form of government "facilities, equipment and employees" relates to an alleged measure that is not identified in the European Communities' panel request, and therefore falls outside of the scope of the European Communities' claim. In contrast to the items of the European Communities' panel request relating to NASA subsidies (which cover "facilities", "equipment" and "employees") and DOD subsidies (which covers only "facilities"), the European Communities' panel request makes no reference to DOC providing access to facilities, equipment or employees.[2805]

7.1216 The United States does not dispute that Boeing received funding and/or participated in the consortia of companies that received funding, under each of the eight projects at issue. It is also not in dispute that different segments of Boeing / MD participated in and received funding related to these projects,

---

[2804] European Communities' second written submission, para. 512.
[2805] For a side-by-side comparison of these items of the European Communities' Panel Request, see above, para. 7.1120.

Report of the Panel

including Boeing's LCA division, Boeing's IDS segment, and McDonnell Douglas's "electronic systems" division.[2806]

7.1217 The ATP is administered by the National Institute of Standards & Technology, which is a division of the DOC.

7.1218 The legislation pursuant to which the ATP operates appears to be comprised of three different legal instruments. These are: (i) the so-called "ATP statute"[2807]; (ii) the American Technology Preeminence Act of 1991[2808] ("ATPA") which amended the ATP statute; and (iii) the "ATP Rules".[2809] In addition to the legislation, certain documents set forth certain guidelines and eligibility criteria for participation in the ATP.[2810]

7.1219 The ATP statute indicates that the Advanced Technology Program has the purpose:

> "... of assisting United States businesses in creating and applying the generic technology and research results necessary to-
>
> (1)   commercialize significant new scientific discoveries and technologies rapidly; and
>
> (2)   refine manufacturing technologies.
>
> The Secretary, acting through the Director, shall assure that the Program focuses on improving the competitive position of the

---

[2806] ATP Project Briefs, Projects 90-01-0126 (Solid-State Laser Technology for Point-Source X-Ray Lithography), 91-01-0267 (PREAMP – Pre-competitive Advanced Manufacturing of Electrical Products), 93-01-0089 (CVD Diamond-Coated Rotating Tools for Machining Advanced Composite Materials), 95-01-0108 (Precision Optoelectronics Assembly), 95-02-0036 (Plasma-Based Processing of Lightweight Materials for Motor-Vehicle Components and Manufacturing Applications), 95-12-0024 (An Agent-Based Framework for Integrated Intelligent Planning – Execution), 97-05-0020 (EECOMS: Extended Enterprise Coalition for Integrated Collaborative Manufacturing Systems), and 98-01-0168 (Hot Metal Gas Forming), Exhibit EC-553.

[2807] Omnibus Trade and Competitiveness Act of 1988, Pub. L. No. 100-418, § 5131, Exhibit EC-531 ("OTCA"); OTCA § 5131 is codified at 15 U.S.C. § 278n, as amended, Exhibit EC-532 ("ATP Statute").

[2808] American Technology Preeminence Act of 1991, Pub. L. No. 102-245("ATPA"), Exhibit EC-533.

[2809] National Institute of Standards & Technology Advanced Technology Program Rules, 15 C.F.R. §§ 295.1 *et seq.* ("ATP Rules"), Exhibit EC-534.

[2810] ATP Eligibility Criteria for U.S. Subsidiaries of Foreign-Owned Companies: Legislation, Implementation and Results, NISTIR-6099A, March 2004 ("2004 ATP Eligibility Criteria"), Exhibit EC-535; Guidelines For Proposing Economic Evaluation Studies to The Advanced Technology Program (ATP), NISTIR-5896, November 1996 ("Guidelines for ATP Economic Evaluation Studies"), Exhibit EC-536; Advanced Technology Program: Proposal Preparation Kit, February 2004 ("2004 ATP Proposal Preparation Kit"), Exhibit EC-539; Advanced Technology Program: Proposal Preparation Kit, November 1998, Exhibit EC-540 ("1998 ATP Proposal Preparation Kit"); Advanced Technology Program: Proposal Preparation Kit, December 1997 ("1997 ATP Proposal Preparation Kit"), Exhibit EC-543.

US - Large Civil Aircraft (2nd Complaint)

United States and its businesses, gives preference to discoveries and to technologies that have great economic potential, and avoids providing undue advantage to specific companies. ..."[2811]

7.1220 According to the ATPA, this assistance is designed

"to improve the competitive position of United States industry by supporting industry-led research and development projects in areas of emerging technology which have substantial potential to advance the economic well-being and national security of the United States."[2812]

7.1221 The ATP Rules provide that:

"The purpose of the Advanced Technology Program (ATP) is to assist United States businesses to carry out research and development on high risk, high pay-off, emerging and enabling technologies."[2813]

7.1222 Boeing participated in the eight ATP-funded projects identified in the panel request, and each of these projects is briefly described in a document prepared by the DOC entitled "ATP Project Briefs".[2814] According to the European Communities, these ATP projects fall into three general categories, all of which are applicable to LCA: (i) improving the manufacturing of lightweight composite and metal structures and materials, (ii) improving electronics components, and (iii) improving manufacturing efficiency and supply chain logistics. Various segments of Boeing and MD have participated in and received funding related to these projects, including Boeing's commercial aircraft division, Boeing's space and defence division, and McDonnell Douglas's electronic systems division.[2815]

[2811] ATP Statute, Exhibit EC-532, § 278n(a).

[2812] ATPA, Exhibit EC-533, § 201(b)(2)(C) (concerning Congress's findings and purposes).

[2813] ATP Rules, Exhibit EC-534, § 295.1(a).

[2814] ATP Project Briefs, Projects 90-01-0126 (Solid-State Laser Technology for Point-Source X-Ray Lithography), 91-01-0267 (PREAMP – Pre-competitive Advanced Manufacturing of Electrical Products), 93-01-0089 (CVD Diamond-Coated Rotating Tools for Machining Advanced Composite Materials), 95-01-0108 (Precision Optoelectronics Assembly), 95-02-0036 (Plasma-Based Processing of Lightweight Materials for Motor-Vehicle Components and Manufacturing Applications), 95-12-0024 (An Agent-Based Framework for Integrated Intelligent Planning – Execution), 97-05-0020 (EECOMS: Extended Enterprise Coalition for Integrated Collaborative Manufacturing Systems), and 98-01-0168 (Hot Metal Gas Forming), Exhibit EC-553.

[2815] European Communities' first written submission, para. 792, citing *ATP Project Briefs*, Exhibit EC-553.

DSR 2012:III

1421

Report of the Panel

7.1223 In each of these projects, Boeing participated as a member of a consortium.[2816] It appears that DOC provided all of the funding under the ATP, including all of the funding at issue, through cooperative agreements.[2817]

(c)   Whether a subsidy exists within the meaning of Article 1 of the SCM Agreement

(i)   Arguments of the European Communities

7.1224 In its first written submission, the European Communities argues that DOC directly transfers funds in the form of "grants" to Boeing's LCA division to support research and development, and that this "direct R&D funding" constitutes a financial contribution within the meaning of Article 1.1(a)(1)(i) of the SCM Agreement. The European Communities asserts that DOC also provides ATP recipients "with organizational and technical advice, and makes available federal equipment, facilities, and personnel", and that the provision of these "goods and services" by the U.S. Government constitutes an additional financial contribution within the meaning of Article 1.1(a)(1)(iii) of the SCM Agreement.[2818]

7.1225 Regarding the existence of a benefit within the meaning of Article 1.1(b) of the SCM Agreement, the European Communities argues that the DOC "subsidies" confer "benefits" upon Boeing's LCA division. The European Communities argues that: (i) the financial contributions "relate to the production of all Boeing LCA"; (ii) the financial contributions "provide Boeing's LCA division with advantages on non-market terms"; (iii) "Boeing is not required to pay anything in return" for the funding and support, and "has not been required to repay the US Government for any resulting commercial rewards"; (iv) Boeing has received valuable "knowledge and experience" from the aeronautics R&D, and (v) it is "axiomatic that such R&D funding and support, which provide commercial rewards for nothing in return, are not available on the market".[2819]

(ii)   Arguments of the United States

7.1226 In its first written submission, the United States does not dispute that the payments made to Boeing under the eight projects at issue constitute a financial

---

[2816] United States' first written submission, para. 379; European Communities' second written submission, para. 516.

[2817] European Communities' first written submission, para. 798: United States' first written submission, para. 360 ("ATP is a cost-sharing program. It uses cooperative agreements as funding instruments to assist in financing projects in which private companies, universities, government laboratories, independent research institutions, and/or non-profit organizations participate.")

[2818] European Communities' first written submission, para. 798.

[2819] European Communities' first written submission, paras. 800-802.

US - Large Civil Aircraft (2nd Complaint)

contribution in the form of a direct transfer of funds.[2820] In response to a question from the Panel, the United States accepts the European Communities' characterization of these measures as "grants".[2821] The United States does not respond to the European Communities' argument regarding DOC "facilities, equipment and employees" in either its first or second written submissions.

7.1227 In its first written submission, the United States does not respond to the European Communities' arguments relating to the existence of a benefit to Boeing's LCA division. However, in a response to a question from the Panel, the United States confirms that DOC R&D funding "can be considered a subsidy within the meaning of Article 1 of the SCM Agreement".[2822]

(iii) Evaluation by the Panel

7.1228 The ATP payments at issue were made to "joint ventures" or "consortia" in which Boeing participated.[2823] It is clear from the evidence before the Panel that the ATP funding at issue was provided for R&D that was principally for the joint venture / consortia's own benefit or use. This evidence includes, among other things, the fact that the payments were made pursuant to "assistance instruments" (cooperative agreements), the fact that the declared objective of the ATP is "to improve the competitive position of United States industry"[2824] and "to assist United States businesses"[2825], and the fact that DOC has no independent use for the R&D that was performed.[2826] The United States does not dispute that the payments made to Boeing under the eight "projects" at issue constitute a financial contribution in the form of a direct transfer of funds.[2827] More specifically, the United States accepts the European Communities' characterization of these measures as "grants".[2828] Accordingly, the Panel finds

---

[2820] United States' first written submission, para. 395 ("ATP provides a financial contribution to program participants by directly transferring funds.")

[2821] United States' response to question 194, para. 240 ("the United States explicitly recognizes that under some circumstances – represented in this dispute by ATP cooperative agreements – cost sharing arrangements can and do confer a benefit to the private party recipient when the government's "share" represents a "grant" for purposes of Article 1.1(a)(1)(i).")

[2822] United States' response to question 14, para. 30.

[2823] European Communities' second written submission, para. 516.

[2824] ATPA, Exhibit EC-533, § 201(b)(2)(C) (concerning Congress's findings and purposes).

[2825] ATP Rules, Exhibit EC-534, § 295.1(a).

[2826] United States' response to question 214, paras. 342-344 ("ATP uses cooperative agreements not to purchase any goods or services, but to fund ATP projects without any expectation that the research will improve the operations of ATP, the National Institute of Standards and Technology ("NIST"), or the U.S. Department of Commerce ... Although the program monitors ATP projects, neither the administering agency, NIST, nor the U.S. Government receive any operational improvements, goods, or services in return for the funding that is provided").

[2827] United States' first written submission, para. 395 ("ATP provides a financial contribution to program participants by directly transferring funds").

[2828] United States' response to question 194, para. 240 ("the United States explicitly recognizes that under some circumstances – represented in this dispute by ATP cooperative agreements – cost sharing arrangements can and do confer a benefit to the private party recipient when the government's

DSR 2012:III
1423

Report of the Panel

that the payments involve a direct transfer of funds within the meaning of Article 1.1(a)(1)(i).

7.1229 With respect to the existence of a benefit within the meaning of Article 1.1(b) of the SCM Agreement, we recall the reasoning that led us to find that NASA's R&D contracts and agreements, and certain DOD R&D agreements, confer a benefit within the meaning of Article 1.1(b). In short, the Panel believes that no commercial entity, i.e. no private entity acting pursuant to commercial considerations, would provide payments (and access to its facilities and personnel) to another commercial entity on the condition that the other entity perform R&D activities principally for the benefit and use of that other entity. At a minimum, it is to be expected that some form of royalties or repayment would be required in the event that financial contributions were provided on such terms.[2829] The United States does not dispute that the "grants" provided to the "joint ventures" or "consortia" in which Boeing participated confer a benefit within the meaning of Article 1.1(b) of the SCM Agreement.[2830] Accordingly, the Panel finds that the payments are provided on terms that confer a benefit within the meaning of Article 1.1(b).

7.1230 For these reasons, the Panel finds that the ATP payments at issue are subsidies within the meaning of Article 1 of the SCM Agreement.

> (d)   Whether the subsidy is specific within the meaning of Article 2 of the SCM Agreement
>
> (i)   Arguments of the European Communities

7.1231 In its first written submission, the European Communities argues that ATP subsidies are specific within the meaning of Article 2.1(a) of the SCM

'share' represents a 'grant' for purposes of Article 1.1(a)(1)(i)"). See also, United States' response to question 14, para. 30.

[2829] Recipients of ATP funding are not required to pay royalties. At paragraphs 786-787 of its first written submission, the European Communities explains that:

> "the US Government at one time required ATP participants to give the government a share of the royalties and licensing fees they received on ATP-funded technology, implicitly recognizing that ATP participants were receiving a commercial benefit at public expense. More specifically, the OTCA and initial ATP regulations required ATP participants to share royalties and licensing fees resulting from intellectual property derived from ATP funding with the US Government, "in an amount proportional to the Federal share of the costs incurred by the business or joint venture." This requirement was repealed as of 1992 by the ATPA.
>
> In 2002, DOC proposed various reforms to ATP, one of which was to reinstate a royalty sharing requirement. In particular, DOC suggested that ATP award recipients "pay an annual royalty to the Federal government of 5 percent of any gross revenues derived from a product or invention supported by or created as a result of ATP funding." In making this proposal, DOC noted that "... it is fair and reasonable to require direct repayment based on the initial Federal share if the company is profitable and nets considerable gains from technology developed under ATP." This proposal has not been adopted." (footnotes omitted)

[2830] United States' response to question 14, para. 30.

1424   DSR 2012:III

Agreement. The European Communities argues that "Access to ATP funding is explicitly limited by regulation to only those US companies that perform research into 'high risk, high pay-off, emerging and enabling technologies'". The ATP is therefore specific "to those US enterprises, industries, or group of industries that perform this type of research, including the US LCA industry". The European Communities also argues that the ATP statute specifies that the Program's emphasis is "on solving generic problems of specific industries, and on making those industries more competitive in world markets", and that these "specific industries" include the fields of "high-resolution information systems, advanced manufacturing, and advanced materials". Finally, the European Communities argues that the eight particular ATP projects at issue are limited to funding companies involved in: (i) manufacturing composite and metal structures and materials; (ii) designing, developing, and manufacturing electronics components; and (iii) improving logistics for manufacturing and supply chains. Thus, these ATP subsidies are specific because DOC explicitly limits access to this funding to certain enterprises.[2831]

7.1232 In its second written submission, the European Communities responds to the United States' argument that the ATP is not specific within the meaning of Article 2 of the SCM Agreement by reiterating two of the arguments set forth above: (i) that the ATP as a whole is specific within the meaning of Article 2.1(a) because of the fact that ATP funding is explicitly limited by regulation to "the group of US enterprises or industries that perform research into 'high risk, high pay-off, emerging and enabling technologies'"[2832]; and that (ii) "what is at issue in this dispute are the eight ATP projects in which Boeing participated, and an examination at the *project level* confirms that each of these projects was explicitly limited to a group of enterprises, and therefore each of these projects is *de jure* specific within the meaning of Article 2.1(a)".[2833] In its second written submission, the European Communities explains that it advances these two arguments as arguments in the alternative.[2834]

(ii) Arguments of the United States

7.1233 In its first written submission, the United States argues that the ATP is not specific within the meaning of Article 2 of the SCM Agreement because it provides funding for innovative, high risk technologies "across a wide range of industries and technology sectors"[2835], as reflected in the distribution of projects and funding across a range of sectors, the technologies funded, and the broad eligibility criteria.[2836]

[2831] European Communities' first written submission, para. 803.
[2832] European Communities' second written submission, paras. 520-527.
[2833] European Communities' second written submission, paras. 528-529.
[2834] European Communities' second written submission, para. 530.
[2835] United States' first written submission, para. 396.
[2836] United States' first written submission, paras. 397-405.

Report of the Panel

7.1234 In its second written submission, the United States reiterates that the ATP's focus on research into "high risk, high pay-off, emerging and enabling technologies" does not amount to a limitation to a "group of enterprises or industries" within the meaning of the SCM Agreement, because if it did, the SCM Agreement's specificity requirement would be meaningless.[2837]

(iii)   Evaluation by the Panel

7.1235 To be specific, a subsidy must be provided to a sufficiently limited "group" of enterprises or industries within the meaning of Article 2 of the SCM Agreement. Article 2 requires more than a simple demonstration that less than all of the enterprises or industries within the territory of a Member were eligible to receive the subsidy. In other words, it is not the case that any limitation whatsoever on access to a subsidy establishes specificity. Rather, it must be demonstrated that the subsidy is provided only to a *sufficiently limited* "group of enterprises or industries" in order to be specific within the meaning of Article 2. This interpretation is consistent with past WTO case law, and is also consistent with the understanding of both parties to this dispute.

7.1236 In *US – Upland Cotton,* the panel noted that beyond setting out the rather general requirement that the granting authority or its legislation explicitly limit access to the subsidy to certain enterprises, "Article 2 of the *SCM Agreement* does not speak with precision about when 'specificity' may be found".[2838] The panel in that case continued:

> "At some point that is not made precise in the text of the agreement, and which may modulate according to the particular circumstances of a given case, a subsidy would cease to be specific because it is *sufficiently* broadly available throughout an economy as not to benefit *a particular limited* group of producers of certain products. The plain words of Article 2.1 indicate that specificity is a general concept, and the breadth or narrowness of specificity is not susceptible to rigid quantitative definition. Whether a subsidy is specific can only be assessed on a case-by-case basis."[2839]

7.1237 The panel decision in *US – Upland Cotton* indicates that the specificity analysis turns on a qualitative assessment of the extent to which a subsidy is "*sufficiently* broadly available" throughout an economy, i.e. whether it benefits a "*particular*" limited group of enterprises or industries. The analysis suggests that there is some tipping point, which varies on a case-by-case basis, at which access to the subsidy in issue is no longer considered to be limited to "certain enterprises" but rather is "*sufficiently* broadly available" throughout an economy

---

[2837] United States' second written submission, paras. 119, 122.
[2838] Panel Report, *US – Upland Cotton*, para. 7.1139.
[2839] Panel Report, *US – Upland Cotton*, para. 7.1142 (emphasis added).

1426   DSR 2012:III

US - Large Civil Aircraft (2nd Complaint)

as to be non-specific. In other words, the relevant question is not whether access to the subsidy is limited in any way at all, but rather where it is *sufficiently* limited for the purpose of Article 2 of the SCM Agreement.

7.1238 We further note that neither of the parties in this case, nor any third party in this case, has questioned this interpretation of Article 2 of the SCM Agreement. The European Communities argues that:

> "The critical question in the present case, however, is whether ATP funding is specific to a group of industries or to a group of enterprises. The European Communities has demonstrated that ATP funding is limited to the group of industries or group of enterprises engaged in R&D related to 'high risk, high pay-off, emerging and enabling technologies.' That is, the common relation or purpose, or similarity, amongst this group of industries or group of enterprises is that they engage in a specific type of R&D. It is clear that ATP funding is ... available only for the sub-set of US-produced goods that can be considered 'high risk, high pay-off, emerging and enabling technologies.' This sub-set represents a *sufficiently limited* portion of the US economy.
>
> Thus, ATP is not a subsidy that is '*sufficiently broadly* available throughout {the US} economy {so} as not to benefit a particular limited group of producers of certain products,' and consequently, ATP is specific within the meaning of Article 2.1 of the SCM Agreement."[2840]

7.1239 Along the same lines, the United States refers to a "limitation on the group that is *restrictive enough* to make it 'specific'".[2841]

7.1240 In the light of the foregoing, we consider that the term "group" in Article 2 of the SCM Agreement means *a sufficiently limited group*. This is how we use the term "group" in our evaluation of the European Communities' arguments. As the complaining party, the European Communities bears the burden of demonstrating that the subsidies provided to Boeing under the ATP are specific within the meaning of Article 2. The European Communities advances three arguments. We address these in turn.

> *The ATP Rules refer to U.S. companies that perform research and development on "high risk, high pay-off, emerging and enabling technologies"*

7.1241 The European Communities emphasizes that according to the ATP Rules, the purpose of the Program is "to assist United States businesses to carry out *research and development on high risk, high pay-off, emerging and enabling*

[2840] European Communities' comments on United States' response to question 48, paras. 177-178.
[2841] United States' response to question 142, para. 123.

DSR 2012:III   1427

Report of the Panel

technologies".[2842] For the following reasons, we do not believe that U.S. enterprises or industries that perform research and development on "high risk, high pay-off, emerging and enabling technologies" constitute a sufficiently limited group of enterprises or industries within the meaning of Article 2 of the SCM Agreement.

7.1242 First, limiting funding to R&D into "high risk, high pay-off, emerging and enabling technologies" does not on its face appear to be a significant limitation to any group of enterprises or industries in the United States. Second, there is nothing in the relevant provision of the ATP Rules to suggest that this language operates as a significant limitation:

> "§ 295.1 Purpose.
>
> (a)   The purpose of the Advanced Technology Program (ATP) is to assist United States businesses to carry out research and development on high risk, high pay-off, emerging and enabling technologies. *These technologies are*:
>
> (1)   High risk, because *the technical challenges make success uncertain*;
>
> (2)   High pay-off, because when applied *they offer significant benefits to the U.S. economy*; and
>
> (3)   Emerging and enabling, because they offer *wide breadth of potential application and form an important technical basis for future commercial applications*." [2843]

7.1243 Along the same lines, other provisions of the ATP Rules suggest that this condition does not operate to limit R&D funding to a limited group of enterprises or industries. For example, section 295.6, which sets forth certain "eligibility criteria", provides that:

> "... The proposed technology must be *highly innovative*. The research must be *challenging*, with *high technical risk*. It must be aimed at *overcoming an important problem(s)* or exploiting a *promising opportunity*. The technical leverage of the technology must be adequately explained. The research must have a strong potential for advancing *the state of the art* and contributing significantly to *the U.S. scientific and technical knowledge base.*
> ..."[2844]

[2842] ATP Rules, Exhibit EC-534, §§ 295.1(a), 295.6.

[2843] *Ibid* (emphasis added).

[2844] *Ibid* (emphasis added).

7.1244 Third, the evidence before the Panel regarding the manner in which ATP funding has actually been expended further confirms that U.S. companies that perform research into "high risk, high pay-off, emerging and enabling technologies" are not a limited group of enterprises or industries:

- Since the programme began making project awards in 1990, it has made 768 project awards that extend across the fields of advanced materials and chemicals, biotechnology, electronics, computer hardware, and communications, information technology, and manufacturing.[2845]

- The 768 ATP projects include 168 in the field of advanced materials and chemicals, 190 in biotechnology, 167 pertaining to electronics, computer hardware, and communications, 156 in the information technology sector, and 87 pertaining to manufacturing of various types.[2846] Each of these sectors potentially comprises multiple industries and enterprises. For example, the manufacturing sector covers health care manufacturing such as digital radiology, photonics manufacturing, automobile manufacturing, and environmental technology manufacturing, among a host of other industries.

- The specific technologies that have resulted from ATP projects include, among others, animal and plant biotechnology, automobile manufacturing, bimolecular and biomimetic materials, computer hardware, diagnostic and therapeutic biotechnology, environmental technologies, imaging and image processing, intelligent control, marine biology, materials handling, nanotechnology, optics and photonics, and semiconductors.[2847]

- The ATP has disbursed more than $2.3 billion in funding since 1990.[2848] The total $2.3 billion of ATP funding from 1990 to 2004 has been similarly broadly distributed: $488 million has gone to projects in advanced materials and chemicals; $449 million to biotechnology; $576 million to electronics, computer hardware, and communications; $504 million to information technology; and $252 million to manufacturing.[2849]

7.1245 Fourth, we note that this language is found only in the ATP Rules. As noted above, the ATP statute states in more general terms that the ATP has the purpose:

[2845] ATP Awards Summary Data - Awards 475 (Technology Area by Year), Factsheet 3.B1, Sept. 2004, Exhibit US-151.

[2846] *Ibid.*

[2847] ATP Funded Technologies, Exhibit US-152.

[2848] Historical Statistics on Applications and Awards, Factsheet 3.A1 (Sept. 2004), Exhibit US-153.

[2849] ATP Awards Summary Data - Funding (Technology Area by Year), Factsheet 3.B2 (Sept. 2004), Exhibit US-168.

Report of the Panel

"... of assisting United States businesses in creating and applying the generic technology and research results necessary to-

(1)   commercialize significant new scientific discoveries and technologies rapidly; and

(2)   refine manufacturing technologies.

The Secretary, acting through the Director, shall assure that the Program focuses on improving the competitive position of the United States and its businesses, gives preference to discoveries and to technologies that have great economic potential, and *avoids providing undue advantage to specific companies. ...*"[2850]

7.1246 In sum, the evidence before us leads us to conclude that the reference to "high risk, high pay-off, emerging and enabling technologies" in the ATP Rules does not operate to limit subsidies granted under the ATP to a "group of enterprises or industries" within the meaning of Article 2 of the SCM Agreement.

The ATP statute refers to "solving generic problems of specific industries"

7.1247 The European Communities asserts that the ATP statute says that the Program's emphasis is "on solving generic problems of *specific industries*, and on making those industries more competitive in world markets".[2851] The European Communities also asserts, along the same lines, that the ATPA indicates that "these specific industries" include the fields of "high-resolution information systems, advanced manufacturing, and advanced materials".[2852]

7.1248 We believe that these statements are taken out of context. First, regarding the reference to "solving generic problems of specific industries", the provision of the ATP statute that European Communities relies on reads in relevant part:

"Under the Program established in subsection (a) of this section, and consistent with the mission and policies of the Institute, the Secretary, acting through the Director, and subject to subsections (c) and (d) of this section, may—

(1)   aid industry-led United States joint research and development ventures (hereafter in this section referred to as 'joint ventures') (which may also include universities and independent

---

[2850]   ATP Statute, Exhibit EC-532, § 278n(a) (emphasis added).
[2851]   ATP Statute, Exhibit EC-532, § 278n(b)(1)(B).
[2852]   ATPA, Exhibit EC-533, § 201(b)(1)(F).

1430   DSR 2012:III

research organizations), including those involving collaborative technology demonstration projects which develop and test prototype equipment and processes, through—

(A)   provision of organizational and technical advice; and

(B)   participation in such joint ventures by means of grants, cooperative agreements, or contracts, if the Secretary, acting through the Director, determines participation to be appropriate, which may include (i) partial start-up funding, (ii) provision of a minority share of the cost of such joint ventures for up to 5 years, and (iii) making available equipment, facilities, and personnel,

provided that *emphasis is placed* on areas where the Institute has scientific or technological expertise, *on solving generic problems* of specific industries, and on making those industries more competitive in world markets ..." (emphasis added)

7.1249 Reading this provision in full, it is clear that it does not limit ATP funding to "specific industries", within the meaning of Article 2 of the SCM Agreement or otherwise.

7.1250 Second, the ATPA does not list "high-resolution information systems, advanced manufacturing, and advanced materials" as the "specific industries" that are eligible to receive ATP funding. The provision that the European Communities cites makes clear that these are illustrative of the fields of research that ATP funds. Section 201(b)(1)(F) states:

"(F)   it is vital that industry within the United States attain a leadership role and capability in development, design, and manufacturing *in fields such as* high-resolution information systems, advanced manufacturing, and advanced materials".[2853]

The eight projects at issue are each limited to a group of enterprises or industries

7.1251 Finally, the European Communities argues, in the alternative, that *each of the eight projects* at issue was limited to a "group of enterprises or industries".

7.1252 In the Panel's view, specificity must generally be analysed at the level of the subsidy programme pursuant to which individual payments are provided (where the subsidy take the form of a payment, and where it is provided pursuant to a wider programme), and not at the level of each individual payment taken in isolation, absent one or more reasons as to why an analysis at the level of the entire programme is not appropriate. To take a simple example, assume that a

---

[2853] *Ibid.*

Report of the Panel

government provides a $100 grant to every enterprise in every industry in its territory, including company A. This would appear to be a textbook example of a subsidy that is not specific under Article 2 of the SCM Agreement. It would seem absurd to reason that the subsidy provide to company A is nonetheless specific under Article 2 because access to *that* subsidy, i.e. the *payment* to A taken in isolation, was limited to one company – i.e. to company A.

7.1253 The panel in *Japan – DRAMs* sought to avoid interpreting Article 2 of the SCM Agreement in such a way as to lead to this result:

> "... if an investigating authority were to focus on an *individual transaction*, and that transaction flowed from a *generally available support programme* whose normal operation would generally result in financial contributions on pre-determined terms (that are therefore not tailored to the recipient company), that individual transaction would not, in our view, become 'specific' in the meaning of Article 2.1 *simply because it was provided to a specific company*."[2854]

7.1254 Of course, the foregoing only applies where an individual payment is made pursuant to and flows from a broader, identifiable subsidy programme. To the extent that a financial contribution is not provided as part of any broader, identifiable subsidy programme, then specificity must necessarily be analysed at the level of the individual payments. In addition, as noted above, there may be one or more reasons as to why an analysis at the level of an entire programme is not appropriate. In this regard, the United States agrees that "it is not the case that specificity must always be examined at the highest level of aggregation of the activities of the granting authority" and that "it may be appropriate to analyze specificity at a lower level".[2855] The United States argues that this is a "fact-specific inquiry", and that "the complaining party must provide a reasoned basis for performing the analysis at that level".[2856] The European Communities seems to agree with these propositions.[2857]

7.1255 We have concluded above that the European Communities has failed to demonstrate that the ATP as a whole is specific under Article 2 of the SCM Agreement. Therefore, we consider the relevant question to be whether the

---

[2854] Panel Report, *Japan – DRAMs (Korea)*, para. 7.374 (emphasis added). In *Japan – DRAMs (Korea)*, the main issue with respect to Article 2 was whether it was appropriate to analyse certain debt restructuring transactions with Hynix at the level of those individual restructurings (in which case it was axiomatic that the subsidies were specific to Hynix), or rather at the level of the broader framework legislation. Korea argued that the broader framework legislation (the "CRPA") was the "relevant program" for the purposes of the Article 2 analysis (which, if correct, would have likely led to a finding that the subsidy provided to Hynix was not specific.) The same issue, involving the same transactions, was addressed by the panel in *EC – Countervailing Measures on DRAM Chips*.
[2855] United States' response to question 50, para. 143.
[2856] *Ibid.*
[2857] European Communities' comments on United States' response to question 50, para. 185.

European Communities has provided one or more reasons for examining specificity at the level of the individual projects at issue, rather than at the level of the entire ATP. Having carefully considered the evidence before us, we conclude that the European Communities has failed to identify any basis for doing so in the case of the ATP. We therefore conclude that, in the absence of any reasoned basis for conducting the specificity analysis at the level of the individual projects, the specificity analysis must be conducted at the level of the entire ATP. We recall that we have already rejected the European Communities' argument that the ATP as a whole is specific.

7.1256 In sum, we find that the European Communities has failed to demonstrate that the subsidies provided to Boeing under the ATP are specific within the meaning of Article 2 of the SCM Agreement.

(e) Conclusion

7.1257 **For these reasons, the Panel finds that the payments that DOC made to joint ventures / consortia in which Boeing participated through the Advanced Technology Program constitute subsidies within the meaning of Article 1 of the SCM Agreement. However, the Panel finds that the European Communities has not demonstrated that these subsidies are specific within the meaning of Article 2 of the SCM Agreement.**

5. *NASA/DOD intellectual property right waivers/transfers*

(a) Introduction

7.1258 The European Communities argues that NASA and DOD "transfer" to Boeing certain patent rights and data rights. The scope of the European Communities' claim is limited to these intellectual property rights over research performed *by Boeing* under its R&D contracts and agreements with NASA and DOD. The European Communities argues that this "transfer" of intellectual property rights is a subsidy within the meaning of Article 1 of the SCM Agreement, and is specific within the meaning of Article 2 of the SCM Agreement. The European Communities is unable to estimate the value of this alleged subsidy, but estimates that the value of 5 of the patents "transferred" to Boeing is $726 million over the period 1997-2022 (i.e. the last year when any of the five valued patents are in force).[2858]

7.1259 The United States argues that Boeing's retention of certain intellectual property rights under NASA and DOD R&D contracts and agreements is not a subsidy within the meaning of Article 1 of the SCM Agreement, and is not specific within the meaning of Article 2 of the SCM Agreement.

[2858] Amount of Subsidies to Boeing's LCA Division , Exhibit EC-17; Estimates of Benefits from Patent Waivers/Transfers to Boeing/MD, Exhibit EC-20.

Report of the Panel

(b) The measures at issue

7.1260 The European Communities' panel request[2859] states that NASA provides a subsidy to Boeing by enabling Boeing "to exploit the results" of research programmes "by means including but not limited to the foregoing or waiving of valuable patent rights, the granting of limited exclusive rights data ("LERD") or otherwise exclusive or early access to data, trade secrets and other knowledge resulting from government funded research", by "granting the US LCA industry exclusive or early access to data, trade secrets, and other knowledge resulting from government funded research", and by "allowing the US LCA industry to exploit the results of government funded research, including, but not limited to, the foregoing or waiving of valuable patent rights or rights in data as such".

7.1261 With respect to DOD, the European Communities' panel request[2860] states in similar terms that DOD provides a subsidy to Boeing by enabling Boeing "to exploit the results" of DOD-funded research, "by means including but not limited to the foregoing or waiving of valuable patent rights, and the granting of exclusive or early access to data, trade secrets and other knowledge resulting from government funded research", and "by allowing the US LCA industry to exploit the results of government funded research, including, but not limited to, the foregoing or waiving of valuable patent rights or rights in data as such".

7.1262 The European Communities' panel request indicates that NASA and DOD accord this treatment to Boeing pursuant to the following laws, regulations, and other measures (some of which are specific to NASA, some of which are specific to DOD, some of which concern patents, and some of which concern data rights):

- 35 U.S.C. §§ 200 *et seq.*;
- Memorandum to the Heads of Executive Departments and Agencies: Government Patent Policy, Pub. Papers 248 (18 February 1983);
- Executive Order 12591 (10 April 1987);
- 14 CFR §§ 1245.100 *et seq.*;
- 14 CFR §§ 1274.911 - 1274.914;
- 48 CFR §§ 27.300 *et seq.*;
- 48 CFR §§ 27.400 *et seq.*;
- 48 CFR §§ 227.7100 *et seq.*
- 48 CFR §§ 227.303 *et seq.*;

[2859] WT/DS353/2, items 2(a), 2(f), 2(g), pp. 6, 8, and 9.
[2860] WT/DS353/2, items 3(a), 3(d), pp. 9 and 11.

1434

DSR 2012:III

US - Large Civil Aircraft (2nd Complaint)

- *Requirements for Documentation, Approval, and Dissemination of NASA Scientific and Technical Information*, section 4.5.7.1 (NPG 2200.2A)

7.1263 In response to a Panel question, the European Communities clarifies that it is challenging all patents transferred / waived to Boeing under any and all R&D contracts and agreements that Boeing entered into with NASA and DOD, including but not limited to those entered into under the specific NASA and DOD R&D programmes listed in the European Communities' panel request. According to the European Communities:

"... from the outset of this dispute, the European Communities has been challenging as a specific subsidy the provision of *all* patents to Boeing by NASA and DOD pursuant to *all* NASA and DOD contracts, *even if they derive from programmes that are not being specifically challenged.*"[2861]

7.1264 With respect to the allocation of "*data rights*", the scope of the European Communities' claim is limited to the treatment accorded under NASA R&D contracts and agreements with Boeing containing "Limited Exclusive Rights Data" (LERD) clauses, and to DOD R&D contracts and agreements with Boeing under which DOD acquired only "limited", "government-purpose" rights in the data (as opposed to "unlimited rights data"). The European Communities has explained that it is not otherwise challenging the allocation of data rights under NASA or DOD R&D contracts and agreements with Boeing:

"To be clear, with respect to NASA, the European Communities is challenging as a subsidy the protection of government-funded data rights on behalf of Boeing only pursuant to the Limited Exclusive Rights Data ('LERD') clauses of the ACT, HSR, AST, and R&T Base programs.[2862] The United States acknowledges that, with respect to LERD, 'Boeing and other contractors negotiated to limit the *otherwise unlimited rights that the U.S. government would normally have* in specifically identified data developed in the course of the contracted research.'[2863] Consequently, NASA provides 'goods other than general infrastructure' within the meaning of Article 1.1(a)(1)(iii), as data rights are a type of intellectual property right that NASA would ordinarily own, but which NASA has provided to Boeing through LERD provisions.

[2861] European Communities' response to question 216, para. 386 (emphasis added).

[2862] (*footnote original*) First Written Submission by the European Communities, para. 838.

[2863] (*footnote original*) First Written Submission by the European Communities, para. 352 (emphasis added).

DSR 2012:III

1435

Report of the Panel

> With respect to provision of data rights by DOD, the European Communities is challenging the practice of providing data rights to Boeing in instances where the Government has funded, at least in part, the R&D resulting in those rights.[2864] During the term of the data rights, the Government 'may not use, or authorize other persons to use, technical data ... for commercial purposes,' while the rights of Boeing to this data is unlimited.[2865]" [2866]

7.1265 With respect to "trade secrets", which appears to be a subset of data rights, the scope of the European Communities' claim is limited to NASA.[2867]

(c)   Arguments of the European Communities

7.1266 In its first written submission, the European Communities argues that the transfers of valuable intellectual property rights to Boeing, including patents, rights to trade secrets, and rights to data, by NASA and DOD, constitute financial contributions within the meaning of Article 1.1(a)(1) of the SCM Agreement. According to the European Communities, such transfers constitute a provision of goods within the meaning of Article 1.1(a)(1)(iii). In this regard, the European Communities explains that the term "good" is defined as "{p}roperty or possessions", that patents and the other rights at issue are generally considered intellectual *property* and are covered as such by the TRIPS Agreement, and that United States law explicitly states that "patents shall have the attributes of personal *property*". [2868] The European Communities argues, in the alternative, that these intellectual property right transfers constitute the "foregoing of government revenue" that is "otherwise due" within the meaning of Article 1.1(a)(1)(ii), as entities making use of a government's intellectual property rights "would ordinarily need to pay license fees for such use". For example, when an entity seeks to use technology patented by NASA or DOD, it must ordinarily negotiate a license requiring, *inter alia*, payment of royalties.[2869]

7.1267 In its second written submission, the European Communities responds to the United States' argument that NASA and DOD patent and data rights transfers/waivers do not constitute a financial contribution because under U.S. patent and copyright law, the rights retained by the contractor and its employees "belong to them in the first place".[2870] With respect to patent rights, the European Communities argues that, under the applicable law and regulations, the

---

[2864] (*footnote original*) First Written Submission by the European Communities, para. 839.

[2865] (*footnote original*) First Written Submission by the European Communities, para. 839, citing 48 C.F.R. § 227.7103-5(b)(4), Exhibit EC-590; First Written Submission of the United States, para. 353.

[2866] European Communities' second written submission, paras. 546-547.

[2857] European Communities' first written submission, para. 833.

[2858] European Communities' first written submission, para. 841.

[2859] European Communities' first written submission, para. 842.

[2870] United States' first written submission, paras. 324, 355-356.

1436

DSR 2012:III

patent rights are neither "guaranteed to the contractor and its employees," nor did they ever "belong{} to them in the first place". The European Communities reviews the policies and practice of both NASA and DOD in order to demonstrate that, absent a waiver, the patent owner is the U.S. Government, not the contractor.[2871] The European Communities argues that the same is true of the data rights it challenges. In this regard, the European Communities clarifies that it is only challenging as a subsidy the protection of government-funded data rights on behalf of Boeing pursuant to the Limited Exclusive Rights Data ("LERD") clauses in the case of NASA, and DOD's practice of providing data rights to Boeing in instances where the government has funded, at least in part, the R&D resulting in those rights.[2872]

7.1268 Regarding the existence of a benefit within the meaning of Article 1.1(b) of the SCM Agreement, the European Communities argues that NASA/DOD "intellectual property right waivers/transfers" confer "benefits" on Boeing's LCA division. The European Communities argues that: (i) the financial contributions "relate, at least in part, to the production of all Boeing LCA"; (ii) the financial contributions "provide Boeing's LCA division with advantages on non-market terms"; (iii) "Boeing is not required to pay anything in return" for these intellectual property right waivers/transfers; (iv) Boeing has received valuable "knowledge and experience" from the aeronautics R&D, and (v) these are rights that Boeing "would not be able to obtain on the market without purchasing or licensing them for fair market value, and therefore represent "free" property rights for Boeing".[2873]

7.1269 In its second written submission, the European Communities responds to the United States' arguments regarding benefit. First, the European Communities argues that a WTO Member cannot avoid all disciplines of the SCM Agreement by simply asserting without any support that every aspect of that contract was market-based and negotiated at arms-length.[2874] Second, the intellectual property provision/waiver policies, as adapted for large businesses like Boeing, were implemented in order to "improve the productivity of the U.S. economy, create new jobs, and improve the position of the U.S. in world trade", at least according to the President of the United States; they were *not* implemented because the government "was having a hard time finding contractors to take the Government's money".[2875] Third, the European Communities argues that the allocation of intellectual property rights under NASA/DOD R&D contracts and agreements deviates from normal commercial practice because "{g}enerally, when private corporations fund other entities to carry out research on their

---

[2871] European Communities' second written submission, paras. 538-541.
[2872] European Communities' second written submission, paras. 546-547.
[2873] European Communities' first written submission, paras. 849-851.
[2874] European Communities' second written submission, paras. 549-550, 552.
[2875] European Communities' second written submission, paras. 551, 559.

Report of the Panel

behalf, they retain full rights to any intellectual property created".[2876] In support of that assertion, the European Communities refers to an article on intellectual property rights and stem cell research[2877] and a Declaration of Regina Dieu, Legal Counsel in the Airbus SAS Industrial procurement Legal Department, which states that when Airbus funds and R&D project it exclusively and solely owns any and all Intellectual Property generated or acquired in connection with and during the performance of the R&D project.[2878] In addition, the European Communities refers[2879] to an article on collaborative research[2880], a WIPO Training Course[2881] and a contract concluded by Boeing with the National Institute for Aviation Research at Wichita State University.[2882]

7.1270 Regarding specificity, the European Communities argues that NASA and DOD intellectual property right waivers/transfers are specific within the meaning of Article 2.1(a) of the SCM Agreement. The European Communities argues that the legislative authority for NASA's R&D programmes (pursuant to which the intellectual property is created) derives from the Space Act, which limits those programmes to those industries that can satisfy the objectives of that Act. Accordingly, NASA's intellectual property right transfers, which all derive from NASA-funded R&D, are specific to the enterprises that participate in aeronautics and space-related R&D. Likewise, DOD's intellectual property right transfers all derive from DOD-funded R&D, which is specific to the group of defense-related industries capable of conducting these specialized activities.[2883] The European Communities also argues that the intellectual property rights transfers are de facto specific under Article 2.1(c) of the SCM Agreement, on the basis of Boeing's share of NASA and DOD R&D contracts.[2884]

7.1271 In its second written submission, the European Communities responds to the United States' rebuttal arguments on specificity by reasoning that it is not relevant if other U.S. government agencies follow the same practices as NASA and DOD with regard to the allocation of intellectual property rights. The European Communities argues that "{i}t is important to recall that Article 2.1(a) provides two options (as reflected by use of the word "or") by which the complainant may demonstrate *de jure* specificity – i.e. the complainant can show *either* that "the granting authority ... explicitly limits access to a subsidy to

---

[2876] European Communities' second written submission, para. 553.

[2877] Sean M. O'Connor, "Intellectual Property Rights and Stem Cell Research: Who Owns the Medical Breakthroughs?" 39 New Eng. L. Rev. 665 (2005), Exhibit EC-1212, p. 669.

[2878] Declaration of Regina Dieu, 8 November 2007, Exhibit EC-1178.

[2879] European Communities' second written submission, paras. 553-556.

[2880] Rochelle Cooper Dreyfuss, "Collaborative Research: Conflicts on Authorship, Ownership and Accountability", 53 Vand. L. Rev. 1161 (2000), Exhibit EC-1228, p. 1212.

[2881] WIPO-MOST, "Intermediate Training Course on Practical Intellectual Property Issues in Business", 13 November 2003, Exhibit-EC 1229, pp. 42-43.

[2882] Contract Between Boeing Commercial Airplane Group Wichita Division and Wichita State University, Contract No. 000051728, 4 November 2002, Exhibit EC-1231.

[2883] European Communities' first written submission, paras. 852-853.

[2884] European Communities' first written submission, paras. 854-855.

1438   DSR 2012:III

certain enterprises" *or* that "the legislation pursuant to which the granting authority operates, explicitly limits access to a subsidy to certain enterprises". The European Communities explains that the "second option does not, however, refer to the "legislation pursuant to which the *subsidy programme* operates," but it refers instead to the "legislation pursuant to which the *granting authority* operates". The European Communities reiterates that "the granting authorities at issue here are NASA and DOD, and they operate pursuant to their own sets of laws and regulations, such as the NASA Space Act".[2885]

(d)   Arguments of the United States

7.1272 The United States argues that NASA and DOD patent and data rights transfers/waivers do not constitute a financial contribution because under U.S. patent and copyright law, the rights retained by the contractor and its employees "belong to them in the first place".[2886] Thus, NASA and DOD do not provide any "contribution" to Boeing, financial or otherwise. Rather, it is Boeing that transfers certain intellectual property rights to NASA and DOD under the R&D contracts and agreements at issue when it grants the government a royalty-free license to use any inventions and data produced under the contract or agreement. Regarding patent rights, the United States argues that the European Communities' allegation that DOD and NASA made a financial contribution by "transferring" or "waiving" of patent rights fails on several counts. At the most basic, "it is the inventor that holds the patent right in the first place", and the only possible "transfer of rights" as a result of the contract begins with the inventor and proceeds to the government, and not *vice versa*. In addition, the European Communities is mistaken in asserting that the assignment of patent rights under a government contract is the provision of a good under Article 1.1(a)(1)(iii) of the SCM Agreement or the foregoing of government revenue otherwise due under Article 1.1(a)(1)(ii) of the SCM Agreement.[2887] Regarding data rights, the United States argues along the same lines that there cannot be a "provision" for purposes of Article 1.1(a)(1)(iii) when the government confirms the data generator's rights and provides nothing additional, and as DOD and NASA merely allowed Boeing to retain the intellectual property rights to which it was entitled under general copyright law, the agencies did not "forego any revenue" within the meaning of Article 1.1(a)(1)(ii).[2888]

7.1273 The United States reiterates this argument in its second written submission, arguing that "the EC assertion that the Government conveyed intellectual property rights to Boeing reverses what actually occurred – that Boeing conveyed intellectual property rights to the Government".[2889] The United

---

[2885]   European Communities' second written submission, para. 577.
[2886]   United States' first written submission, paras. 324, 355-356.
[2887]   United States' first written submission, para. 317.
[2888]   United States' first written submission, para. 356.
[2889]   United States' second written submission, paras. 100-105.

DSR 2012:III

Report of the Panel

States reiterates that intellectual property rights are not goods within the meaning of Article 1.1(a)(1)(iii) of the SCM Agreement, such that even if there were a "transfer" of intellectual property rights from NASA/DOD to Boeing, such a "transfer" would not constitute a provision of "goods" within the meaning of that provision.[2890]

7.1274 Regarding the existence of a benefit, the United States argues in its first written submission that even if the Panel were to conclude that there is a financial contribution, "the treatment identified by the EC does not confer a benefit". The United States argues that the value of the patent rights is incorporated in the exchange of value that the government and contractor agree upon in negotiating the initial contract.[2891] The United States further argues that "even if considered in isolation, the patent clauses in U.S. government contracts indicate a rough balance between the parties".[2892] The United States also takes issue with the European Communities' attempt to derive benefit under Article 1.1(b) of the SCM Agreement based on an *ex post facto* consideration of the value of the intellectual property rights under certain contracts and agreements.[2893] In its second written submission, the United States argues that the European Communities has provided no support for its assertion that the allocation of intellectual property rights under NASA and DOD R&D contracts and agreements is contrary to what market participants would have negotiated at arms-length according to relevant market benchmarks.[2894]

7.1275 Regarding specificity, the United States argues that NASA/DOD intellectual property rights "transfers" are not specific within the meaning of Article 2 of the SCM Agreement. According to the United States, the treatment of which the European Communities complains – i.e. the retention by NASA contractors of their patent rights – arises under the NASA procurement regulations and the patent waiver regulations, which in turn look to the policy established in the Presidential Memorandum of 18 February 1983 and Executive Order 12591. The United States explains that those authorities "apply generally to all federal departments and agencies", and "the substantive treatment" in question is not specific to aeronautics and space R&D but rather is "the same as the treatment of all contractors under U.S. government R&D contracts". In the United States' view, nothing in Article 2.1(a) or (b) suggests that "the use of agency-specific procedures detracts from the general availability of the substantive treatment it affords". The United States argues that this point applies with even greater force to DOD.[2895] The United States also responds to the European Communities' arguments regarding de facto specificity, arguing that the European Communities has failed to demonstrate that Boeing obtained a

---

[2890] United States' first written submission, para. 331; United States' response to question 127.
[2891] United States' first written submission, paras. 326-328.
[2892] United States' first written submission, paras. 326-329.
[2893] United States' first written submission, paras. 330-331.
[2894] United States' second written submission, paras. 106-107.
[2895] United States' first written submission, paras. 335-336.

1440   DSR 2012:III

disproportionate share of R&D funding from NASA and DOD.[2896] In its second written submission, the United States reiterates that "the law and the 1983 Presidential Memorandum make access to this treatment available to *all* government R&D contractors, without limitation to a specific enterprise or industry or group of enterprises or industries".[2897]

(e) Evaluation by the Panel

(i) Patent rights

7.1276 The Panel does not consider it necessary to resolve the issue of whether the allocation of patent rights under NASA/DOD R&D contracts and agreements constitutes a financial contribution that confers a benefit within the meaning of Article 1 of the SCM Agreement, because in the Panel's view it is clear that the allocation of patent rights under NASA and DOD contracts and agreements is not specific to a "group of enterprises or industries" within the meaning of Article 2 of the SCM Agreement. The reason is that the allocation of patent rights is uniform under all U.S. government R&D contracts, agreements, and grants, in respect of all U.S. government departments and agencies, for all enterprises in all sectors. In all cases, the contractor / partner / recipient owns any inventions (i.e. patent rights) that it conceives in the course of performing research funded by the U.S. Government; however the U.S. Government receives a royalty-free, "government use/purpose" license to use the subject invention.

7.1277 Prior to 1980, the United States had a general policy of taking all rights to patents over inventions produced by contractors under federally-funded R&D contracts (and then granting nonexclusive licenses to any applicant, including the contractor, that wished to use the subject invention).[2898] In 1980, the U.S. Government changed its policy governing the allocation of patent rights under federally-funded R&D contracts, and started granting government contractors ownership of patents over any invention that they produced with federal funding under R&D contracts (with the government receiving a limited "government use" license to use the subject invention without having to pay the Contractor any royalties.) Originally, the new policy applied only to non-profit organizations and small business firms. The policy was subsequently extended so as to accord the same treatment to encompass all government contractors, regardless of size and profit/non-profit status.

7.1278 The policy was implemented through a number of different legal instruments. For present purposes, five different legal instruments are relevant:

[2896] United States' first written submission, paras. 338-339.

[2897] United States' second written submission, para. 108.

[2898] European Communities' first written submission, para. 806; United States' first written submission, para. 314.

Report of the Panel

(a)   the so-called **Bayh-Dole Act**, which implemented the policy in 1980, and which is codified in 35 U.S.C. §§ 200-212 (entitled "Patent Rights in Inventions Made with Federal Assistance")[2899];

(b)   a 1983 **Presidential Memorandum** to the heads of executive departments and agencies (entitled "Government Patent Policy") that extended the scope of the policy to encompass all government contractors, regardless of size and profit/non-profit status[2900];

(c)   a 1987 **Executive Order** (entitled "Facilitating access to science and technology") into which the terms of the 1983 Presidential Memorandum were eventually incorporated[2901];

(d)   the corresponding **general federal regulations** implementing the Bayh-Dole Act, the 1983 Presidential Memorandum, and the 1987 Executive Order, which are found at 48 C.F.R. §§ 27.300-27.306 (entitled "Patent Rights Under Government Contracts")[2902];

(e)   the **NASA-specific regulations** (entitled "Patents and Other Intellectual Property Rights", with Subpart 1 entitled "Patent Waiver Regulations") embodied in 14 C.F.R. §§ 1245 implementing this policy[2903].

7.1279 The rationale behind the rules governing the allocation of patent rights in U.S. government-funded R&D contracts and agreements is set out in the **Bayh-Dole Act** (which applies only to non-profit organizations and small business firms) under the heading "Policy and Objective" (§ 200):

"It is the policy and objective of the Congress to use the patent system to promote the utilization of inventions arising from federally supported research or development; to encourage maximum participation of small business firms in federally supported research and development efforts; to promote collaboration between commercial concerns and nonprofit organizations, including universities; to ensure that inventions made by nonprofit organizations and small business firms are used in a manner to promote free competition and enterprise without unduly encumbering future research and discovery; to promote the commercialization and public availability of inventions made in the United States by United States industry and labor; to ensure that the Government obtains sufficient rights in federally supported inventions to meet the needs of the Government and protect the public against nonuse or unreasonable use of

---

[2899] Exhibit EC-558.
[2900] Exhibit EC-560.
[2901] Exhibit EC-561.
[2902] Exhibit EC-559.
[2903] Exhibit EC-572.

1442   DSR 2012:III

inventions; and to minimize the costs of administering policies in this area."

7.1280 The 1983 **Presidential Memorandum** that extended Bayh-Dole treatment to all contractors regardless of size and profit/non-profit status was accompanied by a "fact sheet" which explained that:

"Inventions developed under Government support constitute a valuable national resource. With appropriate incentives, many of these inventions will be further developed commercially by the private sector. The new products and processes that result will improve the productivity of the U.S. economy, create new jobs, and improve the position of the U.S. in world trade. The policy established by the Memorandum is designed to provide such incentives."

7.1281 The 1987 **Executive Order** entitled "Facilitating access to science and technology" reads in relevant part:

"Section 1. Transfer of Federally Funded Technology.

(a) The head of each Executive department and agency, to the extent permitted by law, shall encourage and facilitate collaboration among Federal laboratories, State and local governments, universities, and the private sector, particularly small business, in order to assist in the transfer of technology to the marketplace.

(b) The head of each Executive department and agency shall, within overall funding allocations and to the extent permitted by law:

...

(4) promote the commercialization, in accord with my Memorandum to the Heads of Executive Departments and Agencies of February 18, 1983, of patentable results of federally funded research by granting to all contractors, regardless of size, the title to patents made in whole or in part with Federal funds, in exchange for royalty-free use by or on behalf of the government."

7.1282 The general and NASA-specific implementing regulations (i.e. (d) and (e) above) articulate the rationale behind the allocation of patent rights in similar terms.

Report of the Panel

7.1283 The rules governing the allocation of patent rights under U.S. government-funded R&D contracts and agreements have remained essentially unchanged since the passage of the Bayh-Dole Act.[2904]

7.1284 The U.S. laws and regulations referred to above grant government contractors the option to retain title, with some limitations, to inventions that arise from a funding agreement with the U.S. Government.[2905] Contractors receive patent rights covering technologies "conceived or first actually reduced to practice in the performance of work" under "any contract, grant, or cooperative agreement entered into between any Federal agency ... and any contractor for the performance of experimental, developmental, or research work funded in whole or in part by the Federal Government".[2906]

7.1285 These patent rights authorize the contractor to prevent all other entities from exploiting the technologies claimed by the patent, and allow the company to license the technology to others in exchange for compensation. Specifically, a U.S. patent accords the rights to "exclude others from making, using, offering for sale, or selling" the invention in the United States or "importing" the invention into the United States, for a limited period of time (i.e. currently a minimum of 20 years from date of application).[2907] In addition, as the owner of the patent, the contractor also has the right to assign, or transfer by succession, the patent and to conclude licensing contracts with third parties. However, there is a limitation on the contractor providing an exclusive license to third parties: "any products embodying the subject invention or produced through the use of the subject invention {must} be manufactured substantially in the United States".[2908]

7.1286 The U.S. Government receives "a nonexclusive, nontransferable, irrevocable paid-up license to practice or have practiced for or on behalf of the United States any subject invention throughout the world".[2909] The U.S. Government patent rights take the form of a license to use the invention for any "government use," which includes use of the patent by any government contractor engaged in "government business". This license does not extend to any right to develop patented technology for commercial sale.[2910] The U.S. Government also obtains certain "march-in" rights, a provision that empowers

---

[2904] United States' first written submission, para. 319.

[2905] European Communities' first written submission, para. 810 (citing 35 U.S.C. § 202(a), Exhibit EC-558, and 48 C.F.R. § 27.302, Exhibit EC-559).

[2906] European Communities' first written submission, para. 811 (citing 35 U.S.C. § 201(e) and (b), Exhibit EC-558).

[2907] European Communities' first written submission, para. 812 (citing 35 U.S.C. § 154(a)(2), Exhibit EC-562, and 35 U.S.C. § 271(a), Exhibit EC-563).

[2908] European Communities' first written submission, para. 815 (citing 35 U.S.C. § 204, Exhibit EC-558).

[2909] European Communities' first written submission, para. 813 (citing 35 U.S.C. § 202(c)(4), Exhibit EC-558, and 48 C.F.R. § 27.302(c), Exhibit EC-559).

[2910] European Communities' first written submission, para. 813.

1444

DSR 2012:III

US - Large Civil Aircraft (2nd Complaint)

the Federal agency to compel the contractor, in certain limited circumstances, to grant a license to applicants on terms that are reasonable under the circumstances, or to grant the license itself. No U.S. government department or agency has ever exercised these march-in rights for any patent under any contract.[2911]

7.1287 The Space Act provides that any invention made pursuant to a contract with NASA "shall be the exclusive property of the United States, and if such invention is patentable a patent therefore shall be issued to the United States" unless waived by NASA.[2912] To comply with President Reagan's 1983 **Executive Memorandum** referred to above, NASA formulated regulations under which it generally waives its patent rights to large companies, such as Boeing, for inventions developed pursuant to NASA-funded research.[2913] Pursuant to these **NASA-specific regulations**, NASA waives such rights in order to, in part, "promote early utilization, expeditious development and continued availability of {the} new technology for commercial purposes ...".[2914] The NASA patent waiver regulations permit requests for waivers at two points in time: (i) in advance of the invention, as to any and all of the inventions that may be made under a contract; and (ii) after the reporting of an invention, subsequent to the invention being made.[2915]

7.1288 When NASA waives patent rights, it formally executes this waiver through an "instrument of waiver", which states, for example, as follows:

> "{t}he Administrator waives the property rights of the United States Government in the United States of America and in the following countries: ..., and hereby conveys to the waiver recipient the entire right, title, and interest in and to each invention which may be conceived or first actually reduced to practice in the performance of work under the above-identified contract ...."[2916]

7.1289 The regulations provide a general presumption that a timely waiver request will be granted to U.S. companies "unless the {NASA Inventions and Contributions} Board finds that the interests of the United States will be better

---

[2911] European Communities' first written submission, para. 814.

[2912] 42 U.S.C. § 2457(a), Exhibit EC-571.

[2913] 14 C.F.R. §§ 1245.100 et. seq., § 1245.103, Exhibit EC-572. The regulations do not apply to small business firms or non-profit organizations, which are governed by the U.S. patent law provisions on government transfer of patents (35 U.S.C. §§ 200-212, Exhibit EC-558). See also, 14 C.F.R. § 1245.101, Exhibit EC-572.

[2914] 14 C.F.R. § 1245.103(a), Exhibit EC-572. As with patents transferred pursuant to the U.S. patent laws, the patent rights waived by NASA pursuant to their regulations are not unlimited, as NASA retains the right to use the patented technology for itself, or to issue compulsory licenses through "march-in" rights.

[2915] 14 C.F.R. §§ 1245.104, 1245.105, Exhibit EC-572.

[2916] NASA, Instrument of Waiver (Domestic and Foreign Rights), Structures and Materials Technology for Aerospace Vehicles, Exhibit EC-1227.

DSR 2012:III

1445

Report of the Panel

served by restricting or eliminating all or part of the rights of the contractor" in certain enumerated situations.[2917] The regulations address the situations in which patents might not be waived, including instances when "the contractor is not located in the United States or does not have a place of business in the United States".[2918] According to a study by the National Bureau of Economic Research, by the early 1980s patent "waivers were essentially automatically granted" by NASA.[2919]

7.1290 According to the United States, the patent rights clauses that NASA and DOD use in their R&D contracts and agreements are "standardized for both agencies".[2920] NASA maintains different clauses for large and medium contractors, as opposed to small businesses, universities, and other research institutions, but the clauses are standard as to each group.[2921] The NASA procurement regulations require the insertion of one of two different clauses, 1852.227-70 (New technology) and 1852.227-71 (Requests for waiver of rights to inventions), into NASA contracts with medium and large contractors.[2922] These are among the numerous standardized clauses incorporated by reference in NASA R&D contracts and agreements.[2923]

7.1291 Unlike NASA, DOD does not have its own detailed regulations regarding patent transfers to large companies. Instead, DOD generally relies on the relevant portion of the Bayh-Dole Act and the 1983 Executive Memorandum expanding the policy to large business firms[2924], as well as the corresponding general regulations implementing these instruments.[2925] The relevant provision of the Bayh-Dole Act is 35 U.S.C. § 202(a), as expanded to large businesses by the 1983 Executive Memorandum, which provides that a contractor "may ... elect to retain title to any {government-funded} invention", unless DOD decides

---

[2917] 14 C.F.R. § 1245.104(b), Exhibit EC-572. See also, § 1245.105(b)(1), Exhibit EC-572.

[2918] 14 C.F.R. § 1245.104(b)(1), Exhibit EC-572.

[2919] National Bureau of Economic Research, Evidence from Patents and Patent Citations on the Impact of NASA and other Federal Labs on Commercial Innovation, May 1997, Exhibit EC-574, p. 8.

[2920] United States' first written submission, para. 328.

[2921] United States' first written submission, para. 328, footnote 436.

[2922] United States' first written submission, para. 322.

[2923] See e.g. NASA Contract NAS1-18889 with Boeing Commercial Airplanes for Research and Development in Advance Technology Composite Aircraft Structures, 12 May 1989, Exhibit EC-329, p. 10, incorporating NASA/FAR Supplement clause number 18-52.227-70 entitled "New Technology (APR 1988)".

[2924] The U.S. patent law provisions regarding "patent rights in inventions made with federal assistance", codified at 35 U.S.C. §§ 200-212, apply to any "Federal agency". 35 U.S.C. § 201(a), Exhibit EC-558. "Federal agency" is defined as "any executive agency as defined in section 105 of title 5, and the military departments as defined by section 102 of title 5". *Ibid.* In turn, Section 102 of title 5 provides that the military departments consist of the Army, Navy, and Air Force. 5 U.S.C. § 102, Exhibit EC-581.

[2925] 48 C.F.R. §§ 27.300-27.306, Exhibit EC-559. These provisions, which are part of the Federal Acquisition Regulation ("FAR") System, apply to "all executive agencies," which is defined to include DOD. 48 C.F.R. § 1.101 (purpose of FAR), Exhibit EC-582; 48 C.F.R. § 2.101 (defining "executive agency"), Exhibit EC-583.

1446 DSR 2012:III

US - Large Civil Aircraft (2nd Complaint)

to remove this possibility under certain circumstances.[2926] The DOD could opt to remove the choice of "election", for example, "in exceptional circumstances when it is determined by the agency that restriction or elimination of the right to retain title to any subject invention will better promote the policy and objectives of this chapter".[2927]

7.1292 As noted above, according to the United States, the patent rights clauses that NASA and DOD use in their R&D contracts and agreements are "standardized for both agencies".[2928] According to the United States, DOD uses standardized clauses in all of the contracts it signs, and "equivalent clauses" in agreements.[2929] This aspect of U.S. law, along with the terms of the 1983 Executive Memorandum, is generally implemented by DOD through incorporating certain contract clauses into R&D contracts. In the case of R&D contracts with medium or large business, DOD uses standard clause 52.227-12 (Patent Rights – Retention by the Contractor (Long Form).[2930] As with the patent provisions of NASA contracts, these are among the numerous standardized clauses incorporated by reference into the contracts.[2931]

7.1293 In the Panel's view, NASA's agency-specific regulations for implementing this U.S. Government-wide policy cannot, for the purposes of Article 2 of the SCM Agreement, be analysed in isolation from the broader policy and legal framework that they implement. There are a number of problems with the European Communities' approach of restricting the specificity analysis to the measure through which NASA implements this U.S. Government-wide policy. First, the approach to specificity advocated by the European Communities would lead to anomalous results. For instance, if a granting authority were to introduce a broadly available subsidy through a single piece of legislation, on the European Communities' approach this subsidy would not be specific within the meaning of Article 2. However, if the granting authority were to introduce exactly the same broadly available subsidy, but were to extend it to each industry by passing separate pieces of legislation, this would result in a finding of specificity if the complainant defined the measure under challenge as only one of the pieces of legislation. As the United States points out in its submissions, the European Communities is perhaps conflating the "issue of an element of a claim (whether a measure is a subsidy) and the evidence (what needs to be shown to establish the claim)".[2932] The approach advocated by the

---

[2926] 35 U.S.C. §§ 200-212, "Patent Rights in Inventions Made with Federal Assistance", § 202(a), Exhibit EC-558.

[2927] 35 U.S.C. § 202(a), Exhibit EC-558.

[2928] United States' first written submission, para. 328.

[2929] United States' first written submission, para. 338.

[2930] United States' first written submission, para. 321.

[2931] See e.g. Air Force Contract F33615-91-C-5716 with Boeing regarding Design and Manufacturing of Low Cost Composite Fuselage, 24 July 1991, Exhibit EC-507, p. 27 (incorporating by reference FAR contract clause 18-52.227-12 entitled "Patent Rights – Retention by the Contractor (Long Form) (JUN 1989)".)

[2932] United States' comments on European Communities' response to question 34, para. 116.

DSR 2012:III

1447

Report of the Panel

European Communities means that the specificity analysis is dependent upon how the complaining party chooses to define the measure it is challenging.

7.1294 For these reasons, the Panel finds that, assuming *arguendo*[2933] that the allocation of patent rights under NASA/DOD R&D contracts and agreements with Boeing involves a subsidy within the meaning of Article 1 of the SCM Agreement, the European Communities has failed to demonstrate that any such subsidy is specific within the meaning of Article 2 of the SCM Agreement.

(ii) Data rights and trade secrets

7.1295 The Panel will now address the European Communities' argument that the allocation of data rights (including trade secrets) constitutes a specific subsidy. We will begin with an explanation of the types of "data rights" challenged by the European Communities in this dispute, namely, "Limited Exclusive Rights Data" and "limited" government rights data treatment. We then address the question of whether the European Communities has provided any evidence of such treatment outside of the context of the eight NASA R&D

[2933] In *China – Publications and Audiovisual Products*, the Appellate Body offered the following guidance on the use of *arguendo* assumptions by panels:

"We observe that reliance upon an assumption *arguendo* is a legal technique that an adjudicator may use in order to enhance simplicity and efficiency in decision-making. Although panels and the Appellate Body may choose to employ this technique in particular circumstances, it may not always provide a solid foundation upon which to rest legal conclusions. Use of the technique may detract from a clear enunciation of the relevant WTO law and create difficulties for implementation. Recourse to this technique may also be problematic for certain types of legal issues, for example, issues that go to the jurisdiction of a panel or preliminary questions on which the substance of a subsequent analysis depends."

Appellate Body Report, *China – Publications and Audiovisual Products*, para. 213.

We have relied upon the *arguendo* assumption that the allocation of patent rights is a subsidy within the meaning of Article 1 of the SCM Agreement and proceeded directly to the issue of specificity under Article 2 of the SCM Agreement for the following reasons. First, the question of whether the allocation of patent rights under NASA/DOD R&D contracts and agreements with Boeing constitutes a financial contribution, whether in the form of a provision of goods within the meaning of Article 1.1(a)(1)(iii) of the SCM Agreement or otherwise, is a potentially difficult one; in contrast, the question of whether the alleged subsidy is specific is more straightforward. (On the question of whether the allocation of patent rights under NASA/DOD R&D contracts and agreements with Boeing involves a financial contribution in the form of a "provision" of "goods" or otherwise, see European Communities' first written submission, paras. 841-842; United States' first written submission, paras. 317-325 and 331; European Communities' second written submission, paras. 536-548; United States' response to question 127, and the European Communities' related comments; Australia's oral statement, paras. 28-34; Canada's written submission, paras. 3-9.) In other words, we have relied upon this *arguendo* assumption to "enhance simplicity and efficiency" in our decision-making. Second, having found that the alleged subsidy is not specific under Article 2, our reliance upon this *arguendo* assumption creates no issues or difficulties from the point of view of the "implementation" of DSB recommendations and rulings. Third, the question of whether or not the allocation of patent rights constitutes a subsidy does not "go to the jurisdiction" of the Panel. Finally, the substance of our analysis under Article 2 does not depend on whether the measures at issue are properly characterized as subsidies within the meaning of Article 1.

1448

DSR 2012:III

US - Large Civil Aircraft (2nd Complaint)

programmes and 23 DOD RDT&E programmes that it has challenged. We then address the question of whether the LERD and "limited" government data rights treatment accorded to Boeing under the challenged programmes can be analysed and found to constitute a separate, additional financial contribution in the light of our already having found that the payments and access to facilities provided to Boeing under the same set of contracts and agreements constitute subsidies on the basis of, *inter alia*, the LERD and "limited" government rights data treatment being challenged.

7.1296 As a general rule, contractors own all technical data (i.e. data rights) produced with U.S. government funding, and may use these for their own commercial purposes. As with patents, the U.S. Government receives a royalty-free "license"[2934] to use the technical and scientific data produced with government funding in the performance of the research. A DOD publication cited by both parties in this case explains:

> "'IP deliverables' refers to the contractual obligation to deliver IP that has a predetermined content and format. The Government may own the delivered physical medium on which the IP resides, but generally it will not own the IP rights. 'License rights' refers to the Government's ability to use, reproduce, modify, and release the delivered IP. ... As a general rule under Government contracts, the contractor-developer is allowed to retain ownership of the technical data and computer software it developed; and the Government receives only a license to use that technical data and computer software. DOD does not 'own' the technical data and computer software included in deliverables, even if the Department paid for 100 percent of the development costs. The scope of the license depends on the nature of the technical data and computer software, the relative source of funding for development, and the negotiations between the parties."[2935]

7.1297 The 1987 **Executive Order**, referred to above, appears to articulate the rationale behind the rules governing the allocation of data rights under U.S. government contracts and agreements. As noted above in the context of the discussion of patent rights, the 1983 Presidential Memorandum that extended the scope of the Bayh-Dole Act policy to encompass all U.S. government

---

[2934] See e.g. United States' first written submission, para. 216, explaining that under its R&D contracts, NASA receives "an irrevocable paid-up license to use the data and any inventions developed under the contract"; United States' first written submission, Section VI.C, entitled "The Allocation of *License Rights* to Data Under NASA and DoD Contracts is Not a Financial Contribution, Does Not Convey a Benefit, and is Not Specific".

[2935] Office of the Under Secretary of Defense for Acquisition, Technology and Logistics, Intellectual Property: Navigating Through Commercial Waters, Issues and Solutions When Negotiating Intellectual Property With Commercial Companies, 15 October 2001 ("DOD Intellectual Property Guide"), Exhibit EC-557, pp. 1-3 and 1-4.

DSR 2012:III

1449

Report of the Panel

contractors, regardless of size and profit/non-profit status, was eventually incorporated into law through a 1987 Executive Order entitled "Facilitating access to science and technology". The scope of this Executive Order was not limited to patent rights. It also established a similar policy in respect of data rights. It reads in relevant part:

"Section 1. Transfer of Federally Funded Technology.

(a) The head of each Executive department and agency, to the extent permitted by law, shall encourage and facilitate collaboration among Federal laboratories, State and local governments, universities, and the private sector, particularly small business, in order to assist in the transfer of technology to the marketplace.

(b) The head of each Executive department and agency shall, within overall funding allocations and to the extent permitted by law:

...

(6) cooperate, under policy guidance provided by the Office of Federal Procurement Policy, with the heads of other affected departments and agencies in the development of a uniform policy permitting Federal contractors to retain rights to software, engineering drawings, and other technical data generated by Federal grants and contracts, in exchange for royalty-free use by or on behalf of the government."

7.1298 "Data rights" apply to so-called "technical data". "Technical data" means "recorded information (regardless of the form or method of the recording) of a scientific or technical nature (including computer databases and computer software documentation)".[2936]

7.1299 The provisions governing data rights are set out across different provisions of the *Federal Acquisition Regulation* and other U.S. laws, regulations, and policies.[2937] Section 52.227-14(b) ("Rights in Data—General – Allocation of Rights") of the *Federal Acquisition Regulation* states that "the Government shall have unlimited rights in— Data first produced in the performance of this contract ...", and that "{t}he Contractor shall have the right to ... Use, release to others, reproduce, distribute, or publish any data first

---

[2936] See e.g. 48 C.F.R. § 52.227-14(a) ("Rights in Data—General"), Exhibit US-103.
[2937] In its Panel Request (WT/DS353/2), the European Communities refers to "48 CFR §§ 27.400 *et seq*". In their submissions, the parties have referred to numerous other provisions of United States laws, regulations and policies concerning data rights.

1450   DSR 2012:III

US - Large Civil Aircraft (2nd Complaint)

produced or specifically used by the Contractor in the performance of this contract ...".

7.1300 Generally, any data delivered under an R&D contract funded solely by the government is "unlimited rights data". This means that the license acquired by the U.S. Government gives it "unlimited rights" to use the technical data "as it sees fit, both inside and outside of the government", i.e. to "use, disclose, reproduce, prepare derivative works, distribute copies to the public, and perform publicly and display publicly, in any manner and for any purpose, and to have or permit others to do so".[2938]

7.1301 Where the contractor "contributes resources"[2939] toward a project, the U.S. Government may agree to forego or curtail some of the rights that it would otherwise enjoy under its "unlimited rights" license. In this sense, under the general acquisition regulations "the source of funds" used to produce the data dictates, in the first instance, the scope of the license that the U.S. Government receives with respect to data rights. The U.S. Government may acquire "limited rights" in data that embody trade secrets or are commercial or financial and confidential or privileged, "to the extent that such data pertain to items, components or processes developed at private expense". Thus, "limited rights" data refers to data developed at "private expense", i.e. not with government funding under a contract. The government may explicitly contract for the delivery of such proprietary data, although it would acquire only "limited rights" in such data. Where the government acquires "limited rights" data, it may use the data for its own internal purposes, it may not disseminate the data outside the government without the express consent of the contractors.

7.1302 In certain NASA contracts (apparently under the ACT, HSR, AST, and R&T Base Programs), NASA used a special "limited exclusive rights data" ("LERD") clause. The clauses limited the otherwise "unlimited rights" in data that the U.S. Government would normally have in the data developed in the course of the contracted research.[2940] The LERD clauses granted U.S. companies exclusive rights to exploit critical technologies developed under certain NASA contracts for at least five years from the date the data was reported. Technologies were categorized as "sensitive" and protected through LERD restrictions if they were considered to affect the competitive position of U.S. industry.[2941] The NASA contracts that contained LERD clauses involved "joint funding situation{s}", i.e. contractors were "contributing a significant amount of their own resources to contract research efforts".

7.1303 With respect to so-called "trade secret" protection, where contractors produce technical data in the performance of a contract with NASA which

---

[2938] United States' first written submission, para. 350.

[2939] United States' first written submission, para. 351.

[2940] European Communities' second written submission, para. 546 (agreeing with the explanation found at United States' first written submission, para. 352.)

[2941] See above, footnote 2545.

DSR 2012:III

1451

Report of the Panel

qualifies as trade secret information, it may be entitled to "trade secret" protection if it is the product of "cost-sharing".[2942] NASA's regulations provide that "{i}n the performance of a contract, grant, or cooperative arrangement, usually which is cost-shared[2943], the "contractor, grantee, or partner may produce technical data which qualifies as trade secret information". If such data is properly marked by its originator, NASA agrees to protect it from disclosure as long as the data remains trade secret information. In addition, the Space Act provides that if NASA employees develop information that constitutes a trade secret through joint research with a contractor, such research may be protected for a period of up to five years.[2944] A number of NASA's Space Act Agreements with Boeing (in which Boeing contributed some of its own resources to the projects) contained provisions "to maintain any data that was generated in confidence for at least 2 to 5 years".[2945]

7.1304 With respect to DOD, when valuable technical data is developed through research that is "jointly-funded" by DOD and the contractor, the U.S. Government generally "may release or disclose" the data outside the Government only for "government purposes", i.e. "government purpose rights". The U.S. Government may, however, "use, modify, release, reproduce, perform, display or disclose" such jointly-funded data "within the government without restriction". The term for these "government purpose rights" is negotiable, with five years being the baseline, subject to negotiation between the parties. DOD regulations state that "{l}onger periods should be negotiated when a five-year period does not provide sufficient time to apply the data for commercial purposes". During the term of the "government purpose rights", the U.S. Government "may not use, or authorize other persons to use, technical data marked with government purpose rights legends for commercial purposes". The contractor, however, can use this data for its own purposes during this time, or license it to others.[2946]

7.1305 In this case, the European Communities has not provided any evidence of such treatment outside of the context of the eight NASA R&D programmes and 23 DOD R&D project elements that it has challenged. This raises the question of whether the LERD and "limited" government data rights treatment accorded to Boeing under the challenged programmes can be analysed and found to

---

[2942] United States' first written submission, para. 343.

[2943] The European Communities reads this language as providing for trade secret protection even where there is *no* cost sharing; according to the European Communities, the words "usually which is cost shared" applies only to the third item listed, i.e. "cooperative agreements", and not to the first two items, i.e. "contract, grant". See European Communities' second written submission, para. 543.

[2944] European Communities' first written submission, paras. 835-836 (quoting Requirements for Documentation, Approval, and Dissemination of NASA Scientific and Technical Information (STI), NPR 2200.2A, 12 August 2004, Exhibit EC-587, section 4.5.7.1.2.)

[2945] See above, footnote 2545.

[2946] European Communities' first written submission, para. 819 (citing 48 C.F.R. §§ 227.7100 - 227.7103-17, Exhibit EC-590, § 227.7103-4(a)(1)). See also, United States' first written submission, para. 353.

1452

DSR 2012:III

constitute a separate, additional financial contribution, given the Panel's findings that the payments and access to facilities provided to Boeing under the same set of contracts and agreements constitute subsidies by virtue of, *inter alia*, the LERD and "limited" government rights data treatment being challenged.

7.1306 The Panel has put several questions to the European Communities on this issue, in an attempt to understand how it could be that the allocation of intellectual property rights under NASA/DOD R&D contracts could constitute a separate, additional financial contribution given the fact that the European Communities has already challenged the payments made to Boeing under those same contracts and agreements. Question 28 to the European Communities reads:

> "The European Communities argues that the 'direct R&D funding' and support that Boeing allegedly received under the NASA and DOD R&D programmes at issue constitute subsidies, on the basis that Boeing 'is not required to pay anything in return' for those financial contributions. According to the European Communities, because Boeing is 'not required to pay anything in return' for this funding and support, the entirety of those financial contributions to Boeing's LCA division can be considered to confer benefits. The European Communities also claims that Boeing's acquisition/retention of rights over the intellectual property that it develops under these NASA/DOD R&D programs constitutes an additional subsidy. Does this not amount to double-counting the subsidies provided to Boeing under the NASA/DOD R&D programmes at issue?"

7.1307 The Panel sought further explanation from the European Communities. Questions 218 and 219 to the European Communities read:

> "218. At para. 103 of its Comments on EC RPQ1, the United States argues that '{f}or patents issued as a result of work done under contracts related to the eight NASA programs and 23 DOD RDT&E PEs listed in its first written submission, the EC's treatment of patent rights leads to double counting because it treats the value of the research work and the value of any patent rights that result as separate from one another when, in fact, they arise from the same transaction.' How does the European Communities respond?
>
> 219. Assume that a government and a firm enter into a contract, pursuant to which the government agrees to pay the contractor $100 to carry out certain R&D, and pursuant to which the government further agrees to waive any resulting intellectual property rights in favour of the contractor. Assume that the value of the resulting intellectual property rights is estimated to be $50.

Report of the Panel

> Under what circumstances could a panel conclude that there were two financial contributions, and that the total amount of the subsidy was $150?"

7.1308 The Panel also posed a question to Australia with a view to clarifying its position on this issue. Question 13 to Australia reads:

> "At para. 24 of its Oral Statement, Australia states that it agrees with the European Communities that the treatment of the fruit of the R&D under the *SCM Agreement* 'may be separate to the issue of funding' by the United States government to Boeing to conduct R&D. At para. 29 of its Oral Statement, Australia states that the treatment of intellectual property rights under a government contract 'would not necessarily constitute an additional financial contribution (over and above the government funding)'. At para. 32 of its Oral Statement, Australia argues that '{t}he financial contribution would be limited to the assistance provided by way of government funding' of R&D activities. At para. 33 of its Oral Statement, Australia states that '{i}t may be the case that the treatment of the intellectual property rights under a particular government contract could be considered an additional financial contribution'.
>
> (a)   Is it Australia's position that the treatment of intellectual property rights under a government R&D contract could constitute an 'additional' financial contribution 'over and above' the government funding provided to the contractor pursuant to the contract, or is it Australia's position that the financial contribution 'would be limited to the assistance provided by way of government funding'?
>
> (b)   If Australia's position is that the treatment of intellectual property rights under a government R&D contract could in certain circumstances constitute an 'additional' financial contribution 'over and above' the government funding provided to the contractor, please explain what those circumstances are. For example, assume that a government and a firm enter into a contract, pursuant to which the government agrees to pay the contractor $100 to carry out certain R&D, and further agrees to waive any resulting intellectual property rights in favour of the contractor. Assume that the value of the resulting intellectual property rights is estimated to be $50. Under what circumstances could a panel conclude that there were two financial contributions, and that the total amount of the subsidy was $150?"

7.1309 As is clear from the general thrust of our questions to the European Communities and Australia, we have considerable difficulty accepting the

1454   DSR 2012:III

premise that the NASA/DOD payments and access to facilities, equipment and employees provided to Boeing under R&D contracts and agreements can be treated as one financial contribution, and that Boeing's retention of certain intellectual property rights over the results of the research that it performs pursuant to those same contracts could be treated as a separate, additional financial contribution. It seems to us to be self-evident that this kind of analysis involves double-counting. Put somewhat differently, this kind of analysis involves an attempt to treat the allocation of intellectual property rights under NASA/DOD R&D contracts and agreements both as a term upon which other financial contributions (i.e. the payments and access to facilities, equipment and employees) are provided for the purpose of showing that those other financial contributions confer a benefit, and then as a separate, additional financial contribution. In order to avoid any misunderstanding, we emphasize that we are not confronted with a situation in which a government makes payments to an enterprise to perform R&D and, in addition, transfers intellectual property rights to that enterprise that have arisen out research that was performed with different funding; rather, we are dealing here with a situation in which the intellectual property at issue arises from the R&D that the enterprise receiving the funding used the government funding to perform.

7.1310 Having carefully reviewed the European Communities' and Australia's responses to our questions, we find no clear explanation of how the payments and access to facilities, equipment and employees provided to Boeing under R&D contracts and agreements could be treated as one financial contribution, and how Boeing's retention of certain intellectual property rights over the results of the research that it performs pursuant to those same contracts could be treated as a separate, additional financial contribution.

7.1311 Accordingly, we find that the European Communities has failed to demonstrate that the allocation of data rights under NASA/DOD R&D contracts and agreements constitutes a separate, additional financial contribution under Article 1.1(a)(1) of the SCM Agreement.

(f) Conclusion

7.1312 **For these reasons, the Panel finds that the European Communities has not demonstrated that the allocation of intellectual property rights under NASA/DOD R&D contracts and agreements with Boeing constitutes a specific subsidy within the meaning of Articles 1 and 2 of the SCM Agreement.**

6. *NASA/DOD Independent Research & Development (IR&D) and Bid & Proposal (B&P) reimbursements*

(a) Introduction

7.1313 The European Communities argues that both NASA and DOD reimburse Boeing for its own independent LCA-related R&D ("IR&D") that is not related to any specific contract, as well as for R&D undertaken by Boeing in connection

Report of the Panel

with bidding on NASA/DOD R&D contracts (bid and proposal costs, or "B&P"). The European Communities argues that NASA/DOD IR&D/B&P reimbursements are subsidies within the meaning of Article 1 of the SCM Agreement, and are specific within the meaning of Article 2 of the SCM Agreement. The European Communities estimates that NASA/DOD provided $5.9 billion in IR&D/B&P reimbursements to Boeing over the period 1991-2006, and argues that $3.1 billion of that total should be treated as a subsidy to Boeing's LCA division.[2947]

7.1314 The United States argues that NASA/DOD IR&D/B&P reimbursements to Boeing are not a subsidy within the meaning of Article 1 of the SCM Agreement, and are not specific within the meaning of Article 2 of the SCM Agreement. In addition, the United States argues that the European Communities has overestimated the amount of any subsidy. In this regard, the United States points out that the European Communities' estimate of the amount of the subsidy assumes that 100 per cent of the IR&D performed by Boeing and reimbursed by NASA and DOD through cost-shared R&D contracts with IDS was LCA-related.

(b)   The measures at issue

7.1315 The European Communities' panel request[2948] states that NASA and DOD subsidize Boeing by "providing NASA Independent Research & Development, and Bid & Proposal Reimbursements". The European Communities' panel request indicates that NASA and DOD accord this treatment to Boeing pursuant to the following laws, regulations, and other measures (some of which are specific to NASA, some of which are specific to DOD):

- 14 CFR § 1274.204(g);
- 10 U.S.C. § 2372;
- 48 CFR § 31.205-18;
- 48 CFR § 231.205-18;
- 48 CFR §§ 9904.420 *et seq.*;
- *Department of Defense Directive Regarding IR&D, Number 3204.1* (10 May 1999);
- *DOD Appropriations Acts*

7.1316 Through the IR&D/B&P programme, as elaborated through federal statutes and regulations[2949], NASA and DOD pay aerospace and defense

---

[2947] NASA/DOD IR&D/B&P Subsidies to Boeing LCA Division, Exhibit EC-24, p. 1.

[2948] WT/DS353/2, items 2(c) and 3(a)(ii), pp. 8 and 10.

[2949] Independent Research and Development and Bid and Proposal Costs: Payments to Contractors, 10 U.S.C. § 2372, Exhibit EC-594; Independent Research and Development and Bid and Proposal Costs: Payments to Contractors, 10 U.S.C. § 2372 (version in effect from FY 1993-FY 1994), Exhibit EC-595; Independent Research and Development, 10 U.S.C. § 2372 (version in effect FY 1991-FY

1456   DSR 2012:III

contractors, including Boeing, for their incurred independent research and development expenditures and bid and proposal costs.[2950] IR&D expenditures consist of money spent on: (i) basic research, (ii) applied research, (iii) development, and (iv) systems and other concept formulation studies.[2951] B&P costs are defined as costs incurred in preparing, submitting, and supporting bids and proposals (whether or not solicited) on potential government or non-government contracts.[2952] These payments are made under certain government R&D contracts ("cost-based" procurement contracts), although the IR&D and B&P payments are not related to the underlying contract.[2953] Rather, these expenses are treated as reimbursements of ordinary indirect "costs" (e.g. overhead expenses). Primary control of IR&D activities rests with the contractors, who are free to determine both the amount and focus of their IR&D activities.[2954] Federal law requires that IR&D regulations "may not include provisions that would infringe on the independence of a contractor to choose which technologies to pursue in its independent research and development program".[2955] Contractors maintain rights to the intellectual property developed as a result of their independent research and development, and such rights do not include any government interest.[2956]

7.1317 The *Defense Federal Acquisition Regulation* imposes various limitations with respect to the allowability of DOD IR&D/B&P costs for major contractors like Boeing.[2957] Among other things, IR&D/B&P costs for major contractors are

---

1992), Exhibit EC-596; Independent Research and Development and Bid and Proposal Cost Federal Acquisition Rule, 48 C.F.R. § 31.205-18, Exhibit EC-597; Independent Research and Development and Bid and Proposal Cost Defense Acquisition Rule, 48 C.F.R. § 231.205-18, Exhibit EC-598.

[2950] The statutory authority for this funding derives from the NASA Appropriations Acts, Exhibit EC-285, and the DOD Appropriations Acts, Exhibit EC-403.

[2951] 48 C.F.R. § 31.205-18, Exhibit EC-597, § 31.205-18(a) (defining "independent research and development (IR&D)"); Defense Contract Audit Agency Contract Audit Manual, DCAAM 7640.1, Chapter 7, 23 February 2006, Exhibit EC-599, para. 7-1501.

[2952] 48 C.F.R. § 31.205-18, Exhibit EC-597, § 31.205-18(a) (defining "bid and proposal (B&P) costs"); Defense Contract Audit Agency Contract Audit Manual, DCAAM 7640.1, Chapter 7, 23 February 2006, Exhibit EC-599, para. 7-1501.

[2953] See CRA International, The United States Independent Research & Development (IR&D) and Bid & Proposal (B&P) Reimbursement Program and Its Benefits to The Boeing Company, December 2006, Exhibit EC-5, pp. 3-4, 11-13.

[2954] DOD Independent Research & Development, Program Report, May 2002, Exhibit EC-602, p. 1.

[2955] Independent Research and Development and Bid and Proposal Costs: Payments to Contractors, 10 U.S.C. § 2372, Exhibit EC-594, para. (f).

[2956] Michael E. Davey and Dahlia Stein, Congressional Research Service Report for Congress, DOD's Independent Research and Development Program: Changes and Issues, 17 December 1993, Exhibit EC-604, p. 20.

[2957] "Major contractor" means "any contractor whose covered segments allocated a total of more than $11,000,000 in IR&D/B&P costs to covered contracts during the preceding fiscal year". Independent Research and Development and Bid and Proposal Cost Defense Acquisition Rule, 48 C.F.R. § 231.205-18 (a)(iii), Exhibit EC-598. "Covered contract" in that provision means "a DOD prime contract {or subcontract} for an amount exceeding the simplified acquisition threshold, except for a fixed-price contract without cost incentives". *Ibid.*, at (a)(i). "Covered segment" means "a product division of the contractor that allocated more than $1,100,000 in independent research and

Report of the Panel

limited to those for projects that are of "potential interest" to DOD.[2958] By law, DOD considers that activities intended to "{s}trengthen{} the ... technology base of the United States" and "{e}nhance the industrial competitiveness of the United States" to be R&D activities that are of "potential interest".[2959]

7.1318 Under the Cost Accounting Standards that govern the reimbursement of IR&D/B&P costs, which are elaborated further below, IR&D/B&P expenses must be allocated among business segments based on the beneficial or causal relationship between the IR&D cost and those segments. If a cost has a beneficial relationship to multiple business segments, it will be allocated proportionately to all. In such case, the U.S. Government only reimburses the portion of the total costs.[2960]

(c) Arguments of the European Communities

7.1319 Regarding the existence of a financial contribution, the European Communities argues in its first written submission that "IR&D and B&P reimbursements directly transfer funds from NASA and DOD to Boeing. These transfers constitute financial contributions within the meaning of Article 1.1(a)(1)(i) of the *SCM Agreement*".[2961] According to the European Communities, these reimbursements are "outright grants".[2962] In its second written submission, the European Communities attempts to rebut the United States' argument that NASA/DOD IR&D/B&P reimbursements fall outside of the scope of Article 1.1(a)(1) because they are elements of the price paid to Boeing pursuant to R&D contracts that are "purchases of services". The European Communities argues, among other things, that "'just because government contractors may account for IR&D reimbursement as "part of the purchase price of a good or service," and the US Government approves of this practice, does not mean that they are, in fact, part of the purchase price of a good or service". In the European Communities' view, IR&D/B&P reimbursements are paying Boeing for the same type of activity, regardless of whether they are "tacked onto" a contract that is purchasing goods or services.[2963]

---

development and bid and proposal (IR&D/B&P) costs to covered contracts during the preceding fiscal year". *Ibid.*, para. (a)(ii).

[2958] Independent Research and Development and Bid and Proposal Cost Defense Acquisition Rule, 48 C.F.R. § 231.205-18, Exhibit EC-598, para. (c)(iii).

[2959] Independent Research and Development and Bid and Proposal Costs: Payments to Contractors, 10 U.S.C. § 2372, Exhibit EC-594, at (g); Independent Research and Development and Bid and Proposal Cost Defense Acquisition Rule, 48 C.F.R. § 231.205-18, Exhibit EC-598, at (c)(iii)(B); Department of Defense Directive Regarding IR&D, Number 3204.1, 10 May 1999, Exhibit EC-600, at para. 4.1; Defense Contract Audit Agency Contract Audit Manual, DCAAM 7640.1, Chapter 7, 23 February 2006, Exhibit EC-599, section 7-1503.

[2960] Cost Accounting Standard 420, 48 C.F.R. § 9904.420, Exhibit US-1287, subparagraph (e).

[2961] European Communities' first written submission, para. 875.

[2962] European Communities' first written submission, para. 880.

[2963] European Communities' second written submission, paras. 589-592.

1458   DSR 2012:III

US - Large Civil Aircraft (2nd Complaint)

7.1320 Regarding the existence of a benefit within the meaning of Article 1.1(b) of the SCM Agreement, the European Communities argues that "NASA and DOD IR&D/B&P Program subsidies" confer "benefits" on Boeing's LCA division. The European Communities argues that: (i) the financial contributions "relate, at least in part, to the production of all Boeing LCA"; (ii) the financial contributions "provide Boeing's LCA division with advantages on non-market terms"; (iii) "Boeing is not required to pay anything in return" for this IR&D/B&P Program funding; (iv) IR&D/B&P reimbursements are "outright grants that reimburse Boeing for IR&D and B&P expenses it has already incurred related to improving, developing, and producing its entire line of LCA products", and thus essentially represent "free" money for Boeing"; and (v) it is "axiomatic that such reimbursements are not available on the market".[2964]

7.1321 In its second written submission, the European Communities responds to the United States' arguments regarding the existence of a benefit.[2965] The European Communities emphasizes that the kinds of R&D costs that may be reimbursed through IR&D/B&P include costs related to R&D projects that "enhance the industrial competitiveness of the United States" or "strengthen the technology base of the United States". According to the European Communities, it "is clear that an entity operating pursuant to market considerations would *not* agree, and would certainly *not* actively seek out, to reimburse independently-incurred costs of companies because those costs '{e}nhance the industrial competitiveness of the United States' or '{s}trengthen{} the ... technology base of the United States'". The European Communities argues that this "is particularly true given the global nature of markets for technology, where the position of the United States relative to other countries makes no difference to a company that can seek out technology anywhere in the world". The European Communities explains that when Boeing identifies its own suppliers, it selects them based on the technology, capabilities, and price that they offer, *not* because they are located inside or outside the United States, and *not* because purchasing goods or services from those suppliers could make them more competitive relative to other suppliers. In the European Communities' view, reimbursements of a company's internal costs on the bases that those costs "{e}nhance the industrial competitiveness of the United States" or "{s}trengthen{} the ... technology base of the United States" are completely foreign to market transactions in which adequate remuneration has been negotiated.

7.1322 The European Communities also responds to the United States' argument that the applicable IR&D/B&P cost accounting requirements require Boeing and other government contractors with multiple business segments to allocate the costs of IR&D/B&P projects that are beneficial to multiple segments on a *pro rata* basis across those segments, such that the government does not reimburse the contactor for the portion allocated to its commercial segments. The European

---

[2964] European Communities' first written submission, paras. 878-880.
[2965] European Communities' second written submission, paras. 594-614.

DSR 2012:III

1459

Report of the Panel

Communities argues that: (i) this does not necessarily exclude the possibility that IR&D/B&P expenses that Boeing initially considered to only have military relevance (and therefore allocated entirely to IDS contracts with DOD and NASA) could turn out to have unexpected benefits, in later years, for Boeing's LCA division; and (ii) the Panel cannot be sure that Boeing actually allocates its IR&D/B&P costs in this manner.[2966]

7.1323 The European Communities submits that NASA/DOD IR&D/B&P reimbursements are specific within the meaning of Article 2 of the SCM Agreement. The European Communities argues that IR&D/B&P reimbursements are allowed only for those enterprises in the research-based "defense and aerospace industries" that enter into contracts with NASA and DOD, and are capable of conducting specified activities: (i) basic research, (ii) applied research, (iii) development, and (iv) systems and other concept formulation studies.[2967] In addition, with respect to DOD, "major contractors" are explicitly limited to receiving IR&D/B&P reimbursements on certain projects, namely those that are "of potential interest to DOD".[2968] With respect to NASA, only entities that support NASA's mission may enter into contracts with NASA, and, consequently, be reimbursed for IR&D/B&P expenses.[2969] The European Communities argues that NASA/DOD IR&D/B&P reimbursements are also de facto specific, because in practice a wide range of government contractors are not eligible to receive NASA or DOD IR&D/B&P reimbursements. In this regard, the European Communities asserts that Boeing and a few other aerospace and defense contractors have received a predominant and disproportionate share of IR&D/B&P reimbursements.[2970] In its second written submission, the European Communities responds to the United States' rebuttal arguments on specificity by reasoning that it is not relevant if other U.S. government agencies follow the same practices regarding IR&D/B&P reimbursements. The European Communities argues that it "is simply not in dispute that the "granting authorities" at issue, with respect to the challenge of IR&D/B&P reimbursements, are NASA and DOD", and that the United States does not dispute that if a contractor does *not* receive contracts from NASA or from DOD, they will *not* receive IR&D/B&P reimbursements from NASA or DOD. The European Communities states that the "granting authority" is "not the entirety of the United States Government", thus, the extent to which other "granting authorities" within the United States follow similar, or different, practices, is irrelevant to an analysis of specificity for the subsidies provided by the granting authorities of NASA and DOD.[2971]

[2966] European Communities' second written submission, paras. 608-609.
[2967] European Communities' first written submission, para. 881.
[2968] European Communities' first written submission, para. 883.
[2969] European Communities' first written submission, para. 884.
[2970] European Communities' first written submission, paras. 886-889.
[2971] European Communities' second written submission, para. 617. See also, paras. 618-619.

1460

DSR 2012:III

(d) Arguments of the United States

7.1324 In its first written submission, the United States argues that NASA/DOD IR&D/B&P reimbursements are not "grants". Rather, they are part of the price paid for purchases of goods or services pursuant to government contracts. To the extent that they are reimbursed through a government contract for services, such reimbursements fall outside of the scope of Article 1.1(a)(1) of the SCM Agreement because they are simply part of the price paid to Boeing pursuant to R&D procurement contracts that are "purchases of services".[2972]

7.1325 The United States argues that the European Communities has failed to demonstrate that IR&D/B&P reimbursements provide a benefit to Boeing's LCA division. The United States' principal argument, as developed in its second written submission, oral statements, and responses to questions, is that the applicable IR&D/B&P cost accounting requirements require Boeing and other government contractors with multiple business segments to allocate the costs of IR&D/B&P projects that are beneficial to multiple segments on a pro rata basis across the segments, such that the government does not reimburse the contactor for the portion allocated to its commercial segments.

7.1326 Regarding specificity, the United States argues that the IR&D and B&P regulations place no limitation on the industries or enterprises that may claim IR&D or B&P as an overhead cost allocable to cost-based contracts. The only requirements for specific reimbursement are that the company have a cost-based contract with a U.S. government agency, and that the company has in fact incurred expenses for research and development or bid and proposal activities that are not required in the performance of any other contract and that they are allocable, reasonable, and not otherwise unallowable.[2973] The United States further argues that even if IR&D and B&P reimbursements were restricted to "defense and aerospace industries", this is too broad a category of industries to be characterized as a "group of enterprises or industries" within the meaning of Article 2[2974], and that Boeing has not received a disproportionate share of IR&D/B&P reimbursements.[2975]

7.1327 In its second written submission, the United States reiterates that "the treatment of IR&D costs is not limited to particular industries, because 48 C.F.R. § 31.205-18 (which the EC recognizes as 'IR&D/B&P Federal Acquisition Rule') requires *all* government agencies to include IR&D/B&P costs in the acquisition price on cost-based contracts with *all* contractors".[2976] The United States argues that Article 2.1(a) defines an alleged subsidy as specific only if the granting authority or the legislation under which it operates "limits access to a subsidy to certain enterprises". With regard to IR&D and B&P, the "legislation

---

[2972] United States' first written submission, para. 284.
[2973] United States' first written submission, para. 304.
[2974] United States' first written submission, paras. 306-307.
[2975] United States' first written submission, paras. 308-309.
[2976] United States' second written submission, para. 89.

Report of the Panel

pursuant to which the granting authority operates" for purposes of Article 2.1(a) is, as the European Communities acknowledges, 48 C.F.R. § 31.205-18. This provision is part of Chapter 1 of Title 48 of the Code of Federal Regulations, which sets out the Federal Acquisition Regulations ("FAR") applicable to all U.S. agencies. Thus, it applies "to all acquisitions, by all agencies, with all contractors", and does not limit access to a specific enterprise or industry or group of enterprises or industries. The United States indicates that these provisions "are the sole authority for NASA's reimbursement of IR&D and B&P costs".[2977]

(e) Evaluation by the Panel

(i) The Panel's understanding of the nature of the claim of the European Communities and the scope of the measures at issue

7.1328 While the European Communities frames this claim in terms of "NASA/DOD" IR&D and B&P reimbursements, by the European Communities' estimate[2978], DOD accounts for 95 per cent of the payments to Boeing, and NASA only accounts for 5 per cent of the payments made to Boeing. Thus, the European Communities' claim appears to be predominantly about DOD IR&D/B&P reimbursements.

7.1329 The European Communities' claim appears to relate to NASA and DOD IR&D/B&P reimbursements to *Boeing's military segment*, i.e. IDS, through cost-based procurement contracts with IDS. Together with its first written submission, the European Communities submitted a detailed report prepared by CRA International entitled "The United States Independent Research & Development (IR&D) and Bid & Proposal (B&P) Reimbursement Program and Its Benefits to The Boeing Company".[2979] This 86-page report provides a detailed overview of the IR&D/B&P programme (including its history, governing structure, and rules and regulations), its impacts on industry, and its impact on Boeing in particular. Because there is no publicly available information on the amount of IR&D/B&P reimbursements made to individual military contractors, this report also develops and applies a methodology for estimating the value of IR&D reimbursements made to the Boeing company. Importantly, the CRA estimate, upon which the European Communities relies, is based on the assumption that

---

[2977] United States' second written submission, para. 91.

[2978] European Communities response to question 29, para. 98.

[2979] CRA International, The United States Independent Research & Development (IR&D) and Bid & Proposal (B&P) Reimbursement Program and Its Benefits to The Boeing Company, December 2006, Exhibit EC-5.

1462   DSR 2012:III

US - Large Civil Aircraft (2nd Complaint)

"the entirety of Boeing's IR&D reimbursements are derived from contracts performed by Boeing's defense and space business unit, now called Integrated Defense Systems (IDS)."[2980]

7.1330 Finally, the scope of the European Communities' claim is limited to "IR&D/B&P *reimbursements with respect to* dual-use *technologies applicable to Boeing's commercial aircraft*".[2981] More specifically, the European Communities asserts that IR&D/B&P reimbursements "relate, *at least in part*, to *the production of all Boeing LCA*, and they provide Boeing's LCA division with advantages on non-market terms".[2982] The European Communities asserts that IR&D/B&P reimbursements "*reimburse Boeing for IR&D and B&P expenses* it has already incurred *related to improving, developing, and producing its entire line of LCA products*".[2983] In its second written submission, the European Communities makes clear that:

> "... the IR&D and B&P reimbursements at issue in this dispute *are limited to those that benefit the commercial aircraft division of Boeing*. The European Communities is not challenging as a subsidy the entire IR&D/B&P reimbursement system of NASA and DOD, or any IR&D and B&P reimbursements that legitimately lead to developments *exclusive to the military and space technology* and products purchased by NASA and DOD."[2984]

7.1331 Thus, it is the Panel's understanding that the measures that the European Communities is challenging are NASA and DOD reimbursements, through cost-shared procurement contracts with IDS, of IR&D/B&P expenses that "relate to the production of ... Boeing LCA", i.e. that "reimburse Boeing for IR&D and B&P expenses ... related to improving, developing, and producing its ... line of LCA products".

> (ii)   Whether the European Communities has established the existence of the measures it is challenging

7.1332 U.S. law requires Boeing to allocate a share of the costs of any IR&D/B&P projects benefiting both its military segment (IDS) and its commercial segment (Boeing's LCA division) to each of those segments on a

---

[2980] *Ibid.*, p. 31.

[2981] European Communities' first written submission, para. 871 (emphasis added); CRA International, The United States Independent Research & Development (IR&D) and Bid & Proposal (B&P) Reimbursement Program and Its Benefits to The Boeing Company, December 2006, Exhibit EC-5, p. 26.

[2982] European Communities' first written submission, para. 878 (emphasis added).

[2983] European Communities' first written submission, para. 880 (emphasis added).

[2984] European Communities' second written submission, para. 602 (emphasis added).

Report of the Panel

"pro rata" basis. In the Panel's view, this fact means that the European Communities has failed to establish the existence of the measure it is challenging, namely, NASA and DOD reimbursement, through cost-shared procurement contracts with IDS, of IR&D/B&P expenses that "relate to the production of ... Boeing LCA", i.e. that "reimburse Boeing for IR&D and B&P expenses ... related to improving, developing, and producing its ... line of LCA products".

7.1333 In its 86-page report, CRA International does not say very much about the IR&D/B&P cost accounting requirements that apply to military contractors, like Boeing, that have both a military and a commercial business segment. In the context of its discussion of the rules and regulations of the IR&D/B&P programme, CRA International merely notes:

> **"3.4.4. Cost Accounting Standards (CAS)**
>
> CAS 420 provides detailed criteria and instructions for the allocation of IR&D/B&P costs to a given company's contracts. The objective of the regulation is to ensure that all allocations of IR&D/B&P costs to government contracts are conducted using a consistent and equitable method that accurately reflects the fraction of such costs borne by each business unit, and in turn, by each covered contract."[2985]

7.1334 In its first written submission, the United States explains how the IR&D/B&P cost accounting requirements operate:

> "The EC also fails to realize that even if research is properly characterized as IR&D, it will not be eligible for U.S. government reimbursement unless it is passed along to the government as part of a cost-based contract. Under the Cost Accounting Standards, IR&D expenses are allocated among business segments based on the beneficial or causal relationship between the IR&D cost and those segments. If a cost has a beneficial relationship to multiple business segments, it will be allocated proportionately to all.
>
> This principle has several implications. If IDS conducted research applicable only to civil aircraft, Boeing would not be allowed to allocate the cost to IDS's government contracts, as IDS only performs military and space business for the government. Boeing would instead be required to allocate the entire cost of the R&D to BCA. Because BCA has no cost-based contracts with the

---

[2985] CRA International, The United States Independent Research & Development (IR&D) and Bid & Proposal (B&P) Reimbursement Program and Its Benefits to The Boeing Company, December 2006, Exhibit EC-5, p. 23.

1464

DSR 2012:III

government, these costs would be passed along to BCA's commercial customers, and not be subject to reimbursement by the government.

Second, if a military IR&D project was 'directly beneficial to Boeing's LCA operations,' as the EC mistakenly contends, Boeing would be required to allocate that cost to IDS and BCA 'on the basis of the beneficial or causal relationship between the IR&D and B&P costs and the final cost objectives.' Thus, the portion of that IR&D project related to BCA would not be allocated to IDS, and would not be subject to reimbursement in an IDS cost-based contract. The portion allocated to BCA could not be included in a cost-based contract because BCA has no such contracts. Instead, that portion of the cost would be passed along to commercial customers through BCA's overhead. Thus, 'dual-use research' included in IR&D costs will be reimbursed only to the extent of the military benefit of the research."[2986]

7.1335 In its second written submission, the United States advances this argument not in connection with the existence of a benefit to Boeing's LCA division, but rather as a threshold issue regarding the *existence of the measure being challenged.* Under the heading "The EC Has Failed to Establish That DoD or NASA IR&D or B&P Reimbursements Covered Research for Large Civil Aircraft"[2987], the United States argues that the European Communities "has provided no credible evidence that NASA or DoD actually included research related to large civil aircraft research in IR&D and B&P reimbursements".[2988] The United States again summarizes the applicable U.S. government accounting rules that govern the allocation of IR&D/B&P costs to different "segments" of government contractors (such as Boeing's LCA division and IDS within Boeing)[2989], and Boeing's own accounting rules.[2990] In responding to the European Communities' argument that R&D to "{s}trengthen the technology base of the United States" and "{e}nhance the industrial competitiveness of the United States" may be treated as an IR&D expense, the United States emphasizes that there are other types of R&D that may be reimbursed, but that:

"... the critical point is that *to the extent such research benefitted Boeing's large civil aircraft operations, it would have to be allocated to those operations, and would not be eligible for DoD reimbursement of IR&D or B&P.* Therefore, there is no support

---

[2986] United States' first written submission, paras. 294-296.
[2987] United States' second written submission, Section V.A.
[2988] United States' second written submission, para. 78.
[2989] United States' second written submission, para. 80.
[2990] United States' second written submission, para. 81.

Report of the Panel

for the EC allegation that IR&D reimbursements for projects under the "strengthen the technology base" or "industrial competitiveness" rubrics would reduce the costs of the large civil aircraft division."[2991]

7.1336 The United States concludes that:

"... the evidence shows that U.S. law does not allow Boeing to use IR&D or B&P reimbursements to fund large civil aircraft research or to fund the share of common research that is attributable to large civil aircraft."[2992]

7.1337 In its second oral statement, the United States addresses this question in connection with the existence of a benefit, but its argument seems to again concern the very existence of the measure being challenged:

"We have shown that DoD regulations actually prohibit the conduct that the EC alleges to be a subsidy. Namely, where IR&D or B&P expenses relate to both military and civil transactions, DoD will reimburse only a share of those expenses proportionate to the military transactions.

The EC's IR&D expert, Mr. Keevan, agrees with this assessment. In particular, he agrees that if a known civil application exists at the time an IR&D expense for military technology is incurred, DoD regulations require allocation of a proportionate share of that expense to Boeing's civil transactions.

...

... it is clear that DoD regulations require the outcome that the EC identifies as conferring no benefit to large civil aircraft – proportionate sharing of any "dual use" IR&D between the company's civil and military operations."[2993]

7.1338 The United States has provided the Panel with the full text of the relevant cost accounting standards.[2994] The provision is included as part of the *Federal Acquisition Regulation* (FAR). Section 9904.420 ("Cost Accounting Standard 420") is entitled "Accounting for independent research and development costs and bid and proposal costs". It contains subsections on its "purpose",

---

[2991] United States' second written submission, para. 82 (emphasis original).

[2992] United States' second written submission, para. 84.

[2993] United States' non-confidential oral statement at the second meeting with the Panel, paras. 72-73 and 77.

[2994] 48 C.F.R. § 9904.420-40(e), Exhibit US-131; Cost Accounting Standard 420, 48 C.F.R. § 9904.420, Exhibit US-1287.

1466   DSR 2012:III

"definitions", "fundamental requirements", "techniques of application", and "illustrations".

7.1339 With respect to "purpose", subsection 9904.420-20 states:

> "The purpose of this Cost Accounting Standard is to provide criteria for the accumulation of independent research and development costs and bid and proposal costs and for the allocation of such costs to cost objectives based on the beneficial or causal relationship between such costs and cost objectives. Consistent application of these criteria will improve cost allocation."

7.1340 Subsection 9904.420-30 defines a number of key concepts, including "Allocate", "Bid and Proposal Cost", Business unit", "Independent Research and Development", and "Segment".

7.1341 Subsection 9904.420-40 sets forth certain "fundamental requirements", including the following:

> "(d)   The IR&D and B&P cost pools of a home office shall be allocated to segments on the basis of the beneficial or causal relationship between the IR&D and B&P costs and the segments reporting to that home office.

> (e)   The IR&D and B&P cost pools of a business unit shall be allocated to the final cost objectives of that business unit on the basis of the beneficial or causal relationship between the IR&D and B&P costs and the final cost objectives."

7.1342 Subsection 9904.420-50 explains some of the "techniques of application":

> "(e)   The costs of IR&D and B&P projects accumulated at a home office shall be allocated to its segments as follows:

>> (1)   Projects which can be identified with a specific segment(s) shall have their costs allocated to such segment(s).

>> (2)   The costs of all other IR&D and B&P projects shall be allocated among all segments by means of the same base used by the company to allocate its residual expenses in accordance with 9904.403; provided, however, where a particular segment receives significantly more or less benefit from the IR&D or B&P costs than would be reflected by the allocation of such costs to the segment by the base, the Government and the contractor may agree to a special allocation of the IR&D or B&P costs to such

Report of the Panel

segment commensurate with the benefits received. The amount of a special allocation to any segment made pursuant to such an agreement shall be excluded from the IR&D and B&P cost pools to be allocated to other segments and the base data of any such segment shall be excluded from the base used to allocate these pools.

(f) The costs of IR&D and B&P projects accumulated at a business unit shall be allocated to cost objectives as follows:

(1) Where costs of any IR&D or B&P project benefit more than one segment of the organization, the amounts to be allocated to each segment shall be determined in accordance with paragraph (e) of this subsection."

7.1343 In addition to providing the Panel with the applicable IR&D/B&P regulations, the United States has also submitted two statements by Boeing officials on the same point.

7.1344 First, the United States has submitted an "affidavit" of David Ramey, Corporate Director of Business Operations for The Boeing Company.[2995] With regard to the IR&D/B&P accounting regulations that govern the allocation of costs in firms with multiple business segments, Mr. Ramey states:

"1. ... I have personal knowledge of the way in which the company accounts for the activities and costs charged to the U.S. Government under its NASA and DOD contracts.

2. While both the BCA segment and the IDS segment must account for their various costs – including Independent Research and Development costs – according to general accounting standards (subject to audit by various tax and securities authorities), Boeing's IDS business segment must also comply with the U.S. Government's Cost Accounting Standards (CAS). These rules are set forth in the Federal Acquisition Regulations, which are codified in Volume 48 of the U.S. Code of Federal Regulations and further amplified in the Defense Contract Audit Agency (DCAA) Contract Audit Manual.

3. The CAS regulations require, among many other things, that IR&D expenditures be allocated to various segments (i.e. IDS and BCA) on the basis of the 'beneficial or causal relationship' to the business of the segment. In practice, Boeing operationalizes

---

[2995] Affidavit of David Ramey, Exhibit US-1340.

1468

DSR 2012:III

US - Large Civil Aircraft (2nd Complaint)

this accounting rule as follows: (1) the costs of an IR&D project identified, planned and executed by a single segment for the benefit of its own business are born fully by that segment; and (2) the costs of an IR&D project identified and planned by each segment for the benefit of both of their respective business, and executed by {Phantom Works} on behalf of both, are accumulated in the 'enterprise-wide common pool' and allocated between the two segments according to the relative value-added base of each segment. These designations are reviewed annually, and if an IDS IR&D project is identified as having prospective value for BCA {i.e. Boeing's LCA Division}, it will be reassigned to the enterprise-wide common pool.

4.   This methodology is specifically envisioned in 48 CFR § 9904.420-50 and it has been approved by DOD. Our compliance with this methodology is audited on an ongoing basis by contracting officers, contract administration officials and DCAA, and is ultimately subject to scrutiny by the DOD Inspector General. Non-compliance can result in severe penalties, including non-payment, recoupment by the government of unallowable costs, suit under the False Claims Act, and debarment from future government contracting."

7.1345 Second, the United States has submitted another "affidavit" from David C. Bullock, Vice President and CFO for Engineering, Operations and Technology at The Boeing Company.[2996] In his affidavit, Mr. Bullock states, with regard to Boeing's Phantom Works unit, that:

"{W}here Phantom Works does Independent Research and Development (IR&D) that has applicability to multiple business operations, the costs of this R&D are allocated per U.S. government regulations among the benefiting business operations; any portion allocated to Boeing's civil aircraft operations is covered fully by the company's commercial revenues (and not reimbursed as overhead on the company's U.S. government cost-based contracts)."

7.1346 Given the apparent significance of these cost accounting requirements, the third set of questions put the following detailed question to the United States:

"362. It is the Panel's understanding that, under U.S. government accounting rules, IR&D and B&P costs may be allocated to a 'segment' of a contractor only if the costs bear a 'beneficial and

---

[2996] Affidavit of David C. Bullock, Exhibit US-1284.

DSR 2012:III

1469

Report of the Panel

causal relationship' to that segment (US Second Written Submission, para. 80, citing 48 C.F.R. §9904-420-40 (Exhibit US-131); 48 C.F.R. § 9904.418-40(c) (Exhibit US-1141)).

(a)   What does 'beneficial and causal relationship' mean in this context?

(b)   How does Boeing determine whether IR&D and B&P costs incurred by IDS bear a 'beneficial and causal relationship' to Boeing's LCA segment?

(c)   The United States indicates that IR&D and B&P 'may' be allocated to Boeing's LCA segment 'only if' the costs bear a beneficial and causal relationship to that segment. Does this mean that Boeing is not required to allocate IR&D / B&P costs to its LCA segment even where there exists a 'beneficial and causal relationship'?

(d)   Does Boeing have a financial incentive to allocate only a small share of its IR&D / B&P costs to its LCA operations?"

7.1347 In its response to this question, the United States confirmed, among other things that "costs typically have a beneficial relationship to a segment if they advance one of the activities of that segment".[2997] The United States confirmed that "{d}etermining whether IR&D and B&P costs incurred by IDS bear a 'beneficial or causal relationship' to Boeing's large civil aircraft is part of Boeing's requirement to maintain an accounting system and related internal controls to ensure compliance with the Cost Accounting Standard 420".[2998] The United States further explained that:

"Boeing's IR&D review process does not retroactively reallocate IR&D costs when one segment decides that it is interested in an IR&D project conducted by another. Sometimes this practice will allow IDS to use the results of an IR&D project funded in whole or in part by BCA, and sometimes BCA will get the advantage of an IR&D project funded in whole or in part by IDS. Given that civil technology is generally ahead of military technology in areas where there is overlap, the net flow from BCA to IDS is likely to be larger in volume than the flow from IDS to BCA."[2999]

The United States reiterated that:

[2997]   United States' response to question 362, para. 191.
[2998]   United States' response to question 362, para. 192.
[2999]   United States' response to question 362, para. 194.

1470   DSR 2012:III

US - Large Civil Aircraft (2nd Complaint)

> "the federal acquisition regulations permit the allocation of IR&D and B&P to a single segment, *i.e.*, IDS or BCA, if and only if the costs bear a beneficial or causal relationship only to that segment. Conversely, if IR&D and B&P costs do not bear a beneficial or causal relationship to a particular segment, the regulations prohibit allocation of any of the costs to that segment. If an IR&D project is identified with more than one specific segment of Boeing (for example, with BCA and another segment), the cost of the project must, in accordance with CAS 420-50(e)(2), be 'allocated among all segments by means of the same base used by the company to allocate its residual expenses in accordance with 9904.403...'[3000]
>
> .... once a beneficial or causal relationship exists, allocation is mandatory."[3001]

7.1348 The European Communities does not dispute that the applicable regulations require Boeing to allocate IR&D/B&P benefiting both of its segments across its military and commercial segments on a *pro rata* basis. Rather, it advances the following two arguments.

7.1349 First, the European Communities argues that this does not necessarily exclude the possibility that IR&D/B&P expenses that Boeing initially considered to only have military relevance (and therefore allocated entirely to IDS contracts with DOD and NASA) could turn out to have unexpected benefits, in later years, for Boeing's LCA division. The European Communities submits an expert statement by William T. Keevan, an expert in IR&D/B&P accounting, in support of that position.[3002] In his expert statement, Mr. Keevan, agrees with the United States that if an expected civil application exists at the time an IR&D expense for military technology is incurred, DOD regulations require allocation of a proportionate share of that expense to Boeing's civil transactions. However, Mr. Keevan explains that such allocation would not occur if civil uses are "unknown" or "unexpected" at the time the research is conducted, but "are determined in a later year to have produced information or results useful to its commercial aircraft business".[3003] However, it is only in such an "unexpected use" situation that IDS would be reimbursed by for the full cost of R&D benefiting both IDS and Boeing's commercial segment. In our view, this "unexpected use" argument is not sufficient to establish the existence of the measure.

[3000] *(footnote original)* 48 C.F.R. § 9904.420-50(e)(2), Exhibit US-131.

[3001] United States' response to question 362, para. 195.

[3002] William T. Keevan, "Independent Research & Development Reimbursements: Commentary on Selected Issues Raised by the United States' First Written Submission in DS353," November 2007, Exhibit EC-1179.

[3003] *Ibid.*, p. 5.

DSR 2012:III

1471

Report of the Panel

7.1350 Second, the European Communities argues that the Panel cannot be sure that Boeing actually allocates its IR&D/B&P costs in this manner. Specifically, the European Communities argues that:

> "... to the extent that Boeing takes a position in its own accounting procedures that is consistent with the arguments advanced in this dispute, then not only will it *not* be allocating potentially dual-use technology funded by Boeing IDS to the final cost objectives of Boeing Commercial, but it *will* be allocating potentially dual-use technology funded by Boeing Commercial to the final cost objectives of Boeing IDS."[3004]

7.1351 The "arguments advanced in this dispute" by the United States are that very little DOD R&D has actual or potential "dual use" applications, i.e. the United States argues that very little DOD R&D is LCA-related. In our view, this second argument by the European Communities does not suffice to establish the existence of the measure. It cannot be presumed that Boeing does not comply with the applicable cost accounting requirements. Moreover, even if the Panel were to assume that Boeing does not comply with the applicable cost accounting requirements, this does not change the fact that the U.S. Government has these legal requirements in place. As the panel in *US – Export Restraints* observed:

> "... the existence of a financial contribution by a *government* must be proven by reference to the action of the *government*. To determine whether a financial contribution exists under subparagraph (iv) solely by reference to the *reaction of affected entities* would mean in practice that a different standard would apply under that provision as compared to the standard under subparagraphs (i)-(iii), which involves *consideration of the action of the government* first. Similarly, we do not see how the reaction of *private entities* to a given governmental measure can be *the basis on which the Member's compliance with its treaty obligations under the WTO is established.*"[3005]

7.1352 The cost accounting requirements reviewed above are the same for both IR&D costs and B&P costs.[3006] In the light of the evidence before the Panel regarding the IR&D/B&P cost accounting regulations, we conclude that the European Communities has failed to establish the existence of the measure it is challenging. More specifically, we conclude that the European Communities has

---

[3004] European Communities' second written submission, para. 609.

[3005] Panel Report, *US – Export Restraints*, para. 8.34.

[3006] See e.g. European Communities' second written submission, para. 611 ("... the Cost Accounting Standards at issue here are those for "{a}ccounting for independent research and development costs and bid and proposal costs", and there is generally no distinction between cost accounting standards for IR&D and B&P").

1472

DSR 2012:III

failed to establish that NASA and DOD reimburse, through cost-shared procurement contracts with IDS, IR&D/B&P expenses that: "relate to the production of ... Boeing LCA", i.e. that "reimburse Boeing for IR&D and B&P expenses ... related to improving, developing, and producing its ... line of LCA products".[3007]

7.1353 For these reasons, the Panel concludes that the European Communities has not demonstrated the existence of the measure challenged.[3008]

(f) Conclusion

7.1354 **For these reasons, the Panel finds that the European Communities has not demonstrated that NASA/DOD reimburse Boeing for IR&D/B&P expenses that relate to the production of Boeing LCA, and has therefore failed to establish the existence of the measures that allegedly constitute a specific subsidy under Articles 1 and 2 of the SCM Agreement.**

7. *Department of Labor (DOL) 787 worker training grants*

(a) Introduction

7.1355 In 2004, the Department of Labor ("DOL") awarded a $1.5 million grant to a group of entities known as the "Triad Partnership". The European Communities alleges that the purpose of the DOL grant was to cover the costs of training current and future workers for development and production of the 787, and labels it the "787 Worker Training Grant". The European Communities argues that this grant is a specific subsidy under Articles 1 and 2 of the SCM Agreement, and allocates the full amount of the grant (i.e. $1.5 million) to Boeing's LCA division.

7.1356 The United States does not deny that the DOL made the grant, or that it is a subsidy under Article 1 of the SCM Agreement. However, the United States argues that the grant is a subsidy to the Edmonds Community College, and not a subsidy to Boeing. In this regard, the United States disputes that the purpose of the grant was to train workers for the 787, and refers to it as the "Edmonds Community College Grant". In addition, the United States disputes that the subsidy is specific under Article 2 of the SCM Agreement.

(b) The measures at issue

7.1357 In 2004, the DOL awarded a $1.5 million grant to a group of entities known as the "Triad Partnership". These entities include, among others,

---

[3007] European Communities' first written submission, paras. 871, 878, 880; European Communities' second written submission, para. 602.

[3008] In the Panel's view, the European Communities' failure to establish that NASA/DOD reimburse Boeing for IR&D/B&P expenses that "relate to the production of ... Boeing LCA" could alternatively be analysed in terms of the European Communities' failure to demonstrate that any of the alleged subsidy should be allocated to Boeing's LCA division.

Report of the Panel

Edmonds Community College, Everett Community College, the Snohomish Workforce Development Council, the Snohomish Economic Development Council, Boeing, and other Snohomish County aerospace manufacturing supplier industries.[3009] The money was received by, and used by, Edmonds Community College. The European Communities' panel request[3010] states that:

> "The US Department of Labor transfers economic resources to the US LCA industry on terms more favourable than available on the market or not at arm's length, through the Aerospace Industry Initiative, an element of the President's High Growth Training Initiative, under the authority of the Workforce Investment Act, Pub. L. No. 105-220 (1998), by granting to Edmonds Community College in the State of Washington funds for the training of aerospace industry workers associated with the Boeing 787."

(c) Whether a subsidy exists within the meaning of Article 1 of the SCM Agreement

(i) Arguments of the European Communities

7.1358 The European Communities argues that "DOL funding to Triad and Boeing" for training 787 workers provides a direct transfer of funds and, specifically, a grant, within the meaning of Article 1.1(a)(1)(i) of the SCM Agreement.[3011]

7.1359 Regarding the existence of a benefit within the meaning of Article 1.1(b) of the SCM Agreement, the European Communities argues that the "DOL 787 worker training grants" confer "benefits" on Boeing's LCA division. The European Communities argues that: (i) the financial contributions "relate to the production of the 787"; (ii) the financial contributions "provide Boeing's LCA division with advantages on non-market terms"; (iii) "Boeing is not required to pay anything in return for these DOL worker training grants"; and (iv) "Boeing would no doubt incur the full cost of training its 787 workers on the market".[3012]

(ii) Arguments of the United States

7.1360 The United States argues that the grant constitutes a financial contribution, but not to Boeing's 787 programme, as the European Communities contends, because it was awarded to Edmonds Community College and not to Boeing.[3013]

[3009] United States' first written submission, para. 410.

[3010] WT/DS353/2, item 5, p. 12.

[3011] European Communities' first written submission, para. 910.

[3012] European Communities' first written submission, paras. 913-915.

[3013] United States' first written submission, para. 413.

1474 DSR 2012:III

US - Large Civil Aircraft (2nd Complaint)

7.1361 The United States also argues that Boeing received no benefit from the Department of Labor grant because not only was the grant given to Edmonds Community College, rather than to Boeing, but it was not actually used to provide training to Boeing employees. In this regard, the European Communities' portrayal of the grant to Edmonds Community College as "worker training grants" that "relate explicitly to training 787 workers" is inaccurate.[3014]

(iii)   Evaluation by the Panel

7.1362 Both parties agree that the challenged measure provides a subsidy within the meaning of Article 1 of the SCM Agreement. More specifically, both parties agree that the challenged measure involves a financial contribution in the form of a grant within the meaning of Article 1.1(a)(1)(i) of the SCM Agreement, and both parties agree that this financial contribution confers a benefit within the meaning of Article 1.1(b) of the SCM Agreement. The Panel sees no reason to disagree, and notes that the funding was identified as a "grant" by the Department of Labor itself.[3015]

7.1363 In the Panel's view, the question of whether some or all of the subsidy should be allocated to Boeing's LCA division is an issue that relates to the amount of the subsidy, rather than the existence of a financial contribution or benefit within the meaning of Article 1 of the SCM Agreement.[3016] If the Panel finds that the subsidy is specific within the meaning of Article 2 of the SCM Agreement, it will address the parties' arguments and evidence on this question. However, if the Panel finds that the subsidy is not specific within the meaning of Article 2, then it need not address the question of how much of the (non-specific) subsidy should be allocated to Boeing's LCA division.

(d)   Whether the subsidy is specific within the
meaning of Article 2 of the SCM Agreement

(i)   Arguments of the European Communities

7.1364 In its first written submission, the European Communities advances two arguments in support of its position that the subsidy is specific within the meaning of Article 2 of the SCM Agreement. First, the European Communities argues that the Triad Grant (which it refers to in the plural as "grants", notwithstanding that there appears to have been only one grant) is specific by virtue of the limited group of entities, including Boeing, that are part of the Triad Partnership. The European Communities explains that numerous government publications and the Notification of the Grant Award make clear that the grant to

---

[3014] United States' first written submission, paras. 414-416.

[3015] See e.g. Edmonds Community College Grant Notification, Exhibit EC-622, p. 1 ("The Grantee is approved for this project up to $1,475,045 as specified in the attached Statement of Work with an additional increment of $725,045").

[3016] See above, paras. 7.35-7.36 of this Report.

DSR 2012:III   1475

Report of the Panel

the Triad Partnership is used to train workers associated with the Boeing 787 supply chain, and the key partner in the project is the Boeing Company. For example, the Triad Partnership grant proposal states that the "primary target for this training effort is development of the workforce necessary for aerospace manufacturers in building the Boeing 7E7" including "Boeing and Boeing aerospace suppliers". In this regard, the grants are targeted at the aerospace industry, and particularly benefit Boeing, and the Statement of Work, for example, explains that the grants will be used to meet Boeing's particular needs".[3017] Second, the European Communities asserts that the "grant is also specific under Article 2.1(a) because it is a part of a larger government programme that targets only certain industries, including the aerospace industry".[3018]

7.1365 In its second written submission, the European Communities responds to the United States' arguments that the broader government programme that the Triad Grant is part of – i.e. the High Growth Job Training Initiative – is not specific. The European Communities argues that the United States misses the point that the measure at issue is the DOL's $1.5 million grant to Edmonds Community College, not the entire High Growth Job Training Initiative. According to the European Communities, the fact remains that "the grant at issue was explicitly limited to the aerospace industry (i.e. Boeing and Boeing's aerospace suppliers), and it is therefore *de jure* specific pursuant to Article 2.1(a) of the *SCM Agreement*".[3019]

(ii)   Arguments of the United States

7.1366 In its first written submission, the United States advances two arguments relating to specificity. First, the United States argues that the even if the Triad Grant is analysed in isolation from the broader programme that it is part of, it "is not specific to the aerospace industry or Boeing". Rather, the beneficiaries of this grant alone could extend well beyond the aerospace industry and Boeing.[3020] Second, the United States argues that the Department of Labor grants awarded pursuant to the High Growth Job Training Initiative are not specific under Article 2.1. To begin, they are not specific within the meaning of Article 2.1(a) because they are not explicitly limited to "certain enterprises". Rather, these grants are "broadly available" across 14 diverse industry sectors that cover a significant portion of the U.S. economy, such as health care, financial services, information technology, energy, manufacturing, retail, and transportation. Within these sectors, the grants may be used for a variety of purposes across

---

[3017] European Communities' first written submission, paras. 916 and 919.
[3018] European Communities' first written submission, para. 917.
[3019] European Communities' second written submission, paras. 628-629.
[3020] United States' first written submission, paras. 419-421.

1476   DSR 2012:III

US - Large Civil Aircraft (2nd Complaint)

many sub-sectors. The grants are in no way *de jure* specific to either Boeing or the aerospace industry.[3021]

(iii) Evaluation by the Panel

7.1367 The European Communities argues that the Triad Grant is specific by virtue of the limited group of entities, including Boeing, that are part of the Triad Partnership. If the relevant question for the purposes of Article 2 was whether the Triad Grant would be specific if examined in isolation from the broader High Growth Job Training Initiative programme pursuant to which it was provided, the answer would surely be yes. Among other things, the "High Growth Job Training Initiative Grantee List" says that the "Target Industry" for the Triad Grant is "Aerospace".[3022] However, the grant at issue was provided pursuant to a wider programme. In this regard, we note that the European Communities panel request indicates that the grant to Edmonds Community College was made through the Aerospace Industry Initiative, "an element of the President's High Growth Training Initiative".[3023] Thus, to establish specificity, we consider that the European Communities must either advance a reasoned explanation as to why it is not appropriate to analyse specificity at the level of the broader programme, or demonstrate that the broader programme (i.e. the "High Growth Job Training Initiative") is specific. The European Communities' statement that "the measure at issue is the DOL's $1.5 million grant to Edmonds Community College, not the entire High Growth Job Training Initiative" does not suffice as a reasoned explanation for examining the Triad Grant in isolation. Thus, we turn to the question of whether the High Growth Job Training Initiative Program is specific.

7.1368 In the Panel's view, the European Communities has failed to make a prima facie case that the "High Growth Job Training Initiative" is specific under Article 2 of the SCM Agreement. While it is true that the Program "targets only certain industries, including the aerospace industry"[3024], the industries "targeted" are too broad (e.g. "advanced manufacturing" as 1 of 14 "industries") to support a finding of specificity.

7.1369 The legislative basis for the High Growth Job Training Initiative is 29 U.S.C. § 2916a. The legislation provides in relevant part:

> "(1) In general
>
> The Secretary of Labor shall use funds available under section 1356(s)(2) of title 8 to award grants to eligible entities to provide job training and related activities for workers to assist them in

---

[3021] United States' first written submission, para. 417.

[3022] High Growth Job Training Initiative Grantee List, Exhibit US-171, p. 6.

[3023] WT/DS353/2, item 5, p. 12.

[3024] European Communities' first written submission, para. 917.

DSR 2012:III   1477

Report of the Panel

obtaining or upgrading employment *in industries and economic sectors identified pursuant to paragraph (4) that are projected to experience significant growth* and ensure that job training and related activities funded by such grants are coordinated with the public workforce investment system.

(2)   Use of funds

(A)   Training provided

Funds under this section may be used to provide job training services and related activities that are designed to assist workers (including unemployed and employed workers) in gaining the skills and competencies needed to obtain or upgrade career ladder employment positions *in the industries and economic sectors identified pursuant to paragraph (4).*

(B)   Enhanced training programs and information In order to facilitate the provision of job training services described in subparagraph (A), funds under this section may be used to assist in the development and implementation of model activities such as developing appropriate curricula to build core competencies and train workers, identifying and disseminating career and skill information, and increasing the integration of community and technical college activities with activities of businesses and the public workforce investment system to meet the training needs *for the industries and economic sectors identified pursuant to paragraph (4).*

(3)   Eligible entities

Grants under this section may be awarded to partnerships of private and public sector entities, which may include—

(A)   businesses or business-related nonprofit organizations, such as trade associations;

(B)   education and training providers, including community colleges and other community-based organizations; and

(C)   entities involved in administering the workforce investment system established under title I of the Workforce Investment Act of 1998 {29 U.S.C. 2801 et seq. }, and economic development agencies.

US - Large Civil Aircraft (2nd Complaint)

(4)   High growth industries and economic sectors

For purposes of this section, the Secretary of Labor, in consultation with State workforce investment boards, shall identify *industries and economic sectors that are projected to experience significant growth, taking into account appropriate factors, such as the industries and sectors that-*

(A)   are projected to add substantial numbers of new jobs to the economy;

(B)   are being transformed by technology and innovation requiring new skill sets for workers;

(C)   are new and emerging businesses that are projected to grow;

or

(D)   have a significant impact on the economy overall or on the growth of other industries and economic sectors.

(5)   Equitable distribution

In awarding grants under this section, the Secretary of Labor shall ensure an equitable distribution of such grants across geographically diverse areas. ..." [3025]

7.1370 The Program is administered by the Department of Labor's Employment and Training Administration (ETA). In accordance with the legislation reproduced above, the ETA identified 14 different "high growth industries and economic sectors". These include: Advanced Manufacturing, Aerospace, Automotive, Biotechnology, Construction, Energy, Financial Services, Geospatial Technology, Health Care, Homeland Security, Hospitality, Information Technology, Retail, and Transportation.[3026]

7.1371 Pursuant to the High Growth Job Training Initiative, the Department of Labor has awarded 156 grants totalling over $288 million to entities in the 14 industry sectors covered by the initiative.[3027] The recipients of these grants include state and local workforce investment systems; community colleges; health care associations and organizations; trade groups in industries such as geospatial information and technology, nanotechnology, manufacturing,

---

[3025] 29 U.S.C. § 2916a, Exhibit US-1294 (emphasis added).
[3026] The President's High Growth Job Training Initiative Fact Sheet, Exhibit US-170.
[3027] High Growth Job Training Initiative Grantee List, Exhibit US-171.

DSR 2012:III   1479

Report of the Panel

automotives, and construction; and state and local labour, employment, and community development agencies, among others.[3028]

7.1372 The projects funded by the grants cover various topics such as literacy, building arts, long-term care workforce challenges, hospice care, mine training, supply chain logistics, training individuals with disabilities for employment in the financial services sector, biotechnology workforce development, machine shop skills training, food and beverage manufacturing, and integrated systems technology.[3029]

7.1373 Exhibit US-171 provides the following data regarding the breakdown of grants funded under the High Growth Job Training Initiative programme:

"Target Industry"	Number of Grants
Advanced Manufacturing	31
Aerospace	7
Automotive	12
Biotechnology	17
Construction/Skilled Trades	9
Energy	11
Financial Services	5
Geospatial	6
Health Care	29
Hospitality	4
Information Technology	3
Retail	3
Transportation	4

7.1374 For these reasons, the Panel finds that the European Communities has failed to demonstrate that the subsidy is specific within the meaning of Article 2 of the SCM Agreement.

(e)   Conclusion

7.1375 **For these reasons, the Panel finds that the payment that the Department of Labor made to Edmonds Community College under the High Growth Job Training Initiative is a subsidy. However, the Panel finds**

[3028] *Ibid.*

[3029] *Ibid.*

1480

DSR 2012:III

that the European Communities has not demonstrated that the subsidy is specific within the meaning of Article 2 of the SCM Agreement.

8. *FSC/ETI and successor act subsidies*

(a) Introduction

7.1376 The European Communities argues that the "FSC/ETI and successor act Subsidies" are subsidies within the meaning of Article 1 of the SCM Agreement, and are specific within the meaning of Article 2 of the SCM Agreement. The European Communities estimates that the amount of the subsidy to Boeing's LCA division through 2006 in the form of FSC/ETI tax breaks is $2.199 billion.

7.1377 The United States accepts that the measures at issue are subsidies within the meaning of Article 1, and are specific within the meaning of Article 2. The United States also accepts the European Communities' estimate that the amount of the subsidy to Boeing's LCA division through 2006 in the form of FSC/ETI tax breaks is $2.199 billion. However, the United States disputes the European Communities' assertion that Boeing will continue to receive FSC/ETI benefits after 2006.

(b) The measures at issue

7.1378 The European Communities characterizes the measures at issue as "FSC/ETI and successor act subsidies". In its description of these measures, the European Communities discusses the original provisions of the U.S. Internal Revenue Code relating to foreign sales corporations, the *FSC Repeal and Extraterritorial Income Exclusion Act of 2000*, the *American Jobs Creation Act of 2004* and the *Tax Increase Prevention and Reconciliation Act of 2005*.[3030, 3031]

[3030] European Communities' first written submission, paras. 923-945.

[3031] In its request for establishment of a panel in this dispute, the European Communities submits that:

> "The US Government transfers economic resources to the US LCA industry through the federal tax system, and in particular through the following tax measures:
>
> a. Sections 921-927 of the Internal Revenue Code (prior to repeal) and related measures establishing special tax treatment for "Foreign Sales Corporations" ("FSCs");
>
> b. FSC Repeal and Extraterritorial Income Exclusion Act of 2000, Pub. L. No. 106-519; and
>
> c. American Jobs Creation Act of 2004, Pub. L. No. 108-357."

Request for the Establishment of a Panel by the European Communities, WT/DS353/2, p. 12 (23 January 2006).

Report of the Panel

> (i) Provisions of the U.S. Internal Revenue Code relating to foreign sales corporations[3032]

7.1379 A Foreign Sales Corporation ("FSC") was a corporation created, organised, and maintained in a qualified foreign country or U.S. possession outside the customs territory of the United States under the specific requirements of Sections 921-927 of the U.S. Internal Revenue Code.[3033] A FSC obtained a U.S. tax exemption on a portion of its "foreign trade income", which meant the gross income of a FSC attributable to "foreign trading gross receipts". Foreign trading gross receipts meant the gross receipts of any FSC that were generated by qualifying transactions, which generally involved the sale or lease of "export property".[3034] A portion of the "foreign trade income" was deemed to be "foreign source income not effectively connected with a trade or business in the United States" and was therefore not taxed in the United States. This untaxed portion was referred to as the "exempt foreign trade income". The remaining portion was taxable to the FSC. Dividends paid by the FSC out of exempt and non-exempt income to the shareholder (ordinarily, the "related supplier") generally qualified for a full dividends-received deduction. In addition to the exemption from income taxation of a portion of the FSCs foreign trade income, the FSC measure also allowed U.S. parents of FSCs to defer paying taxes on certain "foreign trade income" that would normally be subject to immediate taxation and to avoid paying taxes on dividends received from their FSCs related to "foreign trade income".

[3032] The European Communities submits that "the primary legal provisions constituting the FSC measure are sections 245(c), 921 through 927, and 951(e) of the United States Internal Revenue Code". European Communities' first written submission, para. 923, footnote 1615. A detailed description of the FSC provisions is contained in Panel Report, *US – FSC*, paras. 2.1-2.8, 7.95-7.97 and Appellate Body Report, *US – FSC*, paras. 11-18.

[3033] Exhibit EC-623. A FSC had to meet certain requirements of foreign presence. For example, a FSC had to maintain an office outside the customs territory of the United States, which office had to be equipped to transact the FSC's business. Also, in order for a FSC, other than a small FSC, to be treated as having foreign trading gross receipts for the taxable year, the management of the corporation during the taxable year had to take place outside the United States, and the corporation could have foreign trading gross receipts from any transaction only if economic processes with respect to the transaction took place outside the United States.

[3034] With certain exceptions, export property was:
- property held for sale or lease;
- manufactured, produced, grown, or extracted in the United States;
- by a person other than a FSC;
- sold, leased, or rented for use, consumption, or disposition outside the United States; and
- with no more than 50 per cent of its fair market value attributable to imports.

(ii)   FSC Repeal and Extraterritorial Income
        Exclusion Act of 2000[3035]

7.1380 On 15 November 2000, the United States enacted the *FSC Repeal and Extraterritorial Exclusion Act of 2000* ("ETI Act") in response to the findings made with respect to the FSC provisions by the panel and the Appellate Body in *US – FSC*.[3036] The ETI Act (i) repealed the provisions in the U.S. Internal Revenue Code relating to taxation of FSCs, subject to certain transition and grandfather provisions and (ii) introduced an exclusion from income taxation of "extraterritorial income".

7.1381 First, the ETI Act specified that, in general, the amendments made by the Act "shall apply to transactions after September 30, 2000". In addition, no new FSCs could be created after that date. However, in the case of a FSC in existence on 30 September 2000, Section 5(c) (1) of the ETI Act provided that the amendments made by the Act did not apply to any transaction in the ordinary course of trade or business involving a FSC which occurred: (i) before 1 January 2002; or (ii) after 31 December 2001, pursuant to a binding contract between the FSC (or any related person) and any unrelated person that was in effect on 30 September 2000.

7.1382 Second, the ETI Act allowed for the exclusion from taxation of certain income of a U.S. "taxpayer". Such income - "extraterritorial income" that was "qualifying foreign trade income" – could be earned with respect to goods only in transactions involving qualifying foreign trade property. The ETI Act defined "extraterritorial income" as the gross income of a taxpayer attributable to "foreign trading gross receipts", i.e. gross receipts generated by certain qualifying transactions involving the sale or lease of "qualifying foreign trade property" not for use in the United States. "Qualifying foreign trade income" under the ETI Act meant, with respect to any transaction, the amount of gross income which, if excluded, would result in a reduction of the taxable income of the taxpayer from such transaction equal to the greatest of: (i) 30 per cent of the foreign sale and leasing income derived by the taxpayer from such transaction; (ii) 1.2 per cent of the foreign trading gross receipts derived by the taxpayer from the transaction, or (iii) 15 per cent of the foreign trade income derived by the taxpayer from the transaction. "Qualifying foreign trade property" meant property: "(A) manufactured, produced, grown or extracted within or outside the United States ; (B) held primarily for sale, lease or rental, in the ordinary course of trade or business for direct use, consumption, or disposition outside the United States; and (C) not more than 50 per cent of the fair market value of which was attributable to: (i) articles manufactured, produced, grown, or

---

[3035] FSC Repeal and Extraterritorial Income Exclusion Act of 2000, United States Public Law 106-519, 114 Stat. 2423 (2000). Exhibit EC-625. A detailed description of the provisions of this Act is contained in Panel Report, *US – FSC (Article 21.5 – EC)*, paras. 2.1-2.8 and Appellate Body Report, *US – FSC (Article 21.5 – EC)*, paras. 12-14.

[3036] Panel Report, *US – FSC*, para. 8.1(a); Appellate Body Report, *US – FSC*, paras. 177(a) and 178.

DSR 2012:III   1483

Report of the Panel

extracted outside the United States; and (ii) direct costs for labour (determined under the principles of Section 263A) performed outside the United States".

7.1383 The ETI Act's definitions of qualifying foreign trade property and foreign trading gross receipts - which determined income that qualified as extraterritorial income, foreign trade income and qualifying foreign trade income - thus contained at least two requirements that had to be satisfied in order for a taxpayer to qualify for the exclusion from taxation: (i) a requirement that a good produced within or outside the United States be held primarily for sale, lease or rental, in the ordinary course of trade or business for direct use, consumption, or disposition outside the United States; and (ii) a requirement that no more than 50 per cent of the fair market value of such property be attributable to articles manufactured, produced, grown, or extracted outside the United States, and direct costs for labour performed outside the United States.

(iii)   American Jobs Creation Act of 2004[3037]

7.1384 On 22 October 2004, the United States enacted the *American Jobs Creation Act of 2004* ("AJCA") in response to the findings made by the Panel and the Appellate Body in *US – FSC (Article 21.5 – EC)*.[3038] Section 101 of the AJCA ("Repeal of exclusion for extraterritorial income") repealed the provisions in Section 114 of the Internal Revenue Code relating to the exclusion from income taxation of extraterritorial income. The effective date of this repeal was 31 December 2004. However, a "transitional rule for 2005 and 2006" in Section 101(d) of the AJCA allowed U.S. taxpayers to claim 80 per cent of ETI tax benefits with respect to certain transactions in 2005 and to claim 60 per cent of ETI tax benefits with respect to certain transactions in 2006. In addition to this time-limited transitional rule, the AJCA indefinitely grandfathered the ETI scheme in respect of certain transactions. Specifically, Section 101(f) ("Binding Contracts") of the AJCA provided that Section 101 of the AJCA did not apply to any transaction in the ordinary course of a trade or business which occurred pursuant to a binding contract (i) which was between the taxpayer and an unrelated person and (ii) which was in effect on September 17, 2003, and at all times thereafter. Moreover, Section 101 of the AJCA did not repeal Section 5(c)(1) of the ETI Act, which indefinitely grandfathered FSC subsidies in respect of certain transactions entered into pursuant to binding contracts in effect on 30 September 2000.[3039]

[3037] American Jobs Creation Act of 2004, Pub. L. No. 108-357, §101. Exhibit EC-626. The provisions of the AJCA are described in greater detail in Panel Report, *US – FSC (Article 21.5 – EC II)*, paras. 2.13-2.17.

[3038] Panel Report, *US – FSC (Article 21.5 – EC)*, paras. 9.1(a), 9.1(b), 9.1(e); Appellate Body Report, *US – FSC (Article 21.5 – EC)*, paras. 256(b), 256 (f), 257.

[3039] Above, para. 7.1381.

1484   DSR 2012:III

(iv) Tax Increase Prevention and Reconciliation Act of 2005[3040]

7.1385 On 17 May 2006, the United States enacted the *Tax Increase Prevention and Reconciliation Act of 2005* ("TIPRA") in response to the findings of the Panel and the Appellate Body in *US – FSC (Article 21.5 – EC II)*.[3041] Section 513 of the TIPRA is entitled "Repeal of FSC/ETI Binding Contract Relief". Section 513(a) of the TIPRA ("FSC Provisions") repeals the provision in Section 5(c)(1)(B) of the ETI Act that allowed for the continuation of FSC benefits in respect of transactions occurring pursuant to a binding contract in effect on 30 September 2000. Section 513(b) of the TIPRA ("ETI Provisions") repeals the provisions in Section 101(f) of the AJCA that allowed for the continuation of ETI tax benefits in respect of transactions occurring pursuant to a binding contract in effect on 17 September 2003. Section 513(c) of the TIPRA provides that "{t}he amendments made by this section shall apply to taxable years beginning after the date of the enactment of this Act".

(c) Whether a specific subsidy exists within the meaning of Articles 1 and 2 of the SCM Agreement

(i) Arguments of the European Communities

7.1386 The European Communities argues that "{t}he US Government provides financial contributions to those companies eligible for the FSC/ETI tax regime, including through the associated transitional and grandfather provisions in successor legislation" and that these financial contributions are covered by Article 1.1(a)(1)(ii) ("government revenue that is otherwise due is foregone or not collected") of the SCM Agreement.[3042]

7.1387 The European Communities submits, in this respect, that the FSC measure provides for three tax exemptions that operate together to shield income from taxation that would otherwise be taxed in the absence of the FSC measure. First, it exempts FSCs from paying taxes on a portion of their foreign trade income. Second, the FSC measure allows U.S. parents of FSCs to defer paying taxes on certain foreign trade income. Third, the FSC measure allows U.S. parents of FSCs to avoid paying taxes on dividends received from their FSCs related to "foreign trade income". Thus, these three exemptions, taken together, involve the foregoing of revenue that is otherwise due because absent the FSC measure, the tax liability of FSCs and their U.S. parents would be higher.[3043]

[3040] Tax Increase Prevention and Reconciliation Act of 2005, Pub. L. No. 109-222, § 513, Exhibit EC 627.

[3041] Panel Report, *US – FSC (Article 21.5 – EC II)*, para. 8.1; Appellate Body Report, *US – FSC (Article 21.5 – EC II)*, para. 100(b).

[3042] European Communities' first written submission, para. 952.

[3043] European Communities' first written submission, para. 953.

Report of the Panel

7.1388 The European Communities submits that the exclusion of "qualifying foreign trade income" from taxation under the ETI measure similarly shields certain income of U.S. taxpayers from taxation. Under the ETI measure only "qualifying foreign trade income" of a U.S. taxpayer is non-taxable. Such "qualifying foreign trade income" is determined on the basis of highly selective qualitative and quantitative requirements such as the "use outside the United States" requirements and the "foreign articles/labour limitation". In the absence of the ETI measure, U.S. taxpayers would be required to include in their income, and hence pay taxes on, such "qualifying foreign trade income". The ETI measure therefore results in the foregoing of revenue that is otherwise due because absent the ETI measure the tax liability of US corporations would be higher.[3044]

7.1389 The European Communities argues that the ETI Act and the AJCA maintain the FSC and ETI subsidies with respect to transactions based on certain pre-existing binding contracts and that the TIPRA did not completely terminate this flow of subsidies. Thus, the transitional and grandfather provisions of the ETI Act and the AJCA continue to provide financial contributions within the meaning of Article 1.1(a)(1)(ii) of the SCM Agreement based on the original FSC and ETI measures.[3045]

7.1390 The European Communities argues that the FSC/ETI tax breaks, including their continuation through transitional and grandfather provisions, confer benefits on Boeing's LCA division within the meaning of Article 1.1(b) of the SCM Agreement. The tax breaks relate to the production of Boeing LCA and provide Boeing's LCA division with advantages on non-market terms. Since Boeing is not required to pay anything in return for these FSC/ETI tax breaks, the entirety of the financial contributions to Boeing's LCA division can be considered to confer benefits.[3046]

7.1391 The European Communities argues that the FSC and ETI measures, including their continuation through successor legislation, are deemed to be specific within the meaning of Article 2.3 of the SCM Agreement because these measures are prohibited subsidies contingent in law upon export performance within the meaning of Article 3.1(a) of the SCM Agreement.[3047]

(ii)   Arguments of the United States

7.1392 The United States "does not dispute that FSC/ETI benefits are a financial contribution that confers a benefit and is specific".[3048]

[3044] European Communities' first written submission, para. 954.
[3045] European Communities' first written submission, para. 956.
[3046] European Communities' first written submission, para. 959.
[3047] European Communities' first written submission, para. 962.
[3048] United States' first written submission, para. 422.

1486   DSR 2012:III

US - Large Civil Aircraft (2nd Complaint)

(iii)   Evaluation by the Panel

7.1393 Before proceeding to an evaluation of whether the measures at issue are specific subsidies, the Panel finds it useful to set out its understanding of the nature of the claims made by the European Communities[3049] and of the scope of the measures challenged by the European Communities.

7.1394 First, as to the nature of the claims advanced by the European Communities, the Panel notes that these claims concern the FSC/ETI subsidies as used by a particular entity, Boeing. The European Communities asserts that "{t}hrough the US federal government's foreign sales corporations ('FSC') and extraterritorial income ('ETI') tax exemptions and exclusions, *Boeing has received over $2 billion in specific subsidies*".[3050] The European Communities also alleges that the FSC and ETI tax breaks confer benefits within the meaning of Article 1.1(b) of the SCM Agreement *on Boeing's LCA division*. In response to a panel question, the European Communities explains that "its challenge to the continuing FSC/ETI scheme does not aim at requiring the United States to withdraw all continuing effects of the scheme generally, but only *the benefit accruing to Boeing/McDonnell Douglas and the adverse effects caused thereby*".[3051] Thus, the claims of the European Communities pertain to FSC and ETI tax exemptions and exclusions specifically in relation to Boeing.[3052]

7.1395 Second, as to the scope of the challenged measures, the Panel notes that the European Communities, in its legal analysis of why these measures constitute subsidies, refers to the measures as "the FSC/ETI tax regime, including ... the associated transitional and grandfather provisions in successor legislation"[3053], "FSC/ETI tax breaks, including their continuation through transitional and grandfather provisions"[3054] and "FSC and ETI measures, including their continuation through successor legislation".[3055] As noted above, in describing the factual background to its claims, the European Communities summarizes the provisions of the U.S. Internal Revenue Code relating to foreign sales corporations, the ETI Act, the AJCA and the TIPRA. We find the following statements of the European Communities particularly instructive to understand how the European Communities' legal claim relates to each of these different measures.

7.1396 In its first written submission, the European Communities states that:

> "the ETI Act and the AJCA maintain these FSC and ETI subsidies with respect to transactions based on certain pre-existing long term

---

[3049] The European Communities makes claims with respect to the FSC/ETI and succesor act subsidies under Article 3 of the SCM Agreement, on the one hand, and Articles 5 and 6, on the other.

[3050] European Communities' first written submission, para. 921 (emphasis added).

[3051] European Communities' response to question 59, para. 207 (emphasis added).

[3052] See also above, para. 7.150.

[3053] European Communities' first written submission, para. 952.

[3054] European Communities' first written submission, para. 959.

[3055] European Communities' first written submission, para. 962.

DSR 2012:III   1487

Report of the Panel

binding contracts, and the flow of these subsidies was not completely terminated pursuant to the TIPRA. In so doing, the transitional and grandfather provisions of the ETI Act and the AJCA continue to provide financial contributions based on the original FSC and ETI measures within the meaning of Article 1.1(a)(1)(ii) of the *SCM Agreement*".[3056]

7.1397 In its second written submission, the European Communities refers to "the Foreign Sales Corporation ('FSC') and extraterritorial income ('ETI') tax breaks, as maintained through the FSC Repeal and Extraterritorial Income Exclusion Act of 2000 ('ETI Act'), American Jobs Creation Act of 2004 ('AJCA'), and Tax Increase Prevention and Reconciliation Act of 2005 ('TIPRA')".[3057]

7.1398 In its statement at the second meeting of the Panel, the European Communities explains that it "is not challenging 'TIPRA' as a separate measure, and it has no interest in doing so given that TIPRA actually repeals certain aspects of FSC/ETI. Rather, it is challenging the FSC/ETI measures listed in the Panel Request, to the extent that they provided and, despite TIPRA, continue to provide subsidies to Boeing."[3058]

7.1399 In sum, it is our understanding that: (i) the claims of the European Communities pertain to, on the one hand, the tax advantages allegedly enjoyed by Boeing under the original legislation relating to the treatment of foreign sales corporations and the ETI Act and, on the other, the continuation of those tax advantages under the transition and grandfather provisions contained in the ETI Act and the AJCA; and (ii) the European Communities relies on the TIPRA as evidence that the subsidies provided under the "binding contracts" grandfather provisions of the ETI Act and the AJCA have not been completely repealed.

7.1400 It is not in dispute that during the period 1989-2006 Boeing received tax exemptions and exclusions under the FSC and ETI legislation, including under transition and grandfather provisions of successor legislation. The Panel notes that the parties agree that these tax exemptions and tax exclusions provided to Boeing are financial contributions within the meaning of Article 1.1(a)(1)(ii) of the SCM Agreement that confer a benefit within the meaning of Article 1.1(b) and are specific within the meaning of Article 2 of the SCM Agreement.

7.1401 With respect to the existence of a subsidy under Article 1, the Panel also notes the findings made in this regard by the panels and the Appellate Body in *US – FSC, US – FSC (Article 21.5 – EC)* and *US – FSC (Article 21.5 – EC – II)*.

[3056] European Communities' first written submission, para. 955 (emphasis original).

[3057] European Communities, second written submission, para. 631.

[3058] European Communities, non-confidential statement at second meeting of the Panel with the parties, para. 78. Thus, rather than making a *claim* in respect of the TIPRA, it appears that the European Communities discusses this measure only for the purpose of pre-empting an argument that the measures at issue have been repealed.

1488   DSR 2012:III

7.1402 First, the panel in *US – FSC* made findings regarding Sections 921-927 of the Internal Revenue Code and related measures establishing special tax treatment for FSCs.[3059] The panel found that certain "exemptions identified by the European Communities under the FSC scheme" were financial contributions under Article 1.1(a)(1)(ii) of the SCM Agreement because they involved the foregoing of revenue which was otherwise due[3060] and conferred a benefit within the meaning of Article 1.1(b) of the SCM Agreement.[3061] The Appellate Body upheld the panel 's findings that the FSC exemptions were financial contributions within the meaning of Article 1.1(a)(1)(ii).

7.1403 Second, the panel in *US – FSC (Article 21.5 – EC)* made findings with respect to the ETI Act. The panel found that the ETI Act's exclusion from gross income of certain "extraterritorial income" gave rise to a financial contribution in the form of a foregoing of government revenue that was otherwise due within the meaning of Article 1.1(a)(1)(ii)[3062] and that this financial contribution conferred a benefit, such that a subsidy within the meaning of Article 1.1 existed.[3063] The Appellate Body upheld the panel's findings that the ETI measure involved a financial contribution through the foregoing of government revenue otherwise due[3064]

7.1404 Third, in *US – FSC (Article 21.5 – EC – II)*, the panel found that the United States, by enacting Section 101 of the AJCA, maintained the prohibited FSC and ETI subsidies through transition and grandfather clauses in section 101 of the AJCA.[3065] The Appellate Body upheld this finding.[3066]

7.1405 Regarding specificity, we further note that, in addition to the agreement of the parties on this issue, Article 2.3 of the SCM Agreement provides that subsidies that are contingent upon export performance within the meaning of Article 3 of the SCM Agreement shall be deemed to be specific. In *US – FSC, US – FSC (Article 21.5 – EC)* and *US – FSC (Article 21.5 – EC II)*, the FSC/ETI subsidies at issue were found to be export contingent. In addition, this Panel finds further below[3067] that the measures at issue are export contingent. Accordingly, we conclude here that they are specific within the meaning of Article 2 of the SCM Agreement.

7.1406 For these reasons, the Panel finds that tax exemptions and tax exclusions provided to Boeing under the FSC and ETI legislation, including the transition and grandfather provisions of the ETI Act and the AJCA, constitute specific subsidies within the meaning of Articles 1 and 2 of the SCM Agreement.

[3059] Panel Report, *US – FSC*, para. 11.
[3060] Panel Report, *US – FSC*, para. 7.102.
[3061] Panel Report, *US – FSC*, para. 7.103.
[3062] Panel Report, *US – FSC (Article 21.5 – EC)*, para. 8.43.
[3063] Panel Report, *US – FSC (Article 21.5 – EC)*, para. 8.48.
[3064] Appellate Body Report, *US – FSC (Article 21.5 – EC)*, para. 106.
[3065] Panel Report, *US – FSC (Article 21.5 – EC II)*, para. 7.65.
[3066] Appellate Body Report, *US – FSC (Article 21.5 – EC II)*, para. 96.
[3067] See below, paras. 7.1450-7.1464.

Report of the Panel

(d)   Amount of the subsidy to Boeing's LCA division

(i)   Arguments of the European Communities

7.1407 The European Communities estimates that the amount of the subsidy to Boeing's LCA division through 2006 in the form of FSC/ETI tax breaks is $2.199 billion.[3068]

7.1408 The European Communities argues that the TIPRA[3069] repeals certain aspects of the grandfathering of FSC and ETI tax breaks for tax years beginning after 2006 but does not end the flow of all FSC/ETI benefits after 2006. The European Communities asserts, in the light of a memorandum from the Internal Revenue Service's Office of Chief Counsel[3070], that Boeing will continue to benefit from the FSC/ETI benefits. Specifically, Boeing will continue to receive certain FSC/ETI benefits to the extent that Boeing recognizes revenue after 2006 that (i) is derived from a firm order or option exercised prior to the end of 2006, where (ii) such order or exercised option was made pursuant to a binding contract that qualifies under either the "FSC binding contract rule" of the ETI Act or the "ETI binding contract rule" of the AJCA.[3071] While the financial contributions from the FSC/ETI measures continue to apply after 2006, the European Communities has been unable to provide an estimate of the future value of those subsidies to Boeing's LCA division.[3072]

7.1409 The European Communities submits that there is no support for the argument of the United States that Boeing will not take advantage of the FSC/ETI subsidies after 2006. The statement in Boeing's 2006 annual report relied upon by the United States[3073], is not dispositive of what Boeing may or may not do as of 1 January 2007 with regard to the FSC/ETI breaks. First, the statement that "2006 will be the final year for recognizing any export tax benefits" is based on the text of the TIPRA and does not take into account the implications of the December 2006 Internal Revenue Service memorandum which interpreted the TIPRA as repealing the FSC/ETI binding contract rules only prospectively. Second, the auditors report and the CEO/CFO certifications are limited to "material" facts or to "the circumstances under which such statements were made". In other words, the statements made in the annual report do not necessarily reflect the full implications of the December 2006 Internal Revenue Service memorandum, as those implications may not have been entirely

---

[3068] European Communities' first written submission, para. 957; International Trade Resources LLC, FSC/ETI Tax Benefits Provided to U.S. Large Civil Aircraft Producers, Exhibit EC-12. The European Communities asks the Panel to adopts this estimate as the best information available and, as appropriate, draw adverse inferences due to the United States' non-cooperation in the information gathering process. European Communities' first written submission, para. 958.

[3069] See above, para. 7.1385.

[3070] Office of Chief Counsel, Qualification for FSC Benefits and ETI Exclusions, Internal Revenue Service Memorandum Number AM 2007.001, 22 December 2006, Exhibit EC-628, p.6.

[3071] European Communities' first written submission, para. 945.

[3072] European Communities' first written submission, para. 957.

[3073] See below, para. 7.1423.

1490   DSR 2012:III

known or understood at the time Boeing issued its annual report. The European Communities notes that the United States has not submitted a certified and enforceable statement from a Boeing official stating that regardless of the interpretation issued by the Internal Revenue Service in its December 2006 memorandum, Boeing will disclaim all FSC/ETI tax breaks after 2006.[3074] The European Communities argues that given how easy it would be for someone at Boeing to author a one or two paragraph affidavit to defend the United States' position on post-2006 FSC/ETI tax benefits to Boeing – something that Boeing has done to defend other claims on a number of other occasions – the fact that Boeing and the United States have not submitted such an affidavit must be taken into account by the Panel when evaluating the European Communities' claims.[3075]

7.1410 In response to a Panel question, the European Communities stresses that it includes within the scope of this dispute the financial contributions and benefits that Boeing continues to receive after 2006. The statement in paragraph 957 of its first written submission that "the financial contributions from FSC/ETI continue to apply after 2006, although the European Communities has been unable to provide an estimate of the future value of those subsidies to Boeing's LCA Division" indicates simply that the European Communities does not have sufficient information to value the FSC/ETI benefits to Boeing after 2006. Thus, it is indeed necessary for the Panel to reach a conclusion on whether Boeing will continue to receive financial contributions and benefits under the FSC/ETI-related measures after 2006.[3076]

7.1411 Regarding the statement by Boeing, submitted by the United States in its response to a panel question, that Boeing "did not receive any benefits from FSC or successor legislation after 31 December 2006", the European Communities asserts that this statement does not indicate that Boeing does not plan to recognise benefits from FSC or successor legislation in its tax filings after 20 July 2009, the date of the signed statement. The European Communities recalls in this regard that it is clear from the Internal Revenue Service memorandum of 22 December 2006 that Boeing may continue to receive certain FSC/ETI benefits after 2006. Because the type of revenue in respect of which Boeing can continue to receive the FSC/ETI benefits can be recognised after 20 July 2009, the benefits from FSC and successor measures can likewise be realised after that date. The United States and Boeing have not presented any evidence to rebut this understanding. The European Communities also points out that the United States' response to this question has no impact on the amount of the FSC/ETI subsidies at issue, as the European Communities has never

---

[3074] European Communities' second written submission, paras. 635-637.
[3075] European Communities' comments on United States' response to question 226, paras. 282-284.
[3076] European Communities' response to panel question no. 30, paras. 99-100.

Report of the Panel

attempted to provide an estimate of the future value of those subsidies to Boeing's LCA division.[3077]

(ii) Arguments of the United States

7.1412 The United States does not dispute the European Communities' estimate of FSC/ETI benefits related to large civil aircraft during the period 1989-2006.[3078]

7.1413 The United States rejects the contention of the European Communities that Boeing will continue to receive certain FSC/ETI benefits after 2006. In this connection, the United States refers to a statement in Boeing's 2006 annual report.[3079] Since the European Communities has presented no reason to disbelieve this certified statement by Boeing's officers the Panel should conclude that Boeing ceased receiving FSC/ETI benefits as of 31 December 2006. Accordingly, with regard to any claims of threat of serious prejudice, FSC/ETI benefits should not enter into the analysis.[3080]

7.1414 The United States argues that the European Communities does not contest that Boeing has stated that it will not use the FSC/ETI subsidy after the 2006 tax year. Instead, the European Communities focuses on a memorandum issued by an Associate Chief Counsel of the Internal Revenue Service with regard to the eligibility for FSC/ETI benefits in some circumstances. As evidence, that general evaluation should not supersede the conclusion reached by Boeing with regard to its specific tax situation that it will not use that subsidy in the future. In addition, the European Communities has ignored a statement at the beginning of the memorandum, saying "This advice may not be used or cited as precedent".[3081]

7.1415 The United States considers that, in the light of the fact that the European Communities excludes any FSC/ETI benefits that Boeing will receive after 2006 from its calculations and in the light of Boeing's statement that it will not receive such benefits after 2006, there is no need for the Panel to make a finding as to whether Boeing will continue to receive such benefits after 2006.[3082] In response to the argument of the European Communities that the Panel should apply adverse inference to estimate the value of FSC/ETI benefits after 2006 in the light of "the US non-cooperation with Annex V and otherwise", the United

---

[3077] European Communities' comments on United States' response panel question 369, paras. 202-206.

[3078] United States' first written submission, para. 422. The United States observes that it does "not agree with all aspects of the EC calculation, but the EC's estimate is sufficient for purposes of Article 6, given that the general magnitude of a subsidy, and not its precise percentage incidence, is the focus of the analysis under that article". United States' first written submission, para, 422, footnote 576.

[3079] United States' first written submission, para. 423; Boeing Annual Report (2006), Exhibit US-126, p. 55.

[3080] United States' first written submission, para. 425.

[3081] United States' non-confidential statement at first meeting of the Panel with the parties, para. 25.

[3082] United States' response to question 30, para. 79.

1492 DSR 2012:III

States asserts that it has submitted all of the information on this topic available to it namely the statement in Boeing's 2006 annual report that it will not receive FSC/ETI benefits after the 2006 tax year. No party can submit unavailable evidence and the absence of that evidence supports only the conclusion that the party has cooperated to the best of its ability.[3083]

7.1416 The United States submits that there are many forms of evidence in addition to affidavits. The United States in this instance has chosen to rely on a statement in Boeing's financial report stating that it will not take advantage of FSC/ETI benefits after 2006. The European Communities has provided no evidence to the contrary. Its only rebuttal is to assert that Boeing would be eligible for that subsidy. However, eligibility and actual use are two very different concepts. Even if the European Communities had proven that Boeing would qualify for FSC/ETI benefits on the basis of the Internal Revenue Service memorandum, that would not constitute evidence that the company actually will use those benefits.

7.1417 In response to a Panel question whether Boeing received any FSC benefits after 31 December 2006, the United States indicates: "No, Boeing did not receive any FSC benefits after December 31, 2006"[3084] In support of this answer, the United States submits a statement by Boeing's Vice-Director for Tax.[3085]

(iii)   Evaluation by the Panel

7.1418 The European Communities estimates that the amount of the FSC/ETI subsidies to Boeing's LCA division during the period 1989-2006 is $2.199 billion. The European Communities has provided a detailed explanation of the methodology used in deriving this figure.[3086] The United States has indicated that it does not dispute the estimate by the European Communities of FSC/ETI benefits related to large civil aircraft during the period 1989-2006.

7.1419 In the light of the explanation provided by the European Communities of the methodology used for deriving its estimate of the amount of FSC/ETI subsidies to Boeing during the period 1989-2006 and the statement of the United States that it does not dispute the European Communities' estimate, the Panel estimates that the amount of FSC/ETI subsidies to Boeing's LCA division in the period 1989-2006 is $2.199 billion.

[3083] United States' comments on European Communities' response to question 30, para. 112.

[3084] United States' response to question 369, para. 225.

[3085] Statement of James H. Zrust, Exhibit US-1341.

[3086] International Trade Resources LLC, FSC/ETI Tax Benefits Provided to U.S. Large Civil Aircraft Producers, Exhibit EC-12. At paragraph 3, ITR explains that "...Boeing and MD received a total of $2,284 million in FSC/ETI benefits during the period from 1989 through 2005. Of this amount, approximately $2,059 million was related to sales of LCA. In addition, ITR estimates that Boeing will receive a further $140 million in LCA-related FSC/ETI benefits in 2006. Thus, Boeing's total LCA-related FSC/ETI benefits from 1989 through 2006 is estimated to be $2,199 million."

DSR 2012:III

Report of the Panel

7.1420 While there is no disagreement between the parties on the characterization of the FSC/ETI tax advantages provided to Boeing through 2006 as specific subsidies and on the amount of these subsidies, they disagree on the question of whether Boeing will continue to receive FSC/ETI benefits in the post-2006 period.

7.1421 The Panel notes that the factual evidence provided by the European Communities in support of its assertion that Boeing will continue to receive FSC/ETI benefits after 2006 consists of an Internal Revenue Service memorandum that sets forth a prospective interpretation of the TIPRA repeal date. Specifically, the European Communities relies on the following passage from this memorandum:

> "The TIPRA repeal date repeals the {FSC and ETI} binding contract rules for taxable years that begin after May 17, 2006. Because the binding contract rules apply on a transaction-by-transaction basis, we interpret the TIPRA repeal date as repealing the binding contract rules prospectively, on a transaction-by-transaction basis, for transactions entered into during a taxable year that begins after May 17, 2006. In other words, the binding contract rules {continue to} apply to certain transactions, but only if such transactions are *not* entered into in a taxable year that begins *after* May 17, 2006."[3087]

7.1422 The analysis in this memorandum is of a general nature and does not specifically relate to Boeing.

7.1423 The Panel notes that with its first written submission the United States provided a statement from Boeing's 2006 annual report:

> "On May 17, 2006, the Tax Increase Prevention and Reconciliation Act of 2005 was enacted, which repealed the FSC/ETI exclusion tax benefit binding contract provisions of the American Jobs Creation Act of 2004. Therefore, 2006 will be the final year for recognizing any export tax benefits. The 2006 effective tax rate was reduced by 5.8% due to export tax benefits."[3088]

7.1424 At a later stage of this proceeding, the United States also submitted a statement of Mr. James H. Zrust, the Vice President of Tax of The Boeing Company, dated 20 July 2009, who "confirm(s) that Boeing did not receive any FSC benefits after 31 December 2006".[3089]

[3087] Qualification for FSC benefits and ETI Exclusions, Office of Chief Counsel, Internal Revenue Service Memorandum Number AM 2007-001, 22 December 2006, Exhibit EC-628, p. 6.

[3088] Boeing Annual Report (2006), Exhibit US-126, p. 55.

[3089] Statement of James H. Zrust, Exhibit US-1341. The statement indicates that Mr Zrust has "personal knowledge of The Boeing Company's... and Boeing Commercial Airplanes' ... tax issues,

1494   DSR 2012:III

US - Large Civil Aircraft (2nd Complaint)

7.1425 Therefore, while it may be true, as argued by the European Communities on the basis of the December 2006 memorandum of the Internal Revenue Service, that it is possible in certain circumstances for a company to continue to benefit from the FSC/ETI measure through the prospective interpretation of the TIPRA repeal provision, this must be weighed against other evidence before the Panel that suggests that Boeing has not actually used this possibility.[3090]

7.1426 Moreover, the assertion of the European Communities that Boeing will continue to benefit from FSC/ETI tax exemptions and tax exclusions in the post-2006 period is inconsistent with the fact that a document submitted by the European Communities on the amounts of subsidies in the period 1989-2006 and 2007-2024 indicates that the amount of FSC/ETI subsidies in the period 2007-2024 is $0.[3091] [3092] This document explicitly states that "{t}he benefits from FSC/ETI after 2006 are zero due to the repeal of the grandfather provisions relating to FSC/ETI."[3093]

7.1427 In any event, the Panel is not convinced that it is necessary to make a finding as to whether Boeing will continue to receive FSC/ETI benefits. In our view, the European Communities has not adequately explained how such a finding is relevant to the Panel's evaluation of the European Communities' claims of present serious prejudice and threat of serious prejudice or to its claim of the existence of prohibited subsidies. In this regard, the Panel finds the response of the European Communities to question 30 unpersuasive. In this question, the Panel sought a clarification from the European Communities as to why it was necessary for the Panel to reach a conclusion on whether Boeing will receive FSC/ETI benefits after 2006, given that the European Communities had not included any future amounts of FSC/ETI benefits in the estimate of the overall amount of FSC/ETI subsidies at issue in this dispute. In its response to this question, the European Communities states that it "includes within the scope of this dispute" the FSC/ETI benefits that Boeing continues to receive after 2006. The Panel considers that the statement that the European Communities "includes within the scope of this dispute" FSC/ETI benefits that Boeing will

---

including issues with respect to the Foreign Sales Corporation... Extraterritorial Income Exclusion Act ...and successor legislation."

[3090] We consider that the mere fact that, as argued by the European Communities, Boeing has not explicitly stated that it does not plan to recognise benefits from FSC or successor legislation in its tax filings after 20 July 2009 is not sufficient to conclude that Boeing will actually use FSC/ETI benefits after July 2009.

[3091] Amount of Subsidies to Boeing's LCA Division, Exhibit EC-17, pp. 1,5.

[3092] We also note that data provided by the European Communities indicates that the "magnitude" of the FSC/ETI subsidies during the reference period (2004-2006) is $0. International Trade Resources LLC, Calculating On A Per-Aircraft Basis the Magnitude Of The Subsidies Provided to US Large Civil Aircraft, Table 4: Subsidy Magnitude by Subsidy Program, Exhibit EC-13.

[3093] Amount of Subsidies to Boeing's LCA Division, Exhibit EC-17, p.7. While the European Communities argues that the non-inclusion of future amounts of FSC/ETI subsidies is due to a lack of information resulting from an absence of cooperation by the United States, we see nothing in this document that suggests that future amounts of FSC/ETI subsidies could not be calculated because of a lack of cooperation by the United States.

DSR 2012:III

Report of the Panel

receive post-2006 is too vague and abstract to clarify how those benefits are relevant to the claims of the European Communities. We note, in this regard, that the European Communities acknowledges that whether or not Boeing continues to receive FSC/ETI post-2006 does not affect its estimate of the overall amount of FSC/ETI subsidies to Boeing.

7.1428 Therefore, the Panel does not consider it necessary to reach a conclusion as to whether there is sufficient evidence before it to support the European Communities' contention that Boeing will continue to receive FSC/ETI benefits in the post-2006 period.

(e) Conclusion

7.1429 **For these reasons, the Panel finds that: (i) tax exemptions and tax exclusions provided to Boeing under the FSC and ETI legislation, including the transition and grandfather provisions of the ETI Act and the AJCA, constitute specific subsidies within the meaning of Articles 1 and 2 of the SCM Agreement; and (ii) the amount of FSC/ETI subsidies to Boeing's LCA division in the period 1989-2006 can be estimated to be \$2.199 billion.**

9. *Summary of conclusions on whether the measures at issue constitute specific subsidies within the meaning of Articles 1 and 2 of the SCM Agreement*

7.1430 In this section of our Report, we have examined whether the measures challenged by the European Communities constitute specific subsidies within the meaning of Articles 1 and 2 of the SCM Agreement, as well as the amount of any such subsidies that is allocable to Boeing's LCA division.

7.1431 We have found that a number of the measures challenged by the European Communities do constitute specific subsidies:

(a) State of Washington and municipalities therein

    (i) the Business and Occupation ("B&O") tax reduction provided for in Washington House Bill 2294 ("HB 2294");

    (ii) the B&O tax credits for preproduction development, computer software and hardware and property taxes provided for in HB 2294;

    (iii) the sales and use tax exemptions for computer hardware, peripherals and software provided for in HB 2294;

    (iv) the City of Everett B&O tax reduction;

    (v) workforce development programme and employment resource center;

(b) State of Kansas and municipalities therein

    (i) the property and sales tax abatements provided to Boeing pursuant to Industrial Revenue Bonds ("IRBs") issued by the State of Kansas and municipalities therein;

1496

DSR 2012:III

(c) State of Illinois and municipalities therein

    (i) the reimbursement of a portion of Boeing's relocation expenses provided for in the *Corporate Headquarters Relocation Act* ("CHRA");

    (ii) the 15-year Economic Development for a Growing Economy ("EDGE") tax credits provided for in the CHRA;

    (iii) the abatement or refund of a portion of Boeing's property taxes provided for in the CHRA;

    (iv) the payment to retire the lease of the previous tenant of Boeing's new headquarters building;

(d) National Aeronautics and Space Administration (NASA)

    (i) the payments made to Boeing pursuant to procurement contracts entered into under the eight aeronautics R&D programmes at issue;

    (ii) the access to government facilities, equipment and employees provided to Boeing pursuant to procurement contracts and Space Act Agreements entered into under the eight aeronautics R&D programmes at issue;

(e) Department of Defense (DOD)

    (i) the payments made to Boeing pursuant to assistance instruments entered into under the 23 RDT&E programmes at issue;

    (ii) the access to government facilities provided to Boeing pursuant to assistance instruments entered into under the 23 RDT&E programmes at issue;

(f) FSC/ETI

    (i) the tax exemptions and tax exclusions provided to Boeing under FSC/ETI legislation, including the transition and grandfather provisions of the ETI Act and the AJCA.

7.1432 However, we have concluded that the European Communities has ***not demonstrated*** that the following measures constitute ***specific subsidies*** within the meaning of Articles 1 and 2 of the SCM Agreement, and/or that any amount of the alleged specific subsidy should be allocated to Boeing's LCA division:

(a) State of Washington and municipalities therein

    (i) the sales and use tax exemptions for construction services and equipment provided for in HB 2294;

    (ii) the leasehold tax exemptions provided for in HB 2294;

    (iii) the property tax exemptions provided for in HB 2294;

    (iv) the I-5 and SR 527 expansion projects, the construction of a rail-barge transfer facility and the expansion of the South Terminal by the Port of Everett;

Report of the Panel

- (v) the waiver of 747 LCF landing fees at Paine Field;
- (vi) the freezing of rates charged to Boeing of certain utility services;
- (vii) the provision of coordinators in connection with Project Olympus;
- (viii) tax and other incentives related to the 747 LCF;
- (ix) the assumption by Washington State of costs of MSA-related legal proceedings;

(b) State of Kansas and municipalities therein
- (i) the payments made to Spirit Aerosytems arising from the issuance of Kansas Development Finance Authority Bonds ("KDFA") bonds;

(c) DOD
- (i) the payments made to Boeing pursuant to procurement contracts entered into under the 23 RDT&E programmes at issue;
- (ii) the access to government facilities provided to Boeing pursuant to procurement contracts entered into under the 23 RDT&E programmes at issue;

(d) NASA/DOD
- (i) the allocation of intellectual property rights under NASA and DOD R&D contracts and agreements entered into with Boeing;
- (ii) the reimbursement of independent R&D and bid and proposal ("IR&D/B&P") expenses under NASA and DOD R&D contracts and agreements with Boeing;

(e) Department of Commerce
- (i) the payments made to joint ventures / consortia in which Boeing participated through the Advanced Technology Program;

(f) Department of Labor
- (i) the payment made to Edmonds Community College under the High Growth Job Training Initiative.

7.1433 With respect to the amount of the specific subsidies found to exist, we have estimated that the amount of these subsidies to Boeing's LCA division was at least $5.3 billion over the period 1989-2006:

1498
DSR 2012:III

US - Large Civil Aircraft (2nd Complaint)

Amount of subsidies to Boeing's LCA division over the period 1989-2006[3094]

Government(s) or Government Agency	Measures found to constitute specific subsidies within the meaning of Articles 1 and 2	Amount of the subsidy to Boeing's LCA division over the period 1989-2006
State of Washington and Municipalities therein	- Business and Occupation ("B&O") tax reduction provided for in Washington House Bill 2294 ("HB 2294") - B&O tax credits for preproduction development, computer software and hardware and property taxes provided for in HB 2294 - sales and use tax exemptions for computer hardware, peripherals and software provided for in HB 2294 - City of Everett B&O tax reduction - workforce development programme and employment resource center	$77.7 million
State of Kansas and Municipalities therein	- property and sales tax abatements provided to Boeing pursuant to Industrial Revenue Bonds ("IRBs") issued by the State of Kansas and municipalities therein	$476 million
State of Illinois and Municipalities therein	- reimbursement of a portion of Boeing's relocation expenses provided for in the *Corporate Headquarters Relocation Act* ("CHRA") - 15-year Economic Development for a Growing Economy ("EDGE") tax credits provided for in the CHRA - abatement or refund of a portion of Boeing's property taxes provided for in the CHRA - payment to retire the lease of the previous tenant of Boeing's new headquarters building	$11 million
NASA	- the payments made to Boeing pursuant to procurement contracts entered into under the eight aeronautics R&D programmes at issue - the access to government facilities, equipment and employees provided to Boeing pursuant to procurement contracts and Space Act Agreements entered into under the eight aeronautics R&D programmes at issue	$2.6 billion

---

[3094] For the reasons set out at paragraphs 7.153-7.158 above, the Panel does not take into account any post-2006 subsidy amounts.

Report of the Panel

Government(s) or Government Agency	Measures found to constitute specific subsidies within the meaning of Articles 1 and 2	Amount of the subsidy to Boeing's LCA division over the period 1989-2006
DOD	- the payments made to Boeing pursuant to assistance instruments entered into under the RDT&E Program Elements at issue - the access to government facilities provided to Boeing pursuant to assistance instruments entered into under the RDT&E Program Elements at issue	the amount of the subsidy to Boeing's LCA division is unclear
FSC/ETI	- the tax exemptions and tax exclusions provided to Boeing under FSC/ETI legislation, including the transition and grandfather provisions of the ETI Act and the AJCA	$2.2 billion
Total		at least $5.3 billion

E.   *Whether the FSC/ETI Measures and the Washington HB 2294 Tax Measures Are Prohibited Subsidies within the Meaning of Article 3 of the SCM Agreement*

7.1434 In this section of our Report we examine whether the FSC/ETI measures challenged by the European Communities and the taxation measures enacted through HB 2294 are prohibited subsidies within the meaning of Article 3.1(a) of the SCM Agreement.

1.   *FSC/ETI and successor act subsidies*

(a)   Introduction

7.1435 The European Communities claims that "FSC/ETI and successor act subsidies" are inconsistent with Articles 3.1(a) and 3.2 of the SCM Agreement.

7.1436 The United States argues that this claim of the European Communities is superfluous and provides no basis for the Panel to make a finding or render a recommendation.

(b)   The measures at issue

7.1437 A description of the measures referred to by the European Communities as "FSC/ETI and successor act subsidies" is provided at paragraphs 7.1378-7.1385 of this Report.

(c)   Arguments of the European Communities

7.1438 The European Communities submits that the subsidies provided by the FSC/ETI measures and successor legislation are contingent in law upon export performance within the meaning of Article 3.1(a) of the SCM Agreement, and therefore inconsistent with the obligations of the United States under Article 3.2. The European Communities recalls that WTO panels and the Appellate Body

1500   DSR 2012:III

US - Large Civil Aircraft (2nd Complaint)

have repeatedly found these tax breaks to constitute WTO-incompatible export subsidies.

7.1439 The European Communities argues that the FSC measure is contingent in law upon export performance within the meaning of Article 3.1(a) because the measure itself provides that the FSC exemptions are available only with respect to "foreign trade income", which arises from the sale or lease of "export property" or the provision of related services. Such "export property" is explicitly limited to goods manufactured, produced, grown or extracted in the United States that are held for direct use, consumption or disposition outside the United States i.e. exports. The existence and amount of the FSC subsidy therefore depends upon the existence of income arising from the exportation of U.S. goods or the provision of related services, based on the text of the FSC measure itself. Consequently, these subsidies are contingent in law upon export performance within the meaning of Article 3.1(a).[3095] This is confirmed by item (e) of the Illustrative List of Export Subsidies in Annex I to the SCM Agreement, which lists the following as an illustrative export subsidy: "The full or partial exemption remission, or deferral specifically related to exports, of direct taxes or social welfare charges paid or payable by industrial or commercial enterprises."[3096]

7.1440 The European Communities argues that the ETI scheme is contingent in law upon export performance within the meaning of Article 3.1(a) because the words of the ETI Act make it clear that, at least in certain defined situations, the ETI subsidy is conditioned upon exportation. The ETI measure allows U.S. taxpayers to exclude only their "extraterritorial income" that is "qualifying foreign trade income" from taxation.[3097] Such income is derived from the sale of "qualifying foreign trade property", which is generally property produced within or outside the United States that is sold for use outside the United States i.e. exports, in those instances when the property is produced within the United States. Thus, with respect to goods produced within the United States, the ETI tax exclusion is available only in the instances when such goods are exported outside the United States. As the ETI Act itself makes exporting a precondition to qualify for the subsidy with respect to goods produced in the United States, the ETI subsidies are contingent in law upon export performance within the meaning of Article 3.1(a).[3098],[3099]

7.1441 The European Communities submits that by maintaining the FSC and ETI subsidies through the grandfather provisions of the ETI Act and the AJCA, the United States continues to grant subsidies based on the original FSC and ETI

[3095] The European Communities cites the Panel Report, *US – FSC*, paras. 7.106-7.108 and the Appellate Body Report, *US – FSC*, para. 121.

[3096] European Communities' first written submission, paras. 966-967.

[3097] ETI Act, § 3(a), IRC §§ 114(a)-(b), Exhibit EC-625.

[3098] The European Communities cites the Panel Report, *US – FSC (Article 21.5 – EC)*, paras. 8.60-8.75 and the Appellate Body Report, *US –FSC (Article 21.5 – EC)*, paras. 113-120.

[3099] European Communities' first written submission, para. 968.

DSR 2012:III

1501

Report of the Panel

measures that are contingent in law upon export performance within the meaning of Article 3.1(a). The inconsistency of these measures with Article 3.1(a) was confirmed by the panel and Appellate Body reports in *US – FSC (Article 21.5 – EC II)*. The European Communities contends that the export contingent subsidy continues to be available, especially to companies such as Boeing, because of the manner in which the U.S. Internal Revenue Service has interpreted the TIPRA repeal date.[3100]

7.1442 In its response to a panel question as to whether the European Communities' claim that the FSC/ETI measures are contingent upon export performance within the meaning of Article 3.1(a) is properly before this Panel[3101], the European Communities argues that its claim in this dispute is different from any claim that has previously been litigated before a WTO panel or the Appellate Body. Although the Appellate Body has stated in *Canada – Aircraft* that "adverse effects are presumed" for "cases that involve prohibited export subsidies", prior disputes involving the FSC/ETI scheme did not involve claims or findings of adverse effects within the meaning of Article 5 of the SCM Agreement. Because the European Communities bases the "specificity" aspect of its actionable subsidy claim with respect to FSC/ETI on Article 2.3 of the SCM Agreement, which requires a finding that the subsidy is a prohibited subsidy, the European Communities establishes that the FSC/ETI scheme is a prohibited subsidy. The European Communities recalls in this connection that the Panel in *US – Upland Cotton* found that Brazil had failed to meet its burden of presenting a prima facie case that the FSC/ETI regime was an export subsidy, despite prior Panel and Appellate Body rulings to that effect.[3102]

7.1443 The European Communities also submits that with respect to the export subsidy claim, as such, there has never been a final resolution of at least one aspect of the particular claim at issue in this dispute – namely, whether the FSC/ETI scheme (and its violation of Article 3.1) continues today in the light of (i) TIPRA, which repealed certain aspects of the grandfathering of FSC and ETI

[3100] European Communities' first written submission, paras. 969-970 and 944-945.

[3101] Panel Question 58:

> "In its first written submission, the European Communities recalls that "WTO panels and the Appellate Body have repeatedly found these tax breaks to constitute WTO-incompatible export subsidies" (e.g. para. 964 and footnote 1684). In *US – Shrimp (Article 21.5 – Malaysia)*, the Appellate Body clarified that Appellate Body Reports that are adopted by the DSB must be treated by the parties to a particular dispute "as a final resolution to that dispute". In *EC – Bed Linen (Article 21.5 – India)*, the Appellate Body clarified that an unappealed finding included in a panel report that is adopted by the DSB must likewise be treated "as a *final resolution* to a dispute between the parties in respect of the *particular* claim and the *specific* component of a measure that is the subject of that claim". On that basis, the Appellate Body concluded that a particular claim "was not properly before the Panel". Is the European Communities' claim, i.e. that "subsidies provided by the FSC/ETI measures and successor legislation are contingent in law upon export performance" ...properly before this Panel?"

[3102] European Communities' response to question 58, paras. 201-202.

1502

DSR 2012:III

US - Large Civil Aircraft (2nd Complaint)

tax breaks for tax years beginning after 2006 (which, in Boeing's case, is the 2007 calendar year); and (ii) the 22 December 2006 memorandum from the Internal Revenue Service Office of Chief Counsel indicating that FSC/ETI benefits continue beyond 2006.[3103] Finally, the European Communities argues that it is clear that a Member may choose to challenge a subsidy as being both a prohibited subsidy under Part II of the SCM Agreement and an actionable subsidy under Part III of the SCM Agreement.[3104]

7.1444 In response to the argument of the United States that the TIPRA is a future measure outside the terms of reference of the Panel, the European Communities points out that its panel request expressly includes "any relevant subsequent amendments thereof or successor acts", a formulation that surely covers TIPRA to the extent that it is relevant to this proceeding. More fundamentally, the European Communities is not challenging TIPRA as a separate measure, and it has no interest in doing so given that TIPRA actually repeals certain aspects of FSC/ETI. Rather, the European Communities is challenging the FSC/ETI measures listed in the panel request, to the extent that they provided and, despite TIPRA, continue to provide subsidies to Boeing.[3105]

7.1445 The European Communities considers that the United States' acknowledgement that FSC/ETI-related benefits to Boeing are specific does not obviate the need for the Panel to address the European Communities' claim that the FSC/ETI-related benefits to Boeing are inconsistent with Article 3.1(a).[3106]

7.1446 In response to a panel question, the European Communities states that it does not believe that it is effectively asking the Panel to adjudicate whether the United States has failed to comply with the recommendations and rulings of the DSB in *US - FSC*. However, this issue is immaterial because, in any event, there is no legal bar in the DSU to a complaining Member preferring the route of fresh panel proceedings, as opposed to proceedings under Article 21.5 of the DSU.[3107]

(d)   Arguments of the United States

7.1447 The United States does not contest that the FSC/ETI measures, including as applied to Boeing, constituted export subsidies that were prohibited under Article 3 of the SCM Agreement.[3108]

[3103] European Communities' response to question 58, para. 203.

[3104] European Communities' response to question 58, paras. 204-206.

[3105] European Communities' non-confidential statement at second meeting of the Panel with the parties, paras. 77-78.

[3106] European Communities' response to question 264, para. 466.

[3107] European Communities' response to question 265, para. 467.

[3108] United States' non-confidential statement at first meeting of the Panel with the parties, para. 25 ("The United States does not contest that FSC/ETI was an export subsidy"); United States' response to question 58, para. 163; United States' response to question 60, para. 167; United States' response to question 266, para. 457.

DSR 2012:III

1503

Report of the Panel

7.1448 In response to a panel question[3109], the United States argues that the European Communities' claim that FSC/ETI measures and successor legislation are contingent in law on export performance is superfluous and provides no basis for the Panel to make a finding or render a recommendation. There is no dispute between the United States and the European Communities as to whether FSC or ETI benefits are subsidies prohibited by the SCM Agreement. They are export-contingent subsidies and, therefore, prohibited subsidies inconsistent with the SCM Agreement. The DSB has ruled that this is the case, and has recommended that the United States bring those measures into compliance with the SCM Agreement. Another finding that they are export contingent or another recommendation that they be brought into compliance with the SCM Agreement will add nothing to the force or effect of the earlier rulings or recommendations. Therefore, making such a finding or recommendation would be superfluous. The United States notes, in this regard, that Article 3.7 of the DSU provides that the "aim of the dispute settlement mechanism is to secure a positive solution to a dispute". Given the existing rulings and recommendations, which constitute a final resolution to the *FSC/ETI* dispute between the European Communities and the United States, additional rulings and recommendations would not provide any additional assistance to "secure{ing} a positive solution". For these reasons, the Panel should decline to address the question whether FSC or ETI is a prohibited subsidy.[3110] In response to a panel question, the United States argues that a panel can decide not to address a claim where it will not further the resolution of the dispute. The United States also submits that, in its first written submission, the European Communities asks the Panel to recommend that the United States "withdraw its prohibited subsidies without delay", which would mean that the United States would have an additional period of time in which to withdraw FSC/ETI subsidies to Boeing. As the United States has explained, Boeing has already affirmed that it will not be receiving FSC/ETI subsidies after 2006.[3111]

7.1449 The United States contends that, in its response to question 58, the European Communities for the first time states that it seeks a "final resolution" of the question "whether the FSC/ETI (and its violation of Article 3.1 of the SCM Agreement) continues today in the light of (i) the Tax Increase Prevention and Reconciliation Act of 2005 ('TIPRA')." This claim is not within the Panel's terms of reference and, as a consequence, the DSU does not permit the European Communities to bring these claims before the Panel. The European Communities' request for establishment of a panel does not reference TIPRA. Therefore, although the European Communities might "seek" a "final resolution" of whether TIPRA allows a measure to continue, it did not include TIPRA

[3109] See above, footnote 3101.
[3110] United States' response to question 58, paras. 163-166.
[3111] United States' response to question 266, paras. 457-458.

1504

DSR 2012:III

within the terms of reference of this Panel. Thus, the question of whether TIPRA is inconsistent with the SCM Agreement is not properly before the Panel.[3112]

(e) Evaluation by the Panel[3113]

7.1450 The European Communities requests the Panel to make a finding that "FSC/ETI and successor act subsidies" are contingent upon export performance within the meaning of Article 3.1(a) of the SCM Agreement and that, as a consequence, "through the ... federal FSC/ETI tax breaks, the United States provides prohibited subsidies, in violation of Articles 3.1(a) and 3.2 of the *SCM Agreement*".[3114] In this regard, the European Communities also requests the Panel "to recommend that the United States withdraw its prohibited subsidies without delay, as required by Article 4.7 of the *SCM Agreement*".[3115]

7.1451 There is no substantive disagreement between the parties to this dispute that FSC and ETI tax benefits have been provided to Boeing under provisions of U.S. tax law that were inconsistent with Articles 3.1(a) and 3.2 of the SCM Agreement.

7.1452 The Panel notes the findings made in this regard by the panels and the Appellate Body in *US – FSC*, *US – FSC (Article 21.5 – EC)* and *US – FSC (Article 21.5 – EC II)*.

7.1453 First, the panel in *US – FSC* made findings regarding Sections 921-927 of the Internal Revenue Code and related measures establishing special tax treatment for FSCs.[3116] The panel found that certain "exemptions identified by the European Communities under the FSC scheme" were financial contributions under Article 1.1(a)(1)(ii) of the SCM Agreement because they involved the foregoing of revenue which was otherwise due[3117] and that these exemptions conferred a benefit within the meaning of Article 1.1(b) of the SCM Agreement.[3118] Having found that the tax exemptions were subsidies, the panel also found that they were contingent in law upon export performance within the meaning of Article 3.1(a) of the SCM Agreement.[3119] The Appellate Body upheld the panel 's findings that the FSC exemptions were financial contributions within the meaning of Article 1.1(a)(1)(ii) of the SCM Agreement and that these exemptions were subsidies contingent upon export performance that were prohibited under Article 3.1(a) of the SCM Agreement.[3120]

[3112] United States' Comments on European Communities' response to question. 58, paras. 199-201.

[3113] It is well established that it is possible for a measure to be inconsistent with both Article 3 and Article 5 of the SCM Agreement. Panel Report, *US – Upland Cotton*, para. 7.1193; Panel Report, *Korea – Commercial Vessels*, para. 7.334. The United States does not argue otherwise in this case.

[3114] European Communities' first written submission, para. 1655.

[3115] European Communities' first written submission, para. 1656.

[3116] Panel Report, *US – FSC*, para. 1.1.

[3117] Panel Report, *US – FSC*, para. 7.102.

[3118] Panel Report, *US – FSC*, para. 7.103.

[3119] Panel Report, *US – FSC*, paras. 7.108, 7.130.

[3120] Appellate Body Report, *US – FSC*, paras. 95, 121.

Report of the Panel

7.1454 Second, the panel in *US – FSC (Article 21.5 – EC)* made findings with respect to the ETI Act. The panel found that the ETI Act's exclusion from gross income of certain "extraterritorial income" gave rise to a financial contribution in the form of a foregoing of government revenue that was otherwise due within the meaning of Article 1.1(a)(1)(ii) of the SCM Agreement[3121] and that this financial contribution conferred a benefit, such that a subsidy within the meaning of Article 1.1 existed.[3122] The panel also found that this subsidy was contingent in law upon export performance and was thereby inconsistent with Article 3.1(a) of the SCM Agreement.[3123] Moreover, the panel found that for FSCs in existence as of 30 September 2000, the FSC subsidies continued in operation for one year and that, with respect to FSCs that had entered into long-term binding contracts with unrelated parties before 30 September 2000, the Act did not alter the tax treatment of those contracts for an indefinite period of time. The panel therefore found that the United States had not fully withdrawn the FSC subsidies found to be prohibited export subsidies inconsistent with Article 3.1(a) and had thereby failed to implement the recommendations and rulings of the DSB pursuant to Article 4.7 of the SCM Agreement.[3124] The Appellate Body upheld the panel's findings that the ETI measure involved financial contributions through the foregoing of government revenue otherwise due[3125] and that the ETI measure granted subsidies contingent in law upon export performance within the meaning of Article 3.1(a).[3126] It also upheld the panel's finding that the United States had not fully withdrawn the FSC subsidies found to be prohibited export subsidies under Article 3.1(a) and had thereby failed to implement the recommendations and rulings of the DSB made pursuant to Article 4.7 of the SCM Agreement.[3127]

7.1455 Third, in *US – FSC (Article 21.5 – EC II)*, the panel found that the United States, by enacting Section 101 of the AJCA, maintained prohibited FSC and ETI subsidies through transition and grandfather clauses in section 101 of the AJCA and thereby continued to fail to implement fully the operative DSB recommendations and rulings to withdraw the prohibited subsidies.[3128] The Appellate Body upheld this finding.[3129]

7.1456 As noted above[3130], in its factual description of the "FSC/ETI and successor act subsidies" that are the subject of its complaint under Article 3, the European Communities refers to: (i) the original FSC provisions; (ii) the ETI Act, including its transition and grandfather clauses with respect to the FSC tax

---

[3121] Panel Report, *US – FSC (Article 21.5 – EC)*, para. 8.43.
[3122] Panel Report, *US – FSC (Article 21.5 – EC)*, para. 8.48.
[3123] Panel Report, *US – FSC (Article 21.5 – EC)*, para. 8.75, 8.110.
[3124] Panel Report, *US – FSC (Article 21.5 – EC)*, paras. 8.168-8.170.
[3125] Appellate Body Report, *US – FSC (Article 21.5 – EC)*, para. 106.
[3126] Appellate Body Report, *US – FSC (Article 21.5 – EC)*, para. 120.
[3127] Appellate Body Report, *US – FSC (Article 21.5 – EC)*, para. 231.
[3128] Panel Report, *US – FSC (Article 21.5 – EC II)*, para. 7.65.
[3129] Appellate Body Report, *US – FSC (Article 21.5 – EC II)*, para. 96.
[3130] See above, paras. 7.1379-7.1385.

1506

DSR 2012:III

US - Large Civil Aircraft (2nd Complaint)

benefits; (iii) the AJCA, which repealed the ETI Act but maintained the FSC grandfather clause and provided for new transition and grandfather clauses with respect to the ETI tax benefits; and (iv) the TIPRA, which repealed the grandfather clauses for FSC and ETI tax benefits.[3131] The original FSC provisions were repealed on 30 September 2000 and the ETI Act was repealed on 31 December 2004. With the exception of the TIPRA, all of the legal provisions identified by the European Communities pursuant to which Boeing received FSC and ETI tax benefits have been the subject of panel and Appellate Body reports that have found these measures to be inconsistent with Articles 3.1(a) and 3.2 of the SCM Agreement and that have given rise to a recommendation addressed to the United States pursuant to Article 4.7 of the SCM Agreement that it withdraw the subsidy without delay.[3132]

7.1457 Against this background, the United States, while agreeing that FSC/ETI was a prohibited export subsidy, submits that the European Communities' claim that FSC/ETI measures and successor legislation is contingent in law on export performance is superfluous and provides no basis for the Panel to make a finding or render a recommendation.[3133]

7.1458 Therefore, the question before the Panel is not what should be the correct legal analysis of the FSC/ETI and successor act subsidies under Article 3 of the SCM Agreement. Nor is the question whether the claim of the European Communities is within the Panel's terms of reference.[3134] Rather, the key question before this Panel is whether the Panel should: (i) make a finding under Article 3 of the SCM Agreement that FSC/ETI and successor act subsidies granted to Boeing are inconsistent with Article 3 of the SCM Agreement, based on the reasoning and findings of the panels and the Appellate Body in the FSC/ETI dispute, and make a recommendation under Article 4.7 that the United States withdraw the subsidy without delay; or (ii) refrain from making such a finding under Article 3 and recommendation under Article 4.7 on the grounds

---

[3131] European Communities' first written submission, paras. 923-945.

[3132] Panel Report, *US – FSC*, para. 8.8. At the request of the United States, the DSB agreed to extend the period for the withdrawal of the FSC subsidies from 1 October 2000 until 1 November 2000. The panels in *US – FSC (Article 21.5 –EC) and US – FSC (Article 21.5 – EC II)* held that the original recommendation and rulings made in 2000 remained operative. See e.g. Panel Report, *US – FSC (Article 2.15 – EC II)*, paras. 8.1-8.2.

[3133] United States' response to panel question no. 58, para. 163. The United States qualifies the FSC/ETI measure as a "measure withdrawn based on prior recommendations and rulings of the Dispute Settlement Body". United States' response to question 80, para. 209. It also states that "the DSB has already ruled that this measure was inconsistent with the SCM Agreement, as it provided a prohibited subsidy. The United States has terminated the measure. FSC/ETI is, therefore, not properly at issue in this case." United States' response to question 92, para. 234.

[3134] It is important to note that, with the exception of the TIPRA, the United States does not argue that the claim of the European Communities with respect to FSC/ETI and successor act subsidies is not within the Panel's terms of reference. Rather, the view of the United States that the Panel should not address the claim of the European Communities regarding FSC/ETI and successor act subsidies appears to be based principally on considerations relating to the role of the Panel under Article 3.7 of the DSU.

DSR 2012:III

1507

Report of the Panel

that, as argued by the United States, the DSB has already ruled that the FSC and ETI and successor act subsidies are prohibited subsidies under Article 3 and that "{a}nother finding that they are export contingent or another recommendation that they be brought into compliance with the SCM Agreement will add nothing to the force or effect of the earlier rulings or recommendations".

7.1459 The Panel notes that at the time of its establishment, in February 2006, the original FSC and ETI legislation no longer applied. Pursuant to the provisions of the AJCA, however, ETI tax advantages continued to be available in certain situations. First, transition clauses allowed for the ETI measure to continue (albeit to a more limited extent) with respect to qualifying transactions entered into between 1 January 2005 and 31 December 2006. Second, the AJCA provided for the grandfathering, for an indefinite period, of transactions that occurred pursuant to a binding contract between the taxpayer and an unrelated person, which was in effect on 17 September 2003. Moreover, the AJCA did not repeal or change section 5(c)(1) of the ETI Act, which provided for the grandfathering, for an indefinite period, of FSC tax benefits in respect of transactions entered into pursuant to a binding contract which existed on 30 September 2000. The United States has not contested in this dispute that Boeing has used the transition and grandfather provisions of the AJCA. The Panel therefore finds that at the time of its establishment, the FSC/ETI measures challenged by the European Communities continued to exist insofar as Boeing used the transition and grandfather provisions of the AJCA and ETI Act.

7.1460 The Panel is not persuaded that the existence of the DSB rulings and recommendations in the FSC/ETI dispute, and the steps taken by the United States pursuant to those rulings and recommendations, provide a compelling reason for this Panel not to make a finding under Article 3 of the SCM Agreement with respect to the FSC and ETI tax measures as they applied to Boeing at the time of the Panel's establishment.

7.1461 First, the findings made by the panels and the Appellate Body in the FSC/ETI dispute were in respect of the legislative provisions as such and not in relation to these provisions as applied in particular cases. As explained above[3135], it is the Panel's understanding that in this dispute the European Communities challenges specific FSC/ETI subsidies received by Boeing. The Panel therefore is of the view that the subject matter of the present dispute is not exactly identical to the subject matter of the FSC/ETI dispute.[3136] The Panel also takes into account the fact that in this case, as argued by the European Communities, a

---

[3135] See above, para. 7.1394.

[3136] The Panel notes that, apart from a claim under Article 3 of the SCM Agreement, the European Communities also makes a claim that the FSC/ETI subsidies, together with the other subsidies at issue, cause adverse effects within the meaning of Article 5 of the SCM Agreement. While previous WTO dispute settlement proceedings have addressed the question of whether legal provisions relating to the FSC/ETI measures at issue in this dispute are inconsistent with Article 3 of the SCM Agreement, whether these measures have caused adverse effects within the meaning of Article 5 of the SCM Agreement has never been addressed in WTO dispute settlement.

1508

DSR 2012:III

finding that the FSC/ETI and successor act subsidies are export subsidies within the meaning of Article 3 provides the basis for finding that these subsidies are specific by virtue of Article 2.3 of the SCM Agreement.

7.1462 Second, the Panel is aware that subsequent to its establishment developments have occurred that significantly affect the continued existence of the measures at issue. The transition provisions of the AJCA expired at the end of 2006; the grandfather provisions of the ETI Act and the AJCA were repealed by the TIPRA, which was enacted in 2006; and, as argued by the United States, Boeing has indicated that it will not use any FSC or ETI tax advantages post-2006. Assuming that these developments mean that the FSC and ETI tax measures no longer exist in respect of Boeing, this does not imply that we should not make a finding on these measures. The Panel is of the view that these developments might be relevant to the question of whether it is appropriate to make a *recommendation* but that they are not relevant to determining whether the Panel should make a *finding*. While "the fact that a measure has expired may affect what recommendation a panel may make...it is not, however, dispositive of the preliminary question of whether a panel can address claims in respect of that measure".[3137]

7.1463 In sum, the Panel finds that it is appropriate to make a finding under Article 3 with respect to the FSC/ETI and successor act provided to Boeing. The reasoning and findings of the panels and the Appellate Body in *US – FSC, US – FSC (Article 21.5 – EC)* and *US – FSC (Article 21.5 – EC II)* imply that the application of the FSC/ETI provisions to Boeing is inconsistent with Articles 3.1 and 3.2 of the SCM Agreement. The Panel thus finds that with respect to the tax advantages enjoyed by Boeing at the time of the establishment of the Panel under the transition and grandfather provisions of the ETI Act and the AJCA, the United States acted inconsistently with Articles 3.1(a) and 3.2 of the SCM Agreement by granting subsidies contingent in law upon export performance.

(f) Conclusion

7.1464 **For these reasons, the Panel finds that FSC/ETI measures challenged by the European Communities that were in force at the time of the Panel's establishment are export-contingent subsidies to Boeing's LCA division prohibited under Articles 3.1(a) and 3.2 of the SCM Agreement.**

2. *State of Washington: HB 2294 tax incentives*

(a) Introduction

7.1465 The European Communities argues that the grant of the subsidies under HB 2294 is contingent in fact upon export performance because the grant is tied

---

[3137] Appellate Body Report, *US – Upland Cotton*, para. 272.

Report of the Panel

to actual or anticipated exportation or export earnings. The grant is thereby inconsistent with Article 3.1(a) of the SCM Agreement.

7.1466 The United States contends that the European Communities has failed to establish any "tie" between the grant of the subsidies and anticipated exportation or actual exportation and therefore HB 2294 is not inconsistent with Article 3.1(a) of the SCM Agreement.

(b) Measure at issue

7.1467 We recall that HB 2294 came into effect in December 2003 and is entitled *"An Act Related to Retaining and Attracting the Aerospace Industry to Washington State"*.[3138] A description of HB 2294 is provided at paragraphs 7.41-7.68 of this Report, which addresses the existence of taxation-related subsidies in Washington State. HB 2294 includes five tax measures which the European Communities challenges as subsidies to Boeing's LCA division. The measures include a B&O tax reduction; B&O tax credits; sales and use tax exemptions; a leasehold excise tax exemption; and a property tax exemption. The Panel has found that the B&O tax reduction, the B&O tax credits and the sales and use tax exemption for construction services and equipment are specific subsidies to Boeing.

7.1468 Section 17(1)(a) of HB 2294 provides that the legislation takes "effect on the first day of the month in which the governor and a manufacturer of commercial airplanes sign a memorandum of agreement regarding an affirmative final decision to site a significant commercial airplane final assembly facility in Washington state". Section 17(1)(b) also provides that HB 2294 is "contingent upon the siting of a significant commercial airplane final assembly facility in the state of Washington".

7.1469 A "significant commercial airplane final assembly facility" is defined as:

> "{A} location with the capacity to produce at least thirty-six superefficient airplanes a year."

A "superefficient airplane" is defined as:

> "{A} twin aisle airplane that carries between two hundred and three hundred fifty passengers, with a range of more than seven thousand two hundred nautical miles, a cruising speed of approximately mach .85, and that uses fifteen to twenty percent less fuel than other similar airplanes on the market."

7.1470 The parties to the dispute agree that the 787 meets the definition of a "superefficient airplane".[3139]

[3138] HB 2294, 58th Leg., 2d Spec. Sess. (Wash. 2003), Exhibit EC-54.

[3139] United States' first written submission, para. 686, footnote 887 and European Communities' first written submission, para. 974.

1510 DSR 2012:III

US - Large Civil Aircraft (2nd Complaint)

7.1471 Boeing satisfied the requirements of section 17 of HB 2294 upon signing the Project Olympus Memorandum of Agreement, which confirms that the MSA constitutes an agreement to site the 787 final assembly facility in the City of Everett, as required under HB 2294.[3140] Specifically, the State confirms in the Project Olympus Memorandum of Agreement that the facilities site in Everett "meets the definition of a significant commercial airplane final assembly facility".[3141]

(c)   Arguments of the European Communities

7.1472 The European Communities argues that the subsidies provided by HB 2294 are contingent in fact upon export performance under Article 3.1(a) of the SCM Agreement.[3142]

7.1473 In its first written submission, the European Communities advances its view of the correct legal interpretation of Article 3.1(a) and makes submissions regarding why the subsidies provided under HB 2294 meet the conditions of export contingent subsidies. At this point of its submissions, the European Communities also makes various arguments in the alternative regarding the correct interpretation of Article 3.1(a). Further, in response to Panel questions, the European Communities advances new interpretations of the terms of Article 3.1(a), including an interpretation that it does *not* advocate, and makes new submissions regarding why the subsidies provided under HB 2294 are export contingent.

7.1474 In its first written submission, the European Communities argues that three elements must be established under Article 3.1(a) in order to make out a claim of de facto export contingency. These elements are (i) the required condition (export performance); (ii) the required consequence; and (iii) the required contingent relationship.[3143] We understand the three elements to amount to a restatement of Article 3.1(a), namely that the subsidy ("the required consequence") be contingent upon ("the required contingent relationship") export performance ("the required condition").

7.1475 In relation to the first element, the European Communities submits that the "required condition" in Article 3.1(a) is that the subsidy be conditional on export performance and not just on performance in general.[3144] The European Communities refers to this as a requirement to demonstrate "a *favouring* or discrimination in favour of a product that will inevitably be generally exported or incorporated within an exported product".[3145] The European Communities argues that the subsidy measure in issue in this dispute, namely "HB 2294 and/or

---

[3140] European Communities' first written submission, para. 975.
[3141] Memorandum of Agreement for Project Olympus, 19 December 2003, Exhibit EC-57, para. 975.
[3142] European Communities' first written submission, paras. 971 and 977.
[3143] European Communities' first written submission, paras. 980, 990 and 991.
[3144] European Communities' first written submission, para. 980.
[3145] *Ibid.*

DSR 2012:III   1511

Report of the Panel

the Project Olympus Master Site Agreement", and the instances of its application, demonstrate the existence of the "required condition" (export performance).[3146] This is because, under the terms of HB 2294, only companies that "contribute to a product that will necessarily generally be exported", namely manufacturers of commercial airplanes and their components, benefit from the subsidies under HB 2294.[3147] In this way, HB 2294 acts as a "filter", ensuring that only companies involved in producing a product that will be exported, are eligible for the subsidies.[3148] Further, the European Communities argues that HB 2294 is contingent upon the requirement to establish a capacity to produce at least thirty-six superefficient 787s per year. According to the European Communities, market forecasts indicate that the domestic United States market could not absorb such a production level and that a significant portion of 787 sales would consist of exports.[3149] Finally, the European Communities notes that Boeing is a highly export-oriented company and cites evidence in support of this.[3150]

7.1476 According to the European Communities, the second element that must be established to succeed in an Article 3.1(a) claim is the "required consequence". The European Communities states that "HB 2294 provides for the *grant* of a subsidy ... The consequence required by Article 3.1(a) and footnote 4 ... is thus apparent".[3151] We understand the "required consequence" to be a requirement that a subsidy be granted.

7.1477 Finally, the European Communities submits that the third element, the "required contingent relationship", also exists in relation to HB 2294. We understand the European Communities to be arguing that the second element, the grant of a subsidy, must be contingent upon the first element, namely export performance. The European Communities argues that the required contingent relationship exists because eligibility for the subsidy is contingent upon being a manufacturer of commercial airplanes or components, which are products that will necessarily be exported. Further, HB 2294 is contingent upon building a plant with the capacity to produce at least thirty-six superefficient airplanes per year.[3152]

7.1478 Throughout its first written submission, largely in the footnotes, the European Communities also refers to various alternative arguments that it makes.[3153] In response to Panel questioning regarding how many distinct legal

---

[3146] European Communities' first written submission, para. 980, footnote 1711.

[3147] European Communities' first written submission, para. 980 and European Communities' non-confidential oral statement at the first meeting with the panel, para. 111.

[3148] European Communities' first written submission, para. 989.

[3149] European Communities' first written submission, para. 981.

[3150] European Communities' first written submission, paras. 982-988.

[3151] European Communities' first written submission, para. 990.

[3152] European Communities' first written submission, para. 991.

[3153] European Communities' first written submission, para. 980 footnote 1712; para. 989 footnote 1731; para. 992; para. 996 footnote 1735.

1512

DSR 2012:III

arguments it makes, the European Communities explicitly sets out three legal arguments that it advances, not all of which rely on the three elements referred to in its first written submission.[3154]

7.1479 In answer to question 56, the European Communities sets out its **first legal argument**. The argument relates to one particular component of HB 2294, namely the B&O tax rate reduction. The European Communities argues that the value of the B&O tax rate reduction increases for each additional sale of a Boeing LCA (it is an *ad valorem* subsidy), including export sales.[3155] In other words, the amount of the subsidy is contingent upon sales, including export sales. According to the European Communities, this is sufficient to establish that the subsidy is prohibited within the meaning of the SCM Agreement because under Article 3.1(a) "it is sufficient to demonstrate the existence of a subsidy grant contingent upon sales, regardless of whether such sales occur in the domestic market (the United States) or with respect to exports. That is, there is no need to demonstrate that the subsidy favours exports or is greater in the case of export".[3156] Therefore, in contrast to its first written submission, the European Communities argues that under Article 3.1(a), it is sufficient to demonstrate that the grant of a subsidy is contingent upon performance (sales) and there is no need to demonstrate that it is contingent upon *export* performance or that there is "favouring" of exports.

7.1480 In relation to this first legal argument, although all of the European Communities' submissions relate to export contingency "in fact" rather than "in law", in its second written submission, the European Communities states:

> "{D}uring the meeting of the Panel, the United States effectively admitted that the HB 2294 B&O tax rate reductions are subsidies contingent *in law* or in fact upon export performance." [3157]

7.1481 The European Communities does not provide further submissions regarding export contingency "in law". It is not clear whether, merely by stating the United States has admitted that the B&O tax reduction is contingent in law upon export performance, that the European Communities claims, in relation to its first legal argument, that the subsidy is contingent in law, as well as in fact, on export performance.

7.1482 The European Communities' **second legal argument** is one that it contends the United States has advocated "elsewhere".[3158] The argument relates

---

[3154] European Communities' response to question 56. In particular, not all of its arguments contend that the subsidy must be contingent upon *export* performance, in that there must be a favouring or discrimination in favour of a product that will inevitably be generally exported or incorporated within an exported product, as the European Communities argues in its first written submission. See para. 7.1491 of this Report regarding a fourth legal argument that the European Communities outlines in response to question 56 but does *not* advance.

[3155] European Communities' response to question 56, paras. 190 and 192

[3156] European Communities' response to question 56, para. 190.

[3157] European Communities' second written submission, para. 642 (emphasis added).

DSR 2012:III

1513

Report of the Panel

to HB 2294 in its entirety, rather than to a particular taxation measure, such as the B&O tax reduction. The European Communities argues that if the facts demonstrate that there was the "anticipating of" exports and that the grant of the subsidies under HB 2994 was "tied to" such "anticipating of" exports, then HB 2294 constitutes a measure contingent in fact upon export.[3159] The European Communities notes that the subsidies under HB 2294 were contingent upon siting an assembly facility in Washington that could produce at least thirty-six 787s per year. This amounts to a grant of subsidies contingent in fact upon anticipated export sales of 787s because demand in the United States market was not such that all thirty-six 787s could be sold domestically. Rather, some of the aircraft would need to be exported.[3160] Under this argument, the European Communities asserts that the State of Washington expected or anticipated exports and if this expectation was a part of the consideration or motivation or intent in the provision of the subsidy, this is sufficient to prove the necessary contingent relationship.[3161]

7.1483 The European Communities states that "it is assumed, for the purposes of this second argument, that it is still necessary to demonstrate some element of 'favouring'".[3162] The reference to favouring seems to be a reference to the first element outlined in its first written submission, namely the "required condition" of "export performance" (and not just performance in general), which the European Communities argues requires a demonstration of a "favouring or discrimination in favour of a product that will inevitably be generally exported or incorporated within an exported product".[3163]

7.1484 The European Communities submits that its **third legal argument**:

> "{I}s the same as the second argument, but proceeds on the basis that it is unnecessary to demonstrate any favouring of exports (a point admitted by the United States during the first hearing). "[3164]

7.1485 In support of its second and third legal arguments, the European Communities argues that the facts overwhelmingly demonstrate that production is anticipated to exceed domestic demand and that the only reasonable inference to draw is that some aircraft will be exported.[3165] Further, the enactment of HB 2294 was "tied to" such anticipation. This is because the subsidies were granted contingent upon the creation of a certain capacity and it was anticipated that the

---

[3158] European Communities' response to question 56, para. 193 and European Communities' first written submission, paras. 992-996.

[3159] European Communities' response to question 56, para. 193.

[3160] European Communities' first written submission, paras. 992-996.

[3161] European Communities' non-confidential oral statement at the first meeting with the panel, para. 108.

[3162] European Communities' response to question 56, para. 193.

[3163] European Communities' first written submission, para. 980.

[3164] European Communities' response to question 56, para. 194.

[3165] European Communities' comments on United States' response to question 54, para. 191.

1514

DSR 2012:III

US - Large Civil Aircraft (2nd Complaint)

capacity would entail production and export.[3166] In response to Panel questioning, the European Communities refers to evidence which it alleges demonstrates that the granting authorities were aware of the capacity of the United States' market.[3167]

7.1486 In response to the United States' argument that HB 2294 does not require the airplane assembly facility *actually* to produce thirty-six aircraft, but only to have the *capacity* to produce at that level, and that the European Communities fails to understand this crucial distinction, the European Communities argues that, in the context of the LCA market, the capacity requirement is tantamount to an export requirement.[3168] This is because aircraft manufacturers do not create capacity that will stand idle. Production capacity is decided after a manufacturer knows how many aircraft it will need to produce, based on the orders it has received. If Boeing did not use its capacity the financial consequences would be grave.[3169] Therefore, the capacity requirement is equivalent to a production requirement, which is tantamount to a requirement to export, given the demand levels in the domestic market.[3170]

7.1487 The European Communities characterizes the argument of the United States outlined in the preceding paragraph as an objection to the absence of an *express requirement*, or a legal obligation, to produce or to export.[3171] The European Communities notes that the United States has "elsewhere" taken a different view, namely that there does not need to be a legal obligation to perform, that necessarily involves export sales, in order successfully to argue that a subsidy is contingent in fact upon anticipated exports. The European Communities submits that "it agrees with the general proposition", only on the condition that it be applied consistently in all WTO disputes, which would result in all of the United States' Article 3 claims being rejected in *EC – Aircraft*.[3172] In the alternative, the European Communities argues that the absence of a requirement to export is not fatal to its claim.[3173] The European Communities notes that in arguing that a subsidy is in fact contingent upon export, regardless of what is expressly provided for in the text of the measure, it is necessary to assess the facts of the situation, including the reality of the marketplace, and to draw the reasonable and necessary inferences from those facts.[3174]

[3166] European Communities' comments on United States' response to question 54, para. 192.

[3167] European Communities' response to question 267.

[3168] European Communities' response to question 54, para. 177.

[3169] European Communities' response to question 54, paras. 175-177.

[3170] European Communities' response to question 54, para. 179 and European Communities' non-confidential oral statement at the first meeting with the panel, paras. 101-104.

[3171] European Communities' response to question 54, para. 179 and European Communities' non-confidential oral statement at the first meeting with the panel, para. 102.

[3172] European Communities' non-confidential oral statement at the first meeting with the panel, para. 103 and European Communities' response to question 54, para. 179.

[3173] European Communities' non-confidential oral statement at the first meeting with the panel, para. 104.

[3174] European Communities' comments on United States' response to question 54, para. 189.

DSR 2012:III

Report of the Panel

7.1488 In question 57, the Panel asked the European Communities to clarify whether it is arguing that the granting of the subsidies was tied to "actual" or to "anticipated" exportation. The European Communities' response, which applies to **all three of its legal arguments**, was:

> "{I}n order to be certain that it has made all the necessary arguments, the European Communities submits that each of the relevant measures provides for a subsidy contingent upon *actual* export; or alternatively contingent upon *anticipated* export; or alternatively contingent upon actual *or* anticipated export; or alternatively contingent upon actual *and* anticipated export."[3175]

7.1489 In relation to the correct legal interpretation of "actual" and "anticipated", the European Communities does not submit its own view. Rather, the European Communities characterizes the United States' position as being that the terms mean "real" and "potential" respectively.[3176] The European Communities also notes that another possible interpretation for the terms, although one it does not advocate, is "past" and "future" respectively.[3177] In relation to its **first legal argument**, the European Communities argues that on either interpretation, a claim under Article 3.1(a) can be made out. If the correct interpretation is in accordance with the United States' submissions, the grant of the subsidies is contingent upon "actual" exports, in that the unconditional right to the subsidies only arises when the sale takes place. In the alternative, if the correct meaning of the terms is "past" and "future", the grant of the subsidies is tied to "anticipated" exports because they are in the future.[3178] In relation to its **second and third legal arguments,** the European Communities reasons that if the United States' interpretation of the terms "actual" and "anticipated" is correct, namely "real" and "potential" respectively, under its second and third arguments the tie is to "anticipated" exports. This is because the exports were expected and this was a consideration or motivation in the adoption of HB 2294.[3179] In what is really a reference to its first legal argument, the European Communities continues that HB 2294 also provides for the grant of a subsidy tied to "actual" exports, because the B&O tax reductions are tied to sales.[3180] The European Communities also reasons that if "actual" or "anticipated" means "past" or "future", under its second and third legal arguments the grant of the subsidies is tied to both actual

---

[3175] European Communities' response to question 57, para. 195.

[3176] European Communities' response to question 57, paras. 195, 198-200. However, we note at para. 7.1502 of this Report, that the United States submits that "anticipated" means "expected", rather than "potential".

[3177] European Communities' response to question 57, paras. 195, 198-200. See also, European Communities' response to question 56, paras. 184-189 for the "reference interpretation", that the European Communities does not advocate.

[3178] European Communities' response to question 57, para. 198.

[3179] European Communities' response to question 57, para. 200.

[3180] *Ibid.*

1516   DSR 2012:III

and to anticipated export. They are tied to actual (i.e. to past) exports because admission to the programme is based on a pre-selection criteria that captures companies that contribute to a product that has been exported in the past. They are also tied to anticipated (i.e. to future) exports because of the continuing nature of the programme and because of the B&O tax rate reduction.[3181]

7.1490 In sum, the arguments advanced by the European Communities in response to question 56 can be expressed as:

(a)   HB 2294 is de facto contingent upon export performance because the B&O tax reduction, an *ad valorem* subsidy, is contingent upon sales, including export sales. The European Communities asserts that the grant of the subsidy is tied to "actual" or "anticipated" exportation.

(b)   HB 2294 is de facto contingent upon export performance because its grant was conditioned upon the establishment of a facility with the capacity to produce 36 superefficient airplanes. The subsidies under HB 2294 are tied to "actual" or "anticipated" exportation. The legal test requires some element of "favouring" of exports.

(c)   The final legal argument is the same as the argument in the preceding bullet point, except that no element of "favouring" of exports need be proven.[3182]

7.1491 As well as advancing its three legal arguments, the European Communities provides a "reference interpretation", which it does *not* advance, but which it contends may "assist the Panel in understanding the precise nature of the European Communities' claims".[3183] The "reference interpretation" appears to be an interpretation that contradicts the position taken by the United States' in *EC and certain member States – Large Civil Aircraft* regarding Article

---

[3181] European Communities' response to question 57, para. 199.

[3182] We note that in its non-confidential oral statement at the first meeting with the Panel, the European Communities refers to its "primary argument" and elaborates that HB 2294 acts as a "filter", with the result that the defining characteristic of the companies that are eligible for the subsidy is that they contribute to a product that will necessarily be exported. The European Communities concludes that there is a "clear correlation" between actual or anticipated export performance and eligibility for the benefit. The European Communities reasons that this demonstrates the "condition required" by Article 3.1(a). Although it may be possible to interpret this is as a fourth, distinct argument, which asserts that if those eligible for a subsidy are all exporters, contingency in fact can be found, it is unlikely that this is in fact a fourth argument. The reference to demonstration of the "condition required" indicates that the "filter argument" merely goes to establishing the first element detailed in the European Communities' first written submission ("export performance" as a "required condition", to demonstrate an element of "favouring" a product that will be exported). Further, in its question asking the European Communities to clarify how many legal arguments it is making, the Panel refers to this section of the non-confidential oral statement at the first meeting with the panel. Therefore, presumably if it was an argument distinct to the three arguments advanced in response to question 56, the European Communities would have so indicated in its response to question 56.

[3183] European Communities' response to question 56, paras. 184-189 and European Communities' response to question 270, para. 476.

Report of the Panel

3.1(a). Although not explicitly expressed, the European Communities' purpose in including the "reference interpretation" seems to be to suggest that if the Panel adopts the position in the "reference interpretation", then the same reasoning should apply in *EC and certain member States – Large Civil Aircraft* and lead to the rejection of all of the United States' Article 3 claims in that case. In essence, the European Communities' position would appear to be that if Article 3 is interpreted consistently by this Panel and the panel in *EC and certain member States – Large Civil Aircraft*, the prohibited subsidy claims in each of the cases must either both be successful or both fail.

(d)   Arguments of the United States

7.1492 The United States refutes the European Communities' claim that the tax measures in HB 2294 are prohibited subsidies because they are contingent upon export performance.[3184]

7.1493 According to the United States, in *Canada – Aircraft,* the Appellate Body stated that footnote 4 of the SCM Agreement requires that three substantive factual elements be established by a complaining party seeking to demonstrate that a subsidy is de facto contingent upon export performance. The three elements that must be proved are (i) the granting of a subsidy (ii) that is "tied to" (iii) actual or anticipated exportation or export earnings.[3185] Further, footnote 4 to Article 3.1(a) provides that "the mere fact that a subsidy is granted to enterprises which export shall not for that reason alone be considered to be an export subsidy". In *Canada – Aircraft,* the Appellate Body held that this footnote "precludes a Panel from making a finding of de facto export contingency for the sole reason that the subsidy is granted to enterprises that export".[3186] Therefore, the United States argues that the evidence the European Communities submits in its first written submission regarding the fact that Boeing is an export-oriented company does not meet the relevant legal standard for a claim under Article 3.1(a).[3187] Further, to the extent the European Communities advances an argument that the grant of the alleged subsidy is tied to actual or anticipated export performance because the defining characteristic of the companies that benefit from the subsidy is that they contribute to a product that will necessarily be exported, the United States argues that this demonstrates nothing more than that "a subsidy is granted to enterprises which export". Footnote 4 provides that this reason alone cannot establish the existence of an export contingent subsidy.[3188]

[3184] United States' first written submission, para. 684.
[3185] United States' first written submission, para. 690.
[3186] United States' first written submission, para. 688.
[3187] United States' first written submission, paras. 689-690.
[3188] United States' second written submission, para. 157.

1518   DSR 2012:III

US - Large Civil Aircraft (2ⁿᵈ Complaint)

7.1494 In relation to all three legal arguments[3189] advanced by the European Communities, the United States argues that the European Communities has not proven element (i) identified in *Canada – Aircraft*, namely the granting of a subsidy.[3190] In this regard, the United States relies on the submissions on the existence of a subsidy in relation to Washington taxation measures, found at Part VII.D.2(a) of this Report.

7.1495 The United States refutes the European Communities' **first legal argument**, namely that the B&O tax reduction is a subsidy contingent upon both domestic and export sales and therefore is an export contingent subsidy.[3191] The United States agrees with the European Communities' submission that it is not necessary to demonstrate that a "subsidy favours exports" in order for a claim to be successful under Article 3.1(a). However, according to the United States, this does not imply that a subsidy contingent upon sales is an export contingent subsidy.[3192] The relevant enquiry is whether the granting of the subsidy is tied to actual or anticipated exportation or export earnings. The United States argues, relying on the panel decision in *Canada – Aircraft,* that this is not the same as a tie to mere sales. The United States notes that the European Communities has presented no evidence of a tie between the grant of the subsidy and actual or anticipated exportation or export earnings, for example by presenting evidence that the State of Washington relied on projections of export sales in providing Boeing with the tax treatment in HB 2294.[3193] The United States argues that the possibility that the amount of a subsidy is contingent upon sales, which could include export sales, does not establish the required tie. This is clear from footnote 4 to the SCM Agreement, which provides that "the mere fact that a subsidy is granted to enterprises which export shall not for that reason alone be considered to be an export subsidy".[3194]

7.1496 In relation to the European Communities' **second legal argument**, the United States repeats its position that there is no requirement under Article 3.1(a) to demonstrate some element of "favouring".[3195] With respect to the **second and third legal arguments**, which focus on the fact that HB 2294 was contingent upon Boeing establishing the capacity to produce thirty-six superefficient aircraft, the United States argues that the European Communities has made out none of the three elements set out by the Appellate Body in

---

[3189] Namely, the three legal arguments the European Communities identifies in its response to question 56 and which are summarized at para. 7.1490 of this Report.

[3190] United States' first written submission, para. 691.

[3191] United States' comments on European Communities' response to question 56, paras. 183-188.

[3192] United States' comments on European Communities' response to question 56, para. 184.

[3193] United States' comments on European Communities' response to question 56, para. 186.

[3194] United States' comments on European Communities' response to question 56, para. 187.

[3195] United States' comments on European Communities' response to question 56, para. 189. The "second legal argument" refers to the second argument identified by the European Communities in its response to question 56 and which is included in the summary of arguments at para. 7.1490 of this Report.

Report of the Panel

Canada – Aircraft.[3196] In particular, the European Communities has not proven that (i) there was a granting of a "subsidy" (ii) tied to (iii) actual or anticipated exportation or export earnings.

7.1497 In relation to element (ii), namely the required "tie", the United States notes that in *Canada – Aircraft* the Appellate Body held that the ordinary meaning of "tied to" is to "limit or restrict as to ... conditions" and that a relationship of "conditionality" or "dependence" between subsidy and export performance must be demonstrated. Further, the Appellate Body held that the "tie" is at the very heart of the legal standard in footnote 4.[3197]

7.1498 The focus of the United States' arguments against the European Communities' Article 3 claim is that the European Communities has not demonstrated the required "tie". In this regard, the United States submits that the fact that HB 2294 was tied to the siting of a facility in Washington with the "capacity" to produce thirty-six superefficient airplanes does not establish the relevant "tie".[3198] The United States contends that the European Communities' legal burden is to establish that, while as a legal matter the provision of the tax treatment in HB 2294 was tied to nothing more than production capacity, in fact the tie was to anticipated exportation or export earnings. The United States argues that the European Communities has not met this burden.[3199] It notes that the European Communities equates a tie to production capacity with a tie to export sales on the basis that Boeing will fully utilize its production capacity and that this will result in export sales due to the level of demand in the domestic market. However, the United States emphasizes that in making these arguments, the European Communities relies on mere assumptions and assertions that are not substantiated with adequate evidence.[3200] In fact, the United States argues that the domestic market is capable of absorbing thirty-six planes annually and it refers to past orders for 787s by customers located in the United States to support this assertion.[3201]

7.1499 In its first written submission the United States repeatedly highlights that HB 2294 is contingent on a requirement to build a facility with a *capacity* to produce thirty-six aircraft, rather than a requirement that Boeing *actually produce* thirty-six aircraft.[3202] However, in its answers to Panel questions the United States clarifies that its argument is not based upon the lack of an *express requirement* to export. Rather, the European Communities' claim fails because of

---

[3196] Where the "second and third legal arguments" refer to the second and third arguments identified by the European Communities in its response to question 56 and which are included in the summary of arguments at para. 7.1490 of this Report.

[3197] United States' first written submission, para. 692.

[3198] United States' first written submission, para. 696.

[3199] United States' response to question 55, para. 159.

[3200] United States' second written submission, para. 154 and United States' response to question 54, para. 153.

[3201] United States' second written submission, para. 155.

[3202] United States' first written submission, paras. 688 and 697-698.

1520

DSR 2012:III

the absence of *any* tie, whether in the form of an express requirement or some other form, between the granting of the alleged subsidies and actual or anticipated exportation.[3203]

7.1500 Further, in contrast to the European Communities' assertion, the United States does not argue that the Boeing facility in Everett will stand idle. The United States contends that a finding that the tax measures under HB 2294 are not export contingent subsidies does not rest upon such a proposition.[3204] Rather, the Article 3 claim must fail because a requirement to establish production capacity is an insufficient basis to conclude that HB 2294 is tied to anticipated exports.[3205]

7.1501 In relation to a tie to "anticipated" exportation, the United States contends that even if the State of Washington expected that Boeing would export some of the airplanes manufactured in the final assembly facility cited in HB 2294, the European Communities has not demonstrated that the granting of the HB 2294 tax incentives were tied to this anticipation.[3206] It has not demonstrated that the expectation of exports was the condition upon which the alleged subsidies were granted.

7.1502 In this regard, in relation to the element (iii) identified by the Appellate Body in *Canada – Aircraft,* namely the "actual or anticipated exportation or export earnings", the United States submits that the correct interpretation of "anticipated" was established by the Appellate Body in *Canada – Aircraft* and is "expected" and not "future", as suggested by the European Communities.[3207] It is exportation that is expected to occur but may or may not actually occur.[3208] Further, it is the United States' position that "actual" means "real" and not past, as suggested by the European Communities. It is exportation that has occurred or will in fact occur in the future.[3209]

7.1503 The United States notes that in answer to a Panel question regarding whether the European Communities argues that the subsidies are contingent upon "actual" or "anticipated" exportation, the European Communities "cobbles together another enumerated list of possible arguments" and it does this "in order to be certain that it has made all necessary arguments".[3210] The United States submits that it is unclear what it means for a party to assert arguments in order to be certain that it has made all the necessary ones. The European Communities either has a legal and factual basis for asserting a claim or it does not. In any event, the list of arguments is nonsensical and when the European Communities

---

[3203] United States' comments on European Communities' response to question 54, paras. 176-178.

[3204] United States' response to question 54, para. 154.

[3205] *Ibid.*

[3206] United States' first written submission, para. 698.

[3207] United States' first written submission, para. 693.

[3208] United States' comments on European Communities' response to question 57, para. 196.

[3209] *Ibid.*

[3210] United States' comments on European Communities' response to question 57, para. 194.

Report of the Panel

attempts to explain them, it admits that its explanations "do not exhaust all alternative arguments".[3211] The United States alleges that the European Communities is identifying arguments in extremely cursory terms and imposing upon the Panel the burden of supporting such arguments with legal reasoning. The United States notes that the Appellate Body has previously refused to rule on a "conditional appeal" by the European Communities that "did not set out any specific arguments to support {the} appeal".

7.1504 The United States argues that the assertions made by the European Communities that exports of 787s were "anticipated", in the sense that they were "expected", is based on mere assertion and not supported by any evidence.[3212] Further, the United States contends that the evidence referred to by the European Communities to establish that the grantor of the subsidies was aware of the capacity of the United States' market is not sufficient. Even if it were, awareness on the part of the grantor of the capacity of the United States' market does not establish that the grantor anticipated exports or that there was a tie between any such anticipation and the granting of the alleged subsidies.[3213]

7.1505 Finally, the United States requests that the Panel ignore the "reference interpretation" advanced by the European Communities. This is because the reference interpretation does nothing to elucidate the claims in the dispute. It merely makes veiled references to claims in other disputes, asserts arguments that the European Communities admits it is not making and misstates the legal standard for export contingency.[3214]

(e) Arguments of third parties

(i) Australia

7.1506 Australia advances arguments regarding the correct interpretation of Article 3.1(a) but does not take a position on whether HB 2294 is contingent in fact upon export performance.[3215] In particular, Australia recalls that according to the Appellate Body's finding in *Canada – Aircraft*, three elements must be established in order to prove that a subsidy is contingent in fact upon export performance, namely that (i) the grant of a subsidy (ii) is "tied to" (iii) actual or anticipated exportation or export earnings.[3216]

7.1507 Australia notes that in establishing the second element, namely the "tie", the relationship of contingency "must be inferred from the total configuration of the facts constituting and surrounding the granting of the subsidy, none of which

---

[3211] United States' comments on European Communities' response to question 57, para. 195.
[3212] United States' comments on European Communities' response to question 57, para. 197.
[3213] United States' comments on European Communities' response to question 267.
[3214] United States' comments on European Communities' response to question 270, para. 472.
[3215] Australia's response to question 15.
[3216] Australia's written submission, para. 59.

US - Large Civil Aircraft (2nd Complaint)

on its own is likely to be decisive in any given case".[3217] In Australia's view, such relevant facts could include an analysis of the nature of the product; the design and form of the subsidy; the export propensity of the product; performance requirements or conditions attached to the granting of the subsidy, which could include a requirement to establish a specified production capacity; any distinction between domestic and export sales in relation to repayment requirements of a loan; the level of sales requirements relative to domestic demand; and official statements of the government indicating the intention behind the granting of the subsidy.[3218]

7.1508 According to Australia, the capacity requirement included in HB 2294, considered in the light of estimated demand for the product in the domestic and export markets, is one relevant factor to consider in determining if the grant of the subsidy was "tied to" export performance. However, it is not conclusive of the issue.[3219] Similarly, the export orientation of the recipient of the subsidy is one of several facts that may be considered in determining if a subsidy is contingent upon exports but it cannot be the only fact in support of a finding of export contingency.[3220]

(ii) Canada

7.1509 According to Canada, a subsidy is contingent upon export performance if its grant was tied to or made conditional upon an incentive or requirement to export.[3221] Canada argues that this view is consistent with the reference to export subsidies under Article XVI of the GATT 1994, namely subsidies granted "on the export of any product". In Canada's view, the phrase "on the export" implies a "close connection between the act of exporting and the act of granting a subsidy so as to create a clear incentive to export". Canada argues that where the same terms are used in GATT 1994 and the SCM Agreement they should be read harmoniously where possible.[3222]

7.1510 As context for the interpretation of Article 3.1(a) of the SCM Agreement, Canada also relies upon the draft definition proposals for "export subsidy" canvassed during the Tokyo Round. Although the proposals it relies upon were not ultimately adopted, Canada argues that they demonstrate that the concept of differential treatment of exports over products destined for domestic consumption was central to the negotiators of the Round. Canada knows of no evidence that the language in Article 3.1(a) was designed to negate this notion of differential treatment.[3223] Canada also notes that all of the subsidies in the Annex

---

[3217] Australia's written submission, para. 62, quoting the Appellate Body, *Canada – Aircraft*, para. 167.
[3218] Australia's written submission, para. 63.
[3219] Australia's written submission, paras. 59 and 61.
[3220] Australia's response to question 16.
[3221] Canada's response to question 16, para. 20.
[3222] Canada's response to question 16, para. 22.
[3223] Canada's response to question 16, paras. 23-24.

DSR 2012:III

1523

Report of the Panel

I Illustrative List of Subsidies are either expressly contingent upon exports or differentially benefit exported products over products destined for domestic consumption. The complete absence from the list of any subsidy that is neutral in terms of market orientation provides context for the interpretation of Article 3.1(a) of the SCM Agreement.[3224]

7.1511 In short, in Canada's view, the absence of an incentive or a requirement to export as a condition precedent to the granting of a subsidy means that the subsidy is not export contingent.[3225] Applying this interpretation, Canada argues that the European Communities' reliance upon the capacity condition in HB 2294 falls well short of establishing export contingency. The capacity condition does not require Boeing to make a single export sale or sell more than it otherwise would have in export markets. It does not provide any incentives that could have the effect of distorting Boeing's market orientation in favour of exports.[3226] Canada concludes that "a contingency that can be satisfied without a single export sale (or a sale of any kind) and where the resulting subsidy continues to be provided even if no export sales materialize is an unlikely instrument for promoting exportation or export earnings.[3227] According to Canada, the "more compelling explanation" for the capacity condition in HB 2294 is that Washington State wanted to retain aerospace manufacturing and was not willing to accept a mere token facility. Canada notes that in any event, "inferring intent can be a highly subjective matter, particularly when the intentions at issue are those of a government".[3228]

(iii)   Korea

7.1512 According to Korea, in order to demonstrate that the requisite "tie" exists in establishing export contingency, it is necessary to prove that the subsidy would *not* have been granted *but for* anticipated exportation or export earnings.[3229] Korea notes that the simple fact that Boeing exports many of its airplanes should not be the legal standard for determining whether an export contingent subsidy exists.[3230] The European Communities must prove that the benefit would not have been granted to Boeing if the United States Government had known that no export sales may ensue from the programme.[3231] Korea concludes that "the Panel should not simply look at the export potential or export sales of Boeing; instead it should evaluate the evidence provided by the EC as a whole, and look into the very nature of the HB 2294".[3232]

[3224] Canada's response to question 16, para. 25.
[3225] *Ibid.*
[3226] Canada's written submission, para. 45.
[3227] Canada's written submission, para. 46.
[3228] Canada's written submission, para. 47.
[3229] Korea's written submission, para. 42.
[3230] Korea's written submission, para. 38.
[3231] Korea's written submission, para. 43.
[3232] *Ibid.*

US - Large Civil Aircraft (2nd Complaint)

(f) Evaluation by the Panel

7.1513 The issue before us is whether the tax measures under HB 2294 constitute subsidies contingent upon export performance under Article 3.1(a) of the SCM Agreement, which provides:

> "3.1 Except as provided in the Agreement on Agriculture, the following subsidies, within the meaning of Article 1, shall be prohibited:
>
> (a)   subsidies contingent, in law or in fact[4], whether solely or as one of several other conditions, upon export performance, including those illustrated in Annex I[5] ..."
>
> _____
>
> [4] This standard is met when the facts demonstrate that the granting of a subsidy, without having been made legally contingent upon export performance, is in fact tied to actual or anticipated exportation or export earnings. The mere fact that a subsidy is granted to enterprises which export shall not for that reason alone be considered to be an export subsidy within the meaning of this provision.
>
> [5] Measures referred to in Annex I as not constituting export subsidies shall not be prohibited under this or any other provision of this Agreement."

7.1514 The European Communities' claim is that HB 2294 is de facto contingent upon export performance. In response to an explicit Panel question regarding how many legal arguments it is making, the European Communities advances three arguments. Therefore, we treat the three arguments there outlined as the only three arguments the European Communities advances.[3233]

(a)   HB 2294 is de facto contingent upon export performance because the B&O tax reduction, an *ad valorem* subsidy, is contingent upon sales, including export sales. The European Communities asserts that the grant of the subsidy is tied to "actual" or "anticipated" exportation.

_____

[3233] As indicated at footnote 3182 of this Report, in its first oral statement the European Communities describes its "primary argument" in support of export contingency. The argument is that HB 2294 acts as a "filter", with the result that the defining characteristic of the companies that are eligible for the subsidy is that they contribute to a product that will necessarily be exported. As indicated in footnote 3182 of this Report, it is not clear that this is a separate legal argument, rather than reasoning in support of its other legal arguments. For completeness, we note that if this is intended to be a separate legal argument, it is not a strong one. The argument essentially amounts to a contention that the taxation subsidies are export contingent simply because all of the enterprises to which the subsidies are granted make products that will ultimately be exported. It is clear from the final sentence in footnote 4 to Article 3.1(a) that such an argument cannot support a finding of *de facto* export contingency.

DSR 2012:III   1525

Report of the Panel

(b) HB 2294 is de facto contingent upon export performance because its grant was conditioned upon establishment of a facility with the capacity to produce thirty-six superefficient airplanes. The subsidies are tied to "actual" or to "anticipated" exportation. The relevant legal test requires some element of "favouring" of exports.

(c) The final legal argument is the same as that outlined in (b) above, except that no element of "favouring" of exports need be proven.

7.1515 Although in its second written submission the European Communities asserts that "the United States effectively admitted that the HB 2294 B&O tax rate reductions are subsidies contingent *in law...* upon export performance", nowhere else in its submissions does the European Communities refer to HB 2294 as export contingent in law. In response to a specific question from the Panel regarding how many legal arguments it is making in support of its claim that the subsidies are contingent in fact upon export performance, the European Communities does not assert that it is also advancing legal arguments to support a claim that the subsidies are contingent *in law* upon export performance. Therefore, it is reasonable to conclude that the European Communities' claim relates only to de facto export contingency.

7.1516 Before addressing each of the European Communities' arguments in this case, it is useful to review the way in which Article 3.1(a) of the SCM Agreement has been interpreted in adopted panel and the Appellate Body reports.

7.1517 The Appellate Body interpreted Article 3.1(a) in the context of a de facto export contingency claim in *Canada – Aircraft*.[3234] Both the panel and the Appellate Body held that the evidence demonstrated that the grant of the subsidy was tied to anticipated exportation and therefore was a subsidy contingent upon export performance. The subsidy programme in issue was the Technology Partnerships Canada ("TPC"), which involved the provision of financing for high-technology projects in the Canadian regional aircraft sector. The repayment terms were such that the recipients of the financing were only required to make repayments if they made sales.

7.1518 In interpreting Article 3.1(a), the Appellate Body stated that the "key word" in the provision is "contingent", which means "conditional" or "dependent for its existence on something else".[3235] The Appellate Body noted that *de jure* and de facto contingency are subject to the same legal standard under Article 3.1(a). However, the evidence used to prove each type of contingency is different. Whereas *de jure* contingency is established on the basis of the terms of the relevant legislation or legal instrument, proof of de facto export contingency

---

[3234] Appellate Body Report, *Canada – Aircraft.*
[3235] Appellate Body Report, *Canada – Aircraft*, para. 166.

1526 DSR 2012:III

is "a much more difficult task".[3236] De facto export contingency must be inferred from the "total configuration of facts constituting and surrounding the granting of the subsidy, none of which on its own is likely to be decisive in any case".[3237] The Appellate Body noted that the export-orientation of the recipient could be considered as *a* relevant fact, but could not be the sole fact supporting a finding of export contingency.[3238]

7.1519 The Appellate Body indicated that the satisfaction of the standard for determining de facto export contingency, as set out in footnote 4 to Article 3.1(a), requires proof of three different elements, namely (i) the granting of a subsidy (ii) tied to (iii) actual or anticipated exportation or export earnings.[3239]

7.1520 According to the Appellate Body, the second element, namely "tied to", indicates that a relationship of "conditionality or dependence" must be demonstrated and this second element "is at the very heart of the legal standard in footnote 4".[3240] The Appellate Body equated "tied to" with "contingent upon". It distanced itself from the "but for" test which the Panel had applied in determining if the grant of the subsidy was tied to anticipated exports. The panel had reasoned that the claimant was required to demonstrate that, "but for" the expectation of export sales ensuing from the subsidy, the subsidy would not have been granted. To the panel, this was an effective indicator of a "strong and direct link" between the granting of the subsidy and the creation or generation of export sales.[3241] However, the Appellate Body held that, while the panel was not in error in its overall approach, it was necessary to interpret and apply the language actually used in the treaty, rather than applying a "but for" test.[3242]

7.1521 In relation to the third element, the Appellate Body held that "anticipated" means "expected".[3243] Whether exports were expected at the time of the grant of the subsidy needs to be gleaned from an examination of objective evidence. The Appellate Body emphasized that the second and third elements are distinct enquiries. It is not sufficient to demonstrate that a subsidy was granted with the anticipation that exports would result.[3244] It is necessary to prove that the granting of the subsidy was *tied to* the anticipation of exportation. The Appellate Body stated that this is emphasized by the second sentence of footnote 4, which provides that a finding of export contingency cannot be based solely on the fact that it is "granted to enterprises which export". Merely knowing that a

---

[3236] Appellate Body Report, *Canada – Aircraft*, para. 167.
[3237] *Ibid.*
[3238] Appellate Body Report, *Canada – Aircraft*, para. 173.
[3239] Appellate Body Report, *Canada – Aircraft*, para. 169.
[3240] Appellate Body Report, *Canada – Aircraft*, at 171.
[3241] Panel Report, *Canada – Aircraft*, para. 9.339.
[3242] Appellate Body Report, *Canada – Aircraft*, para. 171, footnote 102.
[3243] Appellate Body Report, *Canada – Aircraft*, para. 172.
[3244] *Ibid.*

Report of the Panel

recipient's sales are export-oriented does not demonstrate, without more, that the granting of a subsidy is tied to actual or anticipated exports.[3245]

7.1522 The Appellate Body agreed with the panel's finding, based on sixteen different factual elements, that the TPC assistance was "contingent ... in fact ... upon export performance", on the basis that the grant of the TPC assistance was tied to anticipated exportation. In reaching this conclusion, the sixteen factual elements relied upon by the Panel in finding that the necessary "tie" existed were that:

- the Canadian aerospace sector *exported a large proportion of its output*, due to the small size of the Canadian domestic market;

- the TPC Business Plan noted that TPC's "approach" in the aerospace and defence sector was to "{d}irectly support the near market R&D projects *with high export potential*";

- section 3.2.3 of the "Terms and Conditions" set forth in the TPC Interim Reference Binder stated that "TPC will provide contributions to specific industrial development projects in order to enable Canadian Aerospace and Defence Industries *to compete fairly and openly on the world competitive stage*";

- the Industry Minister's Message, which was included in the 1996-1997 TPC Annual Report, stated:

  "Aerospace and defense also make a significant contribution to our economic wellbeing. The sector is highly export oriented. Exports accounted for about 70 percent of sales, or $7.4 billion, in 1995. And there is the prospect of real growth in this area. Canada's aerospace sector currently ranks sixth in the world. *With investments from TPC*, and with industry's concerted efforts, *this sector* will be better equipped to compete effectively in the world marketplace and *could grow to fourth place*";

- the TPC Annual Report stated that "{t}he 12 largest firms {in the aerospace and defence sector} account for most of the R&D and shipments, *of which 80 percent are exported.* ... TPC is proud to be an investment partner in this *export-oriented* success story";

- an Industry Canada press release, issued in respect of the $100 million TPC contribution to a specific firm, quoted Industry Minister Manley as stating "{A}erospace is a critical sector for Canada's economy, with exports growing at a rate of 10 per cent per year. *TPC's investment* in these projects will help increase the global competitiveness of this industry, while supporting jobs in

---

[3245] Appellate Body Report, *Canada – Aircraft*, para. 173.

1528

DSR 2012:III

Montreal, in Halifax and across the country, *generating economic growth and export dollars*";

- concerning the $57 million contribution to a firm for the development of the Dash 8-400, the Leader of the Government in the House of Commons and then-Solicitor General of Canada, stated that "{t}hese two outputs of the Dash 8-400 project - the creation of jobs and the *building of exports - are just what the government had in mind when we established Technology Partnerships Canada earlier this year*";

- TPC website material stated that "TPC approved projects are forecasted to *generate sales* of more than $65 billion (*mostly exports*) and create or maintain 13,166 direct and indirect jobs";

- the TPC Applications Kit required applicants to describe "potential broad economic and social benefits, such as: job creation and retention, *increased exports*, new investment...". The Applications Kit also stated that TPC "*invests in projects* that have the potential to create jobs, *generate exports*, launch new industries, and transform or strengthen the competitiveness of industry";

- according to the TPC Interim Reference Binder, the TPC Aerospace and Defence Sector Generic Model Agreement required applicants *to distinguish between domestic sales and exports* when reporting forecast and actual sales;

- the TPC Interim Reference Binder required TPC employees, when completing Project Summary Forms, to explain the reasons for recommending support or rejection of the project. In particular, employees were given the following instructions:

"Strategic Considerations, Benefits, Indicators

In justifying the recommendation in strategic terms emphasise "business results". The following may be considered:

1. Link the project with departmental strategies and priorities as relevant:

> a) Improvement of international competitiveness; *when sales will result directly from the project, report annual sales in terms of domestic and export sales* and any import replacement";

- the "Terms and Conditions" set forth in the TPC Interim Reference Binder stated that TPC will "fill a financial void ... where government action is *required to level the competitive playing field*, at the near-market end of the spectrum"; and that "{c}ontributions under the Aerospace and Defence component

Report of the Panel

will be directed to projects that will maintain and build upon the technological capabilities and production, employment and *export base* extant in the aerospace and defence sector";

- Industry Canada website material concerning TPC "Application information" stated that one factor considered by TPC in determining the need for federal government involvement was whether assistance was required to *level the playing field against international competitors*;

- the TPC Charter stated that "{i}nvestments will be directed to projects that build on and maintain technological capabilities and the production, employment and *export base* of the sector";

- the TPC Business Plan recorded the proportion of the aerospace and defence industry's *revenue allocable to exports*; and

- the TPC contributions identified by Brazil were for the development of specific products, and were provided expressly on the basis of the projected *sales* of those products, the market for which was known to be almost entirely outside Canada; the statistics maintained by TPC, and the public statements about TPC, separately recount, and emphasize, the amount of export sales "generated" by these contributions. [3246]

7.1523 On the basis of this evidence, the panel in *Canada – Aircraft* concluded that the TPC funding was expressly designed and structured to generate sales of particular products, and that the Canadian Government expressly took this into account, and attached considerable importance to, the proportion of those sales for export, when making TPC contributions in the regional aircraft sector. On this basis, the panel concluded that the subsidy was tied to anticipated exportation or export earnings.[3247]

7.1524 In *Australia – Automotive Leather II*, the panel also concluded that the grant of one of the subsidies in issue was contingent in fact upon export performance on the basis that it was tied to anticipated exportation.[3248] The measure was a grant contract between a producer of automotive leather, Howe, and the Australian Government. The contract provided for a series of three grant payments to Howe. The first payment was made immediately after conclusion of the contract, while the other two were to be made on the basis of Howe's performance against sales targets set out in the contract. Under the contract, Howe was required to use its best endeavours to meet the targets.[3249]

[3246] Panel Report, *Canada – Aircraft*, para. 9.340.
[3247] Panel Report, *Canada – Aircraft*, para. 9.341.
[3248] Panel Report, *Australia – Automotive Leather II*.
[3249] Panel Report, *Australia – Automotive Leather II*, para. 2.3

7.1525 The panel held that the terms "contingent" and "tied to", mean "conditional" and require a "close connection" between the grant of the subsidy and export performance.[3250]

7.1526 The panel ultimately concluded that the grant contract was contingent in fact upon export performance because there was a close tie between anticipated exportation and the grant of the subsidies. In reaching this decision, the panel relied upon the following evidence:

- At the time the contract was granted, Howe exported a significant proportion of its production and the Australian Government was aware of this.[3251] In enacting the programme, there was evidence to suggest that the Australian Government was concerned to ensure that Howe remained in business, after losing funding from another government programme. The panel concluded that, in these circumstances, it was clear that anticipated exportation was an important condition in the provision of the assistance. In reaching this conclusion, the panel noted that it was not prohibited from considering the fact that Howe was an exporter. However, this could not be the sole basis for its decision.[3252]

- In order to meet the sales performance targets, Howe would have had to continue, and perhaps increase, its exportation because the Australian market was too small to absorb the level of production set by the targets. Therefore, the sales performance targets were effectively export performance targets.[3253] The Australian Government was aware of this at the time of granting the subsidy and therefore anticipated continued and perhaps increased exports by Howe. Therefore, Howe's anticipated export performance was one of the conditions for the grant of the subsidy.[3254]

- The subsidy was provided only to Howe, the only *exporter* of automotive leather. It was not provided to producers who supplied only the domestic market.[3255]

- At around the same time as the Australian Government entered the grant contract, a settlement was reached between Australia and the United States which required Australia to remove automotive leather from eligibility for two particular programmes. The panel in *Australia - Automotive Leather II* found that the two programmes gave "incentives to Australian companies to export certain products". Further, "Howe earned significant benefits from

---

[3250] Panel Report, *Australia – Automotive Leather II*, para. 9.55.
[3251] Panel Report, *Australia – Automotive Leather II*, para. 9.66.
[3252] *Ibid.*
[3253] Panel Report, *Australia – Automotive Leather II*, para. 9.67.
[3254] *Ibid.*
[3255] Panel Report, *Australia –Automotive Leather II*, para. 9.69.

Report of the Panel

its exports of automotive leather pursuant to those programmes" (although the programmes were not challenged before any dispute settlement panel). The panel reasoned that the Government of Australia entered into the grant contract at least in part to tide Howe over after it had lost eligibility for benefits under those programmes.[3256]

7.1527 As well as challenging the grant contracts, the United States also alleged that a certain loan contract between Howe and the Australian Government was a subsidy tied to anticipated exportation. The panel found that this measure was not export contingent.

7.1528 The measure in issue was a 15-year preferential loan to Howe, which was secured over the assets of the parent company of Howe (ALH).[3257] Although Howe was a highly export oriented company, and despite the fact that it was likely that some of the money to repay the loan would be generated through export sales, the panel found that the element of contingency between the grant of the loan and export performance was not sufficiently established. Important in the panel's conclusion were the following factors:

- there was "nothing in the loan contract that explicitly linked the loan to Howe's production or sales, and therefore nothing in its terms, the design of the loan payment, or the repayment provisions to tie the loan directly to export performance, or even sales performance".[3258]

- it was ultimately up to Howe and its parent company to decide upon the source of funds to be used to repay the loan. The source of funding to repay the loan would not necessarily be export sales and there was nothing to suggest that it was expected at the time the loan contract was entered into that export sales would generate the funds to repay the loan.[3259]

- the loan was secured by a lien on the assets and undertakings of Howe's parent company, ALH, which was ultimately responsible for repayment of the loan. ALH had other businesses and produced other products from which it could generate the funds to repay the loan.[3260]

7.1529 Thus, in *Australia – Automotive Leather II*, the panel found that the Australian Government's loan to a company whose commercial viability was dependent upon exports was, because of its particular terms, not contingent upon export performance.

[3256] Panel Report, *Australia –Automotive Leather II*, paras. 9.63-9.65.
[3257] Panel Report, *Australia –Automotive Leather II*, para. 9.73.
[3258] *Ibid.*
[3259] Panel Report, *Australia –Automotive Leather II*, para. 9.75.
[3260] *Ibid.*

US - Large Civil Aircraft (2nd Complaint)

7.1530 From the preceding overview of adopted reports we gain guidance from the Appellate Body regarding the way in which de facto export contingency must be demonstrated. In particular, proof of three elements is required, namely (i) the granting of a subsidy (ii) tied to (iii) actual or anticipated exportation or export earnings. At least in its first written submission, the European Communities argues that establishing that a subsidy is de facto contingent upon exports involves consideration of (i) the required condition (export performance); (ii) the required consequence (grant of a subsidy); and (iii) the required contingent relationship (between the grant of the subsidy and the export performance). The submissions of the European Communities in this regard amount to a restatement of Article 3.1(a), namely that the grant of a subsidy must be contingent upon export performance. The United States does not contest that this must be the case and nor does the European Communities suggest that the elements listed by the Appellate Body in *Canada – Aircraft*, which set out the criteria established by footnote 4 for demonstrating de facto contingency, are inapplicable. Therefore, in considering whether the European Communities has established on the evidence that HB 2294 is contingent in fact upon export performance, we follow the structure used by the Appellate Body in *Canada – Aircraft*, namely we consider in turn each of the three elements drawn from footnote 4.

7.1531 Before addressing the legal arguments made by the European Communities, we recall in relation to the first element listed by the Appellate Body in *Canada – Aircraft*, namely the requirement to demonstrate that a subsidy has been granted, that we have concluded that certain taxation subsidies have been granted under HB 2294.[3261] Therefore, in analyzing each of the legal arguments of the European Communities, we need consider only the remaining two elements, namely whether the granting of the subsidy was tied to actual or anticipated exportation.

7.1532 In considering whether the granting of the subsidy was tied to anticipated exportation, the Appellate Body cautioned in *Canada – Aircraft* that this requires two distinct enquiries, namely whether there was *anticipated exportation* and whether this anticipated exportation was *tied to* the grant of the subsidy.

7.1533 In its claim regarding "anticipated exportation", the European Communities does not take a position on the meaning of "anticipated". In contrast, the United States submits that "anticipated" means "expected" and not "future" as suggested in the European Communities' "reference interpretation". In this regard, we note that the Appellate Body held in *Canada – Aircraft* that the "dictionary meaning of the word 'anticipated' is 'expected'". The European Communities does not advance any arguments regarding why this Panel should take an approach to the meaning of "anticipated" that is different to that taken by

---

[3261] See para. 7.302 of this Report.

DSR 2012:III   1533

Report of the Panel

the Appellate Body. In *Australia – Automotive Leather II* and *Canada – Aircraft*, whether or not there was "anticipated exportation" was considered from the point of view of the grantor of the subsidy and the relevant enquiry was whether the granting authority expected exports to ensue or arise out of the granting of the subsidy.[3262] However, the Appellate Body cautioned that it is not sufficient to demonstrate that a subsidy is granted in the knowledge, or with the expectation, that exports will result. Something more is required in order to demonstrate that the grant of the subsidy is "tied to" the anticipated exports.

7.1534 In relation to each of its legal arguments, the European Communities' argues that the "tie" may also be to "actual exportation".[3263] The previous cases discussing de facto export contingency have all been cases in which the claim was that the grant of the subsidy was tied to "anticipated", rather than to "actual" exports. Therefore, the Panel has little guidance regarding the correct interpretation of "actual" exportation. The European Communities does not take a position on the meaning of the term "actual" in footnote 4. In its "reference interpretation", which it does not advance, the European Communities suggests that "actual" means "already existing or in the past". In contrast, the United States' position is that "actual" means "real" and does not mean "past". According to the United States, the Spanish and the French versions of the text of the SCM Agreement confirm this interpretation.[3264]

7.1535 We note that in *Canada – Aircraft*, in dismissing Canada's submission that the subsidy was not contingent upon anticipated exportation because the subsidy was "not conditional on exports taking place" and because there were no "penalties if export sales {were} not realized", the panel held that while this argument may have been relevant in determining if the subsidy was tied to *actual* exportation, it was not sufficient to rebut a prima facie case that the subsidy was tied to *anticipated* exportation.[3265] This suggests that, in that panel's view, "actual" exportation is exportation that must be realized or that must actually occur. This approach to the interpretation of "actual" exportation is supported by the ordinary meaning of the term, which is "existing in act or fact; real" and "in action or existence at the time, present; current".[3266] This is opposed to "anticipated" exportation, which is expected but may or may not in fact take place.

7.1536 Having interpreted the meaning of "actual" and "anticipated" exportation, this brings us to the more difficult question of the meaning of "tied to"

[3262] For example, the Panel in *Canada – Aircraft* referred to an expectation of export sales "ensuing from the subsidy", while the Appellate Body in the same case referred to a subsidy granted "with the anticipation that exports *will result*" (para. 172).

[3263] See European Communities' response to question 57, para. 195.

[3264] United States' comments on European Communities' response to question 54, para. 172.

[3265] Panel Report, *Canada – Aircraft*, para. 9.343.

[3266] *Shorter Oxford English Dictionary*, L. Brown (ed.) (Clarendon Press, 1993), Vol. I, p. 23. It is also supported by the ordinary meaning of the term in *Webster's New Encyclopedic Dictionary*, (Könemann, 1993), p. 11, namely "existing in fact" and "really ... carried out".

1534

DSR 2012:III

anticipated exports. The terms of footnote 4 do not provide specific guidance regarding the meaning of "tied to" or the manner in which such a "tie" should be demonstrated. In *Canada – Aircraft*, the Appellate Body held that it is necessary to demonstrate a relationship of "conditionality or dependence". The panels in *Australia – Automotive Leather II* and *Canada – Aircraft* refer variously to a "close tie", a "but for" test, a "strong and direct link" and an "important condition". In its second and third legal arguments the European Communities adopts an interpretation of "tied to" that it contends the United States advocates "elsewhere". In particular, the European Communities argues that a "tie" exists where it can be shown that the expectation of exports was a part of the consideration or motivation or intent of the government in providing the subsidy.

7.1537 In the Panel's view, a "tie" exists where a subsidy is granted *because of* the granting authority's expectation of exports. In circumstances where a contingent relationship between the grant of a subsidy and export performance is not explicit on the face of the relevant legislation, which is the very nature of a de facto export contingency claim, to determine whether the grant of the subsidy was dependent upon the expected exports requires a determination of whether the subsidy was granted because of the granting authority's expectation of exports.

7.1538 We acknowledge that establishing the existence of the "tie" under footnote 4 of Article 3.1(a) by determining whether the subsidy was granted because of the granting authority's expectation of exports could be considered problematic in some respects. The interpretation could lead to the result that two subsidy programmes, which may operate identically and have the same distorting effect in the market, may not necessarily be subject to the same finding regarding de facto export contingency under Article 3.1(a), where the evidence differs regarding the government's reasons in providing the subsidy. Further, in some circumstances, establishing the necessary "tie" through a focus on the reasons for the grant of the subsidy may make circumvention of Article 3.1(a) relatively easy. For example, in *Canada – Aircraft*, the panel and the Appellate Body found that the subsidies in issue were tied to anticipated exportation. Part of the evidence to support this finding included statements in programme documents to the effect that the programme was expected to result in increased exports.[3267] Perhaps an approach that considers the reasons for the grant of the subsidy may encourage governments to be more discrete without necessarily changing their underlying policies. Nevertheless, despite these issues, the Panel is of the view that to determine whether a "tie" exists between the grant of a subsidy and the grantor's expectation of exports, it is necessary to determine whether the subsidy was granted because of the expectation of exports.

[3267] Panel Report, *Canada – Aircraft (Article 21.5 – Brazil)*.

Report of the Panel

7.1539 Before considering the three legal arguments of the European Communities[3268], the Panel notes that in relation to each argument the European Communities refers to a possible requirement under Article 3.1(a) to demonstrate that a subsidy "favours" exports or is greater in the case of exports.[3269] The European Communities' primary position, as enunciated in its first written submission, is that such a requirement does exist. However, the European Communities notes that the United States has "elsewhere" expressed the view that there is no requirement to demonstrate "favouring" and the European Communities adopts this as its alternative position (in its first and third legal arguments).[3270] In its first written submission, the European Communities discusses "favouring" of exports in relation to the requirement under Article 3.1(a) that the subsidy in issue be contingent upon *export* performance and not mere performance. The European Communities then refers to evidence that it alleges demonstrates "a favouring or discrimination in favour of a product that will inevitably be generally exported or incorporated within an exported product".[3271] The European Communities makes similar arguments in its "reference interpretation", which it does not advance, where it notes:

> "Finally, according to the terms of both Article 3.1(a) and footnote 4, the prohibited condition relates to "*export* performance", not mere performance. For a claim to be successful, the evidence must therefore support the conclusion that there is a grant of a subsidy contingent upon specifically export performance. This will generally involve demonstrating some *favouring* of exports. Demonstrating the existence of a measure contingent upon mere performance is insufficient."[3272]

7.1540 To the extent the European Communities is arguing that there is a requirement to demonstrate that a subsidy is contingent upon *export* performance under Article 3.1(a), this should be accepted as there is no basis to read the term "export" out of Article 3.1(a). Export contingency is the very concern addressed by Article 3.1(a) and this is confirmed by footnote 4, which refers

---

[3268] Where the "three legal arguments of the European Communities" refers to the arguments identified by the European Communities in its response to question 56 and which are summarized at para. 7.1490 of this Report.

[3269] The European Communities' submission regarding the "favouring" of exports has some parallels with Canada's third party submission, in which Canada suggests that an export contingent subsidy must lead to the recipient of the subsidy selling more than it otherwise would have in export markets or must provide incentives that could have the effect of distorting Boeing's market orientation in favour of exports (Canada's written submission, para. 45). However, in response to Panel questioning, the European Communities takes the position that whether or not a subsidy provides an incentive that could have the effect of distorting the subsidy recipient's market orientation is immaterial to the analysis of whether a *de facto* export contingent subsidy exists (European Communities' response to question 269, para. 475).

[3270] See European Communities' first written submission, para. 980, footnote 1712.

[3271] European Communities' first written submission, para. 980.

[3272] European Communities' response to question 56, para. 189.

1536   DSR 2012:III

to subsidies tied to actual or anticipated *exportation* or *export* earnings. As established by the Appellate Body in *Canada – Aircraft*, the relevant legal standard to meet to succeed in a claim of de facto export contingency is that (i) the grant of a subsidy (ii) is tied to (iii) actual or anticipated exportation or export sales. The Panel notes that it would be almost impossible to establish the necessary "tie" between a subsidy and actual or anticipated exports in circumstances where there were not some "favouring" of exports, where favouring does not necessarily mean differential treatment of exports compared with domestic sales, but also refers to granting a subsidy to a company because it is expected to export or will actually export.

(i)   European Communities' first legal argument

7.1541 In its response to question 56, the European Communities contends that its "first legal argument" is based on the B&O tax reduction. In particular, according to the European Communities, the B&O tax rate reduction is an export contingent subsidy because it is an *ad valorem* subsidy. Therefore, it is a subsidy contingent upon sales, whether domestic or export sales. In pursuing this argument, the European Communities submits that there is "no need to demonstrate that the subsidy favours exports or is greater in the case of export".

7.1542 As previously indicated, to fall within the terms of Article 3.1(a), the grant of a subsidy must be "tied to" actual or anticipated exportation. However, any form of conditionality or dependence between the B&O tax reduction and exports arises simply because the recipient of the subsidy is an exporter. If this is the case, the B&O tax reduction is contingent upon either domestic or export sales. The European Communities does not make any other submissions regarding why the grant of the B&O tax reduction is "tied to" exportation. Therefore, it is clear that a "tie" between the B&O tax reduction and exportation arises simply because the subsidy is granted to an enterprise that exports. However, the final sentence of footnote 4 to Article 3.1(a) provides that the grant of a subsidy to an enterprise that exports "shall not for that reason alone be considered to be an export subsidy". Therefore, it is clear from footnote 4 that the standard for de facto export contingency is not met.

7.1543 For these reasons, the Panel finds that, based on its first legal argument, the European Communities has not demonstrated that HB 2294 is contingent upon export performance.

(ii)   European Communities' second and third legal arguments

7.1544 The only difference between the European Communities' second and third legal arguments is that the second argument proceeds on the basis that it is necessary to demonstrate some element of "favouring" of exports in a de facto export contingency claim, while the third does not. As indicated previously, the

Report of the Panel

relevant enquiry under Article 3.1(a) is whether there is a contingent relationship between the grant of the subsidy and *export* performance. It would be almost impossible to establish the necessary "tie" between a subsidy and actual or anticipated exports in circumstances where there were not some "favouring" of exports, where favouring does not necessarily mean differential treatment of exports compared with domestic sales, but also refers to granting a subsidy to a company because it is expected to export or will actually export. In the light of this, the remaining issue to be decided in relation to the second and third legal arguments is whether HB 2294 was tied to an "anticipating of exports" and is therefore a measure contingent upon export performance. Although this is the way in which the European Communities expresses the second and third legal arguments, which seems clearly to be an argument that the grant of the subsidies under HB 2294 was tied to *anticipated* exports, in response to a Panel question, the European Communities states that its second and third legal arguments are also arguments in relation to *actual* exports.[3273] Therefore, our analysis considers both a tie to anticipated exportation and to actual exportation.

Grant of a subsidy in fact tied to
anticipated exportation

7.1545 To determine whether HB 2294 was in fact contingent upon export performance, it is necessary to establish whether there was a (i) grant of a subsidy (ii) tied to (iii) anticipated exportation or export earnings. We have previously concluded that in enacting HB 2294, Washington State granted tax reduction, tax credit and tax exemption subsidies.

Whether the grantor of the subsidy anticipated exportation

7.1546 To demonstrate that the grantor of the subsidy anticipated exports, the European Communities presents a range of evidence. The evidence can broadly be described as evidence relating to the export orientation of Boeing and evidence regarding the capacity condition in HB 2294. The following sections of the Report summarize the evidence before the Panel and the final section draws a conclusion about whether the grantor of the subsidy expected exports to arise from the project benefiting from the subsidies, namely assembly of the 787.

Export Orientation of Boeing

7.1547 The European Communities provides a number of documents, including from the Decadal Survey of Civil Aeronautics, from Boeing and from the Aerospace Industries Association, which include statements that the United States aerospace industry has historically made a major contribution to a positive balance of trade for the United States economy.[3274] Further, the Boeing LCA

[3273] European Communities' response to question 57.

[3274] See European Communities' first written submission, paras. 981-982; Boeing Current Market Outlook 2006 (September 2006), Exhibit EC-635; Boeing Current Market Outlook 2003 (June 2003);

1538

DSR 2012:III

division has played a major role in this regard, with an average of 60 per cent of total LCA sales between 1989-2005 being export sales.[3275] The European Communities also provides a transcript from a speech of the Lieutenant Governor of Washington, which includes a statement that Washington is the United States' most trade dependent state and that Boeing accounts for 50 per cent of the State's exports.[3276]

7.1548 In addition to the objective evidence regarding the export orientation of Boeing, the European Communities submits evidence regarding the awareness of the Governor of Washington of the export orientation of Boeing. In one of his speeches, the Governor states:

> "Now more than ever, we must aggressively capitalize on and protect our competitive advantage in trade... Expanding trade and pressing our state's many advantages is even more important as we strive to recover economically...

> "We must...do everything possible to keep our top companies here – including companies that strengthen our international trade. As you know, we are energetically pursuing Boeing 7E7 final assembly. Boeing has historically been a major exporter for our state and for our nation. We want to keep Boeing assembly and supplier jobs right here where they belong...

> "Expanding international trade is part of my plan to create jobs."[3277]

7.1549 Further, a letter written by Governor Locke, entitled "Restatement of Commitments", is appended to the Master Site Agreement. The letter was submitted as a part of the offer by the State of Washington for the 787 manufacturing facilities to be located in Washington. The letter provides:

> "The recent trade mission I led to China is another example of how the state can play a beneficial and significant role in helping keep Boeing and other Washington companies competitive. I met with

---

Exhibit EC-636; Steering Committee for the Decadal Survey of Civil Aeronautics, National Research Council of the National Academies, Decadal Survey of Civil Aeronautics: Foundation for the Future, 2006, Exhibit EC-301; and Civil Aircraft Sales Fuel Record Year for Aerospace, Press Release, Aerospace Industries Association, 13 December 2006, Exhibit EC-639.

[3275] See European Communities' first written submission, para. 986 and International Trade Resources LLC, FSC/ETI Tax Benefits Provided to U.S. Large Civil Aircraft Producers, December 2006, Exhibit EC-12.

[3276] European Communities' first written submission, para. 982 and Speech by Lt. Governor Brad Owen, "Impact of Trade on the Regional Economy", National Forum on Trade Policy, 7 December 2006, Exhibit EC-637.

[3277] European Communities' first written submission, para. 983 and Governor Gary Locke Speech, World Trade Club Annual Dinner, 29 May 2003, Exhibit EC-638.

Report of the Panel

high-level government officials and airline executives for the purpose of promoting the purchase of Boeing airplanes." [3278]

7.1550 Finally, although not referred to in the European Communities' submissions regarding anticipated exportation, we note that Article 10.6.1 of the MSA provides:

"Boeing's production and assembly of the 7E7 Aircraft is market-driven. The commercial aircraft market is *international* and highly competitive. Despite Boeing's extensive investments and good faith efforts to predict markets for the 7E7 Aircraft, Boeing cannot guarantee that those markets will materialize or be sustained as predicted or desired" (emphasis added).

The capacity condition

7.1551 To support its argument of export contingency, the European Communities variously submits that the requirement in HB 2294 that Boeing build a facility with the capacity to produce at least thirty-six superefficient airplanes per year amounted to a requirement to export or created an expectation of exports.[3279] To the extent the evidence of the European Communities is relevant to whether or not there was an expectation that exports would ensue from the project benefiting from HB 2294, it is outlined in the following paragraphs. We note that the European Communities relies on objective evidence regarding the effect of the capacity condition and also refers to the subjective knowledge of the government of this alleged effect.

7.1552 The European Communities submits a number of exhibits to prove that the requirement that Boeing build a facility in Washington with the capacity to produce thirty-six superefficient airplanes will ultimately result, or could be expected to result, in exports. The European Communities' reasoning proceeds in two-steps; first, that once built, the required capacity will be fully utilized and second, that Boeing could not sell 36 superefficient airplanes in the United States market alone and so must export the excess.

7.1553 To support the notion that the requirement to build a facility with the capacity to produce thirty-six aircraft leads to the production of at least thirty-six superefficient airplanes per year, the European Communities reasons that companies do not create production capacity that is intended to stand idle. The European Communities asserts that in the LCA industry, a manufacturer creates its production capacity based on the number of orders already received for the

---

[3278] European Communities' first written submission, para. 984 and Schedule 3 to Project Olympus Master Site Agreement, Restatement of Commitments, 10 November 2003, Exhibit EC-71.

[3279] See e.g. European Communities' response to question 54, para. 177, where the European Communities states that the capacity requirement is tantamount to a requirement to export. Also see European Communities' first written submission, paras. 992-995, where the European Communities submits that the capacity requirement created an expectation of exports.

1540   DSR 2012:III

US - Large Civil Aircraft (2nd Complaint)

airplane in question as well as on orders that it forecasts it will secure.[3280] The requirement that thirty-six superefficient airplane be built was based on Boeing's determination that it would have sufficient orders to produce and deliver thirty-six 787s per year.[3281] In addition, the European Communities argues that if Boeing were to establish the capacity to produce thirty-six aircraft per year it would suffer "grave" financial consequences if it were not to produce at least thirty-six 787s each year.[3282] Establishing the capacity to produce a certain number of aircraft requires not only the building of an assembly facility, but also requires that Boeing have adequate capacity in its supply chain to produce and deliver thirty-six aircraft. This requires order and delivery to the assembly facility of the necessary components. It is difficult to reverse these capacity decisions without suffering "significant financial costs".[3283] Therefore, according to the European Communities, it is "implausible in the extreme" that Boeing would build an assembly facility with the capacity to produce thirty-six 787s per year and then allow that facility to stand idle, or to under-utilize it.[3284] Indeed, the European Communities provides a statement from the Manager of Boeing's 787 programme that, at the time HB 2294 was enacted, Boeing expected to make 1,750 Dreamliners over a period of twenty years, which the European Communities calculates as equivalent to eighty-eight 787s per year, far higher than thirty-six.[3285]

7.1554 The final step in the European Communities' argument that the capacity requirement amounts to an export requirement, or at least could be expected to lead to exports, is that the level of demand in the United States market is incapable of absorbing a production level of thirty-six 787s and therefore, it is necessary for Boeing to export at least some of its production. The European Communities relies upon a declaration by the Head of Market Analysis and Research at Airbus, Mr. Andrew Gordon, to support this contention.[3286] Mr. Gordon analyzes the backlog position of the 787, the historical share and deliveries for aircraft in the 787 class and concludes that it is "extremely unlikely that production of 36 aircraft per year for the 787 could be sustained by the United States market alone".[3287] In particular, Mr. Gordon notes that the 787 orderbook at the end of 2006 included orders for 448 aircraft, of which thirty-eight were for airlines domiciled in the United States. Mr. Gordon excludes from

---

[3280] European Communities' response to question 54, para. 175.

[3281] *Ibid.*

[3282] European Communities' response to question 54, para. 177.

[3283] European Communities' response to question 54, para. 176.

[3284] European Communities' non-confidential statement at the first meeting with the Panel, para. 105.

[3285] See European Communities' non-confidential statement at the first meeting with the Panel, para. 105; Boeing Webcast, The Boeing Company Annual Investors Conference, 23 May 2007, at 787 Program – Mike Bair, Q and A, 00h:24m:38s, Exhibit EC-1149; James Gunsalus, "Investors hope Boeing can avoid delays of its own," International Herald Tribune, 18 June 2007, Exhibit EC-1150; and Boeing 787 Dreamliner Program Fact Sheet, Exhibit EC-340.

[3286] Declaration of A. Gordon Regarding 787 Export Sales, 21 February 2007, Exhibit EC-8.

[3287] Declaration of A. Gordon Regarding 787 Export Sales, 21 February 2007, Exhibit EC-8, para. 8.

DSR 2012:III

Report of the Panel

this figure aircraft ordered by United States-based leasing companies, which supply aircraft on an operating lease basis to customers worldwide, although the European Communities acknowledges that it is unclear to what extent those orders indirectly go to United States airlines. Mr. Gordon notes that delivery of the thirty-eight 787s ordered by United States airlines is expected to take place over a number of years. According to a forecast by Airclaims, the deliveries will take place over six years, with between nine and four deliveries per year over this period.[3288]

7.1555 Mr. Gordon also considers the 2006 "Current Market Outlook" produced by Boeing. The Current Market Outlook includes a statement by Boeing that in North America 1,410 "twin aisle" aircraft will be delivered between 2006-2025.[3289] As this figure includes exports to Canada and aircraft in the twin-aisle category apart from the 787, namely the 767, 777, A330/A340 and A350, Mr. Gordon makes a number of "conservative" assumptions to convert the figure into the number of 787s to be delivered to the United States market between 2006-2025. In particular, Mr. Gordon makes a conservative estimate that 5 per cent of deliveries will be to the Canadian market and that half of the estimated deliveries will be 787s.[3290] This results in a very optimistic estimate of thirty-three deliveries of 787s per year in the United States market.[3291] Using forecasts from the 2005 and 2004 Current Market Outlooks leads to estimates of twenty-nine and twenty-seven respectively.[3292] Finally, Mr. Gordon also uses the 2006 Airbus Global Market Forecast to estimate the level of demand for 787s in the United States market. The Airbus forecast is that the United States will demand 644 aircraft in the 250-300 seat category over 20 years. Using the same conservative assumption of a 50/50 split in demand between 787s and all other 250-300 seat aircraft results in an estimate of approximately sixteen 787 deliveries per year in the United States market. This estimate drops to ten when the 2004 Airbus Global Market Forecast is used.[3293] Mr. Gordon concludes:

> "An examination of the current backlog for the 787 and competing types, as well as recent Boeing and Airbus forecasts, all suggest that deliveries of 36 787 aircraft per year into the US market alone is highly unlikely."[3294]

[3288] Declaration of A. Gordon Regarding 787 Export Sales, 21 February 2007, Exhibit EC-8, para. 4.

[3289] *Ibid.*

[3290] Declaration of A. Gordon Regarding 787 Export Sales, 21 February 2007, Exhibit EC-8, para. 9.

[3291] Declaration of A. Gordon Regarding 787 Export Sales, 21 February 2007, Exhibit EC-8, para. 11.

[3292] Declaration of A. Gordon Regarding 787 Export Sales, 21 February 2007, Exhibit EC-8, para. 12.

[3293] Declaration of A. Gordon Regarding 787 Export Sales, 21 February 2007, Exhibit EC-8, paras. 13-14.

[3294] Declaration of A. Gordon Regarding 787 Export Sales, 21 February 2007, Exhibit EC-8, para. 16.

1542

7.1556 In contrast to this evidence, the United States argues that its domestic market is capable of absorbing "well in excess" of thirty-six superefficient airplanes per year.[3295] The United States refers to documents which suggest that between December 2004 and June 2007, Boeing received orders for 140 787s from customers located within the United States. The United States divides this figure by the number of months between December 2004 and June 2007 to conclude that this results in average sales in the United States market of four 787s per month or 54.2 per year.[3296]

7.1557 The European Communities argues that the United States' evidence is extremely misleading because the United States' figures represent *orders,* rather than *production.*[3297] The European Communities states that, in fact, "Boeing ... began producing the 787 only in 2007 and it reported in April 2007 that its 787 delivery positions were sold out until 2014".[3298] Therefore Boeing will produce the 140 orders between 2007-2014, at an average rate of approximately twenty 787s per year, rather than over the period 2004-2007, as suggested by the United States.[3299] Further, the European Communities objects to the inclusion in the United States' figures of orders placed by United States-based leasing companies. According to the European Communities, the effect of this is that even the estimate of the twenty deliveries to the United States market per year is an overestimate.[3300]

7.1558 As well as submitting evidence that the effect of the capacity condition is to lead to exports, the European Communities makes submissions to support the notion that the Government of the State of Washington was aware of or expected this when it granted the subsidies. In particular, the European Communities asserts that the granting authority was aware of the capacity of the United States market for 787 airplanes.[3301] The European Communities notes that, prior to the enactment of HB 2294, Washington State estimated the value of the B&O tax reduction to Boeing through until 2024. To calculate this, because the B&O tax reduction is an *ad valorem* subsidy, Washington officials necessarily had specific industry information about Boeing's anticipated revenue and sales of LCAs.[3302] Further, the European Communities contends that Washington officials "certainly must have reviewed the most recent versions of Boeing's Current Market Outlook, given Boeing's importance to the state economy".[3303] The Boeing Market Outlook enabled the grantors of the subsidies to conduct the

---

[3295] United States' first written submission, para. 702.
[3296] *Ibid.*
[3297] European Communities' non-confidential statement at the first meeting with the Panel, para. 112.
[3298] European Communities' non-confidential statement at the first meeting with the Panel, para. 113. We assume the reference to "producing" the 787 is a reference to the assembly of the 787.
[3299] European Communities' non-confidential statement at the first meeting with the Panel, para. 112.
[3300] European Communities' non-confidential statement at the first meeting with the Panel, para. 114.
[3301] European Communities' response to question 267.
[3302] European Communities' response to question 267, para. 468.
[3303] European Communities' response to question 267, para. 469.

DSR 2012:III

1543

Report of the Panel

same type of analysis as was conducted by Mr. Gordon, market analyst at Airbus, in order to determine the level of demand for 787s in the United States market.[3304]

7.1559 In response to the European Communities' submissions regarding the awareness of the grantor of the subsidies of the level of demand in the United States market for 787 airplanes, the United States asserts that the European Communities has provided no evidence of any such awareness of the market or anticipation of exportation.[3305] The United States submits that the European Communities' argument that Washington State officials "certainly must have reviewed the most recent versions of Boeing's Current Market Outlook" is a mere assertion. There is no evidence that Boeing provided the Current Market Outlooks to Washington State as part of the decision making process preceding the granting of the subsidies.[3306] Further, there is no evidence that the Washington State officials actually performed the type of calculations required to convert the figures in the Current Market Outlook into an estimation of the number of 787s to be sold in the United States market (by excluding Canada and models apart from the 787 from the figures provided).[3307] The United States also argues that even if the Washington officials estimated the value of the B&O tax reduction to Boeing, this does not indicate an awareness of the capacity of the United States market or an anticipation of exportation.[3308]

Conclusion on "anticipated exportation"

7.1560 In our view, the European Communities has provided adequate evidence to demonstrate that the grantor of the subsidy anticipated exportation.

7.1561 In reaching this conclusion, we accord some weight to the term of the MSA, namely Article 10.6.1, which refers to the fact that the commercial aircraft market is "international". A possible interpretation of this is that the market is one in which sales occur in the global market and not only within the United States. Given that the reference to the "international" nature of the market is found within a term of the MSA, this provides some evidence that the parties to the Agreement, including the State of Washington, expected that the sale of the Boeing 787 would involve exports. However, we do not consider it conclusive evidence because the "international" nature of the market may be a reference to the fact that there are two main players in the commercial aircraft market, one of which is not a United States company.

7.1562 Our conclusion is also based upon the evidence regarding the export orientation of Boeing.[3309] We acknowledge that footnote 4 to Article 3.1(a)

[3304] *Ibid.*

[3305] United States' comments on European Communities' response to question 267, para. 453.

[3306] United States' comments on European Communities' response to question 267, para. 455.

[3307] United States' comments on European Communities' response to question 267, para. 456.

[3308] United States' comments on European Communities' response to question 267, para. 457.

[3309] See paras. 7.1547-7.1550 of this Report.

1544   DSR 2012:III

US - Large Civil Aircraft (2nd Complaint)

indicates that the mere fact that a subsidy is granted to enterprises which export cannot be the sole reason for concluding that an export contingent subsidy exists. However, in *Canada – Aircraft* the Appellate Body held that this second sentence in footnote 4 is a "specific expression of the requirement in the first sentence to demonstrate the "tied to" requirement".[3310] Therefore, while the export orientation of an entity cannot be the only evidence in support of a "tie" between the grant of a subsidy and anticipated exports, and therefore a conclusion that an export contingent subsidy exists, it is relevant information to consider in determining whether exports are anticipated at all. We conclude that the extensive publicly available information presented by the European Communities regarding the export orientation of Boeing provides evidence that the State of Washington anticipated that exports would ensue from the project benefiting from HB 2294, namely assembly of the 787 in Washington. The statements from the Governor of Washington regarding the contribution of Boeing to the State's export performance also indicate that the State of Washington anticipated that exports would arise or continue as a result of the granting of the taxation subsidies under HB 2294. At least one of the statements of the Governor, indicating an expectation that the export performance of Boeing would be promoted under the agreement to site the 787 assembly facility in Washington, is included as a Schedule to the MSA.[3311] Its incorporation in the agreement between the two parties indicates that the statement is more than political rhetoric delivered to promote a subsidy package to a constituency.

7.1563 In the light of this evidence, it would be unrealistic to conclude that the grantor of the subsidies did not have an expectation of exports.

7.1564 In reaching this conclusion, the Panel notes that the evidence submitted by the European Communities in relation to the effect of the capacity condition upon exports seems somewhat equivocal. We note that the European Communities' case that the United States market cannot absorb a production level of 36 787s per year is quite a marginal one. In particular, the estimate of the Airbus analyst that there is a level of demand in the market for 33 superefficient airplanes per year seems relatively close to 36 airplanes per year which the European Communities asserts Boeing will produce. Further, the statements regarding the knowledge of the State of Washington regarding the capacity of the domestic market seem merely to be assertions, without being concrete evidence. Nevertheless, given the statements made in the legal documents associated with HB 2294, upon which both parties rely, regarding the international nature of Boeing's market, and also given the export orientation of Boeing, we conclude that the State of Washington expected exports to ensue from the project benefiting from HB 2294.

[3310] Appellate Body Report, *Canada – Aircraft*, para. 173.
[3311] European Communities' first written submission, para. 984 and Schedule 3 to Project Olympus Master Site Agreement, Restatement of Commitments, 10 November 2003, Exhibit EC-71.

DSR 2012:III   1545

Report of the Panel

7.1565 For these reasons, the Panel finds that the grantor of the subsidy anticipated exportation.

Whether the grant of the subsidy was "tied" to the anticipated exportation

7.1566 The United States argues that the major flaw in the European Communities' Article 3.1(a) claim is that it does not provide sufficient evidence of a "tie" between any expectations of exports and the granting of the subsidies. The evidence relied upon by the European Communities to support its case that there was a "tie" between the enactment of HB 2294 and Washington State's anticipation of exports is principally related to the capacity requirement.[3312] The European Communities contends that the Washington officials envisaged that exports would arise as a result of this requirement and that the granting of the subsidies, by the very terms of HB 2294, was contingent upon, and therefore "tied to", this requirement being met.[3313]

7.1567 In addition to the capacity requirement found in HB 2294, the following evidence could potentially shed some light on whether the subsidies were granted because of anticipated exports:

(a) A speech by the Governor of Washington which included statements suggesting that he wanted to keep Boeing in Washington because of its export performance:

> "We must ... do everything possible to keep our top companies here – including companies that strengthen our international trade. As you know, we are energetically pursuing Boeing 7E7 final assembly. Boeing has historically been a major exporter for our state and for our nation. We want to keep Boeing assembly and supplier jobs right here where they belong."

(b) The letter attached to the Master Site Agreement regarding the Governor's promotion of Boeing sales in China:

> "The recent trade mission I led to China is another example of how the state can play a beneficial and significant role in helping keep Boeing and other Washington companies competitive. I met with high-level government officials and airline executives for the purpose of promoting the purchase of Boeing airplanes."

[3312] See European Communities' first written submission, paras. 991-996.
[3313] European Communities' first written submission, paras. 992-996.

1546   DSR 2012:III

US - Large Civil Aircraft (2ⁿᵈ Complaint)

    (c)   The fact that HB 2294 acts as a filter, such that only companies which produce products that will necessarily be exported may be recipients of the subsidies.[3314]

7.1568 In addition to the evidence cited by the European Communities in relation to its export contingency claim, there is other evidence before us regarding HB 2294, which was submitted by the parties in the context of demonstrating that the tax incentives constitute subsidies under Article 1.1 of the SCM Agreement, but which we consider to be relevant background evidence in determining if the subsidies were granted because of anticipated exportation.

7.1569 The following evidence reveals that at least one of the reasons in granting the tax incentives under HB 2294 was to encourage Boeing to locate its final assembly facility for the 787 in Washington rather than another state because this would have positive effects on the State's economy, particularly its employment rate. Given that Article 3.1(a) of the SCM Agreement provides that a subsidy is prohibited if it is contingent, *whether solely or as one of several other conditions*, upon export performance, the fact that the subsidies were granted to encourage Boeing to locate its assembly facility in Washington in order to increase employment does not rule out the possibility that the subsidies are contingent in fact upon another condition, namely anticipated exports. Nevertheless, we provide a summary of the evidence that indicates that the subsidies were granted to encourage Boeing to locate in Washington as relevant background information to the circumstances surrounding the grant of the subsidies.

-     HB 2294

7.1570 A review of the legislation itself provides some insight regarding the reasons for the introduction of the tax incentives:[3315]

> *"Preamble*: An Act relating to retaining and attracting the aerospace industry to Washington state.[3316]

> *Section 1.* The legislature finds that the people of the state have benefited from the presence of the aerospace industry in Washington state. The aerospace industry provides good wages and benefits for the thousands of engineers, mechanics, and support staff working directly in the industry throughout the state. The suppliers and vendors that support the aerospace industry in turn provide a range of jobs. The legislature declares that it is in the public interest to encourage the continued presence of this industry through the provision of tax incentives. The

---

[3314] For the "filter argument", see European Communities' first written submission, para. 991.

[3315] HB 2294, 58th Leg., 2d Spec. Sess. (Wash. 2003), Exhibit EC-54, p. 20.

[3316] HB 2294, 58th Leg., 2d Spec. Sess. (Wash. 2003), Exhibit EC-54, p. 1.

DSR 2012:III   1547

Report of the Panel

comprehensive tax incentives in this act address the cost of doing business in Washington state compared to locations in other states.[3317]

Section 16. (1)   The legislature finds that accountability and effectiveness are important aspects of setting tax policy. In order to make policy choices regarding the best use of limited state resources the legislature needs information on how a tax incentive is used.

(2)(a) A person {eligible for the incentives under} this act shall make an annual report to the department detailing employment, wages, and employer-provided health and retirement benefits per job at the manufacturing site. The report shall not include names of employees. The report shall also detail employment by the total number of full-time, part-time, and temporary positions. The first report filed under this subsection shall include employment, wage, and benefit information for the twelve-month period immediately before first use of a preferential tax ...or tax exemption or credit...The report is due by March 31st following any year in which a preferential tax rate...is used, or tax exemption or credit... is taken.

(b)   If a person fails to submit an annual report under (a) of this subsection by the due date of the report, the department shall declare the amount of taxes exempted or credited, or reduced in the case of the preferential business and occupation tax rate, for that year to be immediately due and payable. Excise taxes payable under this subsection are subject to interest but not penalties, as provided under this chapter."

- The MSA

7.1571 The MSA confirms that the tax incentives under HB 2294 will be provided to Boeing. It also deals with a range of other alleged subsidies provided by the government to Boeing in the State of Washington. It provides some insight regarding the reasons for the introduction of HB 2294 and the other incentives. It provides:

"*Recital D* The Public Parties recognize that the {final assembly facility for the 787} will have a significant positive impact on the welfare of the community {and} the State including the creation of jobs, increased tax revenues and other benefits, and therefore the

---

[3317] *Ibid.*

1548

Public Parties are desirous of having Boeing locate the {final assembly facility} within the State; and

"Recital E The Public Parties recognize that Boeing can locate the {final assembly facility} in other states and that, by locating its facilities within the State, the citizens and the constituents of the State...will be benefited." [3318]

- The Memorandum of Agreement

7.1572 Section 17 of HB 2294 provides that the legislation becomes effective when the Governor of the State and a manufacturer of commercial airplanes sign a memorandum of agreement regarding an affirmative final decision to site a significant commercial airplane final assembly facility in the State. The MOA is the agreement between the Governor and Boeing under section 17 of HB 2294. It provides:

"Recital C. In order to enhance the desirability of the State as a place to do business and to promote economic growth for the benefit of its citizens, the State legislature passed HB 2294." [3319]

- The House and Senate Floor Debates for HB 2294

7.1573 The European Communities submits an exhibit that is the unofficial transcript of the House and Senate Floor Debate for the third reading of HB 2294.[3320] It provides:

"Representative Pettigrew: {T}his legislation is part of our effort to get the 7E7 built here in our state, As you know we are one of several states that are vying for this opportunity. Where in the past we were very, very confident that we could compete with any region across the country as it relates to aerospace, but what we're finding ourselves – finding out is that we are in the economic fight of our lives.

"What's at stake here is not only the future of Boeing but our state's economy. For decades the aerospace industry has been a stable part of our economy and Boeing has been the centerpiece of that industry...

[3318] MSA, Exhibit EC-58, p. 2.
[3319] Memorandum of Agreement for Project Olympus, 19 December 2003, Exhibit EC-57.
[3320] State of Washington, House and Senate Floor Debates, HB 2294, June 2003, Unofficial Transcript, Exhibit EC-70.

Report of the Panel

"It's about supporting the suppliers that support Boeing. It's about supporting the small businesses that as a result of Boeing succeed. This is about 130, 000 jobs. It's about $700 million to $1 billion in our general fund. This is about keeping our community strong.

"The legislation...represents a good package for us to get the 7E7 here. It provides a number of tax incentives, yes. It helps Boeing be competitive, yes...but there are triggers in it that will allow us to have the accountability for our investment that we want.[3321]

"Senator Rossi: ...we'd like to see the Boeing company stay in the State of Washington.

"This is a tax incentive package, which will hopefully entice the 7E7, the Boeing Company to build it here in the State of Washington...

"The idea is to make sure that we have these jobs in the State of Washington – good paying jobs in the State of Washington.

"The dollar amounts add up to $25 million in this biennium. In the next biennium, $103 million...But look at what the potential is if Boeing leaves. What is the potential? We could lose revenue to the state of about $540 million a year.

"We need to do this. We need to make sure that our hand is strengthened so we can be one of the three finalists, one of the states that will be in the finals to have the 7E7 in their state... We believe that this will make us very competitive.[3322]

"Senator Fairley: That's what this bill is about, keeping Boeing and our identity for Boeing in our state. We like the jobs. We like the company. We like the planes. This bill will help us."[3323]

- Speeches and statements by Governor Gary Locke

7.1574 Aside from the statements of Governor Locke referenced by the European Communities in its prohibited subsidy claim, a number of other

---

[3321] State of Washington, House and Senate Floor Debates, HB 2294, June 2003, Unofficial Transcript, Exhibit EC-70, pp. 1-2.

[3322] State of Washington, House and Senate Floor Debates, HB 2294, June 2003, Unofficial Transcript, Exhibit EC-70, pp. 6-8.

[3323] State of Washington, House and Senate Floor Debates, HB 2294, June 2003, Unofficial Transcript, Exhibit EC-70, p. 9.

statements by the Governor on the record provide relevant background to the introduction of the taxation incentives:

"Press Release from the Office of the Governor, 9 June 2003.

"Gov. Gary Locke today unveiled his tax incentives package to help the state land final assembly of the Boeing 7E7, stressing the huge economic impact the project would have on the state. Locke emphasized that the project would not only create 1,200 jobs directly related to assembling the 7E7, but would also create hundreds of thousands of related jobs...

"The total expected economic impact of building the 7E7, and its derivatives, in Washington state:

- As many as 150,000 jobs, including suppliers and other multiplier effects; and

- As much as $540 million in tax revenue per year...

"This a thoughtful package to address how Boeing will do business in Washington in the future....

"This tax incentives package is critical to the long-term competitiveness and economic vitality of our state...the Action Washington team continues to develop a creative, aggressive proposal to convince the Boeing Company that Washington is the best place for final assembly of the 7E7."[3324]

"Press Release from the Office of the Governor, 9 June 2003.

"We've delivered to Boeing a very strong and compelling package. Now we will leave it to Boeing to make the best possible choice for the 7E7 final assembly. And we know that choice will be Washington!

[3324] News Release, Office of Governor Gary Locke, Gov. Gary Locke Unveils Tax Incentives Package to Help Land Boeing 7E7, Outlines Project's Significant Economic Impact on State, 9 June 2003, Exhibit EC-69.

Report of the Panel

> ...We responded with a dynamic, innovative and creative proposal
> that will prove to Boeing that Washington state is the best place in
> the world to build the 7E7." [3325]

7.1575 In our view, the European Communities has not established that the grant of the subsidies under HB 2294 was "tied to" anticipated exportation.

7.1576 The European Communities' position appears to be that the capacity condition, requiring a location with the capacity to produce at least thirty-six superefficient airplanes to be sited within the State of Washington, is sufficient to establish the required "tie". The European Communities reasons that the capacity condition creates an expectation of exports. Further, given that the grant of the subsidies was contingent upon meeting the capacity condition, the subsidy was "tied to" anticipated exportation. We do not agree that the capacity condition is sufficient to establish the required "tie" between the grant of the subsidy and anticipated exportation.

7.1577 On a generous view of the European Communities' evidence it is possible to conclude that fulfilment of the capacity condition created an expectation of exports. The European Communities relies upon a declaration by Mr. Andrew Gordon, Head of Market Analysis and Research at Airbus, in order to conclude that the United States' market was incapable of absorbing a production level of thirty-six superefficient airplanes per year. Mr. Gordon's estimates of the demand per year for 787 in the United States' market range from four to thirty-three.[3326] Such a large range in itself creates some uncertainty regarding the strength of the estimates. Further, the upper end of the range is close to the capacity condition requirement of 36 superefficient airplanes. Nevertheless, even accepting that the capacity condition could create an expectation of exports, in our view the condition is not sufficient to establish the required "tie". A link between the capacity condition, upon which the grant of the subsidy depended, and expected exports is not explicit within the legislation or anywhere else. Nevertheless, the evidence of Mr. Gordon provides some suggestion that there may be such a link. However, in order to establish a prima facie case of such a tie between the grant of the subsidy and anticipated exportation, in our view, further evidence is required. It is possible that the capacity condition was not in fact included as a pre-condition to the grant of the subsidies in HB 2294 because of anticipated exports. Rather, as the United States argues, the requirement that a "significant" assembly facility be established may have been included because of a concern to create "higher value jobs, tax income, and upstream activity" in

---

[3325] News Release, Office of Governor Gary Locke, Gov. Locke, Business, Labor and Government Leaders Celebrate Delivery of State's 7E7 Proposal at 'Action Washington' Rally, 20 June 2003, Exhibit EC-62.
[3326] See paras. 7.1554-7.1555 of this Report.

1552   DSR 2012:III

Washington State.[3327] Therefore, we require some further corroborating evidence to support the European Communities' case that HB 2294 was granted because of anticipated exports. Our approach in this regard is supported by the Appellate Body's statement in *Canada – Aircraft* that "the relationship of contingency, between the subsidy and export performance, must be inferred from the total configuration of facts constituting and surrounding the granting of the subsidy, none of which on its own is likely to be decisive in any case".[3328]

7.1578 In relation to the additional evidence, aside from the capacity condition, that could potentially support a finding of the required "tie", we attach a relatively low probative value to the statement of Governor Locke, regarding his wish to keep companies that strengthen international trade within the State of Washington, and his consequent energetic pursuit of Boeing. We note that this statement does not explicitly mention the tax incentives. However, we acknowledge that the statement was made on 29 May 2003, less than two weeks before the passing of HB 2294 by the House and Senate on 11 June 2003[3329], which provides some evidence that the taxation-related subsidies were a part of the "pursuit" of Boeing to which he refers. Even if this is the correct interpretation of his statement, in our view it needs to be considered in the context in which it was delivered, namely that of a public official emphasizing the potential benefits of a programme under which significant levels of public revenue were to be foregone.

7.1579 Although Governor Locke's second statement regarding the trade mission he led to China is an attachment to the MSA and therefore a part of the official documentation surrounding the siting of the 787 assembly facility in Washington and the consequent granting of the subsidies, the statement does little to advance the European Communities' argument. The statement does not indicate that Governor Locke was interested in China because it is an export market. The statement indicates that the Governor was aiming to promote Boeing sales, but it does not indicate that he was targeting particular markets by virtue of the fact that they were export markets. In our view, the statement does not indicate that the subsidies were granted because of the expectation of exports.

7.1580 Finally, the European Communities notes that only companies that produce products that will necessarily be exported may be recipients of the subsidies. Although according to footnote 4 of Article 3.1(a), the fact that a subsidy is granted to an enterprise that exports cannot be the sole reason for finding an export contingent subsidy, this is a factor that we can consider, in combination with the other evidence on the record. However, in our view, an

---

[3327] United States' response to question 268, para. 461. The United States argues that requiring a "significant" final assembly facility to be located in Washington gives the State some certainty that its objectives are being met.

[3328] Appellate Body Report, *Canada – Aircraft*, para. 167.

[3329] See HB 2294, 58th Leg., 2d Spec. Sess. (Wash. 2003), Exhibit EC-54 and Governor Gary Locke Speech, World Trade Club Annual Dinner, 29 May 2003, Exhibit EC-638.

Report of the Panel

overall assessment of the evidence leads to the conclusion that the European Communities has not established the required "tie" between HB 2294 and the grantor's anticipation of exportation.

7.1581 The evidence before the Panel in this case falls far short of that before the panel and Appellate Body in *Canada – Aircraft*. In that case, there were sixteen factual elements found within the official documentation associated with the granting of the subsidy that indicated the subsidy was granted because of the expectation of exports. The evidence indicated that the grantor of the subsidies relied upon and attached importance to the expected export performance of applicants for the subsidies. Although there was less evidence before the panel in *Australia – Automotive Leather II*, we note that this decision was never appealed. Further, the decision was made against the background of the Australian Government agreeing by settlement with the United States to remove automotive leather from eligibility for two programmes pursuant to which the exporter in issue earned significant benefits from its exports.[3330] The Australian Government signed the grant contract eight days after automotive leather was excised from the two pre-existing programmes.[3331] Although not always explicit within the panel report, this background seems to have influenced the panel in reaching its decision that the grant contracts were export contingent subsidies.[3332]

7.1582 In relation to the evidence indicating that HB 2294 was granted because of the State of Washington's desire to have assembly of the 787 sited in Washington rather than another State, due to the positive effects this would have on Washington's economy, particularly its employment rate, we recall that Article 3.1(a) of the SCM Agreement provides that a subsidy is prohibited if it is contingent, *whether solely or as one of several other conditions*, upon export performance. Therefore, even if one of the conditions for the grant of the subsidies was that assembly of the 787 occur in Washington in order to increase employment, this does not exclude the possibility of a tie between HB 2294 and anticipated exportation. However, in our view, the clear and convincing evidence indicating that the subsidies were granted because of the State's desire to attract the 787 assembly to the Washington economy in order to boost employment, in comparison to the paucity of evidence suggesting a tie between the grant of the subsidy and anticipated exportation, reinforces our conclusion that the European Communities has not made its case under Article 3.1(a).

[3330] Panel Report, *Australia – Automotive Leather II*, para. 9.65.

[3331] Panel Report, *Australia – Automotive Leather II*, see paras. 2.2 and 2.5 for the date on which the grant contract was signed and the date on which automotive leather was removed from eligibility for the two pre-existing programmes.

[3332] At para. 9.63 the Panel states that it is "taking into consideration" the fact that the Australian Government was providing assistance to the exporter in response to the removal of automotive leather from eligibility for benefits under the two pre-existing programmes. See also, para. 9.65 where the Panel considers the actions of the Australian Government.

1554   DSR 2012:III

7.1583 For theses reasons, the Panel finds that the European Communities has not demonstrated a "tie" between the grant of the subsidies and anticipated exportation or export earnings. Consequently, the Panel finds that the European Communities has not demonstrated that HB 2294 was de facto contingent upon export performance on the basis of being tied to anticipated exportation.

Grant of a subsidy in fact tied to *actual* exportation

7.1584 The majority of the submissions of the European Communities are directed towards establishing that the grant of the taxation incentives was contingent upon *anticipated* exportation. However, in response to a Panel question regarding whether the European Communities is arguing that the grant of the subsidies is tied to "anticipated" or to "actual" exportation, the European Communities responds that:

> "{I}n order to be certain that it has made all the necessary arguments, the European Communities submits that each of the relevant measures provides for a subsidy contingent upon *actual* export; or alternatively contingent upon *anticipated* export; or alternatively contingent upon actual *or* anticipated export; or alternatively contingent upon actual *and* anticipated export." [3333]

7.1585 In its response to the same Panel question, the European Communities provides some explanation of its argument that the grant of the subsidies is tied to "actual" exportation. However, the European Communities admits that its explanation does "not exhaust all the alternative arguments set out" in the preceding paragraph. [3334]

7.1586 In relation to its first legal argument, the European Communities argues, if the correct interpretation of "actual" is "real", as we have found is the case, then the subsidy is tied to actual exports in the sense that it is only when the sale takes place that the unconditional right to the subsidy accrues. [3335] However, for the reasons expressed at paras. 7.1541-7.1543 of this Report, we do not accept the European Communities' first legal argument regarding the B&O tax reduction.

7.1587 In relation to its second and third legal arguments, the European Communities submits that if "actual or anticipated" means "real or potential", then HB 2294 is contingent upon anticipated exports. However, HB 2294 also provides for the grant of a subsidy in fact tied to *actual* exports, "because the B&O tax rate reductions are tied to sales". [3336] Therefore, its submission

---

[3333] European Communities' response to question 57, para. 195.

[3334] European Communities' response to question 57, para. 197.

[3335] European Communities' response to question 57, para. 198.

[3336] European Communities' response to question 57, para. 200. The European Communities also submits an argument that, if the correct meaning of "actual" is "past", then its second and third legal

Report of the Panel

regarding a tie to "actual" exports in relation to its second and third legal arguments again reduces to its argument regarding the B&O tax reduction, which we do not accept.

7.1588 On the arguments presented by the European Communities in response to question 57, we find no basis to make a finding that HB 2294 is in fact tied to actual exportation. The European Communities argues that its explanations in response to this question do not exhaust all the alternative arguments it is making (namely, its arguments that the "subsidy is contingent upon *actual* export; or alternatively contingent upon *anticipated* export; or alternatively contingent upon actual *or* anticipated export; or alternatively contingent upon actual *and* anticipated export"). However, where the European Communities has provided no arguments or evidence to support a claim, we find no basis to uphold it.[3337] For these reasons, the Panel finds that the European Communities has not demonstrated that the subsidies were tied to actual exportation.

7.1589 Consequently, in relation to the European Communities' second and third legal arguments[3338], the Panel finds that the European Communities has not demonstrated that HB 2294 is contingent upon export performance.

---

arguments amount to a claim that the subsidy is tied to actual exportation (European Communities' response to question 57, para. 199). However, as we have rejected this interpretation of "actual", there is no need for us to consider the merits of this argument.

[3337] Although the European Communities does not explicitly make this argument in support of a claim that the subsidies are tied to *actual* exportation, its only other argument that could possibly be interpreted as supporting a claim that HB 2294 is in fact tied to "actual" exportation is the argument that the capacity requirement is tantamount to a requirement to export (European Communities' response to question 54, especially para. 177). If the capacity requirement in fact operates as a requirement to export, perhaps this could be some evidence in support of a tie to exports that will actually occur, rather than to exports that are anticipated to occur. The European Communities argues that if Boeing built a facility with a capacity to produce 36 superefficient airplanes per year, it would produce at this capacity, which would require exportation to occur due to the level of domestic demand for superefficient airplanes. In our view, although it may be logical for Boeing fully to utilize the capacity it has created, it is possible to think of any number of situations where this may not occur. Indeed, Article 10.6.1 of the Master Site Agreement includes a clause that provides:

> "Boeing's production and assembly of the 7E7 Aircraft is market-driven. The commercial aircraft market is international and highly competitive. Despite Boeing's extensive investments and good faith efforts to predict markets for the 7E7 Aircraft, Boeing cannot guarantee that those markets will materialize or be sustained as predicted or desired."

Upon its attention being directed to this clause in a Panel question, the European Communities distances itself from the argument that the capacity requirement is tantamount to a requirement to export and emphasizes that HB 2294 is tied to anticipated export performance (European Communities' response to question 271). Therefore, if the European Communities ever intended to assert that the capacity condition is evidence in support of a tie to actual exportation, on the basis that the capacity condition amounts to a requirement for exports actually to occur, this is not made out on the facts. A contingency that can be satisfied without a single sale being made, and where the resulting subsidy continues to be provided even if no export sales are ever made, does not support the notion that the subsidies in issue are tied to *actual* exportation.

[3338] As advanced in European Communities' response to question 56 and summarized at para. 7.1490 of this Report.

1556

DSR 2012:III

US - Large Civil Aircraft (2nd Complaint)

(g) Conclusion

7.1590 For these reasons, the Panel finds that the European Communities has not demonstrated that the taxation measures enacted under HB 2294 are inconsistent with Articles 3.1(a) and 3.2 of the SCM Agreement.

F. *Whether the United States Causes, through the Use of the Subsidies at Issue, Adverse Effects within the Meaning of Article 5(c) of the SCM Agreement*

1. Introduction

7.1591 The European Communities claims that the United States, through the use of the subsidies to Boeing, causes adverse effects to the European Communities' interests within the meaning of Article 5(c) of the SCM Agreement; i.e. "serious prejudice" to the interests of the European Communities. The European Communities makes what it asserts to be two, independent serious prejudice claims.

7.1592 One claim is that the subsidies to Boeing cause serious prejudice within the meaning of Article 5(c) of the SCM Agreement in the form of "significant price suppression" and "significant lost sales", and a threat thereof, in the world market, within the meaning of Articles 5(c) and 6.3(c) of the SCM Agreement, as well as displacement and impedance in the United States and third country markets, and a threat thereof, within the meaning of Articles 5(c), 6.3(a) and 6.3(b) of the SCM Agreement.[3339] This serious prejudice claim is addressed below in section 2 of this Part of the Report.

7.1593 The other claim is that the United States causes serious prejudice to the European Communities' interests by violating the *Agreement concerning the application of the GATT Agreement on Trade in Civil Aircraft on trade in large civil aircraft* (the 1992 Agreement); specifically, that the United States has violated agreed obligations concerning support to the LCA sector that are set forth in the 1992 Agreement.[3340] According to the European Communities, this alleged violation by the United States of its obligations under the 1992 Agreement constitutes serious prejudice to the European Communities' interest

---

[3339] European Communities' first written submission, para. 1000. In its panel request, the European Communities alleged that the use of the challenged subsidies measures "causes adverse effects – *i.e.*, material injury or threat of material injury to the European Community LCA industry – and serious prejudice including threat of serious prejudice to the interests of the European Communities within the meaning of Article 5(a) and (c) of the *SCM Agreement*"; Request for the Establishment of a Panel by the European Communities, WT/DS353/2, 23 January 2006, p. 13. However, in its submissions to the Panel, the European Communities did not present arguments and evidence concerning material injury under Article 5(a), thereby confining its adverse effects claim to serious prejudice within Article 5(c) of the SCM Agreement; European Communities' first written submission, para. 22.

[3340] European Communities' first written submission, para. 1016.

DSR 2012:III

1557

Report of the Panel

in having its international obligations respected.[3341] This serious prejudice claim is further discussed in section 3 of this Part of the Report.

> 2. *Whether the United States causes serious prejudice to the interests of the European Communities in the form of significant price suppression and significant lost sales, and a threat thereof, in the world market, and displacement and impedance, and a threat thereof, in the United States and third country markets*

> (a) Main arguments of the parties and third parties

> (i) European Communities

7.1594 The European Communities argues that the subsidies to Boeing have resulted in serious prejudice within the meaning of Article 5(c) of the SCM Agreement in the form of "significant price suppression" and "significant lost sales", and a threat thereof, in the world market, within the meaning of Article 6.3(c) of the SCM Agreement, as well as displacement and impedance in the United States and third country markets, and a threat thereof, within the meaning of Articles 6.3(a) and 6.3(b) of the SCM Agreement.[3342]

7.1595 The European Communities seeks to establish its serious prejudice claim by reference to events that occurred between 2004 and 2006 in what it asserts are three specific LCA product markets; namely, the 100-200 seat single-aisle LCA market, the 200-300 seat wide-body LCA market, and the 300-400 seat wide-body LCA market.[3343] The table below sets forth the three LCA product markets identified by the European Communities, the Boeing "subsidized" aircraft and the corresponding Airbus "like" aircraft that are alleged to compete in each LCA product market, and the specific forms of serious prejudice alleged in each LCA product market.

[3341] European Communities' oral statement at the first meeting with the Panel, para. 117.
[3342] European Communities' first written submission, para. 1000.
[3343] European Communities' first written submission, para. 1151.

1558 DSR 2012:III

Structure of the European Communities' serious prejudice arguments in each of the three LCA product markets

LCA Product market	Alleged Boeing "subsidized product"	Competing Airbus "like product"	Serious prejudice alleged
Single aisle LCA with a capacity of approximately 100-200 passengers and a short to medium range	737NG	A320	significant price suppression of the A320 significant lost sales of the A320 displacement and impedance of European Communities' exports of the A320 from various third country markets[3344] threat of significant price suppression with respect to future orders of the A320
Wide-bodied LCA with a capacity of approximately 200-300 passengers and a medium to long or ultra-long range	787	A330, Original A350 and A350XWB-800[3345]	significant price suppression of the A330, Original A350 and A350XWB-800 significant lost sales of A330 and Original A350 displacement and impedance of European Communities' imports of A330 and Original A350 into the United States displacement and impedance of European Communities' exports of A330 and Original A350 from various third country markets[3346] threat of significant price suppression with respect to future orders of A330 and A350XWB-800

[3344] The European Communities argues that the Panel should determine the existence of serious prejudice in the form of significant price suppression, significant lost sales and displacement and impedance on the basis of order data. The European Communities argues, in the alternative, that if the Panel finds that orders (as opposed to deliveries) booked during the 2004-2006 reference period cannot serve as the basis for the European Communities' serious prejudice claim, the arguments and evidence it presents demonstrate threat of significant price suppression, threat of significant lost sales and threat of displacement and impedance of exports with respect to future *deliveries* of the A320; European Communities' first written submission, paras. 1552, 1563.

[3345] The Original A350 LCA family was marketed by Airbus from December 2004 through 2006 but was replaced by the A350XWB family, which Airbus began marketing in July 2006; European Communities' first written submission, para. 1174. See also para 7.1777 of this Report.

[3346] The European Communities argues that the Panel should determine the existence of serious prejudice in the form of significant price suppression, significant lost sales and displacement and impedance on the basis of order data. The European Communities argues, in the alternative, that if

Report of the Panel

LCA Product market	Alleged Boeing "subsidized product"	Competing Airbus "like product"	Serious prejudice alleged
Wide-bodied LCA with a capacity of approximately 300-400 passengers and a long or ultra-long range	777	A340 and A350XWB-900/-1000	significant price suppression of the A340 significant lost sales of the A340 displacement and impedance of European Communities' exports of A340 from various third country markets[3347] threat of significant price suppression with respect to future orders of the A350XWB-900/1000

7.1596 The European Communities argues that the subsidies to Boeing have resulted in significant price suppression, significant lost sales and displacement and impedance of exports and imports of Airbus LCA through two causal mechanisms.[3348] First, the aeronautics R&D subsidies are said to have provided Boeing with valuable technologies, knowledge, experience and confidence in certain key technology areas which enabled Boeing to research, design, develop, produce and sell the technologically innovative 787 years earlier than would otherwise have been possible. This subsidy-enabled availability of an aircraft as technologically innovative as the 787 is said to have adversely affected sales, market share and prices of the competing Airbus LCA in the 200 – 300 seat wide-body product market. Second, the additional cash flow from all of the subsidies at issue in this dispute is said to have enhanced Boeing's ability to reduce the prices of its LCA in competitive sales campaigns with Airbus. The

---

the Panel finds that orders (as opposed to deliveries) booked during the 2004-2006 reference period cannot serve as the basis for the European Communities' serious prejudice claim, the arguments and evidence it presents demonstrate threat of significant price suppression, threat of significant lost sales and threat of displacement and impedance of imports and exports with respect to future *deliveries* of the A330 and A350XWB-800; European Communities' first written submission, paras. 1446, 1469.

[3347] The European Communities argues that the Panel should determine the existence of serious prejudice in the form of significant price suppression, significant lost sales and displacement and impedance on the basis of order data. The European Communities argues, in the alternative, that if the Panel finds that orders (as opposed to deliveries) booked during the 2004-2006 reference period cannot serve as the basis for the European Communities' serious prejudice claim, the arguments and evidence it presents demonstrate threat of significant price suppression, threat of significant lost sales and threat of displacement and impedance of exports with respect to future *deliveries* of the A340 and A350XWB-900/1000; European Communities' first written submission, paras. 1640, 1652.

[3348] For example, the European Communities states that it "demonstrates causation in two different ways. First, it demonstrates that Boeing's prices would be higher but for the US subsidies at issue. Second, it demonstrates that Boeing's product offering, in particular with respect to the 787 in the 200-300 seat LCA market, would be different but for the US subsidies"; European Communities' second written submission, para. 711.

1560

DSR 2012:III

lower Boeing LCA prices are argued to have affected sales, market share and prices of the competing Airbus LCA in each of three LCA product markets.

7.1597 The European Communities thus makes a distinction as to the effects of the subsidies on Boeing's commercial behaviour between the 787, on the one hand, and the 737NG and the 777, on the other. With regard to the 787, the European Communities argues that the nature of the subsidies benefiting Boeing's 787 family reveals that these subsidies have *two principal effects* on Boeing's behaviour. On the one hand, the European Communities argues that *the aeronautics R&D subsidies* have had what the European Communities terms "technology effects" in that they "have helped Boeing develop, launch and produce a technologically-advanced 200-300 seat LCA much more quickly than it could have on its own".[3349] The European Communities argues that it is through their effects on Boeing's development of technologies for the 787 that the aeronautics R&D subsidies cause significant price suppression, significant lost sales, and displacement and impedance suffered by Airbus in the 200-300 seat wide body LCA product market.[3350]

7.1598 On the other hand, the European Communities argues that *all of the subsidies* have what the European Communities refers to as "price effects" in that they have enabled Boeing to charge lower prices for its LCA and capture market share at the expense of Airbus.[3351] The European Communities argues that it is through their effects on *Boeing's prices* of its 737NG, 777 and 787 families of LCA that all of the subsidies in totality cause significant price suppression, significant lost sales, and displacement and impedance suffered by Airbus in the 100-200 seat single-aisle, 300-400 seat wide-body, and 200-300 seat wide-body LCA product markets, respectively.

7.1599 Set forth below is a description of the European Communities' arguments as to (i) the effects of the aeronautics R&D subsidies on Boeing's development of technologies in relation to the 787; and (ii) the effects of the subsidies on Boeing's pricing behaviour with respect to the 737NG, 777 and 787.

[3349] European Communities' first written submission, para. 1343. See also, European Communities' first written submission, paras. 1335,1345.

[3350] European Communities' first written submission, paras. 1334, 1341, 1376 ("In sum, the nature of the US subsidies for the 787, in terms of their structure, design, and operation, helps reveal that their effects have been to: (1) accelerate Boeing's development, launch, production and future delivery of a technologically-advanced 200-300 seat LCA family; and (2) enable Boeing to significantly reduce its sales prices for 787 family LCA. These effects, in turn, cause significant price suppression, significant lost sales, displacement and impedance, and a threat thereof, in the market for the 787 family and competition Airbus LCA.").

[3351] European Communities' first written submission, para. 1229.

Report of the Panel

Effects of the aeronautics R&D subsidies on Boeing's development of technologies in relation to the 787

7.1600 The European Communities identifies the "aeronautics R&D support provided by NASA, DOD and DOC" as being aeronautics R&D support provided by those U.S. government agencies through specific R&D programmes. The NASA-funded aeronautics R&D programmes are: the Advanced Composite Technology (ACT) Program, the High Speed Research (HSR) Program, the Advanced Subsonic Technology (AST) Program, the High Performance Computing and Communications (HPCC) Program, the Aviation Safety Program, the Quiet Aircraft Technology (QAT) Program, the Vehicle Systems Program and the Research and Technology Base (R&T Base) Program.[3352] The DOD-funded aeronautics R&D programme is the Research, Development, Testing, and Evaluation (RDT&E) Program.[3353] The DOC-funded programme is the Advanced Technology (ATP) Program.[3354]

7.1601 According to the European Communities, the aeronautics R&D subsidies, "primarily through NASA and DOD" gave rise to four effects in the 200-300 seat wide-body LCA market; namely, they: (i) accelerated Boeing's development of new and advanced LCA technologies, as well as design and manufacturing processes, thereby enabling Boeing to bring the 787 to market much sooner than it could have on its own[3355]; (ii) limited and delayed Airbus' access to innovative R&D technologies; (iii) increased the marketability of the 787; and (iv) allowed a rapid ramp-up of 787 deliveries.[3356] The European Communities has sought to demonstrate that the aeronautics R&D subsidies provided Boeing with *usable technologies* in key technology areas, as well as *knowledge, experience* and *confidence* toward developing successful commercial technologies and processes.[3357] The European Communities groups these key technologies into six technology areas, the most significant of which concerns composites technologies, primarily the design, development and manufacturing of the 787 composite fuselage and wings.[3358]

[3352] European Communities' first written submission, para. 1257.

[3353] *Ibid.*

[3354] *Ibid.*

[3355] European Communities' first written submission, para. 1345.

[3356] European Communities' first written submission, paras. 1350-1358.

[3357] European Communities' first written submission, para. 1352. According to the European Communities, the knowledge, experience and confidence gained by Boeing through its participation in U.S. government-supported aeronautics R&D programmes enabled Boeing to accelerate its development, production and delivery of the 787 and "is in fact the crux of the causal connection between the U.S. R&D subsidies and the 787", European Communities' first written submission, para. 1356; Annex C, para. 8.

[3358] The remaining five technology areas are: more electric architecture, open systems architecture, enhanced aerodynamics and structural design, noise reduction technologies and health management systems; European Communities' first written submission, paras. 1350-1351.

1562

DSR 2012:III

US - Large Civil Aircraft (2nd Complaint)

7.1602 The European Communities alleges that, pursuant to the NASA's ACT, AST and R&T Base programmes, NASA provided funding and support to Boeing through several R&D contracts and agreements regarding composites research.[3359] In addition, the European Communities contends that Boeing learned about composites technologies relevant to the 787 composite fuselage by participating in a number of projects under DOD RDT&E programmes such as the ManTech Composites Affordability Initiative, the ManTech Advanced Fiber Placement Program, DUS&T High Rate Fiber Placement Program, V-22 Aft Fuselage Demonstration Program, and JSF Prototype Development Program.[3360] According to the European Communities, "{b}ut for these US Government composites R&D programmes, Boeing would not be able to build and promise deliveries of such an advanced 787 aircraft today. Nor would customers be as willing to buy it".[3361]

7.1603 In relation to the other technology areas, the European Communities alleges that Boeing and McDonnell Douglas collaborated with NASA through the AST Program, and with DOD through a number of programmes under the RDT&E Program, in developing more-electric systems for the 787.[3362] The European Communities argues that the open systems architecture on the 787 likely benefited from the knowledge and experience that McDonnell Douglas gained from an R&D contract under the Technology Reinvestment Program under DOD's RDT&E Program, as well as from dual-use research that Boeing conducted pursuant to the JSF Program.[3363] The European Communities argues that, through contracts under the HPCC Program (CAS project), the AST Program (IWD project), HSR Program and R&T Base Program, as well as through dual-use research conducted under the DOD F-22 Program, the JSF

[3359] European Communities' first written submission, Annex C, para. 26. NASA Contract NAS1-18862 with McDonnell Douglas Corporation regarding Innovative Composite Aircraft Primary Structures (ICAPS), 31 March 1989, Exhibit EC-331; NASA Contract NAS1-18889 with Boeing Commercial Airplanes regarding Research and Development in Advance Technology Composite Aircraft Structures, 12 May 1989, Exhibit EC-329; NASA Contract NAS1-18954 with Boeing Aerospace regarding Advanced Composite Fabrication and Testing, 29 August 1989, Exhibit EC-798; NASA Contract NAS1-19349 with Boeing Commercial Airplanes regarding Structures and Materials Technology for Aircraft Composite Primary Structures, 30 September 1991, Exhibit EC-799; NASA Contract NAS1-20546 with McDonnell Douglas regarding Technology Verification of Composite Primary Wing Structures for Commercial Transport Aircraft, 18 September 1995, Exhibit EC-324; NASA Contract NAS1-20553 with Boeing Commercial Airplane Group regarding Technology Verification of Composite Primary Fuselage Structures for Commercial Transport Aircraft, 25 September 1995, Exhibit EC-334; NASA Contract NAS1-99070 with Boeing Commercial Airplane Group regarding Structures and Materials Technology for Aerospace Vehicles, 25 January 1999, Exhibit EC-800.

[3360] European Communities' first written submission, Annex C, para. 46. The European Communities also alleges that Boeing gained substantial experience and confidence using ATL to fabricate wing skin panels pursuant to DOD funding under the F-22, A-6 and B-2 programmes; European Communities' first written submission, Annex C, para. 59.

[3361] European Communities' first written submission, Annex C, para. 22.

[3362] European Communities' first written submission, Annex C, para. 69.

[3363] European Communities' first written submission, Annex C, para. 78.

DSR 2012:III

1563

Report of the Panel

Demonstrator Program and the C-17 Program, Boeing developed knowledge and experience in relation to various technologies, tools and concepts that it used to enhance the aerodynamics and structural design of the 787.[3364] According to the European Communities, Boeing's development of noise reduction technologies used on the 787 was accelerated by knowledge, experience and confidence that Boeing gained through NASA's AST, QAT and Vehicle Systems programmes, and from collaboration with NASA under two Quiet Technology Demonstrator programmes which tested noise reduction technologies developed under the AST, QAT and Vehicle Systems programmes.[3365] The European Communities argues that the aeronautics R&D subsidies created and accelerated the development and application of the health management systems, allowing Boeing to better monitor the health of different parts on the 787, as well as leading to lower maintenance costs on the 787, and providing improved maintenance service.[3366]

7.1604 The European Communities argues that the knowledge and experience that Boeing (and McDonnell Douglas) gained through their work under the NASA contracts and agreements and DOD contracts and agreements provided Boeing (and McDonnell Douglas) with a solid foundation of tangible technologies, as well as knowledge, experience and confidence, which Boeing was able to further develop into an optimal combination of technologies for the 787.[3367] According to the European Communities, even when the technologies applied to the 787 are not the same as those studied under the contracts and agreements with NASA and DOD, the knowledge, experience and confidence that Boeing derived from its work for NASA and DOD provided Boeing with the insight to assess the validity of different design, manufacturing and assembly solutions, and ultimately to come up with the 787 design.[3368] In this sense, the European Communities argues that the Panel should assess the overall, cumulative knowledge effect of Boeing's participation in the NASA and DOD programmes, which according to the European Communities, Boeing was able to leverage in its own related R&D activity.[3369]

[3364] European Communities' first written submission, Annex C, paras. 83-99.

[3365] European Communities' first written submission, Annex C, paras. 100, 103-104.

[3366] European Communities first written submission, para. 1350. European Communities' first written submission, Annex C, paras. 110 - 121.

[3367] European Communities' confidential oral statement at the second meeting with the Panel, para. 8.

[3368] Dominik Wacht, An Analysis of Selected NASA Research Programs and Their Impact on Boeing's Civil Aircraft Programs, November 2006, Exhibit EC-15, p. 76.

[3369] Statement by Patrick Gavin, Tim Sommer, Burkhard Domke, and Dominik Wacht, 8 November 2007, Exhibit EC-1175 (BCI), paras. 23, 27; Statement of Tim Sommer and Dominik Wacht, Exhibit EC-1336 (BCI), para. 27.

1564

DSR 2012:III

> Effects of the subsidies on Boeing's pricing
> behaviour with respect to the 737NG, 777
> and 787

7.1605 In its first written submission, the European Communities identifies 11 categories of subsidies which it argues have affected Boeing's pricing behaviour. These categories are: (i) B&O tax reductions provided by the State of Washington and the City of Everett; (ii) waiver of 747 LCF landing fees; (iii) FSC/ETI federal tax exemptions/exclusions; (iv) tax breaks and other incentives provided by the State of Washington and municipalities therein; (v) tax breaks and bond interest payments provided by the State of Kansas and municipalities therein; (vi) reimbursements, tax breaks and grants provided by the State of Illinois and municipalities therein; (vii) aeronautics R&D support provided by NASA, DOD and DOC; (viii) intellectual property rights waivers/transfers provided by NASA and DOD; (ix) IR&D and B&P reimbursements provided by NASA and DOD; (x) facilities, equipment and employees provided by NASA and DOD; and (xi) worker training grants provided by DOL.[3370]

7.1606 The European Communities estimates that the total amount of subsidies in the above categories that benefited Boeing's LCA division between 1989 and 2006 was $19.1 billion. In addition, the European Communities estimates that Boeing will receive approximately $4.6 billion in subsidies between 2007 and 2024.[3371]

7.1607 The European Communities argues that the Panel should examine the cumulative effects of all of the subsidies.[3372] According to the European Communities, all of the subsidies have a significant nexus with the price effects at issue, in the sense that all of the subsidies have the effect of freeing up cash for Boeing to use to reduce the prices of its aircraft, and it is therefore appropriate to aggregate all of the subsidies for purposes of assessing their price effects.[3373] However, the European Communities has also grouped the above-referenced categories of subsidies into two general categories for purposes of analyzing their effects on Boeing's prices.

7.1608 The first general category consists of subsidies that the European Communities alleges operate to reduce Boeing's marginal unit costs of

---

[3370] European Communities' first written submission, paras. 1233-1278.

[3371] This figure comprises estimates of the future values of the following categories of subsidies: (i) B&O tax rate reductions provided by the State of Washington and the City of Everett; (ii) waiver of 747 LCF landing fees; (iii) tax breaks and other incentives provided by the State of Washington and municipalities therein; (iv) tax breaks and bond interest payments provided by the State of Kansas and municipalities therein; (v) reimbursements, tax breaks and grants provided by the State of Illinois and municipalities therein; (vi) intellectual property rights waivers/transfers provided by NASA and DOD; and (vii) worker training grants provided by DOL; Amount of Subsidies to Boeing's LCA Division, Exhibit EC-17, p. 2.

[3372] European Communities' first written submission, paras. 1070-1073.

[3373] European Communities' second written submission, paras. 669, 671.

Report of the Panel

production and sale of individual LCA.[3374] The European Communities asserts that subsidies within this category operate to lower the taxes and fees paid by Boeing with respect to the production and sale of its LCA, and that the receipt of these subsidies is essentially contingent on the production and sale of individual LCA.[3375]

7.1609 The second general category consists of subsidies that the European Communities argues operate to increase Boeing's non-operating cash flow.[3376] The European Communities notes that subsidies within this category are not linked to production of particular families of Boeing LCA, or to the production or sale of individual LCA.[3377] The European Communities argues that these subsidies are "fungible" and should therefore be treated as the functional equivalent of additional cash flow available to Boeing's LCA division.[3378] Subsidies within this category account for approximately $16.9 billion of the total $19.1 billion in subsidies that the European Communities alleges was received by Boeing between 1989 and 2006.

7.1610 The European Communities' key argument is that, notwithstanding the fact that the majority of the subsidies at issue in this dispute are not directly related to Boeing's production of LCA, Boeing's receipt of subsidies of the magnitudes alleged in this dispute, in the light of the strategic incentives that result from the particular market structure of the LCA market, and Boeing's financial condition, make it reasonable to infer that the subsidies do in fact affect

---

[3374] European Communities' first written submission, para. 1233. The alleged subsidies said to operate in this manner are the Washington State and City of Everett B&O tax reductions, Snohomish County 747 LCF landing fee waivers, and federal FSC/ETI tax exemptions/exclusions; European Communities' first written submission, para. 1306.

[3375] European Communities' first written submission, para. 1234.

[3376] European Communities' first written submission, paras. 1244-1278. Alleged subsidies falling within this category are (i) the aeronautics R&D funding and support provided by NASA, DOD and DOC; (ii) intellectual property right waivers/transfers provided by NASA and DOD; (iii) IR&D and B&P reimbursements provided by NASA and DOD; (iv) the facilities, equipment and employees provided by NASA and DOD; (v) the remaining tax breaks and other incentives provided by the State of Washington and municipalities therein; (vi) the tax breaks and bond interest payments provided by the State of Kansas and municipalities therein; (vii) the reimbursements, tax breaks and grants provided by the States of Illinois and municipalities therein; and (viii) the worker training grants provided by DOL; European Communities' first written submission, para. 244.

[3377] European Communities' first written submission, para. 1279. The European Communities explains, however, that it considers that certain of the subsidies within this second general category; e.g. the "R&D grants provided through NASA's ACT program" "specifically relate, in whole or in part, to the development and production of the 787 family of LCA"; European Communities' first written submission, para. 1277; European Communities' second written submission, para. 702. The amounts represented by these subsidies are allocated to the 787 as part of ITR's calculation of the per-aircraft subsidy "magnitudes"; International Trade Resources LLC, Calculating on a Per-Aircraft Basis the Magnitude of the Subsidies Provided to US Large Civil Aircraft, 20 February 2007, Exhibit EC-13, Table 7.

[3378] European Communities' first written submission, para. 1279.

1566   DSR 2012:III

Boeing's LCA pricing behaviour.[3379] The European Communities argues that the combination of "LCA market factors and dynamics of production" supports a finding that the subsidies to Boeing, even if not explicitly targeted to lowering the costs of production of specific LCA models, nonetheless cause adverse effects to the interests of the European Communities, because they allow Boeing to market its LCA at lower prices than would otherwise be the case.[3380] The European Communities contends that, under the "right conditions of competition – such as the intense duopoly competition existing in the LCA markets – non-price or non-production-contingent subsidies *can* confer the ability to cause adverse effects"[3381] and that "certain tied subsidies may yield similar effects as certain unrestricted subsidies, depending on the context of the specific subsidy at issue; i.e. the specific nature of the subsidy and its magnitude, as well as on the condition of the recipient".[3382]

7.1611 The European Communities has presented various formulations of its analytical framework for evaluating the effects of the subsidies on Boeing's pricing behaviour. Almost all of these formulations refer to the same key factors. These factors are: (i) the nature of the subsidies, in terms of their structure, design and operation; (ii) an economic model developed by Professor Luís Cabral concerning the effect of what he refers to as "development subsidies", which purports to quantify the degree to which Boeing was able to reduce its LCA prices in 2004 – 2006; (iii) the subsidy amounts and "magnitudes"; (iv) the conditions of competition in the LCA markets; (v) the financial condition, or "economic viability" of Boeing's LCA division in the absence of the subsidy amounts; and (vi) selected individual LCA sales campaigns in each of the three LCA product markets, which are alleged to demonstrate the serious prejudice in terms of Airbus' prices and sales.

7.1612 As to the nature of the subsidies at issue, the European Communities argues that the extent to which a particular subsidy enables Boeing to lower its LCA prices depends on the way in which it operates in an economic sense. The European Communities argues that subsidies that operate to reduce Boeing's marginal unit costs have an effect on Boeing's LCA pricing that is commensurate

---

[3379] For example, the European Communities argues: "{T}he nature of the subsidies, combined with their amount and in light of the conditions of competition in the LCA markets, cause adverse effects"; European Communities' second written submission, para. 786; "The availability of {the} magnitude of subsidies for Boeing to price down its LCA in competitive campaigns against Airbus, combined with the nature of those subsidies, Boeing's ability and incentive to use them, as well as other evidence ... supports the conclusion that they cause significant price suppression, significant lost sales, and market share displacement or impedance"; European Communities' response to question 78, para. 305.

[3380] European Communities' first written submission, para. 1303.

[3381] European Communities' non-confidential oral statement at the second meeting with the Panel, para. 107.

[3382] European Communities' response to question 379, para. 435.

Report of the Panel

with their amount.[3383] In other words, the European Communities argues that, for each additional dollar of such subsidies, Boeing is able to reduce the prices of its LCA by an equivalent dollar.

7.1613 The European Communities argues that subsidies that operate to increase Boeing's non-operating cash flow, on the other hand, although not directly tied to production or sales of specific aircraft, also strongly influence Boeing's pricing and investment decisions.[3384] In support of this contention, the European Communities refers to Professor Cabral's economic analysis of the effects on Boeing's LCA pricing of "development subsidies".[3385] Professor Cabral posits that subsidies that are not directly tied to production or sales volume are essentially fungible with cash and would be used by Boeing to (i) distribute to shareholders; (ii) invest in the development of new aircraft; and (iii) "invest" in capturing market share and moving along the learning curve through "aggressive" pricing of new and existing models of LCA.[3386] Professor Cabral conducts an economic modelling exercise which purports to *quantify* the relative proportion of untied subsidy amounts that Boeing would devote to additional investment (in lower pricing of its aircraft and in additional R&D) rather than to payments of dividends to shareholders.[3387] Based on this allocation, Professor Cabral estimates the total annual dollar value of LCA price reductions that have been made possible by the alleged receipt of $19.1 billion in subsidies between 1989 and 2006, for the years 2004 through 2006. Professor Cabral also calculates these annual price reductions in terms of price reductions for the specific Boeing LCA models over the 2004 -2006 period. According to. Professor Cabral, the total of $19.1 billion in subsidies allegedly received by Boeing between 1989 and 2006 translates into the following "price effects", or price reductions per model of Boeing aircraft in 2004 – 2006: [3388]

[3383] European Communities' first written submission, para. 1306. According to the European Communities, this conclusion is supported by standard economic literature showing that cost-reducing subsidies have a 100 per cent pass-through in competitive markets as well as other evidence relating to the effects on Boeing's prices of the FSC/ETI subsidies, and of cost reductions arising from productivity improvements; European Communities' first written submission, paras. 1307-1308, Steven Landsburg, Price Theory and its Applications, South-Western College Publishing, Cincinnati, Ohio, Exhibit EC-725; European Communities' response to question 289, paras. 612-625.

[3384] European Communities' first written submission, para. 1309.

[3385] Professor Cabral describes "development subsidies" as subsidies that are not directly tied to production and sales volume; Luís M. B. Cabral, Impact of Development Subsidies Granted to Boeing, New York University and CEPR, March 2007, Exhibit EC-4, paras. 2-3.

[3386] Luís M. B. Cabral, Impact of Development Subsidies Granted to Boeing, New York University and CEPR, March 2007, Exhibit EC-4, paras. 29, 31; see also, European Communities' first written submission, para. 1313.

[3387] European Communities' first written submission, para. 1321. According to Professor Cabral, Boeing would allocate each extra dollar of untied subsidies in the following manner: 15 cents to dividends to shareholders; 59 cents to "aggressive pricing" of new LCA and sales of new or existing LCA to new buyers; and 26 cents to additional research and development.

[3388] The European Communities generally uses the term "price effects" to refer to the extent to which Boeing has been able to lower its LCA prices as a result of the subsidies. For example, see

---

1568

DSR 2012:III

US - Large Civil Aircraft (2nd Complaint)

Aircraft model	Per-aircraft "price effect" ($ thousands)		
	2004	2005	2006
737 Family	1,009	879	949
767 Family	1,443	1,248	1,354
787 Family	1,539	1,332	1,445
777 Family	2,324	2,010	2,169

7.1614 The European Communities also argues that, in addition to operating to either reduce Boeing's marginal unit costs of production and sale of additional LCA, or to increase Boeing's non-operating cash flow, the subsidies are also "structured" and "designed" to increase Boeing's competitiveness vis-à-vis Airbus, or to increase Boeing's market share at Airbus' expense.[3389]

7.1615 As to the subsidy amounts and "magnitudes", the European Communities estimates that the $19.1 billion in subsidies that it alleges Boeing's LCA division received between 1989 and 2006 translates into a subsidy "magnitude" of $5.1 billion over the 2004 – 2006 period.[3390] Moreover, the European Communities estimates that over the 2004 – 2006 period, "Boeing's LCA division enjoyed, on average, $1.7 billion per annum in benefits from US subsidies" which it contends translates into an average of $2.4 million per each 737NG, $4.6 million

---

European Communities' first written submission, para. 1306, where the European Communities submits that the subsidies that directly reduce the marginal unit costs of Boeing LCA "have a price effect commensurate with their amount... {e}ach of these subsidy dollars has the effect of reducing the price of a Boeing LCA by exactly $1". However, the European Communities also uses this term in a narrower sense, to refer to Professor Cabral's quantification of the amount of subsidy dollars used directly and immediately by Boeing to "aggressively price" its LCA, based on his analysis which treats all subsidies that are not tied to the production of additional units of LCA as fungible with cash (i.e. equivalent to additional non-operating cash to Boeing), and assumptions about the optimal investment strategy of a company like Boeing given the particularities of the LCA market (learning curve, switching costs etc.). For example, see European Communities' first written submission, para. 1332 and figures 22 and 23 (which are the same as the "price effects" calculations made by Professor Cabral in EC-4, Tables 7 and 8).

[3389] European Communities' first written submission, paras. 1066, 1227, 1238, 1240, 1243, 1247, 1249, 1251, 1260-1266, 1272, 1274, 1276.

[3390] European Communities' first written submission, para. 1288. The European Communities also estimates the "magnitudes" of the subsidies to Boeing's LCA division for the 2000 – 2003 period, which it contends understate the degree of subsidization, but nevertheless demonstrate that Boeing was highly subsidized in the past and that distortions in the LCA markets from the subsidies to Boeing were persistent even before 2004; European Communities' first written submission, para. 1289 and Figure 17. The Panel notes that the ordinary meaning of the term "magnitude" (and the meaning of the term as used by panels and the Appellate Body) is broader than the specialized sense in which the European Communities uses it (which is described in para. 7.1616 of this Report). The "magnitude" of something is generally understood as a reference to its size, extent, degree, or numerical quantity or value. The European Communities sometimes also appears to use the term "magnitude" in its ordinary sense; e.g. European Communities' comments on United States' response to question 391, para. 356.

DSR 2012:III

1569

Report of the Panel

per each 787 and \$5.5 million per each 777 sold during that time.[3391] The European Communities argues that "the size of these subsidies alone suggests that they cause Boeing to change its commercial behaviour in the LCA markets".[3392] However, the European Communities also argues that to properly appreciate the importance of the subsidy "magnitudes", the Panel should consider the "magnitude" figures in the context of the conditions of competition in the LCA markets, and in terms of LCA orders from all LCA sales campaigns, as well as from only "competitive" LCA sales campaigns.[3393]

7.1616 The per-LCA subsidy "magnitudes" to which the European Communities refers are primarily based on the total subsidy amounts that the European Communities alleges that Boeing's LCA division received between 1989 and 2006 (i.e. \$19.1 billion) (i) *allocated over time* (with the addition of an "opportunity benefit" to reflect the time value of the funds to Boeing); and (ii) *allocated across the various models of Boeing LCA* (based on aircraft ordered during the allocation period). In other words, the European Communities' annual subsidy "magnitude" estimates represent an allocation of the \$19.1 billion total subsidy "amount" which it alleges was received by Boeing's LCA division between 1989 – 2006, to the 2004 – 2006 period and to the three Boeing subsidized LCA in this dispute.[3394] In addition, as explained in paragraphs 7.155-7.157, the European Communities has included in its calculation of the annual subsidy "magnitudes" between 2004 – 2006, the amounts of recurring subsidies that it estimated Boeing would receive in 2007 – 2009. The calculations were performed by the European Communities' economic consultants, International Trade Resources LLC (ITR).[3395] The European Communities asserts that the

---

[3391] European Communities' non-confidential oral statement at the first meeting with the Panel, para. 142, referring to International Trade Resources LLC, Calculating on a Per-Aircraft Basis the Magnitude of the Subsidies Provided to US Large Civil Aircraft, 20 February 2007, Exhibit EC-13, at para. 2.

[3392] European Communities' non-confidential oral statement at the first meeting with the Panel, para. 142.

[3393] European Communities' first written submission, para. 1298. The European Communities defines a "competitive" sales campaign as one in which both Airbus and Boeing were actively involved, and where Airbus submitted a [***]; European Communities' first written submission, para. 1222. Christian Scherer of Airbus conducted a survey of all Airbus and Boeing orders during the 2000-2006 period and has classified them as being orders resulting from competitive, or non-competitive sales campaigns; see Christian Scherer, Commercial Aspects of the Aircraft Business From the Perspective of a Manufacturer, March 2007, Exhibit EC-11 (BCI), Annex I and Annex II. The European Communities' identification of "competitive" sales campaigns is based on Scherer's survey.

[3394] The subsidy programmes at issue and the corresponding "amounts" (i.e. annual benefit to Boeing's LCA division) represented thereby are set forth in a table prepared by the European Communities: Amount of Subsidies to Boeing's LCA Division, Exhibit EC-17. The European Communities has also provided an exhibit (Exhibit EC-1296) summarizing the various ways in which it derives the relevant "amounts" of each of the disputed subsidy measures listed in Exhibit EC-17. The methodology used to calculate the "amount" of benefit accrued by Boeing's LCA division varies according to the type of subsidy measure.

[3395] International Trade Resources LLC, Calculating on a Per-Aircraft Basis the Magnitude of the Subsidies Provided to US Large Civil Aircraft, 20 February 2007, Exhibit EC-13. ITR calculates the

1570

DSR 2012:III

US - Large Civil Aircraft (2nd Complaint)

methodologies that ITR has used to calculate the subsidy "magnitudes" during the 2004 – 2006 period are based on an allocation principle used by investigating authorities in the United States and European Communities to allocate the full amount of subsidies over imports on an *ad valorem* basis for purposes of assessing countervailing duties.[3396]

7.1617 Set forth below are the subsidy "magnitude" calculations and corresponding subsidization rates made by ITR for the various versions of 737NG, 787 and 777 aircraft on the basis of all orders (i.e. competitive and non-competitive sales):

Magnitude of 737NG Subsidies Per LCA and Subsidization Rates (All Orders)[3397]

Year	737-600		737-700		737-800		737-900	
	Per-LCA Magnitude	Rate	Per-LCA Magnitude	Rate	Per-LCA Magnitude	Rate	Per-LCA Magnitude	Rate
2004	n/a	n/a	$2,028,144	5.83%	$2,607,614	6.27%	$2,784,674	6.33%
2005	n/a	n/a	$1,908,956	6.06%	$2,454,372	6.50%	$2,621,027	6.55%
2006	$1,812,672	6.54%	$2,076,333	6.48%	$2,669,571	6.97%	$2,850,838	6.97%
Average	$1,812,672	6.54%	$2,004,478	6.11%	$2,577,186	6.57%	$2,752,180	6.61%

---

following subsidy "magnitudes" over 2004, 2005 and 2006, respectively: for the 737NG: $2.38 million, $2.26 million and $2.45 million per plane; for the 787: $4.51 million, $4.47 million, and $4.72 million per plane; and for the 777: $5.56 million, $5.27 million and $5.54 million per plane; see European Communities' first written submission, para. 1295.

[3396] European Communities' response to question 275, para. 506; European Communities' comments on United States' response to questions 387 and 388, para. 309.

[3397] European Communities' first written submission, para. 1486, Figure 42; International Trade Resources LLC, Calculating on a Per-Aircraft Basis the Magnitude of the Subsidies Provided to US Large Civil Aircraft, 20 February 2007 , at para. 2, Table 11, and Table 12, Exhibit EC-13. Subsidization rates are based on average price per family, per year, as derived by ITR.

DSR 2012:III

1571

Report of the Panel

Magnitude of 787 Subsidies Per LCA and Subsidization Rates (All Orders)[3398]

Year	787-3		787-8		787-9	
	Per-LCA Magnitude	Rate	Per-LCA Magnitude	Rate	Per-LCA Magnitude	Rate
2004	4,453,362	5.44%	4,453,362	4.99%	5,292,112	5.61%
2005	4,408,130	5.90%	4,408,130	5.41%	5,238,361	5.34%
2006	4,661,172	6.10%	4,661,172	5.62%	5,539,061	5.56%
Average	4,507,555	5.81%	4,507,555	5.33%	5,356,511	5.50%

Magnitude of 777 Subsidies Per LCA and Subsidization Rates (All Orders)[3399]

Year	777-200ER/-200LR		777-300/-300ER	
	Per-LCA Magnitude	Rate	Per-LCA Magnitude	Rate
2004	$4,904,773	3.95%	$5,996,553	4.32%
2005	$4,652,768	4.14%	$5,688,434	4.52%
2006	$5,120,987	4.48%	$6,260,875	4.86%
Average	$4,892,843	4.18%	$5,981,947	4.56%

7.1618 The European Communities argues that the "magnitudes" of the subsidies benefiting the 737NG, 787 and 777 families of LCA are large enough to have adversely affected the respective Airbus LCA in these markets. The European Communities presents diagrams purporting to depict "counterfactual" analyses of A320, A330 and A340 pricing in the absence of subsidization of the 737NG, 787 and 777, respectively, assuming that Boeing uses all of its subsidy benefits to reduce prices for all ordered aircraft by an identical amount.[3400] The European Communities argues that factoring in the "magnitude" of the subsidies benefiting the 737NG, 787 and 777 (whether viewed in terms of all orders or only orders

---

[3398] European Communities' first written submission, para. 1378, Figure 26. International Trade Resources LLC, Calculating on a Per-Aircraft Basis the Magnitude of the Subsidies Provided to US Large Civil Aircraft, 20 February 2007 , at para. 2, Table 11, and Table 12, Exhibit EC-13. No subsidies are allocated to years in which there was no order of a certain model. Subsidization rates are based on average price per family, per year, as derived by ITR. The seating capacity for the 787-3 is assumed to be the same as the seating capacity for the 787-8.

[3399] European Communities' first written submission, para. 1584, Figure 57; International Trade Resources LLC, Calculating on a Per-Aircraft Basis the Magnitude of the Subsidies Provided to US Large Civil Aircraft, 20 February 2007 at para. 2, Table 11, and Table 12, Exhibit EC-13. Subsidization rates are based on average price per family, per year, as derived by ITR.

[3400] European Communities' first written submission, paras. 1396, 1501, 1597.

1572

DSR 2012:III

arising out of "competitive sales campaigns") shows the extent to which the full use of these subsidies has the potential to cause significant price suppression of the competing Airbus' LCA.[3401] The European Communities provides similar "counterfactual" depictions of the subsidy "magnitudes" on Airbus' [***] for the A320, A340 and A330.[3402]

A320 Family Pricing and Counterfactual A320 Family Pricing Including US Subsidization Rate for All 737NG Orders[3403]

[***]

Price Per Seat of A330 Family LCA in Constant Dollars, Compared to Magnitude of 787 Subsidies, All Orders, 2004-2006[3404]

[***]

A340 Family Pricing and Counterfactual A340 Family Pricing Including US Subsidization Rate for All 777 Orders[3405]

[***]

7.1619 The European Communities argues that the conditions of competition in the LCA market are such that Boeing has the incentive to use the subsidies to lower its LCA prices in the three LCA product markets, most particularly in so-called "competitive" sales campaigns. The European Communities argues that Boeing would use subsidies to lower its LCA prices in order to increase sales, thereby reducing its marginal production costs, and ultimately, increasing its profitability. The European Communities identifies the following key characteristics of the LCA market which it argues give rise to this pricing

---

[3401] European Communities' first written submission, para. 1503.

[3402] European Communities' first written submission, paras. 1501, figure 47; 1401, figure 33; 1597, figure 62. The [***]; Christian Scherer, Commercial Aspects of the Aircraft Business From the Perspective of a Manufacturer, March 2007, Exhibit EC-11 (BCI), paras. 48-50.

[3403] European Communities' first written submission, para. 1501, Figure 47. Pricing information in this figure is based on Airbus proprietary data. Estimates of the per-plane magnitude of the subsidies are by ITR.

[3404] European Communities' first written submission, para. 1396, Figure 31. Pricing information in this figure is based on Airbus proprietary data. Estimates of the per-plane magnitude of the subsidies are by ITR.

[3405] European Communities' first written submission, para. 1597, Figure 62. Pricing information in this figure is based on Airbus proprietary data. Estimates of the per-plane magnitude of the subsidies are by ITR.

Report of the Panel

incentive: duopoly structure characterized by heavy price and quality competition, increasing returns to scale, a steep learning curve, switching costs for customers, heterogeneous products, customer specific configurations, high order volumes and small batch outputs and the need for a continuous delivery stream.[3406]

7.1620 The European Communities asserts that economic theory indicates that the structure of competition in the LCA industry gives rise to an inherent incentive for each duopolist to "out-price" its rival, either through aggressive pricing or through additional investment in R&D (which it asserts is economically equivalent to aggressive "value-per-unit" pricing).[3407] Moreover, lower LCA pricing is argued to lead eventually to higher profits, because lower prices imply higher market share, and higher market share implies faster movement down the learning curve (i.e. lower marginal production costs) as well as the realization of economies of scale and scope. The European Communities argues that, by the same token, one duopolist's increased market share will indirectly result in higher marginal costs to its rival, leading to an effective medium to long-term pay off from lower pricing.[3408]

7.1621 The European Communities also presents a counterfactual analysis of Boeing's financial condition and "economic viability" had it not received an alleged $19.1 billion in subsidies between 1989 and 2006. The European Communities argues that, based on an examination of historical financial information pertaining to the "US LCA industry" (i.e. the LCA divisions of Boeing and, prior to 1997, McDonnell Douglas), it is possible to show that Boeing's LCA pricing and product development decisions were contingent on the receipt of the alleged subsidies because, absent the receipt of $19.1 billion in subsidies over the 1989 – 2006 period, the pricing and product development behaviour of the U.S. LCA industry would have been unsustainable and financially irrational. The European Communities argues, based on material relating to the economic viability of Boeing's LCA division absent $19.1 billion in subsidies, that *but for* the alleged subsidies, Boeing would have been forced to behave differently (i.e. increase its LCA prices and develop new aircraft more slowly), or face complete commercial failure.[3409]

[3406] European Communities' comments on United States' response to question 391, para. 334.

[3407] European Communities' comments on United States' response to question 391, para. 335, referring to Professor Cabral's explanation that, as investment in additional R&D leads to higher quality aircraft, R&D expenditures lower the effective price of LCA on a "per-value" unit basis, regardless of any increases in nominal LCA prices. According to Professor Cabral, the "per-value-unit" measure of price is the relevant determinant of market demand; Luís M. B. Cabral, Impact of Development Subsidies Granted to Boeing, New York University and CEPR, March 2007, Exhibit EC-4, para. 72.

[3408] European Communities' comments on United States' response to question 391, para. 335.

[3409] European Communities' second written submission, paras. 715-732. The European Communities also uses the alternative assessment to rebut one of the principal criticisms of the model developed by Professor Cabral, namely, his assumption that Boeing's access to capital markets is not unconstrained. According to the European Communities, if Boeing can be said to enjoy unconstrained access to the

1574

DSR 2012:III

US - Large Civil Aircraft (2nd Complaint)

7.1622 The European Communities argues that significant price suppression of Airbus' LCA is reflected in Boeing's pricing activity, including in six individual LCA sales campaigns described in *Annex E* to its first written submission[3410], three LCA sales campaigns in *Annex D* to its first written submission[3411] and the 2004 Lufthansa campaign as described in *Annex F* to its first written submission. In support of the European Communities' allegations that Airbus lost a number of sales in each of the three LCA product markets since 2002, the European Communities points to evidence from five LCA sales campaigns set forth in *Annex E* to its first written submission[3412], 10 specific LCA sales campaigns in *Annex D* to its first written submission[3413] and three LCA sales campaigns described in *Annex F* to its first written submission.[3414] The European Communities alleges displacement and impedance of exports of Airbus' A320 family LCA from the third country markets of Singapore, Indonesia and Japan in the period 2004-2006. As regards the 200 – 300 seat wide-body LCA product market, the European Communities alleges displacement and impedance of imports into the United States of the A330 and Original A350 (as evidenced by the alleged lost sales campaigns involving Continental and Northwest) and displacement and impedance of exports from the third country markets of Japan, Canada, Australia, Iceland, Ethiopia, Morocco and Kenya. In the 300 – 400 seat LCA product market, the European Communities alleges displacement and impedance of exports from the third country markets of Singapore, New Zealand and Hong Kong.

7.1623 The European Communities also argues that the subsidies benefiting the 737NG, 787 and 777 families of LCA cause a threat of significant price suppression with respect to *future orders* of, respectively, Airbus' A320, A330 and A350XWB-800, and A350XWB-900/1000 families of LCA.[3415] The European Communities argues that the present and future subsidies give rise to a

---

capital markets, this too is an effect of the alleged subsidies. Had Boeing not received the alleged subsidies, the capital markets would not have permitted it to become so highly leveraged and it could not have invested in lower prices and development of new aircraft in the manner in which it did. European Communities' second written submission, para. 760; Luís M. B. Cabral, Response to the U.S. Criticisms of My Analysis of 'The impacts of Development Subsidies Granted to Boeing', 14 November 2007, Exhibit EC-1182, para. 8.

[3410] The sales campaigns in question are: easy Jet (2002); Air Berlin (2004); Iberia (2005); Aegean (2005); Air Asia (2005); Hamburg International (2005).

[3411] The sales campaigns in question are International Lease Finance Corporation (2005), CIT Group (2005) and Air Europa (2005).

[3412] The sales campaigns are: Ryanair (2000 – 2002); Japan Airlines (2005); Singapore Airline Leasing Enterprise (2005); Lion Air (2005) and DBA (2005).

[3413] The sales campaigns are: Continental Airlines (2003-2005); Northwest Airlines (2003-2005); All Nippon Airways (2003-2005); Japan Airlines (2003-2005); Air Canada (2005); Qantas (2004-2005); Icelandair (2005-2006); Ethiopian Airlines (2004-2005); Royal Air Maroc (2004-2005); and Kenya Airways (2005-2006).

[3414] The sales campaigns are: Singapore Airlines (2004); Air New Zealand (2004) and Cathay Pacific (2005).

[3415] European Communities' first written submission, para. 1654.

Report of the Panel

significant likelihood that Airbus will suffer from significant price suppression for the above-referenced families of Airbus LCA, based on the same types of evidence that support its present serious prejudice arguments.[3416]

(ii) United States

7.1624 The United States disputes the European Communities' contentions that Boeing's product development and pricing behaviour was affected by the alleged subsidies. The United States argues that Boeing's product development strategies and pricing were "market driven", that the subsidies in question did not increase Boeing's non-operating cash flow, and that Boeing generated sufficient cash to fund its pricing and product development behaviour. In short, the United States contends that the European Communities has failed to demonstrate that Boeing's commercial behaviour would have been any different in the absence of the subsidies.

7.1625 Set forth below is a description of the United States' rebuttal arguments as to (i) the effects of the aeronautics R&D subsidies on Boeing's development of technologies in relation to the 787; and (ii) the effects of the subsidies on Boeing's pricing behaviour with respect to the 737NG, 777 and 787.

Effects of the aeronautics R&D subsidies
on Boeing's development of technologies
in relation to the 787

7.1626 The United States advances several arguments in response to the European Communities' arguments that the aeronautics R&D subsidies gave rise to "knowledge effects" that were instrumental in the design, manufacture and timing of the 787.

7.1627 First, the United States argues that the materials and basic manufacturing techniques employed by Boeing on the 787 are commercially available. The United States alleges that global suppliers provide significant components for the 787 and in many cases currently supply those or other components to Airbus.[3417] The United States argues that Boeing's use of commercially available materials and technologies purchased from a global supply network in order to develop and manufacture the 787 underscores the point that there was in fact no "technology gap" that prevented Airbus from making the same decision that Boeing made in 2004; namely, to launch a composite aircraft.[3418] According to the United States, the key strategic technology choice made by Boeing for the

---

[3416] The European Communities contends that the suppressed prices for the respective Airbus LCA "provide a strong indication" that prices for those LCA will continue to be suppressed in the future.

[3417] United States' first written submission, para. 931; In this regard, the United States notes that Airbus and Boeing both use the following suppliers: Alenia, Goodrich, Vought, C&D Aerospace, GKN, Spirit, Fischer, Fuji, Latecoere, Messier-Dowty, Fokker, SAAB, CAC, HAC and Hawker de Havilland; United States' first written submission, para. 931, footnote 1146.

[3418] United States' first written submission, para. 937.

1576   DSR 2012:III

US - Large Civil Aircraft (2nd Complaint)

787 was its decision to work with suppliers to leverage their technology and know-how. The United States contends that this is what expanded Boeing's technology base; not the U.S. Government.[3419] In relation to each of the six technology areas in which the European Communities alleges that Boeing was assisted by aeronautics R&D subsidies, the United States describes the problem-solving and innovation on the part of Boeing and its suppliers that it alleges were the true causes of the technological advancements on the 787.

7.1628 Second, in relation to the NASA aeronautics R&D subsidies, the United States argues that any knowledge acquired by Boeing through its R&D contracts and agreements with NASA has been widely disseminated throughout the aerospace industry and forms part of a general, globalized pool of industry knowledge.[3420] Moreover, the lessons learned from composites research, in particular, have been disseminated well beyond the aerospace industry, and have informed the development of composite usages in many industries. The United States claims that this is one reason why Boeing has looked to suppliers and partners outside the aerospace industry for useful experience and innovation.[3421] The United States also argues that, although the European Communities makes much of the experience gained by Boeing employees engaged on NASA R&D projects, including those where the technologies were not considered to be feasible, any "lessons learned" by Boeing, including pitfalls to avoid, were accessible by Airbus.[3422] In this regard, the United States notes that the report by Airbus engineer, Dominik Wacht, cites to many of these publicly available research results, and that several of the NASA and DOD conferences to which Wacht refers were conferences which Airbus not only attended, but in which it was an active participant.[3423]

7.1629 Third, the United States argues that the basic research that Boeing conducted for NASA cannot be compared to the degree of technological refinement, testing and investment required for Boeing to develop the 787. In terms of the nature of the NASA-funded R&D, the United States argues that the nature of the research conducted under NASA contracts and agreements is either technologically irrelevant or too early stage and basic to have a commercial impact, and thus did not accelerate Boeing's decision or ability to build the 787.[3424] The United States notes that NASA has typically aimed at technology research from basic principle observation (TRL 1) through component validation (TRL 6).[3425] Moreover, according to the United States, from the cost perspective, NASA R&D funding does not even begin to approach the level required for LCA development, and is insignificant compared to the costs of

---

[3419] United States' first written submission, para. 938.
[3420] United States' first written submission, para. 931.
[3421] United States' first written submission, para. 947, footnote 1189.
[3422] United States' first written submission, para. 947.
[3423] United States' first written submission, para. 947 and footnote 1191.
[3424] United States' first written submission, para. 932.
[3425] United States' first written submission, para. 946.

DSR 2012:III

Report of the Panel

aircraft development.[3426] The United States here compares the $750 million, which it argues was the amount that Boeing received from NASA under the challenged NASA R&D programmes from 1989 to 2006, with the investment costs associated with developing and launching an aircraft like the 787, including making arrangements to take maximum advantage of supplier expertise. In this regard, the United States notes that Boeing's BCA division spent $2.39 billion in research and development in 2006 *alone*; while it has been reported that Airbus expects to spend $15.4 billion developing the A350XWB.[3427]

7.1630 Fourth, as regards the knowledge effects of alleged DOD aeronautics R&D subsidies, the United States argues that DOD funded-research on aircraft is for military use, designed to fulfil military functions, and gives rise to technologies that are not relevant to commercial civil aircraft, such as stealth technology, flight at supersonic speeds, unmanned flight and the ability to land in harsh environments.[3428] In addition, the United States argues that commercial aircraft production has more stringent certification/maintenance requirements and demands a higher efficiency/production rate than required for military aircraft, meaning that production methods sufficient for military aircraft cannot work for the significantly higher rates of lower-cost commercial aircraft demanded by commercial customers.[3429] The United States contends that, on the contrary, it is technology development within the commercial sector that is proving useful to DOD, and that DOD acknowledges that it relies heavily on industry as a way of accessing innovative technology and knowledge and sharing the costs and associated risks with the commercial sector.

7.1631 In any case, the United States argues that to the extent that DOD-funded technology has a theoretical civil application, it cannot reasonably be used commercially because of U.S. laws and regulations which control the export of all defense articles and services.[3430] The United States here refers to the ITAR which prevents any technologies developed for a military purpose (including items designed, developed, modified or configured for military applications, regardless of the intended end-use of the item) from being exported without a license or applicable exemption.[3431] The United States contends that, because of their military nature, technologies and products developed by Boeing under DOD contracts and agreements are generally subject to the ITAR and require a licence, which is not a commercially feasible proposition for technologies incorporated in LCA which are to be sold to commercial customers around the

---

[3426] United States' first written submission, para. 943.

[3427] United States' first written submission, para. 943 and footnote 1185.

[3428] United States' first written submission, para. 948.

[3429] United States' first written submission, para. 949. In this respect, the United States contends that using materials developed for military aircraft would require completely redesigning their structural properties to conform to commercial requirements, including safety, comfort and reparability.

[3430] United States' first written submission, para. 951.

[3431] United States' first written submission, paras. 951-952.

1578   DSR 2012:III

US - Large Civil Aircraft (2nd Complaint)

world. This, coupled with the difficulty of determining the heritage of every item on a commercial aircraft, and the severe financial and commercial consequences of inadvertently violating the ITAR, led Boeing to declare the 787 to be "ITAR-free" and to ensure that only technologies with a documented civil origin were used on the 787. This requirement also applies to Boeing's suppliers, all of whom must certify that all items and technologies supplied are of non-military origin. According to the United States, the consequence is that none of the alleged DOD-funded technologies are on the 787.[3432]

7.1632 Fifth, the United States notes that although the European Communities has sought to support its "technology effects" causation theory by pointing to similarities between research conducted under NASA and DOD programmes and technology applied to the 787, for the bulk of the challenged programmes, the European Communities "does not even find a semblance of a connection to the 787".[3433] The United States argues that, even as regards the NASA R&D programme that the European Communities argues had the clearest relevance to the 787 – the Advanced Technology Composites Aircraft Structures (ATCAS) programme – most of the technologies studied under ATCAS are fundamentally different to the technologies used on the 787.[3434]

7.1633 Sixth, the United States contends that knowledge, experience and confidence are not the "benefit" conferred by an R&D subsidy, but rather are the natural result of engaging in R&D.[3435] In this regard, the United States argues that the European Communities' theory of "technological benefit" goes beyond the boundaries of Article 1.1(b) of the SCM Agreement.[3436] The architecture of the definition of a subsidy in Article 1.1 is such that the extent of the financial contribution that is found to exist sets the upper bounds of any benefit conferred thereby. The United States considers any knowledge, experience and confidence that Boeing derives from doing the research to be the result of undertaking the research with the funds, goods and services provided by the government, just as it would be the result of undertaking research with the same funds, goods and services received from the market. Such knowledge, experience and confidence is therefore not an element of the financial contribution and cannot be part of any benefit thereby conferred.[3437] The United States does not dispute that Boeing

---

[3432] United States' first written submission, para. 953.

[3433] United States' confidential oral statement at the second meeting with the Panel, para. 22.

[3434] United States' confidential oral statement at the second meeting with the Panel, para. 24.

[3435] United States' response to question 275, para. 484.

[3436] United States' comments on European Communities' response to question 373(b), para. 251.

[3437] United States' comments on European Communities' response to question 373(b), para. 256. The United States argues that the European Communities is essentially asking the Panel to (i) calculate the benefit of funds, goods and services provided to Boeing according to Articles 1.1(b) and 14 of the SCM Agreement based on the adequacy of the remuneration; and then (ii) to double count it, or multiply it by a measure of what Boeing learned as a result of performing the challenged research measures. Yet, when NASA provides the services of employees to outside entities, including Boeing, the "cooperation" with those employees *is* the service provided and the R&D contracts and agreements between NASA and Boeing show that collaboration between the purchaser and supplier

DSR 2012:III

1579

Report of the Panel

gained specific knowledge, experience and confidence from performing R&D in collaboration with NASA and DOD engineers. However, it argues that the European Communities has failed to demonstrate that this knowledge, experience and confidence is a term of the financial contribution that is more favourable than is available in the market.

7.1634 Finally, the United States argues that the European Communities' argument that, through the aeronautics R&D subsidies, the U.S. Government effectively provides Boeing with extra cash that it did not otherwise have to spend to perform the research is at odds with its argument that the result of the government research support is knowledge that Boeing would not otherwise have had.[3438] In other words, the United States argues that it is logically impossible to demonstrate on the basis of a single counterfactual that an R&D subsidy has both "price effects" and "technology effects". According to the United States, a counterfactual analysis of the position absent the receipt by Boeing of the R&D subsidies would be that, *but for* the R&D subsidies, Boeing would have been required to spend additional funds to conduct the R&D that was financed by the subsidies. In this counterfactual world, in which Boeing funded the R&D that was funded by the subsidies, Boeing would still have derived the technologies, knowledge, experience and confidence from the R&D work.

> Effects of the subsidies on Boeing's pricing behaviour with respect to the 737NG, 777 and 787

7.1635 The United States argues that the European Communities has failed to demonstrate that the bulk of the subsidies at issue in this dispute is of a nature that would affect the product development or pricing decisions of Boeing. In this regard, the United States disputes the European Communities' argument that the "nature" of the NASA, DOD and DOC "contractual research payments" to Boeing is such that they represent additional operating cash flow which Boeing is able to invest in lower prices and additional R&D to lower its costs of research, development, production and sale of LCA. The R&D programmes that are said to involve contractual research payments to Boeing had no effect on Boeing's non-operating cash flow, and there is no evidence that Boeing's commercial airplanes division would have spent any more for civil aircraft research in the absence of the subsidies. Moreover, even if Boeing would have incurred increased costs, the European Communities has provided no evidence

---

of research services is a "term" of such transactions consistent with terms available in the market. The United States argues therefore that Boeing is not "better off" as a result of working with NASA engineers than it would be by performing comparable work with comparable engineers in the marketplace; United States' comments on European Communities' response to question 373(b), para. 255.

[3438] United States' comments on European Communities' response to question 375, para. 264; United States' comments on European Communities' response to question 275, para. 485.

1580

DSR 2012:III

that Boeing's prices would have differed.[3439] The United States also considers that the European Communities' argument that most of the subsidies at issue provide non-operating cash flow in fact means that subsidies within that general category are unlikely to affect Boeing's product development or pricing decisions.[3440] In this regard, a central argument made by the United States regarding the nature of an alleged subsidy in an analysis of serious prejudice is that the effects of a subsidy depend upon whether or not the subsidy creates supply or maintains supply that would not otherwise exist.[3441] The United States asserts that whether a subsidy is supply-creating or supply-maintaining depends upon whether the subsidy is "tied to" the development, production or sale of a particular product. If a subsidy that is not tied to the development, production or sale of a particular product is provided to a company that enjoys unfettered access to capital markets, it is unlikely to affect product and pricing decisions, unless the subsidy is such that, absent the subsidy, the company would not be economically viable.

7.1636 The United States argues that Professor Cabral's analysis of the effects of the subsidies on Boeing's LCA prices, which it regards as underpinning the European Communities' "price effects" theory, in addition to being based on the European Communities' inflated estimates of the amounts of subsidies received by Boeing's LCA division, rests on assumptions that are contrary to fact and on dubious methodologies that are at odds with sound economic practice.[3442] The United States also argues that the European Communities' general theory as to how the subsidies affected Boeing's LCA pricing behaviour is inconsistent with the empirical evidence concerning pricing activities of Airbus and Boeing in the LCA markets between 2001 and 2006. In this regard, the evidence shows that Boeing's market share losses to Airbus were greatest in the period when the alleged "price effects" of the subsidies calculated by Professor Cabral were

---

[3439] United States' first written submission, para. 959.

[3440] United States' response to question 370, para 263: "...characterizing an alleged subsidy to a company with unfettered access to capital markets as 'nonoperating cash flow' means that the alleged subsidy is unlikely to affect the recipient's product development or pricing decisions; free cash to a company that has access to capital markets to finance investments it considers worthwhile is, by definition, *not* supply creating or supply maintaining"; see also, United States' response to question 387, para 278: "In this connection, even accepting the EC's characterization of the alleged nonrecurring subsidies as the equivalent of free cash to BCA, the United States has shown that, by its nature, such free cash (i) is untied to the supply or pricing of any particular Boeing large civil aircraft models, and (ii) would not affect the investment or pricing decisions of a company like Boeing, which does not face significant constraints in its access to capital markets."

[3441] United States' response to question 391, para. 304: "the critical part of the U.S. adverse effects argument is that the most important issue regarding the nature of an alleged subsidy is whether it is supply-creating or supply-maintaining"; United States' response to question 391, para. 306: "The key point of the U.S. argument is that because, with the exception of certain low-value tax programs, the alleged subsidies about which the EC complains are not tied to development, production or sale of any large civil aircraft, they are not in any sense supply-creating and thus had no appreciable impact on market pricing."

[3442] United States' first written submission, para. 954.

Report of the Panel

supposedly at their highest, thus disproving the European Communities' claim of a link between the subsidies and Boeing's pricing.[3443] According to the European Communities' theory as to how the subsidies would affect Boeing's pricing behaviour, Boeing should have been led to price aggressively when it was losing market share (i.e. in the period 2000 – 2004). However, the *ad valorem* levels of the total alleged "price effects" calculated by Professor Cabral were *declining* through the period when, according to the United States, Airbus' price undercutting compelled Boeing to respond.

7.1637 The United States disputes the European Communities' calculation of the amounts of subsidies received by Boeing's LCA division between 1989 and 2006. The United States argues that the value of any subsidy benefit to Boeing's LCA division is, by any reasonable measure, a tiny fraction of the amount asserted by the European Communities, and is also insignificant relative to the value of the aircraft on which the alleged subsidies have allegedly been paid.[3444]

7.1638 The United States criticizes the European Communities' allocation of the subsidy amount across the various Boeing LCA models to arrive at per-LCA subsidy "magnitudes" and the derivation of alleged *ad valorem* rates of subsidization, both with respect to the relevance and appropriateness of such an allocation methodology in the present context, as well as the bases on which various subsidies were allocated, and the *ad valorem* rates were calculated.[3445] The United States' key criticisms of the European Communities' subsidy "magnitude" allocations are, first, that they are not required or justified under the SCM Agreement, and are inconsistent with the European Communities' arguments about how the subsidies function. Moreover, the European Communities' effort to allocate subsidy amounts to specific LCA is arbitrary and contradictory given the European Communities' arguments that the vast majority of the alleged subsidies are subsidies that increase Boeing's non-operating cash flow, and are therefore *not* tied to the development, production or sale of LCA.[3446] Second, the United States notes that in *US – Upland Cotton*, the panel rejected the United States' argument that it was under an obligation to precisely quantify the subsidies at issue in its serious prejudice analysis under Part III of the SCM Agreement.[3447] There is similarly no textual basis in the SCM Agreement for the European Communities' approach of calculating an *ad*

[3443] United States' first written submission, para. 713.

[3444] United States' first written submission, paras. 810-812; United States' second written submission, at paras. 171-173.

[3445] United States' first written submission, paras. 813-822; United States' second written submission, at paras. 174-177.

[3446] United States' first written submission, para. 814; United States' response to question 281, para. 478.

[3447] United States' first written submission, para. 813; Panel Report, *US – Upland Cotton*, at para. 7.1179.

valorem rate of subsidization for each type of Boeing aircraft.[3448] Third, the United States questions the relevance of the magnitude calculation, arguing that a simpler and more comprehensible approach would have been to compare the annual subsidy values with the order values for all Boeing LCA in each year.[3449] Moreover, in making the allegation that the magnitude of the subsidies is, of itself, sufficient to demonstrate the causal link between the subsidies and the adverse effects, and in the light of its failure otherwise to show that Boeing's pricing would have been any different without the alleged subsidies, the European Communities has placed the quantification of the alleged subsidies at the center of its adverse effects case.[3450] According to the United States, if the Panel were to agree that a large portion of the value of the European Communities' magnitude calculations is invalid, then "nothing remains of this key element of the European Communities' adverse effects claim, and the Panel should reject the European Communities' adverse effects claim".[3451]

7.1639 As regards the conditions of competition in the LCA markets, and more particularly, the market incentives and other factors that influence Boeing's LCA pricing decisions, the United States submits that Boeing's LCA pricing decisions seek the optimal or "profit-maximizing" price and that, in general terms, Boeing sets it prices at the maximum level that the market will bear. [3452] In setting its LCA prices, Boeing takes into account factors such as: (i) the pricing of Airbus, its competitor; (ii) the strength and elasticity of demand; (iii) Boeing's expectations regarding future market conditions; (iv) Boeing's strategic interests in particular sales campaigns; (v) the implications of a price reduction for future sales and for the residual values of aircraft previously sold; and (vi) changes in Boeing's product-specific fixed and variable costs, as well as in its general costs.[3453] The United States asserts that Boeing's decision to [***] in 2005 – 2006 was compelled by market conditions in the form of steady market share losses to a competitor that priced aggressively, and was unrelated to the subsidies.[3454]

[3448] United States' first written submission, para. 813. According to the United States, the European Communities' CVD-type analysis assumes, rather than proves, its cause and effect conclusion; United States' comments on European Communities' response to question 370, para. 216.

[3449] United States' first written submission, para. 815. The United States does this with respect to FSC/ETI ("the only programme found to be a specific subsidy"), and on that basis, argues that the subsidies have been small and declining in relation to the value of orders since 2000.

[3450] United States' comments on the European Communities' response to question 78, para. 269 at footnote 339. The United States contends that, although a complaining party in an adverse effects case is not required to precisely quantify the amount of the subsidy, the European Communities has organized its case in a way that requires it to demonstrate that it has accurately calculated the amount and magnitude of the alleged subsidies.

[3451] United States' comments on European Communities' response to question 78, para. 268; United States' comments on European Communities' response to question 83, para. 281.

[3452] United States' response to question 86, para. 299.

[3453] United States' response to question 298, para. 522.

[3454] United States' first written submission, HSBI Campaign Annex, para. 10.

Report of the Panel

7.1640 The United States argues that, assuming *arguendo* that the alleged subsidies affect Boeing's non-operating cash flow, the most logical way of assessing the significance of those subsidies is to compare them with Boeing's total non-operating expenditures (rather than revenues) in each year.[3455] In this regard, the United States notes that since 1998, Boeing has effected share repurchases in excess of $14 billion.[3456] The $14 billion in capital returned to shareholders represents funds for which Boeing did not consider that there were more attractive investment opportunities. Based on the European Communities' own theory of causation, the proper counterfactual conclusion is that, in the absence of the alleged subsidies, Boeing would have followed the same pricing practices and pursued the same research objectives that it did, but would have reduced the extent of its share repurchases.[3457]

7.1641 The United States also rejects the European Communities' efforts to demonstrate that Boeing's LCA division would not have been "economically viable" had it maintained the same pricing and product development behaviour in the absence of the subsidies. During the period under consideration, Boeing had excess operating cash flow after it had spent all of the money that it could economically justify on aircraft investments (including research). The United States presents its own analyses of financial data for Boeing's BCA division, which it argues demonstrates that, "even accepting the European Communities' fantastical magnitude calculations, Boeing's profits and cash flow were more than enough to absorb the portions of the Defense Department and NASA budgets that the European Communities wants Boeing to bear".[3458] Moreover, Boeing's internal funds and access to capital markets were more than sufficient to enable Boeing to develop on its own any technology that the European Communities alleges to have been created with government funds.[3459]

7.1642 The United States also refers to the facts of the specific sales campaigns in order to rebut the European Communities' allegations concerning the incentives that Boeing has to use subsidies to price aggressively. Specifically, the United States argues that: (i) Boeing was the incumbent supplier in most of the campaigns and therefore had no incentive to lower its prices, but a strong incentive to respond to Airbus' pricing to retain its customers; (ii) Airbus "systematically" undercut Boeing's prices in order to "flip" the Boeing customer, while the European Communities presents no evidence that Boeing undercut Airbus' price; (iii) once Boeing decided to respond to Airbus' lower pricing (in 2005 and 2006) it recovered market share and profitability, thus demonstrating

---

[3455] The United States argues, therefore, that the European Communities use of Boeing's "net earnings" figures is inconsistent with its causation theory; i.e. that the alleged subsidies have a cash flow effect; United States' second written submission, para. 177.

[3456] United States' second written submission, para. 176.

[3457] *Ibid.*

[3458] United States' comments on European Communities' response to question 78, para. 270.

[3459] United States' first written submission, para. 961.

1584

DSR 2012:III

US - Large Civil Aircraft (2nd Complaint)

that its decision to lower its prices was economically rational[3460]; and (iv) although Boeing did share some of its productivity gains in 2005 and 2006 with its customers (i.e. used cost savings to lower its prices and increase market share), it did so while simultaneously increasing its operating margins, suggesting a temporal link between productivity gains (or costs savings), lower LCA prices and increased operating margins.[3461] By contrast, the United States notes that the average annual subsidy amounts over this period (based on the European Communities' estimates) were 11 per cent lower than during 2001 to 2003.

(iii)   Third parties

Australia

7.1643 Australia considers that it may be relevant to assess the effects of subsidies in terms of the cumulative effects of certain subsidies, as has been advocated by the European Communities. However, in doing so, Australia is concerned that subsidies should only be aggregated where appropriate for an adverse effects claim and that care should be taken to ensure that an appropriate nexus exists between those subsidies, based on the nature of the subsidies, to warrant their aggregation.[3462]

7.1644 Australia considers that it is appropriate for the Panel to consider the nature of the subsidy in assessing the "effect of the subsidy" under Articles 5 and 6.3 and, in this regard, that it is appropriate to allocate over time the alleged non-recurring subsidies in order to assess their effects. [3463] Australia recalls that the April 1985 adopted report of the GATT Committee on Subsidies and Countervailing Measures, entitled Guidelines on Amortization and Depreciation, recognized that "{c}ertain subsidies exist which should be spread over time".[3464] Further, Australia notes that the Appellate Body in *US – Lead and Bismuth II* and *US – Countervailing Measures on Certain EC Products* considered that "an investigating authority may presume that a benefit continues to flow from an untied, non-recurring 'financial contribution'", so long as the presumption was

---

[3460] United States' comments on European Communities' response to question 78, para. 271.

[3461] United States' comments on European Communities' response to question 84, paras. 77-78. The operating margins of Boeing's commercial aircraft division increased from 3.58 per cent to 6.32 per cent to 9.60 per cent in 2004, 2005 and 2006, respectively.

[3462] Australia's written submission, para. 66.

[3463] Australia notes that, although Article 6.1(a) of the SCM Agreement has lapsed, the Report by the Informal Group of Experts to the Committee on Subsidies and Countervailing Measures, in clarifying issues for the purposes of Article 6.1(a), recognized that some subsidies need to be allocated over time depending on their nature and that continuing benefits may be conferred; Australia's response to questions, 14 April 2008, referring to recommendations contained in the Report (G/SCM/W/415/Rev.2) which, Australia notes, have not been adopted by the Committee.

[3464] Australia's response to question 17, 14 April 2008. GATT Committee on Subsidies and Countervailing Measures, Guidelines on Amortization and Depreciation, (SCM/64, BISD 32S/154, para. 1).

DSR 2012:III

1585

Report of the Panel

not irrebuttable.[3465] In addition, the implementation panel in *US – Countervailing Measures on Certain EC Products* examined whether a benefit continues to exist and whether subsidization exists and is likely to continue or recur, specifically citing as relevant context Articles 10, 14, 19.4, 21.1and 21.3 of the SCM Agreement and Article VI:3 of GATT 1994.[3466] Australia also considers that the principle that a non-recurring subsidy may be allocated over time is also supported by the decision of the Appellate Body in *US – Upland Cotton*.[3467]

7.1645 Australia agrees with Brazil that the causation analysis should not depend on whether alleged subsidies can be traced through a subsidy recipient's cash flow statements.[3468] While a subsidy may result in lowering a recipient's costs or increasing its revenue, the SCM Agreement does not require such an analysis, either in terms of the existence of a subsidy under Article 1 or in terms of the effect of the subsidy under Article 6.3.[3469] Moreover, the analysis of serious prejudice under Article 5 and Article 6.3 relates to the interests of another Member as assessed by the effects of the subsidy in the market. Therefore, it is the effects enumerated in Article 6.3 (for example, price undercutting, displacement of imports), and not other factors, that should form the basis of the Panel's causation determination.[3470]

Brazil

7.1646 Brazil disagrees with both the European Communities' and the United States' approaches regarding the cumulation of subsidies.[3471] In Brazil's view, in making its findings under Article 6.3(c), the Panel should cumulate the challenged subsidies on the basis of whether they would result in prices lower than those that would have been charged otherwise (the particular "effects-related variable" under consideration). As a first step in this analysis, the Panel should determine whether, on account of their structure, design, and operation, the challenged subsidies tend to press prices downwards by, for example, reducing costs (whether they be research and development costs, production costs, financing costs, selling costs, or any other relevant costs), by freeing up cash flow, or through any other mechanism. In conducting this test, the Panel should bear in mind that there may be cases in which the effects involved

---

[3465] Australia's response to question 17, 14 April 2008, referring to Appellate Body Report, *US – Lead and Bismuth II*, para 62; Appellate Body Report, *US – Countervailing Measures on Certain EC Products*, para. 84.

[3466] Australia's response to question 17, 14 April 2008, referring to *US – Countervailing Measures on Certain EC Products (Article 21.5 - EC)*, in particular paras. 7.165 to 7.171.

[3467] Australia's response to question 17, 14 April 2008, referring to Appellate Body Report, *US – Upland Cotton*, para. 475.

[3468] Australia's response to question 20, 14 April 2008, referring to Brazil's written submission, at para. 66 and Brazil's oral statement, at para. 19.

[3469] Australia's response to question 20, 14 April 2008.

[3470] *Ibid.*

[3471] Brazil's written submission, para. 46.

1586

DSR 2012:III

overlap.[3472] Brazil also considers that, if the Panel cumulates subsidies in making its findings on price suppression, it should, in order to maintain consistency, cumulate subsidies in making its findings on displacement/impedance and lost sales.[3473]

7.1647 Brazil argues that, if the calculation of the amount of subsidization is not necessary in serious prejudice disputes, the "allocation" or "amortization" over time of alleged non-recurring subsidies is not required to demonstrate whether the "effect" of the subsidies is serious prejudice within the meaning of Articles 5 and 6.3.[3474] Brazil submits that the allocation of the "benefit" resulting from a financial contribution over a particular period may not be a meaningful way of assessing the "effect" of a subsidy for purposes of a serious prejudice dispute and that the relevant allocation period need not necessarily be coincident in time with the effect of a subsidy. Brazil argues that in conducting its serious prejudice analysis, the Panel should consider the conditions of competition in the LCA market.[3475] Boeing and Airbus are the only surviving manufacturers of LCA, and a sale by one is a sale lost to the other. Under these circumstances, adverse effects caused by subsidies are very transparent, with gains to one company corresponding directly to losses by the other.[3476]

7.1648 Brazil further submits that the LCA market is characterized by a small group of customers that place large but infrequent orders involving deliveries of multiple aircraft over extended periods. The useful lives of LCA are also lengthy, extending for up to 20 years or more. This means that, after making a purchase, a customer may not revisit the market to make new purchases for many years. Therefore, subsidies that distort a customer's purchasing decisions have adverse effects that are far greater than in most other sectors.[3477] Brazil also argues that when an airline decides to purchase a subsidized aircraft model within an aircraft family, it will very likely make follow-up orders of the same aircraft model, and an airline that purchases an aircraft model from one producer's aircraft family is more likely to order additional aircraft models from the same family.[3478] Consequently, past subsidies not only distort the market

---

[3472] Brazil's written submission, para. 47.

[3473] Brazil's written submission, para. 48.

[3474] Brazil's response to question 17, 14 April 2008, para. 15.

[3475] Brazil's written submission, para. 24.

[3476] Brazil's written submission, para. 25.

[3477] Brazil's written submission, para. 26.

[3478] Moreover, according to Brazil, an airline that operates aircraft from one manufacturer's family is also more likely to purchase aircraft from a different family produced by the same manufacturer. The reasons include commonality of spare parts, pilot and crew training, special tooling, and ground support equipment, and the fact that airlines tend to order large numbers of aircraft at the same time and to place such orders infrequently; Brazil's written submission, para. 27.

Report of the Panel

when the aircraft benefiting from the subsidies are delivered, but they are also likely to affect future aircraft sales.[3479]

7.1649 Finally, Brazil argues that the nature of aircraft production is such that the continued development of new aircraft and technology is necessary to remain competitive, and the launch of new aircraft requires enormous initial investments in research and development, design, engineering, and testing. To recoup this investment and to generate economies of scale in production, a producer must sell a large number of aircraft. Subsidies, including research and development subsidies, significantly distort competition in the LCA market because they enable a producer to reduce the costs and risks of developing and launching new aircraft, divert internal funds to other uses, and otherwise make decisions that are inconsistent with normal commercial considerations.[3480]

7.1650 Brazil submits that, although the European Communities has decided to present its case by using complex economic models and by tracing cash flows in Boeing's financial statements, the Panel should focus in making its findings on a straightforward causation analysis consistent with that adopted by the original panel and the implementation panel in *US - Upland Cotton*.[3481] According to Brazil, subsidies may cause adverse price effects by freeing up cash flow of the subsidy recipient for use in lowering prices. The evidence and methodologies for demonstrating this "cash flow" effect, however, are not specified in the text of the SCM Agreement, and the fact that the subsidies cannot be explicitly traced through the subsidy recipient's cash flow financial statements should not be determinative of causation. Brazil therefore submits that the Panel's findings regarding the European Communities' claims of adverse price effects not be made contingent on whether the evidence of additional cash flow is found in the financial data of the subsidized producer.[3482]

7.1651 Brazil also considers that the Panel should reject the position that a Member can avoid a finding of serious prejudice by characterizing the alleged subsidies as additional cash flow, and by alleging that the "additional cash flow" was directed to uses other than investment in firm value (such as the payment of dividends or repurchase of shares) on the basis of simple correlations between the payment of dividends, for example, and the "additional cash flow".[3483] Even

---

[3479] Brazil argues for example, that an airline that buys a subsidized Boeing aircraft is less likely to buy an aircraft from Airbus in the future, thus magnifying and prolonging the adverse effects of the subsidies. Brazil's written submission, para. 27.

[3480] Brazil's written submission, para. 28.

[3481] Brazil's oral statement, para. 17.

[3482] Brazil's written submission, para. 66.

[3483] Brazil's oral statement, para. 24. According to Brazil, even if the subsidies consisted of cash or cash-equivalents and were simply redirected to shareholders as dividend payments, these increased dividend payments would send a signal to financial markets of improvement in the company's financial situation and could lower its cost of capital needed for investment. Similarly, if all subsidies were used to reduce a company's debt, which the United States also alleges, this would directly lower a recipient's financial costs and would represent a significant improvement in the company's financial situation at the government's expense. Brazil submits that, when subsidies are used to improve a

1588

DSR 2012:III

if not used to make investments to increase a firm's value, subsidies may be directed to uses that improve a company's financial situation, with the potential for trade-distorting effects in the market. The approach apparently endorsed by the parties in this dispute, to the extent that it neglects this possibility, would open a loophole in the SCM Agreement and does not reflect an appropriate causation analysis.[3484]

7.1652 Brazil disputes the logic of the U.S. argument that Boeing establishes the price of its aircraft based upon what the LCA market would bear, which suggests, in turn, that Boeing's prices would not have been any different absent the challenged subsidies.[3485] According to Brazil, as long as it is demonstrated that the challenged subsidies can potentially depress or suppress world prices, world prices may be lower or not as high as they would have been otherwise. In this context, Brazil considers that arguing that subsidization has no serious prejudice effects in terms of prices where the recipient firm sets its prices at the going world price neglects the obvious point that, absent subsidization, world prices would have been different and the prices charged by the recipient company would also have been different.[3486]

Japan

7.1653 Japan submits that it is not aware of any textual requirement in the SCM Agreement to allocate a non-recurring subsidy. Japan argues that if allocation were always required, it would lead to an unreasonable result that even a benefit which does not exist is always required to be allocated.[3487]

(b) Preliminary considerations relating to the Panel's evaluation of the European Communities' claim under Articles 5(c) and 6.3(a), (b) and (c) of the SCM Agreement.

(i) Interpretational and methodological issues

7.1654 Article 5(c) of the SCM Agreement provides:

" No Member should cause, through the use of any subsidy referred to in paragraphs 1 and 2 of Article 1, adverse effects to the interests of other Members, i.e.:

...

---

company's financial situation, they may enable such company to take actions that have trade-distorting effects and that the market would otherwise not allow, such as maintaining inefficient production capacity; Brazil's oral statement, para. 19.

[3484] Brazil's oral statement, para. 20.

[3485] Brazil's oral statement, para. 24.

[3486] *Ibid.*

[3487] Japan's response to question 17, 14 April 2008.

Report of the Panel

(c) serious prejudice to the interests of another Member".[3488]

7.1655 Article 6.3 of the SCM Agreement reads as follows:

"6.3 Serious prejudice in the sense of paragraph (c) of Article 5 may arise in any case where one or several of the following apply:

(a)   the effect of the subsidy is to displace or impede the imports of a like product of another Member into the market of the subsidizing Member;

(b)   the effect of the subsidy is to displace or impede the exports of a like product of another Member from a third country market;

(c)   the effect of the subsidy is a significant price undercutting by the subsidized product as compared with the price of a like product of another Member in the same market or significant price suppression, price depression or lost sales in the same market;

(d)   the effect of the subsidy is an increase in the world market share of the subsidizing Member in a particular subsidized primary product or commodity as compared to the average share it had during the previous period of three years and this increase follows a consistent trend over a period when subsidies have been granted".[3489]

7.1656 Article 6.3 of the SCM Agreement provides that serious prejudice within the meaning of Article 5(c) may arise where "the effect of the subsidy" is one of the phenomena described in Article 6.3(a) through (d). Article 6.3, however, does not provide extensive guidance as to the sequence of steps to be followed in assessing whether the effect of the subsidy is displacement or impedance of imports, displacement or impedance of exports, or significant price suppression or lost sales, within the meanings of Articles 6.3(a), (b) and (c), respectively. Although Article 6.3 does not use the word "cause", the Panel considers that the sub-paragraphs of Article 6.3 require the establishment of a causal link between the subsidies in question and the particular form of serious prejudice.[3490] This interpretation of Article 6.3 accords with the ordinary meaning of the terms "arise" and "effect"[3491], and finds contextual support in Article 5(c) and Part V of

---

[3488] Footnotes omitted.

[3489] Footnote omitted.

[3490] See also, Panel Report, *US – Upland Cotton*, para. 7.1341; Appellate Body Report, *US – Upland Cotton (Article 21.5 – Brazil)*, para. 372.

[3491] The ordinary meaning of "arise" in this context is "come into existence or notice; present itself, occur", *Shorter Oxford English Dictionary*, L. Brown (ed.) (Clarendon Press, 2002), Vol. I, p. 116. The ordinary meaning of "effect" in this context is "something accomplished, caused or produced; a

1590   DSR 2012:III

US - Large Civil Aircraft (2nd Complaint)

the SCM Agreement. Article 5(c) provides that no Member should *cause* serious prejudice to the interests of another Member through the use of any subsidy. With regard to Part V, the Panel considers that the fact that the more elaborate and precise "causation" and "non-attribution" language found in its trade remedy provisions has not been expressly prescribed for an examination of serious prejudice under Articles 5(c) and 6.3 of Part III of the SCM Agreement suggests that panels have a certain degree of discretion in selecting an appropriate methodology for determining whether the "effect" of a subsidy is any of the phenomena set forth in Articles 6.3(a) through (d).[3492]

7.1657 The European Communities' serious prejudice arguments focus on the effects of the subsidies on Airbus' prices and sales in the three LCA product markets, through their effects on *Boeing's* LCA prices and product offerings. Indeed, the parties agree that determining whether the effect of the subsidies at issue in the dispute is serious prejudice necessitates an economic analysis of how the subsidies affected *Boeing's* commercial behaviour with respect to the pricing and product development of particular LCA.[3493] Both parties express their views on this issue in the form of counterfactual conditional propositions: the European Communities asserts that, *but for* the alleged subsidies, Boeing's commercial behaviour with respect to the pricing and product development of certain LCA would necessarily have been different.[3494] The United States asserts that Boeing's commercial behaviour with respect to the pricing and product development of the LCA at issue would not have been different in the absence of the subsidies.[3495]

---

result, a consequence", *Shorter Oxford English Dictionary,* L. Brown (ed.) (Clarendon Press, 2002), Vol. I, p. 793.

[3492] Appellate Body Report, *US – Upland Cotton,* para. 436. The Appellate Body in *US – Upland Cotton (Article 21.5 – Brazil),* in discussing the approach to causation and non-attribution taken by the compliance panel in that dispute (in the context of a claim of significant price suppression), noted that "a panel has a certain degree of discretion in selecting an appropriate methodology for determining whether the 'effect' of a subsidy is significant price suppression"; Appellate Body Report, *US – Upland Cotton (Article 21.5 – Brazil),* para. 370, quoting from Appellate Body Report, *US – Upland Cotton,* para. 436.

[3493] See, e.g. European Communities' second written submission, para. 646:

"The European Communities agrees with the United States that, in order to cause adverse effects within the meaning of Articles 5 and 6.3, subsidies must cause a change in the commercial behaviour of their beneficiaries to an extent that results in adverse effects ("change in commercial behaviour"). Contrary to the US assertion, however, compelling and credible evidence demonstrates that, but for the US subsidies, Boeing's commercial behaviour today, like in the past, would be very different, in ways that are recognized as causing adverse effects under Articles 5 and 6.3." Footnote omitted.

[3494] European Communities' second written submission, paras. 646, 651.

[3495] United States' non-confidential oral statement at the second meeting with the Panel, para. 144. The parties agree that a "but for" test is an appropriate and permissible causation *methodology* for determining whether the effects of a subsidy is serious prejudice but that this test is not a legal *requirement* under Articles 5 and 6 of the SCM Agreement. See e.g. European Communities' comments on United States' response to question 390, para. 569:

"... the United States and the European Communities both agree that the 'but for' test is a methodology, not a standard, and as such not *required* by Articles 5 or 6.3

DSR 2012:III

1591

Report of the Panel

7.1658 The European Communities indicates that it has adopted a "unitary" approach to establishing causation, under which prices, sales, market share and other indicators of competitive harm are not assessed in isolation, but rather as part of an integrated analysis of causation.[3496] The European Communities explains that, under this approach, which it alleges is the same approach to causation as that adopted by the implementation panel in *US – Upland Cotton*, the existence of the particular market effect that is alleged to constitute serious prejudice is not separated from the analysis of the causal relationship between that serious prejudice effect and the subsidies at issue.[3497] The United States does not object to the Panel's use of a "unitary" or "integrated" approach to determining whether the effects of the subsidies are displacement or impedance, significant lost sales or significant price suppression.[3498] However, the United States argues that whatever approach it adopts, the Panel needs to ensure that other factors that may have affected sales volume and prices, and thus the causal link between the subsidies and the serious prejudice factors, are taken into account.[3499]

7.1659 We recall that in *US – Upland Cotton (Article 21.5 – Brazil)*, the Appellate Body explained that an analysis of price suppression is counterfactual in nature, and that the adoption by the implementation panel in that dispute of a "but for" approach to examining causation is consistent with the definition of price suppression that had been endorsed by the Appellate Body in the original proceedings.[3500] The Panel proposes to adopt a counterfactual approach to determining whether the "effects" of the subsidies at issue in this dispute are

---

of the SCM Agreement. That said, both parties agree that, for purposes of assessing the European Communities' serious prejudice claim, the 'but for' test constitutes an appropriate methodology."

United States' comments on the European Communities' response to question 300, para. 596: "The United States and the EC agree that a 'but for' test is a useful framework, but not an obligatory standard, for analysing causation." The United States observes elsewhere that while it "adopted a 'but for' methodology for much of its rebuttal" of the European Communities' claim, "its observations regarding the lack of coincidence between the alleged subsidies and the alleged serious prejudice is not a but/for analysis, but is still relevant to the Panel's evaluation of the EC claims;" United States' response to question 300, para. 537 and footnote 674. Moreover, both Australia and Brazil argue that the "but for" approach is but one methodology that panels may select in order to determine whether there is the requisite causal relationship between the subsidy and its alleged effect; Australia's response to question 20, 14 April 2008, Brazil's written submission, para. 61, Brazil's oral statement, para. 26. Japan similarly notes that there is no text in the SCM Agreement that clearly provides that a "but for" test is required for an analysis of causation under Article 6.3(c) but submits that the "but for" test is an effective methodology that the Panel may select in order to conduct its causation analysis in this dispute; Japan's response to question 20, 14 April 2008.

[3496] European Communities' confidential oral statement at the second meeting with the Panel, para. 54.

[3497] European Communities' confidential oral statement at the second meeting with the Panel, para. 54; referring to Panel Report, *US – Upland Cotton (Article 21.5 – Brazil)*, paras. 10.46-10.49, 10.243.

[3498] United States' response to question 295, para. 505.

[3499] United States' response to question 295, paras. 505-506; response to question 300, para. 538.

[3500] Appellate Body Report, *US – Upland Cotton (Article 21.5 – Brazil)*, paras. 370-371, referring to Appellate Body Report, *US – Upland Cotton*, para. 433.

displacement or impedance, significant lost sales or significant price suppression. Consistent with the structure of the European Communities' serious prejudice arguments, we conduct this counterfactual analysis first by examining the effects of the subsidies on Boeing's LCA commercial behaviour (i.e. Boeing's prices and product offerings) and secondly by examining the effects of the subsidies, through their effects on Boeing's commercial behaviour, on Airbus' prices and sales in the specific product markets.

7.1660 We recall further that the Appellate Body has stated that Article 6.3(c) requires a panel to ensure that the effects of other factors on prices do not dilute the causal link between the subsidies and the price suppression.[3501] The Appellate Body also stated, however, that Article 6.3(c) leaves some discretion to panels in choosing the methodology to be used to conduct this assessment of the effects of the so-called "non-attribution" factors.[3502] The Panel agrees with the United States that there is no requirement for panels to undertake a separate analytical step to evaluate potential non-attribution factors, and that it is permissible to adopt an analysis that takes these potential non-attribution factors into account simultaneously with the effect of the subsidies and in the context of conditions of competition affecting the market.[3503] Given that our analysis of the effects of the subsidies occurs in two stages; namely, by commencing with an analysis of the effects of the subsidies on *Boeing's* pricing and product offerings, followed by an analysis of the effects of the subsidies, through their effects on Boeing's pricing and product offerings, on *Airbus'* prices and sales, we will undertake our evaluation of possible non-attribution factors relevant to each stage as a part of our causation analysis at that stage. In other words, in conducting our analysis of whether the subsidies affected Boeing's pricing and product offerings, we will also analyze the effects of other factors that are alleged to have affected that behaviour. Similarly, in analyzing the effects of the subsidies on Airbus' prices and sales, we will consider the effect of factors other than Boeing's pricing and product offerings on Airbus' prices and sales in each of the three product markets.

7.1661 We are also mindful that a counterfactual analysis of causation conducted by way of a "but for" approach does not in itself imply a particular standard of causation. In this regard, the Appellate Body has observed:

> "A subsidy may be necessary, but not sufficient, to bring about price suppression. Understood in this way, the 'but for' test may be too undemanding. By contrast, the 'but for' test would be too rigorous if it required the subsidy to be the only cause of the price suppression. Instead, the 'but for' test should determine that price

---

[3501] Appellate Body Report, *US – Upland Cotton (Article 21.5 – Brazil)*, para. 375.
[3502] *Ibid.*
[3503] United States' response to question 295, para. 506.

DSR 2012:III

Report of the Panel

suppression is the effect of the subsidy and that there is a 'genuine and substantial relationship of cause and effect.'"[3504]

7.1662 In adopting a "but for" approach to our analysis of whether the effects of the subsidies are any of the forms of serious prejudice alleged by the European Communities in the manner which we have outlined above, we will determine whether we are satisfied that there is a genuine and substantial relationship of cause and effect between the subsidy in question and the displacement or impedance, significant lost sales, or significant price suppression, as the case may be.

> (ii) The organization of the European
> Communities' serious prejudice arguments

7.1663 It is important to clarify at the outset the distinction between the European Communities' claim that the subsidies to Boeing cause serious prejudice within the meaning of Articles 5(c) and 6.3(a), (b) and (c) of the SCM Agreement, on the one hand, and the arguments and evidence it presents in relation to the effects of the subsidies in the three LCA product markets, on the other.

7.1664 The United States at first appears to have understood the European Communities to be making three separate adverse effects claims; namely, that: (i) alleged subsidies to the 737NG cause adverse effects to the A320; (ii) alleged subsidies to the 787 cause adverse effects to the A330, Original A350 and the A350XWB-800; and (iii) alleged subsidies to the 777 cause adverse effects to the A340 and A350XWB-900/100.[3505]

7.1665 However, the European Communities indicates that it is making a single serious prejudice claim, while structuring its arguments and evidence in support of that claim on the basis of three separate LCA product markets.[3506] According to the European Communities, this approach is consistent with the requirement, under Articles 5 and 6.3 of the SCM Agreement, to assess the causal link between the challenged subsidies and the adverse effects based on actual competition. The European Communities argues that, because the causation assessment must be undertaken on the basis of the competitive relationship between particular subsidized products and particular competing products of the complaining Member that are alleged to have been negatively impacted by the

---

[3504] Appellate Body Report, *US – Upland Cotton (Article 21.5 – Brazil)*, referring to Appellate Body Report, *US – Upland Cotton*, para. 438, and Appellate Body Report, *US – Wheat Gluten*, para. 69.

[3505] United States' first written submission, para. 802.

[3506] European Communities' response to question 63, paras. 220-222. The European Communities also argues that its adverse effects claim is not dependent on its identification of three separate LCA product markets. According to the European Communities, the arguments and evidence equally support findings of serious prejudice (or threat of serious prejudice) to the European Communities' LCA-related interests if the Panel were to assess causation of adverse effects on the basis of alternative market configurations, including a single LCA product market.

1594

DSR 2012:III

US - Large Civil Aircraft (2nd Complaint)

effects of the subsidies, the Panel should assess the existence of adverse effects caused by the subsidies on the basis of arguments and evidence concerning competition between Boeing LCA and competing Airbus LCA in the three separate LCA product markets in which they compete.[3507]

7.1666 The United States has since indicated that it does not object to the way in which the European Communities has chosen to structure and present the arguments and evidence in support of its serious prejudice claim. However, the United States argues that by identifying three specific sets of Airbus LCA, each one of which allegedly competes with an allegedly subsidized Boeing LCA in one of three distinct LCA product markets, the European Communities has, in practical terms, based its serious prejudice claim "entirely on the alleged effects of the alleged subsidies on competition within each of these three separate markets".[3508] According to the United States, the arguments and evidence presented by the European Communities concern three distinct Boeing "subsidized products" and the alleged serious prejudice affecting three corresponding distinct groups of Airbus "like products" *on the basis of competition occurring in three distinct LCA product markets.* The United States considers that arguments and evidence structured on this basis are not capable of establishing a single adverse effects claim pertaining to a "single" large civil aircraft market.[3509]

7.1667 The Panel considers that the European Communities is free to structure and present the arguments and evidence in support of its serious prejudice claim in the manner it has chosen. Based on the structure of Article 6.3 of the SCM Agreement, serious prejudice arises where the effect of the subsidy is any one or more of the phenomena described in paragraphs (a) through (d) of Article 6.3. Provided the effect of the subsidy is found to be one or several of the effects described in paragraphs (a) through (d) of Article 6.3, serious prejudice in the sense of paragraph (c) of Article 5 arises, and the complaining Member will thereby establish that the alleged subsidies have caused adverse effects to the interests of another Member, pursuant to Article 5 of the SCM Agreement. We consider that provided the European Communities demonstrates one of the forms of serious prejudice in paragraphs (a) through (c) of Article 6.3 that it alleges in relation to a particular Boeing subsidized LCA and a corresponding Airbus like

---

[3507] European Communities' response to question 63, para. 220.

[3508] United States' comments on European Communities' response to question 63, para. 218.

[3509] United States' comments on European Communities' response to question 63, paras. 218-219. The United States notes, for example, that the European Communities' allegations regarding displacement or impedance of imports pursuant to Article 6.3(a) pertain to imports of specific asserted "like products" within each of the three asserted product markets. According to the United States, evidence supporting these allegations would not be sufficient to establish displacement or impedance of imports within the meaning of Article 6.3(a) on the basis of a single product market. The United States argues that the European Communities cannot evade its burden under the SCM Agreement to show serious prejudice by grouping products one way for purposes of its claim, and another way for presenting its arguments and evidence; United States' comments on the European Communities' response to question 63, para. 224.

DSR 2012:III

1595

Report of the Panel

product (or significant price suppression or lost sales, in the "same market"), it will establish serious prejudice to the European Communities' LCA-related interests for purposes of Article 5(c) of the SCM Agreement.[3510]

7.1668 Moreover, the Panel does not consider that evidence supporting allegations regarding serious prejudice based on competition between a subsidized product and corresponding like product in an identified market will necessarily always be incapable of supporting an allegation of serious prejudice based on competition in a differently delineated market. In our view, much would depend on the delineation of the markets and the scope of the subsidized and like products. This is not a question that can or should be resolved at an abstract or theoretical level.[3511]

> (iii) Relevant "markets", subsidized products, like products

7.1669 The parties agree that the market for LCA is a global market geographically.[3512] The European Communities delineates the global LCA market into five separate market segments (or product markets) in which particular families of Boeing and Airbus LCA are alleged to compete. These product markets or segments are based on the specific range and seating capacity of LCA:

- Single-aisle aircraft with a capacity of approximately 100 to 200 passengers in a two-class configuration (or the respective cargo equivalent), and a short to medium range;

[3510] We recall that Article 7.8 of the SCM Agreement provides that the remedies for contraventions of Article 5 are that the Member "take appropriate steps to remove the adverse effects" or withdraw the subsidy. In our view, the contemplated remedies would relate to the particular subsidies found to have caused the specific forms of serious prejudice, meaning that an adverse effects claim established on a "narrow" basis under Article 6.3 (e.g. subsidization of one Boeing LCA causing serious prejudice to one group of Airbus "like products") would result in a correspondingly "narrow" remedy.

[3511] The Panel notes, however, that the European Communities agrees generally that, as a result of its delineation of the LCA industry into five separate LCA product markets, and its identification of the three "subsidized" Boeing LCA and three sets of corresponding "like" Airbus LCA in three separate product markets for purposes of its claim, it is implicitly requesting the Panel to confine itself to examining the causal relationships among the above-referenced groups of subsidized and like products. According to the European Communities, while the effects of subsidies benefiting one grouping of subsidized Boeing LCA may "spill over" to Airbus LCA competing in a different LCA product market, such spill-over effects are infrequent. The European Communities asserts such infrequency on the basis that "bundled sales" campaigns (i.e. sales campaigns involving the provision of LCA from more than one LCA product market) represent a relatively small total number of LCA sales campaigns (e.g. 5.7 per cent of sales transactions over the 2004-2006 period); European Communities' response to questions 67 and 68, para. 242.

[3512] European Communities' first written submission, para. 1186; United States' first written submission, para. 877; See also Brazil's third party submission, para. 36 and Brazil's oral statement, para. 27.

1596

DSR 2012:III

- Wide-body aircraft with a capacity of approximately 200 to 300 passengers in a three-class configuration (or the respective cargo equivalent), and a medium to long or ultra-long range;

- Wide-body aircraft with a capacity of approximately 300 to 400 passengers in a three-class configuration (or the respective cargo equivalent), and a long or ultra-long range;

- Wide-body aircraft with a capacity of 400 to 500 passengers in a three-class configuration (or the respective cargo equivalent), and a long range; and

- Super wide-body aircraft with a capacity in excess of 500 passengers in a three-class configuration (or the respective cargo equivalent), and a long range.[3513]

7.1670 For purposes of its serious prejudice claim, the European Communities focuses on three particular LCA product markets, namely, the 100 – 200 seat single-aisle product market, the 200 – 300 seat wide-body product market, and the 300-400 seat wide-body product market. Within these product markets, the European Communities identifies the following three groups of Boeing "subsidized products" and competing Airbus "like products", respectively: (i) the 737NG family of LCA and A320 family of LCA; (ii) the 787 family of LCA and A330/Original A350/A350XWB-800 families of LCA and (iii) the 777 family of LCA and A340/A350XWB-900/1000 families of LCA.[3514] The United States accepts the European Communities' five-way division of the market as the basis for evaluating the European Communities' serious prejudice claim.[3515] The United States considers that a complaining party is accorded considerable latitude in framing the arguments it makes in support of its claims and submits that, as long as the complainant identifies markets or products that are reasonable and coherent, a panel should accept that definition, and should reject a complainant's proposed definition only if it would make a market analysis impossible.[3516] According to the United States, notwithstanding the "serious flaws" in the European Communities' division of the LCA market into five

---

[3513] European Communities' first written submission, para. 1159; Rod P. Muddle, The Dynamics of the Large Civil Aircraft Industry, 2 March 2007, Exhibit EC-10, para. 37.

[3514] European Communities' first written submission, para. 1154.

[3515] United States' first written submission, para. 800. However, the United States notes that it accepts this approach "solely as an organizational matter" akin to a stipulation, or simplifying assumption; United States' response to question 71, para. 194.

[3516] United States' first written submission, para. 800, referring to an argument made by the European Communities before the panel in *Korea – Commercial Vessels*; Panel Report, *Korea – Commercial Vessels*, Annex F-1, para. 33 (Oral Statement of the European Communities at the Second Panel Meeting); response to question 71, para. 196.

Report of the Panel

discrete segments, the subsidized products that it identifies are sufficiently coherent to permit a market analysis.[3517]

7.1671 The Panel is satisfied that the LCA market is a global market geographically. In this regard, we note that Airbus and Boeing actively compete for the business of airlines and leasing companies throughout the world, and receive orders from, and make deliveries to, customers based in almost all geographic areas of the world.[3518] Both Airbus and Boeing display and market their aircraft at air shows that are held around the world and which are attended by a world-wide audience of potential customers and the interested public, while production and support facilities are also situated around the world.[3519] Aircraft financing also occurs on a global level, with financial institutions operating on a global scale.

7.1672 The Panel accepts, for purposes of its analysis of the European Communities' serious prejudice claim, the European Communities' delineation of three product markets, as well as its identification of three groups of "subsidized" Boeing LCA which correspond to three groups of Airbus "like" products. In analyzing the European Communities' claims on this basis, the Panel does not suggest that this is the only, or most appropriate way in which to divide the LCA market or to identify the relevant subsidized products and corresponding like products. Rather, the evidence before us indicates that the European Communities' identification of the relevant product markets and subsidized and like products is but one way in which its serious prejudice arguments could be organized. The European Communities has chosen to organize its serious prejudice arguments in this way and the Panel considers that it is reasonable to examine those arguments on that basis.[3520]

7.1673 The European Communities also argues that each of the identified LCA product markets operates in individual country markets as well as a world

---

[3517] United States' response to question 71, para. 194. The United States also argues that, as responding party, it retains the latitude to frame its own arguments, and that the Panel should consider those arguments; United States' first written submission, para. 800, response to question 71, para. 197.

[3518] European Communities' first written submission, para. 1186.

[3519] European Communities' first written submission, paras. 1186 – 1187. For example, the European Communities notes that even though Airbus has its corporate headquarters in Toulouse, France, it has subsidiary headquarters in Washington, D.C., Tokyo, Dubai and Beijing, along with over 160 offices around the world, 16 sites in Europe and an international presence with its network of suppliers and a customer base that spans the globe. According to the European Communities, while Boeing's corporate headquarters are in Chicago, it similarly has subsidiary headquarters in China and Japan and a support team of over 200 representatives based in 65 different countries.

[3520] The Panel notes in this regard Brazil's arguments that the Panel should afford substantial discretion to the European Communities as complaining party to define the "subsidized product" to which its claims apply, and that, provided the European Communities identifies the "like products" corresponding to the "subsidized products" in accordance with footnote 46 of the SCM Agreement, the Panel should not "second-guess" the complainant; Brazil's third party submission, paras. 31-33, Brazil's oral statement, para. 22.

1598   DSR 2012:III

market geographically.[3521] According to the European Communities, as Articles 6.3(a) and 6.3(b) of the SCM Agreement legally direct panels to assess the evidence of displacement or impedance on the basis of certain country markets, panels assessing claims under these two provisions are required to limit the geographic scope of the markets to the territorial boundaries of the countries at issue.[3522] The United States argues that the European Communities has provided the Panel with no evidence to support its argument that the three product markets it has identified can be divided into separate country markets for purposes of Article 6.3(c) of the SCM Agreement.[3523] The United States asserts that LCA producers easily trade LCA across large distances, that barriers between buyers and sellers are low, and that prices for a sale in one country routinely affect prices for subsequent sales in other countries (factors which point generally to the existence of a global LCA market). According to the United States, a party asserting the existence of a country market for large civil aircraft would have to provide an explanation as to why these sorts of conditions of competition do not preclude the existence of smaller, discrete markets such as country markets.[3524]

7.1674 Although the European Communities argues that "each LCA product market also operates within individual country markets, including the US market and various third country markets"[3525] it does not confine its arguments concerning the existence of significant price suppression or significant lost sales, within the meaning of Article 6.3(c) of the SCM Agreement, to any individual country market.[3526] Therefore, the Panel will assess the European Communities' arguments concerning the existence of significant price suppression and significant lost sales on the basis that each of the three LCA product markets have a worldwide geographical scope. The Panel recalls that Article 6.3(a) and Article 6.3(b) expressly direct us to conduct our examination of displacement and impedance on the basis of national markets; either the market of the

---

[3521] European Communities' first written submission, para. 1151.

[3522] European Communities' response to question 65, para. 232.

[3523] United States' first written submission, para. 877.

[3524] United States' first written submission, para. 878.

[3525] European Communities' first written submission, para. 1190. The European Communities notes that the panel in *US – Upland Cotton* considered that the existence of a world market does not preclude the existence of other relevant geographic markets within the world market. Panel Report, *US – Upland Cotton*, paras. 7.1247-7.1248. The European Communities refers to the following factors in support of its argument that each LCA product market operates within individual country markets: (i) evidence contained in Annexes D, E and F to its First Written Submission, which it asserts illustrates that LCA sales campaigns take place within individual countries; (ii) the fact that airline and leasing companies have "identities" associated with individual countries; (iii) the fact that since 2000, Airbus and Boeing have received orders from customers in 75 and 70 different countries, respectively; and (iv) the fact that airline order and delivery data can also easily be broken down by any country; European Communities' first written submission, para. 1191.

[3526] The European Communities indicates that its arguments concerning the existence of significant price suppression and significant lost sales in each of the three LCA product markets are based on those markets being world markets geographically, European Communities' confidential oral statement at the first meeting with the Panel, para. 91.

Report of the Panel

subsidizing Member for purposes of Article 6.3(a), or third country markets for purposes of Article 6.3(b). In so doing, the Panel is not required to consider whether the European Communities has established the existence of such country markets. Rather, the question for the Panel is whether, based on evidence of sales occurring in those countries, the Panel is satisfied that there has been displacement and impedance of imports or exports within the meaning of Article 6.3(a) and 6.3(b), respectively in any of the three LCA product markets in the particular country market.

7.1675 We note that the European Communities also submits, "in the alternative", that in addition to world and individual country LCA markets, each LCA sales campaign be considered an LCA market.[3527] The Panel agrees with the United States that the concept of a "market" for purposes of Article 6.3(c) of the SCM Agreement requires more than the coming together of a buyer and a seller to consummate a transaction, as such a definition would hold true for almost every transaction in the world, and would reduce the concept of a "market" to a nullity.[3528] We therefore decline to examine the European Communities' serious prejudice arguments on the basis that an individual LCA sales campaign can itself constitute a relevant "market" for purposes of Article 6.3 of the SCM Agreement.

(iv)   Issues pertaining to the temporal scope of
the European Communities' claim

7.1676 The next issue that we address concerns the appropriate period of time over which the Panel should assess the existence of "present" adverse effects, and whether, in making that assessment, the Panel can take into account evidence and data pertaining to earlier periods.

7.1677 The European Communities argues that Articles 5 and 6.3 of the SCM Agreement require that it establish a prima facie case of *present* adverse effects caused by the challenged subsidies under present conditions of competition. According to the European Communities, this demonstration necessitates the assessment of a causal link between the subsidies and *present* adverse effects during a "reference period".[3529] The European Communities requests that the

---

[3527] European Communities' first written submission, para. 1193. The European Communities argues that individual LCA sales campaigns involve buyers (i.e. airlines and leasing companies) and sellers (i.e. Airbus and Boeing) coming together to agree upon prices and terms for a commercial transaction involving the sale of LCA. According to the European Communities, these individual LCA sales campaigns therefore constitute "markets" for purposes of the European Communities' serious prejudice claims under Article 6.3(c) of the SCM Agreement.

[3528] United States' first written submission, para. 885.

[3529] European Communities' first written submission, para. 1074; non-confidential oral statement at the first meeting with the Panel, para. 126.

1600   DSR 2012:III

US - Large Civil Aircraft (2nd Complaint)

Panel assess the existence of present adverse effects over the period 2004 to 2006.[3530]

7.1678 The United States argues that, given the allegations of subsidization from 1989 onwards and the fact that product development cycles in the LCA industry often last decades, the correct approach is to take a longer-term perspective on the European Communities' serious prejudice allegations and market developments.[3531] The United States submits that an "objective assessment" of the matter as required by Article 11 of the DSU requires the Panel to select a "reference period" that is long enough to enable it to distinguish between developments that were the result of the business cycle and those that were related to other factors.[3532] The United States argues that the 2004 – 2006 period proposed by the European Communities does not permit the Panel to make an objective assessment of the matter before it as is required by Article 11 of the DSU [3533] and that the 2001 – 2006 period is the shortest period that would enable the Panel to discharge its obligations in accordance with Article 11 of the DSU.[3534]

7.1679 In our view, while the European Communities as complaining party is able to identify the period of time over which it requests the Panel to assess the existence of serious prejudice, it may not restrict the temporal scope of evidence that the Panel may consider in making that assessment. In accordance with the requirement of Article 11 of the DSU to make an objective assessment, the Panel should evaluate the European Communities' serious prejudice claim on the basis of all of the evidence presented to it, including evidence pertaining to periods prior to 2004, giving due weight to that evidence in terms of its context, relevance, and probative value. Accordingly, in evaluating whether the European Communities has demonstrated that the effects of the subsidies at issue is present serious prejudice within the meaning of Article 6.3 of the SCM Agreement, the Panel will assess whether the European Communities has demonstrated the existence of serious prejudice within the period 2004 to 2006 identified by the European Communities. However, the Panel will not limit the temporal scope of the evidence that it considers in undertaking that assessment, and therefore will take into account all of the relevant evidence submitted in this dispute.[3535]

[3530] European Communities' non-confidential oral statement at the first meeting with the Panel, para. 126.

[3531] United States' comments on European Communities' response to question 370, para. 203.

[3532] United States' response to question 72, para. 201.

[3533] United States' first written submission, paras. 803, 807.

[3534] United States' response to question 72, para. 201.

[3535] The Panel notes in this regard Japan's submission that the Panel should consider all relevant evidence provided to it, regardless of whether that evidence pre-dates, or post-dates the Panel's establishment; Japan's written submission, para. 10.

Report of the Panel

(v) Use of order and delivery data

7.1680 The Panel next considers the parties' arguments concerning the point in time at which the particular forms of serious prejudice may be said to arise, and the type of data that is relevant to demonstrating the existence of a particular form of serious prejudice; namely, data pertaining to LCA "orders" as opposed to data concerning LCA "deliveries".

7.1681 The European Communities argues that orders, as opposed to deliveries, are most relevant for assessing the impact of the subsidies on Airbus. According to the European Communities, sales are won or lost when orders are placed, and consequently, "significant price suppression, significant lost sales, and displacement and impedance are caused by the US subsidies at the time an LCA order is placed by an airline or a leasing company."[3536]

7.1682 The United States argues that prices at the time of order provide the most appropriate basis for discerning price trends and analyzing the effect of a subsidy on price competition between Airbus and Boeing. According to the United States, price competition between LCA mostly occurs in sales campaigns that end with a decision to order aircraft from Airbus or Boeing, and that the price for the purchase of a large civil aircraft is generally determined at that time.[3537] Similarly the United States argues that a "sale" is "lost" at the time when a customer makes a definitive decision to purchase a competitor's aircraft, and that this occurs at the time of order.[3538] In other words, according to the United States, "lost sales" are properly measured at the time of order.

7.1683 However, the United States argues that in assessing claims of displacement or impedance of imports or exports under Article 6.3(a) or 6.3(b) of the SCM Agreement, the terms "imports" and "exports" should be understood to refer to actual deliveries of LCA rather than orders.[3539] This is because the ordinary meaning of the terms "imports" and "exports" includes actual articles or things that cross international borders; namely, deliveries.[3540] The United States submits that orders are, at most, contracts for future imports and exports, and that while they may be relevant for an analysis of threat of displacement or impedance, they do not provide any information about imports and exports that

---

[3536] European Communities' first written submission, para. 1214.

[3537] United States' first written submission, para. 890.

[3538] United States' first written submission, para. 897.

[3539] Japan agrees with the United States that, at least for purposes of this dispute, the terms "imports" and "exports" within Articles 6.3(a) and 6.3(b), respectively, should be interpreted to refer to actual deliveries rather than orders; Japan's written submission, para. 20. Japan also argues that, in an industry such as the LCA industry, in which there is typically a significant lapse of time between the dates of orders and deliveries, it is not reasonable to interpret the terms "imports" and "exports" as encompassing orders, because of the various factors that may break the link between order and delivery (e.g. the orders are often cancelled, their terms are subject to change prior to delivery, and delivery dates are often postponed for extended periods).

[3540] United States' first written submission, para. 903, referring to *New Shorter Oxford English Dictionary*, p. 889 (export defined as "an article that is exported"), p. 1323 (import defined as "something imported or brought in"), Exhibit US-14.

1602

DSR 2012:III

US - Large Civil Aircraft (2nd Complaint)

have actually occurred.[3541] The United States argues that, by framing its displacement and impedance arguments based on order data rather than delivery data, the European Communities has failed to produce sufficient information to demonstrate the existence of current displacement or impedance.[3542]

7.1684 The Panel considers that the parties' arguments raise two issues. The first concerns the time at which the specific serious prejudice phenomena can be said to exist. For example, does significant price suppression occur only at the time at which an LCA is ordered, does it occur at the time the LCA is actually delivered (which the parties agree is, on average, three years after the order), or does the phenomenon continue from order until delivery? The European Communities submits that sales of LCA occur at the time of order, and thus, that the subsidies at issue in this dispute cause adverse effects at the time of order, which is when a price-suppressed, lost, displaced or impeded sale takes place.[3543] However, the European Communities also argues that those adverse effects also continue over a number of years commencing with the time of order, as Airbus' revenues are affected by deliveries of aircraft at significantly suppressed prices, and lost revenues from aircraft that are not delivered due to lost, displaced and impeded sales.[3544]

7.1685 The Panel recalls that LCA are purchased through long term contracts that are frequently worth billions of dollars, involving deliveries of aircraft over many years. The terms and conditions of purchase (e.g. aircraft specification, net price, discounts, non-price concessions and financing arrangements) are set at the time of order. On signing a purchase agreement, customers pay a non-refundable deposit for each aircraft ordered, and the cash flow relating to a specific sale therefore begins with the order of the aircraft.[3545] Following the order there is, in principle, no re-negotiation of the terms and conditions of the purchase contract, and assessment of the profitability of a certain contract prior to delivery, as well as the profit margins actually generated, is based on the terms and conditions established at the time of order.[3546] However, complete payment does not occur until delivery of the aircraft.[3547] Moreover, Airbus and Boeing both provide for escalation of the basic airframe price to account for the time that elapses between negotiation of price at the time of order, and delivery of the aircraft. Price escalation factors can significantly increase the purchase

---

[3541] United States' first written submission, para. 903.
[3542] United States' first written submission, para. 906.
[3543] European Communities' first written submission, para. 1218.
[3544] Ibid.
[3545] Christian Scherer, Commercial Aspects of the Aircraft Business From the Perspective of a Manufacturer, March 2007, Exhibit EC-11 (BCI), para. 25. Manufacturers generally rely on the cash flow generated by the non-refundable deposit for production financing.
[3546] Christian Scherer, Commercial Aspects of the Aircraft Business From the Perspective of a Manufacturer, March 2007, Exhibit EC-11 (BCI), para. 26.
[3547] Christian Scherer, Commercial Aspects of the Aircraft Business From the Perspective of a Manufacturer, March 2007, Exhibit EC-11 (BCI), para. 49.

DSR 2012:III

Report of the Panel

price to be paid.[3548] In the Panel's view, the phenomena of "price suppression" and "lost sales" do not begin and end at the time at which an LCA is ordered. Rather, given the particularities of LCA production and sale, these forms of serious prejudice should be understood to begin at the time at which an LCA order is obtained (or an order is lost), and to continue up to and including the time at which that aircraft is delivered (or not delivered). However, the Panel considers that the ordinary meaning of the terms "imports" and "exports" in Articles 6.3(a) and (b) of the SCM Agreement, respectively, suggests that these forms of serious prejudice arise only on delivery of the aircraft to the customer. Therefore, while an order of an aircraft can be considered to represent a future delivery, and in that regard, constitute evidence of a future import or export that will be displaced or impeded, it does not of itself evidence displacement or impedance of imports or exports within the meaning of Article 6.3(a) or 6.3(b) of the SCM Agreement, each of which contemplate the existence of goods which cross borders, and can therefore only arise at the point at which LCA deliveries take place.

7.1686 The second issue that is raised by the parties' arguments concerning orders and deliveries relates to the type of data that is relevant to demonstrating the existence of specific serious prejudice phenomena such as price suppression, lost sales and displacement and impedance of imports and exports. Because we regard price suppression and lost sales to exist from the time an order for LCA is made, up to and including its delivery, data pertaining to both LCA orders and to LCA deliveries will potentially be relevant to demonstrating the existence of significant price suppression and significant lost sales. [3549] As regards displacement and impedance or imports or exports, the Panel considers that the existence of these serious prejudice phenomena can only be definitely established by relevant delivery data. However, as indicated above, orders for LCA represent, by and large, deliveries that will occur some years subsequently. The Panel therefore considers that evidence concerning orders that occurred in 2004 – 2006 is capable of showing that future imports or exports will be displaced or impeded in the future, and therefore the existence of a threat of serious prejudice. The Panel applies these principles to its assessment of the arguments and evidence presented by the parties.

[3548] *Ibid.*

[3549] Australia argues that the Panel should consider both the status of orders and deliveries. According to Australia, notwithstanding that delivery may not eventuate, orders are an indication of the effect of the subsidies on the industry and the market, through future projected sales and market share. Australia considers that they consequently provide an indication of how current subsidies are likely to affect the market in the future and thus the threat of future serious prejudice; Australia's third party submission, para. 69. Brazil argues that a complainant may satisfy its burden to demonstrate serious prejudice using either order or delivery data, depending on its relevance in the particular circumstances, and that the Panel should refrain from finding that specific forms of serious prejudice under Article 6.3 must be demonstrated using order or delivery data; Brazil's third party submission, paras. 59-60; Brazil's oral statement, para. 28.

1604

DSR 2012:III

(vi) Overview of the LCA industry

7.1687 The Panel undertakes its evaluation of the European Communities' serious prejudice arguments with the foregoing considerations in mind. Before undertaking that evaluation, we consider that it is useful to provide a short overview of key aspects of the LCA industry, in order to provide relevant factual background to our evaluation of the effects of the subsidies.

7.1688 The main participants in the LCA industry are the LCA airframe manufacturers, the airlines that operate LCA, engine manufacturers that supply engines, and leasing companies that purchase LCA from both manufacturers and airlines and lease them out for operation by airlines. Boeing and Airbus are the two major producers of LCA.[3550] The parties agree that the LCA market is presently a duopoly in which both Airbus and Boeing hold a significant share of the market and offer a full line of competitive LCA. Airbus and Boeing each possess a degree of market power, meaning that each manufacturer's decisions regarding the supply and pricing of its products has the ability to influence the pricing of the other, and more generally, the market price for LCA.[3551] Manufacturers of LCA determine both the type and quantity of new LCA produced, although their decisions regarding the type of LCA developed and produced are taken in consultation with major airlines and leasing companies.[3552] The number of LCA ordered and delivered is strictly a function of demand by airlines and leasing companies, as Boeing and Airbus rarely produce speculative LCA.[3553]

7.1689 The customers for new Boeing and Airbus LCA are primarily airlines and leasing companies.[3554] Airlines either purchase LCA outright, finance the purchase of LCA through instruments such as finance leases, or lease the LCA they operate. Airlines can either purchase LCA directly from Boeing or Airbus or acquire used LCA from other airlines or leasing companies. Aircraft leasing

---

[3550] LCA produced by Boeing (including McDonnell Douglas) and Airbus accounted for 90.9 per cent of the world fleet operated as of 31 December 2006; Rod P. Muddle, The Dynamics of the Large Civil Aircraft Industry, 2 March 2007, Exhibit EC-10, para. 16. Other producers of LCA, such as the Russian manufacturer Tupolev, operate only in certain regions and certain specific product categories and do not account for a significant volume of supply.

[3551] The European Communities states that most airlines that operate LCA are Boeing customers, and provides the following figures: of 764 airlines that operate Airbus and/or Boeing aircraft, 645 operate Boeing LCA, 507 operate only Boeing LCA, 119 operate only Airbus LCA; European Communities' non-confidential oral statement at the second meeting with the Panel, para. 96; Airclaims CASE database, Fleet Summary, data query as of 14 may 2007, Exhibit EC-1311.

[3552] Rod P. Muddle, The Dynamics of the Large Civil Aircraft Industry, March 2007, Exhibit EC-10, para 17.

[3553] Rod P. Muddle, The Dynamics of the Large Civil Aircraft Industry, March 2007, Exhibit EC-10, para. 17. Muddle indicates, however, that manufacturers can still influence demand for new aircraft by accelerating or reducing the rate at which airlines replace older, less fuel-efficient aircraft, for example, by offering a fuel-efficient and low priced aircraft.

[3554] A small number of LCA are purchased for corporate or private use.

Report of the Panel

companies are also significant actors in the LCA markets.[3555] Leasing companies operate on both the demand and supply sides of the LCA industry. On the demand side, leasing companies are significant purchasers of LCA, accounting for 17 per cent of orders placed with Boeing and Airbus and approximately 25 per cent of Boeing and Airbus deliveries over the period 2000-2006.[3556] On the supply side, leasing companies offer leased LCA to airlines that may not wish to purchase LCA, thus creating an additional source of supply for airlines and an alternative to the direct purchase of new LCA from Boeing or Airbus and the purchase of used LCA from other airlines. As providers of used leased aircraft, leasing companies are significant actors in the used LCA market, buying used aircraft and leasing them to airlines. Prices obtained from Boeing and Airbus by leasing companies can serve as a form of benchmarking on new aircraft prices.[3557]

7.1690 Engines are the single most expensive component of an LCA, representing between 20 and 30 per cent of its total cost. A choice of engines is available for most LCA models, and LCA customers make their engine choice independently from their negotiations with LCA manufacturers. Engine pricing and other features, when negotiated separately between the LCA customer and engine manufacturers, can determine whether Airbus or Boeing wins a sale from an airline or leasing company customer.[3558] In many cases, neither the airline nor the engine manufacturers disclose the terms of the engine contracts to the airframe manufacturer.[3559]

7.1691 The production of large civil aircraft involves heavy upfront development costs, with a return over a considerably longer period. Aircraft are developed over a period of several years with a view to their being sold over a period of 18 years, on average. The marketing life of an aircraft is largely determined by the life of the technology that defines the model. Once the technology has been superseded, the LCA manufacturer will no longer be able to sell the model without making major capital investments to incorporate the latest

---

[3555] Muddle identifies the following leading leasing companies worldwide : International Leasing Finance Corporation (ILFC) ; GE Commercial Aviation Services (GECAS) ; Singapore Aircraft Leasing Company (SALE) ; Aviation Capital Group ; AerCap ; RBS Aviation Capital ; CIT Group ; Rod P. Muddle, The Dynamics of the Large Civil Aircraft Industry, March 2007, Exhibit EC-10, para. 19.

[3556] Rod P. Muddle, The Dynamics of the Large Civil Aircraft Industry, March 2007, Exhibit EC-10, para. 20. According to Muddle, leasing company sales are especially important for Airbus, with leasing company orders accounting for 20 per cent of Airbus' orders during the period 2000-2006, compared with 14 per cent for Boeing.

[3557] Rod P. Muddle, The Dynamics of the Large Civil Aircraft Industry, March 2007, Exhibit EC-10, para. 26. Muddle notes, however, that prices obtained by leasing companies may not reflect some of the other "non-price" benefits that airlines can receive.

[3558] Rod P. Muddle, The Dynamics of the Large Civil Aircraft Industry, March 2007, Exhibit EC-10, para. 28.

[3559] Rod P. Muddle, The Dynamics of the Large Civil Aircraft Industry, March 2007, Exhibit EC-10, para. 31.

US - Large Civil Aircraft (2nd Complaint)

available technologies.[3560] LCA production is also generally characterized by steep learning curves. [3561] Initial units of a new LCA are produced at a much higher cost than subsequent units will be, once the LCA manufacturer has begun to realize learning curve efficiencies. Learning curve efficiencies are factored into an LCA manufacturer's projected costs at the time of the launch of the new aircraft programme, and manufacturers price initial units of LCA as though they were already at the bottom of the learning curve.[3562] At the time of launch, the LCA manufacturer projects pricing targets for the new aircraft that, over its projected life, must exceed the manufacturer's fully-loaded average production costs by an amount sufficient to justify the investment.[3563]

7.1692 The LCA characteristics demanded by airlines and leasing companies have triggered the development of broadly similar LCA models by Airbus and Boeing. In addition, Airbus and Boeing models are subject to the same rules of physics and economics that largely dictate the design of the aircraft, while operating costs and interior designs of aircraft are similar. Moreover, the costs of manufacture incurred by Airbus and Boeing are increasingly similar and transparent because both manufacturers source material and technology worldwide, often from the same suppliers.[3564]

7.1693 Aircraft acquisitions are not isolated transactions, but rather the key element in an airline's business and strategic plan, and the basis for an airline's commercial success in the marketplace. Thus, every sales campaign involves a unique focus on the needs of the particular airline or leasing company. Such needs, in turn, are informed by the overall business strategy of the airline or leasing company.[3565] In general, the "net flyaway price" of an aircraft consists of the "total aircraft price" less credits and price concessions offered by the LCA manufacturer[3566]; and estimated engine manufacturer discounts and other discounts offered by suppliers of buyer furnished equipment. The "total aircraft

---

[3560] International Trade Resources LLC, Calculating on a Per-Aircraft Basis the Magnitude of the Subsidies Provided to US Large Civil Aircraft, 20 February 2007, Exhibit EC-13, para. 11.

[3561] The learning curve refers to the negative correlation between cumulative output and unit cost: the more aircraft of a given type of LCA produced by a firm, the less it costs to produce the next unit of that aircraft; Luís M. B. Cabral, Impact of Development Subsidies Granted to Boeing, New York University and CEPR, March 2007, Exhibit EC-4, para. 53.

[3562] Jordan and Dorman Report, Exhibit US-3, p. 15.

[3563] United States' first written submission, para. 848.

[3564] Rod P. Muddle, The Dynamics of the Large Civil Aircraft Industry, March 2007, Exhibit EC-10, para. 47.

[3565] Rod P. Muddle, The Dynamics of the Large Civil Aircraft Industry, March 2007, Exhibit EC-10, para. 48; Christian Scherer, Commercial Aspects of the Aircraft Business From the Perspective of a Manufacturer, March 2007, Exhibit EC-11 (BCI), para. 43.

[3566] Concessions provided by the engine manufacturers and suppliers of buyer furnished equipment are negotiated between the customer and the supplier, without the direct involvement of the LCA manufacturer. Pricing offered by engine manufacturers and suppliers of buyer furnished equipment can have a significant impact on the net fly-away price in a manner that is largely unknown to the LCA manufacturers; Christian Scherer, Commercial Aspects of the Aircraft Business From the Perspective of a Manufacturer, March 2007, Exhibit EC-11 (BCI), para. 47.

DSR 2012:III

Report of the Panel

price" in turn, is composed of the basic airframe basic price (catalogue price) plus charges for changes to standard specifications, buyer furnished equipment, supplier furnished equipment and the engine basic list price.

7.1694 In general terms, differences in price, capacity and direct operating cost are the most significant factors that determine the outcome of LCA sales campaigns.[3567] However, the significance of individual factors varies from campaign to campaign, depending on fleet and business plans as well as the strategic goals of the buyers.[3568] Moreover, the value of each factor to an LCA customer may be different than its cost to the LCA manufacturer. During the negotiation phase, customers make extensive technical and economic evaluations of LCA manufacturers' proposals to assess the total cost and anticipated revenue stream (i.e. the overall economic value) presented by a particular proposal. This evaluation involves arriving at an estimate of the present value of costs associated with the acquisition of a new fleet of aircraft (e.g. price, maintenance costs, direct and indirect operating costs, financing, training costs, costs associated with the introduction of new LCA) against the present value of the revenue stream that would be expected to be generated by the proposed fleet. The resultant calculation is the "net present value" (NPV) to the customer of the proposal.[3569] In addition to differences in price, capacity and direct operating cost, various non-price factors generally form part of an overall assessment of the net present value of a particular offer from an LCA manufacturer. Price concessions can offset disadvantages associated with non-price factors. In certain cases, however, offsetting non-price factors through pricing concessions can be very expensive.[3570]

[3567] Rod P. Muddle, The Dynamics of the Large Civil Aircraft Industry, March 2007, Exhibit EC-10, para. 49; Christian Scherer, Commercial Aspects of the Aircraft Business From the Perspective of a Manufacturer, March 2007, Exhibit EC-11 (BCI), para. 43. There is perhaps a difference with respect to purchases by leasing companies. As Scherer notes, unlike airlines, leasing companies own aircraft for financial, rather than operational reasons, and are therefore focussed on price and how that price will relate to leasing rates and profits; Christian Scherer, Commercial Aspects of the Aircraft Business From the Perspective of a Manufacturer, March 2007, Exhibit EC-11 (BCI), para. 36.

[3568] Muddle notes further that the importance of the individual factors also varies between airlines purchasing to satisfy their own demand, leasing companies purchasing to satisfy known demand from particular customers, and leasing companies purchasing to satisfy speculative demand; Rod P. Muddle, The Dynamics of the Large Civil Aircraft Industry, March 2007, Exhibit EC-10, para. 49.

[3569] Christian Scherer, Commercial Aspects of the Aircraft Business From the Perspective of a Manufacturer, March 2007, Exhibit EC-11 (BCI), para. 76. According to Scherer, most disadvantages compared with the proposal of the competing LCA manufacturer can be compensated for by providing additional concessions, subject to profitability constraints. Conversely, every advantage over the competitor's proposal can be used to avoid making additional concessions; Christian Scherer, Commercial Aspects of the Aircraft Business From the Perspective of a Manufacturer, March 2007, Exhibit EC-11 (BCI), paras. 77-78.

[3570] See Rod P. Muddle, The Dynamics of the Large Civil Aircraft Industry, March 2007, Exhibit EC-10, paras. 98-102.

> (vii) European Communities' approach to the nature of the subsidies at issue and their consequent effects on the three products at issue

7.1695 The parties agree that the nature of the subsidies plays an important role in an analysis of whether their effects are any of the forms of serious prejudice alleged in this dispute and both refer to statements of previous WTO panels in support of this proposition. [3571] In *US – Upland Cotton*, the panel stated that "{w}e consider it axiomatic that the nature of the United States subsidies at issue – in terms of their structure, design and operation – is relevant in assessing whether or not they have price suppressing effects."[3572] In *Korea – Commercial Vessels*, the panel stated "{in} conducting this 'but for' analysis, we will certainly be mindful of the nature of the subsidies alleged to be causing price suppression and price depression."[3573] We agree that it is appropriate to consider the nature of a subsidy in order to properly assess its effects.

7.1696 The Panel considers that it is necessary to structure its analysis in a manner that takes into account the fact that, based on the nature of the subsidies at issue, the European Communities makes a distinction as to the effects of the subsidies on Boeing's commercial behaviour[3574] between the 787, on the one hand, and the 737NG and the 777, on the other.

7.1697 With regard to the 787, the European Communities argues that the nature of the subsidies benefiting Boeing's 787 family reveals that these subsidies have *two principal effects* on Boeing's behaviour. On the one hand, the European Communities argues that *the aeronautics R&D subsidies* have had what the European Communities terms "technology effects" in that they "have helped Boeing develop, launch and produce a technologically-advanced 200-300 seat LCA much more quickly than it could have on its own".[3575] On the other hand, the European Communities argues that *all of the subsidies benefiting the 787* have what the European Communities terms "price effects" in that "they provide Boeing with the ability to charge very low prices for such a technologically-advanced LCA".[3576] These price effects arise because "{e}ach of the subsidies either reduces Boeing's marginal unit costs for its 787 family LCA or increases

---

[3571] European Communities' first written submission, para. 1064; United States' first written submission, para. 728.

[3572] Panel Report, *US – Upland Cotton*, para. 7.1289.

[3573] Panel Report, *Korea – Commercial Vessels*, para. 7.616.

[3574] It is important to note that the European Communities generally uses the term "effect" of the subsidies to refer to the alleged *impact of the subsidies on Boeing's commercial behaviour*, not the impact of the subsidies on Airbus's sales and prices.

[3575] European Communities' first written submission, para. 1343. See also, European Communities' first written submission, paras. 1335,1345.

[3576] European Communities' first written submission, para. 1343. See also, European Communities' first written submission, paras. 1340, 1347.

Report of the Panel

Boeing's non-operating cash flow".[3577] The European Communities argues that it is through these technology effects and price effects on Boeing's commercial behaviour that the subsidies cause significant price suppression, significant lost sales, and displacement and impedance suffered by Airbus in the 200-300 seat wide body LCA product market.[3578]

7.1698 With regard to the 737NG and the 777, the European Communities argues that the nature of the subsidies benefiting these two Boeing aircraft reveals that they have *one principal effect* on Boeing's behaviour in that *all of the subsidies benefiting these aircraft* have price effects by providing Boeing with the ability to charge lower prices for these aircraft.[3579] These price effects arise because each of the subsidies either reduces Boeing's marginal unit costs for its 737NG and 777 family LCA or increases Boeing's non-operating cash flow.[3580] The European Communities argues that it is through these price effects on Boeing's behaviour that the subsidies cause significant price suppression, significant lost sales, and displacement and impedance suffered by Airbus in the 100-200 seat single-aisle LCA product market and in the 300-400 seat wide-body LCA product market.[3581]

7.1699 In sum, whereas for all three aircraft at issue the European Communities argues that the subsidies have caused serious prejudice through their impact on Boeing's ability to charge lower prices for its aircraft (price effects), it is only with respect to the 787 that the European Communities argues that certain subsidies at issue also cause serious prejudice through their impact on Boeing's development of technologies (technology effects). The Panel first examines, in subsection (c)(i) below, whether the *aeronautics R&D subsidies* at issue have caused serious prejudice to the interests of the European Communities by reason of their effects on Boeing's development of technologies for the 787. The Panel

---

[3577] European Communities' first written submission, para. 1340.

[3578] European Communities' first written submission, paras. 1334, 1341, 1376 ("In sum, the nature of the US subsidies for the 787, in terms of their structure, design, and operation, helps reveal that their effects have been to: (1) accelerate Boeing's development, launch, production and future delivery of a technologically-advanced 200-300 seat LCA family; and (2) enable Boeing to significantly reduce its sales prices for 787 family LCA. These effects, in turn, cause significant price suppression, significant lost sales, displacement and impedance, and a threat thereof, in the market for the 787 family and competition Airbus LCA.").

[3579] European Communities' first written submission, paras. 1471, 1474, 1565, 1568. See also, European Communities' first written submission, paras. 1476, 1489, 1570 and 1587.

[3580] European Communities' first written submission, paras. 1476, 1570.

[3581] European Communities' first written submission, paras. 1474, 1484 ("In sum, the nature of the US subsidies for the 737NG, in terms of their structure, design, and operation, helps reveal that their effect is to enable Boeing to significantly reduce its sales prices for 737NG family LCA, thereby causing significant price suppression, significant lost sales, displacement and impedance, and a threat thereof, in the market for the 737NG family and competing Airbus LCA."), 1568, 1582 ("In sum, the nature of the US subsidies for the 777, in terms of their structure, design, and operation, helps reveal that their effect is to enable Boeing to significantly reduce its sales prices for 777 family LCA, thereby causing significant price suppression, significant lost sales, and a threat thereof, in the market for the 777 family and competing Airbus LCA.")

1610

DSR 2012:III

US - Large Civil Aircraft (2nd Complaint)

then examines, in subsection (c)(ii), *with respect to all three aircraft at issue*, whether *all of the subsidies* at issue have caused serious prejudice to the interests of the European Communities in that they have had price effects either by reducing Boeing's marginal unit costs for particular aircraft or by increasing Boeing's non-operating cash flow.

7.1700 We recall that we have found that the total amount of subsidies at issue in this dispute is at least \$5.3 billion.[3582] Of that amount, approximately \$2.6 billion relates to the NASA aeronautics R&D subsidies, while \$2.2 billion represents the amount of the FSC/ETI subsidies. Given that these subsidies comprise the vast majority of the total subsidy amount, we consider the effects of these subsidies first. Accordingly, our analysis begins with an evaluation of the effects of the NASA aeronautics R&D subsidies, as part of our consideration of the effects of the aeronautics R&D subsidies more generally, followed by an evaluation of the FSC/ETI subsidies, as part of our consideration of the effects of the tax subsidies that are alleged to operate to reduce Boeing's marginal unit costs of production and sale of individual LCA.

(c)   Evaluation

(i)   Whether the aeronautics R&D subsidies cause serious prejudice to the interests of the European Communities by reason of their effects on Boeing's development of technologies in relation to the 787

7.1701 The Panel recalls that our serious prejudice analysis includes the following measures which we have found to constitute specific subsidies: (i) R&D procurement contracts, assistance instruments and Space Act Agreements with Boeing and McDonnell Douglas that were funded under eight NASA R&D programmes[3583]; and (ii) assistance instruments with Boeing and McDonnell Douglas that were funded under various programmes under the the DOD RDT&E Program.[3584] The Panel has found that not all of the challenged DOD R&D measures constitute specific subsidies. Specifically, the Panel has found that DOD's R&D procurement contracts with Boeing funded under the RDT&E programmes are properly characterized as purchases of services falling outside the scope of Article 1.1(a)(1).[3585] In conducting its analysis of the effects of the

---

[3582] See para. 7.1433 of this Report.

[3583] These programmes are: Advanced Composites Technologies (ACT) Program, Advanced Subsonic Technology (AST) Program, Research and Technology Base (R&T Base) Program, High Speed Research (HSR) Program, Computational Aerosciences Project (CAS) of the High Performance Computing and Communications (HPCC) Program, Aviation Safety Program, Quiet Aircraft Technology (QAT) Program, and Vehicle Systems (VSP) Program.

[3584] As noted in para. 7.1114 of this Report, the European Communities has challenged funding related to "dual use" technologies allegedly provided to Boeing under 13 "general aircraft" programmes, and under 10 "military aircraft" programmes

[3585] See paras. 7.1171 and 7.1187 of this Report.

DSR 2012:III   1611

Report of the Panel

DOD subsidies in accordance with Articles 5 and 6.3 of the SCM Agreement, the Panel is aware of the need to ensure that it considers the effects only of those DOD measures that it has found constitute specific subsidies. The European Communities has, for the most part, presented its serious prejudice arguments regarding the effects of the DOD measures on the basis of the specific DOD "project elements" or programmes under the RDT&E Program, without distinguishing between effects which are attributable to procurement contracts under those programmes and those which are attributable to assistance instruments. While there is evidence on the record linking specific assistance instruments to funding provided through particular RTD&E programmes, there is insufficient evidence of the effects of those assistance instruments as distinct from the effects of the RDT&E programmes (including the effects of procurement contracts funded under those programmes) more generally. However, as noted at paragraph 7.1148 of the Report, the ManTech and DUS&T programmes had the explicit objective of developing "dual use" R&D and were predominantly funded through cooperative agreements or other assistance instruments.[3586] In these circumstances, the Panel considers that it is highly likely that the effects of the ManTech and DUS&T programmes pertain to the effects of assistance instruments funded through those programmes. The Panel is unable to make a similar assumption in relation to the arguments and evidence concerning the effects of the other RDT&E programmes, on the one hand, and the effects of assistance agreements funded under those programmes, on the other. The Panel considers that there is insufficient evidence on the record that those other RDT&E programmes funded predominantly assistance instruments, as opposed to procurement contracts, or a mixture of assistance instruments and procurement contracts. The end result is that the European Communities has not advanced sufficient argument or evidence regarding the effects of assistance instruments funded through RTD&E programmes other than in relation to the ManTech and DUS&T programmes.

7.1702 The European Communities argues that overall, *but for* the aeronautics R&D subsidies, (i) Boeing could not have launched, in April 2004, a 787 family of LCA offering the many operating cost savings and enhancements in passenger comfort that have made it such a commercial success relative to the A330 and Original A350[3587]; and (ii) Boeing could not have contractually bound itself to make significant deliveries of the 787 starting in 2008.[3588] The European

---

[3586] See also United States' response to question 321, para. 22. We note that the United States has identified two procurement contracts that were funded under the ManTech Program; United States' response to question 321, para. 22 at footnote 32. The effects of these procurement contracts have not been taken into account in the Panel's assessment of the effects of assistance instruments funded through the ManTech Program.

[3587] Rather, according to the European Communities, it would have taken Boeing "years longer" as well as much more of its own money to do so; European Communities' first written submission, Annex C, para. 199.

[3588] European Communities' first written submission, Annex C, para. 199.

1612

DSR 2012:III

US - Large Civil Aircraft (2nd Complaint)

Communities considers that the most important of the technical characteristics of the 787 that are "derived from US Government-supported aeronautics R&D subsidies" are its composite fuselage, composite wing and composite manufacturing tools and processes.[3589] In evaluating the merits of these arguments, the Panel will focus primarily on the material pertaining to research conducted by Boeing and McDonnell Douglas under the aeronautics R&D programmes in the field of composites, and the composites technologies applied to the 787, particularly under the ACT, AST and R&T Base programmes, which appear from the evidence to be the most commercially and technologically significant programmes in this regard.

7.1703 The Panel has carefully reviewed the evidence before it regarding the nature of the U.S. federal aeronautics R&D subsidies. The Panel considers that, viewed together with other contextual factors, this evidence supports the argument of the European Communities that these subsidies have had "technology effects" in relation to the 787 and have, through this route of transmission, caused serious prejudice within the meaning of Articles 5 and 6.3 of the SCM Agreement. We explain the basis for that conclusion below.

7.1704 The Panel considers that its analysis of the nature of the U.S. federal aeronautics subsidies at issue needs to be viewed in the context of their overall policy objectives. Numerous statements on record demonstrate that a key objective of these subsidies was the enhancement of the competitiveness and increase of the market share of the U.S. industry, and Boeing in particular, vis-à-vis its international competitors.[3590]

7.1705 For example, NASA's Langley Director has stated:

> "The reason there is a NASA Langley and the other aeronautics centers is to contribute technology to assure the pre-eminence of U.S. aeronautics. When Boeing brings out a flagship product like the 777, that uses as many products of NASA technology as are on this plane, it reaffirms the reason that we exist and is very gratifying to us."[3591]

[3589] European Communities' first written submission, para. 1351. See also, European Communities' first written submission, para. 750, and Annex C, para. 188. The United States refers to composites technology as "the centerpiece of the EC's technology arguments", United States' first written submission, para. 17.

[3590] The Panel recalls that in the context of its analysis of whether the NASA R&D measures at issue constitute purchases of services it has found that a principal purpose of NASA's aeronautics R&D in general, and of the eight aeronautics programmes at issue, is to transfer technology to U.S. industry with a view to improving U.S. competitiveness vis-à-vis foreign competitors.

[3591] Video clip of Langley Director Dr. J.F. Creedon on visit of Boeing 777, Langley Research Center, LV-1998-00023, Exhibit EC-287.

DSR 2012:III

Report of the Panel

7.1706 The U.S. Congressional Budget Office for its part observed:

"The National Aeronautics and Space Administration (NASA) funds the development of technology and systems intended for use in commercial airliners – both subsonic and supersonic – with the explicit objective of preserving the U.S. share of the current and future world airliner market."[3592]

7.1707 More specifically, as regards the ACT Program, a NASA Contractor Report makes the following observations regarding the benefits from NASA funding:

"World dominance in transport aircraft sales by US. industry is threatened by foreign competitors. The lower left corner of Figure 2-1 shows the European consortium, Airbus Industrie, has captured market share at the expense of US manufacturers. Boeing has remained the only US. aircraft manufacturer to meet the Airbus challenge without loss of market share. US. government research funding, such as the NASA ACT program, helps Boeing and other US. aircraft manufacturers to develop advanced technology and remain competitive in world markets.

...

Boeing is the world's largest producer of commercial transport aircraft, maintaining a market share of over 57% for the world and over 80% for the United States. This provides a large benefit to the US. economy. Approximately 75% of Boeing sales are exports, helping to reduce the US. trade deficit. Every $1 billion in US airplane sales creates about 30,000 labor years of work, of which 87% is performed in the US. The Boeing Commercial Airplane Group has spent up to $10 billion a year on goods and services produced by over 5,000 suppliers throughout the United States (see Figure 2-2). Maintenance of the United States aircraft industry's market position is critical for the preservation of high paying skilled jobs, a capable industrial base, and balance of trade."[3593]

7.1708 As regards the AST Program, Wesley L. Harris, NASA Associate Administrator for Aeronautics, stated that "NASA's objective in the Advanced Subsonic Technology (AST) program is to provide U.S. industry with a competitive edge to recapture market share, maintain a strongly positive balance

---

[3592] Reducing the Deficit: Spending and Revenue Options, Congressional Budget Office, March 1997, Exhibit EC-307, p. 152.
[3593] Advanced Technology Composites Fuselage – Program Overview, pp.2-1-2-2, Exhibit EC-330.

1614

DSR 2012:III

US - Large Civil Aircraft (2nd Complaint)

of trade, and increase U.S. jobs."[3594] A NASA contractor report also stated that it evaluates the long-term success of the AST Program in terms of, among other things, "how well it contributes to an increased market-share for U.S. civil aircraft and aircraft component producers".[3595] A study commissioned by NASA of the impact of Integrated Wing Design technologies provides estimates of increases in U.S. manufacturers' sales revenues expected to result from those technologies.[3596] Regarding the R&T Base Program, NASA has stated that this program is "critical to technological pre-eminence in the worldwide aerospace market" and that the goals of this programme are "driven by the need to reduce product costs and capture increased market share".[3597]

Structure and design of the aeronautics
R&D subsidies

7.1709 The aeronautics R&D subsidies are structured as multi-year R&D contracts which are funded through specific aeronautics R&D programmes. The aeronautics R&D programmes have what might be described as overall objectives or purposes, which are sought to be achieved through the attainment of specific technical objectives. The R&D subsidies that comprise the programmes reflect the objectives of the R&D programmes through which they are funded, and to that end, specify their own objectives as well as more specific technical performance goals. The Panel summarizes below evidence regarding the design of the aeronautics R&D programmes at issue. The Panel's review of this evidence shows that NASA consistently and pervasively expresses the objectives of, and motivations behind, its aeronautics R&D programmes in terms of promoting the competitiveness of the U.S. aeronautics industry through technology development leading to superior and lower cost products. The particular areas covered by these R&D programmes appear to have been selected on the basis of their likely contribution toward the commercial development of technologies that were viewed as being of particular strategic importance to the enhancement of the competitiveness of the U.S. industry. Closely related to this, the evidence shows that the R&D was often undertaken at the behest of and in close collaboration with the U.S. industry. While the research performed by Boeing under the NASA R&D programmes was not undertaken directly in the context of the development and production of particular civil aircraft, the NASA

[3594] Statement of Wesley L. Harris, NASA Associate Administrator for Aeronautics, before the House Subcommittee on Technology, Environment, and Aviation, 10 February 1994, Exhibit EC-359, p. 5.
[3595] Eileen Roberts et al., Aviation Systems Analysis Capability Executive Assistant Development, NASA/CR-1999-209119, Logistics Management Institute, March 1999, Exhibit EC-358, p.1-1.
[3596] Abel A. Fernandez, An Impact Analysis of a NASA Aeronautics Research Project: The Integrated Wing Design Project, Exhibit EC-31.
[3597] NASA R&T Base Budget Estimates, FY 2002, Exhibit EC-398, SAT 4.1-4,; NASA R&T Base Budget Estimates, FY 1996, Exhibit EC-398, SAT 4-4.

DSR 2012:III

1615

Report of the Panel

R&D programmes aimed at enhancing Boeing's ability to develop technology for commercial purposes.[3598]

Advanced Composites Technology Program

7.1710 In 1988, NASA launched the ACT Program as a major new programme for composite wing and fuselage primary structures. [3599] The programme was aimed at developing materials, structural mechanics methodology, design concepts and fabrication procedures that offered the potential to make composite structures cost-effective compared with aluminium structures. NASA's ACT Budget Estimates for 1997 described the goal of the ACT Program in the following manner:

> "{T}o increase the competitiveness of the U.S. aeronautics industry by putting the commercial transport manufacturers in a position to expand the application of composites beyond the secondary structures in use today to wings and fuselages by the end of this decade. Industry's resistance to using composites is one of economics. While the current demonstrated level of composites technology can promise improved aircraft performance and lower operating costs through reduced structural weight, it does so with increased manufacturing costs, currently twice the cost of aluminium. The goal of this program is to verify composite structure designs that will have acquisition costs 20-25% less and weigh 30-50% less than an aluminium aircraft sized for the same payload and mission".[3600]

7.1711 Fifteen contracts were awarded by NASA by the first quarter of 1989 to participants that included commercial and military airframe manufacturers (e.g. Boeing, McDonnell Douglas and Lockheed Corporation), materials developers and suppliers, universities and government laboratories.[3601] The ACT Program established primary research teams in the specific technical areas of automated fibre placement, RTM/stitched technologies and textile preforms. Each of these technical areas had a lead airframe contractor: Boeing (Automated Fibre

---

[3598] The Panel emphasizes that because the NASA R&D programmes at issue are clearly linked to industrial and commercial objectives, the R&D programmes at issue do not involve "fundamental research" that until 1 January 2000 was "non-actionable" under the provisions of Article 8 of the SCM Agreement.

[3599] The European Communities identifies NASA's ACT Program, including its continuation through the AST Program and the R&T Base Program as *the most important U.S. government programme* that contributed to Boeing's development of composites technologies for the 787; European Communities' first written submission, Annex C, para. 26. Emphasis added.

[3600] NASA ACT Budget Estimates, FY 1989-FY 1997, Exhibit EC-321, at FY 1997, SAT 4-21.

[3601] John G. Davis, Jr., Overview of the ACT Program, in John G. Davis, Second NASA Advanced Composites Technology Conference, NASA Conference Publication 3154, 4-7 November 1991, Exhibit EC-810, p. 8.

1616　　　　　　　　　　　　　　　　　　　　　　　　　　　DSR 2012:III

US - Large Civil Aircraft (2nd Complaint)

Placement),[3602] McDonnell Douglas (RTM/Stitched)[3603] and Lockheed (Textile preforms).[3604] In addition, various organizations supported generic R&D that was initiated early in the programme.[3605]

7.1712 The contract awarded to Boeing formed the Advanced Technology Composite Aircraft Structures (ATCAS) element of the ACT Program.[3606] The primary objective of ATCAS was "to develop an integrated technology and demonstrate a confidence level that permits the cost- and weight-effective use of advanced composite materials in primary structures of future aircraft with the emphasis on pressurized fuselages".[3607] The contract awarded to Douglas Aircraft Company (subsequently McDonnell Douglas) formed the Innovative Composite Primary Structures (ICAPS) element of the ACT Program.[3608] The overall objective of this contract was to develop and demonstrate technology to manufacture composite primary structures for transport and fighter aircraft representing 1990 technology.[3609]

[3602] Other members of the AFP research team were Hercules, Stanford University, University of Utah, NASA Langley Materials Division and NASA Langley Structural Mechanics Division; John G. Davis, Jr., Overview of the ACT Program, in John G. Davis, Second NASA Advanced Composites Technology Conference, NASA Conference Publication 3154, 4-7 November 1991, Exhibit EC-810, p. 8.

[3603] Other members of the RTM/Stitched research team were Dow Chemical, NASA Langley Materials Division and NASA Langley Structural Mechanics Division; John G. Davis, Jr., Overview of the ACT Program, in John G. Davis, Second NASA Advanced Composites Technology Conference, NASA Conference Publication 3154, 4-7 November 1991, Exhibit EC-810, p. 8.

[3604] Other members of the textile preforms research team were Grumman, Rockwell International, BASF, NASA Langley Materials Division, NASA Langley Structural Mechanics Division and NASA Langley Structural Dynamics Division; John G. Davis, Jr., Overview of the ACT Program, in John G. Davis, Second NASA Advanced Composites Technology Conference, NASA Conference Publication 3154, 4-7 November 1991, Exhibit EC-810, p. 8.

[3605] These organizations were University of Utah, Sikorsky, University of California-Davis, University of Delaware, Northrop, and various NASA divisions; John G. Davis, Jr., Overview of the ACT Program, in John G. Davis, Second NASA Advanced Composites Technology Conference, NASA Conference Publication 3154, 4-7 November 1991, Exhibit EC-810, p. 8.

[3606] In a 1997 NASA Contractor Report, Boeing describes the ATCAS programme as having been initiated in 1989 as NASA Contract NAS1-18889; an integral part of the NASA sponsored ACT initiative. The report then describes Task 2 of Materials Development Omnibus Contract (NASA Contract NAS1-20013) which was awarded in 1993, as extending the ATCAS work. The report states that these two contracts addressed Phases A and B relating to concept selection and technology development. An additional contract (NASA Contract NAS1-20553, referred to as Phase C) was initiated to verify the technology at a large scale; L.B. Ilcewicz et al., Advanced Technology Composite Fuselage—Program Overview, NASA Contractor Report 4734, April 1997, Exhibit EC-808, para. 2-0.

[3607] L.B. Ilcewicz et al., Advanced Technology Composite Fuselage—Program Overview, NASA Contractor Report 4734, April 1997, Exhibit EC-808, para. 4-1.

[3608] The ICAPS Program was implemented as NASA Contract NAS1-18862 with McDonnell Douglas Corporation regarding Innovative Composite Aircraft Primary Structures, 31 March 1989, Exhibit EC-331.

[3609] Specific objectives included (i) development and demonstration of innovative woven/stitched fibre preforms and resin matrix impregnation concepts for transport wing and fuselage structures; (ii) demonstration of advanced tow placement processes for transport fuselage structures; and (iii)

DSR 2012:III

Report of the Panel

7.1713 The ACT Program formally ended in 1995, in the early stages of Phase C of the programme. Phase C of the programme had been envisaged as the designing, building and testing of major components of the airframe and the demonstration the technology readiness for applications in the next generation of subsonic commercial transport aircraft. Although the ACT Program ended in the early stages of Phase C, funding for advanced composites research related to a composite fuselage continued from 1996 to 2000 under the "Materials and Structures" element of NASA's R&T Base Program, while funding for advanced composites research related to composite wings continued from 1996 to 1999 under the "Composites" element of NASA's AST Program.[3610]

Advanced Subsonic Technology Program

7.1714 As explained above, following the termination of the ACT Program in 1995, NASA continued funding the composite wing aspects of that research programme (i.e. ICAPS) through a newly initiated composites element that had been added to the AST Program in 1995.[3611] The element of the AST Program relevant to the European Communities' arguments regarding the aerodynamics and structural design of the 787 is the Integrated Wing Design project (IWD). The element of the AST Program relevant to the European Communities' arguments regarding the "more-electric" architecture of the 787 is the "Fly-by-Light/Power-by-Wire"(FBL/PBW) project and in particular, the Power-by-Wire subtask (PBW).[3612] The element of the AST Program relevant to the European Communities' arguments concerning the noise reduction technologies on the 787 is the noise reduction element of the AST Program.

7.1715 The initial goal of NASA's AST Program was to accelerate the development of key, high-payoff technologies to maintain the performance/cost advantage of U.S. subsonic transport aircraft in the world market, and to ensure their efficient and safe operation in the National Airspace System.[3613] NASA's Budget Estimates for 1998 indicate that one of the indicia of success of the programme is how well NASA contributes to "technology readiness that will

---

demonstration of the use of thermoplastic materials with advanced manufacturing techniques for fighter aircraft fuselage structures.

[3610] NASA ACT Budget Estimates, FY 1989-FY 1997, Exhibit EC-321, at FY 1997, SAT 4-21.

[3611] The FY 1996 NASA AST Budget Estimates state that, in 1996, based on the technology developed in the recently completed Phase B of NASA's ACT Program, the new AST composites element will accelerate the effort to validate the application of composites to commercial transport wings by completing the baseline aircraft and requirements document for composite airframes, candidate materials identification, along with cost and weight trade and sensitivity issues; NASA AST Budget Estimates, FY 1992 - FY 2001, Exhibit EC-357, at FY 1996, SAT 4-42.

[3612] Fly-by-light means replacing the current fly-by-wire control systems with lightweight, highly reliable fiber optical systems that eliminate the concerns of electromagnetic interference associated with fly-by-wire. Power-by-wire involves replacing hydraulics with an electrical power actuation system.

[3613] NASA AST Budget Estimates, FY 1992 - FY 2001, Exhibit EC-357, at FY 1993, RD12-27.

1618

DSR 2012:III

enable U.S. manufacturers to capture a larger share of the world market for civil aircraft".[3614]

7.1716 The objective of the composites element of the AST Program was described as being "to develop and verify at full-scale the composites structures technology, including verification of design concepts, structural materials and manufacturing methods, required for joining composite wings to composite fuselages while saving weight and cost compared to conventional metal commercial transports".[3615] By 1996, the objectives for the composites element of the AST Program were described as follows:

> "The aircraft industry's resistance to using composites is one of economics. While the current demonstrated level of composites technology can promise improved aircraft performance and lower operating costs through reduced structural weight, it does so with increased manufacturing costs, currently twice the cost of aluminium. The goals of the composites element are to reduce the weight of civil transports by 30-50% and their cost by 20-25% compared to today's metallic transports. This translates into a potential 16% direct operating cost-savings to the airlines and increases the competitiveness of the U.S. built transports. In cooperation with industry and the FAA, research is performed to validate the technology for the application of new composites manufacturing techniques, such as through-the-thickness stitching and resin transfer moulding, textile preforms and advanced fiber placement, on transport wings".[3616]

7.1717 NASA described the goals of the IWD project in the following manner:

> "Current approaches to the aerodynamic design of commercial transport rely on methods that develop the design of various wing components independently, which results in an aerodynamic design cycle that is both long and expensive. New design methodology is being developed that treats the wing aerodynamic technologies and components in an integrated manner. To accomplish this, research is being conducted in test/measurement techniques and the aerodynamic disciplines of high-lift,

---

[3614] NASA AST Budget Estimates, FY 1992 - FY 2001, Exhibit EC-357, at FY 1998, SAT 4.1-30.

[3615] NASA AST Budget Estimates, FY 1992 - FY 2001, Exhibit EC-357, at FY 1995, SAT 4-33.

[3616] NASA AST Budget Estimates, FY 1992 - FY 2001, Exhibit EC-357, at FY 1996, SAT 4-38. In 1997, this objective was modified to recognize industry's concern not just with the comparative costs of composites, but also the robustness and reparability of composites. In addition, the weight and cost reduction targets were modified as follows: reduce the weight of civil transports by 10-30 per cent and their cost by 10-20 per cent, translating into a potential five per cent direct operating cost-savings to the airlines; NASA AST Budget Estimates, FY 1992 - FY 2001, Exhibit EC-357, at FY 1997, SAT 4-37.

DSR 2012:III

Report of the Panel

propulsion/airframe integration, wing design and laminar flow control. New concepts, design methodologies, model fabrication and test techniques are being developed to provide industry an integrated capability to achieve increased aircraft performance at lower cost. In addition, the new methodologies will be integrated into a design and testing process that reduces the aerodynamic design cycle time by 25%."[3617]

Further, in 1997, NASA stated that the integrated design and test procedures would:

"{P}rovide an overall reduction in the total aircraft development time of one year compared to an established 1995 baseline product development cycle time. In addition, the new design and test procedures will be used to deliver validated, highly efficient wing designs for cruise and low-speed operation which include the effects of propulsion system integration. This will yield a 4-per cent reduction in Total Airplane Operation Costs (TAROC) relative to established 1995 baseline technology levels."[3618]

7.1718 The FBL/PBW subtask of NASA's AST Program aimed to develop a more-electric systems architecture for civil aircraft. More specifically, it aimed "to develop and demonstrate the technology for a more-electric secondary power system and to provide enough confidence in this technology through testing that the airline industry will begin to transfer this technology into the civil fleet".[3619] NASA AST Budget Estimates indicate that the general goal of the FBL/PBW subtask of the AST Program was to provide lightweight, highly reliable, electromagnetically immune control and power management systems for advanced subsonic civil transport aircraft.[3620]

7.1719 The noise reduction element of the AST Program was a focused technology programme for developing noise reduction technologies for the U.S. commercial aircraft industry to enhance its competitiveness to meet national and international environmental requirements and to facilitate market growth.[3621] The noise reduction element was designed to develop noise reduction technology for source noise reduction, nacelle aeroacoustics, engine/airframe integration, interior noise, and flight procedures to reduce airport community noise, while maintaining high efficiency via systematic development and validation of noise reduction technology.[3622]

[3617] NASA AST Budget Estimates, FY 1992 - FY 2001, Exhibit EC-357, at FY 1996, SAT 4-36.

[3618] NASA AST Budget Estimates, FY 1992 - FY 2001, Exhibit EC-357, at FY 1997, SAT 4-36.

[3619] Power-by-Wire Development and Demonstration for Subsonic Civil Transport, Exhibit EC-366; NASA AST Budget Estimates, FY 1992 - FY 2001, Exhibit EC-357, at FY 1994, RD 9-36.

[3620] NASA AST Budget Estimates, FY 1992 – FY 2001, Exhibit EC-357, at FY 1995, SAT 4-29.

[3621] NASA Memorandum to Research and Focused Branch, at 4, Exhibit EC-365.

[3622] NASA AST Budget Estimates, FY 1992 - FY 2001, Exhibit EC-357, at FY 1996, SAT-4-36.

US - Large Civil Aircraft (2nd Complaint)

7.1720 The NASA AST Budget Estimates for 1998 also note that, with competition from foreign competitors greatly increasing, technology is "critically needed to help preserve the U.S. aeronautics industry market share, jobs and balance of trade".[3623]

7.1721 The AST Program was terminated in 1999 in order to focus resources on high priority national goals like aircraft engine emissions and airport crowding.[3624] The 2000 and 2001 Budget Estimates indicate that, under the AST Program, aggressive technology transition plans were pursued in order to mitigate the significant risk to successful technology transfer to industry as a result of early termination of the programme.[3625]

Research & Technology Base Program

7.1722 As of 1996, funding for work on composite fuselage structures that had previously been allocated to the ACT Program continued under the "Materials and Structures" element of the R&T Base Program (subsequently to become the "Airframe Systems Program" when the R&T Base Program was reorganized in 1997).

7.1723 The element of the R&T Base Program relevant to the European Communities' arguments concerning the aerodynamics and structural design of the 787 is the "aerodynamics research and technology programme". This component of the R&T Base Program was formed in 1992.[3626] The R&T Base Program was reorganized in 1997, after which aerodynamics research was performed across more than one of the components of the programme.[3627]

7.1724 The element of the R&T Base Program relevant to the European Communities' arguments concerning the health management systems on the 787 was the "flight systems research and technology programme".

7.1725 The goal of NASA's R&T Base Program is described by NASA as follows:

> "{T}o serve as the vital foundation of expertise and facilities that consistently meets a wide range of aeronautical and technology challenges for the nation. The program is intended to provide a high-technology, diverse-discipline environment that enables the

---

[3623] NASA AST Budget Estimates, FY 1992 - FY 2001, Exhibit EC-357, at FY 1998, SAT 4.1-30.

[3624] NASA AST Budget Estimates, FY 1992 – FY 2001, at FY 2001, Exhibit EC-357.

[3625] NASA AST Budget Estimates, FY 1992 – FY 2001, Exhibit EC-357, at FY 2000, at FY 2001, SAT 4.1-36.

[3626] NASA R&T Base Budget Estimates, FY 1991 – FY 2004, at FY 1992, Exhibit EC-398, RD 12-3.

[3627] See Dominik Wacht, an Analysis of Selected NASA Research Programs and Their Impact on boeing's Civil Aircraft Programs, November 2006, Exhibit EC-15, p. 126, in which Wacht discusses the programme achievements by aeronautical discipline rather than by programme classification, due to the change in the structure of the programme.

DSR 2012:III

1621

Report of the Panel

development of new, even revolutionary, aerospace concepts and methodologies for applications in industry."[3628]

7.1726 NASA's R&T Base Budget Estimates for 1997 contain the following statement as a strategy for achieving its goals:

"Today, the U.S. leadership position in aeronautics is being seriously challenged by aggressive international competition. Future U.S. competitiveness is dependent upon sustained NASA advances in aeronautics. Critical elements of NASA's contribution to the aviation industry are the flow of new ideas and concepts, the ability to react quickly to unanticipated technical challenges, and the fundamental knowledge produced by the R&T Base."[3629]

7.1727 The objectives of the Materials and Structures element of the R&T Base Program included the development of structures and materials technologies for increasing efficiency, reducing the cost of the next generation of aircraft and increasing the competitiveness of the next generation of aircraft by making available advanced materials for primary airframe and engine structures.[3630] The objective of the Aerodynamics Research and Technology element of the R&T Base Program was to provide new, validated technology applicable to future U.S. military and civil aircraft from subsonic to hypersonic speeds.[3631]

High Speed Research Program

7.1728 NASA's HSR Program was a focused technology development programme intended to enable development of a high-speed (i.e. supersonic) civil transport ("HSCT").[3632] The programme proceeded in two phases, with Phase I commencing in 1990 and Phase II commencing in 1994.[3633] The object of Phase I was to define "HSCT environmental compatibility requirements in the areas of atmospheric effects and community noise and sonic boom, and...establish{ing} a technology foundation to meet these requirements".[3634] The objective of the HSR Program was expressed at the beginning of Phase I as follows :

[3628] NASA R&T Base Budget Estimates, FY 1991 – FY 2004, Exhibit EC-398, at FY 1999, SAT 4.1.2.

[3629] NASA R&T Base Budget Estimates, FY 1991 – FY 2004, Exhibit EC-398, at FY 1997, SAT 4-5. See also, NASA R&T Base Budget Estimates, FY 1991 – FY 2004, Exhibit EC-398, at FY 1998, SAT 4.1-3.

[3630] NASA R&T Base Budget Estimates, FY 1991 – FY 2004, Exhibit EC-398, at FY 1995, SAT 4.7.

[3631] NASA R&T Base Budget Estimates, FY 1991 – FY 2004, Exhibit EC-398, at FY 1995, SAT 4.5.

[3632] "US Supersonic Commercial Aircraft, Assessing NASAs High Speed Research Program", Exhibit EC-319, p. 1.

[3633] NASA HSR Budget Estimates, FY 1991 – FY 2001, Exhibit EC-343, at FY 1994, RD 9-31, and RD 9-33.

[3634] NASA HSR Budget Estimates, FY 1991 – FY 2001, Exhibit EC-343, at FY 1994, RD 9-31.

1622

DSR 2012:III

US - Large Civil Aircraft (2nd Complaint)

"Studies have indicated that, under certain economic conditions with sufficient technology development, future high-speed aircraft could be economically competitive with long-haul subsonic aircraft. Currently, however, critical environmental concerns about atmospheric impact, airport noise, and sonic boom present powerful disincentives to the private sector to pursue such research and technology. The high-speed research program will address the resolution of these barrier environmental issues and develop the basis for evaluating technology advances that can provide the necessary environmental compatibility."[3635]

7.1729 Phase II of the programme was directed at "addressing essential technologies needed by the U.S. aeronautics industry in order to make informed decisions regarding future HSCT development and production".[3636] At the beginning of Phase II, the goal of the HSR Program was expressed as:

"Industry studies…have identified a substantial market for a future high-speed civil transport (HSCT) aircraft to meet the rapidly growing long-haul market…While current technology is insufficient, the studies further indicate that an environmentally compatible and economically competitive HSCT could reach fruition through aggressive technology development and application."[3637]

7.1730 Boeing and McDonnell Douglas were the primary airframe contractors under the HSR Program, with this area of research commencing in Phase II. Although Phase II of the HSR Program was originally planned as an eight year project, the programme was cancelled at the end of 1999. NASA explained this decision in its Budget Estimates:

"In the early 1990's, studies indicated that an environmentally compatible and economically competitive HSCT could be possible through aggressive technology development. Since then, NASA concentrated its investments in the pre-competitive, high-risk technologies. While NASA has continued to be successful and is on track to meet the original program goals, recent market analyses and estimated industry development costs of $15 to $18 billion have made the HSCT considerably less attractive to NASA's industry partners. Cost of development in this amount puts the aircraft industry at significant financial risk. Current analyses indicate that further significant investments in technology development are required to ensure an economically viable HSCT.

[3635] NASA HSR Budget Estimates, FY 1991 – FY 2001, Exhibit EC-343, at FY 1991, RD 12-35.
[3636] NASA HSR Budget Estimates, FY 1991 – FY 2001, Exhibit EC-343, at FY 1994, RD 9-33.
[3637] NASA HSR Budget Estimates, FY 1991 – FY 2001, Exhibit EC-343, at FY 1994, RD 9-31.

DSR 2012:III

Report of the Panel

Consequently, the cost of development has led the major aircraft manufacturer to the conclusion that the introduction of an HSCT cannot reasonably occur prior to the year 2020. For these reasons, industry has reduced their commitment to this area and has scaled back their investments. Given other pressing needs in the Agency in general, and aeronautics in particular, the HSR program will be concluded by the end of FY 1999."[3638]

Computational Aerosciences Project of the High Performance Computing and Communications Program

7.1731 The HPCC Program was designed as a multi-agency effort, with the involvement of all major agencies interested in high speed computing and communications, including NASA, the Department of Energy, the National Science Foundation, the Defense Advanced Research Projects Agency, the Department of Commerce, the National Institutes of Health and the Environmental Protection Agency.[3639] The 1992 Budget Estimates for the HPCC Program describe the goal of NASA's portion of the HPCC as:

"{T}o accelerate the development and application of high-performance computing technologies to meet NASA's science and engineering requirements."[3640]

7.1732 Further, a HPCC fact sheet produced by NASA claims that the goal of the HPCC Program was to:

"{F}oster the development of high-risk, high-payoff systems and applications that will most benefit America...to increase the speed of change in research areas that support NASA's aeronautics, Earth and space missions."[3641]

7.1733 The HPCC Program consisted of four components, one of which was the computational aerosciences project ("CAS"), the component most relevant to the aeronautics industry.[3642] The aim of the CAS project has been described variously as "to significantly shorten the design cycle time for advanced

---

[3638] NASA HSR Budget Estimates, FY 1991 – FY 2001, Exhibit EC-343, at FY 2000, SAT 4.1-29.

[3639] NASA HPCC Budget Estimates, FY 1992 – FY 2003, Exhibit EC-373, at FY 1992, Budget RD 2-12.

[3640] *Ibid.*

[3641] The National Aeroautics and Space Administration's (NASA) High Performance Computing and Communications (HPCC) Program, Exhibit EC-372, at p. 1.

[3642] Dominik Wacht, An Analysis of Selected NASA Research Programs and Their Impact on Boeing's Civil Aircraft Programs, November 2006, Exhibit EC-15, at page 122. The other components of HPCC were the Earth and Space Sciences project, the Information Infrastructure and Technology and Applications component, and the Remote Exploration and Experimentation project; The National Aeroautics and Space Administration's (NASA) High Performance Computing and Communications (HPCC) Program, Exhibit EC-372.

1624

US - Large Civil Aircraft (2nd Complaint)

aerospace products such as future high-speed civil transports"[3643] and to "accelerate the development, availability and use of high-performance computing technology by the U.S. aerospace industry, and to hasten the emergence of a viable commercial market for hardware and software vendors to exploit this lead".[3644] Further, according to the HPCC Budget estimates:

> "CAS targets advances in aeroscience algorithms and applications, system software and machinery that will enable more than 1000-fold increases in system performance early in the twenty-first century. These computational capabilities will be sufficiently characterized such that they can be rapidly integrated into economical design and development processes for use by the U.S. industry. Although CAS does not develop production computing systems, CAS technology and the characterization of existing hardware and software will enable the development of full-scale systems by industry and will make commercial ventures into this area more attractive." [3645]

7.1734 The HPCC fact sheet provides:

> "The U.S. aerospace industry can effectively respond to increased international competition only by producing across-the-board better quality products at affordable prices. High performance computing capability is a key to the creation of a competitive advantage, by reducing product cost and design cycle times; its introduction into the design process is, however, a risk to a commercial company that NASA can help mitigate by performing this research. The CAS project catalyzes these developments in aerospace computing, while at the same time pointing out the future way to aerospace markets for domestic computer manufacturers." [3646]

Quiet Aircraft Technology and Vehicle Systems Programs

7.1735 The QAT Program built upon the noise reduction element of the AST Program.[3647] QAT, along with its predecessor noise reduction element of the

---

[3643] NASA HPCC Budget Estimates, FY 1992 – FY 2003, Exhibit EC-373, at FY 1996, SAT 4-18.
[3644] The National Aeroautics and Space Administration's (NASA) High Performance Computing and Communications (HPCC) Program, Exhibit EC-372, p. 3.
[3645] NASA HPCC Budget Estimates, FY 1992 – FY 2003, Exhibit EC-373, at FY 2000, SAT 4.1-24.
[3646] The National Aeroautics and Space Administration's (NASA) High Performance Computing and Communications (HPCC) Program, Exhibit EC-372, at p. 3.
[3647] NASA QAT Budget Estimates, FY 2001-FY 2007, Exhibit EC-384, at FY 2002, SAT 4.1-75. Beginning with its FY 2003 Budget Estimates, NASA considered the QAT Program to be a component of the Vehicle Systems Program; however, it provided a separate line item for the QAT Program through its FY 2005 Budget Estimates. The European Communities considers the QAT

DSR 2012:III

1625

Report of the Panel

AST Program, focused on "developing noise reduction technology for the US commercial aircraft industry to enhance its competitiveness to meet national and international environmental requirements and to facilitate market growth".[3648]

7.1736 Beginning in 2003, NASA classified the QAT Program as a component of the Vehicle Systems Program. The VSP Program is focused on the development of breakthrough technologies for future aircraft and air vehicles. One of the stated justifications for the VSP Program is as follows:

> "U.S. competitors are targeting aviation leadership as a stated strategic goal. Without careful planning and investment in new technologies, near-term gridlock, constrained mobility, unrealized economic growth, and the continued erosion of U.S. aviation leadership could result."[3649]

Aviation Safety Program

7.1737 The Aviation Safety Program commenced in 2000 with the goal of developing and demonstrating technologies that contribute to a reduction in aviation and accident fatality rates by a factor of five by the year 2007, compared with the 1994 – 1996 average.[3650] Under the Aviation Safety Program, NASA conducts high-payoff research that builds upon and advances the agency's safety-related research capabilities. In particular, the research conducted under this programme encompasses (i) foundational science and discipline-centric research; (ii) multidisciplinary, coupled effects, and component-based research; (iii) sub-system or multidisciplinary integration; and (iv) system level design.[3651]

Industrial Preparedness/Manufacturing Technology Program

7.1738 The DOD ManTech Program is a corporate Air Force programme that establishes and demonstrates advances in manufacturing process technologies, manufacturing engineering systems and industrial practices, and transitions these advancements into weapons systems design, development, acquisition and/or sustainment.[3652] The Air Force ManTech major programme tenets are described as: "improvement of manufacturing processes and technologies; collaboration

---

Program as a separate programme through FY 2005, and excludes figures for the QAT Program accordingly in its analysis of the non-engine LCA components of the Vehicle Systems Program.

[3648] NASA Memorandum to Research and Focused Branch, Exhibit EC-365, at 4.

[3649] NASA Vehicle Systems Budget Estimates, FY 2003 – FY 2007, Exhibit EC-396, at FY 2003, SAT 4-23.

[3650] NASA Aviation Safety Budget Estimates, FY 2000 – FY 2007, Exhibit EC-382, at FY 2000, SAT 4.1-49.

[3651] NASA Aviation Safety Budget Estimates, FY 2000 – FY 2007, Exhibit EC-382, at FY 2007, SAE ARMD 2-7.

[3652] Air Force Industrial Preparedness/Manufacturing Technology Budgets for FY 1993, Exhibit EC-431.

with Government program offices, industry, and academia; investments in technologies beyond reasonable risk level for industry alone; cost-sharing, multiple system/customer applications; potential for significant return on investment; and customer commitment to implement."[3653] The ManTech Program provides cost reduction processes and practices and new manufacturing capabilities applicable to existing as well as new weapon systems under development. The ManTech Program "strives to make superior mission enabling technologies an affordable life cycle reality by expanding access to a capable, responsible, multi-use industrial base with efficiencies comparable to world class enterprises."[3654]

Dual-Use Science and Technology Program

7.1739 DOD Budgets for the DUS&T Program described the programme in the following way:

> "This program allows the Air Force to leverage industry investments in advanced technologies that are mutually advantageous to both the Air Force and industry. One of the program's objectives is to establish a tool for the Air Force to stimulate the development of dual-use technologies that will provide greater access to commercial technologies, and will result in affordable defense systems that maintain battlefield superiority. A key component of the program is the cost sharing requirement from both industry and the Air Force, which affirms commitment to the development effort. Specific projects are determined through annual competitive solicitation(s). A second objective is to use FY 1997 Defense Authorization Act Section 804, Other Transactions Authority, as part of the Dual Use S&T program to educate the Air Force S&T workforce in non-traditional or commercial contracting practices. Technology development areas considered include advanced materials and manufacturing, affordable sensors, advanced propulsion, power and fuel efficiency, information and communications systems, and weapons systems sustainment."[3655]

7.1740 In the light of the weight of the evidence linking the NASA R&D programmes to competitive advantages for the U.S. aeronautics industry, coupled with the amounts involved and period of time over which the assistance

---

[3653] *Ibid.*

[3654] Air Force Industrial Preparedness/Manufacturing Technology Budgets for FY 1993, FY 1996-FY 2007 (PE# 0708011F for FY 1993, FY 1997-FY 2007; PE# 0603771F for FY 1996), Exhibit EC-431.

[3655] Dual Use Science & Technology Budgets for FY 2000-FY 2007 (PE# 0602805F), Exhibit EC-424.

Report of the Panel

was provided, it is very difficult for the Panel to envisage how the aeronautics R&D subsidies to Boeing could *not* have had a meaningful effect on its competitive position in relation to Airbus. The Panel does not consider that it is very realistic to believe that the United States Government would have provided aeronautics R&D subsidies of the magnitude received by Boeing (and McDonnell Douglas) between 1989 and 2006 without those subsidies contributing in a genuine and substantial way to improving Boeing's competitiveness. The objectives of DOD's ManTech and DUS&T programmes are not specifically expressed as being to provide a competitive advantage to the U.S. aeronautics industry. Rather, these programmes have the explicit objective of developing "dual-use" R&D. To that end, they envisage collaboration with industry in developing technologies, including cost reduction processes and practices that have application in the civil sector. In our view, the objectives of these DOD RDT&E programmes suggest that subsidies funded under those programmes contribute to providing Boeing with competitive advantages. Nevertheless, the Panel's conclusion that the aeronautics R&D subsidies have had "technology effects" in relation to the 787 does not rest solely, or even primarily, on the general considerations set out in the preceding paragraphs regarding the structure and design of the R&D programmes at issue. The Panel has also undertaken a detailed examination of the actual operation of the aeronautics R&D subsidies.

Operation of the aeronautics R&D
subsidies

7.1741 As we have already concluded in the context of our analysis of whether the aeronautics R&D subsidies at issue constitute purchases of services, the evidence relating to NASA aeronautics R&D indicates that the work that Boeing performed under its aeronautics R&D contracts and agreements with NASA was principally for its own benefit or use, rather than for the benefit or use of the United States Government (or unrelated third parties).[3656] The aeronautics R&D conducted under the ManTech and DUS&T programmes was funded through cooperative agreements or other cost-shared arrangements and was directed to the development of "dual use" R&D.[3657]

7.1742 We do not consider that the NASA R&D subsidies were directed to general aeronautics research or to research of incidental importance to the development of a product. Had it been so directed, it may be reasonable to doubt whether the subsidies could be considered to have made an integral and enduring contribution to the development of a product. On the contrary, the NASA R&D subsidies the subject of our analysis are precisely focused on those areas which, from a commercial perspective, are considered to be the most crucial to the LCA industry, in the sense that they carry the greatest prospect of creating significant

---

[3656] See para. 7.981 of this Report.
[3657] See para. 7.1148 of this Report.

1628

DSR 2012:III

competitive advantage. These are technologies that promise airline customers lower direct operating costs and those that reduce the time to market.

7.1743 As McDonnell Douglas engineers explained to participants at a NASA/DOD Advanced Composites Technology Conference, "the measure of merit for our technology is DOC {direct operating cost}... It is apparent that a technology which could reduce the cost of the total aircraft and also reduce the weight would have a marked advantage over a technology that saved weight but increased cost by the same percentage."[3658] In the context of Boeing's work under the ACT Program, a Boeing engineer explained, "{t}he biggest thing we need to do is to reduce manufacturing costs. Now we have NASA adhering to the idea that they need to help us with these costs, and not just with the technology itself."[3659] This engineer described the focus of Boeing's work under the ACT Program in the following manner:

> "The main thing we're after is manufacturing productivity and cutting costs, as well as design concepts that produce advantages from a maintenance stand-point. They should also be lightweight, have increased fatigue resistance and better resistance to corrosion .... This is the only way of getting the use of graphite {carbonfibre composite} to be competitive, and has the potential to give operators a drop in direct operating costs of around 9%."[3660]

7.1744 In addition to focussing on technologies that offer lower costs, both to the airframe manufacturer as well as airlines, the research funded under the NASA R&D programmes was also directed towards technologies that reduce the time to market, for example, by reducing development and production cycles. In describing the goals of the IWD project element of the AST Program, NASA said:

> "Currently, the U.S. commercial transport aircraft manufacturing industry is focused on reduced costs and improved time to market through reduced product development cycle time. In cooperation with U.S. industry, NASA is developing efficient, integrated design and test procedures focused on streamlined aerodynamic design cycle times reduced by 50%. This will provide an overall reduction in the total aircraft development time of one year

---

[3658] Mark J. Shuart, Sixth NASA/DOD Advanced Composites Technology Conference, NASA Conference Publication 3294, Vol. I, Part 1, June 1996, Exhibit EC-279, p. 7.

[3659] Guy Norris, "Boeing homes in on carbon-composite production costs," Flight International, 6 September 1995, Exhibit EC-335, quoting Boeing's director of aircraft-structures engineering, Jack McGuire.

[3660] *Ibid.*

Report of the Panel

compared to an established 1995 baseline product development cycle time."[3661]

7.1745 In short, the aeronautics R&D subsidies are focused on particular types of technologies; namely, those that industry considers to be of the greatest potential commercial benefit. Indeed, the focus of the research under the aeronautics R&D programmes on areas of primary strategic importance to the U.S. civil aircraft industry is hardly surprising given that the definition of the scope and programme of research was arrived at in collaboration with industry. For example, NASA reported that during a series of meetings with aviation industry CEOs in late 1996, it was agreed that the dramatic reduction of airplane acquisition cost was a high-priority need. In order to address this need, NASA refocused the IWD, Propulsion and Composite Wing elements of the AST Program "to satisfy the early milestones of a more revolutionary technology to satisfy this goal."[3662]

7.1746 The aeronautics R&D subsidies not only operated as collaborative research projects with and for Boeing, but also complemented Boeing's internal product development efforts. This complementarity between the research that Boeing performed pursuant to the aeronautics R&D subsidies and its own internal R&D efforts is apparent from the length of the research and development cycle in the LCA industry and the timing of Boeing's product development, as well as from the extensive breadth and depth of technologies that are required to produce a superior aircraft and Boeing's collaboration with NASA in specifying and planning the research tasks that it would undertake for NASA and the technical performance goals of the particular R&D subsidies. For example, in a 1992 Boeing conference paper discussing the critical path to development of a composite fuselage that was originally envisaged under the ATCAS element of the ACT Program, the author states that the combined results of the three phases of the ACT Program (originally planned to run from 1989 to 2002), "if combined with Boeing internally funded efforts (e.g. other fuselage section, material and process standards, design manuals, and structural allowables), would prepare Boeing for commitment to a composite fuselage application" by 2002 – 2003.[3663] Indeed, the research that Boeing conducted for NASA on the technologies in question mostly occurred between 1989 and early 2000. Boeing was working on developing a predominantly composite, high-speed aircraft (the Sonic Cruiser) before it shifted its focus in 2000 - 2001 to development of the 7E7/787.[3664] Boeing nevertheless acknowledges that it

---

[3661] NASA AST Budget Estimates, FY 1992 – FY 2001, Exhibit EC-357, at FY 1997, SAT 4-36.

[3662] NASA AST Budget Estimates, FY 1992 – FY 2001, Exhibit EC-357, at FY 1998, SAT 4.1-30. See also, FY 1999, SAT 4.1-36.

[3663] See Larry B. Ilcewicz, "Advanced Composite Fuselage Technology" Third NASA Advanced Composites Technology Conference, NASA CP-3178 Vol 1, 1992, Exhibit EC-1338, at 110.

[3664] United States' second written submission, para. 922; comments on the European Communities' response to question 87, para. 320; Boeing 2002 Annual Report, p. 18, Exhibit US-1230.

1630   DSR 2012:III

adapted the technologies being considered for the Sonic Cruiser for the 7E7/787.[3665]

7.1747 Another important aspect of the operation of the aeronautics R&D subsidies is their role in reducing Boeing's R&D risk. According to NASA, there are large disincentives for private sector investment in long-term, high risk aeronautical R&T. NASA considers that these disincentives stem from the inability of individual companies to fully capture the benefits of these research efforts, as well as the length of the aircraft research and development cycle and investment recoupment period, and the extensive breadth and depth of technologies required to produce a superior aircraft.[3666] As explained in a NASA publication:

> "As aeronautical technology became more complex and expensive, it was also more difficult for individual companies to shoulder the entire financial burden for researching and developing new technology and products by themselves ... For a manufacturer to be willing to invest the money into a new technology, it had to have short-term, concrete payoffs. Industry did not have the capability or incentive to pursue long term or high-risk projects, or research areas with uncertain benefits."[3667]

7.1748 The research conducted under the NASA R&D subsidies occurs through a gradual, iterative process in which failures and abandonment of further development of particular technologies serve as building blocks for newer technologies. In other words, even unsuccessful research generates important knowledge and experience that is applied to subsequent technology developments. This process leads to a gradual reduction of risk as, through a process of trial and error, development efforts are progressively focused on the most promising technologies. NASA introduced a system to categorize technologies according to their level of maturity ("technology readiness level" or TRL), ranging from the highest risk, lowest maturity technology (TRL 1), to the lowest risk, highest maturity technology (TRL 9). NASA's research efforts focus on the development of higher risk technologies up to TRL 6 (prototype demonstration). A 1999 NASA study of the average time taken for technologies to mature from initial concept to marketable product based on NASA's defined TRLs found that, with respect to the airframe technologies selected as part of the study, the average time from TRL 1 to TRL 6 was 11.3 years (with a standard deviation of 3.9), while the average time from TRL 1 to TRL 9 was 16.5 years

---

[3665] Bair Affidavit, Exhibit US-7, para. 10; see also, Boeing 2002 Annual Report, p. 18, Exhibit US-1230.
[3666] NASA R&T Base Budget Estimates, at FY 1997, SAT4.5; at FY 1999, SAT 4.1.3, Exhibit EC-398.
[3667] Airborne Trailblazer, Exhibit EC-288, p. 2.

Report of the Panel

(with a standard deviation of 4.2). [3668] While we do not mean to suggest that it would have taken Boeing as much as 11 years longer to develop the 787 in the absence of the aeronautics R&D subsidies, there is clearly evidence that the development of higher risk technologies up to TRL 6 results in an acceleration of the overall technology development process for an airframe manufacturer like Boeing and would therefore facilitate an earlier product launch than would otherwise have been possible. [3669]

7.1749 The Panel's analysis of the operation of the R&D subsidies has also included a careful review of evidence presented by the parties concerning the technology concepts that Boeing and McDonnell Douglas studied pursuant to the NASA R&D subsidies, on the one hand, and the technologies that are being applied to the 787, on the other. The United States has sought to emphasize the differences between the two. [3670] The European Communities emphasizes the continuities. Appendix VII.F.1 to this Report sets forth a description of the particular technology areas and the parties' arguments pertaining to the technologies developed under the aeronautics R&D programmes and those applied to the 787.

7.1750 The Panel is aware that it is required to undertake an objective assessment of the matter, based on the arguments and evidence presented. In reviewing the parties' arguments and weighing the evidence, the Panel has come to the general conclusion that to focus on the differences between various technologies which may exist at particular points in time would artificially and inaccurately obscure the important links that exist between them. One such link is the fact that the evidence before us is consistent with the technologies properly being viewed essentially as efforts directed to solving enduring technological problems; for example, how to construct a composite barrel fuselage and composite wing in a way that not only reduces the weight of the aircraft but also

---

[3668] Deborah J. Peisen et al., Case Studies: Time Required to Mature Aeronautic Technologies to Operational Readiness, SAIC and GRA, Inc., November 1999, Exhibit EC-795, at p. 11. The study was based on 18 civil aeronautics products from the major aeronautic technology divisions of airframes, propulsion, flight systems and ground systems. The study found that there is considerable variability in the time it takes for technologies to mature, with average maturation times varying by technology type, by the technology's primary benefit or goal, and to a lesser extent, by the need for additional technologies or NASA testing for the successful maturation of the technology. The average for the flight systems technologies selected as part of the study was 21.6 years (with a standard deviation of 15.3) to progress from TRL 1 to TRL 9, and 8.3 years (standard deviation 6.9) from TRL 1 to TRL6.

[3669] Indeed, we recall that the initial goal of NASA's AST Program was to *accelerate the development of key, high-payoff technologies* to maintain the performance/cost advantage of U.S. subsonic transport aircraft in the world market, and to ensure their efficient and safe operation in the National Airspace System; NASA AST Budget Estimates, FY 1992 – FY 2001, Exhibit EC-357, at FY 1993, RD12-27. Emphasis added.

[3670] Affidavit of Alan Miller, Exhibit US-1258, Affidavit of Michael Bair, Exhibit US-7. The United States refers to statements by various Boeing engineers as "affidavits". The Panel's use of the titles assigned to these statements by the United States does not imply that the Panel considers these statements to be affidavits.

1632   DSR 2012:III

US - Large Civil Aircraft (2nd Complaint)

its total cost. Another is that the evidence before us is consistent with a pattern whereby the technology concepts studied under the NASA R&D subsidies and the technologies applied to the 787 are essentially part of the same process in which solutions to technological problems are developed (through a collective exercise of progressive learning through trial and error involving largely the same teams of people over an extended period of time). Viewed from this perspective, we have concluded that technologies that may, at any given moment, be portrayed as discrete and unrelated, are in fact more appropriately regarded as being part of a single process of iterative learning and advancement in pursuit of a common technological goal.

7.1751 For example, the United States argues that the research that Boeing performed under the ATCAS contract did not relate to a single barrel fuselage, but instead to four quadrant, panelized fuselage sections.[3671] The European Communities acknowledges that under ATCAS Boeing designed, built and tested fuselage from four separate panel sections (rather than 360° barrel sections), but contends that the research under ATCAS served as a "roadmap" for Boeing to arrive at the composite fuselage barrel solution that it later applied on the 787.[3672] According to the European Communities, "on the long road to Boeing's successful development of a composite fuselage barrel, ATCAS provided Boeing with quintessential foundational knowledge and technologies, by supporting the achievement of significant milestones in this long-term, step-by-step process."[3673] As the European Communities notes, under ATCAS, Boeing did undertake preliminary costing studies to substantiate the advantages of 360° barrel fuselage sections.[3674] Moreover, the planning timeline originally devised for Boeing's work under the ATCAS contract shows that research into the separate panels was envisaged to precede and ultimately lead to testing of a full barrel fuselage.[3675] The importance of the work on the separate panel sections to the development of a 360° barrel section is also evident from a NASA contractor report which observed that the advantages of a 360° barrel

---

[3671] United States' comments on European Communities' response to question 87, para. 21. Specifically, the United States explains that the ATCAS crown panel was built as a standalone section using outer mould line (OML) tools and inner mould line (IML) cauls to co-cure the skin and stringers, while the 787 fuselage, by contrast, is being built as a single solid piece of composite created and cured around enormous multi-section mandrels which are IML tools (designed by suppliers for Boeing) with OML cauls.

[3672] European Communities' confidential oral statement at the second meeting with the Panel, para. 44.

[3673] European Communities' confidential oral statement at the second meeting with the Panel, para. 44. See also, Dominik Wacht, An Analysis of Selected NASA Research Programs and Their Impact on Boeing's Civil Aircraft Programs, November 2006, Exhibit EC-15, pp. 72-76.

[3674] European Communities' confidential oral statement at the second meeting with the Panel; European Communities' first written submission, Annex C, para. 47.

[3675] Larry B. Ilcewicz, "Advanced Composite Fuselage Technology," Third NASA Advanced Composites Technology Conference, NASA CP-3178 Vol 1, 1992, at 110, Exhibit EC-1338; see also, Dominik Wacht, An Analysis of Selected NASA Research Programs and Their Impact on Boeing's Civil Aircraft Programs, November 2006, Exhibit EC-15, p. 70.

DSR 2012:III

1633

Report of the Panel

could be developed *only after* the complexities of the separate panel sections were better understood.[3676]

7.1752 To take an example from the "more-electric systems" technology area, the European Communities asserts that in [***], the 787 will use electro-mechanical actuators akin to those that McDonnell Douglas studied and developed pursuant to its PBW contract, which was funded through the power-by-wire/fly-by-light subtask of NASA's AST Program.[3677] The United States argues that the flight controls developed by Boeing for the 787 are not the same as the electronic actuation technology that was originally developed under the power-by-wire/fly-by-light subtask of NASA's AST Program, and that the subtask was terminated before any new technology related to advanced power management and distribution systems was built and tested.[3678] The European Communities argues that this subtask of the AST Program enabled McDonnell Douglas to gain knowledge and experience with regard to power system definitions and requirements by designing, fabricating, testing and demonstrating power management and distribution architectures, electrical actuators and starter/generators.[3679] According to the European Communities, all of this knowledge and experience contributed to Boeing's design and development of the more-electric architecture of the 787, particularly its ability to integrate more-electric components into the aircraft. The NASA PBW contract with McDonnell Douglas noted that three prior studies had shown operational, weight and cost advantages for commercial subsonic transport aircraft using all-electric/more-electric technologies in secondary electric power systems.[3680] This is despite the fact that the studies were completed on different aircraft, using different criteria and applying a variety of technologies. The objective of the PBW contract with McDonnell Douglas was expressed as being the development and demonstration of technology for a more-electric secondary power system that would provide enough confidence through testing that industry would begin to transfer the technology to their civil fleet.[3681] In these circumstances, we consider it artificial to suggest that the research into more-electric systems architecture that Boeing and McDonnell Douglas conducted under the aeronautics R&D programmes did not contribute in a genuine and

---

[3676] Larry B. Ilcewicz et al., Advanced Technology Composite Fuselage – Program Overview, NASA Contractor Report 4734, April 1997, p. 6-6.

[3677] European Communities' first written submission, Annex C, para. 71. NASA Contract NAS3-27018 with McDonnell Douglas Aerospace regarding Power-By-Wire Development and Demonstration for Subsonic Civil Transport, 29 September 1993, Exhibit EC-826, at C-5.

[3678] Bair Affidavit, Exhibit US-7, para. 62.

[3679] European Communities' first written submission, Annex C, para. 71.

[3680] NASA Contract NAS3-27018 with McDonnell Douglas Aerospace regarding Power-By-Wire Development and Demonstration for Subsonic Civil Transport, 29 September 1993, Exhibit EC-826, at C-2.

[3681] NASA Contract NAS3-27018 with McDonnell Douglas Aerospace regarding Power-By-Wire Development and Demonstration for Subsonic Civil Transport, 29 September 1993, Exhibit EC-826, at C-2.

1634   DSR 2012:III

substantial way to Boeing's development of more-electric systems for the 787 because, for example, the flight controls for the 787 are not the same electronic actuation technology studied by McDonnell Douglas under the PBW contract.

7.1753 In the Panel's view, it is reasonable to expect that it is necessary to conduct research into many different potential technologies as part of the process of identifying and developing the most promising technologies for commercial application. The fact that much of the research is unsuccessful, or surpassed, or that the precise technology concepts studied under an industry-focused R&D programme at one particular point in the technology development process may not be the same as the technologies that are ultimately applied to a product does not, in our view, necessarily detract from the contribution of that research to the development of a product.

7.1754 We note the statement of a Boeing engineer submitted by the United States expressing the opinion that the research performed by Boeing under the ATCAS contract did not provide any experience or data relevant to the 787 design.[3682] According to this engineer, in designing the 787, Boeing used research and production experience and data from its other commercial airline programmes, particularly the 777, and also invented many new technologies and processes "from scratch" during the course of 787 development. We consider this view to be somewhat exaggerated in the light of other evidence before the Panel concerning the objectives of the R&D subsidies, the length of time over which they operated, the collaboration with Boeing and complementarity with Boeing's own internal R&D efforts and the nature of the technological problems that were the focus of the research. In short, the evidence presented by the United States, assessed along with all of the evidence concerning the nature of the aeronautics R&D subsidies, does not persuade us that the differences between the technology concepts studied under the R&D subsidies and the technologies applied to the 787 are such that it is no longer possible to consider the R&D subsidies as having contributed in a genuine and substantial way to Boeing's development of technologies for the 787.

7.1755 We now address the other main arguments advanced by the United States contesting the importance of the aeronautics R&D subsidies to Boeing's ability to develop and launch the 787 as and when it did.

7.1756 First, the United States argues that the 787 is a product of Boeing's past commercial experience and its significant internal R&D efforts.[3683] However, as should be clear from the Panel's discussion of the operation of the aeronautics R&D subsidies, we consider that this perspective as to the technological origins of the 787 seeks to sever artificially the contribution of earlier significant research efforts which are nevertheless an inherent part of the technology

---

[3682] Affidavit of Alan Miller, Exhibit US-1258, para. 21.
[3683] Affidavit of Alan Miller, Exhibit US-1258, para. 4, 21; Bair Affidavit, Exhibit US-7, paras. 7, 75; Affidavit of Branko Sarh, Exhibit US-1254, para. 15.

Report of the Panel

development process. The Panel considers that its assessment of the effects of the aeronautics R&D subsidies on Boeing's development of technologies for its aircraft should be made on the basis of the cumulative effect of Boeing's decades-long participation in NASA and DOD programmes[3684], taking into account factors such as the specific technical objectives of the R&D programmes and the complementarity and interdependence between the work that Boeing and McDonnell Douglas performed for NASA and Boeing's own internal R&D efforts.

7.1757 The Panel is not, of course, of the view that the technologies applied to the 787 are entirely and exclusively attributable to work that Boeing and McDonnell Douglas conducted for NASA and DOD pursuant to the aeronautics R&D subsidies. The Panel is well aware that, from 2000 onwards, Boeing and its suppliers have made significant investments in R&D in the respective technology areas, first in the context of the development of the Sonic Cruiser, and subsequently, the 7E7/787. Moreover, as regards the technologies on the 787 in particular, the Panel notes that, prior to performing the research under the aeronautics R&D contracts at issue in this dispute, Boeing had already developed expertise in the application of composites in secondary structures, as well as in primary structures such as the 777 empennage. It is also clear that during the 1990s, Boeing suppliers on the 787, such as Kawasaki Heavy Industries and Fuji Heavy Industries were developing expertise in the use of composites in primary aircraft structures contemporaneously with Boeing's development efforts.[3685] The Panel acknowledges that Boeing had also derived valuable knowledge and experience from lessons learned over the course of the 777 and 737NG production programmes.

[3684] The Panel agrees with the European Communities that the real value of the aeronautics R&D subsidies was in having dozens of Boeing engineers immersed in composite design and manufacturing for several years, thus enabling Boeing to leverage the substantial accumulated knowledge and experience in any future composite-related R&D activity; Statement by Patrick Gavin, Tim Sommer, Burkhard Domke, and Dominik Wacht, 8 November 2007, Exhibit EC-1175 (BCI), para. 27; Dominik Wacht, An Analysis of Selected NASA Research Programs and Their Impact on Boeing's Civil Aircraft Programs, November 2006, Exhibit EC-15, p. 67 (stating that the "most important benefit that the ACT program provided to Boeing was the ability for its engineers to gain experience and work under real development program restrictions with clear cost targets".)

[3685] For example, by the mid-1990s, Kawasaki Heavy Industries had designed and built an all composite wing for the Japanese FS-X fighter aircraft. The Japan Aircraft Development Corporation is reported as having contributed 21 per cent to the Boeing 777 project for the design and production of the fuselage, centre wing and wing body fairings for the life of the 777 programme; Richard N. Hadcock, A Chronology of Advanced Composite Applications, in Louis F. Vosteen and Richard N. Hadcock, Composite Chronicles: A Study of the Lessons Learned in the Development, Production and Service of Composite Structures, NASA Contractor Report 4620, November 1994, pp. 35, 49, Exhibit EC-792. Kawasaki Heavy Industries, Mitsubishi Heavy Industries and Fuji Heavy Industries, operating through the Japan Aircraft Development Corporation, are also reported to be building and co-designing approximately 35 per cent of the 787, Dominic Gates, "Boeing Shares Work, but Guards its Secrets", Seattle Times, 15 May 2007, Exhibit EC-1167.

1636

DSR 2012:III

US - Large Civil Aircraft (2nd Complaint)

7.1758 Boeing's technology developments are clearly the product of a variety of factors. Indeed, it is reasonable to assume that at some point in time, the contribution of the NASA-funded research will diminish in relation to other, more recent or revolutionary technological developments that are attributable to other factors, and that it will no longer be possible to characterize the NASA research conducted in the 1990s as having contributed in a genuine and substantial way to new technologies applied to future Boeing LCA. The United States considers that this point had already been reached by 2004. For the reasons that we have set forth above, we do not agree.

7.1759 Second, the United States argues that, to the extent that Boeing considered that any of the research that it performed under the NASA and DOD R&D contracts and agreements was of independent value to its commercial aircraft development, Boeing had the financial capability and ability to conduct that R&D in the absence of any NASA and DOD funding.[3686] Therefore, according to the United States, in the absence of any subsidies, Boeing could and would have funded any R&D necessary for the 787.[3687] As we explain in paragraphs 7.1830-7.1831, we are not persuaded that the European Communities has demonstrated that Boeing inherently lacked the financial means to price and develop its LCA in the manner in which it did. What does, however, appear clear to the Panel is that NASA's role in aeronautical research has been explained precisely on the basis of, among other things, the large disincentives for private sector investment in long term, high risk aeronautical R&D (stemming from the inability of individual firms to fully capture the benefits from the research efforts).[3688] We have no reason to doubt this evidence. That must at the very minimum mean that, as applied in this particular instance, even if Boeing could have eventually achieved through its own resources the gains that in fact accrued to it through NASA's assistance (a matter on which we express no view), it is not reasonable to believe that Boeing could have done so within the time frame, and/or at the lower cost to itself that were the product of the aeronautics R&D subsidies.

7.1760 The aeronautics R&D subsidies in question amount to at least $2.6 billion[3689], a considerable amount of money from the perspective of a government agency. The Panel is aware, however, that this amount perhaps may not appear significant when compared to Boeing's consolidated revenues or R&D expenditures over 1989 - 2006. Indeed, as the United States points out, Boeing repurchased over $16 billion in stock between 1986 and 2006.[3690] However, this sort of numerical comparison presupposes that the effects of the aeronautics R&D subsidies can essentially be reduced to their cash value, a

---

[3686] United States' comments on the European Communities' response to question 187, para. 324.
[3687] *Ibid.*
[3688] NASA R&T Base Budget Estimates, at FY 1997, SAT 4.5; at FY 1999 SAT 4.1.3, Exhibit EC-398.
[3689] See para. 7.1433 of this Report.
[3690] United States' comments on the European Communities' response to question 78, para. 270.

DSR 2012:III

Report of the Panel

proposition that we do not accept. As can be seen from the analysis above, the value to Boeing of the particular aeronautics R&D programmes in question is essentially a function of the technological advancements that those programmes provide. Precisely because the nature of this kind of subsidy is that it is intended to multiply the benefit from a given expenditure, the Panel considers it unlikely that the effects of such expenditure (to the extent that it was successfully deployed) would be reducible to its face amount. The United States' invitation to compare the amounts of the aeronautics R&D subsidies with Boeing's payments to shareholders may be taken also to imply that the ultimate effect of the aeronautics R&D subsidies was merely to increase payments to Boeing's shareholders. The Panel does not accept the proposition that the effect of the aeronautics R&D subsidies was essentially to benefit Boeing's shareholders by replacing funds that Boeing would otherwise have spent on R&D. As we have noted above in paragraph 7.1759, we have no reason to doubt the evidence that there are large disincentives for private sector investment in research of the kind that was conducted under the aeronautics R&D subsidies, and any suggestion that a firm such as Boeing would have conducted such research is subject to the same fundamental objection here. Moreover, we consider that it is implausible that such specifically earmarked and scrutinized R&D funds disbursed over such a period of time were effectively nothing more than a transfer to shareholders.

7.1761 Finally, as regards the United States' general arguments concerning the DOD subsidies, the Panel is not persuaded that technologies developed under the DOD R&D programmes are neither "technologically applicable" to commercial aircraft (because of the different missions and cost-sensitivities of military and commercial aircraft), nor "legally applicable" to commercial aircraft (because of Boeing's decision to ensure that the 787 is "ITAR free").[3691]

7.1762 With respect to the first of these arguments, we have already concluded, in the context of our analysis of whether DOD aeronautics R&D measures constitute a subsidy within the meaning of Article 1 of the SCM Agreement, that the United States has failed to substantiate its assertion that only a minor amount of the R&D conducted by Boeing under the DOD R&D programmes at issue was "technologically applicable" to commercial aircraft. Among other things, the United States' argument that DOD-funded research on military aircraft is designed to fulfil military functions, and does not translate well to the different commercial imperatives of commercial aircraft production (in terms of FAA certification/maintenance requirements and efficiency of production) overlooks the fact that at least some of the DOD programmes, for example, the ManTech Composites Affordability Initiative related to Advanced Fibre Placement, had the explicit objective of funding R&D to be applied towards both military and civil aircraft and emphasized the development of lower cost technologies.

[3691] Bair Affidavit, Exhibit US-7, para. 25.

1638

DSR 2012:III

7.1763 With respect to the second of these arguments, we have already concluded, in the context of our analysis of whether DOD aeronautics R&D measures constitute a subsidy within the meaning of Article 1 of the SCM Agreement, that the United States has failed to substantiate its assertion that the ITAR make it effectively impossible for Boeing to utilize any of the R&D performed under DOD R&D contracts and agreements towards LCA. Among other things, while we accept the United States' assertions that the ITAR restrict Boeing's ability to use certain R&D performed for DOD towards its civil aircraft, and while we accept that Boeing complies with ITAR in general and took steps to ensure that the 787 is "ITAR free", and while we further accept that the situation with respect to the scope and coverage of the ITAR is not entirely clear, the United States has failed to explain how its assertions regarding the ITAR can be reconciled with the fact that some of the R&D funded by DOD – including R&D performed by Boeing under assistance instruments entered into under the ManTech and DUS&T programmes, which were subject to the ITAR – had the *explicit objective* of being applied towards civil aircraft.

7.1764 For the reasons set forth above, we would characterize the NASA R&D subsidies as strategically-focused R&D programmes with a significant and pervasive commercial dimension, undertaken in collaboration with U.S. industry to provide competitive advantages to U.S. industry by funding research into high risk, high pay-off research of the sort that individual companies are unlikely to fund on their own. The DOD R&D subsidies funded through the ManTech and DUS&T programmes under DOD's RDT&E Program are focused on pursuing "dual use" technologies through collaborative efforts with U.S. industry. The aeronautics R&D subsidies are designed to develop and validate new technologies for Boeing to commercialize, and we consider that it would be artificial to treat their contribution as having been exhausted or so diminished as to no longer be making a genuine and substantial contribution to Boeing's development of technologies for the 787.

The conditions of competition

7.1765 A further factor that we consider to be relevant to our evaluation of whether the aeronautics R&D subsidies have caused serious prejudice to the interests of the European Communities by reason of their "technology effects" concerns the particular conditions of competition in the LCA industry. As explained by the United States' economic consultants, NERA Consulting, the real competition between Airbus and Boeing occurs through their respective investments in R&D to build better airplanes:

Report of the Panel

> "The essence of the intense competition between Boeing and Airbus is to design and build better airplanes – improved versions of existing models as well as new models."[3692]

7.1766 In a 2005 Airbus document, Airbus explains that the only way that it was able to penetrate a market that was largely dominated by U.S. manufacturers was to "offer a unique value with its products through innovation":[3693]

> "Airbus has evolved into a formidable competitor in the large civil aircraft (LCA) industry as a result of its careful development of a family of products in response to market demand while pursuing a product development strategy of exploiting both new technologies and the benefits of commonality."[3694]

7.1767 Airbus describes itself as having followed this "product innovation strategy" successfully from its very first product (the A300) and notes that many of Boeing's new aircraft were introduced in response to new Airbus models: the A300/310 was followed by the 767; the A320 was followed by the 737NG; the A340/330 was followed by the 777 and according to Airbus (in early 2005), the 787 project "appears to be a response to the market success of the A330-200".[3695]

7.1768 A NASA publication also points to the importance of competition through technological development, suggesting that it was Airbus' position as a new entrant in the market that led it to compete on the basis of innovation:

> "Airbus Industries, for example, has incorporated more advanced technology into its aircraft, including full flybywire controls, than the U.S. transport aircraft manufacturers have. But the European consortium had more motivation to innovate and less to lose than its U.S. counterparts. Boeing and McDonnell Douglas held such a commanding market position that unless Airbus distinguished itself significantly in some manner, it would be lost in Boeing's shadow."[3696]

7.1769 It is clear to us that the conditions of competition in the LCA industry are such that a subsidy that enhances an LCA manufacturer's ability to develop innovative technologies for application to its aircraft will potentially give rise to a significant competitive advantage to that manufacturer.

[3692] Jordan and Dorman Report, Exhibit US-3, p. 11.

[3693] Airbus, Key Determinants of Competitiveness in the Global Large Civil Aircraft Market: An Airbus Assessment, March 2005, Exhibit EC-719 (BCI), p. 12.

[3694] Airbus, Key Determinants of Competitiveness in the Global Large Civil Aircraft Market: An Airbus Assessment, March 2005, Exhibit EC-719 (BCI), p. 2.

[3695] Airbus, Key Determinants of Competitiveness in the Global Large Civil Aircraft Market: An Airbus Assessment, March 2005, Exhibit EC-719 (BCI), p. 11, footnote 2.

[3696] Airborne Trailblazer, Chapter 1, Exhibit EC-288, p. 4.

US - Large Civil Aircraft (2nd Complaint)

7.1770 The United States argues that the NASA R&D subsidies do not confer a competitive advantage on Boeing vis-à-vis Airbus because NASA-funded research is generally applicable, conceptual research, the results of which are publicly disseminated and therefore widely known and well understood within the global community of engineers and scientists working in a particular area.[3697] Moreover, according to the United States, many of the technologies that the European Communities attempts to link to the research that Boeing and McDonnell Douglas performed for NASA and DOD pursuant to the aeronautics R&D subsidies are supplied by third parties and are commercially available.[3698]

7.1771 The Panel notes that there are restrictions on the dissemination of certain aspects of NASA-funded research results, and that public dissemination does not occur immediately.[3699] Moreover, the nature of the aeronautics R&D subsidies suggests that Boeing gains a significant advantage from performing the R&D work itself, in collaboration with NASA, as well as from conducting research under the R&D subsidies in tandem with its own related R&D efforts. In any case, we do not think that it is very realistic to believe that NASA would so consistently and prominently state that the objectives of the aeronautics R&D programmes were to provide a competitive advantage to U.S. subsonic transport by accelerating the development of key, high payoff technologies if all of the NASA-funded R&D were in fact research that was publicly disseminated and equally available to Airbus. Nor is the Panel persuaded that the critical technologies that Boeing developed in collaboration with its suppliers are equally available to Airbus. The Panel notes that the United States has failed to rebut a critical assertion made by the European Communities in its HSBI submissions and evidence in this regard.[3700]

7.1772 Moreover, the argument that many of the technologies applied to the 787 are commercially available to Airbus from third party suppliers overlooks the importance of the knowledge and experience that Boeing obtained pursuant to

---

[3697] See e.g. Bair Affidavit, Exhibit US-7, paras. 33-34; Affidavit of Branko Sarh, Exhibit US-1254, para. 5.

[3698] Bair Affidavit, Exhibit US-7, paras. 18-20, 58, 61, 64, 66, 69, 73. For example, components of the 787 that relate to its more-electric architecture, such as the starter engines, de-icing system, air conditioning system, secondary flight controls and brakes were supplied to Boeing by third parties, as were certain components relating to the 787's reduced noise, such as the joint-less inlet liners and landing gear. The Panel notes also that the Product Lifecycle Management Tools (including CATIA, DELMIA, ENOVIA and SMARTEAM) are supplied by Dassault.

[3699] For example, certain NASA and DOD contracts with Boeing contained limited access rights such as (i) limited exclusive data rights, (ii) for early domestic dissemination, and (iii) requirements for prior written approval before the release of certain technical information. Although differing in their nature and scope, each of these limited access rights seek to delay the foreign transfer of commercially sensitive information or prevent its public release without prior written approval of NASA or DOD; see European Communities' first written submission, Annex C, paras. 135-159.

[3700] European Communities' second written submission, Full Version HSBI Appendix, para. 4; Statement by Patrick Gavin, Tim Sommer, Burkhard Domke, and Dominik Wacht, 8 November 2007, Exhibit EC-1175 HSBI, at para. 19.

DSR 2012:III

1641

Report of the Panel

the aeronautics R&D subsidies as an integrator of the various technologies. We agree with the following submission by the European Communities:

"The critical question in developing and building LCA is *not* how to *get* the different technologies and design and manufacturing tools. The critical question is how to *use* them. Which tools out of many available tools should be used, in which way, by whom, and at which step of the design and build process? The ability to define and manage the complex interaction of design processes, organization and tools so as to enable the robust development and manufacturing of an aircraft at minimum time and cost is one of the core competencies of an aircraft manufacturer. This is the true challenge LCA integration poses to both Airbus and Boeing, and it is a challenge that Boeing can meet thanks in large part to NASA and DOD funding and support."[3701]

7.1773 The Panel concludes that the aeronautics R&D subsidies contributed in a genuine and substantial way to Boeing's development of technologies for the 787 and that, in the light of the conditions of competition in the LCA industry, these subsidies conferred a competitive advantage on Boeing. The Panel now proceeds to analyse whether the aeronautics R&D subsidies, as a result of this competitive advantage, affected Airbus' sales and prices in the 200 – 300 seat wide-body LCA product market in the 2004 – 2006 period.

> Effects of the aeronautics R&D subsidies
> on Airbus' sales and prices in the 200 – 300
> seat wide-body LCA product market

7.1774 We recall that the European Communities argues that, *but for* the aeronautics R&D subsidies, (i) Boeing could not have launched, in April 2004, a 787 family of LCA offering the many operating cost savings and enhancements in passenger comfort that have made it such a commercial success relative to the A330 and Original A350[3702]; and (ii) Boeing could not have contractually bound itself to make significant deliveries of the 787 starting in 2008.[3703] The Panel is aware that it should proceed with caution in attempting to assess, through the use of counterfactual analysis, how the aeronautics R&D subsidies affected Boeing's development of the 787. However, we are satisfied from the evidence that Boeing's assessment in the late 1990s that route fragmentation would lead to a larger number of lower-volume routes, best served by a mid-sized, extended range aircraft (a commercial assessment unrelated to the subsidies), along with

---

[3701] European Communities' confidential oral statement at the first meeting of the Panel, para. 14.

[3702] Rather, according to the European Communities, it would have taken Boeing "years longer" as well as much more of its own money to do so; European Communities' first written submission, Annex C, para. 199.

[3703] European Communities' first written submission, Annex C, para. 199.

1642

DSR 2012:III

the age of the 767, likely meant that Boeing needed to develop an LCA to replace the 767 in the 200 – 300 seat wide-body product market, and that it would have done so in the early- to mid- 2000s.[3704] The question is what sort of aircraft Boeing could have developed, and when that aircraft could have been launched and first entered into service, in the absence of the aeronautics R&D subsidies.

7.1775 We consider that two scenarios are most likely: Boeing would have developed a 767-replacement that incorporated all of the technologies that are incorporated on the 787, but its launch would have been significantly later than 2004 and it would not have been able to promise first deliveries for 2008, or Boeing would have launched a 767-replacement in 2004 that was technologically superior to the 767, but did not offer the degree of technological innovation of the 787. We do not have to reach any definitive view on which of these outcomes would have occurred. What is clear to us is that, absent the aeronautics R&D subsidies, Boeing would not have been able to launch an aircraft incorporating all of the technologies that are incorporated on the 787 in 2004, with promised deliveries commencing in 2008.

7.1776 The Panel recalls that European Communities alleges that subsidies benefiting the 787 caused the following forms of serious prejudice:

(a)   Significant price suppression of the A330, Original A350 and A350XWB-800;

(b)   Significant lost sales of A330 and Original A350;

(c)   Displacement and impedance of imports into the United States for the A330 and Original A350;

(d)   Displacement and impedance of exports from various third country markets for the A330 and Original A350; and

(e)   Threat of price suppression with respect to future orders of A330 and A350XWB-800.[3705]

7.1777 Before we evaluate the specific market effects of the aeronautics R&D subsidies in this LCA product market, it is useful to recall the events leading to Airbus' development of the A350XWB in 2006. The European Communities asserts that, when Boeing launched the 787 in 2004, Airbus' A330 was the

---

[3704] One could presumably also argue that Boeing would not have launched a new aircraft in this product market and would have continued to offer the 767, however, even the European Communities does not argue this.

[3705] The European Communities also makes an alternate claim, conditional on the Panel disagreeing with the European Communities that all of its serious prejudice arguments should be assessed on the basis of orders rather than deliveries, of threat of significant price suppression, threat of significant lost sales and threat of displacement and impedance of imports and exports with respect to *future deliveries* of A330 and A350XWB-800 LCA; European Communities' first written submission, para. 1342.

Report of the Panel

"undisputed market leader in the 200-300 seat LCA market".[3706] The Panel is satisfied based on the evidence that, at the beginning of 2004, Airbus expected that its A330 would remain the standard for the 200-300 seat LCA market for at least another 10 years of deliveries.[3707] In late 2004, in response to customer demands that Airbus offer an aircraft to match the 787 in terms of operating costs, Airbus designed an aircraft programme that would retain the A330 fuselage, but add a new composite wing and cabin improvements. Then in April 2005, Airbus redesigned that aircraft (now called the A350) to include a composite aft fuselage (but still sharing the same fuselage cross-section as the A330) and to make further improvements to the aerodynamics, increase the maximum take-off weight, add new landing gear and other improvements.[3708] Various models of the Original A350 were marketed from December 2004, however the Original A350 that featured a composite wing and composite fuselage having the same cross-section as the A330 was launched in October 2005.[3709] Evidence before the Panel indicates that, notwithstanding the launch of the Original A350 in October 2005, certain key customers requested that Airbus launch a whole new LCA with technology equivalent to that on the Boeing 787.[3710] Accordingly, in December 2006, Airbus announced the launch of the redesigned A350XWB programme.[3711] First deliveries of the A350XWB-800 were not scheduled to be made until 2013, some five years after promised first deliveries of the 787.[3712]

7.1778 The European Communities argues that Airbus lost a significant number of sales of its A330 and Original A350 to the 787 because of the operating cost advantages of the 787, the fact that Boeing could provide the 787 in a shorter timeframe than Airbus could provide the Original A350, or because of the low

---

[3706] European Communities' second written submission, Full Version HSBI Appendix, para. 10. The United States does not appear to dispute that the A330 was the market leader in this product market prior to the launch of the 787, see e.g. United States' first written submission, para. 981.

[3707] Christian Scherer, Commercial Aspects of the Aircraft Business From the Perspective of a Manufacturer, March 2007, Exhibit EC-11 (BCI), para. 94.

[3708] Christian Scherer, Commercial Aspects of the Aircraft Business From the Perspective of a Manufacturer, March 2007, Exhibit EC-11 (BCI), para. 102.

[3709] Christian Scherer, Commercial Aspects of the Aircraft Business From the Perspective of a Manufacturer, March 2007, Exhibit EC-11 (BCI), para. 103.

[3710] Christian Scherer, Commercial Aspects of the Aircraft Business From the Perspective of a Manufacturer, March 2007, Exhibit EC-11 (BCI), para. 110; United States' second written submission, HSBI Appendix, para. 16; Andrea Rothman and Susan Ray, "Redesign A350, Airbus told", Seattle Post-Intelligencer, 8 April, 2006, Exhibit US-1172; Scott Hamilton, Redesigning the A350: Airbus' tough choice, leeham.net, 4 April 2006, Exhibit EC-1251.

[3711] This family of LCA would span two LCA product markets: the 200-300 seat market (through the A350XWB-800, which would compete directly with the 787-8 and 787-9), and the 300-400 seat market (through the A350XWB-900/1000 which would compete with the 777 family).

[3712] The Panel is of course aware that Boeing was not ultimately able to deliver the 787 in 2008, however, the relevant fact for purposes of our analysis is that in 2004, Boeing believed that it would be able to make its first deliveries in 2008 (and made contractual promises to its customers to this effect).

1644

DSR 2012:III

price of the 787.[3713] The European Communities also argues that, although Airbus tried to compete against the 787 by offering the Original A350 in 2005, because Airbus did not have access to similar R&D subsidies, the Original A350 "fell short of the 787 in terms of technological advancements and delivery schedule".[3714] Moreover, the European Communities contends that the 787's subsidy-enhanced low prices and advanced technologies forced Airbus to lower the prices of its A330 and Original A350 in order to secure orders, thereby causing significant suppression of A330 and Original A350 prices.[3715]

7.1779 In addition, the European Communities argues that, although Airbus was able to launch the A350XWB-800, a technologically-comparable aircraft to the 787, in 2006, prices for the A350XWB-800 were also suppressed by the subsidies to the 787 because [***.][3716]

7.1780 The Panel is satisfied that the European Communities has established that the technological and operating cost advantages of the 787 over the A330 and Original A350, as well as its scheduled delivery dates commencing in 2008, caused Airbus to lose a significant number of sales of its A330 and Original A350 between 2004 and 2006, and significantly suppressed the prices of those aircraft during that period. We are not persuaded, however, that the European Communities has adequately substantiated its argument that the technological and operating cost advantages of the 787, or its 2004 launch and scheduled first delivery date of 2008, has resulted in significant suppression of A350XWB-800 prices. We explain the basis for these conclusions below.

7.1781 First, we accept the proposition that with the launch of a technologically-advanced aircraft, the price of the competing, older technology aircraft can be expected to decline (along with its residual values). We are satisfied that this is what happened to the A330 when the 787 was launched in 2004. We are persuaded that this left Airbus in a position in which it had to lower the price of the A330 in order to try to mitigate its loss of market share to the 787.[3717] We see in the data submitted to us an indication that price trends for the A330

[3713] European Communities' first written submission, paras. 1426-1455; European Communities' second written submission, Full Version HSBI Appendix, para. 10.

[3714] European Communities' first written submission, para. 1410.

[3715] European Communities' first written submission, paras. 1392-1393, 1410-1412.

[3716] The parties do not appear to dispute that the A350XWB-800, unlike the A330 and Original A350, was technologically competitive with the 787; see e.g. European Communities' second written submission, Full Version HSBI Appendix, para. 13.

[3717] See e.g. Christian Scherer, Commercial Aspects of the Aircraft Business from the Perspective of a Manufacturer, March 2007, Exhibit EC-11 HSBI at para. 109. Because customers did not perceive the Original A350 to be as technologically advanced as the 787, its position in the market was similar to that of the A330; European Communities' second written submission, Full Version HSBI Appendix, para. 12; Scott Hamilton, "Redesigning the A350: Airbus' Tough Choice", leeham.net, 4 April 2006, Exhibit EC-1251. The United States asserts that the Original A350 "could not even come close to matching the operating efficiencies of Boeing's 787", United States' first written submission, U.S. Campaign Annex, paras. 7-8.

Report of the Panel

declined after 2004 and that, from its former position as market leader in this product market, it lost market share to Boeing.

7.1782 We note that, as demonstrated in the diagram below, while demand for 200-300 seat wide-body LCA fell in 2002 (largely due to 9/11 and the SARS epidemic), but then rebounded in subsequent years, [***][3718]

Orders for 200-300 Seat LCA vs. Price Per Seat of A330 Family LCA in Constant Dollars, 2000-2006[3719]

[***]

7.1783 Neither party has submitted global market share data based on orders for aircraft in the 200 – 300 seat wide-body LCA product market over the 2000 – 2006 period. However, based on data presented by the European Communities, the Panel has been able to reconstruct the following global market share data for orders of aircraft in the 200 – 300 seat wide-body LCA product market for the period 2000-2006.

Market share in the 200 – 300 seat wide-body LCA market (based on order data) in 2000 - 2006[3720]

Year	Airbus A330 and A350	Airbus Market share	Boeing 767 and 787	Boeing market share
2000	95	91%	9	9%
2001	52	57%	40	43%
2002	24	75%	8	25%
2003	49	82%	11	18%
2004	51	46%	59	54%
2005	129	34%	251	66%
2006	117	40%	173	60%

[3718] European Communities' first written submission, para. 1389; European Communities' response to question 306, para. 784.

[3719] European Communities' response to question 306, para. 784, Figure 3. Pricing information in this figure is based on Airbus proprietary data. Order information is based on Airclaims CASE database, data query as of 19 January 2007, Exhibit EC-3.

[3720] Compiled from data in Airclaims CASE Database, Data Query as of 19 January 2007, 2004 – 2006 Orders, Exhibit EC-1287 and Airclaims CASE Database, Data Query as of 19 January 2007, Exhibit EC-3.

1646   DSR 2012:III

7.1784 The European Communities has illustrated the above market share trends on a graph as follows:[3721]

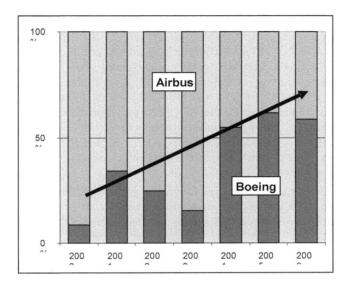

7.1785 The above market share figures show the rather dramatic erosion of Airbus' market share in the 2004 to 2006 period, compared with the 2000 – 2003 period. This erosion of the dominance of the A330 in this product market coincides with the introduction of the 787 in 2004. The evidence concerning the pricing trends for the A330, combined with the market share data, are consistent with what we would expect to occur from the introduction of a technologically-superior aircraft, offering operating cost advantages over older-technology aircraft, for around the same price. Clearly, one would expect that prices of the A330 would fall, and that it would lose market share, even in the face of significantly increased demand in that product market.[3722]

7.1786 Second, we are satisfied that evidence regarding specific sales campaigns that occurred in the 200 – 300 seat wide-body LCA product market between 2004 and 2006 demonstrates that the customer decided to purchase Boeing's 787

[3721] European Communities' confidential oral statement at the first meeting with the Panel, para. 33.
[3722] For example, the United States asserts that the performance gap between the Original A350 and the 787 was too large to bridge through price discounts (implying an erosion in both Airbus' prices and market share). In the Panel's view, the same reasoning is applicable to the A330; United States' first written submission, U.S. Campaign Annex, para. 8. For a concrete example, see the campaign discussed by the United States in its U.S. Campaign Annex at paras. 52-57. The United States explains that, despite Airbus offering extremely large discounts on the Original A350, it could not overcome the 787's value advantages and earlier availability; United States' first written submission, U.S. Campaign Annex, paras. 56-57.

Report of the Panel

family LCA because either (i) it perceived that Airbus' A330 family and Original A350 family LCA were not as capable as Boeing's 787 family LCA in fulfilling its technical or delivery schedule requirements; or (ii) it considered Airbus' A330 family and Original A350 family LCA to be capable of meeting its technical and delivery schedule requirements, but was "swayed by the extremely low pricing offered by Boeing".[3723] In several of the sales campaigns in which the European Communities argues that the customer favoured the 787 owing to its technological features or availability in 2008[3724], it appears that factors other than the performance characteristics of the 787 over the A330 or Original A350, and the 2008 delivery date for the 787, played a significant part in the Boeing sale.[3725] However, the performance characteristics of the 787 and/or its scheduled entry into service in 2008 appear to have been the decisive factors in the outcomes of the Qantas, Ethiopian Airlines and Icelandair campaigns in 2005 and the Kenya Airways campaign in 2006.

7.1787 In the Panel's view, the Qantas, Ethiopian Airlines and Icelandair campaigns in 2005 and the Kenya Airways campaign in 2006, are evidence of sales that Airbus did not secure due to the advanced technological features of the 787, the availability of which at that time was accelerated by the aeronautics R&D subsidies. As such, they are evidence of lost sales that are the effects of the aeronautics R&D subsidies.

7.1788 The Panel notes that the Qantas sale in particular involved an order of 45 787s plus 20 options and a further 50 purchase rights.[3726] HSBI evidence submitted to the Panel supports other evidence indicating that this sales campaign was extremely competitive for various strategic reasons.[3727] Taking into account the size of the order, as well as these various other factors that singled out this campaign as being of particular importance to both Boeing and Airbus, we are satisfied that Airbus' loss of the Qantas sales campaign alone is evidence of a "significant" lost sale. The Panel is therefore satisfied that there is sufficient evidence to support its conclusion that, *but for* the effects of certain aeronautics R&D subsidies, Airbus would have made additional sales of the Original A350, and to that extent, would not have suffered significant lost sales within the meaning of Article 6.3(c) of the SCM Agreement.

[3723] European Communities' first written submission, para. 1427.

[3724] These sales campaigns are: All Nippon Airways (2004); Japan Airlines (2004); Continental Airlines (2004-2006); Icelandair (2005); Northwest (2005); Air Canada (2005); Qantas (2005); Kenya Airways (2006); Ethiopian Airlines (2005); Royal Air Maroc (2005).

[3725] These factors include Boeing's relationship with the airline (Continental Airlines, All Nippon Airways, Japan Airlines), the particular routes to be serviced and range of the aircraft (Northwest, All Nippon Airways, Japan Airlines), the effect of the A340/777 competition and preference of the airline for a mixed fleet (Air Canada), and the failure to submit a formal offer within the time limit specified by the airline (Royal Air Maroc).

[3726] Boeing/ Airbus Press Reports, Exhibit EC-1157, pp. 430-432, 467-469.

[3727] Christian Scherer, Commercial Aspects of the Aircraft Business from the Perspective of a Manufacturer, March 2007, Exhibit EC-11 HSBI, paras. 108-109. See also, Boeing/ Airbus Press Reports, Exhibit EC-1157, pp. 430-432, 467-469.

US - Large Civil Aircraft (2nd Complaint)

7.1789 The market impact of the effects of the aeronautics R&D subsidies on Airbus aircraft were initially felt with the launch of the 787 in 2004, and is reflected in market share data on the basis of *orders* obtained in the 2004 – 2006 period. The European Communities argues that, to the extent that it has identified orders as the cause of displacement or impedance that has not yet resulted in deliveries, future deliveries resulting from those orders are evidence of a *threat* of displacement and impedance.[3728] In this regard, the European Communities argues that the subsidies cause a threat of displacement and impedance of exports from third country markets related to future deliveries of relevant Airbus LCA that result from orders booked in 2004-2006.[3729]

7.1790 The European Communities has presented the following market share data for the relevant third country markets pertaining to the Qantas, Ethiopian Airlines, Kenya Airways and Icelandair campaigns referred to above, based on actual delivery data (for the years up to and including 2006) and projected future deliveries (for the years 2007 onwards) on the basis of actual order data:[3730]

[3728] European Communities' first written submission, paras. 1455-1458, 1466-1468, 1552-1555, 1562, 1640-1643, 1650-1651; European Communities' confidential oral statement at the first meeting with the Panel, para. 90.

[3729] European Communities' first written submission paras. 1455, 1552 and 1640. This argument is part of the European Communities' more general alternative argument that, should the Panel reject the European Communities' use of orders as the basis for its present serious prejudice claim, the subsidies benefiting the relevant Boeing LCAs cause a threat of serious prejudice with respect to future *deliveries* of the "like" Airbus LCA. The Panel notes that Australia also argues that, notwithstanding that delivery of an LCA may not eventuate, orders are an indication of the effect of the subsidies on the industry and the market, through future projected sales and market share. According to Australia, they therefore give an indication as to how current subsidies are likely to affect the market in the future and thus the threat of serious prejudice; Australia's written submission, para. 69.

[3730] Airbus and Boeing Deliveries and Projected Deliveries in the Challenged Markets, Exhibit EC-1173.

DSR 2012:III

Report of the Panel

		Airbus		Boeing	
	2002	2	100%	--	--
	2003	4	100%	--	--
	2004	5	100%	--	--
	2005	3	100%	--	--
	2006	1	100%	--	--
	2007	4	100%	--	--
Australia	2008	4	50%	4	50%
	2009	3	27%	8	73%
	2010	1	10%	9	90%
	2011	--	--	7	100%
	2012	--	--	14	100%
	2013	--	--	3	100%
	2003	--	--	1	100%
	2004	--	--	1	100%
	2005	--	--	1	100%
	2006	--	--	--	--
Ethiopia	2008	--	--	1	100%
	2009	--	--	1	100%
	2010	--	--	3	100%
	2011	--	--	2	100%
	2012	--	--	3	100%
	2001	--	--	3	100%
Kenya	2010	--	--	2	100%
	2011	--	--	4	100%
	2012	--	--	3	100%
Iceland	2010	--	--	2	100%
	2012	--	--	2	100%

7.1791 Given the delay between the order of an aircraft and its delivery, the impact of the aeronautics R&D subsidies on Airbus' sales in these country markets will not be reflected in delivery data until the 787 is delivered, some years after 2006. However, it is clear that at that time, the European Communities will suffer serious prejudice in the form of displacement and impedance of its exports from these third country markets. In these circumstances, the Panel considers that the sales that Airbus has lost due to the effects of the aeronautics R&D subsidies also constitute evidence a threat of of serious prejudice. The Panel is therefore satisfied that, *but for* the effects of certain of the aeronautics R&D subsidies, Airbus would have obtained additional orders for its A330 or Original A350 LCA from customers in third country markets in Australia, Ethiopia, Kenya, and Iceland, and thus would not have suffered the threat of displacement or impedance of its exports from third country markets within the meaning of Article 6.3(b) of the SCM Agreement.

US - Large Civil Aircraft (2nd Complaint)

7.1792 The European Communities has also identified certain sales that Airbus was able to secure by offering [***] in order to offset the technological advantages and operating cost savings offered by the 787.[3731] As we have already indicated, we are satisfied that the technologies applied to the 787 resulted in an aircraft that offered substantial operating cost reductions to its customers, and that the combination of the superior technology and lower operating costs of the 787 clearly affected the comparative value of Airbus' A330 and Original A350, leaving Airbus no other option but to reduce the prices of its aircraft in order to compete.[3732] The evidence concerning the degree of price concessions that Airbus offered in order to secure sales of its A330 and Original A350 indicates that a further effect of the aeronautics R&D subsidies was significant price suppression with respect to the A330 and Original A350.[3733]

7.1793 The European Communities also alleges that a further effect of the aeronautics R&D subsidies is significant price suppression of the A350XWB-800. There is no evidence before the Panel as to price trends for the A350XWB-800, nor has the European Communities presented evidence concerning the actual pricing of the A350XWB in the context of specific LCA sales campaigns. Evidence before the Panel indicates that Airbus regards the A350XWB-800 as being technologically equal, if not superior, to the 787, meaning that there would be no need for Airbus to offer price discounts in order to offset the value of technological innovation of the 787, as was the case with the A330 and Original A350.[3734] The European Communities asserts that [***].[3735] In addition, Airbus' Christian Scherer asserts that, even though the A350XWB is technologically competitive with the 787, it is still at a competitive disadvantage due to the fact that it is not available for delivery until 2013.[3736] Although the Panel considers it quite credible that customers that had previously ordered the Original A350

[3731] European Communities' first written submission, para. 1393; European Communities' second written submission, HSBI Appendix, para. 10.

[3732] The United States argues that Boeing's 787 manufacturing costs have been lowered significantly by using commercially available product life cycle management and design software, sourcing common materials across suppliers, and standardizing customer-selected options; United States' second written submission, HSBI Campaign Annex, para. 22. While the Panel has no reason to doubt that these commercial decisions did result in manufacturing cost savings, we note that one of the major focuses of the aeronautics R&D subsidies was the development of innovative technologies that result in lower direct operating costs to airlines.

[3733] For example, Airbus sold the Original A350 to one customer for significantly less than it had sold the A330 to that same customer several years earlier, European Communities' second written submission, Full Version HSBI Appendix, para. 71.

[3734] See, for example, Christian Scherer, Commercial Aspects of the Aircraft Business from the Perspective of a Manufacturer, March 2007, Exhibit EC-11 (BCI), para. 115; "Airbus goes for extra width", Flight International, 25 July 2006, Exhibit US-302.

[3735] European Communities' first written submission, para. 1424; Christian Scherer, Commercial Aspects of the Aircraft Business from the Perspective of a Manufacturer, March 2007, Exhibit EC-11 (BCI), para. 114.

[3736] Christian Scherer, Commercial Aspects of the Aircraft Business from the Perspective of a Manufacturer, March 2007, Exhibit EC-11 BCI, para. 115.

DSR 2012:III

1651

Report of the Panel

would request, in their negotiations with Airbus, that they receive the same price for an admittedly superior product, we do not consider that it necessarily follows that Airbus had no other option but to accede to such requests, particularly if the A350XWB-800 is regarded as a technologically superior product to the Original A350. We also consider it quite plausible that sales of the A350XWB-800 may be disadvantaged relative to the 787 because the A350XWB-800 will not be ready for delivery until 2013. However, the Panel would require some evidence in this regard in order to make an objective assessment of this issue.

7.1794 The Panel is therefore satisfied, based on the evidence reviewed in the preceding paragraphs, that the aeronautics R&D subsidies contributed in a genuine and substantial way to Boeing's development of technologies for the 787 and that, as a result, *but for* the effects of these subsidies (i) Airbus would have obtained additional orders for its A330 and Original A350 LCA from customers in third country markets Australia, Ethiopia, Kenya and Iceland in 2005 and 2006, and the European Communities would not have suffered the threat of displacement or impedance of exports from third country markets within the meaning of Article 6.3(b) of the SCM Agreement; (ii) Airbus would have made additional sales of the A330 and Original A350 over the same period, and to that extent, would not have suffered significant lost sales in the 200 – 300 seat wide-body LCA product market, within the meaning of Article 6.3(c) of the SCM Agreement; and (iii) prices of the A330 and the Original A350 in the 2004 to 2006 period would have been significantly higher, and to that extent, Airbus would not have suffered significant price suppression in the 200 – 300 seat wide-body LCA product market, within the meaning of Article 6.3(c) of the SCM Agreement.

7.1795 In reaching the above conclusions, the Panel has also taken into account the evidence and arguments advanced by the United States regarding certain factors that, in the view of the United States, explain the difficulties initially experienced by Airbus in competing with the 787 during the 2004 – 2006 period.[3737] We recall that the United States' principal argument in this regard is that Airbus' problems with the Original A350, and its inability to launch the A350XWB earlier than 2006 were not due to its lacking access to key technologies, but because Airbus' resources in the early 2000s were committed to the A380.[3738] According to the United States, Airbus' position in the 200-300

[3737] United States' first written submissions, paras. 916-928; United States' comments on European Communities' response to question 87, para. 310; Interview with Noel Forgeard: "I wanted to limit the costs for Airbus", Süddeutsche Zeitung, 20 May 2006, Exhibit US-1228; Interview with Thomas Enders, "We have made mistakes", Welt am Sonntag, 14 May 2006, Exhibit US-1229; United States' second written submission, HSBI Appendix, para. 12; "Airbus/EADS officials concede Boeing advantage, question A350 viability", Air Transport Daily News, 6 October 2006, Exhibit US-1167; Robert Wall, "A350 Faces Busy Time Until Industrial Launch", Aviation Week & Space Technology, 20 June 2005, Exhibit US-296; Noel Forgeard and the A380, Commercial Aviation Report, January 1 and 15, 2007, Exhibit US-297.

[3738] United States' first written submission, para. 714. During this period, according to the United States, Airbus was also developing the A400M military transport.

1652   DSR 2012:III

seat wide-body market segment was a matter of its strategic choice to focus on mastering the technology of a super-jumbo that was designed to service hub-to-hub routes, while Boeing decided to focus on a smaller, more fuel-efficient point-to-point aircraft that could build on existing, generally available developments in composite technology and reductions in composite costs.[3739] The United States also argues that, having decided to go in a different direction to Boeing, Airbus compounded its own problems after the 787 launch by trying to rush the development of a competing A350 based on a quick reworking of the A330.[3740]

7.1796 In our view, the United States' arguments concerning the effect of the A380 and A400M programmes on Airbus' product development in the 200 - 300 seat product market are not exactly germane. The proper focus of the Panel's analysis is on the effects of the aeronautics R&D subsidies on *Boeing's* product development behaviour, and it is clear to us that the aeronautics R&D subsidies conferred a competitive advantage on Boeing. Even if we were to assume *arguendo* that Airbus had made a strategic decision that risked leaving it commercially vulnerable in the 200 – 300 seat wide-body LCA product market if Boeing decided to launch a new-technology aircraft before 2006, what is of relevance to the Panel's assessment is the role of the R&D subsidies in enabling Boeing to launch a new technology aircraft before 2006 and thereby exploit that vulnerability to Airbus' detriment.

Conclusion

7.1797 In conclusion, the Panel finds that the effect of the aeronautics R&D subsidies is a threat of displacement and impedance of European Communities' exports from third country markets within the meaning of Article 6.3(b) of the SCM Agreement, with respect to the 200-300 seat wide-body LCA product market, and significant lost sales and significant price suppression, within the meaning of Article 6.3(c) of the SCM Agreement with respect to that product market, each of which constitute serious prejudice to the interests of the European Communities within the meaning of Article 5(c) of the SCM Agreement.

[3739] United States' first written submission, para. 714.
[3740] *Ibid.*

Report of the Panel

> (ii) Whether the subsidies at issue in this dispute cause serious prejudice to the interests of the European Communities by reason of their effect on Boeing's pricing behaviour with respect to the 737NG, 777 and 787.

7.1798 As explained above in subsection 2(b)(ii), the difference between the European Communities' arguments in respect of the 787, on the hand, and the 737NG and 777 on the other, is that in the case of the 787, the European Communities submits that there are two principal effects of the subsidies that cause serious prejudice ("technology effects" and "price effects"), whereas in the case of the 737NG and the 777, the European Communities argues that serious prejudice is caused by one principal effect of all the subsidies ("price effects").

7.1799 In subsection 2(c)(i) above, the Panel has found that the aeronautics R&D subsidies, through their effects on Boeing's development of technologies (so-called "technology effects"), have caused serious prejudice to the interests of the European Communities in the 200-300 seat wide-body LCA product market. In this subsection, the Panel examines whether all of the subsidies at issue have caused serious prejudice to the interests of the European Communities by reason of their effect on Boeing's pricing behaviour with respect to 737NG, 777 and 787.

7.1800 The European Communities asserts that the subsidies at issue have "price effects" in that they either reduce Boeing's marginal unit costs or operate to increase Boeing's non-operating cash flow. The Panel first analyzes the effects of the subsidies that are said to reduce Boeing's marginal unit costs before turning to consider the effects of the other subsidies at issue in this dispute on Boeing's pricing, and ultimately, on Airbus' prices and sales in each of the three LCA product markets.

> Effects on Boeing's pricing of subsidies alleged to affect Boeing's marginal unit costs

7.1801 The European Communities has identified three of the challenged measures as operating to reduce the marginal unit costs that Boeing incurs in relation to the production and sale of individual LCA. These measures are (i) the FSC/ETI exemptions and exclusions, (ii) the Washington State and City of Everett B&O tax reductions and (iii) the waiver of landing fees granted by Snohomish County for 747LCFs carrying 787 parts and components to Everett for final assembly.[3741] We recall that the Panel has found that only the FSC/ETI measures and the state and municipal B&O tax reductions are specific

---

[3741] European Communities' first written submission, para. 1233.

1654

DSR 2012:III

subsidies[3742] and we therefore examine the effects of these two subsidies on Airbus' prices and sales in the 2004 – 2006 period.

7.1802 The FSC/ETI subsidies are tax measures that are structured as reductions in Boeing's overall tax liability by excluding a portion of export-related foreign-source income from taxation. The FSC/ETI tax exemptions/exclusions are realized on the delivery of every LCA that Boeing exports, as well as on LCA that Boeing produces and sells to domestic carriers and leasing companies for use predominantly on foreign routes. In other words, the FSC/ETI subsidies directly relate to revenue realized from export LCA sales and operate to reduce the revenues that are subject to taxation, thereby lowering Boeing's taxes and increasing its after-tax profits. As we explain in the Part of this Report in which we make a finding that the FSC/ETI measures are prohibited export subsidies within the meaning of Article 3.1(a) of the SCM Agreement[3743], the U.S. government, through the TIPRA[3744], repealed certain aspects of the grandfathering of FSC and ETI tax breaks for tax years beginning after 2006, and as Boeing will not deliver the 787 to any of its customers before that date, Boeing will not realize FSC/ETI tax exemptions and exclusions in relation to the sale of the 787. Indeed, the European Communities does not suggest that the FSC/ETI subsidies have affected the prices of the 787 and has not allocated the FSC/ETI subsidies to the 787 for purposes of its serious prejudice arguments.[3745] Our analysis of the effects of the FSC/ETI subsidies therefore proceeds on the basis that these subsidies can only have affected Boeing's pricing of the 737NG and 777, and thus can only have had effects in the 100-200 seat single-aisle, and 300-400 seat wide-body LCA product markets, respectively.

7.1803 The Washington State B&O tax subsidies were among the various tax incentives introduced by the Washington State Legislature under House Bill 2294 (HB 2294). Evidence before the Panel indicates that the purpose or intent behind the tax reform package in HB2294 was to reduce Boeing's cost structure and thereby significantly improve Boeing's competitiveness.[3746] The City of Everett's B&O tax reduction was a component of the incentives provided through the MSA. The Ordinance enacting the City of Everett B&O tax reduction states that the B&O tax reduction is intended to create an estimated net present value reduction of approximately $35 million, based on current estimated aircraft production and sales, and a six per cent discount rate over a 20 year period beginning in 2004.[3747] The Washington State B&O tax reductions apply to the production and sale of LCA manufactured in Washington State, and therefore potentially affect the production and sale of the 737NG, 777 and 787 families of Boeing LCA. The City of Everett B&O tax reductions affect the

---

[3742] See paras. 7.1406, 7.212, 7.302, 7.346, 7.516 of this Report.

[3743] See paras. 7.1450-7.1464 of this Report.

[3744] See above, para. 7.1385 of this Report.

[3745] European Communities' first written submission, para. 1230, Figure 15.

[3746] Washington State 7E7 Presentation, slide 9, Exhibit EC-66.

[3747] Everett Ordinance 2759-04 (2004), § 1, Exhibit EC-61.

Report of the Panel

production and sale of LCA manufactured in Everett, and therefore apply to the 777 and 787 families of Boeing LCA.

7.1804 The Panel recalls that in *US – Upland Cotton*, the panel considered that it was entitled, under Articles 5(c) and 6.3(c) of the SCM Agreement, to conduct an integrated examination of the effects of any subsidies with a sufficient nexus with the subsidized product and the particular effects-related variable under consideration.[3748] The panel stated:

> "Thus, in our price suppression analysis under Article 6.3(c), we examine one effects-related variable – prices – and one subsidized product – upland cotton. To the extent a sufficient nexus with these exists among the subsidies at issue so that their effects manifest themselves collectively, we believe that we may legitimately treat them as a "subsidy" and group them and their effects together." [3749]

7.1805 We note that the European Communities has grouped the FSC/ETI subsidies and the B&O tax subsidies together as subsidies that operate to reduce Boeing's marginal unit costs. The United States also submits that the FSC/ETI subsidies and B&O tax subsidies share certain similarities in structure and operation such that it is appropriate that the Panel conduct an aggregate analysis of their effects.[3750] The Panel considers that it is appropriate to aggregate the FSC/ETI subsidies and the B&O tax subsidies for purposes of analyzing their effects. In our view, in order to conduct an aggregated analysis of the effects of subsidies in the context of this dispute, it should be possible to discern from their structure, design and operation that they affect Boeing's behaviour in a similar way.

7.1806 The European Communities has analyzed the FSC/ETI subsidies and B&O tax subsidies as subsidies that are realized on the production and delivery of individual LCA, and which directly reduce Boeing's marginal unit costs for the production and sale of each LCA that benefits from them.[3751] While the United States does not consider that it is accurate to describe the subsidies as reducing Boeing's marginal unit costs[3752], it considers that both subsidies lead to an increase in revenues after the transaction (the sale of an LCA).[3753] In this sense, both subsidies are directly tied to sales of individual LCA. The United States agrees that, as a matter of economics, subsidies that are tied to sales have an impact on those sales.[3754] It also acknowledges that Boeing's LCA prices are

---

[3748] Panel Report, *US – Upland Cotton*, para. 7.1192.
[3749] *Ibid.*
[3750] United States' first written submission, paras. 767, 768.
[3751] European Communities' first written submission, para. 1241.
[3752] United States' first written submission, para. 751.
[3753] United States' first written submission, paras. 751-752.
[3754] United States' comments on the European Communities' response to question 289, para. 540.

1656

DSR 2012:III

affected by, *inter alia*, changes in Boeing's product-specific fixed and variable costs[3755] and endorses the view that product-specific subsidies can have a significant impact on prices and output.[3756]

7.1807 The FSC/ETI subsidies reduce the revenues from certain sales of aircraft on which Boeing is taxed, while the B&O tax subsidies directly reduce the rate at which Boeing's gross revenues from the manufacture of aircraft are taxed. The State of Washington B&O tax is levied on the gross proceeds of sale, gross incomes of a business or the value of products.[3757] The City of Everett B&O tax is a tax on gross revenues which, with respect to manufacturing, are generally treated as the value of products manufactured.[3758] In general terms, the subsidies lower taxes that Boeing pays and thereby increase Boeing's after-tax profits. Both the FSC/ETI and B&O tax subsidies increase the profitability of LCA sales in a way that enables Boeing to price its LCA at a level that would not otherwise be commercially justified. In short, the FSC/ETI subsidies and the B&O tax subsidies, by lowering the taxes incurred in connection with sales of LCA, clearly have a far more direct and immediate relationship to aircraft prices and sales than other subsidies at issue in this dispute, such as the aeronautics R&D subsidies.

7.1808 In addition, we recall that the FSC/ETI subsidies have been the subject of previous WTO dispute settlement and in that context, have been found to be prohibited export subsidies within the meaning of Article 3.1(a) of the SCM Agreement.[3759] We also make a finding in this Report that the FSC/ETI measures are prohibited export subsidies.[3760] The FSC/ETI subsidies not only bear a more direct relationship to Boeing's LCA prices than the aeronautics R&D subsidies, but they are also, by virtue of their very nature as export subsidies, more likely to cause adverse trade effects. We note in this regard that the Appellate Body has stated:

> "There is no logical reason why the Members of the WTO would, in conceiving and concluding the *SCM Agreement*, have granted panels the authority to draw inferences in cases involving actionable subsidies that *may* be illegal *if* they have certain trade effects, but not in cases that involve prohibited export subsidies *for which the adverse effects are presumed.*"[3761]

7.1809 The panel in *Brazil – Aircraft* explained the inherently trade-distorting nature of export subsidies as follows:

[3755] United States' response to question 298, para. 522.

[3756] Stiglitz and Greenwald, On the Question of the Impact of Subsidies on Supply and Prices in the LCA Market, US-1309, para. 4.

[3757] See para. 7.47 of this Report.

[3758] See para. 7.306 of this Report.

[3759] See paras. 7.1452-7.1455 of this Report.

[3760] See para. 7.1464 of this Report.

[3761] Appellate Body Report, *Canada – Aircraft*, para. 202. Emphasis added.

Report of the Panel

> "In our view, the object and purpose of the SCM Agreement is to impose multilateral disciplines on subsidies which distort international trade. It is for this reason that the SCM Agreement prohibits two categories of subsidies - subsidies contingent upon exportation and upon the use of domestic over imported goods - *that are specifically designed to affect trade.*"[3762]

7.1810 In our view, precisely because the FSC/ETI subsidies are contingent on Boeing making export sales, we are entitled to determine, absent reliable evidence to the contrary, that by their very nature, they will have trade distortive effects.[3763]

7.1811 We have previously estimated the amount of FSC/ETI subsidies related to sales of LCA that Boeing and McDonnell Douglas received from FSC and ETI tax exemptions and exclusions from 1989 through 2006 to be approximately $2.2 billion.[3764] The European Communities' consultants, ITR, estimate that, of the $2.2 billion in FSC/ETI subsidies received by Boeing with respect to its sales of LCA between 1989 and 2006, Boeing received approximately $153 million, $142 million and $140 million, respectively, in the years 2004 to 2006.[3765] As set forth in paragraphs 7.254 and 7.353 of this Report, the Panel has estimated that the amount of the State of Washington B&O tax reduction that was received directly by Boeing through 2006 is $13.8 million, while the amount of the City of Everett B&O tax reduction received by Boeing through 2006 is $2.2 million.

7.1812 As discussed in paragraphs 7.155-7.157 of this Report, the European Communities has allocated the full amount of the value of B&O tax subsidies estimated to be received by Boeing in 2007 – 2009 to the period 2004 – 2006 as part of ITR's allocation of subsidy amounts over time, to arrive at estimates of per-LCA subsidy "magnitudes".[3766] Although the Panel does not disagree with the general proposition that the expectation of the receipt of a subsidy may affect a recipient's behaviour, and thus give rise to a market effect prior to its actual receipt, the Panel does not consider that this should automatically lead to the mechanical allocation of amounts of recurring subsidies that reduce Boeing's marginal unit costs back in time by three years. The implication of such an

---

[3762] Panel Report, *Brazil – Aircraft*, para. 7.26. Emphasis added. See also the statement of the arbitrator in *US - FSC (Article 22.6 – US)*: "Export subsidies do, after all, have "adverse effects" on third parties. Systemically speaking they are, as a category of subsidy, more inherently prone to do so than any other". Decision by the Arbitrator, *US – FSC (Article 22.6 – US)*, para. 5.35.

[3763] That being said, as we note below, there is in fact in this case reliable evidence which confirms that determination; see e.g. paras. 7.1806-7.1807, 7.1811, and 7.1817-7.1823.

[3764] See para. 7.1419 of this Report.

[3765] International Trade Resources LLC, Calculating on a Per-Aircraft Basis the Magnitude of the Subsidies Provided to US Large Civil Aircraft, 20 February 2007, Exhibit EC-13, Appendix A, p. 3.

[3766] International Trade Resources LLC, Calculating on a Per-Aircraft Basis the Magnitude of the Subsidies Provided to US Large Civil Aircraft, 20 February 2007. The European Communities' methodology for allocating subsidy amounts to arrive at annual and per-LCA subsidy "magnitudes" is described in paras. 7.1616-7.1617 of this Report.

allocation would be that the subsidy does not give rise to serious prejudice, within the meaning of Article 6.3, in the year of its receipt. As we have explained in paragraph 7.1685, the Panel does not accept this implication. Rather, the Panel considers that given the particularities of LCA production and sale, the effects of the subsidies should be understood to begin at the time at which an LCA order is obtained (or an order is lost) and to continue up to and including the time at which that aircraft is delivered (or not delivered).

7.1813 Moreover, we note that the European Communties' allocation of the post-2006 amounts of B&O tax subsidies estimated to be received by Boeing in 2007 – 2009 to the period 2004 – 2006 arises in the specific context of ITR's allocation of subsidies received by Boeing between 1989 and 2006, over time and across particular models of LCA, for purposes of estimating per-LCA subsidy "magnitudes" and *ad valorem* rates of subsidization for each family of Boeing LCA. ITR's per-LCA subsidy "magnitude" estimates play no part in the Panel's analysis of the effects of the subsidies. We therefore see no reason or need to effectively shift the amounts of recurring subsidies received by Boeing backwards through time for purposes of our serious prejudice analysis in the way in which ITR has done for purposes of its subsidy "magnitude" calculations.

7.1814 The issue before the Panel is whether the availability of FSC/ETI subsidies and B&O tax subsidies enabled Boeing to compete on price in individual sales, and secure sales that it would not otherwise have made, and where it did not win those sales, led to Airbus securing those sales at lower prices than it would otherwise have obtained. The United States argues that the amounts of the FSC/ETI subsidies received by Boeing were too small relative to Boeing's order revenues to have affected Boeing's pricing to a degree that would lead to it winning sales that it would not otherwise have won, or forcing Airbus to win sales only at lower prices than it would otherwise have obtained. It presents the following calculations in this regard:[3767]

[3767] United States' first written submission, para. 815; see also United States' second written submission, para. 175 and footnote 272; United States' comment on European Communities' response to question 229, paras. 418-420; United States' comment on European Communities' response to question 269, para. 469. The European Communities disagrees with the United States' position that the alleged tax benefits were not significant enough to affect Boeing's supply of LCA; European Communities comments on United States' response to question 389, para. 403.

Report of the Panel

Year	Value of orders	FSC/ETI magnitude	Ratio of subsidy to order value
2000	$32,591	$266	1:122
2001	$16,588	$197	1:84
2002	$12,585	$179	1:70
2003	$9,771	$107	1:91
2004	$16,650	$153	1:109
2005	$67,193	$142	1:473
2006	$61,579	$140	1:440

7.1815 ITR criticizes the United States' allocation of FSC/ETI subsidy amounts over order values, which it argues fails to reflect the reality that the FSC/ETI subsidies accrue against aircraft sales revenues, not orders.[3768] ITR notes that the FSC/ETI subsidy is based on a fixed percentage of broadly defined export revenue or earnings, and argues that any *ad valorem* rates of subsidization should be based on the sales revenue against which the subsidies accrued. ITR presents the following table showing FSC/ETI subsidies calculated as a percentage of Boeing's annual revenue from aircraft deliveries between 2000 and 2006:[3769]

Year	Delivery Revenue	FSC/ETI Subsidies	
		Amount	% Delivery Revenue
2000	24,792	266	1.07%
2001	27,251	197	0.72%
2002	22,100	179	0.81%
2003	16,637	107	0.64%
2004	15,905	153	0.96%
2005	14,777	142	0.96%
2006	21,562	140	0.65%

7.1816 We do not consider that either measure is particularly informative or illustrative of the capacity for the FSC/ETI subsidies to have affected Boeing's prices, and by extension, Airbus' prices and sales.

[3768] ITR LLC Response to US Criticisms of ITR Subsidy Magnitude Report, 1 November 2007, Exhibit EC-1181, para. 15.
[3769] ITR LLC Response to US Criticisms of ITR Subsidy Magnitude Report, 1 November 2007, Exhibit EC-1181, para. 16.

1660

DSR 2012:III

US - Large Civil Aircraft (2nd Complaint)

7.1817 It is important to bear in mind that the FSC/ETI subsidies are export subsidies that are designed to increase Boeing's competitiveness through its pricing of LCA for export. The European Communities has provided evidence concerning a sales campaign in 1996 in which an Airbus negotiator states that, owing to Boeing's lower pricing due to its receipt of FSC subsidies, his team was asked by the customer to reduce its price by a further $4 million per aircraft.[3770] The U.S. Trade Representative described the general purpose of the FSC/ETI provisions as being to enhance the international competitiveness of U.S. companies.[3771] A 2003 report on FSC/ETI beneficiaries indicates that, over the six-year period ended in 2002, Boeing was the largest FSC/ETI beneficiary.[3772] Moreover, Boeing itself seems to have regarded the FSC/ETI measures to be an important aspect of its ability to compete. In 2003, Mr. James H. Zrust, Vice President of Tax at Boeing, delivered a statement to the United States Senate regarding the importance of the FSC/ETI tax benefits to Boeing. As Vice President of Tax at Boeing, Mr. Zrust would have been very highly qualified to speak to this issue. In his statement, Mr. Zrust made clear that repealing Boeing's ETI benefits without a "suitable replacement" would have an adverse effect on Boeing's position "vis-a-vis foreign competitors", and stated that while repealing ETI without a suitable replacement would have an adverse impact on the "international competitiveness" of all U.S. exports, it would be "especially devastating to the U.S. aerospace industry".[3773] He spoke about the importance of ETI for "U.S. companies competing against foreign firms, which are often heavily subsidized by their governments".[3774] He reiterated that any repeal of ETI benefits without a suitable replacement would be "particularly detrimental to U.S. competitiveness", and that the loss of a tax benefit that:

> "{A}llows U.S. exporters to compete fairly with European exporters may well translate into a reduction in R&D investments, higher capital costs, and lost market share over time."[3775]

7.1818 These considerations point quite clearly to the significance of the FSC/ETI subsidies to Boeing's ability to compete on price against Airbus. We

---

[3770] Christian Scherer, Commercial Aspects of the Aircraft Business from the Perspective of a Manufacturer, March 2007, Exhibit EC-11 (BCI), para. 56.

[3771] Statement of Robert B. Zoellick, U.S. Trade Representative before the Committee on Finance of the U.S. Senate, 30 July 2002, Exhibit EC-629, at p. 74; WTO's Extraterritorial Income Decision: Hearing before House Comm. on Ways and Means 107th Cong. 35 (2992) (response to questions by Barbara Angus, International Tax Counsel, U.S. Department of the Treasury), Exhibit EC-630, at p. 35.

[3772] European Communities' first written submission, para. 947, Jose Oyola, FSC-ETI Beneficiaries: An Updated Profile, Tax Notes International, 6 October 2003, Exhibit EC-632.

[3773] Statement of James H. Zrust, Vice President of Tax, the Boeing Company, before the Committee on Finance of the U.S. Senate, 8 July 2003, Exhibit EC-631, p. 187.

[3774] Ibid.

[3775] Statement of James H. Zrust, Vice President of Tax, the Boeing Company, before the Committee on Finance of the U.S. Senate, 8 July 2003, Exhibit EC-631, p. 190.

Report of the Panel

have no doubt that the availability of the FSC/ETI subsidies, in combination with the B&O tax subsidies, enabled Boeing to lower its prices beyond the level that would otherwise have been economically justifiable, and that in some cases, this led to it securing sales that it would not otherwise have made, while in other cases, it led to Airbus being able to secure the sale only at a reduced price. We note further that, to the extent that these subsidies have enabled Boeing to win sales from Airbus in the past, they have served to entrench Boeing as the incumbent supplier, thereby putting it at an important switching cost advantage over Airbus in future sales of aircraft of the same family to that same customer.[3776]

7.1819 The FSC/ETI programme was in operation prior to 2000, and it is therefore not possible for the Panel to ascertain the effects of the subsidies from direct observation of market share and pricing trend data over the 2000 – 2006 period. The United States' explanations of factors that it considers explain the prices and performance of Airbus LCA relative to Boeing LCA in the 100 – 200 seat single aisle, and 300 – 400 seat wide-body product markets in the 2004 – 2006 period similarly do not reverse or attenuate the pervasive and consistent pricing advantage that Boeing had in LCA campaigns in the 2001 – 2003 period due to the availability of the FSC/ETI subsidies.[3777]

7.1820 The Panel considers that in these circumstances, it is necessary and appropriate to deduce the effects of the FSC/ETI subsidies and the B&O tax subsidies on Airbus' sales and prices over the 2004 – 2006 period, based on commonsense reasoning and the drawing of inferences from conclusions regarding the nature of these subsides as subsidies that increase the profitability of LCA sales in a way that enables Boeing to price its LCA at a level that would not otherwise be commercially justified, the duration of the FSC/ETI subsidies, as well as from what we understand of the nature of competition between Airbus and Boeing, particularly the price-sensitive nature of certain significant LCA sales campaigns and the pricing advantage afforded to incumbent suppliers through the phenomenon of buyer switching costs. We consider this approach to be consistent with our obligation under Article 11 of the DSU to make an objective assessment of the facts. In this regard, we note that the Appellate Body, in *Canada – Aircraft*, indicated that drawing inferences from facts on the record is a routine and inherent aspect of a panel's discharging its obligation under Article 11 of the DSU:

[3776] Switching costs refer to the costs that buyers who operate one particular family of aircraft must incur to switch to a new supplier (such costs stem from pilot training, aircraft maintenance etc.). See Rod P. Muddle, The Dynamics of the Large Civil Aircraft Industry, March 2007, Exhibit EC- 10, para. 97; Christian Scherer, Commercial Aspects of the Aircraft Business From the Perspective of a Manufacturer, March 2007, Exhibit EC-11 (BCI), para. 53; Jordan and Dorman Report, Exhibit US-3, p. 15.

[3777] E.g. United States' first written submission, paras. 1064-1080, 1138-1155.

1662

DSR 2012:III

US - Large Civil Aircraft (2nd Complaint)

"The DSU does not purport to state in what detailed circumstances inferences, adverse or otherwise, may be drawn by panels from infinitely varying combinations of facts. Yet, in all cases, in carrying out their mandate and seeking to achieve the "objective assessment of the facts" required by Article 11 of the DSU, panels routinely draw inferences from the facts placed on the record. The inferences drawn may be inferences of fact: that is, from fact A and fact B, it is reasonable to infer the existence of fact C. Or the inferences derived may be inferences of law: for example, the ensemble of facts found to exist warrants the characterization of a "subsidy" or a "subsidy contingent ... in fact ... upon export performance". The facts must, of course, rationally support the inferences made, but inferences may be drawn whether or not the facts already on the record deserve the qualification of a *prima facie* case. The drawing of inferences is, in other words, an inherent and unavoidable aspect of a panel's basic task of finding and characterizing the facts making up a dispute."[3778]

7.1821 The other option potentially open to us is to decline to make a serious prejudice finding because of the difficulty of calculating with mathematical certitude the precise degree to which Boeing's pricing of the 737NG and 777 families of aircraft was affected by the FSC/ETI subsidies and B&O tax subsidies. In our view, such an approach would be inconsistent with our obligations under Article 11 of the DSU, as well as contrary to considerations of basic commonsense and reason.

7.1822 The Panel considers that it is reasonable to infer, based on the fact that the effects of the subsidies on Airbus' prices would be most acutely felt in particular sales campaigns of strategic importance to Boeing and/or Airbus, that the effects of the subsidies are therefore significant in the sense that Boeing's success in such sales campaigns necessarily constitutes a significant lost sale to Airbus, and that such sales secured by Airbus in the face of Boeing's reduced prices necessarily constitute sales secured at significantly suppressed prices. It is thus inescapable to also arrive at the conclusion that in law the effects of the subsidies on Airbus' prices and sales constitute significant lost sales and significant price suppression, within the meaning of Article 6.3(c) of the SCM Agreement, as well as displacement and impedance of exports from third country markets, within the meaning of Article 6.3(b).

7.1823 In sum, the Panel is satisfied that the effects of the FSC/ETI subsidies and the Washington State B&O tax subsidies in the 100 – 200 seat single aisle LCA product market were to significantly suppress Airbus' prices in sales in which it competed against Boeing and to cause Airbus to lose significant sales, and to displace and impede European Communities' exports from third country

---

[3778] Appellate Body Report, *Canada – Aircraft*, para. 198.

DSR 2012:III

1663

Report of the Panel

markets in that product market. We are also satisfied that the effects of the FSC/ETI subsidies, the Washington State B&O tax subsidies and the City of Everett B&O tax subsidies in the 300 – 400 seat wide-body LCA product market were to significantly suppress Airbus' prices in sales in which it competed against Boeing and to cause Airbus to lose significant sales, and to displace and impede European Communities' exports from third country markets in that product market.

7.1824 We note that the B&O tax subsidies also apply to the production and sale of the 787. However, there is insufficient evidence before us that would enable us to conclude that these subsidies are of a magnitude that would enable them, on their own, to have such an effect on Boeing's prices of the 787 as would lead to a finding that their effects in the 200 – 300 seat wide-body market were significant price suppression, significant lost sales or displacement or impedance of European Communities imports into the United States or exports to third countries. We recall that we have previously found that the aeronautics R&D subsidies, through their effects on Boeing's development of technologies for the 787, gave rise to serious prejudice in that product market.[3779] However, owing to the very different way in which the aeronautics R&D subsidies operate, we do not consider that it is appropriate to aggregate the effects of the B&O tax subsidies on Boeing's pricing of the 787 with the effects of the aeronautics R&D subsidies on Boeing's development of technologies applied to the 787, as it is clear that the two groups of subsidies operate through entirely distinct causal mechanisms.

> Effects on Boeing's pricing of subsidies
> alleged to increase Boeing's non-operating
> cash flow

7.1825 We now turn to consider the effects of the category of subsidies identified by the European Communities as operating to increase Boeing's non-operating cash flow, thereby allegedly giving Boeing the ability to engage in "aggressive pricing" of its LCA in order to win market share from Airbus. First, the Panel recalls that this group of subsidies comprises all of the challenged measures that the Panel has found to be specific subsidies within the meaning of Articles 1 and 2 of the SCM Agreement, other than the FSC/ETI subsidies and B&O tax subsidies discussed above. In other words, the European Communities purports to include within this category of subsidies the aeronautics R&D subsidies, the Washington State and City of Everett taxation subsidies other than the B&O tax subsidies, the property and sales tax abatements provided to Boeing pursuant to IRBs issued by the State of Kansas and municipalities therein, and the tax credits and other incentives provided to Boeing by the State of Illinois and municipalities therein, each as set forth in paragraph 7.1433 of this Report.

[3779] See para. 7.1797 of this Report.

1664

DSR 2012:III

US - Large Civil Aircraft (2nd Complaint)

The aeronautics R&D subsidies represent the overwhelming majority of the subsidy amount within this category of subsidies received by Boeing between 1989 and 2006.

7.1826 The Panel recalls that it has previously found that the aeronautics R&D subsidies, through their effects on Boeing's development of technologies for the 787, caused serious prejudice to the European Communities in the 200 – 300 seat wide-body LCA product market.[3780] The European Communities' "price effects" causation argument effectively asks the Panel to analyze the effects of the aeronautics R&D subsidies again, this time on the basis that they freed up additional cash which Boeing was able to use to engage in aggressive pricing of its three families of LCA (i.e. the 737NG, 777 and 787) resulting in serious prejudice to the European Communities' interests in the three LCA product markets. We have previously indicated that we do not consider that it is appropriate to reduce the effects of the aeronautics R&D subsidies at issue in this dispute to their cash value.[3781] Moreover, the European Communities has indicated, in response to a question from the Panel, that the Panel should not over-count the effects of the aeronautics R&D subsidies by analyzing their effects in terms of their "knowledge" effects as well as, or in addition to, their "financial" effects.[3782] Having analyzed the effects of the aeronautics R&D subsidies on the basis of their contribution to Boeing's development of technologies for the 787, we consider that it would be over-counting to additionally analyze their effects based on a different understanding of their operation, namely, as freeing up additional cash for Boeing to use to lower the prices of its LCA.

7.1827 When the aeronautics R&D subsidies are subtracted from this category of subsidies that are said to operate by increasing Boeing's non-operating cash flow, the amount remaining is comparatively small, being approximately $550 million. As importantly, the subsidies in this category, unlike the FSC/ETI subsidies and B&O tax subsidies discussed above, are not directly related to Boeing's production or sale of LCA.[3783] Rather, as the European Communities appears to acknowledge, these subsidies are not "explicitly targeted to lowering Boeing's costs of production of specific LCA models".[3784] According to the European Communities, "LCA market factors" and "dynamics of production" combine to support a finding that subsidies of this nature nonetheless allow

---

[3780] Ibid.

[3781] See para. 7.1760 of this Report.

[3782] European Communities' response to question 375, para. 322.

[3783] European Communities' first written submission, para. 1277; European Communities' second written submission, paras. 697-740. Although the European Communities argues that some of the subsidies within this category "specifically relate to the development and production of the 787 family of LCA" and are therefore "tied" to the 787, it uses this concept to denote the allocation of a subsidy amount to particular products, rather than to denote that a subsidy is "tied" to a product in the sense that its receipt is in some way contingent on production or sale of a particular product; European Communities' response to question 374, paras. 297-298, footnote 392.

[3784] European Communities' first wrriten submission, para. 1303.

DSR 2012:III

1665

Report of the Panel

Boeing to market its LCA at lower prices than would otherwise be the case. The European Communities argues that, under the "right conditions of competition – such as the intense duopoly competition existing in the LCA markets – non-price- or non-production-contingent subsidies can confer the ability to cause adverse effects".[3785]

7.1828 Indeed, while the United States has emphasized that subsidies that are not tied to production of a particular product are unlikely to affect production, it has explicitly stated that it agrees with the European Communities that this fact is not determinative.[3786] Thus, it would appear that the parties do not disagree on the proposition that where a subsidy is not tied to production of a particular product, the subsidy may still affect the behaviour of the recipient of the subsidy in a manner that causes serious prejudice, depending upon the context in which it is used. However, an important element of the European Communities' arguments as to why subsidies of this nature would affect Boeing's pricing behaviour relates to the total amount of the subsidies that the European Communities alleges to exist, as well as their allocation over time and across the particular models of LCA to arrive subsidy "magnitudes". One might reasonably expect that a total amount of $19.1 billion in subsidies received between 1989 and 2006 would have a greater potential to affect Boeing's LCA prices than $550 million received over the same period. As we have explained, the Panel is assessing the effects on Boeing's LCA pricing of approximately $550 million in subsidies, the receipt of which is not directly tied to the production or sale of particular LCA. We are not persuaded that subsidies of this nature and of this amount have affected Boeing's prices in a manner that could be said to give rise to serious prejudice to the European Communities' interests.

[3785] European Communities' non-confidential oral statement at the second meeting with the Panel, para. 107. See also, European Communities' response to question 379, para. 435: "certain tied subsidies may yield similar effects as certain unrestricted subsidies, depending on the context of the specific subsidy at issue; i.e., the specific nature of the subsidy and its magnitude, as well as the condition of the recipient."

[3786] United States' comments on European Communities' response to question 301, paras. 601-602:
"The United States also agrees with the EC that the absence of a direct link between subsidies and the development, production, or sale of large civil aircraft 'should not be determinative of the outcome of the Panel's causation analysis'. At the same time, without a direct link between an alleged subsidy and the development, production or sale of large civil aircraft, a complaining member bears the burden of identifying persuasive evidence that the subsidy was used by the recipient in a way that caused the adverse effects at issue, or that, but for' the subsidy, the recipient could not have competed in the market as it did.
Because the bulk of the alleged subsidies in this dispute are, by the EC's own admission, 'untied' to the development, production or sale of any Boeing large civil aircraft, the evidence cited by the EC regarding the ways in which Boeing supposedly used the alleged subsidies is critical to its causation arguments. Yet, that 'evidence' is essentially non-existent ..."

1666

DSR 2012:III

US - Large Civil Aircraft (2ⁿᵈ Complaint)

Other causation arguments made by the
European Communities

7.1829 The European Communities has also, in the context of its arguments that the subsidies caused serious prejudice through their effects on Boeing's LCA prices, presented certain arguments which the Panel does not find persuasive. In particular, the European Communities argues that Boeing's LCA division would not have been "economically viable" had it not received $19.1 billion in subsidies between 1989 and 2006. The European Communities also presents an econometric simulation model that purports to support the European Communities' argument that Boeing would have invested the subsidies in lower LCA pricing and additional investments in R&D. We briefly explain what we consider to be the principal weaknesses in these arguments.

"Economic viability" of Boeing's LCA division in the absence of the subsidies

7.1830 The European Communities' arguments concerning the "economic viability" of Boeing's LCA division between 1989 and 2006 had it not received an alleged $19.1 billion in subsidies initially arose out of its rebuttal of the United States' argument that the subsidies had no effect on Boeing's pricing or product development behaviour. With each successive submission, the parties presented new and more complex financial information concerning the appropriate basis on which to conduct a counterfactual analysis of whether the Boeing LCA division's pricing and product development behaviour would have been possible had it not received an alleged $19.1 billion in subsidies between 1989 and 2006.[3787]

[3787] ITR, Alternative Assessment of the Effect of US Subsidies on the US LCA Industry's Profit and Debt, Exhibit EC-1180; United States' Comments on European Communities' response to question 78, para. 270; European Communities' non-confidential oral statement at the second meeting with the Panel, para. 117; ITR, Economic Viability of Boeing Commercial Airplanes without US Subsidies, 10 April 2008, Exhibit EC-1393, Robert F. Whitelaw, Report on Measuring Economic Viability, 3 April 2008, Exhibit EC-1395 and European Communities' response to question 292; Statement of Ruud Roggekamp, Exhibit US-1321; Greenwald Comments on Whitelaw Economic Viability Report, Exhibit US-1324 and United States' comments on European Communities' response to question 292; Professor David Wessels, The Economic Viability of Boeing's Commercial Aircraft Division (30 July 2009), Exhibit US-1358; Stern Stewart & Co. Comments on Economic Viability Analysis (29 July 2009), Exhibit US-1359 and United States' response to question 370; ITR Report on Reconciliation of EC, Wessels and Stern Analyses of BCA's Economic Viability, 20 August 2009, Exhibit EC-1448; Whitelaw Declaration on Effects of Removal of Cash on WACC and Earnings for Economic Viability Analysis, Exhibit EC-1499; Zarowin Declaration on Treatment of Certain Pension and Other Post-Retirement Obligations, 20 August 2009, Exhibit EC-1450 and European Communities' comments on United States' response to question 370; ITR Report on BCA's Return on Invested Capital, 29 July 2009, Exhibit EC-1429; Declaration of Paul Zarowin, 29 July 2009, Exhibit EC-1431 and European Communities' response to question 378, para. 357; United States' comments on European Communities' response to question 378, and Commentary on ITR's ROIC analysis and the Wessels Economic Viability Reports (Annex A) and Commentary on ITR's ROIC analysis and the Stern Stewart Economic Viability Report (Annex B).

DSR 2012:III

Report of the Panel

7.1831 The parties disagree generally as to the appropriate metric for assessing the "economic viability" of Boeing's LCA division and the appropriate adjustments that should be made to the operating profit figures for Boeing's LCA division as part of that assessment. The Panel recalls that third parties such as Australia and Brazil question whether it is even appropriate for panels to undertake a causation analysis under Articles 5(c) and 6.3 of the SCM Agreement by attempting to trace subsidies through a recipient's cash flow statements. It is not necessary for the Panel to address these issues in order to evaluate the merits of the European Communities' economic viability argument for purposes of this dispute. We recall that all of the economic viability calculations are based on the assumption that Boeing's LCA division received $19.1 billion in subsidies between 1989 and 2006. By contrast, the Panel has found that the amount of subsidies received by Boeing over this period is substantially less than $19.1 billion. Even if the Panel were to accept the adjustments to the operating profit figures for Boeing's LCA division proposed by the European Communities, and even if the Panel were to consider it appropriate to analyze the effects of the aeronautics R&D subsidies on Boeing's behaviour as being equivalent to the effects on Boeing of the receipt of an equivalent amount of unrestricted cash (which we do not), once the amount of the subsidies received by Boeing between 1989 and 2006 is reduced from $19.1 billion to our own estimate of the total amount of the subsidies[3788], the argument that Boeing's LCA division would not have been "economically viable" in the absence of the subsidies unless it altered its prices or product development behaviour becomes untenable, whichever basis for assessing economic viability is used.

Cabral Report

7.1832 The European Communities presents an econometric simulation model by Professor Luís Cabral which seeks to address the question of how the provision of subsidies affects the business decisions of Boeing; specifically, how the receipt of an additional dollar of a particular category of subsidy affects the amount that Boeing chooses to invest in the development of new aircraft, and to price more aggressively.[3789] Professor Cabral's analysis focuses on the effects of a category of subsidies that he refers to as "development subsidies". These are subsidies in which the amount of subsidy does not vary in direct proportion to the number of aircraft produced or sold.[3790] Professor Cabral's analysis is based

---

[3788] See para. 7.1433 of this Report.

[3789] Luís M. B. Cabral, Impact of Development Subsidies Granted to Boeing, New York University and CEPR, March 2007, Exhibit EC-4, para. 1.

[3790] Luís M. B. Cabral, Impact of Development Subsidies Granted to Boeing, New York University and CEPR, March 2007, Exhibit EC-4, paras. 2-3. It appears that the category of subsidies that Professor Cabral refers to as "development subsidies" encompasses the same subsidies that the European Communities analyzes as operating to increase Boeing's non-operating cash flows (as

1668

DSR 2012:III

on a specific economic model of Boeing's behaviour; namely, that when Boeing receives so-called "development subsidies", management seeks to maximize a trade-off between shareholder income and shareholder value, with the result that it directs a certain portion of the subsidy towards dividends, and the remainder towards "investments that increase firm value".[3791] Appendix VII.F.2 to this Part of the Report explains the Cabral model in greater detail, along with the United States' criticisms of the model, and the Panel's evaluation of its principal weaknesses in the context of its use in this dispute.

Conclusion

7.1833 For the foregoing reasons, the Panel concludes: (i) that the effect of the FSC/ETI subsidies and State of Washington B&O tax subsidies is displacement and impedance of European Communities, exports from third country markets within the meaning of Article 6.3(b) of the SCM Agreement with respect to the 100 – 200 seat single-aisle LCA product market, and significant price suppression and significant lost sales within the meaning of Article 6.3(c) in that product market; and (ii) that the effect of the FSC/ETI subsidies, the State of Washington B&O tax subsidies and the City of Everett B&O tax subsidies is displacement and impedance of European Communities' exports from third country markets within the meaning of Article 6.3(b) of the SCM Agreement with respect to the 300 – 400 seat wide-body LCA product market, and significant price suppression and significant lost sales within the meaning of Article 6.3(c) in that product market.

7.1834 The Panel is not satisfied that the European Communities has demonstrated that the Washington State taxation subsidies other than the B&O tax subsidies, or the property and sales tax abatements provided to Boeing pursuant to IRBs issued by the State of Kansas and municipalities therein, and the tax credits and other incentives provided to Boeing by the State of Illinois and municipalities therein, through their effects on Boeing's LCA pricing behaviour, cause serious prejudice to the European Communities' interests in any of the three LCA product markets identified by the European Communities in this dispute.

> Whether the subsidies at issue in this dispute cause a threat of significant price suppression in each of the three LCA product markets

7.1835 In addition to its arguments that the subsidies cause "present" serious prejudice to the European Communities' interests, the European Communities

---

distinguished from the subsidies that the European Communities characterizes as reducing Boeing's marginal unit costs of production and sale of LCA).

[3791] Luís M. B. Cabral, Impact of Development Subsidies Granted to Boeing, New York University and CEPR, March 2007, Exhibit EC-4, para. 5.

Report of the Panel

argues that the subsidies at issue in this dispute cause a threat of serious prejudice with respect to *future orders* of LCA in each of the three LCA product markets.[3792]

Arguments of the European Communities

7.1836 The European Communities' arguments regarding the existencee of a threat of serious prejudice based on future orders of Airubs LCA are structured in the same manner with respect to each LCA product market. The European Communities argues that the present and future subsidies give rise to a significant likelihood that Airbus will suffer from significant price suppression with respect to future orders of each of the competing Airbus LCA families, based on the "same types of evidence" that support the European Communities' present serious prejudice claim.[3793] In this regard, the European Communities contends: (i) Boeing will receive "guaranteed subsidies" benefiting each of its Boeing LCA families in the post-2006 period; (ii) the nature of the subsidies indicates that the "technology effects" (relevant only in relation to the 200 – 300 seat wide-body LCA product market) and "price effects" (relevant with respect to each of the three LCA product markets) will continue in the future; (iii) the magnitude of the past, present and "guaranteed future subsidies" benefiting each of the Boeing LCA families will continue to be very large[3794]; (iv) conditions of competition in the post-2006 period will continue to give Boeing the ability and incentive to use the "subsidy benefits" to "price down" its subsidized LCA families to the detriment of the like Airbus LCA families[3795]; and (v) the already suppressed prices in each of the three Airbus LCA markets at issue, coupled with the nature and magnitude of the subsides, estimated price effects of the subsidies and conditions of competition in each of the three LCA markets give rise to a significant likelihood that Airbus' future orders of "like" LCA products will be at significantly suppressed prices.[3796]

7.1837 According to the European Communities, the suppressed prices for Airbus' LCA (which are caused by subsidies) provide a strong indication that prices will be suppressed in the future. The European Communities considers that the evidence provided in support of its present price suppression arguments is "equally relevant" to its threat of price suppression arguments insofar as it

---

[3792] Specifically, the European Communities argues that the subsidies cause a threat of significant price suppression with respect to *future orders* of: the A330 and A350XWB-800 families of LCA, A320 family of LCA and A350XWB-900/1000 families of LCA; European Communities' first written submission, paras. 1446, 1542 and 1632.

[3793] European Communities' first written submission, paras. 1447, 1542 and 1632.

[3794] European Communities' first written submission, paras. 1450, 1545 and 1635. The European Communities here presents projections of what it claims are per-LCA subsidization magnitudes and *ad valorem* rates for each model of the 787, 737NG and 777 for the years 2007-2010; Figures 36, 37, 53, 54, 69 and 70 of European Communities' first written submission, paras. 1450, 1545 and 1635.

[3795] European Communities' first written submission, para.s 1451, 1546 and 1636.

[3796] European Communities' first written submission, paras. 1452-1454, 1547-1549 and 1637-1639.

1670

DSR 2012:III

US - Large Civil Aircraft (2nd Complaint)

shows already suppressed prices for the Airbus LCA at issue.[3797] Further, the European Communities argues that "having established the existence of serious prejudice from the actionable subsidies, demonstrating the existence of *threat* of serious prejudice from the effects of the same subsidies is a relatively straightforward exercise".[3798]

7.1838 In response to a question from the Panel, the European Communities indicates that it does not agree with the implication that its threat of serious prejudice argument is dependent on it demonstrating the existence of present serious prejudice. The European Communities states that although the evidence relied upon in support of its present and threat of serious prejudice arguments may overlap, the evidence is "being adduced to support different legal conclusions".[3799] Further, in response to a United States' argument, the European Communities contends that its threat of serious prejudice arguments with respect to future LCA orders are not based merely on "the existence of present serious prejudice, and the continuation of that serious prejudice into the future".[3800]

Arguments of the United States

7.1839 The United States argues that the European Communities' threat of serious prejudice arguments rest almost exclusively on the notion that the "technology effects" and the "price effects" alleged in relation to its present serious prejudice claim will "continue".[3801] By asserting that the evidence presented in relation to present serious prejudice demonstrates a threat of serious prejudice on the basis of unsupported assertions that the current situation will "continue" in the future, the European Communities' threat of serious prejudice case does nothing more than repeat the erroneous assertions it made in relation to its present serious prejudice case. The United States argues that the alleged subsidization did not cause present serious prejudice. Therefore, in the absence of any new information from the European Communities, continuation of the existing situation is "likely to lead to more of the same".[3802] In other words, if the Panel does not find the existence of present serious prejudice, the European Communities has provided no basis for finding a threat of serious prejudice.[3803] Further, the United States argues that the European Communities has provided no evidence to support its assertion that the current situation is likely to

---

[3797] European Communities' first written submission, paras. 1453, 1548 and 1638.

[3798] European Communities' first written submission, para. 1148.

[3799] European Communities' response to question 103, para. 544.

[3800] European Communities' comments on United States' response to question 105, para. 414.

[3801] United States' first written submission, paras. 1014, 1103 and 1183.

[3802] United States' first written submission, paras. 1009-1010, 1098-1099 and 1178-1179.

[3803] This is because the European Communities' threat claim is premised on the existence of present serious prejudice and the continuation of that serious prejudice into the future. United States' response to question 313, para. 560.

Report of the Panel

"continue". According to the United States, the situation for Airbus is in fact likely to improve.[3804]

7.1840 In response to the European Communities' argument that the conditions of competition will continue to give Boeing the ability and incentive to use its subsidy benefits to price down its LCA, the United States argues that it has demonstrated in response to the present serious prejudice case that Boeing does not have such an incentive. Further, it asserts that the conditions of competition are evolving in Airbus' favour.[3805] According to the United States, the European Communities' reliance upon the magnitude of the subsidies does not advance its threat of serious prejudice case because the European Communities has grossly overstated the magnitude and price effect figures, both on an absolute and a per-aircraft basis.[3806]

7.1841 The United States also argues that if the Panel finds the existence of present serious prejudice, this warrants the exercise of judicial economy in relation to the European Communities' arguments regarding threat of serious prejudice.[3807] This is because a finding of present serious prejudice triggers the obligation under Article 7.8 of the SCM Agreement for the United States to remove the adverse effects of the subsidy or to withdraw the subsidy. The United States argues that in such circumstances, an additional finding of threat of serious prejudice "will not change the obligation on the subsidizing Member or the recommendation of the Panel".[3808]

Arguments of third parties

Australia

7.1842 Australia argues that a threat of serious prejudice does not constitute a distinct *form* of serious prejudice. According to Australia, footnote 13 to the SCM Agreement makes clear that, whatever the overall scope of serious prejudice may be, that scope includes the concept of threat of serious prejudice within its bounds.[3809] Australia argues that both threat of serious prejudice and the broader concept of serious prejudice can be seen to exist on the same continuum and are defined by the same effects listed in Article 6.3, as elaborated by the rest of Article 6.[3810]

7.1843 Australia considers that the report of the panel in *US - Upland Cotton* suggests that the threat of serious prejudice can be established by an examination

---

[3804] United States' first written submission, paras. 1011, 1100 and 1180.

[3805] United States' first written submission, para. 1015.

[3806] United States' first written submission, paras. 1016, 1104 and 1184.

[3807] United States' response to question 313, para. 559.

[3808] United States' response to question 313, para. 559. The United States contends that its approach is consistent with the reasoning of the Appellate Body in *US – Upland Cotton (Article 21.5 – Brazil)*, para. 244.

[3809] Australia's response to questions, 5 December 2007.

[3810] *Ibid.*

1672   DSR 2012:III

of the likely existence of serious prejudice at some future point in time.[3811] Australia argues that current effects of the subsidies are therefore relevant because, in the absence of a significant change in circumstances, they will indicate the likelihood that the subsidies would continue to cause serious prejudice in the future. Consequently, according to Australia, the same facts may be relevant in establishing both present serious prejudice and threatened serious prejudice.[3812]

7.1844 Australia notes that, although "material injury" is a distinct concept from "serious prejudice" and that the factors to be considered in each determination are set out in Article 15 and Article 6.3 respectively, the Appellate Body has observed that, while provisions that relate to a determination of "injury" rather than "serious prejudice" must not automatically be transposed into Part III of the SCM Agreement, they may nevertheless be relevant.[3813] Australia considers that an examination of whether there is a "change in circumstances" which is "clearly foreseen and imminent" would be relevant to the assessment of a "threat of serious prejudice". However, in Australia's view there is nothing in the Agreement that would *require* that "threat of serious prejudice" must arise from a "change in circumstances" which is "clearly foreseen and imminent".[3814]

Brazil

7.1845 Brazil notes that the term "threat of serious prejudice" is not defined under the SCM Agreement and submits that the Panel may rely upon the "threat of material injury" standard in Article 15.7 broadly to inform its interpretation of "threat of serious prejudice" under footnote 13. Brazil cautions, however, that the Panel should not transpose the standard from Article 15.7 into a standard that is also required to demonstrate "threat of serious prejudice".[3815] Brazil considers that "threat of serious prejudice" within the meaning of footnote 13 arises where the provision of the challenged subsidies is inevitable within the near future on account of the fact that they are already committed (e.g. scheduled), where there are no limits to the recipient's future production and exports of the subsidized good, and where there is evidence that the challenged subsidies have already caused present serious prejudice. In such circumstances, it is reasonable to infer that there will be continuing subsidies, continuing subsidized exports, and continuing serious prejudice.[3816]

[3811] Australia's written submission, para. 67, referring to Panel Report, *US – Upland Cotton*, para. 7.1496.

[3812] Australia's written submission, para. 68.

[3813] Australia's response to question 19, 14 April 2008, referring to Appellate Body Report, *US – Upland Cotton*, para. 438.

[3814] Australia's response to question 19, 14 April 2008.

[3815] Brazil's response to question 19, 14 April 2008, para. 27. According to Brazil, if this had been the intention of the drafters, they would have defined "threat of serious prejudice" by cross-referencing Article 15.7 in footnote 13 or vice versa.

[3816] Brazil's response to question 19, 14 April 2008, para. 28.

Report of the Panel

7.1846 Brazil considers that imposing a requirement to demonstrate a "change in circumstances" in order to establish a threat of serious prejudice would substantially increase the burden of proof for complainants in serious prejudice disputes in a manner not contemplated by the text of the SCM Agreement. However, should the Panel conclude that "threat of serious prejudice" should depend upon a "change in circumstances", an analysis of aircraft orders, for example, could be used to demonstrate a threat of serious prejudice. The fact that these orders are likely to result in actual deliveries would be sufficient under the circumstances to constitute a change in circumstances that is clearly foreseen and imminent.[3817]

China

7.1847 China notes that the relevant provisions of the SCM Agreement are silent on the determination of threat of serious prejudice. It submits that, given the structure of Article 5 and the general framework of the SCM Agreement, Articles 15.7 and 15.8 of the SCM Agreement on the determination of threat of injury provide important guidance. China notes that Article 5 includes both injury and serious prejudice as two parallel adverse effects and submits that, through cross-reference to Part V, footnote 11 to Article 5 clarifies that the concept of "injury" used in Article 5 includes threat of material injury. China argues that footnote 13 to Article 5 stipulates that threat of serious prejudice constitutes "serious prejudice to the interests of another Member".[3818]

7.1848 China submits that the threat of serious prejudice must be clearly foreseen and imminent, and that a finding of such threat must be based on facts and made with special care.[3819]

Japan

7.1849 Japan argues that, although the SCM Agreement does not provide a specific standard for determining "threat" of serious prejudice, the chapeau of Article 15.7 of the SCM Agreement serves as a reference for such a determination. Japan notes that the first sentence of Article 15.7 provides that a determination of "threat ... shall be based on facts and not merely on allegation, conjecture or remote possibility" and that the second sentence of Article 15.7 provides that "threat" arises from a "change in circumstances" which is "clearly foreseen and imminent". Japan argues that not all events that constitute a "change in circumstances" cause "threat" of serious prejudice. According to Japan, the sentence provides that the change of circumstances whose imminency is demonstrated by objective evidence is appropriate for the assessment of the threat of serious prejudice.[3820]

[3817] Brazil's response to question 19, 14 April 2008, para. 29.
[3818] China's oral statement, para. 9. See also, China's written submission, paras. 35-47.
[3819] China's oral statement, paras. 9-14.
[3820] Japan's response to question 19, 14 April 2008.

1674

DSR 2012:III

Conclusion with respect to the European Communities' threat of serious prejudice arguments

7.1850 The Panel notes that the European Communities' arguments concerning the existence of a threat of serious prejudice based on *future orders* of Airbus LCA are made only with respect to threat of *price suppression* within the meaning of Article 6.3(c) and not any other form of serious prejudice.[3821] Its central arguments in support of the existence of a threat of price suppression are that:

(a) the "price effects" and, in the case of the market in which the 787 competes, the "technology effects" of the subsidies *will continue in the future*[3822];

(b) the magnitude of the past, present and guaranteed future subsidies benefiting Boeing LCA *will continue to be very large*[3823];

(c) conditions of competition similar to those that existed in 2004-2006 *will continue to give Boeing the ability and incentive* to use its subsidy benefits to price down its LCA[3824]; and

(d) the *already suppressed prices* for Airbus LCA caused by the subsidies to Boeing provide a strong indication that the *prices will continue to be suppressed* as a result of the United States subsidies.[3825]

7.1851 The Panel recalls its conclusions that the effects of certain of the subsidies is significant price suppression in each of the three LCA product markets.[3826] The European Communities' threat of serious prejudice arguments are based on the continuation into the future of the subsidization and market conditions which the Panel has already found to cause present serious prejudice in the form of significant price suppression. The result of our finding of serious prejudice within the meaning of Articles 5(c) and 6.3 of the SCM Agreement, based on the existence of significant price suppression within the meaning of Article 6.3(c), is that the United States is obligated to take appropriate steps to remove the adverse effects or withdraw the subsidy.[3827] This means that the serious prejudice, or the continuation of the subsidization in the manner which we have found to cause present serious prejudice to the European Communities' interests, will no longer occur, thereby removing the basis for the European Communities' arguments concerning threat of serious prejudice with respect to future orders of Airbus LCA. The Panel considers that in these circumstances, it

---

[3821] European Communities' first written submission, paras. 1446, 1541 and 1631.
[3822] European Communities' first written submission, paras. 1449, 1544 and 1634. Emphasis added.
[3823] European Communities' first written submission, paras. 1450, 1545 and 1635. Emphasis added.
[3824] European Communities' first written submission, paras. 1451, 1546 and 1636. Emphasis added.
[3825] European Communities' first written submission, paras. 1453, 1548 and 1638. Emphasis added.
[3826] See paras. 7.1797 and 7.1833 of this Report.
[3827] See Article 7.8 of the SCM Agreement.

Report of the Panel

is appropriate to exercise judicial economy with respect to this aspect of the European Communities' serious prejudice claim.

7.1852 The Panel recalls that its exercise of judicial economy in this manner is consistent with the panel's decision in *US – Upland Cotton* in which the panel held:[3828]

> "{U}pon required implementation by the United States of this Panel's prohibited subsidy findings and present serious prejudice findings, the basket of measures in question may be so significantly transformed or manifestly different from the measures that are currently in question that it is not necessary to address Brazil's claims of threat of serious prejudice".

7.1853 We also note the Appellate Body's statement in *US – Upland Cotton (Article 21.5 – Brazil)* that "a claim of present serious prejudice relates to the existence of prejudice in the past, and present, and that may continue in the future".[3829] This also supports the notion that the continuation of serious prejudice into the future is caught by the obligation under Article 7.8 of the SCM Agreement, which requires removal of the present serious prejudice which we have found to exist, including that which exists into the future.

(d) Conclusion

7.1854 **In conclusion, the Panel finds:**

(a) that the effect of the aeronautics R&D subsidies is a threat of displacement and impedance of European Communities exports from third country markets within the meaning of Article 6.3(b) of the SCM Agreement with respect to the 200-300 seat wide-body LCA product market and significant price suppression and significant lost sales, within the meaning of Article 6.3(c) of the SCM Agreement, in that product market, each of which constitutes serious prejudice to the interests of the European Communities within the meaning of Article 5(c) of the SCM Agreement.

(b) that the effect of the FSC/ETI subsidies and the State of Washington B&O tax subsidies is displacement and impedance of European Communities' exports from third country markets within the meaning of Article 6.3(b) of the SCM Agreement with respect to the 100 – 200 seat single-aisle LCA product market and significant price suppression and significant lost sales within the meaning of Article 6.3(c) of the SCM Agreement in that product market, each of which constitutes serious prejudice to the interests

---

[3828] Panel Report, *US – Upland Cotton*, para. 7.1503.

[3829] Appellate Body Report, *US – Upland Cotton (Article 21.5 – Brazil)*, para. 244.

of the European Communities within the meaning of Article 5(c) of the SCM Agreement;

(c) that the effect of the FSC/ETI subsidies and the State of Washington and the City of Everett B&O tax subsidies is displacement and impedance of European Communities exports from third country markets within the meaning of Article 6.3(b) of the SCM Agreement with respect to the 300-400 seat wide-body LCA product market, and significant price suppression and significant lost sales within the meaning of Article 6.3(c) of the SCM Agreement in that product market, each of which constitutes serious prejudice to the interests of the European Communities within the meaning of Article 5(c) of the SCM Agreement.

7.1855 The Panel is not satisfied that the European Communities has demonstrated that the Washington State and City of Everett taxation subsidies other than the B&O tax subsidies, or the property and sales tax abatements provided to Boeing pursuant to IRBs issued by the State of Kansas and municipalities therein, and the tax credits and other incentives provided to Boeing by the State of Illinois and municipalities therein, each as set forth in paragraph 7.1433 of this Report, through their effects on Boeing's LCA pricing behaviour, cause serious prejudice to the European Communities' interests in any of the three LCA product markets identified by the European Communities in this dispute.

3. The European Communities' claim that violation of the 1992 Agreement constitutes serious prejudice to the European Communities' interests within the meaning of Article 5(c) of the SCM Agreement

7.1856 In this section of the Report, the Panel considers the European Communities' claim that the United States causes serious prejudice to the European Communities' interests by violating agreed obligations concerning support to the LCA sector that are set forth in the 1992 Agreement.[3830]

(a) Arguments of the parties and third parties

(i) European Communities

7.1857 The European Communities claims that "violation by the United States of the {1992 Agreement} constitutes serious prejudice to the interests of the European Communities within the meaning of Article 5(c) of the SCM Agreement."[3831] On the basis of Article 5(c), which refers to serious prejudice "to the interests of *another* Member", the European Communities contends that

---

[3830] European Communities' first written submission, para. 1016.
[3831] *Ibid.*

Report of the Panel

"{t}he analysis is necessarily bilateral".[3832] The European Communities argues that, "{a}s the United States has breached the terms of that agreement by giving indirect support exceeding the agreed levels, along with prohibited production support, it has violated the rights of the European Communities and this violation must be considered to constitute serious prejudice".[3833]

7.1858 The European Communities explains that the first international agreement related to the LCA sector to which the European Communities and the United States were parties was the Tokyo Round Agreement on Trade in Civil Aircraft (the "1979 Agreement"), which was followed by the bilateral 1992 Agreement.[3834] Both the SCM Agreement and the recast 1979 Agreement entered into force in 1995, as annexed agreements to the WTO Agreement and the 1992 Agreement remained in force between the same parties following the entry into force of the SCM Agreement (together with the recast 1979 Agreement). The European Communities submits that, by regulating the application of the 1979 Agreement, the 1992 Agreement also bound the parties as regards measures concerning LCA potentially falling under the SCM Agreement.[3835]

7.1859 The European Communities notes that in the first recital to the 1992 Agreement, the parties recognized the need to "reduce trade tensions in the area" of large civil aircraft, while in the second recital, they further agreed that the disciplines in the 1979 Agreement shall "be strengthened with a view to progressively reducing the role of government support". Moreover, the parties agreed to detailed disciplines on support "in pursuit of their common goal of preventing trade distortions resulting from direct or indirect government support for the development and production of large civil aircraft."[3836] The European Communities argues that the 1992 Agreement set forth a detailed set of disciplines regarding the use of "indirect support". In particular, each party committed to ensure that indirect support does not confer unfair advantage on LCA manufacturers or lead to distortions in international trade in LCA and agreed that identifiable benefits to the development or production of any LCA derived from indirect support could not exceed, on an annual basis and net of recoupment: (i) three per cent of the commercial turnover of the civil aircraft industry of the Party concerned, or (ii) four per cent of the annual commercial turnover of any one firm in the Party concerned.[3837]

7.1860 The European Communities asserts that regular consultations under the 1992 Agreement took place between it and the United States between 1993-2004, and that many of the issues discussed in the dispute before this Panel were

---

[3832] European Communities' first written submission, para. 1017.
[3833] European Communities' first written submission, para. 1019.
[3834] European Communities' first written submission, paras. 1020 – 1022.
[3835] European Communities' first written submission, para. 1023.
[3836] European Communities' first written submission, para. 1024. 1992 Agreement, Fourth Recital.
[3837] European Communities' first written submission, para. 1025.

1678

DSR 2012:III

US - Large Civil Aircraft (2nd Complaint)

dealt with in these consultations.[3838] As regards "indirect support" under Article 5 of the 1992 Agreement, the European Communities contends that it made repeated inquiries vis-à-vis the United States, and in particular that it complained about government-funded aeronautical R&D as conferring unfair advantage, distorting trade and providing "identifiable benefits" in violation of the terms of the 1992 Agreement.[3839] The European Communities states that the prohibition of "production support" under Article 3 of the 1992 Agreement played a less prominent role in the consultations. According to the European Communities, after the adoption of the Boeing Incentive Package by Washington State, it could not raise the issue of its compatibility with the 1992 Agreement in formal consultations because none were held that year. The European Communities refers to several high-level communications, from European Community Commissioners for Trade to their U.S. counterparts, regarding the United States' compliance with Articles 3 and 5 of the 1992 Agreement.[3840] The European Communities recalls that the United States notified it that it was abrogating the 1992 Agreement on 6 October 2004, on the pretext that the European Communities had breached its obligations on direct support under Article 3.[3841] The European Communities indicates that it did not accept this abrogation and considered the 1992 Agreement to remain in force.[3842]

7.1861 The European Communities alleges that there are "many instances" in which the United States did not comply with the 1992 Agreement.[3843] First, the United States violated Article 5.1 of the 1992 Agreement by failing to take necessary action to ensure that indirect government support did not confer unfair advantage upon LCA manufacturers benefiting from such support and did not take action to prevent such support from leading to distortion in international trade in LCA.[3844] Second, the annual indirect support provided by the U.S. Government, including R&D-related subsidies, exceeded the three per cent threshold set forth in Article 5.2 (a) of the 1992 Agreement.[3845] Third, the subsidies granted by the States of Washington, Kansas and Illinois, as well as the municipalities therein, are inconsistent with Article 3 of the 1992 Agreement, as they conferred benefits on Boeing that reduced its costs, either by foregoing of revenue otherwise due or by taking over costs that would otherwise be funded by Boeing.[3846] The European Communities alleges that because these measures

---

[3838] European Communities' first written submission, para. 1026.

[3839] European Communities' first written submission, paras. 1027-1028.

[3840] European Communities' first written submission, paras. 1028, 1030.

[3841] European Communities' first written submission, para. 1031; Note verbale No. 55 of the US mission to the EU to the General Secretariat of the Council of the EU, 6 October 2004, Exhibit EC-644.

[3842] European Communities' first written submission, para. 1031; Note verbale of the European Commission to US note verbale No. 55 of 6 October 2004, Exhibit EC-645.

[3843] European Communities' first written submission, para. 1032.

[3844] European Communities' first written submission, para. 1033.

[3845] European Communities' first written submission, para. 1034.

[3846] European Communities' first written submission, para. 1035.

DSR 2012:III

Report of the Panel

are not covered by the specific provisions on development support contained in Article 4 of the 1992 Agreement, or indirect support contained in Article 5 of the 1992 Agreement, Article 3 of the 1992 Agreement covers such other production support.[3847]

7.1862 The European Communities argues that the "non-compliance of US subsidies with Articles 3 and 5 of the 1992 Agreement is relevant for the adverse effects analysis in this dispute because of the link between the 1992 Agreement and the GATT/WTO."[3848] The European Communities recalls that the 1979 Agreement was included in the list of covered agreements under Annex IV to the WTO Agreement and submits that footnotes 15, 16 and 24 in the SCM Agreement emphasize the special features of the LCA sector for certain issues under that agreement. The European Communities also recalls that the parties maintained the 1992 Agreement in its original form after the entry into force of the SCM Agreement, and asserts that both sides considered the 1992 Agreement of continuing relevance and continued to organize the bilateral consultations foreseen under the Agreement to discuss the measures covered by it.[3849]

7.1863 The European Communities contends that the 1992 Agreement constitutes "context for the interpretation of the SCM Agreement in this dispute", on the basis that the 1992 Agreement is a "relevant rule of international law", within the meaning of Article 31(3)(c) of the Vienna Convention on the Law of Treaties (Vienna Convention), to be taken into account when interpreting the SCM Agreement in a dispute between the United States and the European Communities. [3850] The European Communities makes two arguments in support of this contention. First, that "rules of international law" in the sense of Article 31(3)(c) of the Vienna Convention may stem from all accepted sources of international law, including other treaty law. In this connection, the European Communities submits that "the 1992 Agreement is a treaty containing legal commitments and concluded in due form between the US and the EC under international law", and further states that "Article 4 {of the 1992 Agreement} had *expressis verbis* established a dynamic link to the GATT/WTO legal order."[3851] Second, that, contrary to the view expressed by the panel in *EC – Approval and Marketing of Biotech Products*, the term "parties" in the text of Article 31(3)(c) of the Vienna Convention refers to the parties to the particular dispute only – and not the entire membership of the WTO.[3852] In support of that proposition, the European Communities refers to the Appellate Body reports in *EC-Poultry*, *EC – Computer Equipment*, *US – Shrimp*, and *United States – FSC (Article 21.5 - EC)*, the panel report in *US – Shrimp (Article 21.5 – Malaysia)*, the practice of other international bodies and tribunals, International Law

---

[3847] *Ibid.*

[3848] European Communities' first written submission, para. 1037.

[3849] European Communities' first written submission, para. 1040.

[3850] European Communities' first written submission, para. 1041.

[3851] European Communities' first written submission, para. 1044.

[3852] European Communities' first written submission, para. 1045.

Commission's 2006 Report of the Study Group on Fragmentation of International Law, contemporary authorities, the drafting history and ILC commentary to the draft of Article 31(3)(c) of the Vienna Convention, and the object and purpose of that provision.[3853]

7.1864 The European Communities submits that the 1992 Agreement is a "relevant rule of international law" to be taken into account when interpreting the SCM Agreement in a dispute between the United States and the European Community, and that "{i}t allows the Panel to have recourse to an additional source of law which reflects in great detail the precise legal positions of the Parties of the dispute with respect to the subject matter before it."[3854] As a consequence, the European Communities requests the Panel to find that "the US subsidies have caused adverse effects to its interests within the meaning of Article 5 of the SCM Agreement because the United States has breached the international obligations it owed to the European Communities under the 1992 Agreement."[3855] The European Communities submits that, "as can be drawn from the preamble and Article 5.1 of the 1992 Agreement, these obligations were specifically set to avoid distortions of international trade in large civil aircraft."[3856] The European Communities "therefore claims that by granting these subsidies, the United States violated its legal rights. This constitutes a particularly severe form of causing serious prejudice to the interests of the European Communities."[3857]

7.1865 The European Communities argues that the concept of "serious prejudice to the interests of another Member" in Article 5(c) of the SCM Agreement is correctly interpreted as covering forms of serious prejudice "not enumerated in Article 6.3".[3858] The European Communities considers that this correct interpretation of the SCM Agreement results from an analysis of the ordinary meaning, context, and object and purpose of the SCM Agreement. The European Communities argues that an examination of the ordinary meaning of the text of Articles 6.3 and 5(c) of the SCM Agreement does not reveal any statement that expressly limits the meaning of "serious prejudice" to the forms enumerated in Article 6.3.[3859] This is confirmed by the term "may" in Article 6.3, particularly when used as an auxiliary verb, as in Article 6.3.[3860] Several dictionary meanings of the term "may" all confirm that this term indicates a "possibility," or similar concept.[3861] The European Communities argues that the possibility in question is

---

[3853] European Communities' first written submission, paras. 1049 – 1053.
[3854] European Communities' first written submission, para. 1054.
[3855] European Communities' first written submission, para. 1055.
[3856] *Ibid.*
[3857] *Ibid.*
[3858] European Communities' response to question 61, para. 209.
[3859] European Communities' response to question 61, para. 211.
[3860] *Ibid.*
[3861] European Communities' response to question 61, para. 211, referring to *Shorter Oxford English Dictionary*, fifth edition (2202), page 1725: "may: ... {h}ave ability or power to ... have the possibility, opportunity ..." etc.

Report of the Panel

not that one of the instances enumerated in Article 6.3 is demonstrated, but that there is no serious prejudice.[3862] Thus, according to the European Communities, the possibility introduced by the term "may" in Article 6.3 can only be the possibility that there are other forms of serious prejudice, in addition to those enumerated in Article 6.3.[3863]

7.1866 The European Communities argues that this view is also supported by context. First, footnote 13 to the SCM Agreement which, as an integral part of Article 5(c), is immediate context, states expressly that the term "serious prejudice" is used in the same sense as in paragraph 1 of Article XVI of the GATT 1994.[3864] Therefore, if something falls within paragraph 1 of Article XVI of the GATT 1994, it constitutes serious prejudice within the meaning of Article 5(c) of the SCM Agreement, even if it is not enumerated in Article 6.3.[3865] Second, the immediate context of footnote 13 further provides that serious prejudice includes threat of serious prejudice and that Article 6.3 at no point refers to threat of serious prejudice. This confirms that "serious prejudice" within the meaning of Article 5(c) includes threat of serious prejudice, even though this is not enumerated in Article 6.3.[3866] The European Communities argues that this confirms that Article 6.3 does not purport to exhaustively enumerate all possible forms of serious prejudice and that such an interpretation is consistent with the object and purpose of the SCM Agreement, which is to provide a remedy for all types of serious prejudice to the interests of another Member resulting from subsidies, within the meaning of Article 1 of the SCM Agreement.[3867]

7.1867 The European Communities argues that, although the 1992 Agreement does not expressly address the question of whether or not Article 6.3 of the SCM Agreement exhausts Article 5(c), it does expressly state that it is enacted in pursuit of the Parties' "common goal" or interest.[3868] In other words, the 1992 Agreement expressly sets out in detail what the interests of the United States and the European Communities are with respect to large civil aircraft, and the manner in which the Parties agree that those interests are to be preserved, particularly with respect to "the role of government support."[3869] Those interests and the means to preserve them reflect partially, but not entirely, the provisions

---

[3862] The European Communities explains that if it is demonstrated that the effect of the subsidy is (for example) to displace imports of a like product of another Member into the market of the subsidizing Member, then serious prejudice has been demonstrated; referring to Panel Report, *US – Upland Cotton*, at para. 7.1389: "We would therefore be permitted to find that serious prejudice has arisen upon fulfillment of the elements in one or more of the paragraphs of Article 6.3."

[3863] European Communities' response to question 61, para. 211.

[3864] European Communities' response to question 61, para. 212.

[3865] *Ibid.*

[3866] European Communities' response to question 61, para. 212.

[3867] European Communities' response to question 61, para. 213.

[3868] European Communities' response to question 61, para. 215, referring to 1992 Agreement, Preamble, penultimate recital.

[3869] European Communities' response to question 61, para. 215.

of Article 6.3 of the SCM Agreement.[3870] Therefore, the very existence of the 1992 Agreement, as well as its overall content, strongly supports the view that the Parties agreed to a set of mutual "interests" in this area, which interests could, by definition, extend beyond those enumerated in Article 6.3, and could be "seriously prejudiced" within the meaning of Article 5(c) of the SCM Agreement.[3871]

(ii) United States

7.1868 The United States contends that the 1992 Agreement does not create legal obligations under the SCM Agreement. The United States submits that the European Communities cites no valid authority for the proposition that its *unilateral* determination that the United States violated the *bilateral* 1992 Agreement constitutes serious prejudice for purposes of the *multilateral* SCM Agreement, and that the European Communities' approach would require the Panel to disregard not only the text of the SCM Agreement but also the relevant articles of the DSU.[3872]

7.1869 The United States advances two arguments as to why the European Communities' claim with respect to the 1992 Agreement should fail. First, the 1992 Agreement is not a "covered agreement" for purposes of the DSU, and the Panel's terms of reference do not permit the Panel to examine a claim based on an alleged breach of that agreement. Second, while the European Communities' claim is based on a theory relating to the rule of treaty interpretation set out in Article 31(3)(c) of the Vienna Convention, what the European Communities really seeks to have the Panel do is apply the 1992 Agreement as substantive law rather than as a basis for interpreting the SCM Agreement.[3873]

7.1870 In relation to the first argument, the United States submits that the 1992 Agreement is not a covered agreement under Article 1.1 of the DSU, and that there is accordingly no basis for the Panel to examine the European Communities' claim. The DSU cannot be used to examine any question of compliance with the 1992 Agreement or the interpretation or application of the 1992 Agreement. In this connection, the United States refers to the Panel's terms of reference in this dispute, which are:

> "{T}o examine, in the light of the relevant provisions of the *covered agreement(s)* cited by the European Communities in

---

[3870] *Ibid.*

[3871] *Ibid.*

[3872] United States' first written submission, para. 1191. The United States further notes that, in responding to the European Communities' arguments with respect to the 1992, Agreement, it does not endorse the European Communities' characterization of the 1992 Agreement or related events. The United States indicates that it does not address in detail the European Communities' characterization of the 1992 Agreement or related events because, in its view, the European Communities' argument is without merit. United States' first written submission, para. 1191, footnote 1436.

[3873] United States' first written submission, para. 1192.

Report of the Panel

document WT/DS353/2, the matter referred to the DSB by the European Communities in that document, and to make such findings as will assist the DSB in making the recommendations or in giving the rulings provided for in *that/those agreement(s)*."[3874]

7.1871 The United States submits that other provisions of the DSU that refer to the "covered agreements", including Article 11 ("the relevant covered agreements"), Article 3.2, ("the covered agreements"), Article 3.4 ("the covered agreements") and Article 19.1 ("a covered agreement") confirm that this claim is outside of the purview of this proceeding.[3875] The United States notes that the European Communities conceded in its request for establishment of a panel that the 1992 Agreement is not a covered agreement.[3876] Because the 1992 Agreement is not one of the covered agreements, there is no basis for the Panel even to reach the European Communities' claim with respect to the alleged breach of the 1992 Agreement.[3877]

7.1872 As regards the European Communities' contention that there is a "link" between the 1992 Agreement and the WTO Agreement because the Uruguay Round included the 1979 Agreement in the list of covered agreements under Annex IV to the WTO Agreement, the United States submits that the European Communities fails to explain the legal significance of a "link", that such a link would have no legal significance, and that in any event, contrary to the European Communities' assertions, the 1979 Agreement is not a "covered agreement" under the DSU.[3878] Appendix 1 to the DSU identifies the 1979 Agreement as a plurilateral agreement that could be subject to the DSU, but that such coverage was made "subject to the adoption of a decision by the parties . . . setting out the terms for the application of the {DSU} to the {1979 Agreement}." No such decision has been adopted; thus, the European Communities' claim that the 1979 Agreement is a "covered agreement" within the meaning of Article 3.2 of the DSU is erroneous.

7.1873 As to the relevance of the 1992 Agreement to the interpretation of the SCM Agreement, the United States recalls at the outset that the European Communities sets forth a claim that the alleged breach of the 1992 Agreement constitutes serious prejudice under the SCM Agreement. In other words, in the European Communities' view, the 1992 Agreement contains substantive obligations relevant to settlement of this dispute; and by allegedly breaching those obligations, the United States has breached an obligation under the SCM Agreement.[3879] However, the European Communities presents its theory by contending that the 1992 Agreement "constitute{s} *context* for the interpretation

---

[3874] WT/DS353/3. Footnote omitted.
[3875] United States' first written submission, para. 1194, footnote 1437.
[3876] United States' first written submission, para. 1194, footnote 1438.
[3877] United States' first written submission, para. 1194.
[3878] United States' first written submission, para. 1194, footnote 1439.
[3879] United States' first written submission, para. 1195.

1684 DSR 2012:III

of the SCM Agreement in this dispute", asserting that Article 31.3(c) of the Vienna Convention is the "legal rule" supporting this claim.[3880] The European Communities' theory is wholly without merit.

7.1874 The United States considers that the European Communities appears to conflate two arguments with respect to the 1992 Agreement. The European Communities first argues that the 1992 Agreement is a source of substantive law, such that a breach of the 1992 Agreement constitutes serious prejudice under the SCM Agreement.[3881] The European Communities then argues that Article 31(3)(c) of the Vienna Convention is the legal rule supporting the view that the 1992 Agreement constitutes "context" for the SCM Agreement. Even if the 1992 Agreement were context for the SCM Agreement, that contention is unrelated to the question whether the 1992 Agreement is a source of substantive law under the SCM Agreement. According to the United States, the European Communities presents these two contentions as if they are part of the same argument.[3882]

7.1875 The United States argues that, in attempting to bring the 1992 Agreement within the Panel's terms of reference, the European Communities is not alleging that the 1992 Agreement assists in interpreting the serious prejudice provisions of the SCM Agreement. Rather, the European Communities is alleging that a breach of the 1992 Agreement itself constitutes serious prejudice under the SCM Agreement.[3883] The European Communities would like the Panel to apply the 1992 Agreement as a matter of substantive law, and its reliance on the customary rule of interpretation reflected in Article 31(3)(c) of the Vienna Convention is misplaced and irrelevant to the Panel's examination of the European Communities' claim. As a result, the Panel need not consider the other flaws in the European Communities' citation to Article 31(3)(c), including the fact that not all WTO Members are parties to the 1992 Agreement, and that neither the United States nor the European Communities is any longer a party to the 1992 Agreement, since it is no longer in force. Moreover, the Panel need not consider whether the 1992 Agreement is "applicable" in the relations between "the parties", since it is no longer in force.[3884]

7.1876 The United States argues that an interpretation of the term "serious prejudice to the interests of another Member" in Article 5(c) of the SCM Agreement to cover forms of serious prejudice not enumerated in Article 6.3 would not be in accordance with customary rules of interpretation of public international law reflected in the Vienna Convention.[3885] The ordinary meaning of Article 5(c) and Article 6.3 of the SCM Agreement, the context, and the

---

[3880] *Ibid.*

[3881] United States' first written submission, para. 1195, footnote 1440.

[3882] *Ibid.*

[3883] United States' first written submission, para. 1196.

[3884] United States' first written submission, para. 1197.

[3885] United States' response to question 61, para. 168.

Report of the Panel

object and purpose of the SCM Agreement make clear that the list of effects enumerated in Article 6.3 is exhaustive and that effects not enumerated do not constitute "serious prejudice" under the SCM Agreement.[3886] The United States notes that neither Article 5(c) of the SCM Agreement, which declares "serious prejudice" to be one of the types of adverse effects covered by Part III of the SCM Agreement, nor paragraph 1 of Article XVI of the GATT 1994 (to which footnote 13 of the SCM Agreement refers) contains a definition of the words "serious prejudice".[3887] However, Article 6 of the SCM Agreement, entitled "Serious Prejudice" does contain a more detailed explanation of the concept of "serious prejudice" as used in Article 5(c) of the SCM Agreement. The chapeau of Article 6.3 states: "{s}erious prejudice in the sense of paragraph (c) of Article 5 may arise in any case where one or several of the following apply." Thus, serious prejudice may arise if one of the forms of serious prejudice enumerated in Article 6.3 is found to exist.[3888] The United States contends that this interpretation of Article 6.3 is further confirmed by the language of paragraph 6.2:

> "Notwithstanding the provisions of paragraph 1, serious prejudice shall not be found if the subsidizing Member demonstrates that the subsidy in question has not resulted in any of the effects enumerated in paragraph 3."[3889]

7.1877 The United States argues that the use of the word "shall" clearly indicates that where none of the effects enumerated in paragraph 3 of Article 6 exists, serious prejudice does not exist and that such an interpretation is also confirmed by the structure of Article 6.[3890] When read together, Articles 6.1, 6.2 and 6.3 originally created two ways for a complaining Member to show serious prejudice.[3891] First, under Article 6.1, prior to its lapsing, the complainant could demonstrate that one of the situations enumerated under Article 6.1(a) through (d) existed. If that was the case, a rebuttable presumption of serious prejudice was established, while Article 6.2 allowed the subsidizing Member to rebut that presumption by demonstrating that the effects enumerated in Article 6.3 did not exist. If the complaining Member was not able to demonstrate that one of the situations in Article 6.1 existed, its second option was to demonstrate that one of the situations in Article 6.3 exists, in which case "serious prejudice .... may arise."[3892] In other words, the structure of Article 6 confirms the interpretation

---

[3886] *Ibid.*

[3887] United States' response to question 61, para. 169.

[3888] United States' response to question 61, para. 170.

[3889] United States' response to question 61, para. 171.

[3890] United States' response to question 61, paras. 171-172.

[3891] United States' response to question 61, para. 172. The United States argues that, although Article 6.1 of the SCM Agreement has lapsed, the panel in *US – Upland Cotton*, para. 7.1377, n. 1487 found that it could nevertheless provide relevant guidance as to the interpretation of Article 6.3.

[3892] United States' response to question 61, para. 172.

1686

DSR 2012:III

following from the ordinary meaning of Article 6.3 and from the context provided to that provision by Article 6.2; namely, that serious prejudice cannot be found to exist unless the complainant demonstrates that one of the effects enumerated in Article 6.3 exists.[3893]

7.1878 The United States submits that the following statement of the panel in *US – Upland Cotton* is directly relevant in this regard and confirms the foregoing analysis of the United States:

> "Article 6.2 serves to clarify that a prerequisite for a finding of serious prejudice is that one of the four effects-based situations in Article 6.3 must be demonstrated. It indicates to us that demonstration that at least one of the four effects-based situations in Article 6.3 exists is a necessary basis to conclude that serious prejudice exists."[3894]

(iii) Third Parties

Australia

7.1879 Australia submits that the concept of serious prejudice in Article 5(c) of the SCM Agreement should not be considered as covering forms of serious prejudice not already enumerated in Article 6.3 of the same agreement. The chapeau of Article 6.3 explicitly links Article 6.3 to Article 5(c) as an elaboration of the forms that serious prejudice may take.[3895] The absence of any reference in Articles 5 and 6 of the SCM Agreement to additional forms of serious prejudice that could trigger the remedies contained in Article 7 favours an exhaustive interpretation of the list set forth in Article 6.3. This silence on additional forms of serious prejudice contrasts strongly with the detail provided in the rest of Article 6 on the further elements relevant to the Article 6.3 examination.[3896] Furthermore, Australia considers that Article 6.2 "serves to clarify that a prerequisite for a finding of serious prejudice is that at least one of the four effects-based situations in Article 6.3 must be demonstrated."[3897] This means that no additional forms of serious prejudice, independent of Article 6.3, can activate the remedies in Article 7 of the SCM Agreement.[3898]

7.1880 Australia argues that there is no legal basis for the European Communities' assertion that the 1992 Agreement constitutes context for the

---

[3893] *Ibid.*
[3894] Panel Report, *US – Upland Cotton*, para. 7.1380.
[3895] Australia's response to questions, 5 December 2007.
[3896] *Ibid.*
[3897] Australia's response to questions, 5 December 2007, referring to Panel Report, *US - Upland Cotton*, para. 7.1380.
[3898] Australia's response to questions, 5 December 2007.

Report of the Panel

interpretation of the SCM Agreement in this dispute.[3899] Under the terms of Article 1 of the DSU, the DSU applies to WTO covered agreements and that, as the 1992 Agreement is not a covered agreement, it does not fall within the scope of Article 7.2 of the DSU and does not constitute applicable law in this dispute. Australia submits that the Appellate Body has made it clear that the DSU operates in relation to covered agreements only and that it is not the function of panels to seek to clarify the provisions of non-covered agreements.[3900]

7.1881 Australia argues that there is a body of WTO case law to support the view that Article 31(3)(c) of the Vienna Convention refers to the rules of international law applicable in the relations between the States which have consented to be bound by the treaty which is being interpreted, and for which that treaty is in force.[3901] The Appellate Body has recognized that Article 31(3)(c) permitted it to seek additional interpretative guidance from general principles of international law.[3902] These principles are rules of international law applicable between the WTO membership as a whole and not a subset of that membership. Australia does not consider that the rules of international law contained in the 1992 Agreement, which is only applicable in the relations between subsets of parties to the SCM Agreement, can be taken into account under Article 31(3)(c) of the Vienna Convention in interpreting the SCM Agreement. More generally, given that the application of Article 31(3)(c) has potentially significant systemic implications for the WTO dispute settlement system, the Panel in this dispute should approach the issue with a degree of caution.[3903]

Brazil

7.1882 Brazil argues that the Panel should reject the European Communities' argument that the subsidies constitute serious prejudice to the interests of the European Communities within the meaning of Article 5(c) of the SCM Agreement because the United States violated its obligations under the 1992 Agreement.[3904]

7.1883 First, the SCM Agreement is the appropriate instrument to address subsidies in the civil aircraft industry in a WTO dispute settlement proceeding. The 1992 Agreement is not a WTO covered agreement, and is outside the Panel's terms of reference. Because the Panel lacks jurisdiction to determine the rights and obligations of the parties under the 1992 Agreement, the Panel

---

[3899] Australia's written submission, para. 71.
[3900] Australia's written submission, para. 71, citing, Appellate Body Report, *Mexico – Taxes on Soft Drinks*, para. 49.
[3901] Australia's written submission, para. 72.
[3902] Australia's written submission, para. 72, referring to Appellate Body Report, *US – Shrimp*, para. 158.
[3903] Australia's written submission, paras. 72-73.
[3904] Brazil's written submission, para. 75; response to questions, 5 December 2007, paras. 7 and 8.

1688

necessarily cannot determine whether the United States violated the substantive provisions of the 1992 Agreement.[3905]

7.1884 Second, because the European Communities is alleging that a violation of the 1992 Agreement is sufficient to succeed on its claim of serious prejudice, it is seeking to apply the 1992 Agreement as substantive law between the parties rather than as context for the interpretation of any particular provision of the SCM Agreement. An appropriate analysis should lead the Panel to find that an alleged substantive violation of the 1992 Agreement cannot constitute "serious prejudice" with the meaning of Article 5(c) of the SCM Agreement.[3906]

7.1885 Third, Brazil objects to the use of the 1992 Agreement to interpret provisions of the SCM Agreement, to the extent that the European Communities is, in fact, attempting to do so. Consistent with the findings of the panel in *EC – Approval and Marketing of Biotech Products*[3907], the reference to "parties" in Article 31(3)(c) of the Vienna Convention must be interpreted to mean all of the parties to the treaty being interpreted, in this case, the SCM Agreement. Brazil considers that a bilateral treaty such as the 1992 Agreement simply does not reflect the common intentions of all WTO Members, and as a result, cannot be used to inform what WTO Members intended when drafting the SCM Agreement. Any other interpretation would lead to absurd and prejudicial results, with third parties seeing their WTO rights affected by a bilateral treaty to which they were not a party and with the provisions of the SCM Agreement potentially being interpreted differently for different WTO Members.[3908] Brazil submits alternatively that, if the Panel interprets the term "parties" in Article 31(3)(c) of the Vienna Convention narrowly to refer to the parties to the 1992 Agreement, any interpretation of the SCM Agreement based on the 1992 Agreement can only apply to the bilateral relations between the United States and the European Communities, as confirmed by Articles 34 and 41(1)(b)(i) of the Vienna Convention.[3909]

Canada

7.1886 Canada argues that read together, footnote 13 of Article 6.2 and Article 6.3 of the SCM Agreement suggest that a panel may only make a finding of serious prejudice if it can establish one of the effects listed in Article 6.3 or the threat of such an effect. However, once having made such a finding, a panel has the flexibility to characterize other effects of the subsidy at issue as a form of

---

[3905] Brazil's written submission, para. 76.
[3906] Brazil's written submission, para. 77.
[3907] Panel Report, *EC-Approval and Marketing of Biotech Products*, para. 7.68.
[3908] Brazil's written submission, para. 78.
[3909] Brazil's written submission, para. 79.

Report of the Panel

serious prejudice, provided those other effects are closely linked to the effects listed in Article 6.3.[3910]

7.1887 Canada submits that footnote 13 to Article 6.2 imports into the SCM Agreement an unbroken chain of meaning for the term serious prejudice, encompassing the concepts set out in Article 6.3, but also recognizing the possibility of additional forms of serious prejudice closely linked to those core concepts.[3911] Article 6.2 appears to suggest that serious prejudice cannot be established if none of the core concepts in Article 6.3 are present. Canada argues that Article 6.3 itself is drafted to permit non-enumerated forms of serious prejudice, while providing particular guidance on the core concepts that have given life to the term serious prejudice since its inception in GATT 1947.[3912]

Japan

7.1888 Japan argues that the text of Article 5 clearly requires a Member to show that serious prejudice was caused "through the *use* of any subsidy {as defined in Article 1}."[3913] Japan considers that the European Communities' arguments concerning serious prejudice do not properly apply the causation test of Article 5. It is the "use of any subsidy" that must be shown to cause serious prejudice. The European Communities has not applied this causation formula as set out in Article 5, but instead argues that the provision of subsidies in excess of commitments under the 1992 Agreement by itself constitutes serious prejudice. This argument is inconsistent with Article 5, which requires a showing that the use of the subsidies at issue is the cause of adverse effects.[3914]

7.1889 Japan also observes that the European Communities appears to alternatively argue that the United States has caused serious prejudice merely by "granting" subsidies in supposed violation of the 1992 Agreement.[3915] Not only is this not the analysis required by the SCM Agreement, but it remains unclear what constitutes the serious prejudice suffered by the European Communities.[3916]

Korea

7.1890 Korea argues that Article 6.3 of the SCM Agreement provides an exhaustive list of instances of serious prejudice as mentioned in Article 5(c) of the SCM Agreement. The terms used in Article 6.3 are definitive in nature, by providing that "{s}erious prejudice...may arise in any case where one or several

---

[3910] Canada's response to questions, 5 December 2007, paras. 7-11. See also, Canada's oral statement, paras. 29-36.

[3911] Canada's response to questions, 5 December 2007, para. 12; Canada's oral statement, para. 30.

[3912] Canada's response to questions, 5 December 2007, para. 12.

[3913] Japan's oral statement, para. 6.

[3914] Japan's oral statement, para. 7.

[3915] European Communities' first written submission, para. 1055.

[3916] Japan's oral statement, para. 8.

1690

DSR 2012:III

of the following apply." Korea argues that the ordinary meaning of this sentence is that, for there to be a serious prejudice, one or more conditions listed in the article must exist. This indicates that what is provided in Article 6.3 is an exhaustive list.[3917] Furthermore, Article 6.3 does not use a term indicating an exemplary nature, such as "including," "*inter alia,*" "for instance," "such as". Rather, Article 6.3 uses the rather broad term "any case" where one or several enumerated conditions apply. This suggests that the drafters attempted to confine the instances of serious prejudice to only these enumerated situations.[3918]

(b)   Evaluation by the Panel

7.1891 The Panel recalls that the practice of judicial economy allows a panel to refrain from making multiple findings that a measure is inconsistent with various provisions when a single, or a certain number of findings of inconsistency, would suffice to resolve the dispute.[3919]

7.1892 The Panel recalls that Article 11 of the DSU provides, in relevant part:

> "...a panel should make an objective assessment of the matter before it, including an objective assessment of the facts of the case and the applicability of and conformity with the relevant covered agreements, and make *such other findings as will assist the DSB in making the recommendations or in giving the rulings provided for in the covered agreements.*" (Emphasis added)

7.1893 The Panel does not consider that making findings in relation to this serious prejudice claim would assist the DSB in making the recommendations or in giving the rulings provided for in the SCM Agreement. The Panel therefore exercises judicial economy with respect to this claim.

[3917] Korea's response to questions, 5 December 2007.
[3918] *Ibid.*
[3919] Appellate Body Report, *Canada – Wheat Exports and Grain Imports*, para. 133.

DSR 2012:III

Report of the Panel

Appendix VII.F.1: Parties' arguments regarding the links between the U.S. Government funded R&D and the specific technologies applied to the 787

A.   INTRODUCTION

1.   The European Communities has sought to demonstrate that the aeronautics R&D subsidies provided Boeing with *usable technologies* in key technology areas, as well as *knowledge, experience* and *confidence* toward developing successful commercial technologies and processes.[3920] It has then sought to demonstrate how those technologies, as well as the knowledge, experience and confidence with respect to various technologies was applied to, or facilitated the development of, the innovative technological features of the 787. The European Communities groups these key technologies into the following six technology areas:

(a)   Composites technologies, primarily the design, development and manufacturing of 787 composite fuselages and wings;

(b)   More-electric architecture;

(c)   Open systems architecture;

(d)   Enhanced aerodynamics and structural design;

(e)   Noise reduction technologies; and

(f)   Health management systems.[3921]

2.   This Appendix first describes the technology areas identified above as they relate to technologies that are applied to the 787. To provide further context to the Panel's analysis, this Appendix next explains its understanding of the process for designing and manufacturing the 787.[3922] Finally, this Appendix provides a summary of the specific arguments made by the parties concerning the links between the research that Boeing conducted under the aeronautics R&D subsidies and the technologies applied to the 787.

[3920] European Communities' first written submission, para. 1352. According to the European Communities, the knowledge, experience and confidence gained by Boeing through its participation in US government-supported aeronautics R&D programmes enabled Boeing to accelerate its development, production and delivery of the 787 and "is in fact the crux of the causal connection between the US R&D subsidies and the 787", European Communities' first written submission, para. 1356; Annex C, para. 8.

[3921] European Communities' first written submission, para. 1350.

[3922] The background factual material presented in this Appendix is based on evidence submitted to the Panel by the parties in the course of these proceedings and therefore generally refers to events or developments that occurred in 2006 as being "recent".

1692

DSR 2012:III

B. DESCRIPTION OF THE RELEVANT TECHNOLOGY AREAS

3. A "**composite**" is a composition of two or more materials on a macroscopic scale, working together to produce material properties that are different to the properties of those elements on their own. Most composites consist of a bulk material (the matrix), a reinforcement, usually in fibre form which is added primarily to increase the strength and stiffness of the matrix, a resin and a curing agent. The resin acts to hold the fibres together and to transfer the load to the fibres in the fabricated composite part. The curing agent (or hardener) acts as a catalyst in curing the resin to a hard plastic. The most common composites appear to be divided into three groups: (i) polymer matrix composites, or fibre-reinforced plastics; these materials use a polymer-based resin as the matrix and a variety of fibres such as glass, carbon and aramid as the reinforcement[3923]; (ii) metal matrix composites, which use a metal such as aluminium as the matrix, reinforced with fibres such as silicon arbide; and (iii) ceramic matrix composites (used in very high temperature environments) which use a ceramic as the matrix reinforced with short fibres such as those made from silicon carbide and boron nitrade.[3924]

4. In general, composites manufacturing processes involve (i) various processes for the combination of the resin, fibre and matrix material; (ii) the "curing" of the composite material in an autoclave, a high-pressure, high-temperature oven; (iii) post-processing, in which machine tools are used to drill holes and cut shapes; and (iv) non-destructive inspection (NDI) testing for faults.[3925] The European Communities alleges that a substantial focus of the U.S. government's composites research efforts was on the first stage of composites manufacturing described in (i) above; i.e. finding the best and most cost-effective way of combining and shaping composite materials.[3926]

5. There are two general and distinct methods for combining and shaping the elements that form the composite material. The first (pre-impregnation) involves combining the resin and fibre *before* shaping that material on a mandrel (a special mould in the shape of the part that is being produced). One example of this first general method involves the combination of resin and curing agent to create a "prepreg" material which is then "impregnated" into the reinforcing fibre, either by dipping the reinforcement through the liquid resin or through the

---

[3923] One example of a polymer matrix composite is the carbon fibre reinforced plastic (CFRP) on the 787 primary structure.

[3924] Tim Sommer et al., Composite Technologies, November 2006, Exhibit EC-14 (BCI), pp. 3-4.

[3925] Nondestructive inspection (NDI) is a wide group of analysis techniques used in science and industry to evaluate the properties of a material, component or system without causing damage. Because NDI does not permanently alter the article being inspected, it is a highly-valuable technique that can save both money and time in product evaluation, troubleshooting, and research. Common NDI methods include thermal, ultrasonic, electromagnetic, radiography and optical methods; Tim Sommer et al., Composite Technologies, November 2006, Exhibit EC-14 (BCI), pp. 48-50.

[3926] European Communities' first written submission, Annex C, para. 41.

Report of the Panel

application of heat or pressure.[3927] The second general method for combining the elements of the composite materials (pre-forming) involves first shaping the fibre into the desired shape, and then combining it with the resin by infusing the resin into the "pre-form", using techniques such as resin film infusion (RFI) or resin transfer moulding (RTM). Resin film infusion involves dry fabrics being arranged in a mould, interleaved with layers of semi-solid resin film. The structure is vacuum-bagged to remove air through the dry fabrics and then heated in an autoclave. The heating allows the resin to melt and flow into the air-free fabrics, before curing. Resin transfer moulding also involves placing dry fabrics in a mould, however they are held together by a binder. A second mould tool is then clamped over the first mould, and resin is injected into the cavity. Once the fabric is fully wet with resin, the resin inlets are closed and the laminate is allowed to cure in an autoclave. Where vacuum pressure is used to assist the infusion of the resin through the fibre, the process is referred to as vacuum-assisted resin infusion.

6.   The aerospace industry has traditionally regarded the use of carbon-fibre reinforced composites (CRFPs) manufactured through pre-impregnation to be extremely expensive, because individually cut pre-pregs needed to be manually applied by highly trained technicians. Automated tape laying (ATL) and automated fibre placement (AFP) technologies presented significant opportunities for cost and efficiency improvements. The ATL and AFP processes are functionally similar, but each is used differently to achieve specific structure construction goals to provide strength or stiffness. In both processes, the fibre is shaped first and then shaped on a mandrel. In both processes, a delivery head mounted on a robotic arm lays or places pre-impregnated tape or fibre on a mandrel. The main difference is that ATL machinery lays tape (which consists of fibres aligned together in a single direction), while AFP lays down multiple tape sections over highly contoured surfaces in multiple fibre axes (i.e. the fibres need not be aligned in a single direction). Tape is wider than individual fibres, meaning that ATL can cover a greater area in a shorter period of time, however, it cannot produce complicated three-dimensional shapes. AFP takes longer to cover the same size area, but can produce shapes with complex three-dimensional curvatures.[3928]

7.   A 1994 NASA report on composites indicates that the first structural composite aircraft components, made from glass fibre reinforced plastics (GFRP) were introduced between 1950 and 1960.[3929] Boron filaments and

---

[3927] The impregnated reinforcements (or prepregs) can take three main forms: woven fabrics, roving and unidirectional tape. Fabrics and tapes are provided as continuous rolls in various widths and lengths. The fabric or tape thickness constitutes one ply in the construction of a multi-ply lay up. The prepreg material is wound onto spools and is used for filament winding, in which the prepreg material is laid down over a mandrel with the resin-coated fibres being laid down in the desired pattern.

[3928] Tim Sommer et al., Composite Technologies, November 2006, Exhibit EC-14 (BCI), pp. 18-31.

[3929] Richard N. Hadcock, "A Chronology of Advanced Composite Applications", in Louis F. Vosteen and Richard N. Hadcock, Composite Chronicles: A Study of the Lessons Learned in the

1694   DSR 2012:III

carbon fibres first became available in about 1965. Their high compression strength and stiffness, in combination with low density, enabled boron fibre reinforced plastics (BFRP) and CFRP to be used instead of aluminium for high performance airplane structures.[3930] Since the mid-1960s, many composite structural components have been designed and produced for U.S. and foreign military aircraft. Much of the advanced composite structures research and development in the United States between the mid-1960s until the mid-1990s has been associated with military aircraft applications.[3931] According to a 1994 report by NASA consultant, Richard Hadcock, U.S. military R&D programmes provided much of the technology base for production of composite structures. Until 1973, the price of boron filaments was less than the price of carbon or graphite fibres, and boron/epoxy also had higher specific strength and stiffness than the carbon/epoxy materials that were then available. For these reasons, BFRP was the advanced composite of choice in the late 1960s.[3932] Some of the major European aircraft companies initiated advanced composite structures development programmes in the early 1970s. These included British Aircraft Company and Hawker Siddeley Aviation (both subsequently part of BAE Systems plc) which were involved in structural development of CFRP components.[3933]

8.   Based on data presented by a NASA consultant, the following military aircraft had at least one part of the fuselage (forward, mid or rear) fabricated from composite materials: MD AV-8B, Bell/Boeing V-22, Northrop B-2, Dassault Rafale C/M, Eurofighter EFA, MD F-18E/F, Lockheed F-22; while the following aircraft used composites for either the covers or substructure of the wing box: MD AV-8B, Grumman A6-E, SAAB Gripen, Bell/Boeing V-22, Northrop B-2A, Dassault Rafale C/M, Eurofighter EFA, MD F-18E/F, Mitsubishi FSX and Lockheed F-22. In addition, composite fuselage pieces or wings were then (in the mid-1990s) being developed for various other military aircraft; e.g. Alphajet, Vought VSTOL A, Grumman VSTOL A, GD F-16XL,

---

Development, Production and Service of Composite Structures, NASA Contractor Report 4620, November 1994, p. 27, Exhibit EC-792. These components included the fins and rudders of the Grumman E-2A. By 1967, the entire airframe of the small Windecker Eagle was made from GFRP. Since then, GFRP has become one of the standard materials for light aircraft and lightly loaded structural components.

[3930] Richard N. Hadcock, "A Chronology of Advanced Composite Applications", in Louis F. Vosteen and Richard N. Hadcock, Composite Chronicles: A Study of the Lessons Learned in the Development, Production and Service of Composite Structures, NASA Contractor Report 4620, November 1994, Exhibit EC-792, p. 27.

[3931] *Ibid.*

[3932] *Ibid.*

[3933] Richard N. Hadcock, "A Chronology of Advanced Composite Applications", in Louis F. Vosteen and Richard N. Hadcock, Composite Chronicles: A Study of the Lessons Learned in the Development, Production and Service of Composite Structures, NASA Contractor Report 4620, November 1994, Exhibit EC-792, pp. 33-34. Other companies included Aeritalia (Italy), SAAB (Sweden), Dassault Aviation (France), Aérospatiale (France, now part of EADS), Fuji (Japan), Kawasaki (Japan), Mitsubishi (Japan) as well as Russian and Ukrainian aircraft companies.

Report of the Panel

Grumman X-29, Dassault Rafale A, BAe EAP, IAI Lavi, Northrop YF-23, Lockheed YF-22, and Rockwell/MBB X-31, GD/MD A-12.[3934] By the mid-1990s, Kawasaki Heavy Industries had designed and built an all CFRP wing for the Japanese FS-X fighter aircraft.[3935] The FS-X (later called the F-2) was developed as a semi-indigenous replacement for the McDonnell Douglas F-4. One of the advancements of this aircraft was its innovative use of co-cured composite structures in a larger wing, enabling the curing and bonding of the wing box and skin to take place in a single process. [3936]

9.   The Airbus A300, which first flew in 1972, incorporated the following composite components: CFRP/GFRP elevators and rudders, CFRP spoilers, nose landing gear doors, and main landing gear leg fairings, GFRP wing upper surface trailing edge panels and AFRP wing-body fairings and flap track fairings.[3937] Use of composites was extended in 1985 by changing the Airbus A310 vertical stabilizer material from aluminium alloy to CFRP, and again in 1987 for the Airbus A320. On the A320, both horizontal and vertical stabilizers are made from CFRP, as well as the elevators, rudder, ailerons, spoilers, flaps, wing leading and trailing edge access and fixed panels, landing gear doors, and engine cowls and doors.[3938] The larger A330/A340 models use composites for similar components. Prior to Boeing's 787, the Airbus A380 had the highest percentage of composite materials on an LCA, including (i) the vertical tail (an area of 1,238 sq. feet, compared to 573 sq. feet for the composite vertical tail area of the 777), (ii) the horizontal stabilizer (an area of 2,207 sq. feet, compared to 1,090 sq. feet for the 777 horizontal stabilizer), (iii) the center wing box (the first use of composites), and (iv) the rear *unpressurized* fuselage section.[3939] Following various design changes between 2005 and 2007, Airbus' A350XWB

[3934] Richard N. Hadcock, "A Chronology of Advanced Composite Applications", in Louis F. Vosteen and Richard N. Hadcock, Composite Chronicles: A Study of the Lessons Learned in the Development, Production and Service of Composite Structures, NASA Contractor Report 4620, November 1994, Exhibit EC-792, p. 35, Table A-2.

[3935] Richard N. Hadcock, "A Chronology of Advanced Composite Applications", in Louis F. Vosteen and Richard N. Hadcock, Composite Chronicles: A Study of the Lessons Learned in the Development, Production and Service of Composite Structures, NASA Contractor Report 4620, November 1994, Exhibit EC-792, p. 35. Fuji was also a major subcontractor under this programme.

[3936] In addition, in 1995, Raytheon launched a six-passenger light business jet (Raytheon 390 Premier I) with an all-composite fuselage. The fuselage was a carbon fibre/honeycomb-sandwich construction, produced in two pieces that were bonded at the aft pressure-bulkhead. The fuselage pieces were formed on a wooden mandrel using automated fibre placement (AFP) processes developed on prototype tow-placement machines supplied by Cincinnati Milacron. Graham Warwick, "Raytheon's First" Flight International (October 4, 1995), Exhibit US-306.

[3937] Richard N. Hadcock, "A Chronology of Advanced Composite Applications", in Louis F. Vosteen and Richard N. Hadcock, Composite Chronicles: A Study of the Lessons Learned in the Development, Production and Service of Composite Structures, NASA Contractor Report 4620, November 1994, Exhibit EC-792, p. 37.

[3938] *Ibid.*

[3939] Bair Affidavit, Exhibit US-7, paras. 51-52. The European Communities points out that a crucial advance of the 787 is its use of [***]; Statement by Patrick Gavin, Tim Sommer, Burkhard Domke, and Dominik Wacht, 8 November 2007, Exhibit EC-1175 (BCI), para. 9.

1696

DSR 2012:III

(launched in December 2006 and scheduled for first delivery in 2013), will be approximately 52 per cent composites by weight.[3940] The fuselage will be constructed from CFRP panels with composite frames, and the wings and empennage will be also be CFRP.[3941]

10.   Boeing started design of both the 757 and 767 models of LCA in the late 1970s.[3942] Boeing used CFRP composites for the elevators, rudders, spoilers, landing gear doors and engine cowlings for both airplanes. The flaps of the 757 were also CFRP. When Boeing introduced the 737-300 in 1985, CFRP composites were selected for the ailerons, elevators, rudder, fairings and engine cowl doors. The 777, which commenced service in 1994, uses CFRP for the control surfaces, floor beams, main landing gear doors, engine nacelles and, most significantly, the entire empennage.[3943] Other composite components on the 777 include the wing-fuselage fairings and wing fixed trailing edge panels. The CFRP horizontal and vertical stabilizers on the 777 are manufactured by Boeing, while many of the other composite components are supplied to Boeing by U.S. and foreign subcontractors. For example, the Japan Aircraft Development Corporation is reported as having contributed 21 percent to the Boeing 777 project for design and production of the fuselage, center wing and wing body fairings for the life of the 777 programme.[3944] Grumman (U.S.) was reportedly awarded a 10-year, $400 million contract to produce the 777 composite inboard flaps and spoilers, Alenia (Italy) was producing the outboard flaps, CASA (Spain, now part of EADS), the ailerons and Rockwell (U.S.), the floor beams.[3945]

11.   A discussion of the application of composites technology on the 787 is included as part of the discussion in Section C of this Appendix.

12.   A "**more-electric**" aircraft uses electrical power to drive secondary mechanical systems, instead of a combination of hydraulic, pneumatic and electrical power.[3946] The 787 is a more-electric aircraft. Unlike existing LCA,

---

[3940] "Qatar Airways Signs MOU for 80 A350XWBs worth $16-18 billion; EIS in 2013", Air Transport World Daily News, 31 May 2007, Exhibit US-1003.

[3941] "Airbus confirms switch to composite frame on A350 XWB," ATW Daily News, 20 September 2007, Exhibit EC-1301.

[3942] The 767 made its first flight in 1981, followed by the 757 in 1982; Richard N. Hadcock, "A Chronology of Advanced Composite Applications", in Louis F. Vosteen and Richard N. Hadcock, Composite Chronicles: A Study of the Lessons Learned in the Development, Production and Service of Composite Structures, NASA Contractor Report 4620, November 1994, Exhibit EC-792, p. 37.

[3943] The "empennage" refers to the tail section of the aircraft. It gives stability to the aircraft and controls the flight dynamics of pitch and yaw.

[3944] Richard N. Hadcock, "A Chronology of Advanced Composite Applications", in Louis F. Vosteen and Richard N. Hadcock, Composite Chronicles: A Study of the Lessons Learned in the Development, Production and Service of Composite Structures, NASA Contractor Report 4620, November 1994, Exhibit EC-792, p. 49.

[3945] *Ibid.*

[3946] Andrew Doyle, "More and more electric," Flight International, 28 August-3 September 1996, Exhibit EC-821, p. 124.

Report of the Panel

electrical systems will be used on the 787 to generate power, as well as to operate components such as the (i) engine starters, (ii) brakes, (iii) de-icing system, (iv) secondary flight controls, and (v) air conditioning systems. The "more-electric" systems architecture of the 787 uses fly-by-wire flight controls[3947], and electrical power instead of pneumatic or hydraulic power to operate a variety of the aircraft's secondary mechanical systems. The 787 will eliminate all of its pneumatic bleed-air systems[3948], while maintaining certain hydraulic systems.[3949] One of the most significant accomplishments of the 787's "more-electric" architecture is the replacement of pneumatic systems with electrical systems. Pneumatic systems are complex, prone to failure, and require frequent maintenance checks.[3950] They entail extracting bleed air (pressurized, hot air) from the aircraft engines and carrying that air via heavy ducts throughout the plane to operate a variety of mechanical systems.[3951] Instead of using these pneumatic systems, each 787 will have four 250 kVA generators on the engines and two 225 kVA generators on the auxiliary power unit to generate power[3952], with no need for ducts that carry bleed air throughout the aircraft.[3953] By replacing bleed air with electric generators as the source of energy, up to 35 per cent less power is extracted from the engines of the 787 than LCA with traditional pneumatic systems.[3954] As bleed air is not diverted from the engines, the high-speed air flowing through the engine can focus on thrust, thereby lowering the 787's overall fuel consumption.[3955]

13. **"Open systems architecture"** relates to the avionics of an aircraft and how onboard systems are installed to interact with each other.[3956] Under a traditional aeronautics model, software runs on customized hardware, with separate computing systems for each function. This means that systems such as radios and displays on the flight deck or entertainment systems in the passenger cabin cannot easily be upgraded. The 787 utilizes a common core computing system based on open systems architecture principles. The open nature of the

---

[3947] Boeing Presentation #16, Exhibit EC-807 (BCI), p. 1.

[3948] Boeing Presentation #3, Exhibit EC-353 (BCI), p. 1; James Wallace, "Introducing ... Boeing's electric 7E7," Exhibit EC-820.

[3949] Elimination of all pneumatic and hydraulic systems would result in an "all-electric" aircraft. Andrew Doyle, "More and more electric," Flight International, 28 August-3 September 1996, 124, Exhibit EC-821. Final CRAD Report, Evaluation of All-Electric Secondary Power for Transport Aircraft, Report Number MDC 91K0418, January 1992, Exhibit EC-822.

[3950] Passing the Value Test: The Boeing Technology Advantage, Boeing Point-to-Point, June 2006, Exhibit EC-784.

[3951] Boeing publication "Point to Point", June 2006, Volume 1 Issue 4, Exhibit EC-784.

[3952] Boeing 787 Dreamliner Program Fact Sheet, Exhibit EC-340.

[3953] James Wallace, "Introducing ... Boeing's electric 7E7," Seattle Post-Intelligencer, 20 May 2004, Exhibit EC-820.

[3954] Boeing 787 Dreamliner Program Fact Sheet, Exhibit EC-340.

[3955] Passing the Value Test: The Boeing Technology Advantage, Boeing Point-to-Point, June 2006, Exhibit EC-784; Meryl Getline, "Dreaming of a more pleasant flight," USA Today, 9 June 2006, Exhibit EC-824.

[3956] European Communities' first written submission, Annex C, para. 79.

architecture is such that all software functions can be run on a central host computing platform using an industry-specified standard interface. The open systems architecture of the 787 makes it possible for Boeing to simply plug in a new component, and let installation software integrate the new equipment with the airplane's central computer system. The software is separable from the host hardware, such that software can be developed by third party providers using the industry standards interface, and runs on the host computing platform without changing the hardware. This will allow for easier upgrade of the airplane functionality over time, and will also alleviate some of the hardware.[3957]

14. **"Enhanced aerodynamics and structural design"** technologies refer to various computer design software codes (CFD codes such as TRANAIR and OVERFLOW as well as "Product Lifecycle Management" tools such as CATIA) and specific aerodynamic and structural improvements to the wings of the 787. CFD codes are computer design software which enable aeronautic engineers to understand the aerodynamic forces acting on an airplane by evaluating the flowfield around the vehicle. Through the use of the CFD codes, engineers are able to quickly and accurately simulate complex airflows about an aircraft. This enables the engineers to arrive at the optimum aerodynamic design for the aircraft, minimizes the number of wind tunnel tests required, and in so doing, speeds up the design process and makes it less costly. CFD codes were first used in aerodynamic design in the 1960s.[3958] Since that time, they have acquired increasing importance in the aerodynamic design process.[3959] Most CFD codes are based upon partial differential equations, known as the Navier-Stokes equations, which show how the velocity, pressure, temperature and density of a moving fluid (both liquids and gases) are related. The CFD codes usually incorporate some simplifications of the equations to reduce the complexity of the computation. A central issue in computational fluid dynamics is how to treat continuous fluids in a discrete manner on a computer so that the model is suitable for numerical evaluation. This is usually done by dividing the space in issue into a grid or mesh. The grid generation process has typically presented a bottleneck in the overall CFD process time.[3960] For complex flow analyses, the task of generating the grid is a labour-intensive and slow process.

15. The European Communities focuses on two codes in its submissions, namely TRANAIR and OVERFLOW. TRANAIR is a CFD code that enables

---

[3957] Bair Affidavit, Exhibit US-7, para. 63.

[3958] Dominik Wacht, An Analysis of Selected NASA Research Programs and Their Impact on Boeing's Civil Aircraft Programs, November 2006, Exhibit EC-15, p. 143.

[3959] Dominik Wacht, An Analysis of Selected NASA Research Programs and Their Impact on Boeing's Civil Aircraft Programs, November 2006, Exhibit EC-15, p. 143; Testimony of Michael Garrett, Director, Airplane Performance, Boeing Commercial Airplanes, Before the United States Senate Committee on Commerce, Science and Transportation, Subcommittee on Technology, Innovation, and Competitiveness, 19 July 2006, Exhibit EC-379, p. 3.

[3960] Dominik Wacht, An Analysis of Selected NASA Research Programs and Their Impact on Boeing's Civil Aircraft Programs, November 2006, Exhibit EC-15, p. 150; Insights "Overflow code empowers computational fluid dynamics", Exhibit EC-1346, p. 2.

Report of the Panel

multipoint design optimization. This means that the design of the aircraft can be optimized for multiple flight conditions and that the aerodynamic objectives can be balanced by other constraints imposed by structures or by manufacturing, for example.[3961] OVERFLOW is a 3-D Navier-Stokes flow solver. It can use an "overset grid scheme", in which grids are generated about individual components, such as a wing or fuselage. The overlapped grids are then tied together to create a grid system about the entire vehicle.[3962] OVERFLOW was developed in the early 1990s by NASA alone and not under contract to Boeing or any other entity.[3963] It was created as part of a collaborative effort between NASA Johnson Space Center and NASA Ames Research Center.[3964]

16.   The CATIA software programme is used by Boeing in the 787 production and assembly process in combination with other software, known collectively as the "Product Lifecycle Management" tools.[3965] These tools, as used on the 787, allow every aspect of the airplane and its manufacturing processes to be designed, built and tested digitally before production begins.[3966] Boeing has standardized the CATIA software package as the basis of its digital design process across the entire company as well as across its global system of partners and suppliers.[3967] The common system allows real-time collaboration among engineers spread throughout the world, all working from a 3-D digital copy of the airplane held on the central Boeing server.[3968] This ensures that all partners in the global team have access to the same product definition data at the same time and avoids the difficulties that arise when data must be translated or exchanged between different computer-aided design tools.[3969] The use of CATIA and other related software throughout the global network means that when the components of the airplane are shipped to the common assembly facility, there is

---

[3961] Dominik Wacht, An Analysis of Selected NASA Research Programs and Their Impact on Boeing's Civil Aircraft Programs, November 2006, Exhibit EC-15, pp. 147-148; Calmar Research Corporation: TRANAIR++, Exhibit US-1235.

[3962] Dominik Wacht, An Analysis of Selected NASA Research Programs and Their Impact on Boeing's Civil Aircraft Programs, November 2006, Exhibit EC-15, pp. 149-152; Insights "Overflow code empowers computational fluid dynamics", Exhibit EC-1346.

[3963] See e.g. Insights "Overflow code empowers computational fluid dynamics", Exhibit EC-1346, p.1 and Affidavit of Douglas Ball, Exhibit US-1257, para. 10.

[3964] Insights "Overflow code empowers computational fluid dynamics", Exhibit EC-1346, p.1.

[3965] Bair Affidavit, Exhibit US-7, para. 66. Boeing uses CATIA in combination with DELMIA, for engineering lean manufacturing processes, ENOVIA for decision support and life-cycle management, and SMARTEAM.

[3966] Bair Affidavit, Exhibit US-7, para. 66.

[3967] See e.g. CRA International Report on IR&D and B&P, Exhibit EC-5, p. 40 and Design News; Beth Stackpole, "Boeing's Brave New World of Product Development; The Global Collaboration Environment lets 787 Partners Design, Build and Test Components and Manufacturing Processes for the Aircraft Digitally, Prior to Physical Production," Design News, 4 June, 2007, Exhibit US-317.

[3968] The Seattle Times, "Boeing shares work, but guards its secrets", Exhibit EC-1167.

[3969] Beth Stackpole, "Boeing's Brave New World of Product Development; The Global Collaboration Environment lets 787 Partners Design, Build and Test Components and Manufacturing Processes for the Aircraft Digitally, Prior to Physical Production," Design News, 4 June, 2007, Exhibit US-317.

less likelihood that the parts will not fit together, or that successive iterations of the manufacturing process will be required.[3970]

17.   The European Communities' allegations in relation to the specific aerodynamic and structural improvements to the wings of the 787 concern (i) the 787's "high-lift" system; and (ii) Boeing"s use of hydraulically actuated spoilers on the 787. The "high-lift" system of an aircraft refers to the elements of the wing that can be extended at the leading or the trailing edge to provide lift, such as the flaps, slats, flaperons and ailerons. CFD analysis for the high-lift components on a wing has traditionally been difficult due to the complex geometry involved.[3971] The difficulty lies in generating a grid to model the fluid flow over the high-lift configuration. Spoilers are small hinged plates that can be used to slow an aircraft, make it descend or generate a rolling motion. Hydraulically actuated spoilers are spoilers that are driven by hydraulic power.

18.   **"Noise reduction technologies"** refer to a group of technologies that reduce the noise generated by an aircraft and, in the case of the 787, involve the chevrons, joint-less acoustic treatment, quiet slats and flaps, low noise landing gear, low weight structures and improved airline performance. Aircraft noise is generated by anything related to the aircraft that creates pressure fluctuations. In most cases, it is some form of flow distortion or turbulent flow. Noise heard on the ground is composed of engine noise and airframe noise. Landing gear noise is a major contributor, along with flap noise, to airframe noise.[3972] During take-off, engine noise is the dominant source of noise and airframe noise less so, while, during landing, both engine noise and airframe noise are important contributors to overall aircraft noise.[3973] NASA research indicates that when an airliner is on approach, air rushing past the complex structure of the lowered landing gear can produce noise almost as loud as that of the engines.[3974] Chevrons are zigzag or saw-tooth shapes at the end of the nacelle[3975], with tips that are bent very slightly into the flow and reduce the jet noise component of the engine noise.[3976] Chevrons reduce jet blast noise by controlling the way that air mixes after passing through and around the engine.[3977] The serrated design

---

[3970] Edward Cone, "Boeing: New Jet, New Way of Doing Business," Eweek.com, 25 April, 2007, Exhibit US-318.

[3971] Dominik Wacht, An Analysis of Selected NASA Research Programs and Their Impact on Boeing's Civil Aircraft Programs, November 2006, Exhibit EC-15, p. 150.

[3972] William H. Herkes, The Quiet Technology Demonstrator Program: Flight Validation of Airplane Noise-Reduction Concepts, AIAA 2006-2720, 8-10 May 2006, Exhibit EC-849.

[3973] This is partly due to the fact that the landing gear is stowed and the flaps are only deployed to a small deflection.

[3974] Results of NASA Aircraft Noise Research, Exhibit EC-390

[3975] A nacelle is the streamlined outer casing of an aircraft engine.

[3976] Jet noise is due to turbulent mixing between jets and the noise generation mechanism is very complex. When the chevrons enhance mixing by the right amount, the total jet noise is reduced. Too much mixing increases the noise, while too little results in no noise reduction benefits; Hushing the roar, Aerospace America, June 2006, Exhibit EC-1342.

[3977] Boeing Team Working to Make Jetliners Quieter, Exhibit EC-391.

Report of the Panel

produces a better mix of engine's exhaust gas and air passing through and around the nacelle, which reduces the exhaust noise that hits the rear of the fuselage, resulting in quieter take-offs.[3978] Joint-less acoustic treatment refers to acoustic nacelle inlet liners. The inlet nacelle surface is usually made of an acoustically absorbent surface. The acoustic absorber (called the acoustic lining) usually consists of a perforated sheet at the surface, behind which is a layer of honeycomb core material, followed by a non-porous back sheet. The depth of the honey comb core and the properties of the perforated face sheet (e.g. hole diameter, sheet thickness, core depth) determine the frequency at which sound is absorbed, with a deeper liner absorbing a lower frequency of sound. Quiet flaps and slats relate to an aircraft's high-lift system. High-lift systems include the flaps and slats used to increase the lift performance of the wing, allowing the airplane to take off and land safely and efficiently. Low-noise landing gear relates to technologies that reduce landing gear noise. The Panel understands the European Communities' reference to "low weight structures" to be a reference to the composites solutions applied throughout the 787[3979] and its reference to "improved airplane performance" to mean that one aspect of overall improved airplane performance is reduced noise, not that improved airplane performance is a specific low noise technology that enables the 787 to be a quiet aircraft.

19. **"Health management systems"** refer to systems that allow for the monitoring of the health of the different parts of an aircraft, including aircraft systems and certain aircraft structures, leading to lower maintenance costs for airline operators.[3980] The 787 will employ health monitoring technologies to monitor aircraft flight systems such as the hydraulic systems and electric braking systems.[3981] Structural health monitoring technologies, including embedded sensors, will also monitor structural health around the 787's cargo doors and landing gear.[3982] Mathematical algorithms and neural networks process the information collected by these sensors.[3983] The health management system of the 787 has "new enabling technologies that turn airplane operating data into actionable information and knowledge."[3984] These new enabling technologies include the "sensors being built into the 787 {that} will track the performance of

---

[3978] Boeing Flight Test Journal, Future Looks Quiet, 20 September 2005, Exhibit EC 393.

[3979] This understanding is confirmed by a Boeing presentation submitted by the European Communities, indicating that the use of composites means that the 787 is lighter, with less thrust and therefore less noise; Larry Craig, "Boeing Noise Technology," Los Angeles World Airports Community Noise Roundtable, 13 September 2006, Exhibit EC-1341.

[3980] European Communities' first written submission, Annex C, paras. 110 - 113. Boeing Presentation #20, Exhibit EC-854 (BCI), p.4.

[3981] Boeing Presentation #3, Exhibit EC-353 (BCI), p. 8.

[3982] Boeing Presentation #19, Exhibit EC-829 (BCI), p. 5.

[3983] Boeing Presentation #19, Exhibit EC-829 (BCI), pp. 1-2. Boeing Presentation #20, Exhibit EC-854 (BCI), p. 5. Boeing, "A golden opportunity to become a lower-cost carrier. Guaranteed. 787 Dreamliner, GoldCare," Exhibit EC-855, p. 3.Boeing Presentation #19, Exhibit EC-829 (BCI), p. 5. Boeing Presentation #3, Exhibit EC-353 (BCI), p. 10.

[3984] GoldCare – The 787 Revolution Now Revolutionizes Service, Boeing Website, Exhibit EC-852.

US - Large Civil Aircraft (2nd Complaint)

different parts and send out alerts if something starts to fail."[3985] These sensors will also help pilots in the cockpit report problems they see.[3986] The information from these sensors can be relayed to the ground via satellite in real-time[3987], which allows Boeing to offer immediate maintenance service to its airline customers and makes regular routine inspections at short intervals less necessary.[3988]

C.   DESIGN, MANUFACTURE AND ASSEMBLY OF THE 787

20.   This section of the Appendix provides some background information regarding the design and manufacture of the fuselage of an aircraft in order to facilitate understanding of the parties' arguments concerning the composite fuselage of the 787. It also describes the process by which the 787 is being constructed; namely, by the outsourcing of certain design and manufacturing functions to key suppliers throughout the world as this aspect of the development and production of the 787 is important to an understanding of certain of the United States' rebuttal arguments.

21.   The fuselage of an airplane (whether constructed from aluminium or from composites) is built around a hollow, cylindrical skeleton, which can be visualized as a birdcage laid on its side. Narrow hoops called "frames" trace the circumference of the cage. "Stringers" run lengthwise, perpendicular to the frames which are used to create stiffness.[3989] Each frame contains openings (mouse holes) that allow the frames to be placed crosswise over the stringers.[3990] To form the smooth, aerodynamic exterior, this lattice is enclosed by "skins" which are attached to the outside of the structure. The skins are less than a quarter of an inch thick in most places.[3991] The fuselage of an aircraft has traditionally been made from several large panels that are bolted together to form a cylinder. However, bolting composite panels together requires that the edges of the panels be made thicker to accommodate the bolts, adding to the weight and necessitating seams and joints that fatigue like their aluminium counterparts and require additional rounds of maintenance.

[3985] Bryan Corliss, "Boeing stressing its 787 'GoldCare' service," HeraldNet, 8 May 2006, Exhibit EC-856. Bill Sweetman, "Boeing, Boeing, Gone?" Aviation & Space, May 2004, Exhibit EC-857.

[3986] Bryan Corliss, "Boeing stressing its 787 'GoldCare' service," HeraldNet, 8 May 2006, Exhibit EC-856.

[3987] Bryan Corliss, "Boeing stressing its 787 'GoldCare' service," HeraldNet, 8 May 2006, Exhibit EC-856. Boeing, "A golden opportunity to become a lower-cost carrier. Guaranteed. 787 Dreamliner, GoldCare," Exhibit EC-855, p. 3.

[3988] European Communities' first written submission, Annex C, para. 113. 7E7 Dreamliner, Structural Health Management Technology Implementation on Commercial Airplanes, undated, Exhibit EC-829 (BCI), p. 18.

[3989] Boeing Bets Big On A Plastic Plane, Chicago Tribune (January 12, 2005), Exhibit US-310, p. 3.

[3990] Tim Sommer et al., Composite Technologies, November 2006, Exhibit EC-14 (BCI), pp. 30, 64-67.

[3991] Boeing Bets Big On A Plastic Plane, Chicago Tribune (January 12, 2005), Exhibit US-310, p. 3.

DSR 2012:III

Report of the Panel

22.   The 787 fuselage is constructed from seamless 360° barrel sections that are pieced together during final assembly. The 360° barrel sections are made from a solid laminate "skin" that is built around a skeleton made up of frames and stringers.   Production of the 360° composite barrel sections involves (i) wrapping the prepreg material around a mould (or mandrel) having the shape of the *inside* surface of the fuselage, referred to as inside mould line (IML) tooling[3992]; (ii) securing the composite-wrapped mandrels with outer mould line cauls (OMLs) to give the desired shape to the outside of the composite fuselage and covering the whole structure with vacuum curing bags; (iii) curing the fuselage sections as a single piece in a pressurized oven; and (iv) after curing, collapsing the internal mandrel and removing it from the stiffened composite structure.[3993]

23.   The frames, stringers and skin of the 787 are all constructed of composite material. The frames of the 787 fuselage are created using a bulk resin infused (BRI) technique, in which the dry carbon fibre pre-form is placed onto a bed of resin in a single open mould. The resin infusion process occurs after the pre-form fibre and the resin are placed under vacuum pressure, and the resin is heated and drawn through the pre-form fiber. The stringers are constructed using a forming process that entails the use of mechanical pressure to form a flat piece of composite material (the stringer charge) into an automated, movable mould. Each such stringer must be tailored for its unique location on the fuselage; thus, once formed, the 787 stringers undergo a multiple axis machine trim, which allows them to be cut into required profiles.[3994] The composite skin is made using AFP processes from Toray T3900 intermediate modulus fibre prepreg material, an epoxy-infused material supplied by Toray Industries (of Japan), which was originally developed and used on the 777.[3995]

24.   In developing the 787, Boeing has shifted responsibility for detailed component design to suppliers, and focuses on systems integration, managing overall requirements, as well as the assembly process. The 787 is essentially assembled from large substructures designed and produced by suppliers. A number of suppliers are risk-sharing partners in the 787 programme, responsible for their own development and production costs and, in some instances, contribution of funds toward overall development and certification costs. Foreign suppliers, especially the Japanese heavy industrial companies and the Italian company Alenia, are reported to play a significant role in the 787

[3992] These are large cylindrical, collapsible mandrels that have the shape of each fuselage section; Affidavit of Alan Miller, Exhibit US-1258, para. 12.

[3993] Affidavit of Alan Miller, Exhibit US-1258, para. 12.

[3994] Affidavit of Alan Miller, Exhibit US-1258, para. 14.

[3995] Bair Affidavit, Exhibit US-7, paras. 49, 57; Affidavit of Alan Miller, Exhibit US-1258, para. 11. According to Boeing's Michael Bair, this material was originally developed and certified for commercial aircraft production (i.e. to meet requirements relating to strength, heat resistance, toughness and stiffness) in May 1990.

US - Large Civil Aircraft (2nd Complaint)

programme.[3996] Analysts' reports in 2007 estimated the development costs for the 787 to be between $7 and 9 billion, about half of which was to be provided by Boeing's risk-sharing suppliers.[3997] In particular, the three Japanese industrial corporations (Kawasaki Heavy Industries, Mitsubishi Heavy Industries and Fuji Heavy Industries), operating through the Japan Aircraft Development Corporation, are co-designing and building approximately 35 per cent of the 787.[3998] The Japanese government has been reported to have provided loans of up to $2 billion to finance the development project.[3999] The Italian government has also been reported to have provided infrastructure support to the Italian risk-sharing supplier, Alenia Aeronautica.[4000] Boeing has been reported as stating that a partner's ability to invest, reducing Boeing's upfront costs, was an important consideration in Boeing's selection of partners, as was the need to ensure engineering talent and technical capacity.[4001]

25.   Completion of sub-assemblies and integration of systems takes place in Everett, Washington, with many components being pre-installed before delivery to Everett. The 787 composite wings are being manufactured by Mitsubishi Heavy Industries.[4002] The horizontal stabilizers are being manufactured by Alenia Aeronautica in Italy, and various parts of the fuselage sections are being built by Alenia in Italy, Vought in Charleston, South Carolina, Kawasaki Heavy Industries and Fuji Heavy Industries in Japan, Alenia in Italy and Spirit Aerosystems in Wichita, Kansas.[4003] The main landing gear and nose landing gear are being supplied by the French company Messier-Dowty, while passenger doors are being made by Latécoère in France, and the cargo, access and crew escape doors by Saab in Sweden.[4004] The integrated avionics platform is designed and supplied by Smiths/GE, while flight controls and other avionics systems are being supplied by Honeywell and Rockwell-Collins.[4005]

[3996] Dominic Gates, Boeing 787: Parts from around world will be swiftly integrated, The Seattle Times, 11 September 2005, Exhibit EC-114.

[3997] R. Aboulafia, Boeing 787 Dreamliner Program Briefing, World Military & Civil Aircraft Briefing, Teal Group, February 2007, Exhibit EC-1170.

[3998] Boeing shares work, but guards its secrets, The Seattle Times, 15 May 2007, Exhibit EC-1167.

[3999] Ibid.

[4000] Boeing shares work, but guards its secrets, The Seattle Times, 15 May 2007, Exhibit EC-1167.

[4001] Boeing shares work, but guards its secrets, The Seattle Times, 15 May 2007, Exhibit EC-1167, quoting Bob Noble, Boeing Vice President responsible for global partners on new programmes.

[4002] Dominic Gates, Boeing 787: Parts from around world will be swiftly integrated, The Seattle Times, 11 September 2005, Exhibit EC-114.

[4003] Ibid.

[4004] Dominic Gates, Boeing 787: Parts from around world will be swiftly integrated, The Seattle Times, 11 September 2005, Exhibit EC-114.

[4005] Bair Affidavit, Exhibit US-7, para. 64.

Report of the Panel

D. ARGUMENTS REGARDING THE RELATIONSHIP BETWEEN THE AERONAUTICS R&D MEASURES AND BOEING'S DEVELOPMENT OF 787 TECHNOLOGIES IN SPECIFIC TECHNOLOGY AREAS

26.   This section of the Appendix sets forth the parties' specific arguments concerning the relationship between work that Boeing performed pursuant to the aeronautics R&D measures and Boeing's development of technologies in the six specific technology areas for application to the 787.

1. Composites technologies, primarily the design, development and manufacturing of 787 composite fuselages and wings

(a)   European Communities

27.   The European Communities alleges that, pursuant to the NASA's ACT, AST and R&T Base programmes, NASA provided funding and support to Boeing through several contracts regarding composites research.[4006] In addition, the European Communities contends that Boeing learned about composites technologies relevant to the 787 composite fuselage by participating in a number of projects under DOD RDT&E programmes such as the ManTech Composites Affordability Initiative, the ManTech Advanced Fiber Placement project, DUS&T High Rate Fiber Placement project, V-22 Aft Fuselage Demonstration Program, and JSF prototype development programme.[4007] According to the European Communities, "{b}ut for these US Government composites R&D programmes, Boeing would not be able to build and promise deliveries of such an advanced 787 aircraft today. Nor would customers be as willing to buy it."[4008]

28.   The European Communities identifies the following characteristics of the construction of the 787 fuselage as "deriving" from knowledge and experience that Boeing gained by participating in U.S. government R&D programmes:

(a)   manufacture of the forward section of the 787 fuselage using Automatic Fibre Placement (AFP) and the centre fuselage sections of the fuselage using Automatic Tape Laying (ATL);

[4006] European Communities' first written submission, Annex C, para. 26: NASA Contract NAS1-18889 regarding Research and Development in Advanced Technology Composite Aircraft Structures, 12 May 1989, Exhibit EC-329; NASA Contract NAS1-18954 regarding Advanced Composite Fabrication and Testing, 29 August 1989, Exhibit EC-798; NASA Contract NAS1-19349 regarding Structures and Materials Technology for Aircraft Composite Primary Structures, 30 September 1991, Exhibit EC-799; NASA Contract NAS1-20553 regarding Technology Verification of Composite Primary Fuselage Structures for Commercial Transport Aircraft, 25 September 1995, Exhibit EC-334; NASA Contract NAS1-99070 regarding Structures and Materials Technology for Aerospace Vehicles, 25 January 1999, Exhibit EC-800.
[4007] European Communities' first written submission, Annex C, para. 46.
[4008] European Communities' first written submission, Annex C, para. 22. Emphasis in original.

1706   DSR 2012:III

(b) production of all of the 787 fuselage sections as 360° barrel sections which are produced on large, rotating, collapsible mandrels and the design of the mandrels with notches for "co-cured" stringers[4009];

(c) the use of resin infused braided fibres to manufacture the frames, which are then bolted to the fuselage skins; and

(d) the design of the cut-outs in the fuselage frames using the same process as on the ATCAS panel.[4010]

29. The European Communities identifies the following characteristics of the 787's composite wings as deriving from U.S. government-supported aeronautics R&D programmes:

(a) Boeing's decision to manufacture the entire wing box (i.e. the wing skins and spars) of the 787 from composite materials as large one-piece structures, which the European Communities alleges stems primarily from the knowledge and experience that Boeing (and McDonnell Douglas prior to its merger with Boeing) gained under NASA's ACT and AST programmes[4011];

(b) Boeing's decision to use ATL techniques for the construction of the wing box, which the European Communities alleges stems primarily from the knowledge and experience that Boeing (and McDonnell Douglas prior to its merger with Boeing) gained under NASA's ACT and AST programmes, as well as DOD RDT&E funding on a number of military aircraft programmes[4012];

30. The European Communities argues that U.S. government-supported research helped Boeing to develop some of the post-processing tools and techniques that it uses to machine the large composite parts for the 787. Its particular allegations are as follows:

(a) Specifications used by Boeing for aligning and drilling holes in multiple layers of composite materials in order to fasten the 787's wings to its fuselage derive from DOD-supported R&D that Boeing conducted for the B-2 programme[4013];

(b) Boeing employs "polycrystalline diamond tools" to drill its composite parts, while it explored similar diamond-coated rotating

---

[4009] European Communities' first written submission, Annex C, para. 44.

[4010] Joint Declaration by Dominik Wacht and Tim Sommer, Exhibit EC-1336 (BCI), para. 23; Dominik Wacht, An Analysis of Selected NASA Research Programs and Their Impact on Boeing's Civil Aircraft Programs, November 2006, Exhibit EC-15, p. 71.

[4011] European Communities' first written submission, Annex C, paras. 56-57.

[4012] European Communities' first written submission,, Annex C, paras. 58-59. The military programmes in question include the F-22, A-6, B-2 and JSF programmes.

[4013] European Communities' first written submission, Annex C, para. 62.

Report of the Panel

tools under the DOC ATP project on CVD Diamond-Coated Rotating Tools for Machining Advanced Materials[4014];

31.   According to the European Communities, as a result of the knowledge and experience in advanced NDI techniques which Boeing obtained under NASA's ACT, AST and R&T Base programmes, as well as under DOD RDT&E programmes (including Materials, Advanced Materials for Weapons Systems, and Ageing Aircraft), Boeing has developed NDI techniques that it uses to detect faults in the composite fuselage and wing parts of the 787 after they have been shaped and cured.[4015]

32.   In relation to Boeing's manufacture of the various fuselage sections of the 787 using AFP and ATL technologies, the European Communities alleges that Boeing studied the application of AFP and ATL techniques to the manufacture of large composite fuselage sections under NASA and DOD programmes, particularly the Advanced Technology Composite Aircraft Structures (ATCAS) element of NASA's ACT Program.[4016] As discussed in paragraph 7.1713 of the Report, the formal ACT Program lasted from 1989 through 1995. Funding for advanced composites research related to a composite fuselage continued from 1996 to 2000 under the "Materials and Structures" element of NASA's R&T Base Program.[4017] The European Communities also alleges that knowledge and experience with respect to AFP and ATL techniques that Boeing gained through its participation in a number of DOD RDT&E programmes; most importantly, the ManTech Composites Affordability Initiative and Advanced Fibre Placement programmes, the DUS&T High Rate Fibre Placement project, the V-22 Aft Fuselage Demonstration Program and the JSF prototype development Program,

---

[4014] European Communities' first written submission, Annex C, para. 63. Composite cutting is different from cutting metal because composites are not homogenous materials; rather, the matrix has different properties from the stronger reinforcement (which is much more difficult to cut). The use of conventional machining techniques to cut composites creates the potential for greater tool wear with significant heat generation, which can be damaging to the composite; Robert B. Aronson, "Cutting Composites," Manufacturing Engineering, March 2006, Exhibit EC-554, p. 2.

[4015] European Communities' first written submission, Annex C, para. 63.

[4016] In a 1997 NASA Contractor Report, Boeing describes the ATCAS programme as having been initiated in 1989 as NASA Contract NAS1-18889, an integral part of the NASA sponsored ACT initiative. The report then describes Task 2 of Materials Development Omnibus Contract (NASA Contract NAS1-20013) which was awarded in 1993, as extending the ATCAS work. The report states that these two contracts addressed Phases A and B relating to concept selection and technology development. An additional contract (NASA Contract NAS1-20553, referred to as Phase C) was initiated to verify the technology at a large scale; L.B. Ilcewicz et al., Advanced Technology Composite Fuselage—Program Overview, NASA Contractor Report 4734, April 1997, Exhibit EC-808, para. 2-0. Airbus' Dominik Wacht also explains that the NASA contracts awarded to Boeing under the ACT Program were grouped together to form the ATCAS programme, which he alleges was aligned with Boeing's independent research efforts focused on the introduction of large scale composites on civil aircraft; Dominik Wacht, An Analysis of Selected NASA Research Programs and Their Impact on Boeing's Civil Aircraft Programs, November 2006, Exhibit EC-15, p. 49.

[4017] NASA ACT Budget Estimates, FY 1989-FY 1997, Exhibit EC-321, at FY 1997, SAT 4-21.

1708   DSR 2012:III

"likely contributed to its decision to use AFP and ATL techniques to manufacture the 787's fuselage skin sections."[4018]

33.   The European Communities argues that "the 360 degree barrel concept for the 787 fuselage sections also derives from Boeing's participation in NASA and DoD programmes."[4019] The European Communities acknowledges that, under ATCAS, Boeing designed, built and tested a fuselage from four separate *panel* sections (rather than 360° barrel sections). However, it contends that the research under ATCAS served as a "roadmap" for Boeing to arrive at the key solution that it later applied on the 787; namely, a composite fuselage barrel.[4020] According to the European Communities, "on the long road to Boeing's successful development of a composite fuselage barrel, ATCAS provided Boeing with quintessential foundational knowledge and technologies, by supporting the achievement of significant milestones in this long-term, step-by-step process."[4021] The European Communities notes that, under ATCAS, Boeing undertook several studies to substantiate the advantages of 360° sections.[4022] The European Communities asserts that there are in fact a number of reasons why 360° barrel sections are "more advantageous" than separate panels, "which Boeing likely learned from its experience in the ATCAS programme."[4023] The European Communities therefore contends that the knowledge and experience that Boeing gained from this ATCAS programme work "led to its ultimate selection of a full barrel concept with design features such as co-cured stringers".[4024] As for the influence of DOD military programmes on Boeing's decision to construct the 787 composite fuselage from 360° barrel sections, the European Communities argues that (i) Boeing gained knowledge and experience in using large, collapsible, rotating mandrels to build the 360° fuselage barrel sections through its participation in the V-22 and JSF programmes; and (ii) that Boeing's "ability to piece together the 360° composite barrel sections during final

---

[4018] European Communities' first written submission, Annex C, para. 46.

[4019] European Communities' first written submission, Annex C, para. 47.

[4020] European Communities' confidential oral statement at the second meeting with the Panel, para. 44.

[4021] *Ibid.*

[4022] European Communities' first written submission, Annex C, para. 47.

[4023] European Communities' first written submission, Annex C, para. 48. The European Communities identifies the most important of these advantages as (i) the fact that large composite barrels enable the manufacturer to reduce the number of parts to make the fuselage, substantially reducing cost and assembly time; and (ii) that the use of large barrels saves approximately 1,500 aluminium sheets and 40,000 – 50,000 fasteners, entailing a far less complex manufacturing process that reduces the need for human labour. The European Communities notes that Boeing itself considers that this translates directly into reduced manufacturing times of between 30 to 40 per cent; European Communities' first written submission, Annex C, para. 48.

[4024] European Communities' first written submission, Annex C, para. 47. The European Communities argues that the U.S. government aeronautics R&D subsidies in question enabled Boeing to confidently take the "last steps" at an acceptable level of risk and cost for the company; European Communities' non-confidential oral statement at the second meeting with the Panel, para. 44.

Report of the Panel

assembly was also "enhanced" by the work Boeing did under the V-22 programme in researching and conducting final assembly of a 360° composite aft fuselage section.[4025]

34. The European Communities argues that Boeing's decision to use braided resin infusion techniques for manufacturing the composite fuselage frames derives from work done under NASA's ACT Program.[4026] In particular, the European Communities contends that the research on resin-infused braided frames which Boeing carried out as part of the construction of the crown fuselage panel under the ATCAS Program, and its conclusion that this was the most cost efficient means of frame fabrication, "likely led to Boeing's decision to use resin-infused braided frames for the 787."[4027] In addition, the European Communities argues that Boeing's decision to bolt "mouse holed" composite fuselage frames to the fuselage skins of the 787 also derives from the knowledge and experience that Boeing gained under the ATCAS Program.[4028] The European Communities contends that the knowledge and experience that Boeing gained from the problems it encountered from the use of bonded (rather than bolted) frames when manufacturing the fuselage crown panel under the ATCAS Program "led to its ultimate decision to use mouse holed bolted frames on the 787."[4029] According to the European Communities, Boeing was able to "optimize" its mouse holed design through its work under the ACT Program.[4030]

35. Finally, the European Communities alleges that the "door and window reinforcements on the ATCAS Program were integrated directly into the skin, similar to the 787 barrel."[4031]

36. The European Communities argues that a number of the technical characteristics of the 787's composite wings derive from R&D conducted under NASA's ACT and AST programmes (particularly the Innovative Composite Primary Structures (ICAPS) and composites elements of those programmes[4032]), as well as DOD RDT&E programmes.[4033] The European Communities notes that under the composite wing element of the AST Program, McDonnell Douglas

---

[4025] European Communities' first written submission, Annex C, paras. 49 and 50.

[4026] European Communities' first written submission, Annex C, para. 53.

[4027] *Ibid.*

[4028] European Communities' first written submission, Annex C, para. 54.

[4029] *Ibid.*

[4030] *Ibid.*

[4031] Joint Declaration by Dominik Wacht and Tim Sommer, Exhibit EC-1336 (BCI), para. 23; Dominik Wacht, An Analysis of Selected NASA Research Programs and Their Impact on Boeing's Civil Aircraft Programs, November 2006, Exhibit EC-15, p. 71.

[4032] The ICAPS element of the ACT Program was implemented as NASA Contract NAS1-18862 with McDonnell Douglas regarding Innovative Composite Primary Structures, 31 March 1989, Exhibit EC-331. When the ACT Program ended prematurely in 1995, funding for advanced composites research related to composite wings continued until financial year 1999 under the AST Program; NASA AST Budget Estimates, FY 1989 - FY 1997, Exhibit EC-357, at FY 1996, SAT 4-42.

[4033] European Communities' first written submission, Annex C, para. 56.

1710

DSR 2012:III

tested a semi-span advanced composite wing.[4034] The manufacturing technology used for the construction of the semi-span composite wing fabricated and tested in the composite wing element of the AST Program was stitched/resin film infusion (S/RFI)[4035], while Boeing used ATL technology to construct 787 composite wings. The European Communities argues that, even though Boeing and McDonnell Douglas used S/RFI techniques to manufacture the AST semi-span composite wing, "this experience nonetheless led Boeing to its ultimate design of the 787's composite wing box and its decision to use ATL to manufacture the 787's wing box components."[4036]

37.   The European Communities argues that U.S. government-supported research has helped Boeing to develop some of the post-processing tools and techniques that it uses to machine the large composite parts for the 787. In particular, it alleges that (i) specifications used by Boeing for aligning and drilling holes in multiple layers of composite materials in order to fasten the 787's wings to its fuselage derive from DOD-supported R&D that Boeing conducted for the B-2 programme[4037]; (ii) Boeing employs "polycrystalline diamond tools" to drill its composite parts, while it explored similar diamond-coated rotating tools under the DOC ATP project on CVD Diamond-Coated Rotating Tools for Machining Advanced Materials[4038]; and as a result of the knowledge and experience in advanced NDI techniques which Boeing obtained under NASA's ACT, AST and R&T Base programmes, as well as under DOD RDT&E programmes (including Materials, Advanced Materials for Weapons Systems, and Ageing Aircraft), Boeing has developed the NDI techniques that it uses to detect faults in the composite fuselage and wing parts of the 787 after they have been shaped and cured.[4039]

(b)   United States

38.   The United States argues that, although the European Communities has sought to support its "technology effects" causation theory by pointing to similarities between research conducted under NASA and DOD R&D programmes and technology applied to the 787, for the bulk of the challenged programmes, the European Communities "does not even find a semblance of a connection to the 787."[4040] The United States argues that, even as regards the NASA R&D programme that the European Communities argues had the clearest

---

[4034] European Communities' first written submission, Annex C, para. 57.

[4035] Michael Karal, AST Composite Wing Program – Executive Summary, NASA/CR-2001-210650, March 2001, Exhibit EC-819, p. 1. This process involves stitching pre-woven dry material together with wing components such as stringers and spar caps, followed by introducing resin just before curing in the autoclave.

[4036] European Communities' first written submission, Annex C, para. 52.

[4037] European Communities' first written submission, Annex C, para. 62.

[4038] European Communities' first written submission, Annex C, para. 63.

[4039] *Ibid.*

[4040] United States' confidential oral statement at the second meeting with the Panel, para. 22.

DSR 2012:III   1711

Report of the Panel

relevance to the 787 – the Advanced Technology Composites Aircraft Structures (ATCAS) Program – most of the technologies studied under ATCAS are fundamentally different to the technologies used on the 787.[4041]

39.   According to the United States, the generic technology concept that Boeing studied under the ATCAS contract was for a panelized fuselage section, which from a technological point of view, differs fundamentally from the seamless 360° barrel sections that Boeing has developed for the 787.[4042] In addition, the United States argues that the key (albeit limited) technology findings of the ATCAS Program were widely known throughout the aerospace engineering community long before Boeing began work on the 787.[4043] In relation to the specific links between knowledge and technologies developed under the ATCAS Program and technologies applied to the 787, the United States argues: (i) that only $26 million was disbursed to Boeing under the ATCAS contract; (ii) that the research done under the ATCAS contract (as acknowledged by Airbus' Wacht) did not relate to a single-barrel fuselage, but instead to four quadrant panelized fuselage sections; (iii) that three sections of the panelized fuselage concept studied under ATCAS were made using a mixed honeycomb core stiffened concept that is a very different technology to the solid laminate technology used on the 787; and (iv) that the one panel studied under ATCAS that was designed using co-cured solid laminate technology which is similar to the 787 fuselage (the ATCAS crown panel) was constructed in a different way to the 787 fuselage sections.[4044]

40.   According to the United States, because of the clear differences between ATCAS and 787 technologies, the only similarity between technologies developed under the ATCAS Program and those applied to the 787 is the co-cured hat stringer used on both the ATCAS crown panel and the 787 fuselage. However, the United States contends that there are significant differences in stringer formation, co-curing methods and load requirements between the two. Specifically, the United States alleges that the ATCAS research was limited to panel sections using only constant gauge stringers, while Boeing had to invent and design methods for creating multi-gauge stringers to manage the changing loads over the length of the 787 composite fuselage.[4045]

[4041] United States' confidential oral statement at the second meeting with the Panel, para. 24.

[4042] *Ibid.*

[4043] United States' confidential oral statement at the second meeting with the Panel, para. 25.

[4044] United States' comments on European Communities' response to question 87, para. 21. Specifically, the United States explains that the ATCAS crown panel was built as a standalone section using outer mould line (OML) tools and inner mould line (IML) cauls to co-cure the skin and stringers, while the 787 fuselage, by contrast, is being built as a single solid piece of composite created and cured around enormous multi-section mandrels which are IML tools (designed by suppliers for Boeing) with OML cauls.

[4045] United States' comments on European Communities' response to question 87, para. 330; Airbus engineers Sommer and Wacht have responded that the fact that the 787 fuselage features multi-gauge stringers, rather than the constant-gauge stringers developed under ATCAS is irrelevant. They contend that the ATCAS structure established basic design data which can then be used to design

1712

DSR 2012:III

US - Large Civil Aircraft (2nd Complaint)

41.   The United States denies that the composite wing developed by Boeing for the 787 was in any way enabled by the research that Boeing and McDonnell Douglas conducted under the NASA R&D programmes. The United States contends that the scope of the NASA composite wing work was very limited, in that it focused on structural issues, but did not fully address the systems integration for pumps, sensors, electrical and thermal integration required for a commercial aircraft design. Moreover, the United States notes that the composite wing designed and tested under the ICAPS element of the NASA ACT Program and then under NASA's AST Composite Wing Program used stitching and resin infusion technologies that were not commercialized by Boeing or McDonnell Douglas, while the 787 composite wings are made using ATL technology.[4046] Finally, the United States alleges that Boeing shared any valuable learning that arose from the NASA composite wing work with visiting personnel from BAE Systems and the U.K. Department of Trade and Industry (DTI) in 1996, which resulted in DTI initiating a carbon wing demonstration project (in which Airbus participated), using a very similar stitched approach for designing and manufacturing.[4047]

42.   In relation to the European Communities' allegations concerning composites manufacturing tools and processes, the United States argues that the composite maintenance and repair processes for the 787 are based on those developed for use on the 777 composite structures and that their development preceded the work that was done under the ATCAS contract.[4048] According to the United States, material selection for the 777 (and later, for the 787) necessitated the development of a repair concept to accommodate that particular material. Moreover, the United States contends that repair concepts in general are widely known and relatively uniform within the aerospace industry, because airlines that own aircraft from multiple manufacturers must be able to efficiently maintain and repair their entire fleet. In this regard, the United States asserts that the "familiarity" of the bolted repair techniques selected for the 777 and 787 which makes them attractive to airlines is in fact a familiarity borne of their origin in use on metallic structures, not studies done with airlines under the ATCAS contract.[4049]

43.   With respect to links to DOD-funded aeronautics R&D, the United States argues that military technologies are not technologically geared toward

---

actual aircraft fuselage sections in which stringer and panel thickness can be adapted to the actual load requirements of each part of the fuselage. According to Sommer and Wacht, the design data established during tests of the ATCAS panel sections *enables* this adaptation; Joint Declaration by Dominik Wacht and Tim Sommer, Exhibit EC-1336 (BCI), para. 23, footnote 44.

[4046] Bair Affidavit, Exhibit US-7, para. 55; Affidavit of Branko Sarh, Exhibit US-1254, para. 13.

[4047] Bair Affidavit, Exhibit US-7, para. 55.

[4048] Affidavit of Alan Miller, Exhibit US-1258, para. 19.

[4049] Affidavit of Alan Miller, Exhibit US-1258, para. 20.

Report of the Panel

commercial aircraft production and design, and that in any case, that Boeing's policy is not to use ITAR-controlled defence technologies on the 787.[4050]

2. More-electric systems architecture

(a) European Communities

44. The European Communities argues that the knowledge, experience, and confidence Boeing gained through (i) the NASA AST Program, in particular, the Power-by-Wire (PBW) subtask of the Fly-by-Light/Power-by-Wire (FBL/PBW) element of that programme; and (ii) the Aerospace Propulsion and Power Technology, and Dual Use Science and Technology programmes under DOD's RDT&E Program, allowed Boeing to develop and use extensive "more-electric" systems on the 787, while maintaining certain efficient hydraulic systems. The European Communities argues that without this more-electric architecture, Boeing would not have been able to obtain the efficiencies and operating cost savings it now guarantees 787 operators, which contribute significantly to the commercial success of the 787.[4051] The European Communities argues that, in addition to any direct application of U.S. Government-supported more-electric technologies on the 787, Boeing's development of the final more-electric architecture of the 787 "surely benefited from the knowledge, experience, and confidence it gained under these programmes."[4052]

45. With respect to the FBL/PBW element of the AST Program, the European Communities argues that McDonnell Douglas gained knowledge and experience with regard to power system definitions and requirements through a NASA contract by designing, fabricating, testing, and demonstrating power management and distribution architectures, electrical actuators, and starter/generators.[4053] The European Communities argues that this knowledge and experience contributed to Boeing's design and development of the more-electric architecture of the 787, particularly as regards Boeing's ability to integrate more-electric components into the 787. According to the European Communities, Boeing's integrative capabilities likely benefited from the knowledge and experience McDonnell Douglas gained under the AST Program with respect to flight actuator designs.[4054] In addition, the European

---

[4050] United States' first written submission, paras. 163-176 and 951-953; Bair Affidavit, Exhibit US-7, paras. 5, 23-32; United States' second written submission, paras. 55-59.

[4051] European Communities' first written submission, Annex C, para. 77.

[4052] *Ibid.*

[4053] European Communities' first written submission, Annex C, para. 71; NASA Contract NAS3-27018 with McDonnell Douglas Aerospace regarding Power-By-Wire Development and Demonstration for Subsonic Civil Transport, 29 September 1993, C-5, Exhibit EC-826. Power-by-Wire Development and Demonstration for Subsonic Civil Transport, Exhibit EC-366.

[4054] European Communities' first written submission, Annex C, para. 71. Dominik Wacht, An Analysis of Selected NASA Research Programs and Their Impact on Boeing's Civil Aircraft Programs, November 2006, Exhibit EC-15, pp. 105-106; Boeing Presentation #16, Exhibit EC-807

1714

DSR 2012:III

US - Large Civil Aircraft (2nd Complaint)

Communities asserts that [***], the 787 will utilize electro-mechanical actuators akin to those that McDonnell Douglas studied and developed pursuant to its PBW contract.[4055]

46.   The European Communities argues that a number of specific aspects of the 787's more-electric architecture derive from knowledge and experience that Boeing gained from dual-use research that it conducted pursuant to the Aerospace Propulsion and Power Technology, and Dual Use Science and Technology programmes under DOD's RDT&E Program. In this regard, the European Communities argues first, that Boeing's use of electrically actuated brakes on the 787 stems from its "existing military experience."[4056] According to the European Communities, this experience consists, *inter alia*, of work that McDonnell Douglas performed pursuant to a 1992 contract with the United States Air Force with regard to Electrically Actuated Brake System ("ELABRAT") technology.[4057] Second, the European Communities argues that Boeing's decision to maintain and improve certain hydraulic systems, thereby making the 787 a "more-electric" (as opposed to all-electric) aircraft, also stems from its dual-use DOD-supported military aircraft research. The European Communities explains that the 787 maintains some hydraulic actuation, but uses an innovative 5,000 psi operating pressure, as opposed to the 3,000 psi on older Boeing LCA like the 777[4058] and argues that this is precisely the same concept that Boeing studied, developed, and used for its DOD-funded JSF demonstrator. The European Communities indicates that, unlike Lockheed Martin, which used electro-hydrostatic actuators for its JSF concept, Boeing used a 5,000 psi hydraulic system because "modern 5,000-psi hydraulics systems compare better than EHAs in terms of cost, weight and supportability."[4059]

(b)   United States

47.   The United States argues that Boeing's decision to use a more-electric architecture for the 787 became possible because of a critical Boeing design innovation as well as supplier innovations.[4060] According to the United States, by using larger starter generators supplied by Hamilton Sundstrand, Boeing and its

---

(BCI), p. 3; Power-by-Wire Development and Demonstration for Subsonic Civil Transport, Exhibit EC-366.

[4055] Power-by-Wire Development and Demonstration for Subsonic Civil Transport, Exhibit EC-366.

[4056] European Communities' first written submission, Annex C, para. 75; Boeing Presentation #3, Exhibit EC-353 (BCI), pp. 5-7.

[4057] Air Force Contract F33615-92-C-3406 with McDonnell Douglas Corporation regarding Electrically Actuated Brake System (ELABRAT), 29 September 1992, Exhibit EC-827; Boeing Presentation #16, Exhibit EC-807 (BCI), p. 9; Boeing Presentation #3, Exhibit EC-353 (BCI), p. 9.

[4058] Boeing Presentation #3, Exhibit EC-353 (BCI), pp. 5-7; Boeing Presentation #16, Exhibit EC-807 (BCI), pp. 6-8; Boeing Presentation #18, Exhibit EC-823 (BCI), p. 3.

[4059] European Communities' first written submission, Annex C, para. 76; James W. Ramsey, "Power-by-Wire," Avionics Magazine, 1 May 2001, Exhibit EC-828.

[4060] United States' first written submission, para. 941.

DSR 2012:III   1715

Report of the Panel

suppliers have been able to design non-pneumatic systems aimed at fuel and energy efficiency to power the aircraft's de-icing system, air conditioning and electronically-actuated brakes.[4061] The United States argues that the most significant developments with respect to more-electric technology in the 787 are the "no-bleed" environmental control system (e.g. air conditioning), supplied by Hamilton Sundstrand and the anti-ice/de-ice system, supplied by Ultra Electronics Holdings and GKN Aerospace.[4062] In addition, the United States notes that the electro-mechanical actuators used in the spoilers are supplied by Smiths, the primary flight control actuation system (both the hydraulic and electric elements) is supplied by Moog, and the electrically-actuated brakes are supplied by Goodrich and Messier-Bugatti.[4063] Moreover, according to the United States, these companies all provide similar systems to Airbus.

48.   The United States contends that the advances in electric motor technology that are the key to the more-electric aircraft are, in large part, due to increasing demand in a broad range of industries, and that both Boeing and Airbus are benefiting from the billions of dollars in technology investments being made for applications such as hybrid cars, electric trains and efficient power generation and distribution methods for commercial and residential power.[4064]

49.   The United States argues that Boeing's switch to more-electric systems has also been driven by another key supplier innovation, namely, the "no-bleed" engine, which is available through engine makers GE and Rolls Royce.[4065] The United States asserts that the new engine technology accounts for at least one-third of the increased operating cost efficiencies of the 787, and that Airbus will benefit from supplier engine experience on the 787 as it has selected Rolls Royce to provide the Trent XWB engine series for the A350XWB.[4066]

50.   As regards the European Communities' allegations concerning knowledge and experience that Boeing obtained from McDonnell Douglas' work under the FBL/PBW element of the AST Program, the United States asserts that the FBL/PBW subtask was terminated before any new technology related to advanced power management and distribution systems was built and tested, and that in any case, the flight controls developed by Boeing for the 787 are not the same as the electronic actuation technology that was originally envisioned under that terminated programme.[4067] In relation to Boeing's use of a 5,000 psi hydraulic system that the European Communities alleges is the same concept

---

[4061] United States' first written submission, para. 941; Bair Affidavit, Exhibit US-7, para. 53; Joseph Ogando, "Boeing's 'More Electric' 787 Dreamliner Spurs Engine Evolution", Exhibit US-314.

[4062] Bair Affidavit, Exhibit US-7, para. 58.

[4063] *Ibid.*

[4064] Bair Affidavit, Exhibit US-7, para. 59; Joseph Ogando, "Boeing's 'More Electric' 787 Dreamliner Spurs Engine Evolution", Exhibit US-314.

[4065] United States' first written submission, para. 941; Bair Affidavit, Exhibit US-7, para. 58.

[4066] United States' first written submission, para. 941; "Fully Optimised for the Airbus A350XWB family", Rolls-Royce.com, Exhibit US-316.

[4067] Bair Affidavit, Exhibit US-7, para. 62.

US - Large Civil Aircraft (2nd Complaint)

that Boeing studied, developed, and used for its DOD-funded JSF demonstrator, the United States asserts that the first 5,000 psi hydraulic system used in a commercial aircraft was actually designed and supplied by Eaton for the Airbus A380.[4068]

3. Open systems architecture

(a) European Communities

51. The European Communities argues that the open systems architecture on the 787 likely benefited from the knowledge and experience that McDonnell Douglas gained pursuant to a 1996 contract on the VMS Integrated Technology for Affordable Life Cycle Cost ("VITAL") program under DOD's Technology Reinvestment Project. The European Communities indicates that work pursuant to this contract aimed to reduce the Life Cycle Cost (LCC) of current and future military *and commercial* aircraft by developing the necessary building blocks for an open and affordable Vehicle Management System (VMS). The European Communities indicates that under this contract, McDonnell Douglas, *inter alia*, "define{d} generic VMS open architecture specifications," worked on interface standards, and demonstrated "plug and play" interchangeability.[4069]The European Communities argues that these are key elements of the 787's open systems architecture.[4070] The European Communities notes that the contract stipulates that "the VITAL team shall perform a research and development program designed to *develop and mature* the affordable Vehicle Management System technologies .... {T}he principal purpose of this agreement is for the VITAL Team to provide its *best research efforts in the support and stimulation of advanced research and technology development* and not the acquisition of property or services for the direct benefit or use of the Government."[4071]

52. The European Communities also argues that the open systems architecture on the 787 likely benefited from dual-use research Boeing conducted pursuant to the JSF Program. The European Communities explains that open systems architecture was in fact an emphasis of the JSF Program from the very beginning, and that Boeing successfully implemented an open systems architecture on its JSF design.[4072] The European Communities asserts that

---

[4068] Bair Affidavit, Exhibit US-7, para. 61.

[4069] Navy Contract N00019-96-H-0118 with McDonnell Douglas Corporation, Statement of Work, Exhibit EC-830, pp. 1-2.

[4070] Boeing Presentation #3, Exhibit EC-353 (BCI), p. 13; Passing the Value Test: The Boeing Technology Advantage, Boeing Point-to-Point, June 2006, Exhibit EC-784.

[4071] European Communities' first written submission, Annex C, para. 184. Navy Contract N00019-96-H-0118 with McDonnell Douglas Corporation, 15 May 1996,Exhibit EC-830, p. 3. Emphasis added.

[4072] JSF X-32 and X-35, International Air Power Review, Volume 1 (2001), Exhibit EC-455, pp. 60-61; John D. Morocco, "Admiral Believes Navy JAST Also Could Fill USAF Need," Aviation Week

---

DSR 2012:III   1717

Report of the Panel

Boeing specifically studied integrating avionics into a core processor that utilizes open architecture as part of its DOD-supported JSF development programme and that this experience likely contributed to its ability to utilize open systems architecture on the 787.[4073] Relying on a statement by a Boeing official in a press report, the European Communities asserts that Boeing would *not be as far ahead on many of its programs* without the experience gained on the JSF program and the many technologies and processes developed and validated on it, such as open systems architecture.[4074]

53.   Finally, in response to the United States' argument that components were purchased by suppliers, the European Communities argues that for the common core of the 787's open system architecture, Boeing still retains the overall integration responsibility.[4075]

(b)   United States

54.   The United States argues that the open systems architecture of the 787 is based on Boeing's decision to rely on supplier technical expertise in identifying the best systems for the aircraft. The United States indicates that the common core of this system, an integrated common data network that runs the aircraft's systems, is provided by Smiths/GE, in partnership with Rockwell Collins and Honeywell. According to the United States, the fiber optic Ethernet system used to run the 787's central processing is not only available commercially, but a version of it has been designed by Rockwell Collins for use on the A380's Integrated Modular Avionics system, a data network that relies on separate computers rather than on a central core.[4076] Finally, the United States asserts that the "plug-in" elements are available on the market, such as the integrated standby flight display purchased from Thales and the flight control electronics purchased from Honeywell.[4077]

---

and Space Technology, 24 April 1995, Exhibit EC-831, p. 22; Air Power for the 21st Century, Boeing Photo Release, 25 February 2000, Exhibit EC-832.

[4073] Boeing Demonstrates JSF Avionics Multi-Sensor Fusion, Boeing News Release, 9 May 2000, Exhibit EC-833.

[4074] William Cole, "The value of lessons learned," Boeing Frontiers Online, December 2003/January 2004, Exhibit EC-464, quoting Frank Statkus, former JSF Program Manager. Emphasis added.

[4075] Statement by Patrick Gavin, Tim Sommer, Burkhard Domke, and Dominik Wacht, 8 November 2007, Exhibit EC-1175 (BCI), para. 21, citing Boeing 787: Integration's Next Step, Avionics Magazine, 1 June 2005.

[4076] Unites States' first written submission, para. 941 citing James W. Ramsey, "Integrated Modular Avionics: Less is More," Avionics Magazine (Feb. 1, 2007), Exhibit US-321.

[4077] Unites States' first written submission, para. 94; Bair Affidavit, para. 64.

1718   DSR 2012:III

4. Enhanced aerodynamics and structural design

(a) European Communities

55. The European Communities argues that, through participating in four NASA aeronautics R&D programmes, namely HPCC (CAS project), AST (IWD project), HSR and R&T Base programmes, Boeing *used* and *enhanced* CFD codes, in particular OVERFLOW and TRANAIR. More specifically, the European Communities argues that, under the CAS project that was part of the HPCC Program, the OVERFLOW CFD code, which was originally developed by NASA, was further enhanced.[4078] TRANAIR was developed by Boeing under a contract that precedes the existence of the NASA R&D programmes at issue in this dispute. The European Communities' arguments therefore focus on the contributions to the design of the 787 arising out of NASA contracts under which the TRANAIR code was enhanced.

56. According to the European Communities, the research carried out under the IWD project (AST Program) resulted in the capability to develop highly optimized, high performance wings at substantially reduced development time and cost.[4079] The European Communities argues that under the Airframe Technology contract awarded to Boeing in 1994 as part of the HSR Program, Boeing further refined CFD methods, including enhancing TRANAIR and integrating OVERFLOW into the overall design process.[4080] Finally, although the R&T Base Program was of a more general nature than the other NASA programmes, spanning a wide array of technical domains, the European Communities argues that this programme nevertheless provided the basic scientific and engineering understanding underpinning further enhancements of the CFD and design codes.[4081]

57. According to the European Communities, this led to direct application of the codes in the design process for the 787 and also provided Boeing employees with "knowledge, experience and confidence", which "surely benefited" the final aerodynamic and structural design of the 787.[4082] In this regard, the European Communities submits that, as well as gaining the "explicit knowledge", or the "tangible data...recorded in...software codes", Boeing also accrued "tacit knowledge" as a result of its work on the CFD codes.[4083] According to the

---

[4078] Dominik Wacht, An Analysis of Selected NASA Research Programs and Their Impact on Boeing's Civil Aircraft Programs, November 2006, Exhibit EC-15, pp. 142, 145.

[4079] Dominik Wacht, An Analysis of Selected NASA Research Programs and Their Impact on Boeing's Civil Aircraft Programs, November 2006, Exhibit EC-15, pp. 85-87.

[4080] Dominik Wacht, An Analysis of Selected NASA Research Programs and Their Impact on Boeing's Civil Aircraft Programs, November 2006, Exhibit EC-15, p. 112.

[4081] Dominik Wacht, An Analysis of Selected NASA Research Programs and Their Impact on Boeing's Civil Aircraft Programs, November 2006, Exhibit EC-15, p. 145.

[4082] European Communities' first written submission, Annex C, para. 99.

[4083] Statement by Patrick Gavin, Tim Sommer, Burkhard Domke, and Dominik Wacht, 8 November 2007, Exhibit EC-1175 (BCI), para. 32.

Report of the Panel

European Communities, only when experienced personnel use the CFD codes in an appropriately integrated manner in the overall design process, will the design cycle time reductions promised by CFD codes be achieved.

58. The European Communities argues that Boeing applied the knowledge and experience that it gained with respect to computer-assisted design and manufacturing tools from DOD supported dual-use research to the 787.[4084] In this regard, the European Communities submits that Boeing developed "advanced 3-D modelling and simulation techniques under the F-22 programme" and that these techniques "became the basis for the Computer-Aided Three-Dimensional Interactive Application ("CATIA") design and manufacturing tools, which Boeing is now making use of in designing and building the 787".[4085] The European Communities also alleges that the 787 team is using the same CATIA-based digital design approach as Boeing used in designing the JSF demonstrator.[4086]

59. In response to the United States' argument that the CATIA software was developed by, and is commercially available from, the French company Dassault, the European Communities argues that Boeing gained "tacit and explicit knowledge" regarding "which design tool should be used in which way, by whom, and at which step of the design process".[4087] The European Communities argues that under certain DOD RDT&E programmes (JSF and F-22), Boeing gained experience regarding how to use the CATIA software and how to integrate it into the design process, which Boeing then applied to the 787 design and assembly process.

60. The European Communities argues that NASA funding and support under the IWD project of the AST Program provided Boeing with the ability and confidence to integrate the aerodynamic, structural and systems design aspects of the design of a wing in order to reduce design cycle time and cost, while at the same time improving the wing's aerodynamics and structural design.[4088] The European Communities also argues that (i) the hydraulically actuated drooped spoilers on the 787 are "precisely the same concept that Boeing used on the C-17, a programme for which Boeing received billions of dollars in dual-use funding from DOD"; (ii) the "slimmer wings" used on the 787 arise out of NASA and DOD composites R&D programmes; and (iii) the simplified trailing edge for the 787's wings is the result of a combination of improved CFD tools and the integrated design techniques developed under the IWD project.[4089]

[4084] European Communities' first written submission, Annex C, para. 90.
[4085] *Ibid.*
[4086] *Ibid.*
[4087] Statement by Patrick Gavin, Tim Sommer, Burkhard Domke, and Dominik Wacht, 8 November 2007, Exhibit EC-1175 (BCI), paras. 39-40.
[4088] European Communities' first written submission, Annex C, para. 92; Dominik Wacht, An Analysis of Selected NASA Research Programs and Their Impact on Boeing's Civil Aircraft Programs, November 2006, Exhibit EC15, pp. 94-98.
[4089] European Communities' first written submission, Annex C, paras. 96-98.

1720

DSR 2012:III

(b) United States

61. The United States argues that the cornerstone of the efficiency gains achieved under the 787 programme is Boeing's extensive use of digital data which was achieved in partnership with the French supplier, Dassault.[4090]

62. The United States argues that the CFD codes enhanced under the NASA programmes "are not the same codes that Boeing uses in its product design process".[4091] Rather, the NASA codes are generic CFD codes that are publicly available. The United States argues that Boeing was required to enhance the generic codes so that they would "fit its own product design processes".[4092] Moreover, the United States asserts that the versions of TRANAIR that Boeing developed with NASA funds are publicly available, and that it has been possible to commercially license the TRANAIR code since 2004.[4093] According to the United States, OVERFLOW was developed by NASA alone, is widely used by both NASA and industry and can be commercially licensed. The United States also denies that OVERFLOW was developed or enhanced under any contract between Boeing and NASA.

63. The United States denies that the R&D work that Boeing performed under NASA's HSR Program and the IWD element of the AST Program is linked to the technologies developed for the 787. According to the United States, the HSR Program was aimed at developing concepts for a supersonic passenger aircraft, and the results of such research have no applicability to the challenges of designing the 787, which is a subsonic aircraft that flies under very different conditions, and accordingly, is designed with a different fundamental structure to the high speed civil transport aircraft studied under the HSR Program.[4094] In relation to the use of CFD codes as part of the IWD element of the AST Program, the United States acknowledges that one CFD code used under the IWD contract demonstrated a slight improvement in design time, and was disseminated to industry, but contends that Boeing subsequently invested its own funds outside of the contract to achieve an additional significant time reduction relative to the time reduction achieved under the IWD contract.[4095] Moreover, the United States argues that the reduction in design cycle time related to the code does not affect the overall 787 development cycle because it is not in the critical path sequence of work that determines the total development cycle time for the aircraft.[4096]

[4090] Bair Affidavit, Exhibit US-7, para. 18.

[4091] United States' non-confidential oral statement at the second meeting with the Panel, para. 22.

[4092] *Ibid.*

[4093] United States' comments on the European Communities' response to question 87, para. 327; US Department of Defense Website, DOD 101, An Introductory Overview of the Department of Defense, "What We Do", Exhibit EC-1234, p. 4.

[4094] Affidavit of Douglas Ball, Exhibit US-1257, paras. 4, 7.

[4095] Bair Affidavit, Exhibit US-7, para. 67.

[4096] *Ibid.*

Report of the Panel

64.   The United States agrees with the European Communities that the computer-aided design and manufacturing tools used on the 787 are fundamental to the improvements in the design process for the 787.[4097] However, the United States contends that these tools are a commercially available suite of technologies, the Product Lifecycle Management Tools (including CATIA, DELMIA, ENOVIA and SMARTEAM), which are purchased from Dassault, and that Airbus France has purchased and implemented the same technology from Dassault.[4098]

65.   The United States agrees with the European Communities as to the importance of integration skills, and specifically, the proposition that it is the ability to define and manage the complex interaction of design processes, organization and tools so as to enable the development and manufacture of an aircraft at minimum time and cost that is one of the core competencies of an aircraft manufacturer.[4099] However, the United States disputes the contention that Boeing performs better as an integrator of commercial technologies and products because of its experience as an integrator on military projects; it asserts that such a contention is at odds with the views of most DOD analysts who consider that DOD should learn more from commercial enterprises, rather than vice-versa.[4100] The United States argues that in any case, Boeing's integration knowledge develops from its role as a prime contractor on most of its DOD *systems production* contracts, and from NASA contracts with Boeing related to the space shuttle, both of which are outside the scope of the aeronautics R&D programmes challenged in this dispute.[4101]

66.   The United States acknowledges that the fundamental structural design of a large commercial aircraft, notably its aerodynamic shape, is the primary responsibility of Boeing, notwithstanding that Boeing conducts much of the work on the 787 in conjunction with suppliers. However, the United States denies that the aerodynamic design of the 787 wing is the result of government funding.[4102] According to the United States, Boeing aerodynamicists review the same NASA-sponsored research as the rest of the world, but the most significant learning is the knowledge developed within the company from over 80 years of commercial aircraft designing.[4103] Moreover, the United States argues that the IWD project explored initial wing design optimization on generic wing

---

[4097]   Bair Affidavit, Exhibit US-7, para. 26.

[4098]   *Ibid.*

[4099]   United States' second written submission, para. 203, referring to European Communities' confidential oral statement at the first meeting of the Panel, para. 14.

[4100]   United States' second written submission, para. 204; Louis Rodriguez, Defense Acquisition: Improved Program Outcomes are Possible, Exhibit US-1151, p. 3.

[4101]   United States' second written submission, para. 205.

[4102]   Bair Affidavit, Exhibit US-7, para. 65.

[4103]   *Ibid.*

1722   DSR 2012:III

US - Large Civil Aircraft (2nd Complaint)

configurations, with little applicability to the specific 787 wing platform or airfoil development.[4104]

67.   In response to the European Communities' arguments concerning the similarities between the high-lift system on the 787 and the C-17, including all of the elements required to power, actuate and monitor the flap and slat system, the United States argues that the connection is that the systems for both aircraft are designed and supplied by the supplier Smiths/GE, a supplier that also provides the high lift system for the Airbus A330, A340 and A380.[4105]

5.   Noise reduction technologies

(a)   European Communities

68.   The European Communities argues that the knowledge, experience, and confidence Boeing gained from US Government-supported R&D, primarily through NASA's AST, QAT and Vehicle Systems programmes, accelerated Boeing's development of noise reduction technologies used on the 787.[4106] The European Communities argues that under the NASA R&D programmes, Boeing and McDonnell Douglas conducted research with respect to noise reduction technologies that are very similar to the noise reduction technologies on the 787.[4107] The noise reduction technologies in question include the following technologies, each of which the European Communities argues derives at least in part from NASA funding and support: (i) low weight structures, (ii) improved airplane performance, (iii) chevrons, (iv) joint-less acoustic treatment, (v) quiet flaps and slats, and (vi) low-noise landing gear.[4108] In addition, the European Communities argues that industry and NASA collaborated on two Quiet Technology Demonstrator (QTD) programmes to test the noise reduction technologies developed under the AST, QAT, and Vehicle Systems programmes.[4109] According to the European Communities, there is no question that these NASA-supported and QTD-tested technologies have benefited Boeing's development of the 787.[4110] The European Communities argues that, *but for*, the aeronautics R&D subsidies, Boeing would not be able to build such an environmentally-friendly 787 aircraft and customers would not be as willing to buy it.[4111]

[4104] Bair Affidavit, Exhibit US-7, para. 67.

[4105] United States' first written submission, para. 941; Bair Affidavit, Exhibit US-7, para. 68.

[4106] European Communities' first written submission, Annex C, para. 100.

[4107] European Communities' first written submission, Annex C, para. 102.

[4108] European Communities' first written submission, Annex C, para. 101.

[4109] "Boeing, Rolls-Royce Work On A Quieter Future For Commercial Aviation," Boeing News Release, 20 November 2001, Exhibit EC-387.

[4110] European Communities' first written submission, Annex C, para. 104.

[4111] European Communities' first written submission, Annex C, para. 100.

DSR 2012:III   1723

Report of the Panel

69.   The European Communities argues that Boeing has been able to develop and apply the noise reduction technologies on the 787 when it did because of the knowledge, experience, and confidence that it gained through participating in NASA's AST, QAT, and Vehicle Systems programmes. The European Communities contends that under these programmes, pursuant to a number of NASA contracts, Boeing and McDonnell Douglas conducted research with respect to such noise reduction technologies as scarfed inlets, chevron nozzles, swept and lean stators, advanced liner treatments, quiet high-lift systems, and quiet landing gear, all of which it alleges are very similar to the noise reduction technologies on the 787.[4112]

70.   The European Communities also argues that Boeing's development of noise reduction technologies for the 787 has benefited from the testing of noise reduction technologies developed under the AST, QAT and Vehicle Systems programmes that occurred pursuant to the two QTD programmes that were undertaken as a collaborative effort between NASA and industry, including Boeing.   The European Communities asserts that, under the initial QTD Program, with NASA sponsorship, Boeing tested technologies such as chevrons and acoustic inlet liners,[4113] while under the QTD2 Program, which NASA funded in part through the QAT portion of its Vehicle Systems Program,[4114] Boeing tested additional technologies such as covered landing gears, redesigned chevrons including shape-memory alloys, and a new acoustic inlet liner for the front of the engine nacelles.[4115]

71.   Finally, the European Communities argues that NASA's work in other technological areas have also had spill-over effects for noise reduction on the 787. First, the composite fuselage, which the European Communities alleges was developed with US Government assistance, provides increased sound attenuation when compared to comparable aluminium structures.[4116] Second, the CFD codes and integrated design concepts, which the European Communities alleges were used and enhanced through the aeronautics R&D subsidies, not only helped

---

[4112] European Communities' first written submission, Annex C, para. 102.

[4113] "Boeing, Rolls-Royce Work On A Quieter Future For Commercial Aviation," Boeing News Release, 20 November 2001, Exhibit EC-387.

[4114] Results of NASA Aircraft Noise Research, Exhibit EC-390.

[4115] Boeing Flight Test Journal, Future Looks Quiet, 20 September 2005, Exhibit EC-393; James Wallace, Boeing makes 'quiet' advances, Seattle-Post Intelligencer, 11 August 2005, Exhibit EC-389; James Wallace, Shhhh! Noise tests for planes in progress, Seattle Post-Intelligencer, 30 November 2005, Exhibit EC-394; Tad Calkins and Walter Polt, "Not so loud," Boeing Frontiers Online, March 2006, Exhibit EC-392; Jia Yu et al., Quiet Technology Demonstrator 2 Intake Liner Design Validation, AIAA 2006-2458, 8-10 May 2006, Exhibit EC-848; William H. Herkes, The Quiet Technology Demonstrator Program: Flight Validation of Airplane Noise-Reduction Concepts, AIAA 2006-2720, 8-10 May 2006, Exhibit EC-849.

[4116] John Gillie, An inch saved might mean an order earned for Boeing, The News Tribune (Tacoma, WA), 18 November 2005, Exhibit EC-338.

1724   DSR 2012:III

Boeing to enhance the aerodynamics and structural design of the 787, but also to reduce its noise.[4117]

(b)   United States

72.   The United States argues that the noise reduction technologies used on the 787 are largely the product of supplier technology, and as such, are available to Airbus.[4118] According to the United States: (i) the engine nacelle chevrons that will dampen engine noise are supplied by GE (as are the improved engines), and were actually first flight tested on an Airbus A321 aircraft; (ii) the joint-less inlet liners were developed and supplied by Goodrich, which is also an Airbus supplier; and (iii) the landing gear was developed and is being supplied by Messier-Dowty, a French company.[4119]

73.   Moreover, the United States argues that the Quiet Technology Demonstrator project was an industry-led effort involving, among others, Boeing, GE and Goodrich. The United States asserts that Boeing has contributed its privately-funded noise database as well as its acoustic array facility for the testing and that the other participants have designed, built and installed their various technologies on an aircraft on loan from an airline for which it was destined, which was then flight-tested in order to generate full-scale data on these in-development technologies.[4120] Of the two tests that have occurred to date, the United States asserts that, while NASA participated in QTD1 in order to gain access to the generated data for use in the validation of its noise prediction codes, it contributed very little money.[4121] The United States contends that in QTD2, NASA "bought its way into the effort" in order to test certain technologies it had developed in partnership with supplier companies, including "toboggan" landing gear fairings developed with Goodrich.[4122]

6.   Health management systems

(a)   European Communities

74.   The European Communities argues that the aeronautics R&D subsidies created, and accelerated the development and application of the health management systems, allowing Boeing to better monitor the health of different parts on the 787, lower maintenance costs on the 787, and provide improved

---

[4117] European Communities' first written submission, Annex C, para. 107.
[4118] United States' first written submission, para. 941.
[4119] Bair Affidavit, Exhibit US-7, para. 69.
[4120] Bair Affidavit, Exhibit US-7, para. 70.
[4121] *Ibid.*
[4122] *Ibid.*

Report of the Panel

maintenance service.[4123] In this respect, the European Communities refers to Boeing's "GoldCare" service, a comprehensive life-cycle management service through which Boeing offers fleet maintenance management and parts support, as well as services for the repair and overhaul of components.[4124] The European Communities argues that Boeing is able to provide GoldCare, in part, because of the integrated vehicle health management system of the 787 that was enabled by the aeronautics R&D subsidies.

75.   The European Communities argues that Boeing gained knowledge and experience regarding health management technologies, as well as confidence in the application thereof, through its participation in U.S. government-supported aeronautics R&D programmes, and that this has enabled it to implement these technologies on the 787 so quickly.[4125] First, the European Communities argues that Boeing conducted research on health management technologies under the NASA R&T Base and Aviation Safety programmes.[4126] The European Communities has submitted various contracts that NASA awarded to Boeing to explore   health   management   technologies.[4127]   Second,   the   European Communities argues that Boeing developed health management technologies pursuant to a number of its DOD RDT&E contracts. The European Communities argues that research into health management and sensor technology conducted under a number of DOD RDT&E programmes has likely benefited the health management system on Boeing's 787. The European Communities refers to research conducted under the Aerospace Flight Dynamics/Vehicle Systems Program, the Aerospace Avionics/Sensors Program and the DUS&T Program. The European Communities argues that under these programmes, McDonnell Douglas and Boeing studied, developed, and patented technologies related to aircraft health monitoring and that Boeing developed techniques that improve damage assessment of advanced composite structures.[4128]

76.   Finally, the European Communities argues that Boeing gained knowledge and experience with respect to advanced NDI techniques under a number of DOD RDT&E programmes, including the Materials, Advanced Materials for Weapons Systems Program, and the Aging Aircraft Program. The European

---

[4123] European Communities first written submission, para. 1350. European Communities' first written submission, Annex C, paras. 110 - 121.

[4124] GoldCare – The 787 Revolution Now Revolutionizes Service, Boeing Website, Exhibit EC-852; "Ready for the upturn," Flight International, 10 January 2003, Exhibit EC-853. Boeing Presentation #20, Exhibit EC-854 (BCI), p. 1.

[4125] European Communities' first written submission, Annex C, para.114.

[4126] NASA Aviation Safety Budget Estimates, FY 2000, Exhibit EC-382, SAT 4.1-51.

[4127] NASA Contract NAS1-00106 with The Boeing Company regarding Flight Critical Systems Research, 2000, Exhibit EC-858, Section C.1, Article 2.3; NASA Contract NAS1-99070 with Boeing Commercial Airplane Group regarding Structures and Materials Technology for Aerospace Vehicles, 25 January 1999, Exhibit EC-800, p. 4; and US Patent No. 6,920,790, Exhibit EC-579.

[4128] European Communities' first written submission, Annex C, para.116 and European Communities' second written submission, para. 423; CRA RDT&E Report, Exhibit EC-7, Appendix A, pp. 15, 21-24.

1726

DSR 2012:III

US - Large Civil Aircraft (2nd Complaint)

Communities argues that working under these R&D programmes, Boeing gained the confidence to apply advanced NDI techniques for the health management of the 787. Further, the European Communities argues that the sensors and other specific health management technologies researched pursuant to DOD-supported military aircraft R&D facilitate the use of NDI on the 787.[4129]

(b)   United States

77.   The United States argues that the 787 health management systems derive primarily from Boeing's own proprietary 777 technology, developed 15 years earlier and supplied by Honeywell.[4130] In addition, Boeing engineer Michael Bair explains that the on-board health management/crew information system on the 787 is a "plug-in" element of the "more electric" architecture.[4131]

78.   Bair argues that the "Aircraft Health Monitoring services" that Boeing offers for the 787 is the same basic service that Boeing offers for all models of its aircraft. He alleges that the service was first developed in 1991/1992, and has been in production on both the 777 and 747 airplanes since 2004. According to Bair, the 787's health management system is more extensive simply because the "more electric architecture" allows for monitoring of more system components. Bair asserts that Boeing has not deployed Structural Health Monitoring capability on the 787 and that structural inspections for the 787 will be accomplished using normal visual inspection methods. According to Bair, the maintenance benefits that the 787 offers to airline customers are simply the result of meeting design requirements and validating these design requirements through a comprehensive testing program.[4132] Finally, Bair argues that the virtual "Crack Closure Technique" is commercially available through a company formerly known as ABACUS, now called Simulia, which is part of Dassault Systemes.[4133] He notes, in addition, that Boeing has no contracts under the Integrated Vehicle Health Management Program and that data generated from that project have, however, been made widely available, as was the data generated by the Flight Critical Systems Research Program.[4134]

[4129] European Communities' first written submission, Annex C, paras. 117-120.
[4130] United States' first written submission, paras. 937 and 941; Bair Affidavit; Exhibit US-7, paras. 71-74.
[4131] Bair Affidavit, Exhibit US-7, para. 71.
[4132] Bair Affidavit, Exhibit US-7, para. 72.
[4133] Bair Affidavit, Exhibit US-7, para. 73.
[4134] Bair Affidavit, Exhibit US-7, para. 74.

DSR 2012:III

Report of the Panel

Appendix VII.F.2: The Cabral Model

A. OVERVIEW

1.   The purpose of this Appendix is to explain an economic model presented by the European Communities as part of its serious prejudice case and to evaluate key assumptions on which the model is based. The model is constructed by Professor Luís Cabral of the Stern School of Business at New York University.[4135] Professor Cabral states that his report seeks to address the question of how the provision of subsidies affects the business decisions of Boeing; specifically, how the receipt of an additional dollar of a particular category of subsidy affects the amount that Boeing chooses to invest in the development of new aircraft, and to price more aggressively.[4136] The category of subsidies the focus of Professor Cabral's analysis is what he calls "development subsidies". These are subsidies in which the amount of subsidy does not vary in direct proportion to the number of aircraft produced or sold.[4137]

2.   Professor Cabral's analysis is based on a specific economic model of Boeing's behaviour; namely, that when Boeing receives so-called "development subsidies", management seeks to maximize a trade-off between shareholder income and shareholder value, with the result that it directs a certain portion of the subsidy towards dividends, and the remainder towards "investments that increase firm value."[4138] His conclusions about the types of activities that constitute "investments in firm value" are based on particular assumptions about the LCA markets; particularly the nature of LCA production and importance of learning curve efficiencies and switching costs, and the role played by product quality. As discussed further in Section B below, Professor Cabral's model of Boeing's investment behaviour is based on the underlying premise that Boeing's access to capital is constrained, and thus that Boeing's investment behaviour is sensitive to changes in its cash flow (e.g. the receipt of subsidies).

3.   Professor Cabral's analysis is not a unified model of Boeing's pricing and investment behaviour, but rather, two separate models. This is not immediately obvious from the way that the analysis has been presented in this dispute,

---

[4135] Luís M. B. Cabral, Impact of Development Subsidies Granted to Boeing, CEPR and New York University, March 2007, Exhibit EC-4.

[4136] Luís M. B. Cabral, Impact of Development Subsidies Granted to Boeing, New York University and CEPR, March 2007, Exhibit EC-4, para. 1.

[4137] Luís M. B. Cabral, Impact of Development Subsidies Granted to Boeing, New York University and CEPR, March 2007, Exhibit EC-4, paras. 2-3. It appears that the category of subsidies that Professor Cabral refers to as "development subsidies" encompasses the same subsidies that the European Communities analyses as operating to increase Boeing's non-operating cash flows (as distinguished from the subsidies that the European Communities characterizes as reducing Boeing's marginal unit costs of production and sale of LCA).

[4138] Luís M. B. Cabral, Impact of Development Subsidies Granted to Boeing, New York University and CEPR, March 2007, Exhibit EC-4, para. 5.

1728

DSR 2012:III

US - Large Civil Aircraft (2nd Complaint)

although it becomes clear once the Annexes to Professor Cabral's Report are examined in greater detail. Although we refer to the "Cabral model" in this Appendix, we describe the two models that comprise Professor Cabral's analysis separately. For ease of discussion, we refer to the two models that constitute Professor Cabral's analysis as the "Objective Function Model" and the "Price Competition Model".

4.   The main purpose of the **Objective Function Model** is to obtain an estimate of the share of each additional dollar of subsidies that Boeing would devote to payments to shareholders, on the one hand, and to "investment" (in the form of "aggressive pricing of new LCA and mature LCA to new customers, and additional R&D), on the other. Professor Cabral concludes that the allocation would be 15 cents : 85 cents.

5.   The main purpose of the **Price Competition Model** is to determine Boeing's division of the 85 cents in every additional dollar of subsidies that it devotes to "investment" between the following three uses: (i) aggressive pricing of new models of LCA implied by learning curve efficiencies; (ii) aggressive pricing of mature aircraft through the phenomenon of buyer switching costs; and (iii) additional investments in R&D. Professor Cabral finds that, from 85 cents in the dollar that Boeing would "invest": 12 cents goes to aggressive pricing of new models due to the learning curve effect; 47 cents goes to aggressive pricing due to switching costs; and 26 cents goes to additional R&D. Due to the time profile of R&D investments (which Professor Cabral sees as representing future price reductions where price is considered the "effective price on a per-value unit basis"), the 26 cents in R&D investments result in a cumulated net present value of 40 cents when the time period 2007 to 2022 is taken into account.

6.   Based on the above estimates, and on other calculations that are described in greater detail below, Professor Cabral calculates that the total of $19.1 billion in subsidies allegedly received by Boeing between 1989 and 2006 translates into the following "price effects", or price reductions per model of Boeing aircraft in 2004 – 2006: [4139]

[4139] Extracted from the Luís M. B. Cabral, Impact of Development Subsidies Granted to Boeing, New York University and CEPR, March 2007, Exhibit EC-4, para. 89, Table 7. The term "price effects" generally refers to the extent to which Boeing has been able to lower its LCA prices as a result of the subsidies. For example, see European Communities' first written submission, para 1306 where the European Communities submits that the subsidies that directly reduce the marginal unit costs of Boeing LCA "have a price effect commensurate with their amount... {e}ach of these subsidy dollars has the effect of reducing the price of a Boeing LCA by exactly $1" However, the European Communities also uses this term in a narrower sense, to refer to Professor Cabral's quantification of the extent to which subsidy dollars enable Boeing to directly and immediately "aggressively price" its LCA, based on his particular theory that equates all subsidies that are not tied to the production of additional units of LCA as fungible with cash (i.e. equivalent to additional non-operating cash to Boeing), and assumptions about the optimal investment strategy of a company like Boeing given the particularities of the LCA market (learning curve, switching costs etc.). For example, see European

DSR 2012:III

Report of the Panel

Aircraft model	Per-aircraft "price effect" ($ thousands)			*Ad valorem* price effect (%)		
	2004	2005	2006	2004	2005	2006
737 Family	1,009	879	949	2.59	2.47	2.64
747 Family	2,834	2,597	2,986	2.10	1.90	1.95
767 Family	1,443	1,248	1,354	1.78	1.70	1.81
787 Family	1,539	1,332	1,445	1.75	1.67	1.77
777 Family	2,324	2,010	2,169	1.72	1.62	1.72

B.   THE OBJECTIVE FUNCTION MODEL

1.   Structure and Mechanics of the Objective Function Model

7.   The first model presented in the Cabral Report consists of Boeing's objective function. The main purpose of this model is to obtain an estimate of the share of each additional dollar of subsidies that would be devoted to total "investment" in aggressive pricing (in relation to both learning curve and switching cost effects) and in R&D. This value is found to be 85 cents.

8.   Boeing maximizes its "utility" by choosing the optimal combination of dividend payments and investments in future value of the firm (which are the only two uses of funds permitted in the model). The maximization problem is constrained by the condition that dividends plus investment together cannot exceed cash flow from development subsidies and other sources of funds. Boeing's objective function is of the Cobb-Douglas type, where the parameter α specifies the relative "weight" that Boeing's shareholders attach to dividends, so that $(1-\alpha)$ is the weight attached to investments in future firm value.[4140] From the first-order condition for a maximum, Professor Cabral obtains α as an increasing function of (i) Boeing's internal rate of return on investment; and (ii) the ratio between dividends and firm value; two observable variables for which data can be obtained. The objective function is consistent with the assumption that increases in Boeing's cash flow will lead it to increase its level of investment. Professor Cabral notes that his framework depends on the assumption that Boeing's access to capital is constrained. If Boeing had unconstrained access to capital, then according to the Modigliani-Miller theorem, it could be assumed to

---

Communities' first written submission, para. 1332 and figures 22 and 23 (which are the same as the "price effects" calculations made by Professor Cabral in EC-4, Tables 7 and 8).

[4140] Professor Cabral says that the virtue of the Cobb-Douglas functional form is that it embodies the concept of decreasing marginal returns. In other words, it embodies the phenomenon that the additional degree of shareholder satisfaction from dividend payments will decrease as dividend payments increase, and similarly, the additional degree of shareholder satisfaction from increases in firm value decreases as the level of firm value increases. Luís M. B. Cabral, Impact of Development Subsidies Granted to Boeing, New York University and CEPR, March 2007, Exhibit EC-4, paras. 17-18.

1730

DSR 2012:III

US - Large Civil Aircraft (2nd Complaint)

always be investing at optimal levels. In this scenario, an increase in government subsidies would be entirely reflected in higher dividends, and would have no effect on Boeing's investment levels.[4141]

9.   Having determined the respective weights of dividends and investment in Boeing's objective function, Professor Cabral subjects Boeing's utility maximization problem to the "cash flow constraint" that is partly determined by the amount of subsidies received. From this, he is able to calculate the marginal increase in investment for a given marginal increase in "development subsidies" (β) which is approximately 85 per cent.

10.   Professor Cabral's calibration of the model parameters is as follows:

- To estimate the value of α (the relative weight that Boeing shareholders attach to dividends) Professor Cabral uses (i) data on Boeing's ratio of payments to shareholders, compared with firm value and (ii) an estimate of the internal rate of return on investment for Boeing. Professor Cabral calculates that ratio of payments to shareholders : firm value on the basis of Boeing's publicly reported annual payments to shareholders and its market capitalization. On the basis of publicly-available data, Professor Cabral calculates that Boeing distributed $14.74 billion to shareholders between 2000 and 2006 (in the form of dividend payments and repurchases of stock), which represents an average of $2.1 billion per year. In addition, Professor Cabral calculates that the average market capitalization of Boeing (i.e. Boeing's share price multiplied by the number of outstanding shares) between 2000 and 2006 was $43.59 billion. From these numbers, Professor Cabral calculates that Boeing's "dividend to value ratio" was 4.8 per cent.[4142] Professor Cabral estimates that Boeing's internal rate of return on investment is 10 per cent, which is not a figure derived from Boeing data, but rather, is a mid-range figure from a 1988 study estimating rates of return on R&D capital in the transportation equipment industry.[4143] From these figures, Professor Cabral calculates that the value that Boeing's shareholders

---

[4141] Luís M. B. Cabral, Impact of Development Subsidies Granted to Boeing, New York University and CEPR, March 2007, Exhibit EC-4, para. 22. The Modigliani-Miller theorem is a neo-classical model of firm investment behaviour in which firms make investments to the point that their return on investment equals the market rate. Their optimal investment level is independent of the way in which the investment is financed (e.g. through subsidies, borrowings, cash flow from operations etc.).

[4142] Luís M. B. Cabral, Impact of Development Subsidies Granted to Boeing, New York University and CEPR, March 2007, Exhibit EC-4, para. 40.

[4143] Luís M. B. Cabral, Impact of Development Subsidies Granted to Boeing, New York University and CEPR, March 2007, Exhibit EC-4, para. 41. The rate of 10 per cent appears relatively high. Professor Cabral claims that this is a plausible value for the marginal rate of return, although average rates of return are usually much lower due to high fixed costs; Luís M. B. Cabral, Impact of Development Subsidies Granted to Boeing, New York University and CEPR, March 2007, Exhibit EC-4, para. 42.

DSR 2012:III

1731

Report of the Panel

attach to dividends (α) is approximately 5 per cent and therefore, that they attach a weight of 95 per cent to future increases in firm value.

- To estimate the impact of subsidies on investment (β), Professor Cabral needs data on actual investment spending by Boeing in relation to dividends, and on the response to the marginal rate of return on investment to the investment level. For the former, Professor Cabral uses Boeing data on actual dividend payments and share repurchases from 2000 - 2006 ($2.1 billion) and arrives at his own estimate of Boeing's actual "investments" on the basis of Boeing data on R&D expenditures between 2000 and 2006 ($1.073 billion average annual R&D expenditures) plus his own derivations of investments in "aggressive pricing of new and mature LCA" which he obtains from the **Price Competition Model** ($483 million and $1.936 billion, respectively, discussed in the following section of this Appendix). From these figures, he calculates that Boeing's ratio of dividends to investment is: $2.1 billion : $3.492 billion, or approximately 0.60.[4144] Professor Cabral obtains his estimate for the value of the elasticity of the marginal rate of return on investment to the investment level from a 2000 study of the elasticity of marginal return to investment of a portfolio of patents. Professor Cabral also refers to "evidence from other manufacturing industries" which he claims suggests that the greater the amount of resources devoted to R&D, the lower the marginal returns to investment.[4145] From this information, Professor Cabral selects a value of -0.2.

11.   On the basis of the foregoing, Professor Cabral arrives at the estimate that 85 cents of each additional dollar of subsidies is spent on three types of "investment". He estimates the precise allocation of the 85 cents of each additional subsidy dollar across these three forms of investment using the Price Competition Model which is described in Section C of this Appendix.

2.   U.S. Criticisms and Professor Cabral's responses

12.   The United States criticizes Professor Cabral's reasoning on the following general grounds: (i) Professor Cabral's reliance on what the United States considers to be the European Communities' "grossly overstated" calculation of the magnitude of the subsidies; (ii) the structure of Professor Cabral's model, in that it does not accurately reflect business decision-making by a company like Boeing; (iii) the key theoretical assumption on which it is predicated (i.e. that Boeing's investment decisions depend on its cash flow) which the United States

---

[4144] Luís M. B. Cabral, Impact of Development Subsidies Granted to Boeing, New York University and CEPR, March 2007, Exhibit EC-4, para. 45.

[4145] Luís M. B. Cabral, Impact of Development Subsidies Granted to Boeing, New York University and CEPR, March 2007, Exhibit EC-4, paras. 46-47.

1732   DSR 2012:III

US - Large Civil Aircraft (2nd Complaint)

considers to be invalid in the light of Boeing's unconstrained access to capital markets; and (iv) assumptions of fact which the United States alleges find no support in empirical evidence (e.g. that Boeing's sales in 2004 – 2006 involved significant switching costs or that its production during 2004 – 2006 involved significant learning curve gains, and that Boeing's only discretionary use of non-operating cash is payments to shareholders or "investment" in "aggressive pricing").[4146]

13.   The United States argues that the flawed assumptions underlying Professor Cabral's model dictate the results that he purports to demonstrate; namely, that the untied subsidies cause Boeing to lower its LCA prices.[4147]   The United States argues, therefore, that Professor Cabral's analysis can provide no support for the European Communities' attempt to establish a genuine and substantial link between the alleged subsidies and the alleged serious prejudice. These alleged flawed assumptions, as well as more technical criticisms of the calibrations of certain of the parameter values, are discussed in greater detail by the U.S. economic consultants, Professor Bruce Greenwald of the Columbia Business School and Drs. James Jordan and Gary Dorman of NERA Economic Consulting.

14.   As part of the European Communities' Second Written Submission, Professor Cabral submitted an additional report in response to the U.S. criticisms of his analysis.[4148] In this Report, Professor Cabral addresses criticisms of his model. Professor Cabral concludes that the United States and its consultants are unjustified in their criticisms of his report, and that none of those criticisms undermine the validity of the methodology that he employed, or its conclusion that the subsidies Boeing received led Boeing to lower its LCA prices.[4149] The U.S. criticisms and Professor Cabral's responses to those criticisms are summarized in greater detail below.

(a)   Assumption that Boeing's access to capital is constrained

15.   Professor Greenwald's central criticism of Professor Cabral's model is its assumption that Boeing's access to capital is constrained. He argues that, having assumed this fundamental premise, against the weight of the evidence, Professor Cabral then embeds his conclusions in other "assumptions". Professor Greenwald says that, while markets may be imperfect and firms may make less than optimal decisions, "as long as firms have largely unconstrained access to capital, non-specific subsidies which amount to fixed transfers – the kind of

---

[4146] United States' response to question 90, para. 224.

[4147] United States' comments on the European Communities' response to question 383, paras. 354-355.

[4148] Luís M. B. Cabral, Response to the U.S. Criticisms of my Analysis of "The impacts of Development Subsidies Granted to Boeing", 14 November 2007, Exhibit EC-1182.

[4149] Luís M. B. Cabral, Response to the U.S. Criticisms of my Analysis of The impacts of Development Subsidies Granted to Boeing", 14 November 2007, Exhibit EC-1182, para. 60.

DSR 2012:III   1733

Report of the Panel

subsidy at issue in the Cabral Report – will not affect firm investment decisions."[4150] According to Professor Greenwald, funds that flow from transfers (i.e. subsidies) will simply substitute for funds that flow from other sources (e.g. borrowing) and investment decisions will remain unaffected.[4151] Professor Greenwald argues that a company like Boeing, which has relatively little debt and which regularly repurchases large amounts of its stock, is obviously not subject to the sort of investment constraints that are the foundation of Professor Cabral's model.[4152] NERA makes a similar criticism, stating that the assertion that increases in a firm's internal cash flow lead to higher levels of firm investment is *not* clearly supported in the research literature.[4153] NERA argues, moreover, that Professor Cabral does not empirically show whether subsidies are correlated with increases in investment for Boeing.

16.   Professor Cabral responds with several reasons why, in his view, the U.S. arguments that Boeing's investment decisions do not depend on variations in its cash flow are implausible. First, he argues that, to the extent that Boeing is not financially constrained, this is itself a result of the subsidies.[4154] Second, he argues that the balance between dividends and investments that increase firm value depends not just on whether a firm faces financial constraints, but also on market imperfections (e.g. information asymmetries between firms and financial markets have a significant impact on a firm's behaviour).[4155] According to Professor Cabral, given such additional factors, a firm will find it optimal to balance its various objectives with the constraints imposed on it by various sources of funds. Moreover, Professor Cabral argues that the fact that Boeing is able to borrow funds does not imply that Boeing is "financially unconstrained" in the sense understood by the Modigliani-Miller theorem. According to Professor Cabral, the costs associated with different sources of funds and the

---

[4150] Greenwald Paper, Exhibit US-8, pp. 1-2.

[4151] Greenwald Paper, Exhibit US-8, p. 2.

[4152] Professor Greenwald also disagrees with Professor Cabral as to the interpretation of the economic literature on the question whether firms' investment decisions are sensitive to changes in their cash flow. Professor Greenwald asserts that the empirical literature generally concludes that, while many firms are constrained in their access to capital, and do adjust their investment levels in response to current cash flows, firms like Boeing (with low debt levels and high dividend/share repurchase levels) are not; Greenwald Paper, Exhibit US-8, p. 2.

[4153] Jordan and Dorman Report, Exhibit US-3, p. 5.

[4154] Professor Cabral considers what Boeing's debt-to-equity ratios would have been had it financed an amount equivalent to the amount of subsidies over 1989 – 2006 through increases in debt and foregoing share repurchases. He concludes that Boeing could not have sustained such debt, and that it therefore could not have made the investments that were financed by the subsidies; Luís M. B. Cabral, Response to the U.S. Criticisms of my Analysis of The impacts of Development Subsidies Granted to Boeing", 14 November 2007, Exhibit EC-1182, paras. 6-8.

[4155] Professor Cabral argues that, contrary to the assumptions underlying the Modigliani-Miller theorem, because of asymmetries of information (e.g. firms having better knowledge that investors of the risks and potential returns from investments), as well as taxation, and the possibility of financial distress, various sources of funds are *not* equivalent; Luís M. B. Cabral, Response to the U.S. Criticisms of my Analysis of The impacts of Development Subsidies Granted to Boeing", 14 November 2007, Exhibit EC-1182, para. 11.

1734   DSR 2012:III

US - Large Civil Aircraft (2nd Complaint)

market signals associated with such choices, may lead a firm to choose sources or uses for its capital that would not otherwise represent the cheapest source or optimal use.[4156] Professor Cabral concludes therefore that, in terms of its investment behaviour, "the firm effectively behaves according to a function of the sort I considered in my model."[4157] Third, he argues that, consistent with this reasoning, statements by Boeing executives and empirical data contradict the U.S. theory.[4158]

17.   Professor Cabral contends that, if Boeing had not invested any of its subsidies, but had instead distributed them to shareholders through dividends and repurchases, one would expect a substantial correlation between the historical levels of subsidies, on the one hand, and dividends and share repurchases, on the other. Moreover, Professor Cabral argues that one would expect to find *no* significant correlation between dividends and share repurchases (which would vary with the amount of subsidies) and the level of firm value that results from investments (which would not vary with the amount of subsidies).[4159] Professor Cabral asserts that, contrary to what would be expected if the U.S. arguments were true, there is *no* statistically significant correlation between subsidies and dividends plus share repurchases, while there *is* a clear correlation between firm value and dividends plus share repurchases. According to Professor Cabral, these trends fit closely with his model, and suggest that Boeing does optimally trade-off the benefits of currently distributed cash, future investments and the costs of obtaining funds.[4160]

(b)   Assumption that Boeing maximizes a Cobb-Douglas function.

18.   Professor Greenwald argues that it is not appropriate to assume that Boeing maximizes a Cobb-Douglas function of dividends and investment related to market value. He explains that, for example, a consumer who maximizes a Cobb-Douglas objective function over consumption levels of goods spends a constant fixed proportion of his income on each type of good, regardless of the relative prices of the goods, or the consumer's level of income. Therefore, if the

---

[4156] Luís M. B. Cabral, Response to the U.S. Criticisms of my Analysis of The impacts of Development Subsidies Granted to Boeing", 14 November 2007, Exhibit EC-1182, para. 13.

[4157] Luís M. B. Cabral, Response to the U.S. Criticisms of my Analysis of The impacts of Development Subsidies Granted to Boeing", 14 November 2007, Exhibit EC-1182, para. 5.

[4158] Cabral points to various statements of Boeing executives which he considers to indicate that, consistent with the objective function in the Cabral model, Boeing management balances direct value (i.e. dividends and share repurchases) and indirect value (investments in the firm), and that Boeing management is sensitive to cash flow.

[4159] Luís M. B. Cabral, Response to the U.S. Criticisms of my Analysis of The impacts of Development Subsidies Granted to Boeing", 14 November 2007, Exhibit EC-1182, para. 18.

[4160] Luís M. B. Cabral, Response to the U.S. Criticisms of my Analysis of The impacts of Development Subsidies Granted to Boeing", 14 November 2007, Exhibit EC-1182, paras. 19-20. Moreover, Professor Cabral argues that his model appropriately captures this trade-off through a reduced-form objective function.

DSR 2012:III

Report of the Panel

price of one good doubles, the consumer would not increase the proportion of his income allocated to that good, but rather, would halve his consumption of that good. Professor Greenwald says that this particular, widely known property of the Cobb-Douglas utility function makes it highly unsuitable as a description of how a firm like Boeing would make its investment decisions in reality. Moreover, Boeing's actual behaviour strongly argues against the assumption that subsidies are always proportionately divided between dividends and investments.[4161]

19.   Professor Cabral agrees with Professor Greenwald that the Cobb-Douglas functional form has had limited success in modeling demand curves, however, he states that he does not use the Cobb-Douglas functional form to model the trade-off faced by Boeing in its choice of dividends versus investment. According to Professor Cabral, the Cobb-Douglas functional form provides a useful and accurate approximation of the way Boeing actually balances investments that increase firm value and current returns to its shareholders (without meaning to imply that Boeing expressly uses such a model to make its investment decisions), a fact which is confirmed by the relative stability of Boeing's ratio of dividends to firm value.[4162]

20.   Professor Cabral argues that the value of the ratio of dividends and investments to firm value that he calculated as part of his model is in any case quite close to the value one would obtain from estimating the value of the same ratio on the basis of 2000-2006 historical data, showing that the functional form that he chose was appropriate. He also argues that he performed extensive sensitivity analyses as part of his original report, in order to ensure that his results did not depend critically on the value of key parameters, and found that they do not.[4163]

(c)   Static model that places unrealistic restrictions on Boeing's sources and uses of cash

21.   According to NERA, while Professor Cabral's Objective Function Model is based on a line of research that asks how a firm manages its sources and uses of cash in order to maximize the value of its equity, it departs from the approach of the models in that literature "by placing unrealistic restrictions on the sources and uses of cash", with such restrictions driving the results of the model.[4164] NERA notes that the model allows (i) only two uses of Boeing's cash; namely, dividends and investment, (ii) only three forms of investment; namely, R&D price reductions, learning curve price reductions and switching cost price

---

[4161] Greenwald Paper, Exhibit US-8, p. 3.

[4162] Luís M. B. Cabral, Response to the U.S. Criticisms of my Analysis of The impacts of Development Subsidies Granted to Boeing", 14 November 2007, Exhibit EC-1182, paras. 22-30.

[4163] Luís M. B. Cabral, Response to the U.S. Criticisms of my Analysis of The impacts of Development Subsidies Granted to Boeing", 14 November 2007, Exhibit EC-1182, para. 26.

[4164] Jordan and Dorman Report, Exhibit US-3, p. 4.

1736   DSR 2012:III

US - Large Civil Aircraft (2nd Complaint)

reductions, and does not consider other uses of cash (e.g. repayment of debt, acquisitions, contributions to the corporate pension fund, payments for operating expenses and interest). Moreover, NERA argues that Professor Cabral's model does not incorporate the effect of other sources of cash (e.g. Boeing's profits, changes in net working capital, cash from asset sales, access to external financing, the issuance of stock). According to NERA, these restrictions essentially ensure the result that whenever Boeing receives a subsidy, it increases its investment spending.[4165]

22.   NERA also claims that investment models in the literature are multi-period and dynamic, in which firms continually respond to current and expected economic and firm-specific conditions by adjusting sources and uses of cash in order to maximize equity value.[4166] NERA argues that, by contrast, Professor Cabral's model is static – producing the "completely unrealistic" result that Boeing makes the same decision about the use of its subsidy cash every year from 1989 to 2006 (i.e. that it invests 85 per cent of each subsidy dollar), regardless of the business cycle and other factors affecting its sources and uses of funds.[4167] NERA considers that, although the Cabral model is specified as a maximization problem in which firm equity is maximized, it is an unrealistically restricted problem, because in the model, Boeing gets to make only one decision; the allocation of cash between dividends and investment. According to NERA, the Cabral model, "by assumption rather than by a well-specified theory backed up by empirical analysis" imposes a dividend/investment trade-off on Boeing in which Boeing does not have enough money to carry out a desired investment programme.[4168]

23.   Professor Cabral's response to criticisms that his model unrealistically concludes that Boeing allocates a constant proportion of subsidy (85 per cent) to investments every year, regardless of general economic conditions or the business cycle, is to note that his calculations are of "average impact", and that, although they may be too high or two low in particular years, "on average they are about right and represent a reasonable approximation of reality."[4169] To demonstrate, Professor Cabral notes that if he divides 2000 – 2006 into two sub-periods, the differences in resulting parameter values are minimal (instead of 85 per cent of the subsidy going to investment, he calculates that 87 per cent goes to investment in 2000 – 2003 and 83 per cent in 2004 – 2006). He notes that in

---

[4165] Ibid.

[4166] NERA provides some examples of the types of financial constraints that are considered in the literature and built into the models, or used in empirical testing. NERA argues that the Cabral model contains none of this rich literature which allows the models in the literature to capture the degree of financial constraint of a firm, nor is it based on an empirical analysis to determine whether Boeing should be modeled as though it is materially financially constrained; Jordan and Dorman Report, Exhibit US-3, p.9

[4167] Jordan and Dorman Report, Exhibit US-3, p. 5.

[4168] Jordan and Dorman Report, Exhibit US-3, p. 8.

[4169] Luís M. B. Cabral, Response to the U.S. Criticisms of my Analysis of The impacts of Development Subsidies Granted to Boeing", 14 November 2007, Exhibit EC-1882, para. 43.

DSR 2012:III   1737

Report of the Panel

these two sub-periods, economic conditions for the LCA industry were sharply different.[4170]

(d)   Assumption that in-kind subsidies and direct subsidies are functionally equivalent.

24.   Professor Greenwald disputes Professor Cabral's assertion that the value of in-kind (i.e. non-cash) subsidies can be measured by the cost that Boeing would have to incur to achieve the effective value provided by the in-kind subsidies. According to Professor Greenwald, the problem with this assertion is that it assumes that the cost of achieving the same effective value as the in-kind subsidies can be defined independently of other variables (e.g. Boeing's financial condition, level of cash subsidies, prices of labor and other inputs, output levels), when in general, it cannot.[4171] Professor Cabral responds that, on the contrary, NASA is more likely better able to do what it does than Boeing, and that his assumption therefore effectively underestimates the effect of the in-kind subsidies provided by NASA.[4172]

(e)   Assumption that Boeing's preference for dividends is comparable with its total market value.

25.   Aside from the use of a Cobb-Douglas function, Professor Greenwald also faults Professor Cabral's use of dividends (which are annual flows of funds) with total market value of the company (a stock, the value of which is fixed at any moment in time) in the same function.[4173] Professor Greenwald alleges that, as a result, Professor Cabral is able to assert that, because annual dividends are a small fraction of the company' market value, Boeing will devote a comparably small fraction of any additional cash flow to dividends. Professor Greenwald says that Professor Cabral should have either had Boeing maximize a function of dividends and *changes* in market value, or a function of a net present value of dividends and the market value of the firm.[4174] In response to this criticism, Professor Cabral acknowledges the importance of making the distinction between stocks vs. flows, but demonstrates that a re-writing of his analysis using the flow equivalent of firm value along with dividends (or vice-versa) does not change the results.[4175]

[4170] Luís M. B. Cabral, Response to the U.S. Criticisms of my Analysis of The impacts of Development Subsidies Granted to Boeing", 14 November 2007, Exhibit EC-1182, para. 44.

[4171] Greenwald Paper, Exhibit US-8, p. 5.

[4172] Luís M. B. Cabral, Response to the U.S. Criticisms of my Analysis of The impacts of Development Subsidies Granted to Boeing", 14 November 2007, Exhibit EC-1182, para. 33.

[4173] Greenwald Paper, Exhibit US-8, p. 3.

[4174] Greenwald Paper, Exhibit US-8, p. 4.

[4175] Luís M. B. Cabral, Response to the U.S. Criticisms of My Analysis of 'The Impacts of Development Subsidies Granted to Boeing', 14 November 2007, Exhibit EC-1182, paras. 21-30. Professor Cabral argues that with current firm value being equivalent to a corresponding perpetual

1738   DSR 2012:III

(f) Criticisms of Professor Cabral's estimation of values of certain parameters

26. NERA also criticizes Professor Cabral's estimation of the values of certain parameters. For example, NERA considers that the parameters that Professor Cabral estimates to measure the relative importance of dividends versus other investment opportunities to shareholders (i.e. the parameters that are key to yielding the result that Boeing would allocate 15 cents of each additional dollar to dividends and 85 cents to investments) are either (i) counter-intuitive, in that they imply that, as the rate of return of a potential investment increases, Boeing will invest less and return more to shareholders; (ii) not based on Boeing empirical data; or (iii) not found in the general literature regarding firm investment behaviour and appear to be unique to the Cabral model.[4176] Moreover, NERA argues that Professor Cabral's estimate that Boeing would devote 85 cents of each dollar of subsidy to additional investment seems extraordinarily high for a company like Boeing, which has all the hallmarks of a financially unconstrained firm (e.g. large corporation with access to global capital markets, a diverse set of individual and institutional shareholders, and widespread coverage by bond rating firms and stock analysts).[4177] NERA argues that there are no signs that Boeing had a shortfall of cash during the period of Professor Cabral's analysis; on the contrary, Boeing's financial data indicates that, even if the alleged cash subsidies were taken away, Boeing still generated more than enough cash to fund its investment programme.[4178]

27. This leads to NERA's next criticism of Cabral's model, which is that Professor Cabral fails to empirically test its validity, both as a model for predicting the investment behaviour of firms, and also as a model of how Boeing would invest any subsidies. According to NERA, Professor Cabral's model is particularly in need of empirical testing because of (i) its basic structure, which is unlike other economic models of firm investment behaviour; and (ii) its dubious implications, including that shareholders would prefer higher dividends when a firm's expected return on investments *increases* and that a firm like Boeing is so financially constrained that it would increase investment spending by 85 per cent of any subsidy.[4179]

28. Professor Cabral responds by noting the actual stability of this ratio in Boeing data between 1989 and 2006 and regressing firm value on dividends, obtaining a coefficient that is close to his model estimate. Finally, with respect to the United States' observation that his model would imply higher dividend payments in face of investment opportunities offering higher returns, Professor Cabral explains the difference between model calibration, to which the

---

annuity, it can be shown that the objective function used would only change by a multiplicative constant that does not affect the outcomes of the model.

[4176] Jordan and Dorman Report, Exhibit US-3, pp. 10-11.
[4177] Jordan and Dorman Report, Exhibit US-3, p. 11.
[4178] *Ibid.*
[4179] Jordan and Dorman Report, Exhibit US-3, p. 12.

Report of the Panel

relationship implied by the United States should be applied, and comparative statics that show the response of a model to an exogenous change on its equilibrium values. Professor Cabral explains that the above relationship between dividends and the marginal rate of return to investment is the result of a "reverse engineering" process involved in model calibration that seeks to derive model parameters that are consistent with historical data. In other words, a high marginal rate of return on investment implies a high weight placed by the firms on dividends, or else the firm would have invested up to a higher level, resulting in a lower marginal return on investment. Conversely, Professor Cabral shows that the comparative static outcome from a positive profitability shock is a higher investment level, not a higher level of dividends, featuring as a multiplicative factor in his model.[4180]

29.   Professor Cabral dismisses as inappropriate NERA's criticism that he failed to empirically test his model using real world data. Professor Cabral explains that he addresses the absence of certain Boeing data by including a sensitivity analysis, which determines how variations in the estimates of certain data would affect his ultimate calculations of price effects resulting from his model. Professor Cabral notes his conclusion from that analysis was that even if there were significant changes in the relevant parameters, this would not substantially alter the model's results.[4181]

C.   THE PRICE COMPETITION MODEL

1.   Structure and mechanics of the Price Competition Model

30.   As previously mentioned, the main purpose of this second model is to determine Boeing's division of subsidies between the three types of investment: (i) "aggressive pricing" due to learning curve efficiencies; (ii) "aggressive pricing" due to buyer switching costs; and (iii) R&D expenditures.[4182]

31.   Professor Cabral chooses a standard Hotelling model of price competition in a duopoly market as his basic framework. The essential features of the Hotelling model are that competition between the two competitors is on the basis of price (rather than quantities) and that the products are differentiated. The more differentiated the products, the less likely it is that producers will compete the prices down to average cost (the competitive outcome of the Bertrand model of price competition). While Professor Cabral uses the basic Hotelling

---

[4180] Luís M. B. Cabral, Response to the U.S. Criticisms of my Analysis of The impacts of Development Subsidies Granted to Boeing", 14 November 2007, Exhibit EC-1182, paras. 34-41.
[4181] Luís M. B. Cabral, Response to the U.S. Criticisms of my Analysis of The impacts of Development Subsidies Granted to Boeing", 14 November 2007, Exhibit EC-1182, para. 58.
[4182] As noted in the discussion of the Objective Function Model, the values of the first two are plugged into the parameters for the Objective Function Model to arrive at the conclusion of the Objective Function Model that 85 cents of every additional subsidy dollar will be applied to investments to increase firm value.

1740   DSR 2012:III

framework, he introduces an additional variable that denotes product quality or "value" (z). One important feature of Professor Cabral's model is that increases in product quality lead to increases in nominal prices, but *decreases* in quality-adjusted prices. In other words, when a firm increases its product quality, Professor Cabral assumes that it will raise its price by less than the inherent value of the rise in product quality. Professor Cabral does not explain why or how this rather mechanical outcome of his definition of "quality-adjusted price" is necessarily consistent with the optimal behaviour of a firm. In addition, Professor Cabral uses a fixed 2:3 relationship between prices and cost reductions, based on the simplest set up of the Hotelling model.

32.   Professor Cabral considers that Boeing engages in essentially three types of "investment": interpreting the concept of "investment" as a "current expenditure that increases future profits".[4183] The first two types relate to "aggressive pricing" of new and mature models of aircraft. The third is development (and pre-development) expenditures to create new aircraft or increase the value of aircraft that it is in the process of developing, which are discussed further in (c) below.

(a)   "Aggressive pricing" of new aircraft implied by learning curve efficiencies

33.   According to Professor Cabral, aggressive pricing of *new models* of aircraft (i.e. aircraft at early stages of production) leads to higher sales in the current year and, through the dynamics of the learning curve, leads to lower production costs in future years.[4184] The "learning curve" refers to the negative correlation between cumulative output and unit cost: the more aircraft of a given type produced by a firm, the less it costs to produce the next unit of that aircraft.[4185]

34.   Professor Cabral sets out to estimate the dollar value of Boeing's investment in aggressive pricing while moving down the learning curve. He considers that the learning curve is defined by three elements: (i) the cost of the first unit of production; (ii) the steepness of the learning curve; and (iii) the number of units after which learning ceases. Professor Cabral notes that previous research on aircraft manufacturing suggests that the learning curves are very steep, thus creating an incentive for LCA producers to price aggressively to generate more sales and move more rapidly down the learning curve in order to reduce per-unit production costs. His calculations are based on the assumption that the learning curve is particularly steep over the first 100 units of any LCA

[4183] Luís M. B. Cabral, Impact of Development Subsidies Granted to Boeing, New York University and CEPR, March 2007, Exhibit EC-4, para. 27.
[4184] *Ibid.*
[4185] Luís M. B. Cabral, Impact of Development Subsidies Granted to Boeing, New York University and CEPR, March 2007, Exhibit EC-4, para. 53.

Report of the Panel

model and that Boeing strategically prices as though its costs for these aircraft produced at the steep part of the learning curve were the costs for aircraft produced at the bottom of the learning curve (i.e. approximately the 200th unit).[4186]

35.   Since the learning curve portrays cost as a function of learning by increasing output, Professor Cabral links this "cost function" to pricing using a formula defining the "break-even" level of output (which he estimates at 300 units, based on reports of the break-even points for the A380, A350 and 787).[4187] Using, among other parameter estimates, data on Boeing average annual aircraft sales and development expenditures between 2000 and 2006, he then calculates the remaining unknown parameter; i.e. the cost of the first unit. He is then able to calculate the highest possible cost of production to Boeing, when it does not take into account the effect of learning curve efficiencies, and the lowest possible cost of production, when the learning curve is flat.[4188]

36.   Professor Cabral estimates that for an "average Boeing aircraft" during the production stage of the first 100 units, the learning curve implies pricing that is \$9.53 million lower per plane.[4189] This estimate is based on an "average" Boeing aircraft (i.e. number of seats, price and number of annual deliveries) which he calculates from data on Boeing's aircraft deliveries and estimated market prices (based on a discount of 45.75 per cent from published list prices) for the various models of Boeing aircraft.[4190] Professor Cabral also estimates that 13.5 per cent of aircraft sold by Boeing are "new" in the sense that Boeing is still moving down the steep portion of the learning curve.[4191] In other words: 13.5 per cent of 378 average annual deliveries of planes involved \$9.53 million of learning curve-related cost reductions. Professor Cabral therefore concludes that

---

[4186] Luís M. B. Cabral, Impact of Development Subsidies Granted to Boeing, New York University and CEPR, March 2007, Exhibit EC-4,para. 59.

[4187] Luís M. B. Cabral, Impact of Development Subsidies Granted to Boeing, New York University and CEPR, March 2007, Exhibit EC-4, para. 57.

[4188] The difference between these two figures would exaggerate the average loss if learning curve effects were ignored, because producers would still produce more than one unit, price each unit according to cost and move down the learning curve. Therefore, Professor Cabral assumes that Boeing would price its aircraft somewhere in the middle of the learning curve, as an average up to a point where the cost reductions become less steep (this he assumes to be at 100 units, without offering a justification for this assumption); Luís M. B. Cabral, Impact of Development Subsidies Granted to Boeing, New York University and CEPR, March 2007, Exhibit EC-4, para. 60.

[4189] Luís M. B. Cabral, Impact of Development Subsidies Granted to Boeing, New York University and CEPR, March 2007, Exhibit EC-4, para. 60.

[4190] Luís M. B. Cabral, Impact of Development Subsidies Granted to Boeing, New York University and CEPR, March 2007, Exhibit EC-4, para. 52. The result is that Professor Cabral's "average Boeing aircraft" has a seating capacity of 190, a market price of \$54.7 million and 378 annual deliveries.

[4191] Luís M. B. Cabral, Impact of Development Subsidies Granted to Boeing, New York University and CEPR, March 2007, Exhibit EC-4, para. 70.

1742   DSR 2012:III

US - Large Civil Aircraft (2nd Complaint)

Boeing's annual "investment" in "aggressive pricing" due to the learning curve is $483 million.[4192]

(b)   "Aggressive pricing" implied by buyer switching costs

37.   Professor Cabral considers that the "investment" nature of increasing current sales through aggressive pricing is also present for *mature aircraft* through the phenomenon of buyer switching costs. Switching costs refer to the costs that buyers who operate one particular family of aircraft must incur to switch to a new supplier (such costs stem from pilot training, aircraft maintenance etc.). Professor Cabral states that, to the extent that a buyer will be in the market for the same family of planes in the future, having previously bought from one supplier increases the chances that the same supplier will be chosen the next time around. For this reason, Professor Cabral claims that it makes strategic sense for Boeing to aggressively price its mature LCA models to *new customers*.[4193]

38.   Professor Cabral estimates the dollar amount of subsidies targeted at new buyers of Boeing aircraft who may become repeat buyers in the future. He does this by interpreting the Hotelling demand function as a "probability of making a repeat sale", and solving this function with respect to switching costs (expressing other variables in terms of a demand elasticity and likelihood of switching, taking values for these parameters from other LCA studies and his own estimates, respectively). [4194] Professor Cabral therefore estimates in percentage terms how much higher prices would be if switching costs were not taken into account by Boeing. He calculates that switching costs induce price discounting of 25 per cent on *current sales* when Boeing sells to new customers, in order to lock in those new customers who would then face switching costs if they were to order from Airbus in future. Since pricing to take account of switching costs applies to new buyers, he also estimates the average share of Boeing's annual sales that are to airlines that have not previously bought from Boeing an aircraft of the same family *and generation*. Based on Boeing 2000 – 2006 data, that percentage is 37.4 per cent.[4195] Cabral therefore concludes that 37.4 per cent of 378 annual aircraft deliveries involved discounts of 25 per cent from the average

---

[4192] Luís M. B. Cabral, Impact of Development Subsidies Granted to Boeing, New York University and CEPR, March 2007, Exhibit EC-4, para. 60.

[4193] Luís M. B. Cabral, Impact of Development Subsidies Granted to Boeing, New York University and CEPR, March 2007, Exhibit EC-4. Professor Cabral considers that the strategic benefit from subsidizing sales of mature aircraft is also true, "if to a lesser extent" for ongoing buyers (i.e. existing customers).

[4194] Luís M. B. Cabral, Impact of Development Subsidies Granted to Boeing, New York University and CEPR, March 2007, Exhibit EC-4, para. 65. Profesor Cabral says that his estimate that there is 25 per cent probability of switching sellers is consistent with the observation of demand patterns for wide-body aircraft.

[4195] Luís M. B. Cabral, Impact of Development Subsidies Granted to Boeing, New York University and CEPR, March 2007, Exhibit EC-4,para. 67.

DSR 2012:III

Report of the Panel

market price of $54.7 million. This corresponds to an average annual "investment" in "aggressive pricing" through switching costs of $1.936 billion.[4196]

(c)   R&D expenditures can be considered equivalent to future price reductions where price is considered the "effective price on a per-value unit" basis

39.   Professor Cabral considers that, where subsidies are applied to investments in aggressive pricing of new planes (learning curve), or of mature aircraft to new customers (switching costs), their impact is "immediate".[4197] However, the impact of a portion of each subsidy dollar is that is applied to investments in R&D is "only felt in terms of future pricing."[4198] He reasons that greater investments in R&D will lead to a higher quality aircraft, and thus, to a "greater buyer willingness to pay".[4199] According to Professor Cabral, if nominal LCA prices were to remain constant, this would mean that the "effective price on a per value unit basis" would be lower. In other words, higher R&D expenditures lead to higher nominal prices, but lower prices on a per value unit basis.[4200] Professor Cabral concludes that for a given unit of "aircraft value", Boeing is thus able to charge a lower "price".[4201] On the basis of Boeing data for the years 2000 – 2006, he determines average annual spending on R&D to be $1.073 billion.[4202] As noted above, the price impact of annual R&D spending is felt in terms of pricing over the whole lifetime of an aircraft design. The total price impact of R&D subsidies in a given year then depends on the R&D subsidies provided in this and previous years.[4203]

[4196] Luís M. B. Cabral, Impact of Development Subsidies Granted to Boeing, New York University and CEPR, March 2007, Exhibit EC-4, para. 68.

[4197] Luís M. B. Cabral, Impact of Development Subsidies Granted to Boeing, New York University and CEPR, March 2007, Exhibit EC-4, para. 69.

[4198] Luís M. B. Cabral, Impact of Development Subsidies Granted to Boeing, New York University and CEPR, March 2007, Exhibit EC-4, para. 72.

[4199] Ibid.

[4200] Ibid.

[4201] Cabral also considers that the per value unit price (or "corrected price") is the relevant determinant of market demand, a conclusion he attempts to demonstrate formally.

[4202] Luís M. B. Cabral, Impact of Development Subsidies Granted to Boeing, New York University and CEPR, March 2007, Exhibit EC-4, para. 45, Table 2.

[4203] Luís M. B. Cabral, Impact of Development Subsidies Granted to Boeing, New York University and CEPR, March 2007, Exhibit EC-4, para. 85, Table 5.

US - Large Civil Aircraft (2nd Complaint)

2. U.S. Criticisms and Professor Cabral's responses

(a) Professor Cabral's theory of how Boeing would behave is at odds with empirical evidence regarding Boeing's actual pricing strategies between 2000 and 2006

40. The United States argues that the implications of Professor Cabral's theory about how Boeing would have operated in the LCA markets are not borne out by the events that actually occurred in the markets. The United States submits that, over the 2000 - 2006 period, Boeing's share of the global LCA market measured by volume of deliveries *dropped* from 61 to 47 per cent, indicating that, far from pricing "aggressively", Boeing was being systematically *under priced* by Airbus, which gained the market share that Boeing lost.[4204]

41. According to the United States, Boeing in fact *resisted* pressure to reduce its prices in response to Airbus' price undercutting until 2004, when it could no longer sustain the consequent market share losses. The United States argues that Boeing resisted the pressure to reduce its prices for so long because of the significant long-term costs entailed in price reductions, which tend to condition the market for lower prices. In this regard, the United States makes a further criticism of Professor Cabral's analysis; namely, that Professor Cabral assumes that "aggressive pricing" increases firm value, without accounting for the negative consequences to the value of the business.[4205]

42. In response to these criticisms, the European Communities argues that the Cabral model does not analyze the absolute levels of deliveries or market shares held by Boeing and Airbus, but the *marginal* pricing effects on order pricing of additional subsidies to Boeing. The European Communities says that the question whether or not the marginal pricing effects on order pricing lead to Boeing actually gaining or losing market share at any point in time is not answered by the model, and is not relevant to assessing the model's accuracy.[4206]

(b) Nature of pricing incentives related to "learning curve efficiencies"

43. The United States agrees with Professor Cabral that significant learning curve efficiencies occur over production of the first one hundred or so units of a new aircraft.[4207] However, the United States argues that Professor Cabral is

---

[4204] United States' first written submission, para. 858.

[4205] United States' first written submission, para. 859. The United States argues that a robust analysis of a firm's propensity to invest its cash in "aggressive pricing" instead of distributing it to shareholders would have to factor into the analysis the costs of aggressive pricing in terms of profit margin reductions and the impact of a reduction in profit margins on the market value of the firm.

[4206] European Communities' second written submission, para. 781.

[4207] The United States notes that it has "serious reservations" about Cabral's conclusion that learning curve efficiencies *only* occur over the first 100 units produced, but assumes *arguendo* for purposes of

---

DSR 2012:III

1745

Report of the Panel

wrong to assert that an LCA producer will lower its prices *in a campaign-specific context* to achieve learning curve gains. According to the United States, learning curve efficiencies are factored into a producer's projected costs at the *time the launch decision is made*.[4208] At this time, the producer projects pricing targets for the new aircraft that, over its projected life, must exceed the producer's fully-loaded average production costs by an amount sufficient to justify the investment.[4209] According to the United States, these pricing projections account for concessions that are routinely granted to launch customers before the volume of production is sufficient to generate learning curve efficiencies. The United States argues that, because the learning curve is factored into the pricing targets at the time the programme is launched, there is no expectation of subsequent, campaign-specific learning curve adjustments to price.[4210]

44.   The United States also considers that Professor Cabral is wrong to assert that learning curve efficiencies apply to the production of the first 100 units of each (or any) *subsequent variants* of a new model.[4211] The United States argues that, of the 2,640 Boeing LCA deliveries between 2000 and 2006 that form the basis for Professor Cabral's analysis, *none* involved significant learning curve gains; i.e. the production of each major model delivered between 2000 and 2006 had exceeded 100 before the year 2000.[4212] The United States argues that, between 2000 and 2006, Boeing's learning curve investment in the pricing of these sales was in fact "zero", or "close to zero", not $438 million per annum, as calculated by Professor Cabral.[4213]

45.   NERA also argues that, although there is no dispute that there are "substantial" learning curve effects associated with the manufacture of LCA, they have no direct effect on LCA pricing.[4214] NERA agrees that LCA manufacturers price initial units of LCA as though they were already at the bottom of the learning curve, however, NERA argues that this is a feature of the nature of production and competition in the industry, and would occur whether or not an LCA manufacturer had received subsidies.[4215] According to NERA,

---

this discussion, that the assumption is not incorrect; United States' first written submission, para. 848, footnote 1043.

[4208] United States' first written submission, para. 848.

[4209] *Ibid.*

[4210] United States' first written submission, para. 848. The United States refers to a statement of Clay Richmond, Vice President of Revenue Management at Boeing Commercial Airplanes, who states that, "{w}hile included in Boeing's program cost projections, learning curve efficiencies are not separately factored into pricing in individual sales campaigns", Statement of Clay Richmond, Exhibit US-275, para. 3.

[4211] United States' first written submission, para. 847.

[4212] United States' first written submission, para. 853.

[4213] *Ibid.*

[4214] Jordan and Dorman Report, Exhibit US-3, p. 13.

[4215] NERA argues that the intense competition between Airbus and Boeing to launch successful new models means that they *must* price on a forward-looking basis; they cannot hope to succeed by

1746   DSR 2012:III

US - Large Civil Aircraft (2nd Complaint)

Professor Cabral's analysis implicitly assumes that, in the absence of the subsidies, Boeing would not have priced as though it were at the bottom of the learning curve, and that, if Boeing had received a lower amount of subsidies, it would have raised its LCA prices to initial customers.[4216] NERA identifies this as a fundamental flaw in Professor Cabral's analysis.

46.   NERA also criticizes Professor Cabral's quantification of the learning curve price reductions in that it is based on there being steep learning curve effects for the first 100 units of every *version* of each Boeing LCA model built between 1989 – 2006 (e.g. the Boeing 737-600, 737-700, 737-800 and 737-900 were each assumed to experience steep learning curve effects during the production of the first 100 units of each version).[4217] NERA considers that this does not reflect the reality of the LCA business. For example, NERA notes that, given that all four current versions of the 737 are assembled in the same factory, and share a common wing, fuselage, cockpit and most other components, there is no reason to expect that each of the four versions of each LCA model benefits separately from learning curve effects that are particularly steep during the first 100 units.[4218]

47.   The European Communities responds to these criticisms in the following manner. First, in relation to the criticism that learning curve effects are factored into the pricing targets at the time of launch of an LCA programme, and not in the context of campaign-specific adjustments to price, the European Communities notes that the Boeing expert on whom the United States relies for its statement that learning curve efficiencies are not separately factored into pricing individual sales, but rather, are included in Boeing's programme cost projections, far from contradicting Professor Cabral's reasoning, confirms that Boeing has an incentive to (and does) offer additional launch concessions for the initial aircraft sold under a programme.[4219] According to the European Communities, the level of interest that Boeing has in convincing the market that demand is significant and thereby moving down the learning curve is impacted by the subsidy funds that it has available to justify accepting lower margins on particular sales.[4220]

48.   Second, the European Communities rejects the U.S. criticism that learning curve efficiencies do not also apply to the first 100 units of subsequent *variants* of LCA models. The European Communities submits that "available evidence" demonstrates that learning curve effects benefit the entire production

---

charging higher prices to launch customers to reflect the higher costs of producing those initial airplanes; Jordan and Dorman Report, Exhibit US-3, p. 15.

[4216] Jordan and Dorman Report, Exhibit US-3, p. 15.

[4217] *Ibid.*

[4218] *Ibid.*

[4219] European Communities' second written submission, para. 771. The European Communities identifies the Boeing expert as James Hayes, Boeing's Director for 787 Pricing, but the Boeing expert is Clay Richmond (see United States' first written submission, paras. 847-848).

[4220] European Communities' second written submission, para. 771.

DSR 2012:III   1747

Report of the Panel

life of an aircraft, and that additional learning curve effects apply to new models within an aircraft family. On this basis, the European Communities argues that Professor Cabral's estimate of the percentage of Boeing aircraft that benefited from learning curve effects during the 2000 to 2006 period is therefore reasonable.[4221]

(c)   Estimation of the degree to which prices are affected by buyer switching costs

49.   The United States acknowledges that, unlike the impact of learning curve efficiencies, the phenomenon of switching costs does arise in the sales campaign-specific context. However, the United States argues that Professor Cabral mistakenly ascribes switching costs to sales in which switching costs did not arise; thereby greatly exaggerating the frequency with which Boeing considers a price concession for switching cost reasons. According to the United States, switching costs occur when an airline decides to buy a new supplier's current generation aircraft, instead of buying additional current generation aircraft from the incumbent supplier. The United States says that, in contrast, price concessions relating to switching costs do not factor in sales of (i) a new type of LCA (e.g. the 787); (ii) a *new generation* of a type of aircraft that an airline already operates (e.g. the purchase of a 737-800 by an airline that operates 737-300s); or (iii) a *new variant* of a type of aircraft that an airline already operates (e.g. the purchase of a 737-800 by an airline that operates 737-700s).[4222]

50.   The United States argues that Professor Cabral mistakenly assigns switching costs to all purchases by airlines that have not bought aircraft of the same *generation* and family before, and therefore estimates that 37.4 per cent of Boeing's sales are to new customers of that particular aircraft family.[4223] According to the United States, an analysis of the 2,644 deliveries made by Boeing during 2000 – 2006 shows that no more than 120 (i.e. only 4.5 per cent) involved the type of switching costs that could have led Boeing to make switching cost price concessions.[4224]

[4221] European Communities' second written submission, para. 772. The European Communities argues that, in any event, Professor Cabral's sensitivity analysis demonstrated that even where the share of aircraft benefiting from learning curve effects was significantly lower than the model parameter, the overall impact to his conclusions was negligible.

[4222] United States' first written submission, para. 855; referring to the Statement of Clay Richmond, para. 6, Exhibit US-275.

[4223] United States' first written submission, para. 854.

[4224] United States' first written submission, paras. 851, 85,; referring to the Statement of Clay Richmond, para. 8, Exhibit US-275; United States' comments on the European Communities' response to question 95, para. 244. In addition, the United States argues that, where Boeing was the incumbent, the evidence shows that it resisted price concessions, and as a result, lost major sales campaigns to Airbus on price, despite the costs that those airlines incurred in switching to Airbus.

1748   DSR 2012:III

51. In addition, the United States argues that Professor Cabral's understanding of the nature of the pricing incentives related to switching costs is at odds with the realities of the LCA industry.[4225] According to the United States, Professor Cabral conceives of the price incentives related to future switching costs as being based on a link between the probability of future switching and *current price discounts*. The United States argues that, in reality, the question whether a current buyer switches suppliers in the future will depend more than anything on whether, at that future time, the challenging supplier offers a discount large enough to offset the customer's switching cost. The challenging supplier's ability to offer such a discount in the future is not affected by historical data on the probability of switching across suppliers. Therefore, according to the United States, a supplier has no incentive to offer current discounts based on the historical probability data that Professor Cabral uses.[4226]

52. NERA agrees with Professor Cabral that there can be switching costs associated with purchasing LCA, whether for replacement or fleet growth. However, NERA says that the magnitude of these costs will vary widely depending on the existing fleet of the airline and the new airplane alternatives under consideration.[4227]

53. Moreover, NERA considers that Professor Cabral's formula for estimating that switching costs induce price discounting of 25 per cent when selling to new buyers is overly simplistic, not based on data relating to any actual Boeing price concessions offered to any customer in a sales campaign, and fails to take account of the complexities of competition between Airbus and Boeing in which each sales opportunity generates an individualized sales campaign targeted at the circumstances of the particular customer.[4228] In this regard, NERA notes that during the 2004 – 2006 "reference period", Boeing delivered 973 airplanes of which 37.4 per cent (i.e. 364 planes) would, based on Professor Cabral's methodology, be assumed to involve switching cost price reductions. NERA considers this to be an unrealistic assumption given that 366 deliveries were made to long-time operators of Boeing airlines or to leasing companies, neither of which would have been affected by switching costs.[4229]

54. NERA also argues that Professor Cabral's analysis necessarily implies that, in the absence of the subsidies, Boeing would not have priced as it did in order to offset prospective buyers' switching costs (and as a corollary, that had Boeing received one less dollar of subsidy, it would have raised its prices to new customers). NERA considers that such an assumption ignores the intense

---

[4225] United States' comments on the European Communities' response to question 95, para. 243.

[4226] *Ibid.*

[4227] Jordan and Dorman Report, Exhibit US-3, pp. 15-16. The authors note, for example, that there is typically substantial commonality across versions of a model that are of the same generation (e.g. Boeing 737 family, or the Airbus A320 family) and there can also be commonality across models, such as between the A330 and A340.

[4228] Jordan and Dorman Report, Exhibit US-3, pp. 15-16.

[4229] Jordan and Dorman Report, Exhibit US-3, p. 17, footnote 14.

Report of the Panel

competition between Airbus and Boeing in their LCA campaigns to prospective customers.[4230]

55.   The European Communities makes the following points in response to these criticisms. First, the European Communities disagrees that no switching costs could arise when an airline orders a new generation of a type of aircraft that an airline already operates. In this regard, the European Communities contends that customers have publicly affirmed that switching costs from moving to a new generation of one producer's aircraft can be even greater than those of changing from one producer to another.[4231] Second, the European Communities argues that the United States has misrepresented the relevance of switching costs in Professor Cabral's model. According to the United States, Professor Cabral's model focuses on Boeing considering in its current pricing decisions the possibility of future switching costs that would be incurred by an airline (i.e. as a justification for Boeing to offer lower prices to a customer today).[4232] From this perspective, switching costs can be relevant in sales of a new type of LCA, or new generations of existing LCA, because there is the possibility of locking in the customer for future sales. In addition, the European Communities argues, the related U.S. criticism that the share of Boeing sales that involved switching costs was dramatically less than Professor Cabral's assumption (4.5 per cent compared to 37.4 per cent) similarly misses the point. In any case, the European Communities argues that Professor Cabral's sensitivity analysis shows that even if the share of aircraft sales affected by switching cost considerations were different from his estimate, the impact on his overall result is negligible.[4233]

(d)   R&D expenditures as future price reductions

56.   NERA criticizes Professor Cabral's attempt to convert Boeing's R&D expenditures on commercial airplanes into price reductions. According to NERA, the essence of the intense competition between Boeing and Airbus is to design and build better airplanes (improved versions of existing models as well as new models). Yet, according to NERA, Professor Cabral's implicit assumption is that, in the absence of the subsidies, Boeing would not have made the same investments in R&D.[4234]

[4230] Jordan and Dorman Report, Exhibit US-3, p. 17.

[4231] European Communities' second written submission, para. 775, footnote 1179. The European Communities refers to an article in which the easyJet CEO said that easyJet faced higher switching costs in adding Boeing 737-700 aircraft to its existing line of 737-300s than it would in adding Airbus A319 models to its fleet. Part of the switching costs involved in moving from one Boeing generation to the next was the fact that 30 per cent of easyJet pilots were only certified to fly one or other of the 737 types; "Easy Does It" Airline Business, 12 January 2002, Exhibit EC-1247.

[4232] European Communities' second written submission, paras. 776-778.

[4233] European Communities' second written submission, para. 778.

[4234] Jordan and Dorman Report, Exhibit US-3, p. 18. The United States also independently makes this argument. The United States contends that neither the European Communities nor Professor

1750   DSR 2012:III

US - Large Civil Aircraft (2ⁿᵈ Complaint)

57.   NERA notes Professor Cabral's conclusions that, over the 1989 – 2006 period, subsidies to Boeing have resulted in "R&D price reductions" by Boeing of $4.43 billion (plus an additional $2.41 billion for 2007 – 2022). NERA considers that this could only be true where either: (i) those R&D expenditures would not have been productive investments for Boeing absent the subsidies, but Boeing had no alternative productive investments, so it made them anyway; or (ii) such R&D expenditures would have been productive investments for Boeing absent the subsidies, but Boeing lacked the necessary capital to make them, absent the subsidies.[4235] NERA argues that there is no logical or empirical basis for either proposition.

(e)   Choice of the Hotelling model of oligopoly behaviour as representative of the nature of price competition between Airbus and Boeing

58.   The United States argues that Professor Cabral's choice of a Hotelling model for his analysis of duopoly pricing between Airbus and Boeing is badly flawed (although it stresses that the flawed modeling assumption described above would invalidate Professor Cabral's results even if his choice of a Hotelling model were correct).[4236] According to the United States, the most egregious flaw in the choice of the Hotelling model for an analysis of price competition between Airbus and Boeing is that under the Hotelling/Bertrand models, each competitor makes a *single, simultaneous price offer*. According to the United States, this is at odds with the nature of pricing in the LCA market, where there is typically a *vigorous sequence of competing price bids*.[4237] The United States argues that the correct pricing model for the LCA market is what is known as a "repeated Bertrand competition". The United States contends that the literature of repeated Bertrand pricing generally concludes that any rational price outcome (from monopoly to competitive) is a *possible* equilibrium outcome of this form of oligopoly competition and that the actual outcome in any concrete case will depend on factors such as the competitive attitudes and cultures of the competitors. The United States notes that Professor Cabral's "highly deterministic pricing model" is completely at odds with this conclusion.[4238]

59.   Professor Greenwald also criticizes the assumptions made regarding the basic model of price competition underlying Professor Cabral's conclusions. He argues that Professor Cabral's model assumes that prices cannot be tailored to individual airlines, either because, in a sales campaign, neither Boeing nor Airbus has knowledge of an airline's preferences when setting price, or because

---

Cabral has proven that the government funding that Boeing received for R&D work that it carried out was for work that Boeing would otherwise have carried out on its own, and in amounts that Boeing would otherwise have spent on its own; United States' first written submission, para. 841.

[4235] Jordan and Dorman Report, Exhibit US-3, p. 19.
[4236] United States' comments on the European Communities' response to question 382, para. 342.
[4237] United States' comments on the European Communities' response to question 382, para. 347.
[4238] United States' comments on the European Communities' response to question 382, para. 348.

DSR 2012:III   1751

Report of the Panel

they are somehow constrained to keep their prices the same for all airlines.[4239] Professor Greenwald considers that this assumption bears no relationship to the reality of extended bidding by Airbus and Boeing for individual orders, their respective knowledge of well-established airline preferences, or "painstakingly negotiated" final sales contracts. Professor Greenwald argues that, in a market characterized by individual bargaining with airlines with well-known preferences, the final price each airline pays depends on whether its preference for one LCA manufacturer over the other makes it a Boeing or Airbus buyer. Professor Greenwald also explains that a realistic model would need to account for this reality and that such a model would have been simpler than Professor Cabral's model.

60.   In response, Professor Cabral notes that his model considered the impact of subsidies on an "average" buyer of Boeing and Airbus aircraft, rather than a model incorporating LCA pricing tailored to specific customers.[4240] However, this latter type of model would have resulted in greater mathematical complexity. Moreover, modeling one single buyer with an average preference therefore provides a good approximation of the average price and of the average impact of subsidies on prices as explicitly as modeling the entire distributions of buyer types.[4241] Professor Cabral also observes that the repeated Bertrand model of price competition suggested by the United States may not be appropriate for the LCA market because there is no evidence of collusion between Airbus and Boeing that would require that their interaction be modelled as a repeat game.[4242]

D.   EVALUATION OF THE CABRAL MODEL

1.   Preliminary considerations regarding the Panel's evaluation of the Cabral model

61.   The Cabral model is a particular type of empirical simulation model which is known as a "calibrated model". Economists create calibrated models by assuming the existence of a relationship between different variables; for example, the relationship between subsidies and prices. They also make assumptions about the nature of that relationship, which is reflected in the parameters of the model. Calibration of the model involves choosing values for

---

[4239] Greenwald Paper, Exhibit US-8, p. 5.

[4240] Luís M. B. Cabral, Response to the U.S. Criticisms of my Analysis of The impacts of Development Subsidies Granted to Boeing", 14 November 2007, Exhibit EC-1182, para. 54. Such a model would consider the following factors: sellers' costs, the component of the buyer's preference that is known by the sellers, and the component of the buyer's preference that is known only by the buyer.

[4241] Luís M. B. Cabral, Response to the U.S. Criticisms of my Analysis of The impacts of Development Subsidies Granted to Boeing", 14 November 2007, Exhibit EC-1182, paras. 54-55.

[4242] Luís Cabral, Investment and Pricing Behaviour Model: Literature Review of Theories Dealing with Strategic Interaction in Duopolies, July 2009, Exhibit EC-1435, para. 30.

1752   DSR 2012:III

the parameters that ensure that the model assumptions and the observed data are consistent. Calibrated models can be distinguished from estimated econometric models which use statistical techniques (i.e. regression analysis) to test the validity of the assumptions on which the model is based.

62.   In evaluating the Cabral model in the context of the European Communities' causation arguments, it is important to note that, while the Cabral model may indicate that a causal link between the subsidies and the "event" (in this case, the price of Boeing LCA) is logically possible, it does not of itself indicate how plausible this logical possibility actually is. In other words, Professor Cabral's model necessarily *assumes* (on the basis of the assumptions embedded in the model) that there is a positive relationship between the receipt of the subsidies and the lower Boeing prices: It does not, however, purport to test that proposition. However, if the Panel were to accept the assumptions embedded in the model (including those made regarding the values of the different parameters), then the Cabral model could assist in *quantifying* the impact of the subsidies on Boeing's prices.

2.   The role of the Cabral model in the European Communities' "price effects" arguments

63.   In its first written submission, the European Communities introduces the Cabral Report by saying that, in addition to ITR's calculations of the "magnitudes" of the subsidies benefiting Boeing aircraft, it relies on Professor Cabral's work to "demonstrate that during 2004-2006, the US subsidies caused Boeing's 787, 737NG and 777 prices to be significantly lower."[4243] Later in that submission, the European Communities says that its causation argument; namely, that Boeing has a strong *incentive* to use a portion of the additional non-operating cash flow from the $16.9 billion in untied subsidies to lower its LCA prices is *confirmed* by Professor Cabral's analysis.[4244] The European Communities then describes Professor Cabral as providing an "economic analysis of *why* US subsidies received by Boeing that are not directly tied to production or sales volumes of specific aircraft ... strongly influence Boeing's investment and pricing decisions."[4245] The European Communities describes the conclusions of Professor Cabral's model as being that subsidies that increase Boeing's non-operating cash flow have a direct and substantial effect on Boeing's investment and pricing behaviour.[4246] This suggests that the European Communities seeks to use Professor Cabral's model as additional evidence in support of its causation argument (that the subsidies caused Boeing to lower its LCA prices) as well as to quantify the extent of the price reductions.

[4243]   European Communities' first written submission, para. 1007.
[4244]   European Communities' first written submission, para. 1309.
[4245]   European Communities' first written submission, para. 1309. Emphasis added.
[4246]   European Communities' first written submission, para. 1309.

Report of the Panel

64.   In its second written submission, the European Communities describes the report prepared by Professor Cabral as "offer{ing} quantitative estimates" of the extent to which subsidies that increase Boeing's non-operating cash flow led Boeing to lower its LCA prices.[4247] However, it then describes Professor Cabral's contribution in the following terms:

> "In his report, Professor Cabral developed a model to determine how Boeing spends additional cash, *i.e.*, how it allocates the subsidy funds it receives between investments in future firm value and distributions to shareholders. He *concluded* that the majority of the US subsidies are channeled into investments in firm value, *and* result in price effects of approximately the same magnitude as the amount of the subsidies."[4248]

65.   The European Communities' discussion of the Cabral Report in its second written submission concludes with the statement that the "price effects *determined* by Professor Cabral, therefore, stand and support the EC arguments and other evidence demonstrating the adverse effects caused by the US subsidies."[4249]

66.   As indicated by the foregoing, the Cabral Report appears to be relevant to the European Communities' causation arguments in two ways. The first is to support its general (and critical) argument that Boeing used the subsidies to lower its LCA prices (i.e. supporting the European Communities' principal contentions that the conditions of competition in the LCA market, coupled with the magnitude of the subsidies, created incentives, opportunities and the ability for Boeing to lower its LCA prices). The second is to quantify the extent to which the subsidies flowed through to lower Boeing LCA prices. Moreover, Professor Cabral's analysis of the ways in which a firm like Boeing will use subsidies that are not directly tied to the production or sale of specific LCA mirrors and provides the theoretical underpinnings of the European Communities' key arguments about why and how, given the pricing incentives related to LCA production and sale, and the nature of competition in the LCA market, Boeing will use a significant portion of the subsidies to lower the prices of its LCA and increase market share.

3.   **Principal weaknesses of Professor Cabral's model as support for the European Communities' arguments that Boeing uses the subsidies to lower the prices of its LCA**

67.   The Panel here sets forth what we see as the principal flaws in Professor Cabral's analysis of the ways in which the category of subsidies that he identifies

---

[4247] European Communities' second written submission, para. 753.
[4248] European Communities' second written submission, para. 753. Emphasis added.
[4249] European Communities' second written submission, para. 785. Emphasis added.

1754   DSR 2012:III

as development subsidies allegedly affect Boeing's LCA pricing behaviour. The Panel does not address the many criticisms made by the United States and its consultants of Professor Cabral's estimates of particular parameters, as in our view, these factors primarily affect the quantification of the "price effects".

(a)   Consistency with Boeing's pricing behaviour in the LCA markets between 2000 and 2006

68.   In the Panel's view, the most apparent weakness in Professor Cabral's analysis, in so far as it purports to *demonstrate* that Boeing would use a significant proportion of each additional dollar of subsidy to engage in aggressive pricing of its LCA, is the fact that it is not supported by empirical evidence concerning Boeing's actual pricing behaviour between 2000 and 2006. The Panel recalls that Professor Cabral's theory as to the way in which the receipt of "development subsidies" would affect Boeing's pricing behaviour is that Boeing would directly and immediately apply a significant proportion of any such subsidies that it receives in any year to "investments" in aggressive pricing in order to capture market share from Airbus. The Panel accepts evidence that Boeing changed its pricing policy in late 2004/2005 and became much more "aggressive" on price. Indeed, the Panel notes that the European Communities' version of events in the LCA markets between 2000 and 2006 is that Boeing suddenly became much more aggressive on price in late 2004, with the appointment of a new sales manager and a clear change in pricing policy.[4250] However, the very suggestion that Boeing could suddenly decide to change its policy and become more aggressive on price in 2004/2005 (using the subsidies to do so) appears to contradict Professor Cabral's theory about how Boeing would optimally be applying additional dollars of subsidies to "investments" in aggressive pricing, unless it were possible to show that from 2004/2005 onwards, the amount of subsidies paid to Boeing increased significantly (which it did not).

69.   When asked by the Panel to explain this apparent inconsistency, the European Communities replied that Cabral's model reflects Boeing's "average" behaviour with respect to its use of the subsidies over the 2000 – 2006 period. According to the European Communities, the fact that post-2004, Boeing used a greater portion of subsidies than previously is consistent with a model that assesses Boeing's "average" behaviour during 2004 – 2006.[4251] The European Communities also does not dispute that Boeing may contribute its own funds –

[4250] European Communities' confidential oral statement at the first meeting with the Panel, paras. 53 and 75-76; Christian Scherer, Commercial Aspects of the Aircraft Business from the Perspective of a Manufacturer, March 2007, Exhibit EC-11 (BCI), para. 117. Both parties appear to accept that Boeing adopted a more aggressive pricing policy in late 2004 or early 2005 (they disagree somewhat as to the precise timing). See, for example, United States' comments on the European Communities' response to question 86, para. 307.

[4251] European Communities' response to question 86, para. 394.

Report of the Panel

in addition to the subsidies it receives – to invest in lower pricing. According to the European Communities, Boeing's 2004 decision to dramatically reduce its pricing for, *inter alia*, the 737NG was made possible partly by "greater use of these subsidies" and partly by Boeing's decision to use its own funds to reduce prices.[4252] The European Communities argues that, for purposes of assessing the European Communities' arguments and evidence, it does not matter which of the two factors made the greatest contribution to Boeing lowering its prices – what is important is the "marginal effect of the US subsidies on Boeing's price."[4253]

70. The United States argues that this explanation by the European Communities merely illustrates the contradictions between reality and theory. The United States recalls that the European Communities, in its first written submission, argued that the price effects that increase Boeing's non-operating cash flow are *immediate and direct* for both the case of investment in aggressive pricing of new planes (via pricing down the learning curve) and for aggressive pricing of sales of mature aircraft.[4254] The United States argues that, in its attempt to explain the consistency of Professor Cabral's analysis with post-2004 market events, the European Communities admits that Boeing may significantly change its distribution of the amount of the alleged non-operating cash flow benefit among various spending options. The United States notes that it is *only* through Professor Cabral's assumption that Boeing uses any subsidy cash in a *fixed proportion* between investments leading to lower LCA prices and payments to shareholders that Professor Cabral can claim that the alleged subsidies that increase Boeing's non-operating cash flows will *always* affect Boeing's prices. Otherwise, Professor Cabral's model would provide no reason why, at any given time, the proportion of the subsidy invested in lower pricing would not be zero, and the proportion passed onto shareholders would not be 100 per cent.[4255] Thus, according to the United States, Professor Cabral's model positively precludes that Boeing may invest a somewhat higher percentage of its subsidies in pricing down its LCA in some years, but not in others.

71. The United States also argues that if Professor Cabral's theory that "aggressive pricing" is a rational "investment" were true, one would have expected that in 2000 – 2004 Boeing would have been pricing aggressively to take market share from Airbus, instead of resisting price reductions and losing market share. The European Communities argues that subsidies to Boeing also caused adverse effects during the 2001 – 2003 period, however, a number of factors "prevented Boeing from maximizing the effects of these subsidies to increase its market share at Airbus' expense."[4256] These factors included: Boeing's poor customer relationships, the fact that its order book was dominated

---

[4252] European Communities' response to question 86, para. 396.

[4253] European Communities' response to question 86, para. 397.

[4254] United States' comments on the European Communities' response to question 86, para. 303; referring to European Communities' first written submission, para. 1322.

[4255] United States' comments on the European Communities' response to question 86, para. 304.

[4256] European Communities' response to question 85, para. 390.

1756

DSR 2012:III

US - Large Civil Aircraft (2nd Complaint)

by distressed U.S. airlines, Boeing's failure to launch new LCA and its decision to compete with leasing companies. The European Communities says that, by late 2004, "these factors had changed, and the full effects of the subsidies were again felt by Airbus."[4257]

72.   The Panel is persuaded by the United States' criticism of the Cabral model in this regard. To the extent that Professor Cabral's analysis purports to demonstrate, not just that it is "logically possible" that Boeing used the "development subsidies" to lower the prices of its LCA, but that Boeing *actually did* use the subsidies to lower the prices of its LCA, we would expect that the implications of Professor Cabral's theory about how Boeing would behave in the LCA markets would, at least to some degree, be borne out by events that occurred in those markets. Professor Cabral himself said, in his discussion of the various models of oligopoly behaviour that he could have potentially chosen for the basis of his model, that while it may be difficult to choose a model based on purely theoretical grounds, one can ask whether their assumptions are reasonable given the industry at issue and whether their predicted outcomes are consistent with the reality of that industry and the actual market outcomes.[4258] The Panel considers that the same can be said of Professor Cabral's model, and we do not consider that his model and its predicted outcomes are consistent with the evidence as to pricing behaviour and market share in the LCA industry between 2000 and 2006.[4259]

(b)   Are "untied" subsidies the functional equivalent of additional cash to Boeing?

73.   Professor Cabral's analysis rests on the assumption that "in kind" subsidies such as the NASA R&D subsidies are fungible with cash.[4260] The European Communities and Professor Cabral both argue that this is because the R&D subsidies lower Boeing's costs of conducting R&D and thereby free up additional cash that Boeing can use to engage in aggressive pricing. We are not persuaded that the nature of the particular aeronautics R&D subsidies at issue in this dispute, particularly in the light of NASA's role in supporting long-term, high risk aeronautical R&T, is such that it is appropriate to analyse the effects of

---

[4257] European Communities' response to question 85, para. 391.

[4258] L. Cabral, Investment and Pricing Behaviour Model: Literature Review of Theories Dealing with Strategic Interaction in Duopolies, July 2009, Exhibit EC-1436, para. 11.

[4259] See also paras. 74 and 75 in (c) below.

[4260] Luís M. B. Cabral, Impact of Development Subsidies Granted to Boeing, New York University and CEPR, March 2007, Exhibit EC-4, p. 41; Luís M. B. Cabral, Response to the U.S. Criticisms of my Analysis of The impacts of Development Subsidies Granted to Boeing", 14 November 2007, Exhibit EC-1182, paras. 32-33. The Panel observes that the proof of the fungibility of "in-kind" subsidies with cash contained in Annex A.2 of Professor Cabral's March 2007 report is simply a rewriting of the budget constraint of the firm in a highly abstract model.

Report of the Panel

the aeronautics R&D subsidies as being equivalent to the receipt of additional cash.[4261]

(c)   Cabral's theory as to how the subsidies influence Boeing's pricing of its LCA is at odds with evidence as to how Boeing sets its LCA prices

74.   Even assuming that it is appropriate to analyse the effects of the aeronautics R&D subsidies as cost savings that generate additional cash for Boeing, the Panel is not persuaded that such cost savings influence Boeing's LCA pricing in the way suggested by Professor Cabral. Both Airbus and Boeing officers acknowledge that the LCA prices they set relate to the development costs for a particular LCA programme.[4262] However, Professor Cabral's analysis does not indicate how a reduction in Boeing's general costs (e.g. a reduction in Boeing's general R&D costs) would affect the development costs for a specific LCA programme. Moreover, as shown by the evidence, the nature of the LCA market is such that LCA prices are also influenced by the prices of competing LCA.[4263] In short, we consider that the relationship between cost savings arising from the receipt of development subsidies and LCA prices is less direct than is suggested by Professor Cabral.

75.   A similar criticism relates to Professor Cabral's analysis of the effects of learning curve efficiencies on Boeing's LCA pricing. The United States asserts that, because learning curve efficiencies are factored into a producer's projected costs at the time of the launch of an aircraft programme, there is no basis for any expectation of subsequent, campaign-specific learning curve adjustments to price. The Panel is satisfied that the evidence submitted by the United States in support of this assertion is credible and consistent with other evidence as to how Boeing sets prices for its LCA.[4264]

[4261] See also paras. 7.1760, 7.1831 of the Report.

[4262] See, e.g. Statement of Clay Richmond, Exhibit US-275 HSBI; According to Richmond, at the time of the decision to launch an LCA programme, Boeing bases its pricing on (i) the price it believes the LCA will command over its lifetime, and (ii) the projected volume of sales for that LCA, against (iii) the costs of the LCA programme (including non-recurring investments and recurring costs such as anticipated learning curve efficiencies). Richmond says that once the launch decision is made, pricing is "market driven" in the sense that Boeing aims to achieve the highest market value for its products in light of market conditions. See also Christian Scherer, Commercial Aspects of the Aircraft Business from the Perspective of a Manufacturer, March 2007, Exhibit EC-11 (BCI), para. 105.

[4263] See, e.g. Christian Scherer, Commercial Aspects of the Aircraft Business from the Perspective of a Manufacturer, March 2007, Exhibit EC-11 (BCI), para. 105; Greenwald Paper, Exhibit US-8, p. 6. European Communities' second written submission, Full Version HSBI Appendix, para. 86: "As a profit maximizer, Airbus has no incentive to offer very low pricing. Thus, in competitive sales campaigns, Airbus pricing is, to a large extent, the result of Boeing's behaviour."

[4264] See, e.g. Statement of Clay Richmond, Exhibit US-275 HSBI; Jordan and Dorman Report, Exhibit US-3, pp. 14-15.

1758

DSR 2012:III

4. Conclusion

76. In conclusion, Professor Cabral's model does not support the existence of a causal link between the receipt by Boeing of "development subsidies", and lower Boeing LCA pricing. The Panel is not convinced that the assumptions underlying Professor Cabral's model are an appropriate representation of Boeing's actual commercial behaviour. As we are unable to accept the assumptions on which the model is based, we do not consider the model to provide evidentiary support for the European Communities' argument that Boeing's receipt of the subsidies enables it to lower the prices of its LCA.

VIII. CONCLUSIONS AND RECOMMENDATION

A. Conclusions

8.1 We recall that in this dispute, the claims of the European Communities with respect to the challenged measures fall into two categories. First, the European Communities claims that two of the alleged subsidies, namely the tax breaks provided by the U.S. Federal Government pursuant to legislation concerning foreign sales corporations and exclusion of extraterritorial income and the tax incentives provided by the State of Washington under the legislation adopted in 2003, are prohibited under Articles 3.1(a) and 3.2 of the SCM Agreement. Second, the European Communities claims that all of the alleged subsidies are actionable under the SCM Agreement and that by using these subsidies the United States causes adverse effects to the interests of the European Communities, in violation of Article 5(c) of the SCM Agreement.

8.2 With respect to the European Communities' prohibited subsidy claims under Articles 3.1(a) and 3.2 of the SCM Agreement, we conclude that:

    (a)   the FSC/ETI measures that have been challenged by the European Communities and that were in force at the time of the Panel's establishment are inconsistent with Articles 3.1(a) and 3.2 of the SCM Agreement;

    (b)   the European Communities has not demonstrated that the Washington State tax measures provided for in HB 2294 are inconsistent with Articles 3.1(a) and 3.2 of the SCM Agreement.

8.3 With respect to the European Communities' adverse effects claims under Article 5(c) of the SCM Agreement:

    (a)   we conclude that the United States causes serious prejudice to the interests of the European Communities within the meaning of Articles 5(c) and 6.3(b) and 6.3(c) of the SCM Agreement in that:

        (i)   the effects of the NASA and DOD aeronautics R&D subsidies are significant price suppression, significant lost sales and threat of displacement and impedance of exports

Report of the Panel

from third country markets, with respect to the 200 – 300 seat wide-body LCA product market;

(ii)   the effects of the FSC/ETI subsidies and the B&O tax subsidies provided by the State of Washington under HB 2294 are significant price suppression, significant lost sales and displacement and impedance of exports from third country markets, with respect to the 100-200 seat single-aisle LCA product market;

(iii)   the effects of the FSC/ETI subsidies and the B&O tax subsidies provided by the State of Washington under HB 2294 and by the City of Everett are significant price suppression, significant lost sales and displacement and impedance of exports from third country markets, with respect to the 300-400 seat wide-body LCA product market;

(a)   we exercise judicial economy with respect to the European Communities' claim that violation of the 1992 Agreement constitutes serious prejudice to the European Communities' interests within the meaning of Article 5(c) of the SCM Agreement.

8.4   Under Article 3.8 of the DSU, in cases where there is an infringement of the obligations assumed under a covered agreement, the action is considered prima facie to constitute a case of nullification or impairment. We conclude that, to the extent that the United States has acted inconsistently with the SCM Agreement, it has nullified or impaired benefits accruing to the European Communities under that Agreement.

B.   Recommendation

8.5   Article 4.7 of the SCM Agreement provides that, having found a measure in dispute to be a prohibited subsidy:

> "the Panel shall recommend that the subsidizing Member withdraw the subsidy without delay. In this regard, the panel shall specify in its recommendation the time period within which the measure must be withdrawn."

8.6   The Panel has found that the European Communities has demonstrated that FSC/ETI and successor act subsidies to Boeing are export subsidies that are prohibited under Articles 3.1(a) and 3.2 of the SCM Agreement. As to whether the Panel should make a recommendation under Article 4.7 of the SCM Agreement with regard to the subsidies which it has found to be prohibited under Article 3, there are two basic considerations that the Panel needs to take into account. First, the FSC/ETI measure in force at the time of the Panel's establishment has been substantially changed during the course of the present proceedings and indeed it appears that the measure is no longer in force with

1760

DSR 2012:III

respect to Boeing.[4265] The Panel considers that it is well established in WTO dispute settlement practice that when a measure has expired, it is appropriate for a panel to refrain from making a recommendation with respect to such a measure.[4266] Second, to the extent that FSC/ETI tax benefits remained applicable to Boeing at the time of the establishment of this Panel, pursuant to the transition and grandfather clauses of the AJCA, the Panel notes that the panel and Appellate Body reports in *US – FSC (Article 21.5 – ECII)* concluded that the recommendation made by the panel in *US – FSC* remained operative. The Panel considers it important not to disturb this recommendation. A new recommendation under Article 4.7 of the SCM Agreement would not add to the legal force of the existing recommendation. The findings made in prior cases regarding the legal provisions as such necessarily imply that the application of these provisions in individual cases was also inconsistent with Article 3. The obligation of the United States to withdraw the prohibited subsidies at issue thus also entails an obligation to cease applying the measures in individual cases. If anything, a new recommendation could detract from the legal force of the existing obligation insofar as it would give rise to a new period for implementation.[4267]

8.7 In the light of the foregoing, the Panel refrains from making a recommendation under Article 4.7 of the SCM Agreement. To the extent that the United States has not already withdrawn the FSC/ETI export subsidies to Boeing, the Panel notes the conclusion of the Panel in *US - FSC (Article 21.5 – ECII)*, which was upheld by the Appellate Body, that the recommendation made by the Panel in the dispute in *US – FSC* continued to be "operative".[4268]

8.8 Article 7.8 of the SCM Agreement provides that:

> "Where a panel report or an Appellate Body report is adopted in which it is determined that any subsidy has resulted in adverse effects to the interests of another Member within the meaning of

---

[4265] We note that the European Communities argues that there has been no "final resolution" as to whether FSC/ETI benefits will continue. We also note, however, that this issue is limited to certain transactions that are authorized under the TIPRA provisions as interpreted in the December 2006 memorandum of the Internal Revenue Service and that the European Communities has not provided sufficient evidence that Boeing has actually made use of those provisions.

[4266] See, for example, Appellate Body Report, *US – Certain EC Products*, paras. 81-82. The panel in *EC – Approval and Marketing of Biotech Products* concluded that "WTO jurisprudence supports the inference that panels are to avoid making recommendations which would apply to measures that are no longer in existence or have been amended." Panel Report, *EC – Approval and Marketing of Biotech Products*, para. 7.1316.

[4267] A recommendation by this Panel under Article 4.7 of the SCM Agreement would provide the United States with a new period within which to withdraw the subsidy provided to Boeing. The implication would be that while the United States has since November 2000 been under an obligation to withdraw the FSC measures at issue, with respect to the application of those measures to Boeing, the obligation to withdraw the subsidy would come into existence only upon completion of the present proceeding. Such a result would be fundamentally illogical.

[4268] See, for example, Panel Report, *US – FSC (Article 21.5 – ECII)*, para. 8.2.

DSR 2012:III

1761

Article 5, the Member granting or maintaining such subsidy shall take appropriate steps to remove the adverse effects or shall withdraw the subsidy."

8.9   Accordingly, in the light of our conclusions with respect to adverse effects set out above, we recommend that, upon adoption of this Report, or of an Appellate Body report in this dispute determining that any subsidy has resulted in adverse effects to the interests of the European Communities, the United States "take appropriate steps to remove the adverse effects or ... withdraw the subsidy".

8.10   Article 19.1 of the DSU provides that a panel "may" suggest ways in which a recommendation could be implemented. It is well established that Article 19.1 does not oblige panels to make a suggestion. In this case, neither party has requested that the Panel make any such suggestion. Accordingly, we make no suggestions concerning the steps that might be taken to implement this recommendation.

US - Large Civil Aircraft (2nd Complaint)

ANNEX A*

UNITED STATES - MEASURES AFFECTING TRADE IN LARGE CIVIL AIRCRAFT

Request for Consultations by the European Communities

ADDENDUM

The following communication, dated 27 June 2005, from the delegation of the European Communities to the delegation of the United States and to the Chairman of the Dispute Settlement Body, is circulated in accordance with Article 4.4 of the DSU.

———————

The European Communities refers to the United States' statement at the meeting of the Dispute Settlement Body ("DSB") on 13 June concerning the European Communities' request for the establishment of a Panel in the above case, where you asserted that 13 of the 28 subsidy programs referenced in the panel request were not listed in the consultation request of 6 October 2004 (circulated as document WT/DS/317/1 on 12 October 2004) and cannot be the subject of panel proceedings.

The European Communities cannot agree with this contention but is prepared to pursue consultations on the issues raised in these proceedings in order to clarify and, if possible, resolve them, it being understood that this is without prejudice to the European Communities' legal position and rights.

Accordingly, the European Communities hereby requests consultations with the United States pursuant to Articles 4.1, 7.1 and 30 of the *Agreement on Subsidies and Countervailing Measures* ("*SCM Agreement*"), Article XXIII:1 of the General Agreement on Tariffs and Trade 1994 ("GATT 1994") and Article 4 of the Understanding on Rules and Procedures Governing the Settlement of Disputes ("DSU"). These consultations will be a continuation of those held on 5 November 2004 pursuant to the request for consultations of 6 October 2004.

The measures that are the subject of this request are prohibited and actionable subsidies provided to US producers of large civil aircraft[1] ("US LCA

———————

* This communication was originally circulated on 1 July 2005 as WT/DS317/1/Add.1-G/L/698/Add.1-G/SCM/D63/1/Add. 1. On 4 December 2006, a corrigendum was issued to add "second complaint" at the end of the title of the document and to add "WT/DS353/1" to the document number.

DSR 2012:III

1763

Report of the Panel

industry"), and in particular the Boeing Company and the McDonnell Douglas Corporation, prior to its merger with Boeing, including related legislation, regulations, statutory instruments and amendments thereto. The measures currently include the following:

1. STATE AND LOCAL SUBSIDIES

US States and local authorities, where production and headquarter facilities of the US LCA industry are located, transfer in various ways economic resources to the US LCA industry. Such States and local authorities include, but are not limited to, those in the States of Washington, Kansas and Illinois.

These economic resources transferred to the US LCA industry include numerous financial incentives and other advantages effectuated, for example, through tax breaks, bond financing, fee waivers, lease arrangements, corporate headquarters relocation assistance, research funding, infrastructure measures and other benefits.

2. NASA SUBSIDIES

The National Aeronautics and Space Administration ("NASA") transfers economic resources to the US LCA industry, *inter alia*, by:

(i)   allowing the US LCA industry to participate in research programmes, making payments to the US LCA industry under those programmes, or enabling the US LCA industry to exploit the results thereof by means including but not limited to the foregoing or waiving of valuable patent rights, the granting of limited exclusive rights data ("LERD"), or otherwise exclusive or early access to data, trade secrets and other knowledge resulting from government funded research. The following are examples of such NASA programmes:

- High Speed Research Program;
- Advanced Subsonic Technology Program;
- Aviation Safety Program/Aviation Safety & Security Program/Aviation Security & Safety Program;
- Quiet Aircraft Technology Program;
- High Performance Computing and Communications Program;

---

[1]   In accordance with the *1992 Agreement between the European Communities and the Government of the United States of America concerning the application of the GATT Agreement on Trade in Civil Aircraft on trade in large civil aircraft*, large civil aircraft ("LCA") includes all aircraft as defined in Article 1 of the GATT Agreement on Trade in Civil Aircraft, except engines as defined in Article 1.1(b) thereof, that are designed for passenger or cargo transportation and have 100 or more passenger seats or its equivalent in cargo configuration. Boeing produces or markets the following families of LCA: 717, 737, 747, 757, 767, 777, and 787.

- Research & Technology Base Program;
- Advanced Composites Technology Program;
- Vehicle Systems Program;
- Materials and Structures Systems Technology Program;
- Aircraft Energy Efficiency Program, including Composite Primary Aircraft Structures, Transport Aircraft Systems Technology, and Advanced Composite Structures Technology Programs;

(ii)   NASA Personnel and Institutional Support Costs Dedicated to US LCA Industry R&D;

(iii)   NASA Independent Research & Development, and Bid & Proposal Reimbursements;

(iv)   Use by the US LCA industry of research, test and evaluation facilities owned by the US Government, including NASA wind tunnels, in particular the Langley research centre;

(v)   NASA procurement contracts.

3.   DEPARTMENT OF DEFENSE SUBSIDIES

The Department of Defense ("DOD") transfers economic resources to the US LCA industry, *inter alia*, by:

(i)   allowing the US LCA industry to participate in DOD-funded research, making payments to the US LCA industry for such research, or enabling the US LCA industry to exploit the results thereof by means including but not limited to the foregoing or waiving of valuable patent rights, and the granting of exclusive or early access to data, trade secrets and other knowledge resulting from government funded research, through, for example:

- Research, Development, Testing and Evaluation Programs;
- Independent Research & Development, and Bid & Proposal Reimbursements;

(ii)   use by the US LCA industry of test and evaluation facilities owned by the US Government, including the Major Range Test Facility Bases;

(iii)   procurement contracts including those for the purchase of goods from the US LCA industry for more than adequate remuneration, including in particular but not limited to the US Air Force contract with the Boeing corporation for the purchase of certain spare parts for its Airborne Warning and Control System (AWACS) aircraft, the Boeing KC-767A Tanker Program (lease contract), the National Polar-orbiting Operational Environmental Satellite System-Conical Microwave Imager Sensor, Boeing, the C-22 Replacement Program (C-40), Boeing, the KC-135 Programmed Depot Maintenance, Boeing/Pemco, the C-40 Lease and Purchase Program, Boeing, the C-130 avionics modernisation upgrade

Report of the Panel

program, the C-17 H22 contract (Boeing BC-17X) and the US Navy contract with Boeing for the production and maintenance of 108 civil B-737 and their conversion into long-range submarine hunter Multi-Mission Aircraft.

The EC is also concerned about pending legislation, in particular draft amendment (Section 817 – Prohibition on Procurement from Beneficiaries of Foreign Subsidies) to the FY06 Defense Authorisation bill (HR 1815) (Hunter Amendment).

4. DEPARTMENT OF COMMERCE SUBSIDIES

The Department of Commerce ("DOC") transfers economic resources to the US LCA industry, *inter alia*, by allowing the US LCA industry to participate in the National Institute of Standards & Technology ("NIST") Advanced Technology Program, making payments to the US LCA industry under this research programme, or enabling the US LCA industry to exploit the results thereof by means including but not limited to the foregoing or waiving of valuable patent rights, the granting of exclusive or early access to data, trade secrets and other knowledge resulting from government funded research.

5. DEPARTMENT OF LABOR SUBSIDIES

The US Department of Labor transfers economic resources to the US LCA industry through, *inter alia,* the Aerospace Industry Initiative, an element of the president's High Growth Training Initiative, by granting to Edmonds Community College in the State of Washington funds for the training of aerospace industry workers.

6. FEDERAL TAX SUBSIDIES

The US Government transfers economic resources to the US LCA industry through the federal tax system, and in particular the following tax measures:

Sections 921-927 of the Internal Revenue Code (prior to repeal) and related measures establishing special tax treatment for "Foreign Sales Corporations" ("FSCs"), including individual applications; the FSC Repeal and Extraterritorial Income Exclusion Act of 2000, Pub. L. No. 106-519, including individual applications; and the American Jobs Creation Act of 2004, Pub. L. No. 108-357 including individual applications.

The European Communities considers that these measures are inconsistent with the obligations of the United States under the following provisions:

(1)   Articles 3.1 (a) and (b) and 3.2 of the *SCM Agreement*;

(2)   Article 5 (a) and (c) of the *SCM Agreement*;

1766   DSR 2012:III

(3)   Article 6.3 (a), (b), and (c) of the *SCM Agreement*;

(4)   Article III:4 of the GATT 1994.

The European Communities is of the view that the measures referred to above are inconsistent with these provisions as such and as applied.

These measures are subsidies because in each instance there is a financial contribution by the US, State or local government and a benefit is thereby conferred within the meaning of Article 1.1(a) and (b) of the *SCM Agreement*. Each of them is specific to the US LCA industry within the meaning of Article 2 of the *SCM Agreement*.

The subsidies listed above are *de jure* or *de facto* export contingent, and contingent on the use of domestic over imported goods. The use of these measures causes adverse effects, *in particular*, serious prejudice or a threat of serious prejudice to the interests of the European Communities and material injury or threat of material injury to the European Community LCA industry:

- The effect of the measures is significant price undercutting by subsidized products of the US LCA industry as compared with the price of the European Community LCA products, or a threat thereof in violation of Articles 5(c) and 6.3(c) of the *SCM Agreement*;

- The effect of the measures is significant price depression and price suppression in the markets for LCA products or a threat thereof in violation of Articles 5(c) and 6.3(c) of the *SCM Agreement*;

- The effect of the measures is significant lost sales in the markets for LCA products or a threat thereof in violation of Articles 5(c) and 6.3(c) of the *SCM Agreement*;

- The effect of the measures is to displace or impede exports of European Community LCA products in the US market or a threat thereof in violation of Articles 5(c) and 6.3(a) of the *SCM Agreement*;

- The effect of the measures is to displace or impede exports of European Community LCA products in third country markets or a threat thereof in violation of Articles 5(c) and 6.3(b) of the *SCM Agreement*;

- The effect of the measures is material injury to the European Community LCA industry or a threat thereof in violation of Article 5(a) of the *SCM Agreement*.

- The Hunter Amendment would also be incompatible, *inter alia*, with Article 23 of the DSU and Article 32 of the *SCM Agreement*.

Articles 4.2 and 7.2 of the *SCM Agreement* together require that requests for consultations include a statement of available evidence with regard to: (1) the existence and nature of the subsidies in question, and (2) the adverse effects to the interests of the European Communities. The available evidence is listed in the Annex to this letter. It combines the available evidence already contained in the letter of 6 October 2004 and additional evidence on the existence and nature of the subsidies that has become available since then.

The European Communities reserves the right to request the United States to produce further information and documents regarding the measures in question and their effect on the interests of the European Communities. The European Communities also reserves the right to address additional measures and claims under other WTO provisions.

My authorities look forward to receiving in due course a reply from the United States to this request. The European Communities is ready to consider with the United States mutually convenient dates to hold consultations in Geneva.

ANNEX

STATEMENT OF AVAILABLE EVIDENCE

The evidence set out below is evidence available to the European Communities at this time regarding the existence and nature of the subsidies subject to this dispute, and the adverse effects caused by them to the interests of the European Communities. It is further supported by business confidential internal Airbus documents that are summarized below. The European Communities reserves the right to supplement or alter this list in the future, as required.

(a) Existence and Nature of the Subsidization

The evidence currently available to the European Communities includes the following documents. The European Communities' request for consultations describes in more detail the nature of these subsidies.

H.B. 2294, 58th Leg., 2d Spec. Sess. (Wash. 2003)

Final Bill Report, H.B. 2294

Memorandum of Agreement for Project Olympus between the Boeing Company and the State of Washington, dated as of 19 December 2003, *available at* http://www.effwa.org/pdfs/boeing_olympus.pdf

Project Olympus Master Site Development and Location Agreement between the Boeing Company and the State of Washington, dated as of 19 December 2003, *available at* http://www.effwa.org/pdfs/boeing_olympus.pdf

First Amendment to Project Olympus Master Site Development and Location Agreement between the Boeing Company and the State of Washington, dated as of 19 December 2003, *available at* http://www.effwa.org/pdfs/ boeing_amended.pdf

News Release, Office of Governor Gary Locke, *Gov. Gary Locke Unveils Tax Incentives Package to Help Land Boeing 7E7, Outlines Project's Significant Economic Impact on State*, 9 June 2003, *available at* http://www.governor.wa.gov/press/press-view.asp?pressRelease=1372&newsType=1

Bryan Corliss, *7E7 Perks Go to Boeing*, HeraldNet, 20 December 2003, *available at* http://www.heraldnet.com/stories/03/12/20/17926878.cfm

Action Washington, Boeing 7E7 Site Agreement: Tax Adjustment Package, 6 December 2004, *available at* http://dir.cted.wa.gov/DesktopModules/Documents/DocumentsView.aspx?tabID=0&alias=ActionWA&lang=en&ItemID=146&MId=116&wversion=Staging

News Release, Office of Governor Gary Locke, *Gov. Locke, Business, Labor and Government Leaders Celebrate Delivery of State's 7E7 Proposal at 'Action Washington' Rally*, 20 June 2003, *available at* http://www.governor.wa.gov/press/press-view.asp?pressRelease=1379&newsType=1

News Release, Office of Governor Gary Locke, *Gov. Gary Locke Credits States Aggressive Proposal, Unified Effort in Winning 7E7 Bid*, 16 December 2003, *available at* http://www.governor.wa.gov/press/press-view.asp?pressRelease=1491&newsType=1

David Ammons, *Boeing 7E7 Deal Includes Perks*, The Olympian, 22 January 2004, *available at* http://www.theolympian.com/home/news/20040122/business/19223_Printer.shtml

Our View: Sweet Boeing Deal Leaves a Sour Taste, King County Journal, 22 January 2004, *available at* http://www.kingcountyjournal.com/sited/story/html/154305

Press Release, Evergreen Freedom Foundation, *Details of Boeing Agreement Revealed*, 21 January 2004, *available at* http://www.effwa.org/press_releases/2004_01_21a.php

Open Letter to Washington Legislators from Bob Williams, President of EFF, 15 October 2004, *available at* http://www.effwa.org/commentaries/2004_10_15.php

John Gillie, *A Smooth Landing for the 7E7*, The News Tribune, 20 December 2004, *available at* http://www.thenewstribune.com/business/aerospace/story/4356715p-4127928c.html

Action Washington, *available at* http://dir.cted.wa.gov/portal/alias__ActionWA/lang__en/tabID__63/DesktopDefault.aspx

State of Washington, House and Senate Floor Debates, HB 2294, 10-11 June 2003

Executive Message Video, 20 June 2003, *available at* http://dir.cted.wa.gov/DesktopModules/Documents/DocumentsView.aspx?tabID=0&alias=ActionWA&lang=en&ItemID=177&MId=115&wversion=Staging

Washington State and the Boeing Company: Working Together for the Boeing 7E7 Dreamliner, Continuing Support and Collaborative Actions, September Presentation, Greenville, SC (September 2003)

Project Management Services Contract Between State of Washington Employment Security Department and Accenture, LLP, ESD Contract No. 05-415-PS, 5 May 2005, and related exhibits

Boeing's 747 Large Cargo Freighter Development on Plan, 22 February 2005, *available at* http://www.boeing.com/news/releases/2005/q1/nr_050222g.html

Snohomish County Airport, Aircraft Rate Schedule, effective 1 April 2002

Aircraft Models and Weights for Reporting All-Cargo Data to FAA, CY 2003 FAA ACAIS, February 2005, *available at* http://www.faa.gov/arp/planning/stats/2005/Cy04CargoAircraftEnc2.pdf

Joint Use Agreement between Snohomish County and the Boeing Company with regard to Boeing's use of the Snohomish County Airport (Paine Field), dated 17 June 1966, and all subsequent amendments and letter agreements in relation thereto, including those dated 14 July 1969, 25 August 1999, 7 December 2000, 17 December 2002, and any amendments pursuant to the Project Olympus Master Site Agreement

Port of Everett, Rail/Barge Transfer Facility, *available at* http://www.portofeverett.com/boeingrailbarge.shtml

Port Commission authorizes staff to go out to bid on Rail-Barge Facility, Port of Everett Press Release, 26 May 2005, *available at* http://www.portofeverett.com/press/2005_05_26BidRailBarg.shtml

City of Everett Ordinance 2759-04 (2004), amending Chapter 3.24 of the Everett Municipal Code

Boeing Major Production Facilities, Everett, Washington, *available at* http://www.boeing.com/commercial/facilities/

Spreadsheets of top Everett manufacturing companies as compiled by the City of Everett Mayor's Office

Economic Revitalization and Reinvestment Act, S.B. 281, 2003 Sess., Reg. Sess., § 1(e) (Kan. 2003)

Supplemental Note on S.B. 281, *available at* http://www.kslegislature.org/supplemental/2004/SN0281.pdf

Richard Williamson, *Kansas Lands Piece of Jet, but Boeing May not Use the Bonds*, The Bond Buyer, 24 November 2003

Caroline Daniel, *Boeing Eyes Highest Handout in Bid to Soar Above Europe*, The Financial Times, 16 June 2003

Steve Painter, *Boeing Wichita Lands State Bonds*, The Wichita Eagle, 22 May 2003

Jean Hays, *Tweaks to Boeing Bill Pass Senate*, The Wichita Eagle, 7 May 2003

Chris Grenz, *Boeing Banking on State*, The Topeka Capital-Journal, 20 April 2003

Kansas Department of Commerce, Legislative Session Track for S.B. 281, *available at* http://kdoch.state.ks.us:82/NewsApp/news_legislative_updates_bill_display.jsp?id=1049378817480

Steve Painter and Molly McMillin, *State Sees Bonds as Boeing's Best Shot*, The Wichita Eagle, 2 April 2003

Kansas Development Finance Authority, Financial Statements Years Ended June 30, 2003 and 2002, and Independent Auditors' Report, *available at* http://www.kdfa.org/admin/UPLOADS/FinalAuditReport-FY2003.pdf

Now You Know: Who Received Incentives? The Wichita Eagle, 11 July 2004

City of Wichita, *IRB Overview, "Industrial Revenue Bond Issuance in the State of Kansas,"* *available at* http://www.wichita.gov/Business/EconomicDevelopment/IRB/IRBOverview.htm

Minutes of Meetings of the Wichita City Council, 1995-2005, *available at* http://www.wichitagov.org/Government/MinutesAndAgendas/CityCouncil/

Lillian Zier Martell, The Wichita Eagle, 10 November 1999

David Dinell, *City approves Boeing industrial revenue bonds*, 7 November 2002, *available at* http://wichita.bizjournals.com/wichita/stories/2002/11/04/daily44.html

Karen Pierog, *Wichita Council OKs Tax Break for Boeing*, Reuters News Service, 10 November 1999

Council approves Boeing bonds, Wichita Business Journal, 14 November 2000, *available at* http://wichita.bizjournals.com/wichita/stories/2000/11/13/daily21.html

City of Wichita Industrial Revenue Bond Policy, Resolution No. R-98-151, *available at* http://www.wichita.gov/NR/rdonlyres/5C4F7504-A681-47EC-8369-F1AD7C400FAE/0/Industrial_Revenue_Bond_Policy_06d.pdf

Wichita City Council Ordinance Nos. 46-401 (2004), 45-914 (2003), 45-495 (2002), 45-133 (2001), 44-811 (2000), 44-428 (1999), 44-102 (1998), 43-642 (1997), 43-325 (1996), 42-949 (1995), 42-553 (1994), 42-228 (1993), 41-916 (1992), and 41-592 (1991)

Bond transcripts for industrial revenue bonds issued on behalf of Boeing by the City of Wichita since 1979

Letters of intent for Industrial Revenue Bonds issued to the US LCA industry pursuant to actions of the Wichita City Council taken on 17 May 2005, 13 July 2004, 9 November 1999, 13 February 1996, 24 March 1992, 5 December 1989, 21 December 1982, 9 June 1981, and 23 October 1979

Tax Abatement Cost-Benefit Analyses for US LCA-industry industrial revenue bonds performed by the Center for Economic Development and Business Research, W. Frank Barton School of Business, Wichita State University

Council approves Onex IRBs, Wichita Business Journal, 17 May 2005, *available at* http://wichita.bizjournals.com/wichita/stories/2005/05/16/daily16.html

K.S.A. §§ 12-1740 *et seq.*, as amended

K.S.A. §§ 79-201 *et seq.*, as amended, and Article 11, Section 13 of the Constitution of the State of Kansas

K.S.A. §§ 79-3601 *et seq.*, as amended

Boeing Commercial Airplanes, Wichita Division, "Wichita Overview," *available at* http://www.boeing.com/commercial/wichita/commercial.htm

List maintained by the City of Wichita that contains information about all IRBs issued by the City of Wichita since 1979

City of Wichita/Sedgwick County Economic Development Incentives Policy, *available at* http://www.wichita.gov/NR/rdonlyres/5C4F7504-A681-47EC-8369-F1AD7C400FAE/0/Industrial_Revenue_Bond_Policy_06d.pdf

The City of Wichita Industrial Revenue Bond Policy, Resolution No. R-98-151

Property Tax Exemption Orders issued by the Kansas Board of Tax Appeals for property owned by or leased to the Boeing Company from FY 1985 to present

Property Tax Exemption Applications filed with the Kansas Board of Tax Appeals by the Boeing Company from FY 1985 to present

Kansas Department of Revenue Ruling No. 19-1996-1, 1 July 1989

Kansas Private Letter Ruling No. P-2001-098, 30 September 2001

Kansas Private Letter Ruling No. P-1999-44, 26 February 1999

Funding provided by the State of Kansas, Kansas Technology Enterprise Corporation ("KTEC"), and the Federal Government to the National Institute for Aviation Research at Wichita State University for collaborations with the US LCA industry, as detailed in the National Institute for Aviation Research, 2003 Annual Report

Economic Development for a Growing Economy Tax Credit Act, Illinois Public Act 91-476, as amended

35 Ill. Comp. Stat. §§ 10/5 *et seq.*

35 Ill. Comp. Stat. §§ 5/211 *et seq.*

Corporate Headquarters Relocation Act, Illinois Public Act 92-0207, 20 Ill. Comp. Stat. §§ 611/1 *et seq.*

35 Ill. Comp. Stat. § 200/18-165

Ordinance of the County of Cook, Illinois, Approving Execution of a Tax Reimbursement Payment Agreement with the Boeing Company (2001)

Ordinance of the City of Chicago, Illinois, Approving Execution of a Tax Reimbursement Payment Agreement with the Boeing Company (2001)

The Boeing Company – Corporate Headquarters Relocation Grant Application (10 December 2001), prepared for the Illinois Department of Commerce and Community Affairs

John O'Connor, *Chicago's Boeing Incentives May Be Cut*, Denver Post, 24 May 2001

Tax Reimbursement Payment Agreement Between the City of Chicago and the Boeing Company, 1 November 2001, attached as Exhibit A to An Ordinance of the City of Chicago, Illinois Approving Execution of a Tax Reimbursement Payment Agreement with the Boeing Company (ordinance *available at* http://egov.cityofchicago/webportal/COCWebPortal/COC_Editorial/ Boeing.txt)

Tax Reimbursement Payment Agreement Between the County of Cook and The Boeing Company, 1 November 2001

Boeing amended certification of real estate taxes paid in accordance with the Lease Agreement (attached to Boeing's 23 July 2003 request for Tax Reimbursement from the County of Cook)

Boeing certification of real estate taxes paid in accordance with the Lease Agreement (2 December 2003) (attached to Boeing's 29 January 2004 request for Tax Reimbursement Payment from the City of Chicago)

Statement of Robert Kunze (Deputy Commissioner, Department of Planning and Development, City of Chicago), Report of the Committee on Finance, Board of Commissioners of Cook County, 12 September 2001, *available at* http://www.co.cook.il.us/secretary/CommitteePages/Meeting%20Reports/Financ e%20Committee/2001/09-12-01.htm

Meeting of the Cook County Board of Commissioners: Post Agenda Report, 29 September 2001, *available at* http://www.cookctyclerk.com/agendas/ 2001/092001/092001meeting.pdf

Boeing Moving Headquarters to Chicago, 14 May 2000, *available at* http://www.spaceandtech.com/ digest/sd2001-19/sd2001-19-001.shtml

City of Chicago, Office of City Comptroller, *Order Payment Voucher*, No. PV08030801779

City of Chicago, Office of City Comptroller, *Order Payment Voucher*, No. PV08040800041

City of Chicago, Office of City Comptroller, *Order Payment Voucher*, No. PV08040801118

City of Chicago, Office of City Comptroller, *Order Payment Voucher*, No. PV08040800574

Cook County, Bureau of Finance, *Cashier's Check 461492*, 25 May 2004

Cook County, Bureau of Finance, *Cashier's Check 456646*, 23 December 2003

Boeing Headquarters Relocation Projected Cost/Benefit Analysis

Lease Termination Compensation Agreement between 100 North Riverside, LLC and the City of Chicago, 15 January 2003

Jack Lyne, *US$63 million in Incentives, Last-Second Space Deal Help Chicago Land Boeing*, June 2001, *available at* www.conway.com/ssinsider/incentive/ti0106.htm

Press Release from The Boeing Company, Boeing Begins World Headquarters Operations in Chicago (4 September 2001), available at http://www.boeing.com/news/releases/2001/q3/nr_010904z.htm

Press Release from the Office of Illinois Governor George Ryan (10 May 2001), available at http://www.state.il.us/gov/press/01/may/0510boeing.htm

Ron Starner and Mark Arend, "Behind Boeing's Flight Plan: Why the New Chicago Headquarters is Just Part of the Story," Site Selection Magazine, September 2001, available at http://www.siteselection.com/issues/2001/sep/p572

Illinois Economic and Fiscal Commission, Corporate Incentives in the State of Illinois (August 2001)

Memo to Honorable Members of the General Assembly from Pam McDonough, Director, Department of Commerce and Community Affairs, regarding the Corporate Headquarters Relocation Act (23 May 2001)

State of Illinois, 92nd General Assembly, House of Representatives, Transcription Debate, 69th Legislative Day, 31 May 2001

Jeff McCourt and Greg LeRoy, Good Jobs First, *A Better Deal for Illinois: Improving Economic Development Policy* (January 2003), available at http://www.heartland.org/Article.cfm?artId=12828

Corporate Headquarters Relocation Act Master Agreement between The Illinois Department of Commerce and Community Affairs and The Boeing Company (27 March 2002)

Marc J. Lane, *It Pays to Invest in State's Homegrown Technology*, 24 Crain's Chicago Bus. 11, 2001 WL 7067142

Reports of Job Creation/Retention and Capital Improvements Expenditures for several years

EDGE Tax Credit Report of Annual Compliance for Year Ending 12/31/2003

Report of the Committee on Finance, Board of Commissioners of Cook County (12 September 2001), *available at* http://www.co.cook.il.us/secretary/ CommitteePages/Meeting%20Reports/Finance%20Committee/2001/09-12-01.htm

Hearing Charter, *The Future of Aeronautics at NASA: Hearing Before the House Subcomm. on Space and Aeronautics of the Comm. on Science*, 16 March 2005

Statement of Dr. J. Victor Lebacqz, NASA Associate Administrator for Aeronautics Research, before the House Subcommittee on Space and Aeronautics, 16 March 2005

Achieving Aeronautics Leadership, NASA Aeronautics Strategic Enterprise Plan, 1995-2000, April 1995

Statement of Dr. John M. Klineberg, Chair, Committee to Review NASA's Aeronautics Technology Program, Aeronautics and Space Engineering Board, Division on Engineering and Physical Sciences, National Research Council, the National Academies, before the House Subcommittee on Space and Aeronautics, 16 March 2005

NASA Langley Research Center, Economic Impact, Fiscal Year 1998

Joseph R. Chambers, *Concept to Reality: Contributions of the NASA Langley Research Center to US Civil Aircraft of the 1990s* (2003)

Minutes of the NASA Advisory Council, Aerospace Technology Advisory Committee, and Technology and Commercialization Advisory Committee

Federal Support for US Aeronautics Industry: Hearing Before the House Subcomm. on Government Activities and Transportation of the Comm. on Government Operations, 102nd Cong. 182 (1992)

FY98 Budget for NASA: Hearing Before the Senate Subcomm. on Science, Technology and Space of the Comm. on Commerce, Science and Transportation, 105th Cong. (1997), Federal News Service, 24 April 1997

Competitiveness of the Aerospace Industry: Hearing on S. 419 Before the Senate Comm. on Commerce, Science, and Transportation, 103rd Cong. 80-81 (1993)

The Clinton Administration's Initiative to Promote a Strong Competitive Aviation Industry, January 1994

Joe Cobb, *Clinton's Welcome Plan to Improve Air Travel*, Heritage Foundation Reports, 28 January 1994

Report of the Panel

Competition in the US Aircraft Manufacturing Industry: Hearing before the House Subcomm. on Aviation of the Comm. on Transportation and Infrastructure, 107th Cong. 4 (2001)

Jeffrey L. Ethell, *Fuel Economy in Aviation*, NASA SP-462

NASA's Aeronautics Program: Hearing Before the Senate Subcomm. on Science, Technology and Space of the Comm. on Commerce, Science and Transportation, 107th Cong. (2001), FDCH Political Transcripts, 24 April 2001

Innovations in Aircraft Design, *available at* http://www.sti.nasa.gov/tto/spinoff1997/t1.html

Statement of Billy M. Glover, Director of Environmental Performance Strategy, Boeing Commercial Airplanes, before the House Subcommittee on Aviation of the Committee on Transportation and Infrastructure, 5 June 2003

Dawn C. Jegley and Harold G. Bush, *Structural Response and Failure of a Full-Scale Stitched Graphite-Epoxy Wing*, AIAA Paper No. 2001-1334-CP

Randy Tinseth, *Boeing Innovations in Technology and Airplane Design*, April 2004

National Aeronautics and Space Act of 1958, Pub. L. No. 85-568

NASA Appropriations Acts, P.L. 94-116 (FY 1976); P.L. 94-378 (FY 1977); P.L. 95-119 (FY 1978); P.L. 95-392 (FY 1979); P.L. 96-103 (FY 1980); P.L. 96-526 (FY 1981); P.L. 97-101 (FY 1982); P.L. 97-272 (FY 1983); P.L. 98-45 (FY 1984); P.L. 98-371 (FY 1985); P.L. 99-160 (FY 1986); P.L. 99-500 & P.L. 99-591 (FY 1987); P.L. 100-202 (FY 1988); P.L. 100-404 (FY 1989); P.L. 101-144 (FY 1990); P.L. 101-507 (FY 1991); P.L. 102-139 (FY 1992); P.L. 102-389 (FY 1993); P.L. 103-124 (FY 1994); P.L. 103-327 (FY 1995); P.L. 104-134 (FY 1996); P.L. 104-204 (FY 1997); P.L. 105-65 (FY 1998); P.L. 105-276 (FY 1999); P.L. 106-74 (FY 2000); P.L. 106-377 (FY 2001); P.L. 107-73 & P.L. 107-117 (FY 2002); P.L. 108-7 (FY 2003); P.L. 108-199 (FY 2004); P.L. 108-447 (FY 2005)

Basis of NASA FY 1976-FY 2006 Funding Requirements, including sections relevant to the Aircraft Energy Efficiency ("ACEE"), Materials and Structures Systems Technology ("MSST"), Advanced Composites Technology ("ACT"), High Speed Research ("HSR"), Advanced Subsonic Technology ("AST"), High Performance Computing and Communications ("HPCC"), Aviation Safety/Aviation Safety & Security/Aviation Security & Safety ("Aviation Safety"), Quiet Aircraft Technology ("QAT"), Vehicle Systems, and Research and Technology Base ("R&T Base") Programs, as well as Research and Program Management ("R&PM"), and Institutional Support

Basis of NASA ACEE FY 1976-FY 1987 Funding Requirements

Basis of NASA MSST FY 1988-FY 1995 Funding Requirements

Basis of NASA ACT FY 1996-FY 1997 Funding Requirements

Basis of NASA HSR FY 1990-FY 2001 Funding Requirements

Basis of NASA AST FY 1992-FY 2001 Funding Requirements

Basis of NASA HPCC FY 1991-FY 2003 Funding Requirements

Basis of Aviation Safety FY 2000-FY 2006 Funding Requirements

Basis of NASA QAT FY 2000-FY 2006 Funding Requirements

Basis of NASA Vehicle Systems FY 2003-FY 2006 Funding Requirements

Basis of NASA R&T Base FY 1991-FY 2004 Funding Requirements

Basis of NASA R&PM FY 1976-FY 2003 Funding Requirements

Basis of NASA Aerospace Institutional Support FY 2002-FY 2005 Funding Requirements

48 C.F.R. § 31. 205-18

14 C.F.R. § 1274.204(g)

48 C.F.R. §§ 9904.420 *et seq.*

Requirements for Documentation, Approval, and Dissemination of NASA Scientific and Technical Information, section 4.5.7.1 (NPG 2200.2A)

48 C.F.R. §§ 27.400 *et seq.*

L.B. Ilcewicz, P.J. Smith, C.T. Hanson, T.H. Walker, S.L. Metschan, G.E. Mabson, K.S. Willden, B.W. Flynn, D.B. Scholz, D.R. Polland, H.G. Fredrikson, J.T. Olson, and B.F. Backman, The Boeing Company, Seattle, WA, NASA/CR 4734, *Advanced Technology Composite Fuselage—Program Overview*, April 1997

Robert H. Kinder, Douglas Aircraft Company, N95-29030, *Impact of Composites on Future Transport Aircraft*

John Quinlivan, N95-29031, *Challenges and Payoff of Composites in Transport Aircraft: 777 Empennage and Future Applications*

R.H. Liebeck, D.A. Andrastek, J. Chau, R. Girvin, R. Lyon, B.K. Rawdon, P.W. Scott, R.A. Wright, McDonnell Douglas Aerospace, Long Beach, CA, NASA/CR-195443, *Advanced Subsonic Airplane Design & Economic Studies*, April 1995

L.B. Ilcewicz, T.H. Walker, K.S. Willden, G.D. Swanson, G. Truslove, S.L. Metschan, and C.L. Pfahl, The Boeing Company, Seattle, WA, NASA/CR-4418, *Application of a Design-Build Team Approach to Low Cost and Weight Composite Fuselage Structure*, 1991

Individual Budgets for DOD Project Related Elements of US Navy, Army, and the Defense Research Projects Agency

10 U.S.C. §§ 2511, 2521

DOD Appropriations Acts P.L. 101-511 (FY 1991); P.L. 102-172 (FY 1992); P.L. 102-396 (FY 993); P.L. 103-139 (FY 1994); P.L. 103-335 (FY 1995); P.L. 104-61 (FY 1996); P.L. 104-208 (FY 1997); P.L. 105-56 (FY 1998); P.L. 105-262 (FY 1999); P.L. 106-79 (FY 2000); P.L. 106-259 (FY 2001); P.L. 107-117 (FY 2002); P.L. 107-248 (FY 2003); P.L. 108-87 (FY 2004); P.L. 108-287 (FY 2005)

RDT&E US Civil Aircraft Related Project Element Budgets for FY 1991-FY 2005, including: Defense Research Sciences (PE# 0601102F), Materials (PE# 0602102F), Aerospace Flight Dynamics\Vehicle Technologies (PE# 0602201F), Aerospace Propulsion (PE# 0602203F), Aerospace Sensors (PE# 0602204F), Dual Use Applications\Science & Technology (PE# 0602805F), Advanced Materials for Weapon Systems (PE# 0603112F), Flight Vehicle Technology (PE# 0603205F), Aerospace Structures\Technology Dev/Demo (PE# 0603211F), Aerospace Propulsion & Power Technology (PE# 0603216F), Flight Vehicle Technology Integration (PE# 0603245F), RDT&E For Aging Aircraft (PE# 0605011F), Manufacturing Technology/Industrial Preparedness (PE# 0603771F/0708011F/0708011N), C-17 (PE# 0401130F/0604231F), CV-22 (PE# 0401318F), Joint Strike Fighter (PE# 0603800F/0603800N/0603800E/0604800F/0604800N), AV-8B Aircraft (PE# 0604214N), Comanche (PE# 0604223A), F-22 (PE# 0604239F), B-2 Advanced Technology Bomber (PE# 0604240F), V-22 (PE# 0604262N), A-6 Squadron (PE# 0204134N), F/A-18 Squadrons (PE# 0204136N), Dual Use Applications Program (including its predecessor, the Technology Reinvestment Project)

DOD RDT&E Budget Item Justification, Exhibits R-2, FY 1991-FY 2006

DOD FY 1991-FY 2006 Budgets for RDT&E Programs (Exhibit R-1), DOD Component Summary

Department of Defense Office of the Inspector General, "Major Range and Test Facility Base," D-2004-035, 8 December 2003

Report of 15 February 2005 of the General Accountability Office (GAO) of the United States' Government to the Secretary of Defense, Contract Management, The Air Force Should Improve How It Purchases AWACS Spare Parts, GAO-05-169.

Management Accountability Review of the Boeing KC-767A Tanker Program, Office of the Inspector General of the Department of Defense, 13 May 2005, Report No OIG-2004-171, available at: http:/www.dodig.osd.mil/tanker.htm.

Daily Briefing, 15 April 2005

GAO says problems justify rebidding C-130 contract

By Amy Klamper, CongressDaily, available at: http://www.govexec.com/dailyfed/0405/041505cdam2.htm

E-Mails Detail Air Force Push for Boeing Deal

Pentagon Official Called Proposal Lease of Tankers a "Bailout", Report Finds

By R. Jeffrey Smith, Washington Post, Tuesday 7 June 2005; A01

Holes in the Tanker Story

Washington Post, Monday, 20 June 2005; A14

Factual information and various statements covering, among other things, the "Tanker Deal" available at http:/www.pogo.org/p/x/archivecontractover.html (Project on Government Oversight website)

Report of 14 April 2005 of the General Accountability Office (GAO) of the United States' Government, Air Force Procurement, Protests Challenging Role of Biased Official Sustained, GAO-05-436T, available at: http:/www.gao.gov/new.items/d05436t.pdf

Congressional Budget Office (CBO) Report, Letter of Douglas Holtz-Eakin, Director addressed to the Honorable Don Nickles, Chairman of the Committee on the Budget United States Senate dated 26 August 2003 and related documents available at: http:/www.cbo.gov/showdoc.cfm?index=4494&sequence=0

Statement of The Honorable Joseph E. Schmitz, Inspector General, Department of Defense before the Airland Subcommittee, Senate Committee on Armed Services on "Air Force Acquisition Oversight", 14 April 2005 available at: http://armed-services.senate.gov/statemnt/2005/April/Schmitz%2004-14-05.pdf

DOD Follow-Up on Boeing Probe Results in 8 Contracts Referred to IG, in particular the National Polar-orbiting Operational Environmental Satellite System-Conical Microwave Imager Sensor, Boeing, the C-22 Replacement Program (C-40), Boeing, the KC-135 Programmed Depot Maintenance, Boeing/Pemco, the C-40 Lease and Purchase Program, Boeing, the upgrade to the avionics of the C-130J aircraft, the C-17 H22 contract, the Boeing KC-767A tanker program, the contract for the purchase of certain spare parts for the Airborne Warning and Control System (AWACS) aircraft and Pentagon statement on DCMA Identified Questionable Contracts, BNA of 15 February 2005.

FY06 Defense Authorisation bill (HR 1815), House Armed Services Committee Chairman Duncan Hunter's amendment (Section 817 – Prohibition on Procurement from Beneficiaries of Foreign Subsidies) adopted by the US House on 25 May 2005.

Jeanne Rapley, *Testing for Private Industry: A Legal Perspective*, powerpoint presentation, 17 March 1997, *available at* http://www.dtc.army.mil/apbi/ 1997/legal97/index.html

AEDC, "Commercial Success Stories," *available at* http://www.arnold.af.mil/ aedc/commercial/commercial.pdf

10 U.S.C. § 2681

10 U.S.C. § 2539b

NAWCAD, "Commercial Service Agreements (CSAs)," *available at* http://nawcadcounsel.navair.navy.mil/CSAs.htm

US General Accounting Office, "Aerospace Testing: Promise of Closer NASA/DOD Cooperation Remains Largely Unfulfilled," GAO/NSIAD-98-52, March 1998

US Department of Labor Employment & Training Administration News Release, *US Secretary of Labor Elaine L. Chao Announces Nearly $1.5 Million to Train Washington Workers for Careers in the Aerospace Industry*, 5 November 2004, available at http://www.doleta.gov/whatsnew/new_ releases/november052004-Washington.cfm

Notification of Award for Grant No. AN-14571-05-60 to Edmonds Community College, 4 February 2005

Workforce Investment Act of 1998, Pub. L. No. 105-220 (1998)

Statement of Work for Grant No. AN-14571-05-60 to Edmonds Community College, undated

35 U.S.C. §§ 200 *et seq.*

48 C.F.R. §§ 27.300 *et seq.*

Memorandum to the Heads of Executive Departments and Agencies: Government Patent Policy, Pub. Papers 248 (18 February 1983)

Executive Order 12591 (10 April 1987)

14 C.F.R. §§ 1274.911 – 1274.914

48 C.F.R. §§ 1827.301 *et seq.*

48 C.F.R. §§ 227.303 *et seq.*

48 C.F.R. §§ 227.7100 *et seq.*

Contract No. NAS1-20267

19 C.F.R. § 351.524(b) (1998)

NASA Langley Research Center, High-Speed Research Program: Technology Transfer Control Handbook (April 1998)

National Research Council, Committee on High Speed Research, US Supersonic Commercial Aircraft: Assessing NASA's High Speed Research Program (1997)

James Schultz, "HSR Leaves Legacy of Spinoffs," Aerospace America, September 1999

United States notification to the WTO Committee on Subsidies and Countervailing Measures, G/SCM/N/3/USA/Suppl.1 (19 November 1998)

United States Updating and New and Full Notification to the WTO Committee on Subsidies and Countervailing Measures, G/SCM/N/48/USA (2 July 2002)

Aviation Systems Analysis Capability, Executive Assistant Development, NASA/CR-1999-209119, Logistics Management Institute, March 1999

Testimony to the Subcommittee on Technology, Environment, and Aviation of the US House of Representatives, 10 February 1994, Federal Document Clearing House, 1994 WL 214062

Advanced Subsonic Technology Program, Technology Transfer Control Handbook (August 1998)

Federal News Service, Hearing of the Science, Technology and Space Subcommittee of the Senate Commerce, Science and Transportation Committee, 24 April 1997

Flight International, 11 August 1999

NASA HPCC, Status of Ames Sponsored HPCC NASA Research Announcements

NASA HPCC, Computational Aerospace Sciences ("CAS") Project Description

NASA HPCC, Computational Aerospace Sciences NASA HPCC 1999 Brochure

NASA HPCC, Mission Description

NASA Budget Estimates for FY 1993-FY 2003, NASA Mission Support, Research and Program Management

NASA News, Boeing Names New Airplane Wing Composites Development Center

35 U.S.C. §§ 154, 271

NASA Property Rights in Inventions, 42 U.S.C. §§ 2457 *et seq.*

NASA Patent Waiver Regulations, 14 C.F.R. §§ 1245 *et seq.*

Evidence from Patents and Patent Citations on the Impact of NASA and other Federal Labs on Commercial Innovation, National Bureau of Economic Research (May 1997)

General Information Concerning Patents, published by USPTO

Sylvia K. Kraemer, NASA's Director of Policy Development Office of Policy and Plans, Monopolies, and the Cold War: The Origins and Consequences of NASA Patent Policy, 1958-1998 (October 1999)

NASA Office of Policy and Plans, Value of Patent Rights Waived by NASA

US Patent No. 6,497,389

US Patent No. 6,126,110

US Patent No. 6,053,050

US Patent No. 6,014,606

US Patent No. 5,971,252

US Patent No. 6,138,895

US Patent No. 5,953,231

US Patent No. 5,931,107

US Patent No. 5,902,535

US Patent No. 5,242,523

US Patent No. 5,893, 535

US Patent No. 5,909,858

US Patent No. 5,899,413

US Patent No. 5,740,984

US Patent No. 5,681,013

Independent Research and Development and Bid and Proposal Costs: Payments to Contractors, 10 U.S.C. § 2372

Independent Research and Development and Bid and Proposal Cost Federal Acquisition Rule, 48 C.F.R. § 31.205-18

Independent Research and Development and Bid and Proposal Cost Defense Acquisition Rule, 48 C.F.R. § 231.205-18

Department of Defense Directive Regarding IR&D Number 3204.1 (10 May 1999)

Internal Revenue Service National Office Technical Advice Memorandum, Private Ruling 8633004 (unpublished), 1986 PLR LEXIS 2296 (9 May 1986)

Defense Contract Audit Agency Contract Audit Manual, DCAAM 7640.1, January 2001

DOD Independent Research & Development, Program Report (May 2002)

Assessing the Impact of Regulatory and Legislative Changes to the Independent Research and Development Program, Prepared for Office of the Director, Defense Research & Engineering Acquisition and Technology, DOD (14 March 1997)

Michael E. Davey & Dahlia Stein, Congressional Research Service Report for Congress: DOD's Independent Research and Development Program: Changes and Issues (17 December 1993)

10 U.S.C. § 2324(l)(1) (version in effect from FY 1995-FY 2001)

10 U.S.C. § 2306a (version in effect FY 1991-FY 1992)

10 U.S.C. § 2324(m)

48 C.F.R. § 16.301-3(a)(1)

48 C.F.R. § 12.207

48 C.F.R. §§ 37.602-4, *et seq.*

48 C.F.R. § 36.207(a)

48 C.F.R. § 216.104-70(b)(2), (c), (d)(2)

48 C.F.R. § 235.006(b)(i)

48 C.F.R. § 35.006(c)

Defense Contract Audit Agency, Independent Research and Development and Bid and Proposal Costs Incurred by Major Defense Contractors (Multiple Reports for Fiscal Years 1989 through 2004)

GSA Contract Database

Congressional Office of Technology Assessment, Competing Economies: Government Support of Large Civil Aircraft Industries of Japan, Europe and the United States (Washington, 1991)

Dual Use Technology 1995 Report

BC-17X Background Information

US Department of Defense News Release: Technology Reinvestment Project Announces FY 94 Selections, 25 October 1994

Commerce Business Daily, "Technology Reinvestment Project Program Announcement," 21 October 1994

Anne Kellogg, "Clinton Administration to Diversify Defense Under Attack," The Hartford Courant, 11 May 1996, p. A9

Richard Burnett, "Defense Conversion Faces Own War; The Program Has Come Under Attack by Congress as Lawmakers Search for Prime Budget Cuts," Orlando Sentinel, 15 October 1995, p. H1

Potomac Institute for Policy Studies, A Review of the Technology Reinvestment Project, 30 January 1999

National Defense Authorization Act for Fiscal Year 1997, 10 U.S.C. § 2511

Defense Acquisition Reform: Hearing before the Subcommittee on Acquisition and Technology of the Senate Committee on Armed Services, 105th Congress, 19 March 1997 (Statement of Hon. Paul G. Kaminski, Under Secretary of Defense for Acquisition and Technology)

Dual Use Science and Technology Program Web Site, at Fact Sheet hyperlink

FY02 Air Force Dual Use Science & Technology Annual Competition: Updated FY 02 Solicitation Schedule

Department of Defense, Report to Congress on the Activities of the DOD Office of Technology Transition, January 1998

Department of Defense, Dual Use Science & Technology Report to Congress, March 1999, Appendix C

DOD Research & Development Contracting Definitions, 48 C.F.R. § 235

Omnibus Trade and Competitiveness Act of 1988, Pub. L. No. 100-418, codified at 15 U.S.C. § 278n

American Technology Preeminence Act of 1991, Pub. L. No. 102-245

National Institute of Standards & Technology Rules, 15 C.F.R. §§ 295.1 *et seq.*

NISTIR-6099, Connie K.N. Chang, ATP Eligibility Criteria for US Subsidiaries of Foreign-owned Companies: Legislation, Implementation and Results, Chapter 1

NISTIR-5896, Rosalie Ruegg, Guidelines For Proposing Economic Evaluation Studies to The Advanced Technology Program (ATP), Chapter 1.4

Slides by Marc G. Stanley, Acting Director of ATP (ATP Awards to Date by Technology Area (1990-2001))

US Secretary of Commerce, A Progress Report on the Impacts of an Industry-Government Technology Partnership

NISTIR-6491, Jeanne W. Powell and Karen L. Lellock, Development, Commercialization, and Diffusion of Enabling Technologies: Progress Report (2000)

Slides About the ATP Proposers' Conference (1999)

Replies to Questions Posed by Chile, the European Community, Mexico and Poland Regarding the New and Full Notification of the United States, G/SCM/Q2/USA/20 (7 April 1999)

NIST Overview of the Advanced Technology Program

Statements of US Senators Danforth and Hollings Regarding ATP Program, 140 Cong. Rec. S2851 (11 March 1994), Cong. Rec. S2763 (10 March 1994)

Historical Statistics on Awards/Winners (1990 – 5 September 2002)

ATP Project Briefs, Projects 93-01-0089 (CVD Diamond-Coated Rotating Tools for Machining Advanced Composite Materials), 95-12-0024 (An Agent-Based Framework for Integrated Intelligent Planning – Execution), 95-01-0108 (Precision Optoelectronics Assembly), 91-01-0267 (PREAMP – Pre-competitive Advanced Manufacturing of Electrical Products), 97-05-0020 (EECOMS: Extended Enterprise Coalition for Integrated Collaborative Manufacturing Systems), and 98-01-0168 (Hot Metal Gas Forming)

Sections 921-927 of the Internal Revenue Code (prior to repeal) and related measures

FSC Repeal and Extraterritorial Income Exclusion Act of 2000, Pub. L. No. 106-519

American Jobs Creation Act of 2004, Pub. L. No. 108-357

(b)   Serious Prejudice to the Interests of the European Communities

The European Communities has voluminous evidence that the subsidies granted to the US LCA industry have caused and continue to cause adverse effects through significant price suppression or depression of prices of LCA worldwide, significant price undercutting and significant lost sales by the Community industry in the market for LCA.

The evidence available includes the following materials:

Information regarding Airbus products, including at http://www.airbus.com/en/aircraftfamilies/ and http://www.boeing.com/commercial/flash.html, and related links and company information

Airbus and Boeing documents describing aircraft in terms of range and seats

Boeing pricing, order and delivery data, including at http://www.boeing.com/commercial/prices/ and http://active.boeing.com/commercial/orders/userdefinedselection.cfm

Airbus order and delivery data, including at http://www.airbus.com/en/corporate/orders_and_deliveries/ (and in internal business confidential sources)

Airbus marketing material analysing the competitive relationship between the various Airbus and Boeing products

Airclaims, Client Aviation System Inquiry data (paid access database)

Boeing Current Market Outlook, various editions (including at http://www.boeing.com/commercial/cmo/index.shtml)

Airbus Global Market Forecast, various editions (including at http://www.airbus.com/store/mm_repository/pdf/att00003033/media_object_file _GMF2004_full_issue.pdf)

"Bouncing Boeing," The Economist, 13 June 1998

Report of the Panel

"Airbus Eclipses Boeing, Sets Order Book Record," Aviation Week and Space Technology, 10 January 2000

"Boeing increases base price for commercial aircraft by 5 percent," Seattle Times, 10 July 1998

Cumulative Deliveries for the Boeing 737 Family since 1974

"Airbus bets the company," The Economist, 18 March 2000

"Boeing, Banking on a big bird," The Economist, 12 March 1994

"Wall Street frets over Boeing," Airline Business, August 1998

"Just in time, not just in case; Boeing's push for production casts," Air Transport World, April 1994

"Boeing hit by 737 problems," Financial Times, 23 April 1998

"Airbus, Boeing in costs dogfight," Financial Times, 12 July 1994

"USA: Strong gains expected from Boeing commercial unit," The Seattle Times, 14 January 2000

"USA: Software City starts to find major bugs in reality," Independent, 5 December 1998

"USA: City – what's bugging Boeing," Sunday Telegraph, 6 September 1998

"USA: Boeing sold below cost, study suggests," The Seattle Times, 4 March 1999

"Fearful Boeing," The Economist, 27 February 1999

"Boeing to Revive Plans for Larger Super Jumbo," Seattle Times, 9 September 1998

"Medium Residual Values of 747 Buoyed by A3XX Delay," Aircraft Value News, 13 April 1998

"A340-500/600 Nears Go-Ahead," Aviation Week and Space Technology, 11 August 1997

"Too Big to Fly?," Washington Post, 4 May 1997

1790

DSR 2012:III

Airbus press releases (including at http://www.airbus.com/en/presscentre/pressreleases/)

Boeing press releases (including at http://www.boeing.com/news/releases/archive2004.html, and for earlier years included in website archives)

Press releases by Airbus and Boeing customers

Commission Decision of 30 July 1997 declaring a concentration compatible with the common market and the functioning of the EEA Agreement, OJ L 336/16 (8 December 1997)

Moody's Investors Service, Global Aerospace/Defense – Industry Outlook January 2002

Society General, Aerospace and Defense Industry Report, June 2002

Aircraft Value News, various editions

Aviation Week & Space Technology, various editions

Air Transport World, various editions

Airline Business, various editions

Citigroup Smith Barney, Boeing analyst reports

Credit Suisse First Boston, Boeing analyst reports

JP Morgan, Boeing analyst reports

Wachovia Securities, Boeing analyst reports

Society of British Aerospace Companies, Has the Business model for commercial aviation changed permanently post September 11th?

US International Trade Commission, Investigation No. 332-414, Publication 3433, June 2001

US Department of Commerce, International Trade Administration, "The US Jet Industry: Competition, Regulation, and Global Market Factors Affecting US Producers," March 2005

Statement by Airbus that it has also gathered substantial evidence of a business confidential nature (*e.g.*, internal memoranda, communications to and from actual and potential airline and leasing company customers, and internal analyses of campaigns), which confirms the existence of injury, market displacement or impediment, price suppression, depression and undercutting as well as lost sales.

ANNEX B*

UNITED STATES - MEASURES AFFECTING TRADE IN LARGE CIVIL AIRCRAFT

Request for the Establishment of a Panel by the European Communities

The following communication, dated 20 January 2006, from the delegation of the European Communities to the Chairman of the Dispute Settlement Body, is circulated pursuant to Article 6.2 of the DSU.

On 6 October 2004 the European Communities ("EC") requested consultations in the above matter with the United States ("US") pursuant to Articles 4.1, 7.1, and 30 of the *Agreement on Subsidies and Countervailing Measures* ("*SCM Agreement*"), Article XXIII:1 of the General Agreement on Tariffs and Trade 1994 ("GATT 1994"), and Article 4 of the *Understanding on Rules and Procedures Governing the Settlement of Disputes* ("DSU").[1] Consultations were held on 5 November 2004 but failed to resolve the dispute.

At the meeting of the Dispute Settlement Body ("DSB") on 13 June concerning the request for establishment of the panel in the above case[2] the US asserted without any explanation that 13 of the 28 subsidy programs referenced in the panel request were not listed in the consultation request of 6 October 2004 and could not be the subject of panel proceedings. The EC did not agree with this unfounded contention but expressed its readiness to continue consultations in order to clarify and resolve the issues, it being understood that this was without prejudice to the EC's legal position and rights. Accordingly, the EC on 27 June 2005 requested a continuation of the consultations held on 5 November 2004.[3]

The requested continued consultations were held on 3 August 2005 but failed to resolve the dispute.

Regrettably, the US decided to use its unfounded procedural objections further to undermine the Annex V proceeding initiated in this matter by the DSB on 23 September 2005. In particular, the US decided not to provide answers on measures that the US unilaterally determined to be outside the scope of the

---

* This communication was originally circulated on 23 January 2006 as WT/DS317/5. On 4 December 2006, a corrigendum was issued to add "second complaint" at the end of the title of the document and to add "WT/DS353/2" to the document number.

[1] Circulated as document WT/DS317/1 on 12 October 2004.

[2] Circulated as document WT/DS317/2 on 3 June 2005.

[3] Circulated as document WT/DS317/1/Add.1 on 1 July 2005.

Report of the Panel

dispute. In addition, the US repeatedly blocked endeavours by the EC to have the Panel rule authoritatively on the scope of the dispute.

As a result, the EC has been deprived of its rights under the *SCM Agreement* to obtain the necessary information with respect to approximately half of the measures involved. This has seriously undermined the due process rights of the EC and its ability to prepare its case against the US.

To resolve this situation, the EC, in good faith and in an effort to resolve the dispute efficiently, hereby requests that a panel be established pursuant to Article 6 of the DSU; Article XXIII:2 of GATT 1994; and Articles 4, 7, and 30 of the *SCM Agreement* (to the extent that Article 30 incorporates by reference Article XXIII of GATT 1994) to consider the matter described below. This request is without prejudice to the EC's position that all the measures described below are already properly before the Panel that was established on 20 July 2005. The EC has already contacted the US in order to discuss how most efficiently to follow up on this request in the light of the developments described above and is prepared to continue these discussions with a view to ensuring a prompt and positive solution to this dispute.

* * * * * * *

This dispute concerns prohibited and actionable subsidies provided to and benefiting the US producers of large civil aircraft[4] (the "US LCA industry"), including, in particular, the Boeing Company ("Boeing") and McDonnell Douglas Corporation prior to its merger with Boeing. The measures are currently reflected in and derive from the following:

1. State and Local Subsidies

US States and local authorities, where research, development, production and headquarter facilities of the US LCA industry are located, transfer in various ways economic resources to the US LCA industry.

These economic resources include numerous financial incentives and other advantages effectuated, for example, through tax breaks, bond financing, fee waivers, lease arrangements, corporate headquarters relocation assistance, research funding, infrastructure measures and other benefits.

Such States and local authorities include, but are not limited to the States of Washington, Kansas and Illinois and local authorities therein.

---

[4] In accordance with the *1992 Agreement between the European Communities and the Government of the United States of America concerning the application of the GATT Agreement on Trade in Civil Aircraft on trade in large civil aircraft*, large civil aircraft ("LCA") includes all aircraft as defined in Article 1 of the GATT Agreement on Trade in Civil Aircraft, except engines as defined in Article 1.1(b) thereof, that are designed for passenger or cargo transportation and have 100 or more passenger seats or its equivalent in cargo configuration. Boeing produces or markets the following families of LCA: 717, 737, 747, 757, 767, 777, and 787.

1794

DSR 2012:III

a. *State of Washington*

Governmental authorities in the State of Washington, including municipalities and public bodies therein, such as Snohomish County, the Port of Everett, and the City of Everett, provide to the US LCA industry an incentive package of measures benefiting the development, production and sales of US LCA. These incentives include but are not limited to tax and other advantages reflected in or pursuant to, *inter alia*:

- Washington House Bill No. 2294 (2003);

- Memorandum of Agreement for Project Olympus between Boeing and the State of Washington of 19 December 2003;

- The Master Site Development and Location Agreement between Boeing and the State of Washington of 19 December 2003;

- The First Amendment to the Master Site Development and Location Agreement of 2 February 2004, and any subsequent amendments; and

- City of Everett Ordinance 2759-04 (2004), amending Chapter 3.24 of the Everett Municipal Code.

b. *State of Kansas*

Governmental authorities in the State of Kansas, including municipalities and public bodies therein, such as Sedgwick County, the City of Wichita, and local school districts, provide incentives, including bond financing, tax benefits and other advantages, to the US LCA industry, *inter alia*, through the following:

- Bond financing and payments pursuant to the Economic Revitalization and Reinvestment Act – Kansas Senate Bill No. 281 (2003), codified at K.S.A. §§ 74-50,136 *et seq.* (2004), as reflected in, *inter alia*:

  - A Resolution of the Kansas Development Finance Authority Declaring an Intent to Issue its Revenue Bonds to Finance a Project on behalf of Mid-Western Aircraft Systems, Inc., adopted 9 June 2005;

  - Incentive Agreement Between the Kansas Department of Commerce and Spirit Aerosystems Inc., dated as of 30 June 2005, signed by Spirit Aerosystems Inc. on 7 October 2005 and 10 October 2005, signed by the Kansas Department of Commerce on 11 October 2005;

  - State of Kansas, State Finance Council Resolution No. 05-544, 18 October 2005; and

  - Bond Resolution No. 222 Authorizing the Kansas Development Finance Authority To Issue Its Kansas Development Finance Authority Revenue Bonds (Spirit AeroSystems, Inc. Project) (adopted 5 December 2005).

Report of the Panel

– Property and sales tax abatements pursuant to K.S.A. § 79-201a, as amended, K.S.A. § 79-3606, as amended, and K.S.A. § 79-3640, as amended, associated with Industrial Revenue Bonds ("IRBs") issued for the financing of US LCA industry projects by the City of Wichita pursuant to K.S.A. §§ 12-1740 *et seq.*, as amended, including, but not limited to, those authorized by the following Ordinances of the Wichita City Council:

- Wichita City Council Ordinance No. 46-818 authorizing $80 million in IRBs for Spirit Aerosystems, Inc., dated 15 November 2005;

- Wichita City Council Ordinance No. 46-817 authorizing $29 million in IRBs for Boeing, dated 15 November 2005;

- Wichita City Council Ordinance No. 46-401 authorizing $67 million in IRBs for Boeing, dated 16 November 2004;

- Wichita City Council Ordinance No. 45-914 authorizing $60 million in IRBs for Boeing, dated 18 November 2003;

- Wichita City Council Ordinance No. 45-495 authorizing $96 million in IRBs for Boeing, dated 19 November 2002;

- Wichita City Council Ordinance No. 45-133 authorizing $84 million in IRBs for Boeing, dated 20 November 2001;

- Wichita City Council Ordinance No. 44-811 authorizing $41 million in IRBs for Boeing, dated 21 November 2000;

- Wichita City Council Ordinance No. 44-428 authorizing $155 million in IRBs for Boeing, dated 23 November 1999;

- Wichita City Council Ordinance No. 44-102 authorizing $350 million in IRBs for Boeing, dated 8 December 1998;

- Wichita City Council Ordinance No. 43-642 authorizing $340 million in IRBs for Boeing, dated 25 November 1997;

- Wichita City Council Ordinance No. 43-325 authorizing $194 million in IRBs for Boeing, dated 26 November 1996;

- Wichita City Council Ordinance No. 42-949 authorizing $201 million in IRBs for Boeing, dated 14 November 1995;

- Wichita City Council Ordinance No. 42-553 authorizing $280 million in IRBs for Boeing, dated 15 November 1994;

- Wichita City Council Ordinance No. 42-228 authorizing $292 million in IRBs for Boeing, dated 30 November 1993;

- Wichita City Council Ordinance No. 41-916 authorizing $274 million in IRBs for Boeing, dated 8 December 1992; and

- Wichita City Council Ordinance No. 41-592 authorizing $206 million in IRBs for Boeing, dated 26 November 1991.

1796

DSR 2012:III

Letters of intent for IRBs for the US LCA industry, including, but not limited to, those issued pursuant to actions of the Wichita City Council taken on 17 May 2005, 13 July 2004, 9 November 1999, 13 February 1996, 24 March 1992, 5 December 1989, 21 December 1982, 9 June 1981, and 23 October 1979.

– Funding provided by the State of Kansas, Kansas Technology Enterprise Corporation ("KTEC"), and the Federal Government to the National Institute for Aviation Research at Wichita State University for collaborations with the US LCA industry.

c. *State of Illinois*

Governmental authorities in the State of Illinois, including municipalities and public bodies therein, such as Cook County and the City of Chicago, provide incentives, including tax incentives, relocation assistance and other advantages, to the US LCA industry, including but not limited to:

– Tax credits from the State of Illinois pursuant to the Economic Development for a Growing Economy Tax Credit Act, Public Act 91-0476, as amended, 35 Ill. Comp. Stat. §§ 5/211 *et seq.*, and 35 Ill. Comp. Stat. § 10/5-45;

– Reimbursement of relocation expenses and other benefits from the State of Illinois pursuant to the Corporate Headquarters Relocation Act, Public Act 92-0207;

– Payments from the State of Illinois pursuant to the Illinois Large Business Development Act, Ill. Rev. Stat. 1989, ch. 127, paras. 2710-1 *et seq.*, and 14 Ill. Admin. Code §§ 590.10 *et seq.*

– Payments from the State of Illinois pursuant to the Illinois Industrial Training Program, 20 Ill. Comp. Stat. § 605/605–800, and 56 Ill. Admin. Code §§ 2650.10 *et seq.*

– Payments from the State of Illinois pursuant to the Technology Challenge Grant Program, 20 Ill. Comp. Stat. §§ 700/2001 *et seq.*, and 14 Ill. Admin. Code §§ 545.110 *et seq.*

– Property tax abatements from Cook County pursuant to § 920 of the above-mentioned Corporate Headquarters Relocation Act, Public Act 92-0207, § 18 of the Property Tax Code, 35 Ill. Comp. Stat. §§ 200/1 *et seq.*, as amended, and an Ordinance of the County of Cook, Illinois Approving Execution of a Tax Reimbursement Payment Agreement with the Boeing Company (2001);

– Property tax abatements from the City of Chicago pursuant to § 920 of the above-mentioned Corporate Headquarters Relocation Act, Public Act 92-0207, § 18 of the Property Tax Code, 35 Ill. Comp. Stat. §§ 200/1 *et seq.*, as amended, and an Ordinance of the City of Chicago, Illinois Approving Execution of a Tax

Report of the Panel

> Reimbursement Payment Agreement with the Boeing Company (2001); and

– Payments by the City of Chicago pursuant to the Lease Termination Compensation Agreement between 100 North Riverside, LLC, and the City of Chicago, 13 January 2001.

2. NASA Subsidies

The National Aeronautics and Space Administration ("NASA"), acting on the basis of the National Aeronautics and Space Act of 1958, Pub. L. No. 85-568, as amended, transfers economic resources on terms more favourable than available on the market or not at arm's length to the US LCA industry, _inter alia_, by:

a. allowing the US LCA industry to participate in research programmes, making payments to the US LCA industry under those programmes, or enabling the US LCA industry to exploit the results thereof by means including but not limited to the foregoing or waiving of valuable patent rights, the granting of limited exclusive rights data ("LERD") or otherwise exclusive or early access to data, trade secrets and other knowledge resulting from government funded research. The following are examples of such NASA programmes:

(i) _High Speed Research Program_

- NASA Budget Requests for FY 1990 – FY 2001;

- NASA Appropriations Acts, Pub. L. No. 101-144 (FY 1990); Pub. L. No. 101-507 (FY 1991); Pub. L. No. 102-139 (FY 1992); Pub. L. No. 102-389 (FY 1993); Pub. L. No. 103-124 (FY 1994); Pub. L. No. 103-327 (FY 1995); Pub. L. No. 104-134 (FY 1996); Pub. L. No. 104-204 (FY 1997); Pub. L. No. 105-65 (FY 1998); Pub. L. No. 105-276 (FY 1999);

- High Speed Research Program Technology Transfer Control Handbook, April 1998.

(ii) _Advanced Subsonic Technology Program_

- NASA Budget Requests for FY 1992 – FY 2001;

- NASA Appropriations Acts, Pub. L. No. 102-139 (FY 1992); Pub. L. No. 102-389 (FY 1993); Pub. L. No. 103-124 (FY 1994); Pub. L. No. 103-327 (FY 1995); Pub. L. No. 104-134 (FY 1996); Pub. L. No. 104-204 (FY 1997); Pub. L. No. 105-65 (FY 1998); Pub. L. No. 105-276 (FY 1999);

- Advanced Subsonic Technology Program Technology Transfer Control Handbook, August 1998.

US - Large Civil Aircraft (2nd Complaint)

(iii) *Aviation Safety Program/Aviation Safety & Security Program/Aviation Security & Safety Program*

- NASA Budget Requests for FY 2000 – FY 2007;

- NASA Appropriations and Authorization Acts, Pub. L. No. 106-74 (FY 2000); Pub. L. No. 106-377 (FY 2001); Pub. L. No. 107-73 & Pub. L. No. 107-117 (FY 2002); Pub. L. No. 108-7 (FY 2003); Pub. L. No. 108-199 (FY 2004); Pub. L. No. 108-447 (FY 2005); Pub. L. No. 109-108 (FY 2006); Pub. L. No. 109-155 (FY 2007 – FY 2008).

(iv) *Quiet Aircraft Technology Program*

- NASA Budget Requests for FY 2000 – FY 2007;

- NASA Appropriations and Authorization Acts, Pub. L. No. 106-74 (FY 2000); Pub. L. No. 106-377 (FY 2001); Pub. L. No. 107-73 & Pub. L. No. 107-117 (FY 2002); Pub. L. No. 108-7 (FY 2003); Pub. L. No. 108-199 (FY 2004); Pub. L. No. 108-447 (FY 2005); Pub. L. No. 109-108 (FY 2006); Pub. L. No. 109-155 (FY 2007 – FY 2008).

(v) *High Performance Computing and Communications Program*

- NASA Budget Requests for FY 1991 – FY 2003;

- NASA Appropriations Acts, Pub. L. No. 101-507 (FY 1991); Pub. L. No. 102-139 (FY 1992); Pub. L. No. 102-389 (FY 1993); Pub. L. No. 103-124 (FY 1994); Pub. L. No. 103-327 (FY 1995); Pub. L. No. 104-134 (FY 1996); Pub. L. No. 104-204 (FY 1997); Pub. L. No. 105-65 (FY 1998); Pub. L. No. 105-276 (FY 1999); Pub. L. No. 106-74 (FY 2000); Pub. L. No. 106-377 (FY 2001).

(vi) *Research & Technology Base Program*

- NASA Budget Requests for FY 1991 – FY 2004;

- NASA Appropriations Acts, Pub. L. No. 101-507 (FY 1991); Pub. L. No. 102-139 (FY 1992); Pub. L. No. 102-389 (FY 1993); Pub. L. No. 103-124 (FY 1994); Pub. L. No. 103-327 (FY 1995); Pub. L. No. 104-134 (FY 1996); Pub. L. No. 104-204 (FY 1997); Pub. L. No. 105-65 (FY 1998); Pub. L. No. 105-276 (FY 1999); Pub. L. No. 106-74 (FY 2000); Pub. L. No. 106-377 (FY 2001); Pub. L. No. 107-73 & Pub. L. No. 107-117 (FY 2002).

(vii) *Advanced Composites Technology Program*

- NASA Budget Requests for FY 1994 – FY 1997;

- NASA Appropriations Acts, Pub. L. No. 103-124 (FY 1994); Pub. L. No. 103-327 (FY 1995).

(viii) *Vehicle Systems Program*

- NASA Budget Requests for FY 2003 – FY 2007;

DSR 2012:III

1799

Report of the Panel

- NASA Appropriations and Authorization Acts, Pub. L. No. 108-7 (FY 2003); Pub. L. No. 108-199 (FY 2004); Pub. L. No. 108-447 (FY 2005); Pub. L. No. 109-108 (FY 2006); Pub. L. No. 109-155 (FY 2007 – FY 2008).

(ix) *Materials and Structures Systems Technology Program, including advanced composites materials and structures research*

- NASA Budget Requests for FY 1988 – FY 1995;

- NASA Appropriations Acts, Pub. L. No. 100-202 (FY 1988); Pub. L. No. 100-404 (FY 1989); Pub. L. No. 101-144 (FY 1990); Pub. L. No. 101-507 (FY 1991); Pub. L. No. 102-139 (FY 1992); Pub. L. No. 102-389 (FY 1993).

(x) *Aircraft Energy Efficiency Program, including Composite Primary Aircraft Structures, Transport Aircraft Systems Technology, and Advanced Composite Structures Technology Programs*

- NASA Budget Requests for FY 1976 – FY 1987;

- NASA Appropriations Acts, Pub. L. No. 94-116 (FY 1976); Pub. L. No. 94-378 (FY 1977); Pub. L. No. 95-119 (FY 1978); Pub. L. No. 95-392 (FY 1979); Pub. L. No. 96-103 (FY 1980); Pub. L. No. 96-526 (FY 1981); Pub. L. No. 97-101 (FY 1982); Pub. L. No. 97-272 (FY 1983); Pub. L. No. 98-45 (FY 1984); Pub. L. No. 98-371 (FY 1985).

b. providing the services of NASA employees, facilities, and equipment to support the R&D programmes listed above and paying salaries, personnel costs, and other institutional support, thereby providing valuable services to the US LCA industry on terms more favourable than available on the market or not at arm's length:

- NASA Budget Requests for FY 1976 – FY 2007;

- NASA Appropriations and Authorization Acts, Pub. L. No. 94-116 (FY 1976); Pub. L. No. 94-378 (FY 1977); Pub. L. No. 95-119 (FY 1978); Pub. L. No. 95-392 (FY 1979); Pub. L. No. 96-103 (FY 1980); Pub. L. No. 96-526 (FY 1981); Pub. L. No. 97-101 (FY 1982); Pub. L. No. 97-272 (FY 1983); Pub. L. No. 98-45 (FY 1984); Pub. L. No. 98-371 (FY 1985); Pub. L. No. 99-160 (FY 1986); Pub. L. No. 99-500 & Pub. L. No. 99-591 (FY 1987); Pub. L. No. 100-202 (FY 1988); Pub. L. No. 100-404 (FY 1989); Pub. L. No. 101-144 (FY 1990); Pub. L. No. 101-507 (FY 1991); Pub. L. No. 102-139 (FY 1992); Pub. L. No. 102-389 (FY 1993); Pub. L. No. 103-124 (FY 1994); Pub. L. No. 103-327 (FY 1995); Pub. L. No. 104-134 (FY 1996); Pub. L. No. 104-204 (FY 1997); Pub. L. No. 105-65 (FY 1998); Pub. L. No. 105-276 (FY 1999); Pub. L. No. 106-74 (FY 2000); Pub. L. No. 106-377 (FY 2001); Pub. L. No. 107-73 & Pub. L. No. 107-117 (FY 2002); Pub. L.

No. 108-7 (FY 2003); Pub. L. No. 108-199 (FY 2004); Pub. L. No. 108-447 (FY 2005); Pub. L. No. 109-108 (FY 2006); Pub. L. No. 109-155 (FY 2007 – FY 2008).

c. providing NASA Independent Research & Development, and Bid & Proposal Reimbursements:

- 48 CFR § 31.205-18;

- 14 CFR § 1274.204(g);

- 48 CFR §§ 9904.420 et seq.

d. allowing the US LCA industry to use the research, test and evaluation facilities owned by the US Government, including NASA wind tunnels, in particular the Langley Research Center.

e. entering into procurement contracts with the US LCA industry for more than adequate remuneration.

f. granting the US LCA industry exclusive or early access to data, trade secrets, and other knowledge resulting from government funded research pursuant, inter alia, to:

- Requirements for Documentation, Approval, and Dissemination of NASA Scientific and Technical Information, section 4.5.7.1 (NPG 2200.2A);

- 48 CFR §§ 27.400 et seq.

g. allowing the US LCA industry to exploit the results of government funded research, including, but not limited to, the foregoing or waiving of valuable patent rights or rights in data as such, pursuant, inter alia, to:

- 35 U.S.C. §§ 200 et seq.;

- 48 CFR §§ 27.300 et seq.;

- Memorandum to the Heads of Executive Departments and Agencies: Government Patent Policy, Pub. Papers 248 (18 February 1983);

- Executive Order 12591 (10 April 1987);

- 14 CFR §§ 1245.100 et seq.;

- 14 CFR §§ 1274.911 - 1274.914;

- 48 CFR §§ 1827.301 et seq.;

- 48 CFR §§ 27.400 et seq.

3. Department of Defense Subsidies

The Department of Defense ("DOD") transfers economic resources to the US LCA industry on terms more favourable than available on the market or not at arm's length, *inter alia*, by:

Report of the Panel

a. allowing the US LCA industry to participate in DOD-funded research, making payments to the US LCA industry for such research, or enabling the US LCA industry to exploit the results of such research, by means including but not limited to the foregoing or waiving of valuable patent rights, and the granting of exclusive or early access to data, trade secrets and other knowledge resulting from government funded research, through, for example:

(i) A number of Research, Development, Test, and Evaluation ("RDT&E") Programs of the US Air Force, Navy, Army, and the Defense Advanced Research Projects Agency ("DARPA") including, but not limited to:

- Defense Research Sciences (PE# 0601102F)

- Materials (PE# 0602102F)

- Aerospace Flight Dynamics and Aerospace Vehicle Technologies (PE# 0602201F)

- Aerospace Propulsion (PE# 0602203F)

- Aerospace Sensors (PE# 0602204F)

- Dual Use Applications and Dual Use Science & Technology (PE# 0602805F)

- Advanced Materials for Weapon Systems (PE# 0603112F)

- Flight Vehicle Technology (PE# 0603205F)

- Aerospace Structures and Aerospace Technology Dev/Demo (PE# 0603211F)

- Aerospace Propulsion & Power Technology (PE# 0603216F)

- Flight Vehicle Technology Integration (PE# 0603245F)

- RDT&E For Aging Aircraft (PE# 0605011F)

- Manufacturing Technology/Industrial Preparedness (PE#

- 0603771F/0708011F/0708011N)

- C-17 (PE# 0401130F/0604231F)

- CV-22 (PE# 0401318F)

- Joint Strike Fighter (PE#0603800F/0603800N/0603800E/0604800F/0604800N)

- AV-8B Aircraft (PE# 0604214N)

- Comanche (PE# 0604223A)

- F-22 (PE# 0604239F)

- B-2 Advanced Technology Bomber (PE# 0604240F)

- V-22 (PE# 0604262N)

- A-6 Squadrons (PE# 0204134N)

- F/A-18 Squadrons (PE# 0204136N)
- Dual Use Applications Program (including its predecessor, the Technology Reinvestment Project).

These Programmes are currently reflected in, *inter alia*:

- DOD RDT&E Budget Item Justification, Exhibits R-2, FY 1991 – FY 2007;
- DOD FY 1991 – FY 2007 Budgets for RDT&E Programs (Exhibit R-1), DOD Component Summary;
- 10 U.S.C. § 2521 (statutory basis for Manufacturing Technology Program);
- 10 U.S.C. § 2511 (statutory basis for Dual Use Programs);
- DOD Appropriations Acts, Pub. L. No. 101-511 (FY 1991); Pub. L. No. 102-172 (FY 1992); Pub. L. No. 102-396 (FY 1993); Pub. L. No. 103-139 (FY 1994); Pub. L. No. 103-335 (FY 1995); Pub. L. No. 104-61 (FY 1996); Pub. L. No. 104-208 (FY 1997); Pub. L. No. 105-56 (FY 1998); Pub. L. No. 105-262 (FY 1999); Pub. L. No. 106-79 (FY 2000); Pub. L. No. 106-259 (FY 2001); Pub. L. No. 107-117 (FY 2002); Pub. L. No. 107-248 (FY 2003); Pub. L. No. 108-87 (FY 2004); Pub. L. No. 108-287 (FY 2005); Pub. L. No. 109-148 (FY 2006).

(ii) providing Independent Research & Development, and Bid & Proposal Reimbursements.

- 10 U.S.C. § 2372;
- 48 CFR § 31.205-18;
- 48 CFR § 231.205-18;
- 48 CFR §§ 9904.420 *et seq.*;
- Department of Defense Directive Regarding IR&D, Number 3204.1 (10 May 1999);
- DOD Appropriations Acts, Pub. L. No. 101-511 (FY 1991); Pub. L. No. 102-172 (FY 1992); Pub. L. No. 102-396 (FY 1993); Pub. L. No. 103-139 (FY 1994); Pub. L. No. 103-335 (FY 1995); Pub. L. No. 104-61 (FY 1996); Pub. L. No. 104-208 (FY 1997); Pub. L. No. 105-56 (FY 1998); Pub. L. No. 105-262 (FY 1999); Pub. L. No. 106-79 (FY 2000); Pub. L. No. 106-259 (FY 2001); Pub. L. No. 107-117 (FY 2002); Pub. L. No. 107-248 (FY 2003); Pub. L. No. 108-87 (FY 2004); Pub. L. No. 108-287 (FY 2005); Pub. L. No. 109-148 (FY 2006).

b. allowing the US LCA industry to use research, test and evaluation facilities owned by the US Government, including the Major Range Test Facility Bases.

Report of the Panel

    c.   entering into procurement contracts, including those for the purchase of goods, from the US LCA industry for more than adequate remuneration, including in particular but not limited to the US Air Force contract with Boeing for the purchase of certain spare parts for its Airborne Warning and Control System (AWACS) aircraft, the National Polar-orbiting Operational Environmental Satellite System-Conical Microwave Imager Sensor, the C-22 Replacement Program (C-40), the KC-135 Programmed Depot Maintenance, the C-40 Lease and Purchase Program, the C-130 avionics modernisation upgrade program, the C-17 H22 contract (Boeing BC-17X), the US Navy contract with Boeing for the production and maintenance of 108 civil B-737 and their conversion into long-range submarine hunter Multi-Mission Aircraft, the Missile Defense Agency's Airborne Laser (ABL) Program, and the Army's Comanche Program.

    d.   by allowing the US LCA industry to exploit the results of government funded research, including, but not limited to, the foregoing or waiving of valuable patent rights or rights in data as such, pursuant, *inter alia*, to:

- 35 U.S.C. §§ 200 *et seq.*;
- 48 CFR §§ 27.300 *et seq.*;
- Memorandum to the Heads of Executive Departments and Agencies: Government Patent Policy, Pub. Papers 248 (18 February 1983);
- Executive Order 12591 (10 April 1987);
- 48 CFR §§ 227.303 *et seq.*;
- 48 CFR §§ 27.400 *et seq.*;
- 48 CFR §§ 227.7100 *et seq.*

4.   National Institute of Standards & Technology (US Department of Commerce) Subsidies

The US Department of Commerce ("DOC") transfers economic resources to the US LCA industry on terms more favourable than available on the market or not at arm's length, through the Advanced Technology Program operated pursuant to the Omnibus Trade and Competitiveness Act of 1988, Pub. L. No. 100-418, as amended, and the American Technology Preeminence Act of 1991, Pub. L. No. 102-245 and 15 CFR §§ 295.1 *et seq.*, by allowing the US LCA industry to participate in this programme, making payments to the US LCA industry under this programme, or allowing the US LCA industry to exploit the results of this programme, including but not limited to the foregoing or waiving of valuable patent rights, and the granting of exclusive or early access to data, trade secrets and other knowledge resulting from government funded research.

In particular, economic resources are transferred to the US LCA industry through a number of projects, including, but not limited to, the following:

- Project 93-01-0089 (CVD Diamond-Coated Rotating Tools for Machining Advanced Composite Materials);

- Project 95-12-0024 (An Agent-Based Framework for Integrated Intelligent Planning – Execution);

- Project 95-01-0108 (Precision Optoelectronics Assembly);

- Project 91-01-0267 (Pre-competitive Advanced Manufacturing of Electrical Products);

- Project 97-05-0020 (Extended Enterprise Coalition for Integrated Collaborative Manufacturing Systems);

- Project 98-01-0168 (Hot Metal Gas Forming);

- Project 90-01-0126 (Solid-State Laser Technology for Point Source X-Ray Lithography);

- Project 95-02-0036 (Plasma-Based Processing of Lightweight Materials for Motor-Vehicle Components and Manufacturing Applications).

5. US Department of Labor

The US Department of Labor transfers economic resources to the US LCA industry on terms more favourable than available on the market or not at arm's length, through the Aerospace Industry Initiative, an element of the President's High Growth Training Initiative, under the authority of the Workforce Investment Act, Pub. L. No. 105-220 (1998), by granting to Edmonds Community College in the State of Washington funds for the training of aerospace industry workers associated with the Boeing 787.

6. Federal tax incentives

The US Government transfers economic resources to the US LCA industry through the federal tax system, and in particular through the following tax measures:

a. Sections 921-927 of the Internal Revenue Code (prior to repeal) and related measures establishing special tax treatment for "Foreign Sales Corporations" ("FSCs");

b. FSC Repeal and Extraterritorial Income Exclusion Act of 2000, Pub. L. No. 106-519; and

c. American Jobs Creation Act of 2004, Pub. L. No. 108-357.

* * * * * * *

The European Communities considers that the above measures are inconsistent with the obligations of the US under the following provisions:

(1)   Articles 3.1(a), 3.1(b) and 3.2 of the *SCM Agreement*;

(2)   Article 5(a) of the *SCM Agreement*;

(3)   Articles 5(c), 6.3(a), 6.3(b) and 6.3(c) of the *SCM Agreement*;

(4)   Article III:4 of the GATT 1994.

The European Communities is of the view that the above measures, reflected in the US, State, and local statutes, regulations, administrative procedures, and other programmes and policies as listed above, including any relevant subsequent amendments thereof or successory acts, are inconsistent with these provisions as such and as applied.

The measures listed above are subsidies because in each instance there is a financial contribution by the US, State or local government, and a benefit is thereby conferred within the meaning of Article 1.1(a)(1) and (b) of the *SCM Agreement*. They benefit and will continue to benefit in the future the development, production, sale, and export of each of the individual subsidised LCA products of the US LCA industry. Each of the listed subsidies is specific to the US LCA industry within the meaning of Article 2 of the *SCM Agreement*.

The subsidies listed above are *de jure* or *de facto* export contingent, and contingent on the use of domestic over imported goods.

The use of these measures causes adverse effects – *i.e.,* material injury or threat of material injury to the European Community LCA industry – and serious prejudice including threat of serious prejudice to the interests of the European Communities within the meaning of Article 5(a) and (c) of the *SCM Agreement*, because, *inter alia*:

–   The effect of the measures is material injury, or a threat thereof, in violation of Article 5(a) of the *SCM Agreement*;

–   The effect of the measures is a significant price undercutting by subsidised products of the US LCA industry as compared with the price of competing European Community LCA products in the world, European Community, US, and third country markets where US and Community producers compete, or a threat thereof, in violation of Articles 5(c) and 6.3(c) of the *SCM Agreement;*

–   The effect of the measures is significant depression and suppression of the prices of competing European Community LCA products in the world, European Community, US, and third country markets where US and Community producers compete, or a threat thereof, in violation of Articles 5(c) and 6.3(c) of the *SCM Agreement*;

–   The effect of the measures is significant lost sales of competing European Community LCA products in the world, European Community, US, and third country markets where US and

Community producers compete, or a threat thereof, in violation of Articles 5(c) and 6.3(c) of the *SCM Agreement*;

– The effect of the measures is to displace or impede exports of competing European Community LCA products in the US market, or a threat thereof, in violation of Articles 5(c) and 6.3(a) of the *SCM Agreement*;

– The effect of the measures is to displace or impede exports of competing European Community LCA products in third country markets, or a threat thereof, in violation of Articles 5(c) and 6.3(b) of the *SCM Agreement*.

The above measures are neither justified under any provision of a covered agreement, including the *Agreement on Trade in Civil Aircraft*, nor under the 1992 *Agreement between the European Communities and the Government of the United States of America concerning the application of the GATT Agreement on Trade in Civil Aircraft on trade in large civil aircraft*.

The European Communities requests that a panel be established with standard terms of reference, in accordance with Articles 4.4 and 7.4 of the *SCM Agreement* and Article 7 of the DSU.

The European Communities asks that a special meeting of the Dispute Settlement Body be convened on Thursday 2 February 2006 and that this request for the establishment of a panel be placed on the agenda of that meeting.

Finally, the European Communities requests that the DSB, together with the establishment of the panel, initiate the procedures for developing information concerning serious prejudice under Annex V of the *SCM Agreement*. This request is without prejudice to the EC's position that all the measures described above are already properly before the Panel that was established on 20 July 2005 and therefore were covered by the Annex V proceeding initiated by the DSB on 23 September 2005. The EC is prepared to discuss together with the Representative designated by the DSB to serve the function of facilitating the information-gathering process, pursuant to paragraph 4 of Annex V of the *SCM Agreement*, Mr. Mateo Diego-Fernandez, and with the US, how the Annex V process can be pursued most efficiently.

Report of the Panel

ANNEX C

UNITED STATES — MEASURES AFFECTING TRADE IN LARGE CIVIL AIRCRAFT — SECOND COMPLAINT – WORKING PROCEDURES FOR THE PANEL

(revised 13 September 2007)

1.   In its proceedings the Panel shall follow the relevant provisions of the Dispute Settlement Understanding (DSU). In addition, the following working procedures shall apply.

2.   The Panel shall conduct its internal deliberations in closed session. The parties to the dispute, and interested third parties, shall be present at meetings only when invited by the Panel to appear before it. The Panel may open its meetings with the parties to the public, subject to appropriate procedures to be adopted by the Panel after consulting with the parties. The Panel may open the third party session of its first substantive meeting to the public, subject to appropriate procedures to be adopted by the Panel after consulting with the parties and third parties.

3.   The deliberations of the Panel and the documents submitted to it shall be kept confidential. Nothing in the DSU shall preclude a party to a dispute from disclosing statements of its own positions to the public. Members shall treat as confidential information submitted by another Member to the Panel which that Member has designated as confidential. Where a party to a dispute submits a confidential version of its written submissions to the Panel, it shall also, upon request of a Member, provide a non-confidential summary of the information contained in its submissions that could be disclosed to the public.

4.   The Panel may adopt special procedures for the protection of certain confidential information as an annex to these working procedures, following consultation with and opportunity for comment by the parties on any proposed procedures.

5.   Before the first substantive meeting of the Panel with the parties, the parties to the dispute shall transmit to the Panel written submissions in which they present the facts of the case, their arguments and their counter-arguments, respectively.

6.   At its first substantive meeting with the parties, the Panel shall ask the European Communities to present its case. Subsequently, and at the same meeting, the United States will be asked to present its point of view. The parties will then be allowed an opportunity for final statements, with the European Communities presenting its statement first. Third parties will be asked to present their views thereafter at the separate session of the same meeting set aside for that purpose. Upon request, the parties will be allowed an opportunity to make

written comments on the views presented by the third parties at this separate session.

7. All third parties which have notified their interest in the dispute to the Dispute Settlement Body shall be invited in writing to present their views during a session of the substantive meeting of the Panel set aside for that purpose. All such third parties may be present during the entirety of this session.

8. Formal rebuttals shall be made at a second substantive meeting of the Panel. The United States shall have the right to take the floor first, to be followed by the European Communities. The parties shall submit, prior to that meeting, written rebuttals to the Panel.

9. The Panel may at any time put questions to the parties and to the third parties and ask them for explanations either in the course of the substantive meeting or in writing. Answers to questions shall be submitted in writing by the date(s) specified by the Panel. Answers to questions after the first meeting shall be submitted in writing at the same time as the written rebuttals, unless the Panel specifies a different deadline.

10. The parties to the dispute and any third party invited to present its views shall make available to the Panel and the other party or parties a written version of their oral statements, preferably at the end of the meeting, and in any event not later than the day following the meeting. Parties and third parties are encouraged to provide the Panel and other participants in the meeting with a provisional written version of their oral statements at the time the oral statement is presented.

11. In the interest of full transparency, the presentations, rebuttals and statements shall be made in the presence of the parties. Moreover, each party's written submissions, including responses to questions put by the Panel, shall be made available to the other party.

12. The parties should provide the Secretariat with an executive summary of the claims and arguments contained in their written submissions and oral presentations. These executive summaries will be used by the Secretariat only for the purpose of assisting the Secretariat in drafting a concise arguments section of the Panel report so as to facilitate timely translation and circulation of the Panel report to the Members. They shall not serve in any way as a substitute for the submissions of the parties. The summaries of the first written submission and rebuttal written submission shall be limited to twenty (20) pages each, and the summaries of the oral statements at the meetings will be limited to five (5) pages each. The Panel may vary these page limits. Third parties are requested to provide the Panel with executive summaries of their written submissions and oral presentations, of no more than five (5) pages each. The executive summaries shall be submitted to the Secretariat within ten days of the original submission or presentation concerned. Paragraph 0 shall apply to the service of executive summaries.

13. A party shall submit any request for preliminary ruling not later than its first submission to the Panel. If the complaining party requests such a ruling, the

Report of the Panel

respondent shall submit its response to the request in its first submission. If the respondent requests such a ruling, the complaining party shall submit its response to the request prior to the first substantive meeting of the Panel, at a time to be determined by the Panel in light of the request. Exceptions to this procedure will be granted upon a showing of good cause.

14. Each party shall submit all factual evidence to the Panel no later than during the first substantive meeting, except with respect to evidence necessary for purposes of rebuttals or answers to questions. Exceptions to this procedure will be granted upon a showing of good cause. The other party shall be accorded a period of time for comment, as appropriate, on any new factual evidence submitted after the first substantive meeting.

15. The parties to the dispute have the right to determine the composition of their own delegations. The parties shall have the responsibility for all members of their delegations and shall ensure that all members of the delegation act in accordance with the rules of the DSU and the Working Procedures of this Panel, particularly in regard to confidentiality of the proceedings. The parties as well as third parties shall provide a list of their delegation before each meeting to the Secretary to the Panel, Mr. Hiromi Yano (e-mail: hiromi.yano@wto.org).

16. To facilitate the maintenance of the record of the dispute, and to maximize the clarity of submissions, in particular the references to exhibits submitted by parties, parties shall sequentially number their exhibits throughout the course of the dispute. For example, exhibits submitted by the European Communities could be numbered EC-1, EC-2, etc. If the last exhibit in connection with the first submission was numbered EC-5, the first exhibit of its next submission thus would be numbered EC-6.

17. Following issuance of the interim report, the parties shall have the time, as established by the timetable of the Panel, to submit written requests to review precise aspects of the interim report and to request a further meeting with the Panel. The right to request such a meeting must be exercised no later than at that time. Following receipt of any written requests for review, if no further meeting with the Panel is requested, the parties shall have the opportunity, within a time-period specified by the Panel, to submit written comments on the other party's written requests for review. Such comments shall be strictly limited to responding to the other party's written request for review.

18. The following procedures regarding service of documents shall apply:

    a. Each party and third party shall serve all of its written submissions (including any separate requests for preliminary ruling and responses thereto), executive summaries and written versions of oral statements, directly on all other parties, and on third parties as appropriate, and confirm that it has done so at the time it provides those submissions to the Secretariat.

    b. The parties and third parties should provide their submissions to the Secretariat by 5:30 p.m. on the deadlines established by the Panel, unless a different time is set by the Panel.

c.   Unless the Panel indicates otherwise, the parties and third parties shall provide the Secretariat with ten paper copies of each of their written submissions. These copies shall be filed with the Dispute Settlement Registrar, Mr. Ferdinand Ferranco (office 2150).

d.   The parties and third parties shall provide electronic copies of all submissions to the Secretariat at the time they provide their submissions, if possible in a format compatible with that used by the Secretariat. If the electronic version is provided by e-mail, it shall be addressed to DSRegistry@wto.org, and copied to XXXXX@wto.org,, XXXXX@wto.org, XXXXX@wto.org, XXXXX@wto.org and XXXXX@wto.org. If the electronic version is provided by diskette or CD, four copies shall be delivered to Mr. Ferdinand Ferranco (office 2150).

e.   The Panel will endeavour to provide the parties with an electronic version of the descriptive part, the interim report and the final report, as well as of other documents as appropriate. When the Panel transmits to the parties or third parties both paper and electronic versions of a document, the paper version shall constitute the official version for the purposes of the record of the dispute.

Report of the Panel

ANNEX D

**UNITED STATES — MEASURES AFFECTING TRADE IN LARGE
CIVIL AIRCRAFT — SECOND COMPLAINT, (WT/DS353) –
ADDITIONAL WORKING PROCEDURES FOR DS353 –
PROCEDURES FOR THE PROTECTION OF BUSINESS
CONFIDENTIAL INFORMATION AND HIGHLY
SENSITIVE BUSINESS INFORMATION
("BCI/HSBI PROCEDURES")**

(Last revised 11 February 2011)

I.   GENERAL

The following Procedures apply to all business confidential information ("BCI")
and highly sensitive business information ("HSBI") on the Panel record. These
Procedures do not diminish the rights and obligations of the parties to request
and disclose any information within the scope of the *SCM Agreement* and Article
13 of the *DSU*.

II.   DEFINITIONS

For the purposes of these Procedures,

1.   **"Approved Persons"** means:

   (a)   Representatives or Outside Advisors of a Party, or Employees of
         the Secretariat, when designated in accordance with these
         procedures;

   (b)   Panel members; and

   (c)   PGE members or experts appointed by the Panel who in the
         opinion of the Panel require access to BCI and/or HSBI.

2.   **"Business Confidential Information"** or **"BCI"** means any business
information that a Party or Third Party has "Designated as BCI" regardless of
whether contained in a document provided by a public or private body because it
is not otherwise available in the public domain. Each Party and Third Party shall
act in good faith and exercise restraint in designating information as BCI, and
will endeavour to designate information as BCI only if its disclosure would
cause harm to the originators of the information.

3.   **"Conclusion of the Panel Process"** means the earliest to occur of the
following events:

   (a)   pursuant to Article 16.4 of the DSU, the Panel report is adopted by
         the DSB, or the DSB decides by consensus not to adopt the report;

(b) a Party formally notifies the DSB of its decision to appeal pursuant to Article 16.4 of the DSU;

(c) pursuant to Article 12.12 of the DSU, the authority for establishment of the Panel lapses; or

(d) pursuant to Article 3.6 of the DSU, a mutually satisfactory solution is notified to the DSB.

4. **"Designated as BCI" means:**

(a) for printed information, text that is set off with bold square brackets in a document clearly marked with the notation 'BUSINESS CONFIDENTIAL INFORMATION' and with the name of the Party or Third Party that submitted the information;

(b) for electronic information, characters that are set off with bolded square brackets (or with a heading with bolded square brackets on each page) in an electronic file that contains the notation 'BUSINESS CONFIDENTIAL INFORMATION', has a file name that contains the letters "BCI", and is stored on a storage medium with a label marked 'BUSINESS CONFIDENTIAL INFORMATION' and indicating the name of the Party or Third Party that submitted the information; and

(c) for uttered information, declared by the speaker to be "Business Confidential Information" prior to utterance.[1]

5. **"Designated as HSBI" means:**

(a) for electronic information, in characters that are set off with double bolded square brackets (or a heading with double bolded square brackets on each page) in an electronic file that contains the notation 'HIGHLY SENSITIVE BUSINESS INFORMATION', has a file name that contains the letters "HSBI", and is stored on a storage medium with a label marked 'HIGHLY SENSITIVE BUSINESS INFORMATION' and indicating the name of the Party or Third Party that submitted the information; and

(b) for uttered information, declared by the speaker to be "Highly Sensitive Business Information" prior to utterance.[2]

5*bis.* **"Designated Reading Room"** means a room, located on the premises of the WTO, where a Third Party BCI Approved Person may use to access Party's submission that contains Party-BCI.

6. **"Electronic information"** means any information stored in an electronic form (including but not limited to binary-encoded information).

---

[1] The erroneous failure by a speaker to make such a prior declaration shall not affect the designation of the BCI in question.

[2] The erroneous failure by a speaker to make such a prior declaration shall not affect the designation of the HSBI in question.

Report of the Panel

7. **"Employee of the Secretariat"** means a person employed or appointed by the Secretariat who has been authorized by the Secretariat to work on the dispute, and includes translators and interpreters as well as any transcribers present at Panel meetings involving BCI and/or HSBI.

8. **"Highly Sensitive Business Information"** or **"HSBI"** means any business information regardless of whether contained in a document provided by a public or private body that a Party or Third Party has "Designated as HSBI" because it is not otherwise available in the public domain and its disclosure could, in the Party's or Third Party's view, cause exceptional harm to its originators. Each Party and Third Party shall act in good faith and exercise the utmost restraint in designating information as HSBI. Each Party and Third Party may at any time designate as non-BCI/HSBI or as BCI information designated by that Party or Third Party as HSBI.

(a) The following categories of information may be Designated as HSBI:

(i) information indicating the actual selling or offered price of any large civil aircraft (LCA) manufacturer's products or services,[3] and, except as provided in subparagraph (d)(i) below, any graphs or other use of the data which reflect the movement of prices, pricing trends or actual prices of an LCA model or a family of LCA;

(ii) information gathered or produced in the context of LCA sales campaigns;

(iii) information concerning market forecasts, analyses, business plans and share/business valuations generated by LCA producers, consultants or investment banks with regard to LCA products; or

(iv) information concerning an LCA manufacturer's costs of production, including but not limited to data regarding pricing by suppliers.

(b) Each Party and Third Party may also designate as HSBI other categories of business information that is not otherwise available in the public domain and the disclosure of which could, in the Party's view, cause exceptional harm to its originators.

---

[3] This category includes (but is not limited to) information on individual LCA prices, prices per seat, or information allowing the operating cost per seat of an LCA to be determined, calculated or reflected; the negotiated or offered prices for the airframe; all concessions offered or agreed to by an LCA manufacturer including financing, spare parts, maintenance, pilot training, asset value and other guarantees, buy back options, remarketing arrangements or other forms of credit support. This category shall also include the actual pricing information relating to any number of individual LCA offers and prices (including concessions) aggregated by model or other category.

1814

DSR 2012:III

US - Large Civil Aircraft (2nd Complaint)

(c)   Each Party and Third Party shall Designate as HSBI any information described in subparagraph (a) that pertains to LCA produced by an LCA manufacturer headquartered within the territorial jurisdiction of either of the Parties.

(d)   The following categories of information may not be Designated as HSBI:

(i)   aggregated pricing data for a particular LCA model or family of LCA within a particular market that is indexed (i.e., does not reflect actual prices but rather movements in prices off a base of 100 for a particular year). Such data shall be treated as BCI;

(ii)   general legal conclusions based on HSBI (e.g., that HSBI demonstrates that a producer engaged in price undercutting). Such conclusions shall be treated as neither BCI nor HSBI; and

(iii)   intergovernmental agreements and government decisions, other than information described in subparagraph (a).

(e)   Information may not be Designated as HSBI simply because it is subject to bank secrecy or banker-client confidentiality.

(f)   In case either Party objects to the designation of information as HSBI under paragraphs 8(a)-(e), the dispute shall be resolved by the Panel. If the Panel disagrees with designation of information as HSBI, the submitting Party or Third Party may either designate it as BCI, as non-BCI/HSBI or withdraw the information. The Panel shall either destroy such information or return it to the submitting Party or Third Party. Each Party or Third Party may at any time designate as non-BCI/HSBI or as BCI information previously designated by that Party or Third Party as HSBI.

9.   **"HSBI Approved Person"** means Approved Persons specifically designated by the Parties, the Panel or the Director-General of the WTO or his designee as having the right to access HSBI (according to the procedures laid down in Section IV), as well as the Panel members.

10.   **"HSBI location"** means a room to be kept locked when not occupied and the access to which shall be possible only for HSBI Approved Persons, located:

(a)   for the HSBI submitted by the United States, the European Communities, and any Third Parties, on the premises of the WTO (Centre William Rappard, Rue de Lausanne 154, Geneva, Switzerland);

(b)   for HSBI submitted by the United States, on the premises of the United States Mission to the European Union in Brussels;

(c)   for HSBI submitted by the European Communities, on the premises of the Delegation of the European Commission to the United States in Washington;

DSR 2012:III   1815

Report of the Panel

> (d) for HSBI submitted by a Third Party, on the premises of its Geneva Mission to the WTO, should that Third Party so wish.

11. **"Locked CD"** means a CD-ROM that is not rewritable.

12. **"Outside Advisor"** means a legal counsel or other advisor of a Party or Third Party, who:

> (a) advises a Party or Third Party in the course of the dispute;
>
> (b) is not an employee, officer or agent of an entity or an affiliate of an entity engaged in the manufacture of LCA, the provision of supplies to an entity engaged in the manufacture of LCA, or the supply of air transportation services; and
>
> (c) is subject to an enforceable code of professional conduct that includes an obligation to protect confidential information, or has been retained by another outside advisor who assumes responsibility for compliance with these procedures and is subject to such a code of professional conduct.

> For purposes of this paragraph, outside legal counsel representing an LCA producer headquartered in the territory of one of the Parties or Third Parties in connection with these proceedings or outside consultants who have been retained by such counsel to provide advice with regard to these proceedings are not considered agents of an entity listed in subparagraph (b).

13. **"Panel"** means the DS353 Panel composed on 22 November 2006.

14. **"Party"** means the European Communities or the United States.

14*bis*. **"Party-BCI"** means BCI originally submitted by a Party.

15. **"Representative"** means an employee of a Party or Third Party.

16. **"Sealed laptop computer"** means a laptop computer having (software and hardware) characteristics considered necessary by the submitting Party for protection of HSBI, provided that it has software installed that permits such HSBI to be searched and printed in accordance with paragraph 42. However, HSBI may not be edited on the sealed laptop computer.

17. **"Secure site"** means a facility to be kept locked when not occupied and the access to which shall be possible only for Approved Persons, located:

> (a) in the case of the Panel, PGE members or experts appointed by the Panel in accordance with paragraph 1(d), and the Secretariat, on the premises of the WTO (Centre William Rappard, Rue de Lausanne 154, Geneva, Switzerland);
>
> (b) in the case of the European Communities, the offices of External Relations Team of the Legal Service of the European Commission (Rue de la Loi 200, Brussels, Belgium), the offices of Directorate General for Trade of the European Commission (Rue de la Loi 170, Brussels, Belgium), the offices of the Permanent Delegation of the European Communities to the International Organisations in

1816   DSR 2012:III

Geneva (Rue du Grand-Pré 66, 1202 Geneva, Switzerland), and three additional sites specified in accordance with subparagraph (d);

(c)   in the case of the United States, the offices of the General Counsel of the Office of the United States Trade Representative (600 17th Street, NW, Washington, DC, USA), the Office of Defense Procurement and Acquisition Policy, Office of the Undersecretary of Defense for Acquisition, Technology & Logistics, the Pentagon, Arlington, VA, USA, the Mission of the United States to the World Trade Organization (11, route de Pregny, 1292 Chambésy, Switzerland), and three additional sites specified in accordance with subparagraph (d); and

(d)   three sites other than a government office that are designated by each Party for use by its Outside Advisors; provided that the identity of those sites has been submitted to the other Party and the Panel, and the other Party has not objected to the designation of that site within ten days of such submission.

(e)   Any objections raised under subparagraph (d) may be resolved by the Panel.

18.   **"Stand-alone computer"** means a computer that is not connected to a network.

19.   **"Stand-alone printer"** means a printer that is not connected to a network.

20.   **"Third party"** means a Member having notified its interest in the dispute to the DSB pursuant to DSU Article 10.

21,   **"Third Party BCI Approved Person"** means a representative or Outside Advisor of a third party granted access to BCI pursuant to paragraphs 25 and 32, 32bis and 37bis.

III.   SCOPE

22.   These procedures apply to all BCI and HSBI received by an Approved Person as a result of the Panel process *and to all BCI reviewed, in accordance with these procedures, by a Third Party BCI Approved Person.*

23.   Unless specifically otherwise provided herein, these procedures do not apply to a Party's or Third Party's treatment of its own BCI and HSBI.

IV.   DESIGNATION OF APPROVED PERSONS

24.   At the latest on 23 February 2007, each Party shall submit to the other Party and Third Parties, and to the Panel, a list of the names and titles of any Representatives and Outside Advisors who need access to BCI submitted by the other Party and/or Third Parties and whom it wishes to have designated as

Report of the Panel

Approved Persons, along with any clerical or support staff that would have access to the BCI. On that list, each Party shall indicate which Approved Persons need access to HSBI submitted by the other Party and/or Third Parties and whom it wishes to have designated as HSBI Approved Persons.

25. There shall be no Third Party HSBI Approved Persons. The designation of Third Party BCI Approved Persons shall be governed by paragraph 32.

26. Each Party shall keep the number of Approved Persons as limited as possible. Each Party may designate no more than a total of 37 Representatives and 20 Outside Advisors as "HSBI Approved Persons".

27. The Panel Members, any PGE members or experts appointed by the Panel in accordance with paragraph 1(d) shall have access to BCI and HSBI. The Director-General of the WTO, or his designee, shall submit to the Parties and Third Parties, and the Panel, a list of the employees of the Secretariat who need access to BCI and/or HSBI.

28. Unless a Party objects to the designation of an Outside Advisor of the other Party or an Employee of the Secretariat, the Panel shall designate those persons as Approved Persons. A Party also may object within ten days of becoming aware of information that was not available to the Party at the time of the filing of a list under paragraphs 24 or 27 that would suggest that designation of an individual is not appropriate. If a Party objects, the Panel shall decide on the objection within ten working days.

29. An objection may be based on the failure to satisfy the definition of "Outside Advisor" or on any other compelling basis, including conflicts of interest.

30. The Parties or the Director-General of the WTO, or his designee, may submit amendments to their lists at any time, subject to the overall limits set out in paragraph 26 and to objections for the addition of new Approved Persons in accordance with paragraph 29.

V. BCI

31. Only Approved Persons and Third Party BCI Approved Persons may have access to BCI submitted in this proceeding. Third Party BCI Approved Persons may not have access to Party-BCI other than that included in the body of the submissions.[4] Approved Persons and Third Party BCI Approved Persons shall use BCI only for the purposes of this dispute. No Approved Person shall disclose BCI, or allow it to be disclosed, to any person except another Approved Person or Third Party BCI Approved Person. No Third Party BCI Approved

---

[4] "Body of the submissions" includes Appendixes and Annexes of submissions, but does not include exhibits.

1818

DSR 2012:III

Person shall disclose BCI, or allow it to be disclosed, to any person except another Approved Person or Third Party BCI Approved Person.

32.   Each Third Party that wants to access Party-BCI contained in the first submission of a Party shall submit to the Parties and the other Third Parties, and to the Panel, a list of the names and titles of any Representatives and Outside Advisors (including clerical or support staff) who need access to such BCI and whom it wishes to have designated as Third Party BCI Approved Persons. Each Third Party shall keep the number of Third Party BCI Approved Persons as limited as possible. Each Third Party may designate no more than a total of 5 Representatives and Outside Advisors as Third Party BCI Approved Persons.

32bis. Unless a Party objects to the designation of an Outside Advisor of a Third Party, the Panel shall designate those persons as Third Party Approved Persons. A Party also may object within ten days of becoming aware of information that was not available to the Party at the time of the filing of a list under paragraph 32 above that would suggest that designation of an individual is not appropriate. If a Party objects, the Panel shall decide on the objection within ten working days. An objection may be based on the failure to satisfy the definition of "Outside Advisor" or on any other compelling basis, including conflicts of interest.

33.   A Party shall make no more than one copy of any BCI submitted by the other Party or a Third Party for each Secure site provided for that Party in paragraph 17.

34.   Parties may incorporate BCI in internal memoranda for the exclusive use of Approved Persons. Any memorandum and the BCI it contains shall be marked in accordance with paragraph 4.

35.   BCI submitted pursuant to these procedures shall not be copied, distributed, or removed from the Secure site, except as necessary for submission to the Panel.

36.   The treatment in a Party's submissions to the Panel of any BCI shall be governed by the provisions of this paragraph, which shall prevail to the extent of any conflict with the other provisions of the Working Procedures (including these Procedures) relating to BCI.

(a)   Parties may incorporate BCI in submissions to the Panel, marked as indicated in paragraph 4. In exceptional cases, parties may include BCI in an appendix to a submission.

(b)   Unless the Panel informs the Parties otherwise, a Party submitting a submission or appendix containing BCI shall also submit, within a time period to be set by the Panel, a version redacting any BCI. This shall be referred to as the "Non-BCI Version";

(c)   A Non-BCI Version shall be sufficient to permit a reasonable understanding of its substance. In order to prepare such a Non-BCI Version:

Report of the Panel

(i) A Party may request the Party that originally submitted the BCI, as soon as possible, to indicate with precision portions of documents containing BCI that may be included in the non-BCI Version and, if necessary to permit a reasonable understanding of the substance of the information, produce a Non-BCI summary in sufficient detail to achieve this aim.

(ii) Upon receipt of such a request, the Party that originally submitted the BCI shall, as soon as possible, indicate with precision portions of documents containing BCI that may be included in the Non-BCI Version and, if necessary to permit a reasonable understanding of the substance of the information, produce a Non-BCI summary in sufficient detail to achieve this aim.

(iii) The Panel shall resolve any disagreement as to whether the Party that originally submitted the BCI failed to indicate with sufficient precision portions of documents containing BCI that may be included in the Non-BCI Version and to produce, if necessary, a Non-BCI summary in sufficient detail to permit a reasonable understanding of the substance of the information, and may take appropriate action to ensure that the provisions of this paragraph are satisfied.

(d) The responding Party may designate the personal offices of up to four of its Approved Persons as additional Secure sites for the sole purpose of storing and permitting review of the BCI versions of the Parties' submissions to the Panel. All of the protections applicable to BCI under these procedures, including the storage rules in paragraph 39, shall apply to such submissions. BCI exhibits may not, however, be stored at these locations. The addresses of these locations (including room number) shall be notified to the Panel and the complaining Party.

37. Any document containing BCI shall not be copied in excess of the number of copies required by the Approved Persons. All copies of such documents shall be consecutively numbered. The making of electronic copies shall be avoided whenever possible. Such documents may be transmitted electronically only by using secure e-mail. If a Party or Third Party submits to the Panel an original document that cannot be transmitted electronically, it shall on the day of submission deliver a copy of that document to the first secure site listed for the Parties/Third Parties in paragraph 17.

37*bis*. Notwithstanding paragraph 19 of the Working Procedures,[5] the following procedures apply to the access by Third Parties to a Party's submission that contains Party-BCI.

---

[5] Concerning service of documents.

1820

DSR 2012:III

(a) A Party's Submission containing Party-BCI shall not be serviced to Third Parties unless both Parties agree otherwise.

(b) Third Party BCI Approved Persons may view Party-BCI contained in a Party's first written submission only in a Designated Reading Room. Third Party BCI Approved Persons may not bring into that room any electronic recording or transmitting devices. Third Party BCI Approved Persons may not remove a Party's first written submission containing Party-BCI from that room, but may take handwritten notes of the Party-BCI contained therein. Such notes shall be used exclusively for this dispute (that is, DS353). Each person viewing a Party's first written submission containing Party-BCI shall complete and sign a log identifying the submission the person reviewed. The WTO Secretariat shall maintain such log until one year after the Conclusion of the Panel Process. Before entering and when leaving the room, Outside Advisors who are Third Party BCI Approved Persons may be subject to appropriate controls.

(c) If a Third Party BCI Approved Person removes from the Designated Reading Room a handwritten memo in accordance with subparagraph (b) above, that Third Party BCI Approved Person shall store the memo only in a locked security container. Such memo shall be appropriately protected against improper inspection and eavesdropping when being consulted and will be transmitted in sealed heavy duty double envelopes only. The content of such memo shall not be incorporated, electronically or in handwritten form, into the Non-BCI Version, as defined in paragraph 36(b).

(d) All Third Parties that have designated Third Party BCI Approved Persons must inform the Panel and both Parties, by a date set by the Panel, the identity of the specific room (including the address and the room number) in which the locked security container, as referred to in subparagraph (c) above, is located.

(e) If a Third Party BCI Approved Person removes from the Designated Reading Room a handwritten memo in accordance with subparagraph (b) above, such memo shall not be copied in excess of the number of copies required by the Third Party BCI Approved Persons. All copies of such documents shall be consecutively numbered. The making of electronic copies of such memo shall be prohibited.

(f) A Third Party may not incorporate into the body of its submission any Party-BCI . If a Third Party wishes to refer to any Party-BCI, the relevant arguments including such BCI should be incorporated into a separate Appendix. Such Appendix shall not be serviced to other Third Parties.

Report of the Panel

(g) On the date determined by the Panel as the deadline to make the Third Party submission, a Third Party shall service its submission only to the Parties and to the Panel. The submission shall be serviced to the other Third Parties only after the Parties have confirmed that the submission does not contain or disclose Party-BCI. A Party shall make this confirmation or otherwise advise of any necessary change to the relevant Third Party within 2 working days of receiving the submissions of Third Parties.

38.   A Party or Third Party that wishes to submit or refer to BCI at a Panel meeting shall so inform the Panel and the other Party, and Third Parties as appropriate. The Panel shall exclude persons who are not Approved Persons or, as appropriate, Third Party BCI Approved Persons from the meeting for the duration of the submission and discussion of BCI.

39.   Approved Persons shall store BCI only in locked security containers. BCI shall be appropriately protected against improper inspection and eavesdropping when being consulted and will be transmitted in sealed heavy duty double envelopes only. All work papers (*e.g.*, draft submissions, worksheets, etc.) containing BCI shall, when no longer needed, be shredded or burned consistent with normal government practice for destroying sensitive documents.

40.   The Panel shall not disclose BCI in its report, but may make statements or draw conclusions that are based on the information drawn from the BCI.

VI.   HSBI

41.   Unless otherwise provided below, HSBI shall be subject to all the restrictions in Section V applicable to BCI.

42.   HSBI shall be submitted to the WTO in electronic form, using locked CDs or two Sealed laptop computers connectable to 19" - 21" monitors. HSBI shall be stored at the HSBI location indicated in paragraph 10(a) and shall be made available for viewing and use by HSBI Approved Persons pursuant to paragraph 45 below. Each Party shall maintain an additional copy (electronic or hard) of the HSBI it submits to the WTO for access by HSBI Approved Persons acting on behalf of the other Party in the HSBI location listed in paragraph 10 located within the other Party's territory. A Stand-alone printer may be used to make hard copies of any HSBI. Such hard copies shall be made on distinctively colored paper. Such hard copies shall either be stored in a safe at the relevant HSBI location, or destroyed at the end of the relevant working session.

43.   If a Third Party submits HSBI, it shall notify the Parties of the fact that such submission has been made.

44.   Except as otherwise provided in these procedures, HSBI shall not be stored, transmitted or copied either in written or electronic form.

45.   HSBI Approved Persons of a Party may view HSBI on the Sealed laptop computer submitted by the other Party /a Third Party or, in the case of HSBI submitted on Locked CDs on a Stand-alone computer, only in a designated room

1822   DSR 2012:III

US - Large Civil Aircraft (2nd Complaint)

at one of the HSBI locations indicated in paragraph 10, unless otherwise mutually agreed by the Parties. The designated room shall be available to HSBI Approved Persons from 9:00 a.m. to 5:00 p.m. during official working days at the respective HSBI location, except at the location indicated in paragraph 10(a) where the room will be available at any time, including weekends, to the Panel and the PGE members or experts appointed by the Panel in accordance with paragraph 1(d), and to HSBI Approved Persons designated by the Director-General of the WTO or his designee. HSBI Approved Persons may not bring into that room any electronic recording or transmitting devices. HSBI Approved Persons may not remove HSBI from that room, except in the form of handwritten notes or aggregated information generated on a Stand-alone computer. In either case, such notes or information shall be used exclusively for this dispute in connection with which the HSBI has been submitted. Each person viewing the HSBI in the HSBI location shall complete and sign a log identifying the HSBI that the person reviewed or, alternatively, such a log can be generated automatically. Each Party shall, for the HSBI location within its territory referenced in paragraph 10, maintain such log until one year after the Conclusion of the Panel Process. Before entering and when leaving the room, Outside Advisors who are HSBI Approved Persons may be subject to appropriate controls. Viewing of HSBI at the location indicated in paragraph 10(a) by HSBI Approved Persons designated by the Parties shall be conducted under the observation of a WTO security guard or employee.

46.   No Approved Person shall disclose HSBI to any person except another HSBI Approved Person, and then only for the purpose of this dispute.

47.   HSBI may be processed only on Stand-alone computers. Any memorandum containing HSBI shall not be transmitted electronically, whether by e-mail, facsimile, or otherwise.

48.   A Party or Third Party that wishes to submit or refer to HSBI at a Panel meeting shall so inform the Panel and the other Party, and Third Parties as appropriate. The Panel shall exclude persons who are not HSBI Approved Persons from the meeting for the duration of the submission and discussion of HSBI.

49.   All HSBI shall be stored in a safe at the relevant HSBI location.

50.   The treatment in a Party's submissions to the Panel of any HSBI shall be governed by the provisions of this paragraph, which shall prevail to the extent of any conflict with the other provisions of the Working Procedures (including these Procedures) relating to HSBI.

    (a)   HSBI may be incorporated into a separate appendix to, but not the body of, a Party's submission, which shall be referred to as the "Full HSBI Version Appendix" of the appendix;

    (b)   A Party submitting an appendix containing HSBI shall also submit, within a time period to be set by the Panel, a version redacting any HSBI. This shall be referred to as the "Redacted Version Appendix";

DSR 2012:III   1823

Report of the Panel

(c) At the request of a Party, information contained in the Redacted Version Appendix may be treated as BCI, in accordance with the provisions of Section V;

(d) A Redacted Version Appendix shall be sufficient to permit a reasonable understanding of its substance. In order to prepare such a Redacted Version Appendix:

(i) A Party may request that the Party that originally submitted the HSBI, as soon as possible, indicate with precision portions of documents containing HSBI that may be included in the Redacted Version Appendix and, if necessary to permit a reasonable understanding of the substance of the information, produce a non-HSBI summary in sufficient detail to achieve this aim.

(ii) Upon receipt of such a request, the Party that originally submitted the HSBI shall, as soon as possible, indicate with precision portions of documents containing HSBI that may be included in the Redacted Version Appendix and, if necessary to permit a reasonable understanding of the substance of the information, produce a non-HSBI summary in sufficient detail to achieve this aim.

(iii) The Panel shall resolve any disagreement as to whether the Party that originally submitted the HSBI failed to indicate with sufficient precision portions of documents containing HSBI that may be included in the Redacted Version Appendix and to produce, if necessary, a non-HSBI summary in sufficient detail to permit a reasonable understanding of the substance of the information, and may take appropriate action to ensure that the provisions of this paragraph are satisfied.

(e) The Full HSBI Version Appendix shall be kept in an HSBI Location in the form of a locked CD. If that is not practical, the Party may keep it in a locked security container in a Secure Site in the form of a locked CD.

(f) The locked CD containing the Full HSBI Version Appendix shall bear the label marked 'FULL VERSION OF HSBI APPENDIX TO SUBMISSION' and indicate the name of the Party that submitted the HSBI. In addition, the HSBI Appendix itself shall be marked with heading with double bolded square brackets on each page in an electronic file that contains the notation 'FULL VERSION OF HSBI APPENDIX TO SUBMISSION'. The electronic file containing the HSBI Appendix shall have a file name that contains the letters "HSBI VERSION".

(g) The Party shall submit one copy of the Full HSBI Version Appendix to the Panel (c/o the DS Registry), and two copies to the other Party in the form of locked CDs. The Full HSBI Version Appendix shall not be transmitted via e-mail. Parties shall agree

1824

DSR 2012:III

between themselves beforehand on the name of the Approved Person that is to receive the locked CD.

(h)   The Party shall commence transfer of the locked CDs containing the Full HSBI Version Appendix no later than the deadline for the submission concerned, and, at the same time, provide the Panel and the other Party with proof that this has been done.

(i)   No more than one working day in advance of a Panel meeting with the parties, a Party may, exclusively at that Party's Permanent Mission in Geneva, use the locked CD to produce no more than one hard copy of the Full HSBI Version Appendix for each HSBI Approved Person planning to attend that Panel meeting.

(j)   Panelists and the PGE members or experts appointed by the Panel in accordance with paragraph 1(d) and HSBI Approved Persons designated by the Director-General of the WTO or his designee may, exclusively on the WTO premises, produce paper versions of the Full HSBI Version Appendix for the purpose of, and immediately prior to, a Panel meeting with the parties and/or an internal meeting.

(k)   Any hard copy of a Full HSBI Version shall be destroyed immediately upon the conclusion of a Panel meeting with the parties and/or an internal meeting.

(l)   The Panel reserves the right, after consulting the parties, to amend the provisions of this paragraph at any time in order to accommodate situations arising during Panel meetings, and the preparation of the interim report and the final report.

51.   The Panel shall not disclose HSBI in its report, but may make statements or draw conclusions that are based on the information drawn from the HSBI.

VII.   RESPONSIBILITY FOR COMPLIANCE

52.   Each Party and Third Party is responsible for ensuring that its Approved Persons and Third Party BCI Approved Persons comply with these procedures to protect and to return or destroy BCI and HSBI submitted by each Party and Third Party, as well as with enforceable codes of professional conduct to which its approved persons or other outside advisors are subject. The Secretariat is responsible for ensuring that its employees comply with these procedures to protect BCI and HSBI submitted by a Party or Third Party and for adhering to the requirements to provide access in the WTO to Approved Persons and to control the use by HSBI Approved Persons when reviewing the material in the WTO premises. The Panel shall comply with these procedures to protect BCI and HSBI submitted by a Party or Third Party.

VIII. ADDITIONAL PROCEDURES

53. After consulting with the Parties, the Panel may apply any other additional procedures that it considers necessary to provide additional protections to the confidentiality of BCI or HSBI or other types of information not explicitly covered by these Procedures but which the Panel considers may be of assistance in adjudicating the claims before it, including, if necessary, information that the United States internally classifies as "Top Secret", "Secret", or "Confidential".

54. The Panel may, with the consent of both Parties, waive any part of these procedures. Such "waiver" shall be specifically set forth in writing and signed by a representative of both Parties.

IX. RETURN AND DESTRUCTION

55. Before the Conclusion of the Panel Process as defined in paragraphs 3(a), 3(c) or 3(d), the Panel shall fix a period within which, the Panel, any PGE members or experts appointed by the Panel, the Secretariat, the Parties and Third Parties (along with all Approved Persons) shall destroy or return all documents (including electronic material) or other recordings containing BCI to the Party or Third Party that submitted such documents or other recordings. At the same time, the Panel shall fix a period within which the Panel, Secretariat and Parties shall destroy and/or return any electronic material submitted by a Party or Third Party that contains HSBI to the Party or Third Party that submitted it.

56. After the Conclusion of the Panel Process as defined in paragraph 3(b), the Panel will inform the Appellate Body of these procedures and will transmit to the Appellate Body any BCI/HSBI governed by these Procedures. Such transmission shall occur separately from the rest of the Panel record, to the extent possible.

57. The hard drive of all Stand-alone computers and all media used to back up such computers shall be destroyed at the Conclusion of the Panel Process as defined in paragraphs 3(a), 3(c) or 3(d).

ANNEX E

SELECTED RULINGS OF THE PANEL CONCERNING BCI/HSBI PROCEDURES AND THEIR APPLICATION

Contents	Page
Annex E-1 Communication of 4 June 2007	1827
Annex E-2 Communication of 9 July 2007	1833
Annex E-3 Communication of 16 July 2007	1834

ANNEX E-1

COMMUNICATION OF 4 JUNE 2007

United States – Measures Affecting Trade in Large Civil Aircraft
(Second Complaint) (DS353)

1.   The Panel has carefully considered the letter from the European Communities ("EC") dated 23 April 2007, responding to the comments of the United States ("US") concerning designation of certain BCI and HSBI. In support of its approach to the designation of information as HSBI, the EC draws a distinction between (a) information sought to be protected, and (b) documents that reveal such information. According to the EC, the BCI/HSBI Procedures are concerned with the former, and support for this proposition can be found in paragraph 8 of the BCI/HSBI Procedures which refers to "information ... regardless of whether contained in a document...". The EC contends therefore that "publicly available documents may be classified as HSBI if their disclosure (particularly in light of the context in which they are disclosed) would reveal business information not in the public domain that, in the view of the Party submitting the information, could cause exceptional harm to its originators."[1] From this, the Panel understands the EC to be arguing that the "information" which may be protected as BCI or HSBI under the BCI/HSBI Procedures extends beyond information imparted directly in the content of a particular text or speech and comprehends more indirectly the use made of a particular document or utterance, or the context in which a particular document or utterance is obtained, communicated, made or reproduced.

---

[1]   EC Letter dated 23 April 2007, p. 3.

Report of the Panel

2.　　Paragraph 2 of the BCI/HSBI Procedures defines BCI as "any business information that a Party or Third Party has 'Designated as BCI' regardless of whether contained in a document provided by a public or private body *because it is not otherwise available in the public domain"*. Paragraph 8 of the BCI/HSBI Procedures, defines HSBI as "any business information regardless of whether contained in a document provided by a public or private body that a Party or Third Party has 'Designated as HSBI' *because it is not otherwise available in the public domain* and its disclosure could, in the Party's or Third Party's view, cause exceptional harm to its originators." It is clear that a common feature of both BCI and HSBI is that the information so designated is not otherwise in the public domain. The EC interprets the concept of "information" which may be designated as BCI and HSBI under the BCI/HSBI Procedures in a broad manner. Such interpretation leads to the result that, notwithstanding the clear requirement in both paragraphs 2 and 8 that information in the public domain cannot be designated as BCI or HSBI, it would nonetheless be possible to designate information which is in the public domain as BCI or HSBI where one can derive from that information other "information" (in a more abstract sense) which is distinct from the information that is in the public domain. We do not consider this to be a reasonable interpretation of the BCI/HSBI Procedures. The Panel considers that the "information" with which the BCI/HSBI Procedures is concerned is information which is explicitly communicated in a document,[2] as opposed to "information" concerning the use being made of a particular document[3] in the context of the present dispute, or "information" as to how a particular document[4] came into the possession or knowledge of one of the Parties. The Panel considers that this is evident from a reading of paragraphs 2 and 8 of the BCI/Procedures in conjunction with terms "Designated as BCI" and "Designated as HSBI" in paragraphs 4 and 5, respectively, of the BCI/HSBI Procedures. Paragraphs 4 and 5 refer to the means of designating information as BCI and HSBI, respectively. These paragraphs refer to "information" that is in printed form, electronic form or spoken form and clearly show that the BCI/HSBI Procedures were intended to apply to specific sensitive information appearing *within* a document or electronic file, or revealed in the course of speech.

1.　　**The fact that a document is being used by the EC in the context of this dispute**

3.　　In relation to the specific issues for determination by the Panel, the Panel notes that the EC argues as follows (italics in original, underlining added):

---

[2]　Or electronic file or oral statement.

[3]　*Ibid.*

[4]　*Ibid.*

1828　　　　　　　　　　　　　　　　　　　　　　　　　　　　　DSR 2012:III

"In particular, the *information* being protected through the HSBI designation is *the identity of the airlines involved in the sales campaigns selected by the European Communities* as evidencing lost sales, displacement and impedance, and price suppression within the meaning of Article 6.3 of the *SCM Agreement.* While it is true that publicly available documents provide certain information regarding these campaigns, *the fact that campaigns involving these airlines are being used by the European Communities to demonstrate lost sales, displacement and impedance, and price suppression is not information in the public domain.* It is therefore necessary to classify even publicly available documents related to these sales campaigns as HSBI in order to *protect the fact that they are being used by the European Communities in the context of this dispute.*"[5]

4.   It follows from the view we have expressed in paragraph 2 that the Panel does not agree with the EC that "the fact that {a document is} being used by the European Communities in the context of this dispute" in and of itself is the *information* which the BCI/HSBI intends to protect – be it as BCI or HSBI. It is obvious that the fact the EC is using a particular document in this dispute is not "information in the public domain". In fact, unless a party elects to publicly disclose the fact that it is using certain documents as evidence in support of its claims in a dispute, it is *always* the case that the identity of the documents being used by a party in an ongoing dispute is confidential – that is, information not in the public domain.[6] If the EC's argument were correct, it would result in a party being free to designate *any* document in this dispute as BCI or HSBI unless it voluntarily elects to disclose the fact that it is using a specific document in this dispute. Moreover, to accept the EC's arguments on this issue would be tantamount to classifying a core part of its case as HSBI. We do not consider that the BCI/HSBI Procedures were intended to lead to such a result.

2.   Documents obtained on an informal and confidential basis

5.   The EC has also sought to (i) designate as HSBI various presentations made by *Boeing* executives to particular airline clients in the context of sales campaigns, which have been shared with Airbus by those airlines on condition of anonymity; and (ii) designate as BCI presentations made by *Boeing* at airline conferences which have been shared with Airbus by conference organizers on condition of anonymity. According to the EC, "the *information* that the European Communities is trying to protect, by classifying these documents as BCI and HSBI is that Airbus is in possession of these documents and that certain

---

[5]   EC Letter of 23 April 2007, p. 4.
[6]   DSU Article 14.1.

Report of the Panel

airline executives or conference organisers have provided these documents to Airbus."

6. In relation to the information it has sought to designate as HSBI, the EC argues that such information constitutes "information gathered or produced in the context of LCA sales campaigns" within the meaning of subparagraph 8(a)(ii) of the BCI/HSBI Procedures. In addition, the EC argues that failure to designate these documents as HSBI in their entirety (including the titles of the documents) could cause exceptional harm to Airbus and to the airlines and airline executives that provided the documents to Airbus if Boeing were to learn that these documents had been provided to Airbus by the airlines concerned.

7. In relation to the Boeing presentations at airline conferences, which the EC has designated as BCI, the EC contends that if these documents were not classified as BCI in their entirety, the identity of the conference organizers who provided these documents to Airbus would be readily apparent and this disclosure would cause harm to Airbus as well as to the conference organizers in question.

8. The Panel understands that the EC is in effect arguing that the fact of *how* it obtained the document/information is the "information" it seeks to protect under the BCI/HSBI Procedures. It follows from the views we have expressed in paragraph 2 that the Panel rejects this argument. As the Panel stated in its communication of 16 April 2007:

> "The Panel considers that the standard for determining whether {information contained in Boeing documents} is BCI or HSBI relates to the possibility of harm to the "originator" of the information, which in this case is Boeing, in the event of disclosure. In our view, the originator of a document is entitled, through appropriate channels, to waive BCI or HSBI status where it believes that disclosure of the information would not cause the requisite harm, or where it is prepared to accept such harm. The Panel has, at the very least, strong doubts about how it could be that it would be consistent with fundamental fairness for it to rely on documents originated by a private party where that private party was unaware that those documents were even before the Panel (let alone their content) because they were designated as BCI or HSBI by the other party."

3. Exhibit EC-15

9. The EC has sought to defend its designation of exhibit EC-15 as BCI in its entirety on a somewhat different basis. Exhibit EC-15 comprises an analysis, conducted by Airbus aeronautical engineers, of alleged links between various NASA research and development programs and specific Boeing civil aircraft

programs. Concerning exhibit EC-15, the EC states as follows (underlining added):

> "Second, disclosure of any portion of exhibit EC-15, including its conclusions, would cause harm to Airbus. As this is a study conducted by Airbus' engineering department, *it provides valuable insights into the extent of Airbus' aeronautical engineering expertise, for it is that very expertise that provides the basis for the study's conclusions.* Indeed, a Boeing engineer examining this study would be able to ascertain from it how far advanced Airbus' knowledge is with respect to the wide variety of aeronautics technologies covered by the study."[7]

10.   The Panel notes that the conclusions of any expert analysis are necessarily based, at least in part, on the subjective knowledge of the expert, and that such conclusions are therefore inherently revelatory of that expert's subjective state of knowledge. However, it is clear from the approach outlined by the Panel in paragraph 2 that it is incumbent on the EC to specifically identify the Airbus aeronautical engineering expertise, or other Airbus technological information or know-how that is explicit in the document itself.

4.   Concluding remarks

11.   The Panel clarifies that the views we have expressed above do *not* mean that the documents the EC is seeking to protect can be made public by the US. As the parties are well aware, panel deliberations are confidential.

12.   In the light of the above, the Panel directs the EC to submit, ***by Monday 11 June***, properly bracketed versions of all the paragraphs and exhibits raised by the US – including paragraphs 717 and 1361 of the EC submission, which the US identified in footnote 3 of its 10 April letter. In so doing, the EC is directed to perform the re-bracketing in accordance with the Panel's understanding of the HSBI/BCI Procedures as outlined above, as well as indicated in our communication dated 16 April.

13.   Other than paragraphs 717 and 1361, the EC need not resubmit the body (i.e. the 678 page-document) of the submission at this time. The Panel has noted that the EC stated as follows in its letter:

> "The European Communities is willing to re-designate the name and number of exhibit EC-15 as non-BCI in the citations throughout its first written submission."[8]

---

[7]   EC Letter of 23 April 2007, p. 8.
[8]   Page 8 of the 23 April EC letter.

Report of the Panel

The Panel will inform the EC in due course when it must submit a revised version of the body of the submission.

14. *Unless* the EC makes changes to the text of the specific exhibit/paragraph, the Panel requests the EC to submit the re-bracketed exhibits and paragraphs (i.e. Annexes) in a BCI version.[9]

---

[9] That is, the Panel does not, for example, expect the EC to upload the re-bracketed exhibits onto the HSBI laptop. Needless to say, the EC is allowed to redact all information which it deems as HSBI from the BCI version.

1832   DSR 2012:III

ANNEX E-2

COMMUNICATION OF 9 JULY 2007

United States – Measures Affecting Trade in Large Civil Aircraft
(Second Complaint) (DS353)

The Panel confirms receipt of the letter and the documents submitted by the European Communities ("EC") on 18 June, which were submitted in response to the Panel's ruing dated 4 June on the issue of bracketing of certain information. The Panel has also noted the comments of the United States on this issue in its cover letter of the submission made on 6 July. As the parties will recall, this issue was triggered by the comments of the United States ("US"), dated 10 April, on the non-BCI version and on the Redacted Version Appendix submitted by the EC on 3 April.

The Panel hereby suggests that the revised version submitted by the EC on 18 June be deemed as the basis of the non-BCI version to be serviced to the Third Parties. The Panel requests the EC to service the non-BCI version (i.e. with information between brackets being deleted) by close of business on **10 July**.

In addition, in accordance with paragraph 32 of the BCI/HSBI Procedures[1], the Panel proposes that the attached procedures be followed in order for Third Parties to access BCI in the parties' submission. The Panel requests that the parties submit comments, if any, on the attached draft procedures by close of business **11 July**. The Panel understands that once the parties agree on the procedures, the revised BCI version of the body of the submission and the revised Redacted Version Appendix submitted from the EC on 18 June is the document that the Third Parties will be granted access at this point of time. The Panel understands that Third Parties will not be granted access to the "BCI exhibits".

---

[1]   "Additional Working Procedures For DS353 – Procedures for the Protection of Business Confidential Information and Highly Sensitive Business Information".

List of Index

ANNEX E-3

COMMUNICATION OF 16 JULY 2007

*United States – Measures Affecting Trade in Large Civil Aircraft
(Second Complaint) (DS353)*

The Panel informs the Parties and Third Parties that it has amended, after consulting the parties, the BCI/HSBI Procedures[1] as attached in accordance with the original paragraph 32[2] of the BCI/HSBI Procedures.[3]

In accordance with paragraph 32 and paragraph 37*bis*(d) of the amended BCI/HSBI Procedures, the Panel invites Third Parties to submit, if they so wish, the following information to the Panel as well as to the Parties and other Third Parties by close of business of **18 July 2007**.

- A list of the names and titles (including affiliation) of any Representatives and Outside Advisors (including clerical or support staff) who need access to Party-BCI and whom it wishes to have designated as Third Party BCI Approved Persons. (Please note that no more than 5 persons can be designated.)

- The identity of the "specific room" (including the address and the room number) in which the locked "security container", as referred to in paragraph 37*bis*(c) of the amended BCI/HSBI Procedures, is located. (Please note that only one "specific room" can be designated.)

Once the above information is submitted from Third Parties, the Panel invites the Parties to submit any objections based on paragraph 32*bis* of the amended BCI/HSBI Procedures by close of business of **20 July 2007**.

---

[1] "Additional Working Procedures For DS353 – Procedures for the Protection of Business Confidential Information and Highly Sensitive Business Information".

[2] This paragraph has been amended in the attached latest version. See Panel's communication dated 19 February 2007 for the original wording of this paragraph.

[3] Changes are highlighted in the attachment for ease of reference.

1834

DSR 2012:III

For EU product safety concerns, contact us at Calle de José Abascal, 56–1°,
28003 Madrid, Spain or eugpsr@cambridge.org.

www.ingramcontent.com/pod-product-compliance
Ingram Content Group UK Ltd.
Pitfield, Milton Keynes, MK11 3LW, UK
UKHW030655060825
461487UK00011B/946